The Life You Save May Be Your Own

The Life You Save May Be Your Own

AN AMERICAN PILGRIMAGE

Paul Elie

FARRAR, STRAUS AND GIROUX

NEW YORK

Farrar, Straus and Giroux
19 Union Square West, New York 10003

Owing to limitations of space, all acknowledgments for permission to reprint previously
published and unpublished material can be found on pages 553–55.

Library of Congress Cataloging-in-Publication Data
Elie, Paul.
    The life you save may be your own : an American pilgrimage: Flannery O'Connor,
Thomas Merton, Walker Percy, Dorothy Day / Paul Elie.— 1st ed.
        p.   cm.
    Includes index.
    ISBN 0-374-25680-2
    1. American literature—Catholic authors—History and criticism. 2. Christianity
and literature—United States—History—20th century. 3. Catholics—United States—
Intellectual life—20th century. 4. American literature—20th century—History and
criticism. 5. Authors, American—20th century—Biography. 6. Catholics—United
States—Biography. 7. Merton, Thomas, 1915–1968. 8. Day, Dorothy, 1897–1980.
9. Percy, Walker, 1916–90. O'Connor, Flannery, 1925–1964.   I. Title.

PS153.C3 E45 2003
810.9'9222—dc21

                                                                    2002192522

Designed by Jonathan D. Lippincott

1   3   5   7   9   10   8   6   4   2

For Lenora
and the whole family

Contents

On Pilgrimage

I n the photographs, they don't look like people who might make you want to change your life. Flannery O'Connor's black dress and big glasses suggest a pious and dutiful Georgia daughter. Thomas Merton seems to be uncomfortable in his Trappist habit—all the vitality is in the eyes. Walker Percy's face frames a smile, as if he is just another duffer at the country club, nattering on about the Old South. In her castoff overcoat and kerchief Dorothy Day might be a nun or a social worker, not a radical under surveillance by the FBI.

Ordinary people, on the face of it—but for many of us these photographs are icons, ideals in black and white. O'Connor's grim propriety is of a piece with her fiction, a pitiless enactment of the mystery and manners of the South. Merton's unease with his monastic calling kept him always striving for more perfect solitude. Percy's good mood is a great achievement, an escape from the pressures of his family history—inheritance, duty, war, fatal accidents, mortal illness, depression, suicide. Day's overcoat is no better than those given out to the poor men who stand on line outside the Catholic Worker, an emblem of the rough equality of every person under God.

They are writers from the middle of the last century now, who precede us the way Tolstoy and Dostoevsky, Hopkins and Henry James, preceded them. They are solidly canonical, fixed in the lens of literary posterity: anthologies, conferences, monographs, appreciation societies.

Because they prized independence, they are typically seen as great individuals, four figures who came out of nowhere and stood alone. Merton is the monk whose autobiography became a best-seller, spoiling his solitude. Day is the Greenwich Village bohemian who founded the Catholic Worker—newspaper, soup kitchen, and revolutionary headquarters. Percy is the doctor who quit medicine to be a writer, stealthily slipping philosophy into his novels. O'Connor is the comic genius who wrote shockingly about rural prophets and desperadoes before dying of lupus at the age of thirty-nine.

Taken together, their stories are told as episodes in a recent chapter of American religious history, in which four Catholics of rare sophistication overcame the narrowness of the Church and the suspicions of the culture to achieve a distinctly American Catholic outlook.

All of that is true and worth knowing. This book, though, will take a slightly different approach, setting out to tell their four stories as one, albeit one with four points of origin and points of view. It is, or is meant to be, the narrative of a pilgrimage, a journey in which art, life, and religious faith converge; it is a story of readers and writers—of four individuals who glimpsed a way of life in their reading and evoked it in their writing, so as to make their readers yearn to go and do likewise.

What is a pilgrimage? The theme, which is found all through their work (and the work about them), is never defined precisely there; but a pattern of pilgrimage emerges, one that seems to fit Dante and Chaucer, these four writers, and the present age alike.

A pilgrimage is a journey undertaken in the light of a story. A great event has happened; the pilgrim hears the reports and goes in search of the evidence, aspiring to be an eyewitness. The pilgrim seeks not only to confirm the experience of others firsthand but to be changed by the experience.

Pilgrims often make the journey in company, but each must be changed individually; they must see for themselves, each with his or her own eyes. And as they return to ordinary life the pilgrims must tell others what they saw, recasting the story in their own terms.

In the story of these four writers, the pattern of pilgrimage is also a pattern of reading and writing. Dorothy Day could have been speaking for the group when she said the meaning of her life was to live out the imperatives found in the Gospels and in her favorite novels: all four were great readers before they were great writers. Three were Catholic converts, but it was in literature, first of all, that they found religious experience most convincingly described. As they read Dickens and Joyce, Blake and Eliot, Augustine and Kierkegaard, they recognized themselves as people with religious temperaments and quandaries.

Emboldened by books, they set out to have for themselves the experiences they had read about, measuring their lives against the books that had struck them the most powerfully. With the Catholic Worker, Day strove to embody the Gospel story literally on the streets of the Lower East Side. Merton, leaving New York and the modern world for a Trappist monastery in Kentucky, hoped to find there the life of order and purpose described in medieval philosophy. O'Connor, raised a Catholic among Protestants of the Deep South, discovered herself as a writer when she recognized that the people of her part of Georgia were kin to the outsize figures in the Bible. An orphan, a survivor of tuberculosis, a descendant of illustrious melancholics, Percy saw himself as a searcher after life's meaning, like the characters the existentialists wrote about, and he quietly slipped out of the harness of his family history to live in a small town and write fiction, testing his philosophy with his life.

Already, they saw themselves as representative figures, whose concerns were characteristically modern; and already, they were sharpening their skills as writers—trying to describe religious experience, to imagine it, to convey it to the reader as believable, exciting, profound. At first they sought to retell the stories they had read, recasting the European classics for mid-century American life. In time, as they found their own voices and means of approach, religious experience in their work would take on forms no one expected: mystical prayer in an abandoned toolshed in the woods, televised civil disobedience outside City Hall, a survivor's ordeal in a cave in North Carolina, an elderly lady's epiphany at gunpoint by the roadside.

The pilgrimage of these four writers is part of a larger story of the convergence of literature and religion in the twentieth century, the effects of which are still being felt in our own time. It is a story that runs parallel to the modern history of the United States. As James Wood has pointed out, the decline of the Bible's authority in the nineteenth century coincided with the rise of the modern novel, which aspired to have something like a religious authority over the reader. In part, this development led to the defiant heterodoxy of the great modernist writers, who conceived of literature as cult, creed, and dogma, a world unto itself. And yet the Bible, in decline in Europe, retained its authority in America, and perhaps it was only natural that the religiously charged books of early modernity would prompt certain American writers to seek out actual religious experience, and then to set about writing literary work which would have a frankly religious power.

How that happened is complicated, and one way to understand it more precisely is through the notion of the "anxiety of influence," which Harold Bloom applied to the English Romantic poets some years ago. If, as Bloom proposed, a writer in early maturity is beset by the "anxiety of influence" and must "misread" a great precursor in order to attain an original style, it is no surprise that some modern American writers felt the anxiety of influence with a religious intensity—that they brought books to bear on every aspect of their experience, "misreading" their precursors with their lives.

The surprise is that it happened to four American Catholic writers, and happened all at once, and with such intensity that American Catholicism, through their work, came to seem a creative misreading of Catholic Europe. For, on the face of it, their emergence was unlikely, and their careers converged with startling abruptness, so much so that the resemblances among them were overlooked at the time.

When, reviewing George Orwell's *Homage to Catalonia* in 1952, Lionel Trilling complained that the American literary scene lacked "representative figures"—"who live their visions as well as write them, who *are* what they write"—he could not have been further off the mark. Whole groups of representative figures were then emerging: the Jewish American novelists; the Beat poets; the "confessional" poets, led by Robert Lowell; and these four writers, whom a friend suggestively dubbed the School of the Holy Ghost.

The publication in 1948 of Thomas Merton's autobiography, *The Seven Storey Mountain*, had given American Catholics a first-class writer, and spurred Dorothy Day, who had been in the public eye since the thirties, to write her own autobiography. Day's *The Long Loneliness* was published in 1952; so was *Wise Blood*, the first novel by Flannery O'Connor, then twenty-seven years old. Shortly afterward, Walker Percy, struggling with a novel, set it aside and began to write the philosophical essays that led him, indirectly, to *The Moviegoer*, a fresh and vital philosophical novel.

They came to know one another only gradually. On the Georgia dairy farm called Andalusia, at the Abbey of Gethsemani in Kentucky, in the "pleasant nonplace" of Covington, Louisiana, or at the Catholic Worker "houses of hospitality" across the country, they were set apart from literary society, and they sought in their work to make what Faulkner called "oratory out of solitude." At the same time, they thought of writing as an act of communication, an urgent piece of news sent from writer to reader like a message in a bottle. "No matter what the writer may say, the work is always written to someone, for someone, against someone," Percy explained, and as the four of them gained a wide public for their work, they took great satisfaction in the knowledge that, among their readers, they had one another, who (as Percy put it) had a "predicament shared in common."

By 1969 O'Connor and Merton were dead, and Day and Percy were living in the epilogue of the story. Their influence upon subsequent generations, however, has spread far and wide. O'Connor was the first postwar writer published in the Library of America series. There are now enough books about Merton to fill the Abbey of Gethsemani's scriptorium. Day is being considered for canonization as a saint in Rome. With *The Moviegoer*, Percy has begotten a whole strain of keen-eyed, present-tense, disaffected contemporary fiction.

It is in their lives and their work together that their influence is found, and that this telling of their story is meant to explore. Today, as when they were alive, they are representative figures, whose struggles with belief and unbelief are vivid and recognizable. At the same time, as they venture forth together, their story suggests a series of different ways of pilgrimage, with the episodes highlighting patterns that the yearning for religious experience can take, in their time and in ours.

Their work, once the pride of a socially aspirant Catholic populace, is now a point of entry for readers of all kinds—curious, perplexed, indifferent, or altogether hostile to religious experience. Set as it is on the border between life and art, between faith and doubt, it describes that experience with rare clarity and power. What is more—and this, perhaps, is what makes it persuasive—it dramatizes that experience in such a way that the reader enters into it personally through a kind of radical identification with the protagonist. At its best, it is writing that one reads with one's whole life, testing the work against one's own life, and vice versa.

It is writing that invites the reader on a pilgrimage. Because it has to do with questions of belief—questions of how to live—it makes the pattern of pilgrimage explicit. But the way of the pilgrim, so to speak, is a common way of reading and writing. It is not the only way, of course, or the correct way, but it is a way that we actually do read and write, whether or not we acknowledge it. Certain books, certain writers, reach us at the center of ourselves, and we come to them in fear and trembling, in hope and expectation—reading so as to change, and perhaps to save, our lives.

The four of them touched on this idea in their different ways. Merton spoke of it as the mark of wisdom literature, which has a power of "enactment"—the ability to "convey not a system of truths which explain life but a certain depth of awareness in which life itself is lived more intensely and with a more meaningful direction." Percy identified it as "the Delta factor," whereby writer and reader, through the use of a common language, come to understand each other. Day put it into practice each year in the *Catholic Worker*'s "Fall Appeal," in which, begging for funds, she sought to make every reader of the paper feel like a participant in the movement's work. O'Connor pointed toward it in the story that gives this book its title, in which a one-armed handyman named Mr. Shiftlet offers a lady help around the house—and wry insights about the human predicament.

"There's a strange paradox about writing novels," Percy, late in his life, with the others dead and gone, told a group of admirers. "It is precisely this: There's no occupation in the universe that is lonelier, and that at the same time depends more radically on a community, a commonwealth of other writers. . . . As lonely as is the craft of writing, it is the most social of vocations." He was speaking of Herman Melville and Nathaniel Hawthorne, friends and contemporaries in nineteenth-century New England, but he might have been describing this community of mid-twentieth-century Catholic writers.

Their lives, their work, and their significance for us—that is the story this book aspires to tell. Ours is an age suspicious, and rightly so, of religious experience and religious tradition alike—suspicious of forms inherited secondhand from our predecessors, but also skeptical of any claim to firsthand experience of the divine. At the same time, ours is an age suspicious of literature's claim to speak to us directly, to suggest patterns of experience that we might read back into our lives.

In these circumstances, their world seems another world altogether; yet they are still very much alive. They speak to us and invite us to reply, to transpose their stories from their lives to our own. That, if nothing else, is what this telling of their story hopes to accomplish—through their pilgrimage to begin to understand ours, which is already in progress.

The Life You Save May Be Your Own

ONE

Experience

T he night the earthquake struck San Francisco—April 18, 1906—
Dorothy Day was there. Startled awake, she lay alone in bed in the
dark in the still-strange house, trying to understand what was happening and what it meant, for she was confident that it had a meaning, a significance beyond itself.

Some years later she described that night in her autobiography. By then
she was known as an organizer and agitator, a living saint, the prioress of the
Bowery. But she saw herself as a journalist, first of all, and gave a journalist's
eyewitness account of the event, which had brought on the most haunting
of her early "remembrances of God."

"The earthquake started with a deep rumbling and the convulsions of
the earth started afterward, so that the earth became a sea which rocked our
house in a most tumultuous manner. There was a large windmill and water
tank in back of the house and I can remember the splashing of the water
from the tank on top of our roof."

She was eight years old, the third child of four. Her family had moved
from New York to Oakland earlier in the year after her father, a journalist,
found work with one of the local papers. Back in Brooklyn she had shared a
bedroom with their Irish servant girl. Here she shared a room with her baby
sister, who slept in her arms.

"My father took my brothers from their beds and rushed to the front
door, where my mother stood with my sister, whom she had snatched from
me. I was left in a big brass bed, which rolled back and forth on a polished
floor."

Before getting into bed she had knelt at the bedside to say her prayers. Of all her family, she alone was religious: she prayed in school, sang hymns with neighbors, went to church by herself because the others would not go. She was "disgustingly, proudly pious."

In bed, however, she would have nightmares about God, "a great noise that became louder and louder, and approached nearer and nearer to me until I woke up sweating with fear and shrieking for my mother." And that night, alone in the dark on the big rolling bed, shaken by the earth, left behind by her mother and father, she felt God upon her once again, a figure stalking her in the dark.

Or was that night the first time? "Even as I write this I am wondering if I had these nightmares before the San Francisco earthquake or afterward. The very remembrance of the noise, which kept getting louder and louder, and the keen fear of death, makes me think now that it might have been due only to the earthquake. . . . They were linked up with my idea of God as a tremendous Force, a frightening impersonal God, a Hand stretched out to seize me, His child, and not in love."

The earthquake went on two minutes and twenty seconds. Then it was over. The world returned to normal. She got out of bed and went down the stairs and out to the street and looked around.

She was startled all over again by what she saw: buildings wobbling on their foundations, smoke rising from small fires, parents calming strange children and passing jugs of water back and forth. People were helping one another.

For two days refugees from the city came to Oakland in boats across San Francisco Bay, making camp in a nearby park. The people of Oakland helped them—the men pitching tents and contriving lean-tos, the women cooking and lending their spare clothing. What did Dorothy Day do? She stood on the street, watching, and felt her fear and loneliness drawn out of her by what she saw.

"While the crisis lasted, people loved each other," she wrote in her autobiography. "It was as though they were united in Christian solidarity. It makes one think of how people could, if they would, care for each other in times of stress, unjudgingly in pity and love."

A whole life is prefigured in that episode. In a moment in history—front-page news—Dorothy Day felt the fear of God and witnessed elemental, biblical charity, the remedy for human loneliness. All her life she would try to recapture the sense of real and spontaneous community she felt then, and would strive to reform the world around her so as to make such community possible.

From the beginning, she had the gift of good timing, a knack for situating herself and her story in a larger story. Her first significant religious experience took place during the first great event of the American century, a cataclysm in the city named for St. Francis, the patron saint of "unjudging pity and love" for one's neighbor.

Moreover, it took place at a moment of great change (seismic change, one might say) in religion in America, and also in the interpretation of religion—changes to which she would spend the rest of her life responding.

There is little question that America at the turn of the century was a religious place. The question, then as now, was this: religious how?

At the time, the answer to the question was usually theological, grounded in stock ideas about Catholicism and Protestantism that had been developing since the sixteenth century. Catholics (it was thought) were traditional, communal, submissive to higher authority, taking faith at second hand from pope and clergy, whereas the Protestant was individualistic, improvisatory, devoted to progress, bent on having a direct experience of God, obedient to no authority save the Bible and the individual conscience.

From the time of Columbus, according to this scheme, which was accepted by Catholics and Protestants alike, the religious history of America was a running conflict between Catholic missionaries, who saw America as an annex of Catholic Europe, and Protestant pioneers, who saw it as a frontier to be settled according to the directives in the Bible.

In the nineteenth century Protestantism became dominant, and religion in America came to be characterized by the rivalry between different Protestant churches, whose circuit-riding evangelists would travel on horseback from one town to the next, each of them preaching a creed and a way of life that he claimed was more faithful to the Gospel than those his competitors were offering. Thus the country, discovered by Catholics, was settled by Protestants, whose work ethic became the basis of the national character.

Around 1900, however, the situation began to change. Because of immigration from Europe the Roman Catholic Church was suddenly the largest single church in America, with twelve million members. Taken all together, Protestants outnumbered Catholics seven to one, but when they thought of themselves separately, denominationally—as Baptists, Presbyterians, Unitarians, Methodists, and the like—they were outnumbered by Catholics, more of whom arrived each day.

As Catholics settled in New York, Boston, Chicago, San Francisco, New Orleans, and other cities, the emphasis in American religion shifted from village and town to the metropolis. The spectacle of poor, dirty, ill-nourished people making camp on the outskirts of the city—such as the people Dorothy Day saw displaced by the San Francisco earthquake—became a familiar one, the subject of countless cautionary tales told among Protestants. And because so many of those people were Catholics, immigrant Catholics *were* the poor in the Protestant mind, and Protestant leaders, to care for them, devised the "social gospel," which sought to apply the New Testament to modern city life.

Competition between different Protestant churches, then, was overlaid by the competition between Protestants and Catholics, each group a majority that felt like a minority.

At the same time, conventional notions of Catholicism and Protestantism were being upended by the best and the brightest of the Protestant elite, in ways that challenged the standard account of American religious history and the usual understanding of religion generally.

In *The Varieties of Religious Experience* (1902) William James, who had had a religious experience all alone on a mountaintop after a long hike, defined religion as "the feelings, acts, and experiences of individual men in their solitude, so far as they apprehend themselves to stand in relation to whatever they consider the divine." For making the solitary individual the measure of religion, James is generally credited with shifting the study of religion in America away from institutions and toward experience. But his method of jumbling together believers of all sorts was just as important. He assembled his lectures from newspaper clippings about odd religious occurrences, and in his view the familiar distinctions between Protestants and Catholics, poets and saints, self-taught preachers and learned divines, were less telling than those between different religious temperaments: the "sick-souled" and the "healthy-minded," or the "once-born" and the "twice-born."

Meanwhile, James's Harvard colleague Henry Adams was being born again. In France in 1895 Adams, whose chronicle of the history of America ran to nine volumes, had undergone a religious conversion of sorts—not to God or Christ but to a mystical sense of history grounded in the Middle Ages and epitomized by the order and beauty and fixity, the sheer absoluteness, of the great French cathedrals. Declaring himself "head of the Conservative Christian Anarchists, a party numbering one member," Adams wrote two books in which he sought to impress his vision of things upon the reader as boldly as possible. First came *Mont-Saint-Michel and Chartres* (1904), which is not so much a work of history as an imaginative pilgrimage, in which Adams slips into the skin of a French peasant who, in his view, saw and felt and understood life more directly than the stereotypical industrial-age American. Three years later came *The Education of Henry Adams*, Adams's third-person account of himself as a representative American man called Adams—whose problem, as he sees it, is that he is the descendant of pragmatic Enlightenment Protestants rather than of French Catholics, and so grew up with no knowledge of the religious energy that had inspired the cathedral builders of Europe—"the highest energy ever known to man."

Adams turned out to be a more representative man than he could have expected. Over the next twenty years, as *The Education* was read and embraced as a sacred text by the expatriate writers of the Lost Generation, France became, in American writing, a heaven, set in contrast to the hell of capitalist America, and the descent from the age of faith to an era of industry came to be seen as the fall from order to chaos, from civilization to barbarism, from community to an awful alienation.

Thomas Merton was ten years old when he first went back to France, the place of his birth and the setting of his father's paintings. Father and son set out by ship from New York, sailed to London and Calais, went by train to Paris and then to the south of France, the train racing through fields and towns—"over the brown Loire, by a long, long bridge at Orléans," Merton recalled in his autobiography, "and from then on I was home, although I had never seen it before, and shall never see it again."

He was a son of two artists. His parents—Owen Merton from New Zealand, Ruth Jenkins from New York—had met and been married in Paris, and Owen Merton, a landscape painter at a time when the French landscape was on the frontier of art, had gone to the Midi in search of an ideal place to paint. Thomas Merton was born there in 1915, and a brother, John Paul, in 1918. As America entered the world war they all went to New York to stay with Ruth Merton's family. Three years later she entered Bellevue Hospital, with stomach cancer, and she sent her elder son a note from her hospital bed to inform him matter-of-factly that she would never see him again.

Thomas Merton was six years old when his mother died. The next few years were hard ones. His father would go away to paint or to show his work, leaving him and his brother on Long Island with their grandparents. He went to school on and off. He read the Tom Swift books at his grandfather's office in a New York publishing house. He watched W. C. Fields make a movie in a vacant lot. And he prayed, following his father's instructions, asking God "to help him paint, to help him have a successful exhibition, and to find us a place to live."

Then, in the summer of 1925, Owen and Thomas Merton went to France. As they settled one night in a small hotel in an ancient village, "I felt at home. Father threw open the shutters of the room, and looked out on the quiet night, without stars, and said: 'Do you smell the woodsmoke in the air? That is the smell of the Midi.' "

They traveled for several weeks. In *The Seven Storey Mountain* Merton recalls the places they passed through—a bend at the base of a cliff with a castle on top; hayfields running down to the river, crossed by cattle tracks or dirt roads; a gorge with cliffs rising away on both sides, dotted with caves to explore—and describes them with painterly precision, until the point in the story when they reach their destination, the village of St. Antonin, whereupon he reverts to his own language, that of religious experience.

St. Antonin was an ordinary village, encircled by a road where the ancient ramparts had been. The ruined buildings were recognizably medieval, except for the church in the center, which was modern. But it was the plan of the town, not its beauty or its history, that struck Merton most powerfully. He explained, "The church had been fitted into the landscape in such a way as to become the keystone of its intelligibility. . . . The whole landscape, unified by the church and its heavenward spire, seemed to say: this is the meaning of all created things: we have been made for no other purpose than that men may use us in raising themselves to God, in proclaiming the glory of God."

As he writes, twenty years have passed and he is cloistered in the Abbey of Gethsemani, the closest thing to a medieval French village to be found in America. The order and unity of the French village, he believes, are the attributes of the Catholic faith, and their fulfillment is the monastery; the longing he first felt as a boy in France he has satisfied as a Trappist.

There is more to it than that, however. The son of a painter, he describes the village so as to give it the wholeness and harmony and radiance of a landscape painting. He, too, will wind up a painter of landscapes in his way, for in entering a monastery he has sought not just to return to France or the Middle Ages but to enter into the vision he had seen over his father's shoulder in St. Antonin that summer, in which the imperfect world was made perfect in the mind's eye.

The Catholic immigrants who came to America came for good: most of them never returned to the old country. Yet in America, as in Europe, they still clustered by nationality: Irish, German, Italian, Polish, Mexican, *canadien français*. They had their own folkways and old-style devotions, a certain way of kneeling or clasping the hands. Their parish churches went up brick by brick in their neighborhoods: St. Stanislaus for the Poles, St. Philip Neri for the Italians, Our Lady Star of the Sea for the Irish longshoremen. Their processions filled the narrow streets where they were tenemented, the plaster Virgin or patron saint bobbing above a great wave of them during the feast-day parade.

Today those immigrant neighborhoods are romanticized as outposts of the Old World, where community was palpable and the Church was at the center of people's lives. But to the Catholic immigrants—peasants, most of them—those neighborhoods, all gridlike streets and upright tenements, clamorous subways and motorcars, were nothing like the villages where they had once lived, and life in America, for all its promise, was shot through with the sense of what they had left behind. The regional touches in the neighborhoods were secondhand, imitative, brought fully to life only by the memories the immigrants carried around in their heads; and American Catholicism, likewise, was a reconstruction effort, in which religious faith involved remaining faithful to the old country and the old ways, lest they be lost forever.

Thus the Northern cities rose on a bedrock sense of loss, which was covered over with expectation. In the South, meanwhile, the sense of loss was out in the open. The region had been settled—founded—on an ideal of decline and fall, and the Civil War gave this ideal a powerful, biblical warrant. With defeat (the white planters concluded) all was lost: the lives of the young men who had died in the fighting, the free labor of the slaves, the civilization their big houses embodied, their sense of dominion over the territory. Whereas the Northern immigrants recalled a distant homeland, the Southern gentry looked back to a supposedly nobler age.

So it was that even before his father killed himself and his mother drowned, Walker Percy was haunted by loss, beset by the sense that a better time had preceded his, that he was living in the aftermath of his people's story.

The Percys were a self-fashioned great family of the South, and their lineage has fascinated Walker Percy's biographers. They claimed descent from an old Scottish clan. Henry Percy was Shakespeare's model for Harry Hotspur in *Henry IV, Part I*. At the turn of the century LeRoy Percy was elected a U.S. senator from Mississippi.

Percys were melancholy people, and their prominence seems to have compounded their sadness. There was a suicide in nearly every generation. One Percy man dosed himself with laudanum; another leaped into a creek with a sugar kettle tied around his neck. John Walker Percy—Walker Percy's grandfather—went up to the attic in 1917 and shot himself in the head. LeRoy Pratt Percy—Walker Percy's father—committed suicide in 1929 in precisely the same manner.

That branch of the family lived in Birmingham, Alabama, where Walker Percy was born in 1916, the eldest of three boys; but after the suicide Mrs. Percy took her sons to Georgia, where her own family lived. Shortly afterward William Alexander Percy paid them a visit there. His legend preceded him: veteran of the foxholes in the Great War; Harvard-trained lawyer; plantation overseer; poet whose books were published by Alfred A. Knopf in New York; foreign traveler, who was just back from an excursion to the South Seas. "He was the fabled relative, the one you liked to speculate about," Walker Percy recalled. "The fact that he was also a lawyer and a planter didn't cut much ice—after all, the South was full of lawyer-planters. But how many people did you know who were war heroes and wrote books of poetry?"

Will Percy was forty-five years old. His parents, with whom he had lived for some years (he was a confirmed bachelor), had died the previous year, and their big house in Greenville, Mississippi, was empty. He invited Mrs. Percy and her sons to live with him there, and they accepted the invitation.

Three years later Mrs. Percy died in a car accident, driving off the road and into a creek, where she drowned. Walker Percy, now nearly sixteen, was riding in a car not far behind; he leaped out, but bystanders kept him from seeing the accident site firsthand. He and his brothers were now orphans—their mother's accident was a suicide, some said—and William Alexander Percy adopted them.

"Uncle Will" Percy lived up to his legend. He was a tireless pedagogue, expatiating on the novels of Walter Scott and the symphonies of Beethoven. He stood up for "his" Negroes in town in the paternalistic way of the time. In life and poetry alike he was a moralist and self-styled exemplary man, asking those around him, "What do you love? What do you live by?"

He exhorted his adoptive sons to model their conduct on his, and they did so, the eldest son in particular. When he arrived in Greenville (he later claimed) Walker Percy was "a youth whose only talent was a knack for looking and listening, for tuning in and soaking up"; Uncle Will, he said, gave him "a vocation and in a real sense a second self," inspiring him to become a writer.

But Will Percy was not an exemplar for Walker Percy simply because he was a writer. He was also an exemplar of the Percy melancholia. No less than Percy's natural father, he was wracked with a sense of loss; for all his learning, his wide experience of the world, his love of art, his principles and philosophy, the man who paced the parlor of the house in Greenville and recited poetry while a symphony played on the phonograph was no happier than the man who had gone up to the attic in Birmingham one Tuesday afternoon and put a gun to his head.

In the family plot in the cemetery in the center of Greenville there stood a life-size statue of a square-jawed man clad as a medieval knight, in cape and chain mail, hands crossed over a sword. It was a likeness of William Alexander Percy's father, which Will Percy had commissioned as a burial monument, a monument to his ideals and the loss of them.

Some years later, the nature of Will's ideals—and of the loss of them—became clear to the Percy boys, Walker especially. As a boy, it turned out, Will had had a religious conversion. Although he was raised an Episcopalian, his mother had been a Catholic, and she saw to it that he was tutored by nuns and a priest. When he was ten years old, the Catholic faith overwhelmed him in a violent attack like the ones described in the lives of the saints. All of a sudden he was praying mightily, fasting "on the sly," confessing the slightest of sins, and imagining that he was a monk in a cave in a desert. "I wanted so intensely to believe, to believe in God and miracles and the sacraments and the Church and everything. Also, I wanted to be completely and utterly a saint; heaven and hell didn't matter, but perfection did."

Five years later he still wanted to be a priest, but he was sent away to college at the University of the South, as Percy tradition dictated. The school, set atop a mountain in Tennessee, had an Episcopal chapel on the grounds, but one Sunday morning a month Will would mount a horse and ride the ten miles down the mountain to go to Mass at a Catholic church in the valley.

During his sophomore year the news came that his youngest brother had been shot. It was an accident: hunting with a friend, the boy was wounded in the stomach; he died a week later.

One Sunday—before or after, he did not say—Will rode down the mountain to Mass as usual, but when he reached the church he found that his faith was gone. As he rose to go to confession, he recalled, "I knew there was no use going, no priest could absolve me, no church could direct my life or my judgment. . . . It was over, and forever."

Truly, his life was just beginning, but in him the family legacy of nobility and loss had already catalyzed into a tragic worldview. As time went on, he lived a distinctive life—as a bachelor who was also a father, a pillar of the community who was also an artist, an exemplary man who was also (Walker Percy said) "unique" and "one of a kind."

In William Alexander Percy the double aspect of the family legacy was apparent in all its complexity. Looking and listening, aspiring and imitating. Walker Percy evidently glimpsed early on what his own calling would be, although half his life would pass before he fully grasped it and put it into words. He was called at once to uphold the family history and to defy it, at once to emulate it and to diagnose it—to find the way of being a Percy that was distinctly his, so as to break the pattern of melancholy, loss, and violence against the self that ran down the generations.

"When I was five," Flannery O'Connor recalled, "I had an experience that marked me for life. The Pathé News sent a photographer from New York to Savannah to take a picture of a chicken of mine.

"This chicken, a buff Cochin Bantam, had the distinction of being able to walk either forward or backward. Her fame had spread through the press, and by the time she reached the attention of Pathé News, I suppose there was nowhere left for her to go—forward or backward. Shortly after that she died, as now seems fitting."

Compared to an earthquake or a parent's suicide, a chicken's fleeting fame seems hardly revelatory. But this story is the most personal story O'Connor ever told, and, along with the Pathé short, it is the most vivid picture there is of her earliest years.

She was born in 1925 and grew up an only child, adored and precocious, called Mary Flannery. As Catholics, her family were exceptional in Georgia, where Catholics made up only a fraction of the population. As prosperous people, they were exceptional among the Catholics. A relative in Savannah owned the townhouse they lived in there, catty-corner from the Cathedral of St. John the Baptist, and had staked her father in the real-estate business. Her mother's family, the Clines, lived in a grand house in Milledgeville, a morning's drive north, and Mary Flannery went to visit them in the summers, playing between the tall whitewashed columns on the porch steps. Her uncle Bernard had a medical practice in Atlanta but spent weekends in Milledgeville, at a dairy farm on the edge of town.

As Southerners, moreover, they were exceptional in the eyes of people from the North, such as the Pathé cameraman from New York. Mary Flannery O'Connor hadn't asked him to come, but he came into their yard and stuck his camera into her life and gave her the idea that she was up to something out of the ordinary.

The newsreel short was shown in movie houses not long afterward. It opens with the title UNIQUE CHICKEN GOES IN REVERSE. A girl in a black coat and skullcap—a city girl—comes along cradling a chicken in her hands. She sets it down and watches it with eyes full of concentration as it begins to walk, forward and then back. "Odd fowl goes backward to go forward so she can look back to see where she went," says the caption. Then the camera withdraws and the film is suddenly reversed, so the geese and cows walk backward, too.

The episode lasts less than a minute. Yet Mary Flannery O'Connor had been changed by it. She perceived that she had an unusual gift, even if it was just a gift for getting a certain kind of chicken to walk a certain way; and she saw that her challenge in life would be to make the nature of her gift clear to people who wouldn't understand it otherwise.

She began to collect chickens, to give them striking names, to dress them in little outfits she sewed for them. "What had been only a mild interest became a passion, a quest. I favored those with one green eye and one orange one or with overlong necks and crooked combs but nothing in that line turned up. I pondered over the picture in Robert Ripley's book, *Believe It or Not*, of a rooster that had survived thirty days without his head."

She was drawn to what she would call "mystery and the unexpected." It was a mystery why the chicken could walk either forward or backward, not just forward as it was expected to do. The chicken was a freak, a grotesque, and when a cameraman came all the way from New York to Savannah to photograph her just because she had trained it, she was suddenly a kind of freak, too.

When she told the story in an essay thirty years later, she had devoted her life to the aesthetic contemplation of the grotesque.

The grotesque character or freak plays various roles in her work, serving a broad range of dramatic purposes. The freak is an image of human nature deformed by sin, as is the Misfit in "A Good Man Is Hard to Find," or an instance of human nature transformed by God's grace, as Hazel Motes is at the end of *Wise Blood*. The freak is a figure for modern man, like the psychologist Rayber in *The Violent Bear It Away*, reduced by the scientific worldview to an aggregate of tendencies and statistics; or a character deliberately distorted by the author, like the tattooed O. E. Parker in "Parker's Back," so as to startle the unwitting reader to attention.

Finally, the freak stands in for the author. She explained, "It is the way of drama that with one stroke the writer has both to mirror and to judge. When such a writer has a freak for his hero, he is not simply showing us what we are, but what we have been and could become. His prophet-freak is an image of himself."

Solitary, strange, physically weakened, often misunderstood, and yet sustained by a belief, so strong as to be religious, that she was exceptionally gifted, Flannery O'Connor was so unique as to seem to others a kind of freak; and her girlhood encounter with the Pathé cameraman from New York was her conversion to the grotesque and the freakish, the moment in which she came to firsthand experience of the phenomenon she would write about.

From San Francisco the Days moved to Chicago, settling on the South Side and then on Webster Avenue, near Lincoln Park. Dorothy Day did well in high school and won a scholarship to the state university in Urbana, a hundred miles downstate. She had a severe beauty: a jutting chin and cheekbones, big deep-socketed eyes. She had gone ahead and gotten baptized in the Episcopal church in the neighborhood. After school, as she pushed her new baby brother in a carriage toward the park and Lake Michigan, she would hum psalms she'd heard in church to express the joy in life she felt.

Yet she was restless, hungry for the direct experience of life, in, say, a great event like the Russian Revolution, which she had written a term paper about. "Maybe if I stayed away from books more this restlessness would pass," she told a friend. "I am reading Dostoevski and last night I stayed up late and this morning I had to get up early and I feel that my soul is like lead."

Her father, apparently threatened by her independence, forbade the Day children to leave the house alone. So Dorothy would sit in the room called the library and read, day and night: Dostoevsky, Jack London, Frank Norris, Upton Sinclair, the "revolutionist" Peter Kropotkin, *The Imitation of Christ.*

Sinclair's *The Jungle* was set in the slums of Chicago's West Side, and the setting struck her powerfully. Now when she went out to push her brother in his carriage she walked west, right into the world of the novel. She was startled to find that life itself was just as Sinclair had described it. Passing taverns, she imagined scenes from the book taking place inside, and she felt joined to the people whose fictional counterparts she had read about.

"Though my only experience of the destitute was in books," she recalled in her autobiography, "the very fact that *The Jungle* was about Chicago where I lived, whose streets I walked, made me feel that from then on my life was to be linked to theirs, their interests were to be mine: I had received a call, a vocation, a direction in my life."

In September 1914 she left Chicago for college. In Urbana, she made friends with a professor who was a Methodist and passed time with his family, talking about faith. She joined the Socialist Party, but found the meetings boring. She fasted for three days, eating nothing but peanuts, in order to write a personal essay about the experience of hunger.

She was homesick. Alone, missing the baby brother she had helped to raise, she read her way out of her loneliness. "I read everything of Dostoevski," she recalled, "as well as the stories of Gorki and Tolstoi." Fiction became a home away from home, vivid and full of companionship. It comforted her better than religion could, for even as novels gave solace they cried out against injustice.

In 1914 Tolstoy and Dostoevsky were the great novelists of the age just past. Tolstoy had died only in 1910, and in his later years he had become a figure of legend: a man who had renounced novels to write religious parables, who had left his large family and vast estate to wander the country like the archetypal Russian in *The Way of a Pilgrim*—a man "alien to all," Gorky recalled, "a solitary traveler through all the deserts of thought, in search of an all-embracing truth which he has not yet found." Tolstoy called himself a Christian anarchist, but his pacifist, celibate, literal acting out of the Gospel led people to mock him as a "Tolstoyan," and his late works were read not as art but as imaginative statements of the ideals he was striving toward.

Dostoevsky had the opposite reputation. Though he had died in 1881, a generation passed before his books were translated into English. He was thought to have been like one of his hapless characters, a drunkard, gambler, debtor, epileptic, fanatic, ex-convict, and all-around unfortunate man. The events of his life were like real-life parables—the lifting of his death sentence while he stood before a firing squad, his conversion to Christianity in a prison in Siberia—and the religious torments he wrote about had the electric charge of the real thing, of experience that had been thrust upon him against his wishes.

Together Tolstoy and Dostoevsky were the two halves of the Slavic soul: the debased man whose suffering united him to all humanity and made him holy, the highborn man who sought out suffering as a means of enlightenment. Each had struggled with God and put the story into his books, urging his readers to carry on the struggle in their own lives.

Day read them and accepted their challenge. Yet the religious ardor of Russian fiction could not be reconciled with the docile Christianity of Urbana, Illinois, a place as yet untouched by modernism or the Great War. "Both Dostoevski and Tolstoi made me cling to a faith in God, and yet I could not endure feeling an alien in it. I felt that my faith had nothing in common with that of the Christians around me . . . and the ugliness of life in a world which professed itself to be Christian appalled me."

She was eighteen years old. Like a Dostoevsky character, she cursed God, and decided that religion was a crutch for the weak, an opiate of the people.

Her family had left Chicago to return to New York, and she quit school and followed them. New York, full of immigrants, was also the American city where socialism was thriving. There, she would live the life the great Russian novelists had written about.

The next years might have come straight out of *The Possessed*, Dostoevsky's novel about the "cells" of radicals in czarist Russia.

"During that time I felt the spell of the long loneliness descend upon me," Day later wrote. Mornings she would set out on the streets of lower Manhattan, looking for a job with one of the socialist papers. There were no jobs to be found. "In all that great city of seven millions, I found no friends; I had no work; I was separated from my fellows. Silence in the midst of city noises oppressed me. My own silence, the feeling that I had no one to talk to overwhelmed me so that my very throat was constricted; my heart was heavy with unuttered thoughts; I wanted to weep my loneliness away."

In time she got a job with *The Call* and started to write. As she walked the streets, notebook in hand, amid the smells of dirty laundry and rotten food and garbage—"the smell of the grave," she called it—she realized that she didn't want to report on poverty: she wanted to live it firsthand, as the poor did.

She was still reading the Russian novelists, and was "moved to the depths of my being," especially by Dostoevsky. "I read all of Dostoevsky's novels and it was, as Berdyaev says, a profound spiritual experience," she recalled. "The scene in *Crime and Punishment* where the young prostitute reads from the New Testament to Raskolnikov, sensing sin more profound than her own, which weighed upon him; that story 'The Honest Thief'; those passages in *The Brothers Karamazov*; Mitya's conversion in jail, the very legend of the Grand Inquisitor, all this helped to lead me on."

She studied the anarchism of Emma Goldman. She interviewed Leon Trotsky. She went to Webster Hall for the Anarchists Ball and to Madison Square Garden to celebrate the 1917 revolt in Russia, and was caught up in the "mystic gripping melody of struggle, a cry for world peace and human brotherhood" in the midst of senseless world war.

But her comrades said she would never be a good Communist, because she was too religious—a character out of Dostoevsky, a woman haunted by God.

She had gotten a job with *The Masses*, a stylish socialist magazine, but it was shut down by the government. At loose ends, she went to Washington to take part in a rally for women's suffrage. With several dozen others, she was arrested and sentenced to thirty days on a disorderly conduct charge. She was startled by what she saw. The women were kept fifteen to a cell; they rioted, and were locked up in pairs. They went on a hunger strike: twice a day for six days toast and milk were brought, and they refused to eat. They yearned to be let go. There was nothing to do, nothing to read or write with. On the floor, hungry and exhausted, Day and her cellmate passed the time by discussing Joseph Conrad's novels.

"It was one thing to be writing about these things," she recalled, "to have the theoretical knowledge of sweatshops and injustice and hunger, but it was quite another to experience it in one's own flesh."

Now she knew suffering firsthand, as the poor did, and what was more, she knew what it was to feel, as they did, that it was her own fault, a consequence of her own rebellious nature. "I was a petty creature," she told herself, "filled with self-deception, self-importance, unreal, false, and so, rightly scorned and punished."

Brought low, she asked for a Bible, the way Dostoevsky, seventy years earlier, in a prison in Siberia, had asked a guard for a Bible, which he read over and over again until he was a believer.

Three days later a Bible was given to her. She read and read. The ancient words spoke to her, a voice from her childhood, familiar and comforting. "Turn again our captivity, O Lord, as a stream in the south. They that sow in tears shall reap in joy": as she pondered that biblical verse she applied it to the suffragists' plight, and decided that "if we had faith in what we were doing, making our protest against brutality and injustice, then we were indeed casting our seeds, and there was promise of the harvest to come."

She was freed after two weeks. She had been changed—radically changed. Dostoevsky's novels had so taken root in her that she had begun to follow their pattern, to conform her life to the lives he described. But she was not a character out of Dostoevsky, a prisoner of her nature. By nature she was a Tolstoyan, ardent for suffering, free to choose it, and the desolation of jail was an experience that she, inspired by fiction, had actively sought.

Shortly before the Percy brothers moved to Greenville Uncle Will had taken another boy aside at a local country club and asked him to make friends with "some kinsmen of mine."

Shelby Foote was an only child, and his father had died of septicemia (a bacterial infection) a few years earlier. He was thirteen years old, a few months younger than Walker Percy. The house where he lived with his mother and an aunt was not far from Will Percy's house, and during the next few years he all but lived with the Percys, joining the odd family as a kind of fourth brother. He became closer to Walker Percy than Percy's blood brothers were: a best friend, a boon companion, a scold, a rival. And he introduced Percy to modern literature, beginning a conversation about books that would last the rest of their lives.

Percy was already being raised on books by his Uncle Will. He wrote poems "in the manner of" Poe and Blake for his classes, articles for the Greenville High School paper, and the paper's gossip column as well. One piece was about "Africa—Land of Race Problems," another about a soup kitchen in the black section of Greenville, where he found "an ill-sorted array of our darker citizens in a straggling sort of line receiving food." But in those years Foote, more than Percy, was the aspiring writer; and whereas Percy (like his Uncle Will) read the classics, Foote favored modern literature.

In their senior year of high school Percy read *The Brothers Karamazov*.

Perhaps Foote recommended it; perhaps he came to it on his own. In any case, he read the novel straight through over three or four days on the big porch of the house in Greenville, hardly putting it aside to live his own life. His father had killed himself, and here was a book about four brothers who wanted to kill their father; his mother had died in a car crash, and here was a book about the question of whether there can be a God in a world in which innocent people suffer.

A few years later Foote gave his own copy of *The Brothers Karamazov* to Percy at Christmastime, putting an inscription on the flyleaf. The inscribed book suggests the role literature would play in their friendship. For the next fifty years they would have what Percy called "long Dostoevskian conversations" about writing and writers, especially Dostoevsky. Foote would read *The Brothers Karamazov* six times more, exclaiming over it each time; Percy would think of it as the book that had opened the most possibilities for him, for it showed how a novelist could write in response to ideas, combining literature and philosophy.

The book, and the conversations it inspired, also suggested Percy's developing conviction about reading and writing. For him literature would not be a private affair, but the stuff of influence and exchange and dialogue, which the books themselves called forth. The literary life would consist of friendship, and of spirited disagreements over books and their implications.

A photograph taken of the two friends in Greenville suggests the bond that formed between them. Percy is draped over a garden chair—gangly, his hair slicked back, wearing a V-neck sweater and a sports jacket and saddle shoes and dandyish striped socks. Foote, darkly handsome, is next to him, stretched out on a chaise longue. Percy's younger brother Phinizy is to their left, with them and yet, it seems, outside their conversation.

All the while, Percy's biographers report, he was growing expert in science, chemistry in particular. As college approached he had to decide which field to study in greater depth. After reading *The Brothers Karamazov*, he recalled, he was drawn to literature, "but I abandoned it then for science (like Ivan in the book)." A trip to the World's Fair in Chicago—which, Percy later recalled, put forward a "technological vision" of "future happiness"—seemed to confirm his choice. For the next twenty years, like Ivan Karamazov, Percy would see science and art as in opposition in his own life, presenting competing notions of truth and of the meaning of life. At the time, he explained later on, science seemed to have the better answers: clear, logical, verifiable, true at all times and places. But it may be that he chose science, and eventually medicine, for a deeply personal reason as well. There were no scientists or doctors in the Percy lineage. His Uncle Will was a writer. So was his best friend. The two of them were tireless pedagogues, and they doubtless offered as much advice and counsel as Percy could bear. In abandoning literature for science, perhaps he sought to escape their influence — to find a way of life in which, like Ivan Karamazov, he could draw conclusions in light of his own experience, not somebody else's.

Owen Merton, settling in St. Antonin, decided to build a house there; and just as the layout of the village, with its suggestion of a prior order and splendor, had come to define the place, and the Catholic world, in Thomas Merton's mind's eye, so the house came to characterize his life with his father.

Owen bought some land at the foot of a hill called Calvaire, or Calvary. At the top there was an old stone chapel, and the path up was marked with the Stations of the Cross.

Diviners tested for springs on the property. Workmen dug a well. Meanwhile father and son visited the neighboring villages, looking at churches and abbeys as models for their own design. At night, in their rented rooms, Merton would turn the pages of a picture book about France and gaze at the photographs of old churches in it: St. Denis, Chartres, the abbey at Cluny, a Carthusian hermitage clinging to a hillside.

His father sketched a simple dwelling, light, low, square, stone, and surrounded by a garden. "It would have one big room," Merton recalled, "which would be a studio and dining room and living room, and upstairs there would be a couple of bedrooms. That was all."

One day they went to a wedding in the village, followed by a feast in an old barn. At dusk some townsmen led them out behind the barn. There in a pasture was another abandoned chapel. Its stone walls glowed in the waning light. They stood admiring it. "I wonder what it had been: a shrine, a hermitage perhaps? But now, in any case, it was in ruins. And it had a beautiful thirteenth- or fourteenth-century window, empty of course of its glass."

Owen Merton decided to buy the chapel then and there and have it transported to his own land. Out of its ruins they would build their house. Its stones would surround them. Its Gothic arch would loom overhead. Through its window father and son would look out.

In St. Antonin, Merton tasted the direct experience of life. There, he was the hero of the adventure story that was his boyhood. The past was his playground. Life with Father was life itself. And as the house went up, he was a visitor no longer, but a villager like everyone else, a French boy who had found where he belonged. "Sometimes I think I don't know anything except the years 1926–27–28 in France," he wrote in his journal some years later, "as if they were my whole life, as if Father had made that whole world and given it to me instead of America, shared it with me."

St. Antonin, in Merton's writing, is a kind of paradise, and he will spend his adult life trying to recapture the directness and immediacy of experience he had known there. No matter how strenuous his self-denial, his imitation of Christ and the saints, he will never want to be anybody but Thomas Merton, French-born son of a landscape painter. For him the vital religious questions will always be variants of the question: Who am I, and who am I meant to be? In this sense he is a representative, even a typical, modern person, whose strong sense of self is constantly met by the sense that the self and its pre-occupations are unworthy or illusory. His answers will always involve a pledge to devote himself to an ideal way of life, and this way of life will be bound up with an ideal setting: a space, a place, a destination, a habitation. If only he can find the place where he is meant to be, he will tell himself, he will become the person he is called to be—will fulfill his God-given nature.

He will be a mystic of places and spaces. Churches and chapels and monasteries and hermitages will be expressions of his ever-changing religious ideals. In the spirit of a long mystical tradition, he will make them symbols of what mystics call "the interior life." He will write about the soul as a work of sacred architecture, elaborately figured and consecrated; he will write about the religious life as a work in progress, like a cathedral that stands unfinished for a hundred years. Out of poems and essays and auto-biography he will make a religious compound, to which readers can come as if on a pilgrimage, a new place made of remnants of the Catholic past.

The house in St. Antonin was left unfinished. Father and son left for London to attend a show of Owen Merton's landscapes, and never returned. It was a loss Merton felt the rest of his life. "It is sad, too, that we never lived in the house that Father built," he wrote in his autobiography, the book in which he began to complete the structure he and his father had designed. "But never mind! The grace of those days has not been altogether lost, not by any means."

The United States, by then, was in some ways as Catholic as France. In the decades after 1900 the American Catholic population had grown to twenty million, almost a fifth of the U.S. population.

Writers looking for the American past now looked to the Catholic past. D. H. Lawrence interpreted the work of Hawthorne, Melville, and the like as a "complex escape" from the Old World, a search for "something grimmer" than the "new liberty" of enlightened Europe. William Carlos Williams, in *In the American Grain*, related the legend of Père Sebastian Rasles, a French Jesuit missionary whose death, in Williams's telling, spelled the death of the Catholic claim on America—and the death of American Protestantism as well, for without an established church to oppose, Puritanism had grown fatally narrow and self-righteous.

Meanwhile, with American Catholics ever more numerous and more various, the leaders of the church in the United States sought, through various stratagems, to unify them.

The Baltimore Catechism—its very name fragrant with Americanness—instilled the habit of imitation. "Q. Why did God make you? A. God made me to know Him, to love Him, and to serve Him in this world and to be happy with Him forever in the next"—the catechism's question-and-answer presentation of the tenets of the faith oriented Catholic education, and Catholic life generally, around the ritual echo of authority, the adoption of someone else's questions and answers as one's own.

The parochial school system applied the pattern of imitation on a vast scale. By schooling them together, the system gave Catholic children of many nations a common store of knowledge, as well as a common language, English. And by keeping them separate from Protestants the schools made separateness a source of unity and pride, instilling in young Catholics the belief that their way of life was separate from, and superior to, the Protestant one.

The system became so pervasive that it is taken for granted. But its stress on separateness actually was a departure from the usual theological notions of Catholicism and Protestantism. In Europe, where the Catholic Church was present as early as the fourth century, the impulse to separate oneself, to stand apart, was associated with Protestants, and since the time of the Reformation the Catholic Church had seen separatism as the egregious sin of Protestantism, condemning the Protestant churches as wayward children who had spitefully broken off relations.

Now, in North America, it was the Catholics who stood apart. Even as they made their way in society, as shopkeepers and laborers, police officers and politicians, they were taught to cherish separateness as a virtue, the worldly expression of the virtue of purity sought in convents and monasteries.

Separate in their minds and hearts if not in actual worldly fact, Catholics achieved a degree of unity that would have been inconceivable in Europe. It was a unity grounded in a biblical sense of themselves as a chosen people, a people set apart.

As it happened, however, the sense of apartness, the conviction of chosenness, was the defining trait of *all* the religious peoples who went their way outside the American Protestant mainstream: of black Christians, of Jewish immigrants, of Shakers and Quakers, and, after the *Scopes* trial of 1925, of the Protestant fundamentalists of the Deep South.

By the time Mary Flannery O'Connor made her First Holy Communion, then, the Catholic child in America was being raised on a paradox. She belonged to the oldest, biggest, vastest church of them all. Yet she believed that her belonging made her unique. And her sense of uniqueness was a trait she shared, whether she realized it or not, with the believers who were least like herself.

She was six years old when she started at St. Vincent's Grammar School, also on Liberty Square in Savannah, seven when she made her First Communion at the cathedral next door.

Like most Catholic children, she was photographed on First Communion Day, and with her white-lace-trimmed dress, her hair swagged to the side, she looks like a typical Catholic girl of the time, but there is already an alien fierceness in her stare.

If she found the occasion remarkable she never said so in writing. "Stories of pious children tend to be false," she declared later on, and in her work she would steer clear of Catholic girlhood and its rituals and appurtenances, as if she had foreseen all the awful memoirs that would issue from other writers and taken a vow to write no such thing.

The one exception is the short story "A Temple of the Holy Ghost." This story, in which a child comes to grasp the significance of the Eucharist, is not overtly autobiographical, but the child in it, alone among the children in O'Connor's fiction, is a Catholic child, and the quandary the child in the story fights with, the deadly sin the story is meant to dramatize, is the one the author herself would spend all her life fighting.

The girl is an only child, bright and strong-minded. One weekend her two second cousins come from Mayville to stay at her house. They are "practically morons," in the child's estimation. Their names are Joanne and Suzanne, but they call themselves Temple One and Temple Two because a sister at the convent school where they board, seeing them go, has told each of them not to forget that she is a Temple of the Holy Ghost. This means they are to behave themselves with boys.

Joanne and Suzanne want to meet boys, but there are no boys around. As the girls change out of their brown convent-school uniforms the child has a brainstorm: What about the Wilkins boys? The Wilkins boys have a car, and " 'somebody said they were both going to be Church of God preachers because you don't have to know nothing to be one.' "

The boys come that evening to escort the girls to the fair. They bring a guitar and a harmonica, and as the girls sit on a swing and the child spies on them from behind some bushes, the boys serenade the girls with a song that sounds "half like a love song and half like a hymn." It is "The Old Rugged Cross."

The girls take a turn, singing in Latin, in "convent-trained voices," long and slow. Wendell Wilkins says that it must be "Jew singing." What a moron! the child thinks. It is the Tantum Ergo—the hymn sung during the Mass as the priest holds the Eucharist aloft for the people to adore. Everybody knows that.

Then, as the others set out for the fair, the child, left behind, begins to brood. Here the story turns inward, and the narrator's voice becomes tender and confidential, as though the reader is all alone with the child:

She went upstairs and paced the long bedroom with her hands locked together behind her back and her head thrust forward and an expression, fierce and dreamy both, on her face. She didn't turn on the electric light but let the darkness collect and make the room smaller and more private.

At regular intervals a light crossed the open window and threw shadows on the wall. She stopped and stood looking out over the dark slopes, past where the pond glinted silver, past the wall of woods to the speckled sky where a long finger of light was revolving up and around and away, searching the air as if it were hunting for the lost sun. It was the beacon light from the fair.

She could hear the distant sound of the calliope and she saw in her head all the tents raised up in a kind of gold sawdust light.

The child has been to the fair before, and now, seeing it in her mind's eye, she longs to be there, among the "faded looking pictures on the canvas of people in tights, with stiff stretched composed faces like the faces of the martyrs"—and now, in a way at once proud and pious, she longs to be a saint or a martyr herself. Sainthood is out, she reflects, because "she was a born liar and slothful and she sassed her mother" and "was eaten up with the sin of Pride, the worst one"—but she thinks "she could be a martyr if they killed her quick." She imagines herself in the Roman arena among the lions; she tries to pray, and finds herself thanking God that she doesn't belong to the Church of God.

The girls wake her with their laughter. At the fair, they have seen a fat man and a midget and a freak who strode from one side of the stage to the other, saying, "God made me thisaway and if you laugh He may strike you the same way. This is the way He wanted me to be and I ain't disputing His way. I'm showing you because I got to make the best of it."

The child, precocious though she is, doesn't understand, so the girls explain. The freak is a male and a female at once. They have seen it with their own eyes.

The child tries to sleep; and as she drifts off she can see the people gathered in the tent, dressed as for church, and hears the freak declaring each of them is a Temple of the Holy Ghost.

The fairgrounds like a Roman arena; the tent crowded as at a revival meeting; the freak testifying to God's ways—the fair is akin to a religious ritual. But religious how? That is always the question in O'Connor's work; and in its last few pages, the story comes to define religion in the South, grounded in the side-by-side lives of Catholics and Protestants and their odd likenesses in the mind of a child.

The next day, when the girls go back to the convent, the child tags along. The rite of Benediction is under way in the chapel when they arrive—the priest kneeling before the gold monstrance in which the Eucharist is exposed, the nuns in their habits singing the Tantum Ergo. The child goes in and kneels down, sensing that she is in the presence of God, and prays: "Hep me not to be so mean. Hep me not to give her so much sass. Hep me not to talk like I do." And as the Eucharist is upraised, in her imagination she sees the man at the fair and hears him say: "This is the way He wanted me to be."

She has had the meaning of the Eucharist dramatized for her, and has grasped a tenet of her faith for herself as though for the first time.

The theology behind this revelation is complex, but the Baltimore Catechism would have made it familiar to the child. The Eucharist is the Body of Christ, and it represents Christ's taking on of a frail human body and taking on of human suffering on the cross, reminding the child of the hermaphrodite, whose sufferings reduce her pride to piety. And the Eucharist reminds her of her apartness. Although many Protestant churches of the time celebrated a Eucharist of some kind, only Catholics believed Christ was actually present in the consecrated Communion wafer through a sacrifice whereby God became present to them in the Body of Christ so that they might know him directly by taking him into themselves.

There is more to the story, as if O'Connor grasped that someday it would be Catholicism, and not the freakish varieties of human nature, that would need explaining.

When the child leaves the convent, the story goes on, she has the meaning of the episode literally impressed upon her: "The big nun swooped down on her mischievously and nearly smothered her in the black habit, mashing the side of her face into the crucifix hitched onto her belt and then holding her off and looking at her with little periwinkle eyes."

During the drive home the child becomes "lost in thought." As she watches night fall outside the car window she sees the sun — "a huge red ball like an elevated Host drenched in blood" — streaking the sky red like a road in a hillbilly song. It is an image of God, and of the way to God, and an image of Protestantism and Catholicism reconciled on the horizon — but the image of the sun eucharistically looming over all, above and apart, suggests the pride the Catholic child is prone to, the deadliest sin of all.

"When I came back from Washington I worked wherever I could," Day recalled, "living in one furnished room after another, moving from the lower East Side to the upper East Side and then down again to the lower West Side. It was a bitterly cold winter and the rooms I lived in were never adequately heated. We were still at war, and it was the time of heatless Mondays and meatless Tuesdays. There were times when it was pleasanter to spend the night with friends rather than face an ugly sordid room."

She was living what she called a "wavering life." It lasted only a few months — the winter of 1918 — but became crucial to the story later told about her. For that winter was the time she spent in the company of other striving young writers, and in Malcolm Cowley's *Exile's Return*, which would become the definitive memoir of the so-called Lost Generation, she was singled out as one of the wildest of the wild.

Her biographers usually consult Cowley's book just long enough to quote his remark about her as a girl "the gangsters admired" at the saloon because "she could drink them under the table." But his book offers as much insight into her wavering life as her own memoirs do.

The way he tells it, everybody in the Village was caught between contradictory ideals of how to live. They were parochial Greenwich Villagers yet insisted they were "citizens of the world." They pronounced themselves exiles from bourgeois society but yearned to speak for America. They were incurable city people who romanticized rural country life. They were populists, confident in the will of the people, yet fancied themselves an avant-garde.

Those ideals could not be reconciled, and when the war came, says Cowley, "people were suddenly forced to decide what kind of rebels they were"; and for Day the ensuing "war in bohemia" became a war in her own character, a war between a life of experience for its own sake and a life of the experience undertaken for the benefit of others.

She had spent the previous summer in the company of Mike Gold: socialist, journalist, sometime editor at *The Call*, and author, later on, of a novel called *Jews Without Money*. Together they roamed the shores of lower Manhattan and the beaches of Staten Island. They sat up all night in a coffee shop near City Hall talking about how to change the world. They befriended homeless men and brought them to his apartment, allowing them to sleep over. Once when she was sick he snuck into her boardinghouse (men were not allowed) with medicine and hot whiskey and spent the night tending to her at her bedside. They read Tolstoy together and agreed that the answer to her "religious instinct" was Tolstoyan religion, a "Christianity that dispensed with churches or a priesthood."

She was working for another socialist magazine, called *The Liberator*, but the thrill was gone. She rented an apartment on Macdougal Street, above the Provincetown Playhouse, and began to spend her evenings with the theater crowd, especially Eugene O'Neill, the playwright in residence, who was on the cusp of fame and on the rebound from a broken love affair. For a while they spent every evening together. Their place of rendezvous was a saloon on Sixth Avenue named the Golden Swan, which had a room in the back known as the Hell Hole. They would drink with friends till dawn, and then she would walk him to his apartment around the corner. By then he would be dead drunk and shivering with cold. Sometimes she would follow him in and warm him with her body, she recalled, holding him in her arms until he fell asleep, whereupon she would go home.

O'Neill was a lapsed Catholic, and Day thought of him as an Irish Ivan

Karamazov, who had rebelled against God and religion altogether. "If ever a man was haunted by death it was Gene," she later wrote. "Was it Gene himself or some friend of his who told me how he used to swim far out to sea when he lived at Provincetown and how he played with the idea of death in those deep waters in the ocean from which all life springs? But he never would have taken his life because he felt too keenly his own genius, his own vocation, his capacities as a writer to explore and bring to light those tragic deeps of life, the terror of man's fate."

The Hell Hole was a place to escape from the fate of mankind and the cares of life. There was talk of Marxism, but for Day the revolution had lost its spark, for there was no real solidarity between the immigrant poor, who drank to banish the misery of their oppression, and the show people from the Playhouse, who drank to fill the hole left in their lives when the theater was dark. Alcohol brought on a phony camaraderie, an illusion of human brotherhood: the time she brought a couple of homeless men to the saloon for a nightcap, the bartender shooed them out.

Yet in that setting O'Neill brought her to a "consciousness of God." Once they were good and drunk he would start reciting poetry, and Day was struck especially by his rendition of "The Hound of Heaven," by the Catholic convert Francis Thompson. The poem today is an especially dated piece of Victoriana, but its conceit still charms—that God snaps like a hound at the heels of the would-be believer, who will be able to outrun the hound of heaven only so long. "It is one of those poems that awaken the soul, recalls to it the fact that God is its destiny," Day explained later on.

O'Neill knew the poem by heart, all 182 lines of it. "I fled him, down the nights and down the days / I fled him, down the arches of the years," he declaimed. "I fled him, down the labyrinthine ways / Of my own mind; and in the midst of tears / I hid from him"—and it was as though the poem were speaking to her directly.

So it was that at dawn, going home, she found herself stopping at St. Joseph's Church on Sixth Avenue, not far from the Hell Hole, thinking it inevitable that "sooner or later I would have to pause in the mad rush of living and remember my first beginning and my last end."

The first Mass in those days was penitentially early—5 a.m.—and yet there were the working people of the neighborhood hastening toward the church. They clambered up the steps and past the big wooden doors. She did likewise: "What were they finding there? I seemed to feel the faith of those about me and I longed for their faith."

She knelt in a pew near the back and collected her thoughts. She was twenty-one years old. All her life she had been haunted by God. God was behind her. God loomed before her. Now she felt hounded toward Him, as though toward home; now she longed for an end to the wavering life in which she was caught.

St. Joseph's is the oldest Catholic church in Manhattan, low and square, with fieldstone walls, high white pillars, and a portico topped by a cross that stands out starkly against the sky. It is a kind of house blend of old and new, of city and country, of Catholic Europe and leatherstocking America.

Day will come to this church again and again in the next few years. Finally she will come to stay. She is a generation ahead of Merton and Percy and O'Connor, and strides out ahead of them, the eldest and the most precocious, but what she will seek in the Church, and find in the Church, is what each of them will seek and find there: a place of pilgrimage, a home and a destination, where city and world meet, where the self encounters the other, where personal experience and the testimony of the ages can be reconciled.

For the time being, she began to pray. "Perhaps I asked even then, 'God, be merciful to me, a sinner.' " Perhaps she told herself, kneeling there, that "I would have to stop to think, to question my own position: 'What is man that Thou art mindful of him, O Lord?' What were we here for, what were we doing, what was the meaning of our lives?"

TWO

The Downward Path

Merton was reading a Dumas novel at a family friend's home in London when there was a telephone call for him. It was the operator with a telegram, which she read aloud: ENTERING NEW YORK HARBOR. ALL WELL. FATHER. Merton told her she must have reached the wrong person. His father wasn't aboard a ship; he was recovering from surgery in a hospital right there in London. But the operator told him that the telegram *was* from London, and he had to admit that it was the sort of telegram his father would send. All of a sudden he knew that his father wasn't going to recover, and that, at age sixteen, he was going to be an orphan, "without a home, without a family, without a country, without a father, apparently without any friends, without any interior peace or confidence or light or understanding of my own—without God, too, without God, without heaven, without grace, without anything."

Owen Merton died of brain cancer six months later, and Thomas Merton's rebellion began. According to Merton in *The Seven Storey Mountain*, his father's death didn't leave him wounded, bereft, and helpless; it left him independent, accountable to nobody but himself: "And so I became the complete twentieth century man."

He told the story in a chapter of *The Seven Storey Mountain* called "The Harrowing of Hell," chronicling the exploits in his first months as an orphan. On summer break from a school called Oakham, he traveled up the Rhine with a backpack full of philosophy but read the "filthy novels" of Gide and Lawrence instead. Aboard a ship crossing the Atlantic, he declared his love to an American woman twice his age while a Catholic priest looked on. In New York, he ran up a bar bill with some girls from Vassar and Bryn Mawr; he read T. S. Eliot and listened to Duke Ellington; he got caught in a raid on a speakeasy. Back at Oakham, he flirted with the "pseudo-religion" of psychoanalysis and played jazz out his window—"the hottest and loudest records, turning the vic toward the classroom building" to goad the students less adept than he, stuck conjugating Latin verbs. He got a toothache, then gangrene in his foot, whereupon he was carried across the schoolyard on a stretcher "with blankets all up around my face and nothing sticking out but my nose," convinced that he was going to die.

This last image is Merton's *ecce homo*, his view of modern man, whose foot is medicated promptly while his soul is left to rot. But it, like the other imagery in the chapter, seems more extreme than his exploits warrant. The young man Merton is vain, self-absorbed, a reckless seeker after pleasure— but "a man living on the doorsill of the Apocalypse, a man with veins full of poison, living in death"? What led him, looking back, to judge himself so harshly? Why did he loathe his old self so much? What had he done?

We now know that *The Seven Storey Mountain* doesn't tell the whole story. Merton's fierce sense of his own sinfulness was grounded in a particular act, a sexual indiscretion which haunted the backstairs of his memory, and which he wrote about at length in the manuscript of *The Seven Storey Mountain*, but which his Trappist superiors, who scrutinized everything he wrote before it left the monastery, forced him to cut out. The omission distorted the book, made it angular, severe, exaggerated: without a capital sin to confess Merton seems less a Catholic than a puritan, condemning himself to hell for carousing on Fifty-second Street and denouncing all of Western civilization for playing its radios too loudly.

Dorothy Day's *The Long Loneliness* has a similar distance between experience and what she makes of it. The way she tells it, her wayward life frankly doesn't seem so awfully wayward. So she liked to stay up late drinking in the back room of a saloon with her friends. So she was thrown into jail on a bogus charge. Does that make her a sinner who must cry to the heavens begging God to change her life?

She too left out some sexual misadventures. Although no priest scrutinized her manuscript, it was understood that a Catholic writer should not scandalize the so-called simple faithful. So Day euphemized the period as "a time of searching," alluding to "the sadness of sin, the unspeakable dreariness of sin," but insisting that about her own sins "there is little to say." As spiritual autobiography, consequently, her book is an oddity: a conversion story about a woman whose great virtue is not change, but constancy.

Day is a generation older than Merton, but at this stage of their pilgrimage the two are side by side, and their stories echo and answer each other. They are sinning their way to God, as the saying goes, following the downward path to salvation. For a while they will press forward without anyone to guide them, plunging directly into experience. As they hit bottom they will discover God—or, more precisely, their desire for God. Slowly, painfully, faith will follow.

In their literary aspects, their accounts of sin and regeneration are near opposites. Day, born in the nineteenth century, bred on Dickens and Tolstoy, is Victorian in her reticence, untroubled by the need to smooth over some things and leave others out. Merton, a devotee of the modernists and especially James Joyce, writes as if suppression of specifics is a violation of the pattern he is creating, a betrayal of life and art alike.

These differences are telling, for they reveal markedly different approaches to religious experience. Day meanders toward God; Merton throws himself at God headlong. For her, sin is dull and dreary but leaves much of life untouched; grace gathers gradually, as life goes on, and faith, once found, is a path through the territory, the best route to follow. For Merton—the young Merton—sin is everywhere, and his every act tells for or against God; grace erases sin and wipes clean the soul, and the eyes of faith allow him to see the pattern that sin has obscured, the Jamesian figure in the carpet.

The two of them are two distinct religious temperaments, the reformer and the rebel—William James's once-born and twice-born souls turned upside down. The reformer struggles to set her life aright. The rebel renounces one life altogether in order to start over. Although they do not record it in all its details, the experience of sin is crucial, because, for them both, only direct experience of the life of sin—evil, greed, violence, despair—will justify the life of faith that is to follow.

The day he turned eighteen Merton drank champagne in London, then boarded a train for Italy. At Oakham he had discovered the "weird and violent figures" of William Blake and learned something about Blake's eccentric Christian faith; he had read the poems of Gerard Manley Hopkins, the "Jesuit poet." But it was in Rome, by his own account, that he first felt the distinction between religious art and modern art, between the Christian world and the "pagan" one.

One morning he stood alone in the church of Sts. Cosmas and Damian, in the Forum, and gazed up at the Byzantine mosaic of the Last Judgment: Christ coming on gilded clouds, with His head encircled by a halo of glittering shards and His eyes fixed sternly on the viewer below. There and then, for the first time, as Merton tells it in his autobiography, he encountered the image of Christ and responded with religious longing. At the same time, he perceived the faith of the artist—"the ancient craftsman's love of Christ, the Redeemer and Judge of the World."

He decided that he would try to see all the early Christian mosaics in Rome. It was an auspicious decision. In Rome, overgrown with history, Roman and Christian alike, the mosaics seem timeless and otherworldly: bright, distinctly outlined, perfectly preserved, untouchable. In churches full of sculptural tributes to saints and popes and patrons, the mosaics seem dedicated to God alone. They hover over the city like a Platonic ideal, a memory of the time before the fall.

By day he went to the churches, over and over. "And thus without knowing anything about it I became a pilgrim. I was unconsciously and unintentionally visiting the great shrines of Rome, and seeking out their sanctuaries with some of the avidity and desire of a true pilgrim, though not quite for the right reason."

At night, in a pensione, he read and wrote. To understand the mosaics better, he had bought a Bible—the Latin Vulgate; he had also bought "a fancy India-paper edition" of Joyce's *Ulysses*, then available only on the Continent. He read the novel, kept a journal, and started writing a novel of his own.

In *The Seven Storey Mountain*, writing under the influence of Augustine's *Confessions* and its dichotomies between pagan and Christian literature, between the city of man and the city of God, Merton contrasts the two types of art sharply: the novel is "slick and expensive," the mosaics pure and holy. But it seems clear that the two together, not apart, were inspiring in him an artistic ideal that was equal parts Byzantine and modern, Roman and Joycean.

H. G. Wells had compared *A Portrait of the Artist as a Young Man* to a "mosaic of jagged fragments," and in *Ulysses* Joyce had taken the comparison further, arraying thousands of concrete particulars (many drawn from his own experience) as a kind of mosaic of everyday life. Merton plainly took note. Searching for an artistic exemplar after his father's death, he became devoted to Joyce. In journals, in novels, and finally in an autobiography, he would array countless details drawn from his life and comment on them as though from the outside, striving for an art that had the clarity and vividness and particularity of a mosaic and the authority of religious judgment.

One night in the pensione his father appeared at his elbow. In a flash he saw that his soul was corrupt and longed to be free. He cried and cried, calling out to God and to his dead father. And for the first time in his life, he recalled, he prayed, really prayed—prayed to be set free from "the iron tyranny of moral corruption that held my whole nature in fetters."

He left Rome not long afterward, bound for America, then for Cambridge and university. He would be set free. But he would not be set free yet. First he would bottom out; first he would become a father himself, and would feel the stern gaze of Christ the Judge upon him.

Kings County Hospital, Brooklyn, is a vast and imposing place—a compound of several buildings, each of brown brick, with Romanesque windows and a red tile roof, as on a monastery. In the spring of 1918, with a flu epidemic spreading in the city, Dorothy Day, along with her sister, Della, began work as a nurse there. At the hospital, dawn was the beginning of the day, not the end of it. There Day encountered the poor firsthand—changing their sheets, cleaning their bedpans, sponging their bodies, bearing their corpses to the morgue in the end. There, with a Catholic co-worker, she went to Mass. There, she acquired habits of discipline, which another nurse called the "sacrament of duty." Day explained, "If there was a bell that rang at six o'clock, if there was a program for the day laid out and one were forced by community discipline, one's life fell into efficient, orderly lines. One could accomplish not only what work was laid out, but more besides."

Her memoirs suggest that life as a nurse was a sharp break from life as a bohemian in Greenwich Village. But Kings County Hospital was no monastery, and it was there, in fact, that Day brought her bohemian life to fulfillment. She fell in love for the first time, beginning an affair straight out of a Dreiser novel—a pregnancy; a suicide attempt; an abortion—and no sooner was it over than she wrote a novel of her own about it, as if by Village standards the experience wasn't real and true until it was retold as fiction.

She wanted him the moment she laid eyes on him.

He was an orderly in the men's ward. He was perhaps ten years older than she, strongly built, with a nose that had once been broken.

His name was Lionel Moise. Hospital orderly was the latest of his wage-earning exploits. He had been a carnival roustabout, a movie cameraman, a deckhand on a ship. A few months earlier, he told her, he'd been in a seaman's bar on the Brooklyn waterfront when some Mexican sailors gave him sleeping drops and robbed him. When he came to, he was in Kings County Hospital, bruised and beaten. Now he was working to pay off his bill. What he really wanted to do was write for a newspaper.

She told her sister she wanted to "——" him. Then she set to it. She suggested. He resisted. She insisted. He went along.

She told him she loved him, adding that there was no point in pretending he loved her. She didn't care. "You are hard," she told him. "I fell in love with you because you are hard." He was sexually experienced. She was not. "I've never had a virgin before," he told her.

After some time, his bill was paid, and he prepared to leave the hospital. As they parted he slipped a card down the bosom of her starched nurse's dress. It had the address of an apartment he rented in Manhattan.

She showed up there a week later, carrying her possessions.

They made love. In the novel she wrote of "bright flames searing her, leaping up in her again and again until it was almost anguish."

They were together, on and off, for the next year. They quarreled often. He left, or threw her out. She despaired. She told her friends she loved him more than life itself.

At a friend's apartment, where she was staying, she detached the hose from the gas heater and waited for the end. A neighbor, smelling the gas, broke in and revived her.

She returned to him. They reconciled. She declared her love. He warned her to be careful. He told her if she got pregnant he would leave her as soon as she began to show.

She was pregnant. When she began to show she confided in a friend. They reviewed her options. Going home. Entering a home for unwed mothers. Adoption. Abortion. Persuading the father to accept the child. Raising the child on her own.

The friend urged her to carry the child to term.

She wanted Lionel Moise not to know. The next time he told her he was leaving, however, she told him. He told her to get an abortion.

She arranged to have an abortion at an office on the Upper East Side. In those days, a metal instrument was inserted into the uterus, and the fetus was pried loose and then delivered, dead, a short time afterward.

When it was done she slept fitfully, waiting for the pain to subside. A diva on a phonograph record sang an aria in the airshaft. In the novel, she wrote, "She no longer thought of the child. That was over and done with."

She expected Moise to meet her at the office. He didn't arrive. She went to his apartment. He was gone. There was some money and a note. He had kited a check for her, the note explained. She should find somebody to marry, somebody rich, and forget all about him.

She quit her job. Although Kings County Hospital was no monastery, the work there was cloistrally all-consuming; it left her too busy to feel the "human misery" on the ward, too busy at war's end to celebrate the Armistice in the streets, too busy to write. Nursing, she had concluded, was a distraction from her true calling, which, she had determined, was to be a writer.

Those are the reasons she gives in her memoirs, and they square with the themes of her life to that point: the yearning to encounter life firsthand, to move in the stream of history, to find her way not alone but among the masses. But there was more to the story. She left the hospital because she was getting married and going to Europe to write a novel.

The man this time was a rich man, a journalist from the Midwest named Berkeley Tobey. He was forty-two, more than twice as old as she was. He was a founder of the Literary Guild in New York, and lived in an impressive apartment on Washington Square. He had been married before, and would be married again, eight times in all.

They went to London, Paris, and Italy. This trip she does describe in *The Long Loneliness*, but as a solo journey—not a honeymoon but a pilgrimage to the settings of some of her favorite novels, which she makes stand in for her experiences, whatever they were: "In London I walked and took bus rides and explored and thought of De Quincey and Dickens. In Paris it was the same, but there Balzac and De Maupassant and Victor Hugo were my companions."

Italy was different: in Naples and on Capri, with no books to prefigure her experience, she was struck powerfully by Old World poverty, which was not a condition but a way of life, and one more beautiful than the life of poverty in America.

The beauty she saw in Italy, and the unanticipated joy she felt there, she would later strive to recapture in New York, in "the smell of Italian cooking, the sound of buzzing flies, and loud strong voices of my Italian neighbors, the taste of spaghetti and polenta and the sour red wine." She was especially moved by the peasant women, "who carried heavy burdens and worked long hours and were always gracious, with a dignity and a beauty far surpassing that of any other women I have ever seen."

Where was Berkeley Tobey? The marriage was falling apart, and Day later told friends she left Tobey when they got home. But her recollections of Italy have the flavor of authentic solitude: even if she and her husband were still together, in spirit she was already alone.

It would be simple enough to see the marriage and the European sojourn it made possible as Day's ways of escape from New York and the tawdry affair she had had there. But while she was abroad she pondered the affair obsessively and relived it in a novel. Then, finishing the novel, she returned to America on the trail of its protagonist, Lionel Moise, who was in Chicago, working as a writer.

In Europe, Day later recalled, she was indifferent to politics, caught up in her own "joy and heartbreak" as Mussolini, marching on Rome, led the Fascist Party to power. Chicago was different. Chicago was where she had first heard the call to revolution, first felt the pull of poverty. Chicago, her hometown, was home, too, to immigrant workers from all over the world, and there, more than in New York, perhaps, they felt the bonds of brotherhood the labor leaders rhapsodized about. "They were part of a movement, a slow upheaval," Day wrote. "Among them was a stirring and a groping and they were beginning to feel within themselves a power and a possibility."

She rejoined some radical friends, writing articles, rallying with the Wobblies—the International Workers of the World. Yet her everyday work—court reporter, proofreader's aide, library factotum, clerk with Montgomery Ward, secretary to the editor, artist's model—was no more a vocation than nursing had been.

She found that another woman was in love with Lionel Moise. This woman, a shoplifter, an addict, a depressive, lived in a flophouse over the IWW headquarters on Skid Row. One night, when the other woman was feeling unwell, Day stayed at her bedside, the way Mike Gold had done for her. That night the police staged a raid on the flophouse. The Wobblies fled. So did some of the women. Those who remained—Day and her cohort among them—were arrested as "inmates of a disorderly house. Fortunately I did not realize this until later," Day recalled, "so I was able to endure the shame and humiliation of standing there at midnight on the street corner under the gaze of whatever idlers were around at that time of night."

Under the lamppost, she felt like "a girl of the streets" in a stage-show advertisement, and she felt worse when she got to jail. Streetwalkers undressed and cavorted before the police and taunted one prisoner, an alcoholic old woman, for "giving it away" for a drink. A drug addict in withdrawal "beat her head against the bars and howled like a wild animal. I have never heard such anguish, such unspeakable suffering. To see human beings racked, by their own will, made one feel the depth of the disorder of the world."

In *The Long Loneliness*, this second jail episode is the heart of the chapter called "A Time of Searching," and Day spends several pages pondering its effects on her. Getting arrested made her feel ashamed. So did being released, for she was treated more civilly than the actual streetwalkers. But what disturbed her especially was the suspicion, deep down, that she really was the kind of person the police said she was: a loose woman, a woman of questionable morals. "I do not think that ever again, no matter of what I am accused, can I suffer more than I did then of shame and regret, and self-contempt. Not only because I had been caught, found out, branded, publicly humiliated, but because of my own consciousness that I deserved it."

After her release, she left Chicago (and, presumably, any hope of reuniting with Lionel Moise). She had finished writing her novel, and a firm in New York had offered to publish it. When a friend moved to New Orleans, she went along.

They rented an apartment on St. Peter Street, then the boulevard of the French Quarter. The cathedral was nearby—Gothic, with biblical scenes painted in the arches—and Day would go there for Benediction, or evening prayer. Although New Orleans, like Chicago, was a predominantly Catholic city, she did not know a single Catholic there. Alone (or so it seemed to her) in her religious curiosity, she practiced some prayers and devotions taken from a book—a "little manual of prayers" she had bought at a gift shop near the cathedral.

She found work on a newspaper, the New Orleans *Item*—"only at the usual price of the capitalist paper, of writing sensational articles. My first assignment was to work as a taxi dancer in a cheap dance hall on Canal Street and write a series about the lives of the girls"—a taxi dancer being a girl who would dance with a man for money, and who for more money would "go for a ride" with him.

One day she got a call from her publisher in New York. A Hollywood producer had bought the film rights to her novel. Her share was three thousand dollars, far more money than she had ever had.

The novel was published shortly afterward. It was called *The Eleventh Virgin*, and it told the story of the affair and the abortion that brought an end to it. The title, an allusion to the biblical motif of the ten wise and the ten foolish virgins, took the scriptural image of female wisdom and made it into a pun about a common whore. The reviewers were harsh, recognizing that the novel was raw experience, hardly a novel at all.

Most tellings of Day's story present the abortion as the turning point in her life, the experience of sin that spurred her toward God. There is no doubt that, once she was a believer, she thought abortion a grave sin. But if having an abortion changed her own life, she never said so in print. In two memoirs, five other books, and some fifteen hundred articles and columns, all grounded in her conviction that firsthand experience and the art of recording it in prose are vital to religious insight, she never mentioned having an abortion; and her biographers, who knew her personally and who fondly recall their long and far-ranging conversations with her, treat the novel as the most reliable account of the experience, indeed the only one.

Day's reticence is no great surprise. In a sense, one which doubtless made her uneasy, having an abortion made it possible for her, a single woman rather than a young mother, to follow the path marked out for her. About the abortion, then, she generally said nothing. Instead, she described the whole time as a mistake: a waste of her life and a betrayal of her calling as a writer. She never referred to her misbegotten first book by name again; and she declared that if she could have one wish granted, it would be to have every copy of *The Eleventh Virgin* sought out and destroyed.

Merton left Rome religiously curious. He climbed the Aventine Hill and prayed in the church of Santa Sabina, suspecting that the Italian women were watching him. He visited a Trappist monastery in the hills outside Rome and flirted with the idea of being a monk, a man hidden in a cell while the girls he had known "beat on the gates of the monastery crying 'Come out, come out!' " Once back in America—he was to spend the summer in New York—he traveled to the World's Fair in Chicago and roamed the Hall of Religion; he went to a Methodist Sunday service and a Quaker meeting, and at night, lying awake on the sleeping porch of his grandparents' house, he stole glances at a Bible and wished that his uncle were not asleep nearby: he yearned to get out of bed and go down on his knees and pray, if only he were alone.

He recalls those incidents precisely in his autobiography, striving to pinpoint every last figure in the pattern of religiosity that led him to the monastery. His recollections of Cambridge, where he began at Clare College in the fall, are hazy and indistinct by contrast. Partly this is because of all the things he was inclined or compelled to leave out. Partly it is a deliberate literary effect: if his autobiography was inspired by Augustine's *Confessions*, a sounding of past sins in the streambed of memory, it was patterned after the *Divine Comedy*, where each sin is given a characteristic setting, and Merton sought to depict Cambridge as an infernal place, a swirling miasma of decadence and chaos. But partly, it seems, his memories were indistinct because he was not distinctive at Cambridge. He had literally lost himself. He was no longer the French-born son of an artist, no longer an orphan on accidental pilgrimage in Rome; he was just another bright young man grasping after experience wherever he could find it.

What did he do? He drank, smoked, missed morning classes. He played rugby, joined the crew. He "ran with a pack of hearties who wore multicolored scarves around their necks and who would have barked all night long in the shadows of Petty Cury if they had not been forced to go home to bed at a certain time." Monica Furlong in her biography gives a matter-of-fact catalog: he "ran up bills that he could not afford to pay, threw a brick through a shop window, got arrested for riding on the running-board of a car."

Inevitably, he dallied with women. He paid a visit to a figure known as "the freshman's delight," and called on a prostitute in London. Cambridge being mostly a male university, he kept company with working girls. He took a Sandra to a nightclub. He courted a Joan. Late at night, he sneaked women into his rooms through an open window, prompting his landlady to scold him and threaten to tell the college authorities.

He was only a halfhearted member of the crew, but the boathouse on the Cam, he had discovered, was an ideal place for a rendezvous. One night he had an important conversation there. There is no mention of it in his autobiography, but more than thirty years later, as he reviewed his life in his journal on the occasion of his fiftieth birthday, that night, that rendezvous, stood out. "Sitting on the steps of the boat house late at night with Sylvia, when the two fairies came down expecting to get into the boat house, saw us there, turned and hurried away . . ."

She was pregnant. He was the father. They sat at the water's edge, with the sculls racked in the boathouse behind them, and discussed what should be done about it.

In the end Merton's guardian, an English friend of his father's, handled the matter. He summoned Merton to London and gave him a dressing down. He made a payment to the woman's family and got them to pledge confidentiality. He encouraged Merton to go to New York for the summer and, once he was there, wrote him a letter encouraging him not to return— in effect, disowning him.

In New York Merton would make a new life: settling with his grandparents, enrolling at Columbia University, becoming a writer. He never mentioned the prospect of his paternity specifically in the tens of thousands of pages that form his published writing. But the friends he made at Columbia recall his saying that he'd been "sent down" from Cambridge for fathering a child. And he fictionalized his Cambridge misadventures in several novels he wrote as a young man.

One, *The Labyrinth*, contained a central chapter, called "The Party in the Middle of the Night" and frankly imitative of the Nighttown episode of *Ulysses*, in which the protagonist takes part in a mock crucifixion during a party at a nightclub called the Rendezvous.* Another included a fictional account of his last night in England. Because he was an English citizen, in America on a temporary visa, he was required to return to England the next fall in order to emigrate permanently. He spent several weeks there, concluding in London. That last night he sat drinking champagne in a bar in Oxford Circus with a college friend. Once he was drunk he staggered away from the bar to phone his guardian one last time. But first he tried to remember the telephone number—he could not—of a woman he knew in London.

The pregnancy would have been coming to term, and Merton left England with the assumption that he would soon have a son or daughter there. Through his guardian's intercession he would be free to begin a new life in New York, but the memory of the life he had left behind weighed upon him.

---

*Merton's biographer Michael Mott, who describes these manuscripts, gathered evidence that Merton was crucified in some fashion, and that this episode, a firsthand experience of crucifixion, caused him as much regret as his riotous behavior generally, which he later described as "the crucifixion of Christ: in which he dies again and again in the individuals who were made to share in the joy and the freedom of His grace, and who deny Him."

Was it because his child lived (or so he supposed) that he was so determined to renounce his past altogether, so eager to die to the world and be reborn in a monastery?

During the German air raids on London in 1940 he saw a propaganda film depicting the bombing, including the destruction of Oxford Circus, and returned home feeling that he "belonged there, not here," fighting the Nazis instead of preparing to enter a friary. "Bombs are beginning to fall in my life . . . ," he wrote in his journal that night. "I have responsibilities in England, I left my childhood behind there." When he entered the monastery, renouncing all worldly goods, he arranged for some of his savings to go to the nameless person his guardian knew about "if that person can be contacted."

When, seven years later, he wished to begin a new life once more in a Trappist monastery, his child loomed large. His vocation or calling to be a monk, which he regarded as a directive from God, depended on his being childless, a man devoted to God alone. The child was across the Atlantic, unknown to him. There was no hard evidence of his paternity. The best evidence was in the novels he had written. The evening before he set out for the monastery, hoping to stay there for good, he "took the manuscripts of three finished novels and one half-finished novel and ripped them up and threw them in the incinerator."

The child—it was said—died in the Blitz, but the affair was not forgotten. Concluding the Cambridge chapter of his autobiography, Merton addressed a kind of prayer in prose to the Mother of God—a piece of writing addressed indirectly, perhaps, to the mother of his child. "Lady, when on that night I left the Island that was once your England," he declared, "your love went with me, although I could not know it, and could not make myself aware of it. And it was your love, your intercession for me, before God, that was preparing the seas before my ship, laying open the way for me to another country."

With her film money Dorothy Day bought a fisherman's cottage on Staten Island, an hour from Manhattan by bus and ferry. The price was a thousand dollars.

The cottage—the "bungalow," she also called it, or "the little house"—was the first home she made for herself. It figures in all her writing about the twenties, evoked so vividly that, many years later, her associates would speak of the place and the life she lived there as if they had been present themselves.

She would live there four years, and there would be converted from one life to another: from bohemian to anchorite, loose woman to expectant mother, social radical to rosary-praying Catholic.

But in important ways life at the cottage was a further experiment in bohemia, in which Day's ideal of life, an ideal that combined writing and social action, the examples of the great books and the challenges of life unfolding around her, were not rejected but fulfilled.

The cottage was set on a beach, facing away from New York and overlooking a bay which opened onto the Atlantic. On the outside it was small, square, sided in planks, with a tin roof and a stovepipe chimney. Inside it was "furnished very simply," she wrote in her journal at the time, "with a driftwood stove in one corner, plenty of books, comfortable chairs and couches, and my writing table where I can look out at the water all day." A photograph taken of her there shows her aslouch at the table—spare and pale, her face half in shadow, her dark hair cut in bangs—with a typewriter in front of her and lots of books shelved behind.

Life at the cottage was a return to the waterfront life of her childhood: as she had once walked along Lake Michigan in the company of the Psalmist, so to speak, "I spent those first few winters on the beach with Tolstoi, Dostoevski and Dickens." It was a place of solitude and quiet, a retreat from the city and its temptations. Yet it was one of several dozen dwellings on the bay, whose inhabitants formed a colony of artists and drifters and Russian expatriates, people of independent mind.

Her old friend Peggy Baird from the Hell Hole introduced her to the place. While Day was in Europe Baird had married Malcolm Cowley, then a struggling writer, and they had rented an apartment on Bank Street in the Village, but they shared Day's yearning to escape the city.

So did everybody they knew. The literary bohemians, as Cowley depicted them in *Exile's Return*, believed that great literature arose from the satisfaction of two contradictory desires: the desire to be apart from the crowd and the desire to belong to a community of writers. As they reached their middle twenties and found it difficult to subsist on their freelance income in Manhattan, the literary bohemians felt "the desire to escape and the hope of living somewhere under more favorable conditions, perhaps in their own countryside." They had an ideal of rural simplicity and self-sufficiency but couldn't leave New York altogether, for the city was where the work was. A nearby part-time small-town bohemia was needed. So it was that "about the year 1924 there began a great exodus toward Connecticut, the Catskills, northern New Jersey and Bucks County, Pennsylvania. Many of the former expatriates took part in it; and soon the long process of exile-and-return was resumed almost in the form of a mass migration."

Shortly after Day bought her cottage, then, the Cowleys bought one nearby, and soon they were joining her for meals and socializing with her. Unlike Day, they had a water heater, and she never forgot the night when, taking a bath at their cottage, she "luxuriated in the hot water with a cigarette and a copy of [Balzac's] *Cousin Pons* in my hands."

Unlike Day, too, the Cowleys kept their Manhattan apartment, and through them Day was drawn into Village literary society again. In *The Long Loneliness* there is a roll call of the membership: the Cowleys; Kenneth and Lily Burke; Hart Crane, poet, drunk, seer, mystic; John Dos Passos, who was writing a novel of "social realism" called *The Big Money*; Allen Tate, formerly an editor of *The Fugitive* in Nashville; and Caroline Gordon, who had been secretary to the novelist Ford Madox Ford in Paris. "This again was another 'set,' liberal, radical, Bohemian, engaging in literary controversies," Day wrote.

Tate and Gordon were the newest members of the Cowley set, and in time they would have the greatest presence in Day's life. They were natives of Tennessee. Gordon had been home-schooled in Latin and Greek on her family's tobacco farm, then gone to Paris. Tate had studied at Vanderbilt, where, under the influence of one of his professors, John Crowe Ransom, he joined the Fugitives, a group of writers who "met fortnightly to discuss philosophy and read from their own verse" and put out a journal on the side. He began to imitate T. S. Eliot so faithfully that he had to resolve with regret "to avoid, consciously, Eliot's idiom and viewpoint, which in the nature of me are also mine."

Tate and Gordon had come to the city separately after a fitful romance, self-conscious fugitives from the South. Imaginatively, however, they were still in Dixie; at their apartment on Bank Street, across the street from the Cowleys, Tate started writing a biography of Stonewall Jackson, Gordon a novel about life on a farm in Kentucky.

They saw the South (in Eliot's term) as an objective correlative—a mass of tradition, ritual, symbol, and language in which to efface themselves, stripping away the self so that their work might have the implacable authority of objective truth. Eliot had conceived the idea to describe the artistic process, but for Tate and Gordon, as for Eliot himself, the sacrifice of one's talent in the service of tradition was a quasi-religious act, which inevitably led the individual talent to hold all sorts of ideas about how society ought to be organized.

The Cowley set spent their evenings in the Village discussing such ideas exhaustively. Industrial capitalism, they all believed, was a downward path, spelling the destruction of civilization. Against it stood literature, which was a kind of "equipment for living" (the phrase is Kenneth Burke's), a series of experiments in prose and verse that suggested alternative ways of life. As Tate and Gordon joined the conversation, to the schools of thought then current in the Village—Communism, anarchism, distributism—there was added the Fugitives' emerging philosophy of the yeoman farmer, whose simple, self-sufficient life, grounded in a sense of place and of responsibility to others, stood outside the Northern industrial-capitalist system.

They were all engaged in another phase of the war in bohemia, the perpetual conflict between life and art. In later years Day wryly remarked that she had had trouble following the conversation. But the questions her friends were asking—how might the writer take part in the affairs of the day? how could they reconcile the solitude and apartness of the writer's life with concern for the general welfare of society?—were the questions she herself had been asking ever since she was a girl, without finding a convincing answer.

The group had arranged themselves in pairs: Malcolm and Peggy Cowley, Kenneth and Lily Burke, Allen Tate and Caroline Gordon. Day, lacking an apartment in Manhattan, also lacked a mate, until she was introduced to Lily Burke's brother, Forster Batterham.

He moved into her beach cottage shortly after they met. In her autobiography, she presents him grandly as "the man I loved . . . an anarchist, an Englishman by descent, and a biologist." But the details of her portrait make him seem somewhat less grand. He was no scientist; he made gauges in a factory. He was no Englishman, merely of English descent, and had grown up in North Carolina and gone to Georgia Tech. He was not so much an anarchist as a "decentralist and deindustrialist," and his political activity consisted of reading aloud from the *New York Times*. He was fussy and domineering in his preferences, insisting that Day use his brand of toothpaste and drink her coffee black, as he did. Mornings, he tried to teach her a little biology. Having grown up with seven sisters, he was committed above all to his own independence, which he zealously protected.

Their time together would be marked by a series of disagreements. But he was a good man, the first good man Day had fallen in love with. She loved "his integrity and stubborn pride," loved the way he "refused to do other than live from day to day and insisted on his freedom of body and soul." She thought he resembled a figure William James called the "unbribed soul," who refused to join the "general scramble" and held a "manlier indifference" to material things. "When one sees the way in which wealth-getting enters as an ideal into the very bone and marrow of our generation," James had written, "one wonders whether the revival of the belief that poverty is a worthy religious vocation may not be the transformation of military courage, and the spiritual reform which our time stands most in need of."

During the week Batterham worked in the factory and stayed in Manhattan, and when he was on Staten Island he was often gardening or fishing from the side of a rowboat in the bay. Day's most evocative descriptions of her love for him, the ones that have the ring of simple truth, all involve his returning to the cottage after a time away—returning from the city on Fridays, or returning from a solitary night walk on the beach and climbing into bed next to her, lean and cold, "smelling of the sea."

Their companionship, such as it was, seems to have consisted mainly in taking long walks together along the ocean. They would walk for miles, side by side, winter or summer—"no matter how cold or rainy the day, and this dragging me away from my books, from my lethargy, into the open, into the country, made me begin to breathe. If breath is life, I was beginning to be full of it because of him."

She had always been a walker in the city, but during those walks on the beach with Batterham she felt something new and strange: a sudden, strong intuition about the presence of God. She described the feeling at length in her autobiography. Nature, she felt, was evidence of the unity and goodness of created things. The knowledge of nature was the beginning of the knowledge of God. To walk in nature was to walk in God's creation. But Batterham felt differently: "He loved nature with a sensuous passion, and he loved birds and beasts and children because they were not men." Nature, pure, lawful, impersonal, was a refuge from society and a reproach to humanity and its ideas, especially its ideas about God.

This quarrel about God's presence in nature—about "the argument from design," as theologians call it—was the first of their disagreements. The next evidently was a quarrel about marriage.

When she wrote about Batterham, the first thing Day said was that they had a "common-law marriage." It was invariably the first thing she said about him. Her dramatic introduction of him in *The Long Loneliness*, for example, reads, in full, as follows: "The man I loved, with whom I entered into a common-law relationship, was an anarchist, an Englishman by descent, and a biologist." It is a curious passage: a strong, direct, dramatic statement ("The man I loved was an anarchist . . .") has been split in two by the blunt insertion of the bit about marriage.

The details of the marriage, as she related them in her various books and articles, somehow fail to convince. She never says when they entered into it, what led them to do so, how they went about it, or what it meant to them. Although she says in *The Long Loneliness* that she knew Batterham "a long time before we contracted our common-law relationship," it can have been little more than "some months" at most. And although a common-law marriage is usually a financial arrangement between people who live together at length, she says that he "refused to take a role in the affairs of the household or manage the money"—suggesting that he continued to live on his salary from the city, she on her earnings from her writing and what was left of her film advance from Hollywood.

It is unlikely that Batterham would have entered into such a relationship willingly in any case. She depicts him as a man of remote principles, who "had always rebelled against the institutions of the family and the tyranny of love," and who reminded her that their relationship was a "comradeship," nothing more.

A man and a woman become married in the common-law sense by declaring themselves married, and it may be that Day declared them married at some point and he went along. Or it may be that she declared them married some years later, when she wrote *From Union Square to Rome*, the first account of her conversion to Catholicism.

Either way, the marriage she describes was more an arrangement than a union. And either way, she likely wished them to be married for one simple reason: because she had gotten pregnant.

Awkward marital arrangements were common among the bohemians. Caroline Gordon and Allen Tate, for example, had made such an arrangement just when Day was coming to know them. In December 1924 Gordon learned that she was pregnant with Tate's child. She and Tate had split up, and Tate was involved with another woman. He agreed to marry Gordon and then divorce her quietly after the child was born. One day in May 1925 they went to City Hall, got married, and then painstakingly backdated the marriage license to December 27, 1924, to make their child legitimate.

There is no telling how much Day knew about what they had done; but that summer she and Gordon spent an evening together at the beach cottage, along with Batterham, Tate, and the Cowleys. The way Gordon told it four decades later, the sight of the one woman, pregnant, made the other's heart leap. "When Dorothy saw I was pregnant, she said, 'Oh, I hope I am pregnant.' We had a good time in the cottage, staying till one a.m. Her last words were still, 'I hope I am pregnant!' "

Day *was* pregnant, and the discovery led to another disagreement with Forster Batterham. She was surprised and delighted by the pregnancy. She had yearned to have a child but feared she was unable to; and without a child, and the experience of motherhood that accompanied it, she felt incomplete. "My home, I felt, was not a home without one. The simple joys of the kitchen and garden and beach brought sadness with them because I felt myself unfruitful, barren. No matter how much one was loved or one loved, that love was lonely without a child."

Batterham was not delighted. As Day tells it, he didn't want children and thought it wrong to bring a child into a world scarred, as he was, by war and injustice. "His fear of responsibility, his dislike of having the control of others, his extreme individualism made him feel that he of all men should not be a father." Though she doesn't say so, he may have wished she would have another abortion and may have urged her to do so.

It was in the midst of all this storm and strife that Day was overcome by religious ardor. "I am surprised that I am beginning to pray daily," she wrote in her journal in November 1925.

In the journal she described what she felt as gratitude for the child she was carrying and joy in the act of creation. But the feeling, if the dates of the published extracts from the journal are reliable, came well into the pregnancy—the fifth month—at a time when there must have been considerable strife between the expectant mother and the reluctant father.

Batterham was still a part-time comrade. Day was a pregnant woman living in a fisherman's shack without heat or hot bathwater. She had, in a sense, the poverty she had longed for.

Alone there, she filled her time with prayers and improvised devotions.

As she tidied the cottage she prayed to a plaster statue of the Mother of God, turning to face her as she scrubbed or swept. Walking to the post office she prayed the rosary, matching her steps to the repetitions of the Our Father and the Hail Mary. On the beach she sang the Te Deum, the ancient Latin hymn in praise of God who fills heaven and earth with his glory. The bells of a nearby convent seemed to be calling her, and she began to go to Mass on Sundays.

Not so Forster Batterham. During the week there was no obstacle to Day's piety. But Sunday, when they were together, she could not go to Mass without defying him.

This was their final disagreement. When it came to religion Batterham, who so often had so little to say, became "garrulous in wrath." Day recalled, "It was impossible to talk about religion or faith to him. A wall immediately separated us. The very love of nature, and the study of her secrets which was bringing me to faith, cut Forster off from religion."

She never said precisely why Batterham objected so strongly to religion, and the omission is telling. It may be that at the time she was writing, with the Catholic Church set against Communism, the clash between orthodox religion and political radicalism was thought to be inevitable. It may be that Batterham's objections to religion were bound up with his objections to fatherhood, which she didn't wish to rehearse after the fact. Or it may be that, while he serves as a vivid antagonist, he is largely a literary device, and that Day's deepest conflict was with herself—a conflict between her fidelity to her radical background and her desire to set out on a different path.

In *The Long Loneliness* she recalls taking a walk from the cottage to the nearby village of Tottenville, putting her new faith to the test along the way. The scene has all the searching inwardness, the authentic conflict, that the passages about Batterham lack. Why was she praying? she asked herself. Out of weakness? Raw need? "I thought suddenly, scornfully, 'Here you are in a stupor of content. You are biological. Like a cow. Prayer with you is like the opiate of the people.' And over and over again that phrase was repeated jeeringly, 'Religion is the opiate of the people.' 'But,' I reasoned with myself, 'I am praying because I am happy, not because I am unhappy.' I did not turn to God in unhappiness, in grief, in despair—to get consolation, to get something from Him." No, she turned to God in thanksgiving: "I had been passing through some years of fret and strife, beauty and ugliness—even some weeks of sadness and despair. There had been periods of intense joy but seldom had there been the quiet beauty and happiness I had now."

If she was drawn to God out of joy, she was drawn to organized religion out of a wish to share the feeling with others. Batterham was often away, and life as a "sybaritic anchorite" suited her in the abstract but not in fact. Reading Dickens in the cottage every evening she missed bohemian society, even if she had no desire to resume the rounds of parties and conversations and "prohibition drinks" and "the dull, restless cogitations which come after dissipating one's energies." She recalled the predawn Masses at St. Joseph's in Greenwich Village—recalled the working people streaming into the church, awake, focused, full of purpose.

She resolved to have her child baptized a Catholic, "cost what it may." For herself, she prayed for "the gift of faith."

Winter came. She was twenty-eight years old and six months pregnant. "A woman does not want to be alone at such a time. Even the most hardened, the most irreverent, is awed by the stupendous fact of creation." She nailed tight the shutters on the cottage and returned to the city, taking an apartment with her sister, Della, on West Street near the Hudson River, "close to friends, close to a church where I could pray."

To that point in *The Long Loneliness*, Catholicism hardly figures in the story. The Church is still an abstraction. The Sermon on the Mount, the Last Supper; crucifixion and resurrection; the forgiveness of sins, the communion of saints, the resurrection of the body, the life everlasting—all are still in the future.

That is fitting, and artistically shrewd. For this, Day insisted, was the way her conversion went. She hardly knew the Church's teachings. She had gone to Sunday Mass in Tottenville for only a few weeks. Yet she was ready not only to have her child baptized (plenty of bohemian women did that, she says) but to believe for herself. In undertaking baptism on her child's behalf she was claiming the Catholic faith provisionally, at second hand, in the hope that in time it would take hold of her directly.

Why was she so drawn to the *Catholic* Church, which lay outside her own experience? There are several explanations.

At the time the Catholic Church, as Day's father scornfully put it, was the church "of Irish cops and washerwomen." But this, for Day, was part of its appeal. "My very experience as a radical, my whole make-up, made me want to associate myself with others, with the masses, in loving and praising God," she explained, and in her experience the masses were associated with Holy Mother Church. The Catholic Church "had come down through the centuries since the time of Peter, and far from being dead, she claimed and held the allegiance of masses of people in all the cities where I had lived. They poured in and out of her doors on Sundays and holy days, for novenas and missions . . ." While Communism claimed to represent the masses, the masses put their faith in the Church instead. "It may have been an unthinking, unquestioning faith, and yet the chance certainly came, again and again. 'Do I prefer the Church to my own will,' even if it was only the small matter of sitting at home on a Sunday morning with the papers? And the choice was the Church."

The identification of the masses with the Church seemed absolute. As she watched them, she wanted to belong, to know the experience firsthand. Yet she was too bashful to speak to the Catholics at the church in Tottenville or those who lived in nearby cottages on the beach. Alone, at a distance, at one remove from experience, she did what she had always done: she read her way in.

The books she read during her pregnancy, as she tells it, all pointed her in the direction of the Church. William James's *The Varieties of Religious Experience* convinced her that conversion was serious business; and it introduced her to St. Teresa of Avila—mystic, saint, reformer of the Carmelite order of nuns, a strong-willed woman of action she could identify with.

She had read *The Imitation of Christ* in high school; but now, reading it again, she was struck by its simple and direct everyday piety. The author, Thomas à Kempis, was an Augustinian monk and a contemporary of Luther, but before entering a monastery he was in an informal aggregation called the Brethren of the Common Life, and he makes the reader feel a sense of belonging to a larger community as well. His message is simple: Being a Christian means imitating Christ, nothing more, nothing less: "If we desire to have a true understanding of his Gospels, we must study to conform our life as nearly as we can to His," striving to "follow His teachings and His manner of living" as faithfully as possible.

"I read *The Imitation of Christ* a great deal during those months," Day recalled in *The Long Loneliness*. The Psalms, Frank Norris, Dostoevsky, Tolstoy, Dickens, James: ever since she was a girl she had read books in search of a pattern to set against her own experience as a measure and a guide. Lately she had taken the downward path, going out into the wilderness of a life without examples or models. Now she was ready to resume the path of her youth and conform her character and experiences to those she read about. *The Imitation of Christ* simply made the process explicit. It identified her approach to life as religious. It made Christ the model for imitation and the Bible the book of books, at once a devotional text and a guidebook. And it insisted that the process of imitation is a matter of life and death, for in the end, Thomas à Kempis wrote, we shall be judged not by what we have read but by what we have done.

Day knew what she would do: she would imitate Christ by imitating the Catholic masses—their poverty, their dignity, their communal spirit, their devotion to church and family, their special generosity to the brother who was down on his luck.

That ideal image of the masses was not one she conceived herself. It was one she read in the papers. All during the time she was turning religious, the press was telling the story of two Italians whose Christlike acts of self-sacrifice made her yearn to be like them.

Sacco and Vanzetti were anarchists, immigrants, tradesmen living in Massachusetts. They were riding a streetcar one morning when police arrested them as suspects in a killing at a factory nearby. They were carrying revolvers and anarchist tracts; they were associated with an anarchist who had died mysteriously while in FBI custody. Although the evidence against them was shaky they were charged with murder, tried, convicted, and sentenced to death.

That was in 1920. For seven years, while Dorothy Day went through a "time of searching" in New York and Chicago and New Orleans, in Europe and on Staten Island, Sacco and Vanzetti were in jail near Boston; and as they sat behind bars, workers around the country, and middle-class radicals and bohemians as well, came to know their story. They insisted that they were innocent and were being punished because they were poor, were radicals, were Italians. They were atheists, too, but they described their situation in religious terms. Vanzetti described Sacco as "a man who gave all, who sacrificed all for mankind." Of himself he said, "If it had not been for these things I might have lived out my life talking at street corners to scorning men." Jail had become "our career and our triumph."

"These men were Catholics, inasmuch as they were Italians," Day later wrote. "Catholics by tradition, but they had rejected the church." In the press, they were secular saints, and by 1925 they were beginning to look like martyrs as well.

Day returned to Manhattan, and there, in the last months of her pregnancy, she prepared for childbirth by reading childbirth scenes by the great writers: Tolstoy, Sinclair, O'Neill, Galsworthy.

She was reading an Agatha Christie mystery in the bathtub when the first contractions came. "[I] was thrilled, both by the novel and the pain, and thought stubbornly to myself, 'I must finish this book.' And I did, before the next one struck fifteen minutes later."

Then her sister Della hailed a taxi and they went to Bellevue Hospital, smoking cigarettes on the way.

A vast brick edifice on the East Side, Bellevue was the largest hospital in the world, and it accepted patients from all social classes and all walks of life. Arriving, Day, still a journalist first of all, took note of the other women in the waiting room the way she had once observed the other women in jail.

As the pains came more swiftly and sharply she compared the experience to what she had read, and resented the presumption of the great novelists, so many of whom were men. " 'What do they know about it, the idiots,' I thought. And it gave me pleasure to imagine them in the throes of childbirth. How they would groan and holler and rebel."

As if to right the wrong, she made her account of her own childbirth one of the most carefully worked-over passages in all her writing, a controlled fury of surreal imagery. "Earthquake and fire swept my body. My spirit was a battleground on which thousands were butchered in a most horrible manner. Through the rush and roar of the cataclysm which was all about me, I heard the murmur of the doctor and the answered murmur of the nurse at my head. In a white blaze of thankfulness I knew that ether was forthcoming." It was as though the struggles of the bohemians and the masses, which she had spent her twenties writing about, were now taking place deep inside her.

Then the "harsh winter" was over and spring had come. Her child was a daughter.

"If I had written the greatest book, composed the greatest symphony, painted the most beautiful painting or carved the most exquisite figure, I could not have felt the more exalted creator than I did when they placed my child in my arms," she wrote.

In a sense, the struggle between life and art was settled once and for all. As a new mother, she joined to the masses as never before—for childbirth is "a joy all women know, no matter what their grief at poverty, unemployment, and class war." She was not a painter or sculptor, not a "book writer." She was a journalist, who wrote from her own experience. So she sat up in bed and wrote an article for *The New Masses* about the birth of her child— "to share my joy with the world."

She named the child Tamar Teresa, after Teresa of Avila and the Hebrew word for palm tree. It was a good name for an actress or dancer, she thought.

A young mother reading the *Daily News* in the next bed thought the name referred to Thérèse of Lisieux, the "Little Flower." Day didn't know that saint, but as she heard her story—Thérèse had died of tuberculosis in a convent in 1897, the year Day was born—she decided that it was fine with her. So her daughter would have two patron saints: a strong-willed Spanish abbess and a bourgeois French girl.

She returned to the cottage on Staten Island, set on having her daughter baptized. But she didn't know how to go about it. In the end she hailed a nun walking on the side of the road and asked her what to do. The nun, a "simple old" Sister of Charity named Sister Aloysia, volunteered to come and catechize her at the cottage, asking, "How can your daughter be brought up a Catholic unless you become one yourself?"

The nun came three times a week and drilled Day in the catechism, as Batterham had done with biology. " 'And you think you are intelligent!' she would say witheringly. 'What is the definition of grace—actual grace and sanctifying grace? My fourth-grade pupils know more than you do!' "

Day plays up the comedy in these episodes, exploiting the conflict between unwitting new mother and the bred-in-the-bone Catholics she encountered. But at the time, radical that she was, she still had specific objections to the "Church of Rome." Ever since the French Revolution the Church had stood with the collapsing monarchies of Europe and against populism and democracy. The Church was made up of the masses, but whenever the masses stood up for their rights the Church found herself on the other side. The Church's priests and nuns worked hard, but they were no saints: they lived comfortably on the money the masses put in the collection plate every Sunday.

On Staten Island the Sisters of Charity lived on an estate which had been donated to the Church by a captain of industry, Charles Schwab. Day invariably walked by the place on her way to Tottenville. "I could never pass it without thinking of Schwab's career as the head of the Bethlehem Steel Corporation, of his work in breaking the Homestead strike, of how he, to this day, refuses to recognize unions of workers. . . . I could not but feel that his was tainted money which the Sisters had accepted. It was, I felt, money which belonged to the workers. He had defrauded the worker of a just wage. His sins cried to heaven for vengeance. He had ground the faces of the poor."

For Day "that estate was one of my stumbling blocks." In *From Union Square to Rome* she cites the teaching that the Church is holy even if its members are not—the argument that the sins of its people actually prove the Church's holiness, for the Church could not have persisted so long amid such sinfulness were it not divine. But it seems unlikely that she knew this argument so early. "I could only console myself with Christ's words that the greatest enemies would be those of the 'household.' I felt, too, that there were going to be many obstacles put in my path, and that this in a strange way was one of them."

Where was Forster Batterham? Away, apparently. He enjoyed being a father, as it turned out, but detested the religious turn his comrade had taken. As the baptism approached a gloom came over the cottage, especially as Day prepared to go to Mass on Sunday mornings. Whenever Sister Aloysia showed up Batterham stormed out, "greeting her through clenched teeth" like the village atheist in a Russian novel.

The day of the baptism was grim. Mother and child went to the church in Tottenville, joined by some neighbors from the beach colony, as well as a distant cousin and her husband, whom Day had asked to be the child's godparents, since they were the only Catholics she knew. Batterham went along, too. But when, with the child baptized—Day says nothing of the rite—they returned to the cottage, he left the group and took his boat onto the bay. He pulled up some traps he had set; he brought in lobsters, enough for everybody. Then, as the lobsters were boiled and a salad was made, he and Day quarreled again. "He had thought of the baptism only as a mumbo jumbo, the fussy and flurry peculiar to woman. . . . And then he had become angry with some sense of the end to which all this portended."

Another year and a half would pass before they separated for good. But it seems that Batterham made a resolution that day. Did he decide to leave her, or to let her go? Did she leave him, or drive him away? Was it faith that divided them, or the pressure of a marriage that was not a real union in the first place?

They had one more ordeal to endure together, one last stage of their descent. On August 11, 1927, Sacco and Vanzetti, held captive seven years in Charles Town Prison, were scheduled to die in the electric chair.

Sacco and Vanzetti themselves had seen their case as an occasion to spread the anarchist gospel, and as their prospects wound down and their appeals were denied, their plight (Malcolm Cowley remarked) drew together American intellectuals as an ad hoc community and then divided them again. Here were two peasant rebels on the front pages of all the papers—their anarchism a direct challenge to American industrial capitalism, their charm and heroic sanctity a refutation of the idea of the immigrant masses as unwashed, unlettered, undignified; and in them the opposed forces in society—the radicals and the bohemians, the intellectuals and the masses, the life of art and the life of politics—were reconciled.

They died in stages, each one more excruciating than the one before. A high-born judge rejected a last stay of execution, holding all anarchists in contempt of court. The Reverend Billy Sunday preached that if the men were guilty they should get the "juice" and quick.

The radicals and the masses alike grew more enraged by the day, and in the end several thousand of them made a pilgrimage to Boston to stage a final protest on Boston Common, and then to keep a noisy vigil outside the walls of the prison where the condemned men awaited death.

Day and Batterham were not there. They had stayed behind on Staten Island, taking care of Tamar Teresa, now nearly eighteen months old. But they were, in their different ways, deeply affected by the whole affair, and in a sense, Day suggests in *The Long Loneliness*, the execution put an end to their marriage.

For Batterham the execution of two good and innocent men was proof of the cruelty of humankind and the wickedness of human society. He had never met Sacco and Vanzetti, but as an anarchist he identified with them as with brothers or relatives from the old country. So he retreated, hiding in his boat or in his books, refusing to eat or to talk, except to his daughter. It was as if *he* had been sentenced to death.

Day saw it differently. As she walked the beach, she was struck, and moved, by the solidarity she felt with the two men; and she pondered the mystery of her own and the public's identification with them. While the press tagged them as anarchists, she saw Sacco and Vanzetti as Catholic radicals. Although they had rejected the Church as adults they had been baptized into it as children, just as her daughter had, and had been brought up in its embrace. They were native Catholics now resident elsewhere, and their native faith was so strong that they instinctively understood their fate in Catholic terms, at once a victory and a sacrifice.

And yet the Church proper was against them, indifferent to their fate. She asked herself, "Where were the Catholic voices crying out for these men?" As a girl she had read the lives of the saints and had felt the same attraction-repulsion she felt now, the same yearning for sanctity and dissatisfaction with sanctity as the Church presented it. "I could see the nobility of giving one's life for the sick, the maimed, the leper. . . . But there was another question in my mind. Why was so much done in remedying evil instead of avoiding it in the first place? . . . Where were the saints to try to change the social order, not just to minister to the slaves, but to do away with slavery?"

Now, standing by as Sacco and Vanzetti went to the electric chair, she wanted to be like them. So she would break up her marriage and divide her family to embrace the church Sacco and Vanzetti had rejected—to lay claim to the solidarity those poor men could afford to cast off, like rich men their garments, so fully did they take it for granted.

"The day they died, the papers had headlines as large as those which proclaimed the outbreak of war," she recalled. "All the nation mourned. All the nation, I mean, that is made up of the poor, the worker, the trade unionist— those who felt most keenly the sense of solidarity—the very sense of solidarity which made me gradually understand the doctrine of the Mystical Body of Christ whereby we are the members of one another."

All week she had paced the cottage. Now she went outside and walked down to the beach, sidling up to the shoreline and the water. In the Church, she believed, she would know the masses firsthand. Believing, she would belong. So she hoped, she prayed, she cast her doubts aside, and then she leaped—into the crowd.

Winter came. She shuttered the cottage and returned to New York.

One day after Christmas she went downtown and boarded the ferry to Staten Island. She sat on the deck writing in her journal. The sea was choppy. The air was foggy. The occasion felt forced and cheerless. She felt she was being "too precipitate. I had no sense of peace, no joy, no conviction even that what I was doing was right. It was just something that I had to do, a task to be gotten through. A most consuming restlessness was upon me so that I walked around and around the deck of the ferry, almost groaning in anguish of spirit. Perhaps the devil was on the boat."

On Staten Island she went to the church in Tottenville. She made her confession and was baptized—"conditionally," as it is said, since she had been baptized in the Episcopal church as a teenager. Even baptism, which the Church regards as the occasion of new life, built on an experience she'd had before.

It was December 28, 1927. She was thirty years old, "a Catholic at last though at that moment I never felt less the joy and peace and consolation which I know from my own later experiences religion can bring."

She and Batterham separated sometime afterward. She says nothing about it in *The Long Loneliness*. The best account of their parting is a black-and-white illustration by Fritz Eichenberg, whose portraits of saints and martyrs illustrated the *Catholic Worker*. It is night, and she is barefoot, on the beach, standing in tall grass, wearing a dress that reveals her to be narrow-waisted and curvaceous. Her back is turned, for she is watching a boat on the water, hewing to the horizon, as if sailing away. Over her shoulder she holds her child, who gazes at the reader with imploring eyes.

The stock market crashed; a slump set in, and brought on, for Day, another time of searching. She was a Catholic, a writer, a single mother, an unemployed worker, mystically a member of the Body of Christ but in everyday fact more alone than ever.

THREE

Seeking the Real

With the Depression there came a great migration, a quasi-biblical wandering. It was a movable pilgrimage which scattered people to many destinations in fulfillment of the fundamental human needs. Fifteen million people were unemployed, and as times got harder more and more of them went from farm to farm, from one city to the next, from their native region north and west, seeking work, food, shelter, prospects, a new life altogether.

No sooner had they taken to the road than a multitude of writers and photographers set out to interpret their condition. Today the story of these "documentary workers" is as well known as that of the people they documented. Unemployed, they worked on assignments for agencies like the Federal Writers Project, and in a few years created a fixed image of American poverty and at the same time a fresh model for realism in twentieth-century American art—prosaic in style, collaborative in approach, invested with this-worldly mysticism of the everyday. The aim, as defined by James Agee, a late and reluctant practitioner, was to shift the emphasis "from the imagined, the revisive, to the effort to perceive simply the cruel radiance of what is."

Agee and his photographer-partner, Walker Evans, worked for *Fortune* magazine, not for the federal government, and collaborated "in distant harmony" rather than side by side; but they were representative figures, whose obsessions refracted those of their contemporaries.

This is especially true of their focus on the South. Among documentary workers, the South was the mirror of Northern industry and progress—a remote and antique place, indubitably real, with its own way of thinking and speaking and worshipping and segregating the races; and they went there to quarry its rich deposits of real life.

When in Mississippi, they invariably visited at William Alexander Percy's place in Greenville. "He was a literary figure and something of a spokesman for the South," Walker Percy recalled. "As a consequence, his house became a standard stopover for all manner of folk who had set forth to make sense of this mysterious region—poets, journalists, sociologists, psychiatrists."

The house stood at State and Percy streets, hard by the Mississippi River, which had overflowed its banks in 1927, flooding the ground floor. To visitors, perhaps, it seemed an archetypal Southern manor. In fact, as Percy recalled, it was an odd hybrid: a manor house which, after the flood, had been remade to resemble an Italian villa, reflecting the taste of Will Percy, who thought of Taormina, in Sicily, as a kind of earthly paradise.

Uncle Will was most at home there while listening to records on a giant Capeheart phonograph. Walker Percy, a loner in his own way, was left to roam the place. For him it became a site of experience and exploration. It had an elevator, an attic full of Will's war gear, a large library, and "dozens of . . . odd, angled-off rooms serving no known purpose." And as visitors came, it became a large and eccentric household—fluid of boundary, racially mixed, intensely social, full of strangers and kin brought together by their passion for the South.

The house is where Percy and Shelby Foote came to see literature as social, the stuff of running conversation. It was full of writers and artists. Langston Hughes came to give a speech in town. William Faulkner showed up for tennis, too drunk to play. Carl Sandburg "broke out his guitar and sang, not too well, for hours." A journalist paid a visit to ask Uncle Will for advice and wound up establishing a newspaper in town. A man with an inheritance made the house into a one-man writer's colony, staying two years to finish a novel. A psychiatrist, down from New York for three weeks on a grant, turned his visit into a working holiday.

This was Harry Stack Sullivan, then one of the best-known psychiatrists in America. Percy recalled his visit vividly. The grant obliged Sullivan to gain an understanding of race relations in Mississippi, but he knew that was impossible. So he identified the place in the house "where the traffic was heaviest and the race relations the liveliest"—the pantry, "a large room with bar, between kitchen and dining room, between the white folks in the front and the cook and her friends and friends of her friends in the back"—and sat there for hours every afternoon, drinking and talking, watching and listening.

Percy, meanwhile, was watching the psychiatrist. Sullivan's "knack for looking and listening, for tuning in and soaking up" was a kind of documentary scrutiny, something very different from Uncle Will's agitated moralizing. Percy saw in Dr. Sullivan a man as nonchalant and watchful as he was, and made of him a role model: the diagnostician in disguise, who situated himself in an in-between place and carried out his diagnosis from behind a pitcher of martinis.

The Depression coincided exactly with Flannery O'Connor's childhood, and although she was never poor herself she would later depict the poor as insightfully as any documentary worker.

At first the slump touched her only indirectly. Her father was a "real-estate man," buying and renting properties in Savannah, and while the business suffered the O'Connor family's own circumstances were not diminished. At age eleven, having transferred from the cathedral school to the Sacred Heart school a few blocks away, Mary Flannery was chauffeured there each day in her cousin Kate's limousine. The other girls stared. Once again she was a freak in her way.

Her father, then in his thirties, was witty and dashing. When he was at home he was a kindred spirit, even a playmate: the time she dreamed up an imaginary society and dubbed herself Lord Flannery O'Connor, she crowned him the King of Siam. But as the Depression grew worse he was away more and more often. First he was off giving speeches to local assemblies of the American Legion, the veterans' group, which had elected him State Commander. Then he was up in Atlanta, working as a "zone appraiser" for the Federal Housing Administration.

For a time the whole family lived in Atlanta, but O'Connor was unhappy in school there, so it was arranged that during the week her father would stay alongside two of his brothers-in-law in a rooming house in Atlanta while she and her mother moved into the mansion in Milledgeville.

The household where the women talk among themselves while the man of the house is gone—a familiar setting of her fiction—is a setting O'Connor knew early. Separated from her father, she was not only an only child and a wise child but a solitary one, and one suddenly living among women— mother, grandmother, assorted aunts—who were not at all solitary.

She didn't mind being an only child. Her sense of herself—unique, apart, adamant, hard to satisfy—was already highly developed, and her imagination offered plenty of company.

She sewed clothes for her chickens. She read the books precocious children read, scrawling comments in the margins as if to impose her view of the books on the books themselves, already spelling words the way they sounded, not the way they looked. On *Little Men*: "First rate. Splendid." On *Alice in Wonderland*: "Awful. I wouldn't read this book." She kept a journal, printing a warning on the cover: MIND YOUR OWN BIDNIS.

She thought and thought. Perhaps she did the things the wise children in her stories do: looked out the window wistfully like the child in "A Temple of the Holy Ghost," sat with a "look of complete absorption" like the child in "A View of the Woods," watched poor people come to the house to ask for work, as in "A Circle in the Fire," reading rapidly on the porch at nightfall "to catch the last light."

There is no telling whether she did those things. But the story of the wise child who is led to contemplate the poor people around her will recur again and again in her work, even as the wise child becomes an adult. She is inside. They are out. They are poor. She is not. But people not known first-hand and experientially can be known imaginatively. If she can come to know them through her imagination, she will have some company in her solitude. So she will sit in the bedroom window (as in "A Circle in the Fire") and watch them come closer and closer, imagining that they are "going to walk on through the side of the house."

Dorothy Day spent her first months as a Catholic at loose ends in Manhattan—working, reading, writing, praying, going to Mass and confession, caring for her daughter, and observing the effects of the Depression on the poor people of the city, whose lives had been hard enough in the supposedly roaring twenties.

Whereas her reception into the Church had been grim, her confirmation was "a joyous affair." This time it was not a late December morning but a bright spring Sunday—the seventh Sunday after Easter, or the feast of Pentecost. This time she was not alone but in a recognizable community—"a large group of adults" who advanced toward the altar "to the sweet singing of the nuns" and stood solemnly as a bishop daubed their brows with holy oil.

Pentecost marks the day when the Holy Spirit—the Holy Ghost—descended in "tongues of flame" on the disciples, anointing them by fire and inspiring them to speak in tongues "as the Spirit gave them power to express themselves." It is thought of as the "birthday" of the Church, but it would serve aptly as the feast day for religious writers. All the relevant themes are there. A calling, or vocation, begins in a dramatic experience, coming upon the believer in wind and flame. It is bound up with language, and can be communicated to others. And it must be communicated in one's own way. The community speaks many languages, and its members are faithful to their own vocations only if they find the distinctive voices in which to express themselves.

Baptized and confirmed, finally as Catholic as anybody else, Day set out to find her own voice and her own calling. Like the poor, and the people who wrote about them, she went on the move, looking for work.

She had rented rooms from some friends on Fourteenth Street so as to be near to the Church of Our Lady of Guadalupe, where she liked to worship—a small Mexican church between Seventh and Eighth avenues, no wider or grander than a railroad flat. The West Side was different, she thought, lacking in hospitality compared to the Jewish ghetto on the Lower East Side, where neighbors would drop by to talk or invite you to share a meal. When she caught pneumonia and had to stay in bed for a few days, none of her neighbors came by—and there, "surrounded by the ordinary American with his desire for privacy, for going his own way . . . where each one was isolated from the other, each afraid another would ask something from him," she grew fearful that she might die and not be missed by anybody.

She wrote articles. She raised funds for a socialist group called the Anti-Imperialist League and did clerical work for the Fellowship of Reconciliation, a Protestant peace group. She took a job cooking for some priests on Staten Island. With her money running out, she wrote a play and submitted it to Pathé Films, part of MGM. When they sent her a letter inviting her to come to Hollywood—she was the next Chekhov, they said—she went west.

She rented an apartment, bought a secondhand Model T, and reported to the MGM lot in Culver City, but there was no work for her. She spent her days smoking cigarettes and waiting for the mail, her nights caring for Tamar and a sick friend. "I was lonely," she recalled, "deadly lonely."

When her contract expired, she returned to New York. Then she moved again, this time to Mexico City. To pay her way she got an assignment from *Commonweal*, a Catholic magazine, to document conditions in the country—"to see what it was like to live under a persecution."

In *The Long Loneliness* Day says she went to Mexico to avoid "an occasion of sin"—probably, the temptation to move back in with Forster Batterham. But why Mexico? The answer seems clear: Mexico was a Catholic country. Having left her comrade for the Church, she would immerse herself in Catholic life instead. She had witnessed the complex and ardent piety of the Mexicans at Our Lady of Guadalupe on Fourteenth Street, but after three years as a Catholic she had no firsthand experience of the community of the faithful poor that had made her yearn to be a Catholic in the first place. The Church, far from being the church of the poor, seemed to her to be the church against the poor, aligning itself with the powers and principalities of American society.

The individual Catholic was little better. "Catholics believe that man is the temple of the Holy Ghost, that he is made to the image and likeness of God," she later wrote, but she wondered whether "we really believe it, when we see our fellows herded like brutes in municipal lodging houses, tramping the streets and the roads hungry, working at starvation wages or under an inhuman speed-up, living in filthy degraded conditions." The scandal of Christianity was the fact that so many Christians fail to imitate Christ—who "affront Christ in the Negro, in the poor Mexican, the Italian, yes, and the Jew."

Surely it would be different in Mexico. There the Church was inescapable, woven into the fabric of society. And yet there, since the socialist revolution of the previous year, Catholic churches were being shut and priests persecuted. There, the Church was the oppressed, not the oppressor. There, God willing, she would have a direct encounter with the people whose faith she professed to share.

Mexico did strengthen Day's ideal of the Church as the church of the people, as she evidently hoped it would. The peasants cared for one another and for her. Though the Church was outlawed, holy days were observed out of respect to "the will of the people." Religion was basic to them, as she observed in describing the complex Mexican sign of the cross, which was concluded with a kiss to the hand. "The sign of the cross is the most natural gesture of these people," she reported, her journalistic detachment disguising her own longing.

She wrote half a dozen pieces about Mexico, describing her life there with a young child in colorful terms. Although she was indeed living among the poor, as a middle-class American she lived relatively well: rooms in Mexico City and a stone house on ten acres in the Santa Anita lagoon; a servant and a landlady who insisted on helping with the housework; long days to roam the city or play with her daughter or to "write outside with my typewriter propped up on a stone wall where melons and squashes are ripening in the sun."

Their favorite thing to do was to go on a pilgrimage—a "pil'mage," Tamar Teresa called it. For Day a pilgrimage was devotion and reportage at once. For her daughter it was a kind of holiday—"very delightful bus rides, and in general a spirit of festivity."

One day they went on pilgrimage to the shrine of Our Lady of Guadalupe just outside Mexico City, "not as far as the Bronx is from lower Broadway." The shrine is set on the spot where, it is said, the Virgin Mary appeared to the native peasant Juan Diego in 1531 and left her image printed indelibly on his cloak, presaging the conversion of the Mexican people to Catholicism. There was a replica of the cloak in the tiny church on Fourteenth Street. Now Day would stand in the spot where Juan Diego had stood. Now she would see his resplendent cloak with her own eyes.

Mother and daughter came upon the shrine, a chapel atop a hill encircled by an open-air market and a carnival with a Ferris wheel and a merry-go-round; went up the "slippery cobbled steps"; entered the hushed chapel; daubed some holy water on her forehead, coming down the steps; took in the view of the city; then went back down. " 'And oh, the tiniest baby church!' Teresa shouted, looking across the street where the littlest and humblest of chapels has been erected in honor of Juan Diego. There is room for only eight or ten people in it and it is the width of its doors which always stand open."

There is some question about how long Day stayed in Mexico: a year is unaccounted for, apart from a trip to Florida, where her parents were living. And there is some question about the reasons for her return. Perhaps she spent the missing year with Batterham, her daughter's father, after all, who may have lived in the beach cottage while she was gone. Perhaps Mexico was *too* Catholic, the religion unquestioned and all-pervasive, when she felt that one's faith should set one apart.

When she returned to New York, in May 1932, the Depression was at its most intense. "No smoke came from the factories. Mortgages on homes and farms were being foreclosed, driving more people to the city and loading them onto the already overburdened relief rolls. In New York long, bedraggled breadlines of listless men wound along city streets. On the fringes, by the rivers, almost every vacant lot was a Hooverville, a collection of jerry-built shanties where the homeless huddled in front of their fires."

In that passage, written thirty years later, Day employs the somber imagery of Depression-era documentary work. But poverty was not all bad, and she herself was not depressed. There was "an air of excitement and impending social change"; as she walked from the public library in midtown to her apartment on the Lower East Side, she recalled, the city seemed a kind of heaven.

She was conducting research for a new book. Though she supported herself as a journalist, she still "dreamed in terms of novels," and that summer, cut off from other Catholics, divided by faith from her radical friends, she dreamed herself into action through a novel—"a social novel with the pursuit of a job as the motive and the social revolution as its crisis." Like *The Eleventh Virgin*, the new book would be autobiographical, centering on her own struggle—"the struggle between religion and otherworldliness, and communism and this-worldliness, replete with a heroine and hero and scores of fascinating characters."

She had kept on writing for the Catholic magazines, and in the fall of 1932, when unemployed workers organized a series of marches on Washington—a factory workers' march, a farmers' march, a march of unemployed workers on a hunger strike—she secured assignments to go along to the capital and write about them.

The marches, as it turned out, were the most dramatic episode in her newspaper career so far. She had stayed behind on Staten Island when Sacco and Vanzetti were executed. Now she was part of a pilgrimage right out of *The Grapes of Wrath*, a caravan of trucks and cars moving from church to labor hall en route to Washington, to the strains of the "Internationale."

Outside Washington the procession was halted by police. A standoff began. As the workers waited at the roadside, many of them on hunger strike, others just plain hungry, reporters from the daily newspapers, needing a story overnight, aroused fear of a Communist uprising.

The standoff lasted three days. Then, surrounded by police, the "ragged horde" entered the capital, waving flags and shouting slogans.

Day stood watching, as she had done in Oakland after the earthquake when she was eight, and once again she had a religious insight. She felt "joy and pride in this band of men and women mounting in my heart, and with it a bitterness too that since I was a Catholic, with fundamental philosophical differences, I could not be out there with them." How odd the Church was! "How self-centered, how ingrown, how lacking in sense of community" she herself was! Though she was writing about the marches, suddenly journalism counted for nothing. Nor did her efforts as a single mother. Ever since she had become a Catholic, she concluded, she had squandered her life, living for herself only. "My summer of quiet reading and prayer, my self-absorption seemed sinful as I watched my brothers in their struggle, not for themselves but for others.

"How our dear Lord must love them, I kept thinking to myself. They were His friends, His comrades, and who knows how close to His heart in their attempt to work for justice."

The Catholic University of America was nearby, and after the march was finished Day went there. It was December 8—the feast of the Immaculate Conception—and the university was erecting a shrine dedicated to the Immaculate Conception, a kind of rival to the National Cathedral, an Episcopal place. The shrine was still unfinished, obscured by scaffolding and drop cloths.

She entered the shrine and knelt down and began to pray. She was now thirty-five years old and still in search of a calling. Fiction was not it; novels were not social enough—not real enough. She sought something else. Anguished, in tears, she "offered up a special prayer"—a prayer "that some way would open up for me to use what talents I possessed for my fellow workers, the poor."

She had become a radical and a journalist so as to know the experience of poverty, but she hardly knew any poor people. Likewise, in becoming a Catholic she had joined the immigrant masses, but "as I knelt there, I realized that after three years of Catholicism my only contact with active Catholics had been through articles I had written. . . . I still did not know personally one Catholic layman." She was still alone, and that was the root of her anguish.

The story has it that Peter Maurin was waiting for her at her apartment when she returned from Washington, and that "the *Catholic Worker* was conceived in that meeting."

It is a story straight out of the lives of the saints, and Day told it that way in *The Long Loneliness* and elsewhere. But she silently corrected it in *Loaves and Fishes*, her chronicle of the movement.

She was at home on a weekday afternoon, working on her novel. Her sister-in-law, who was pregnant and living with her, along with her brother, answered the door. An odd old man walked right in "and started talking at once—casually, informally, almost as though he were taking up a conversation where it had been left off. There was a gray look about him: he had gray hair, cut short and scrubby; gray eyes; strong features; a pleasant mouth; and broad hands with short fingers, evidently used to heavy work, such as with a pick and shovel. He wore the kind of clothes that have so lost their shape and finish that it's impossible to tell whether they are clean or not."

He was Peter Maurin—"a genius, a saint, an agitator, a writer, a lecturer, a poor man, and a shabby tramp, all at once."

Usually, the story of their encounter emphasizes the way they complemented each other—his philosophy enriching her practical experience, his knowledge of Catholic "social teaching" adding to the insights she'd gleaned from newspapers and novels. But at first his philosophy was beside the point. There and then, all she had was her first impressions, which were striking. Although he pronounced his surname with the stress on the first syllable, he was obviously French, and he looked like the poor men on the march, which pleased her: "I like people to look their part—if they are workers to look like workers, and if they are peasants to look like peasants." Poor, an immigrant, a worker, a real live bred-in-the-bone Catholic, an émigré from the Europe of the last century, a walk-on from a novel by Dickens or Tolstoy or Balzac—he was the kind of character she had read about.

Supposedly he was loath to talk about himself, but his personal history, which Day later documented with the thoroughness of a WPA scribe, was as complex as her own. Born in 1877, he grew up with twenty-one brothers and sisters on a farm in the south of France, where the dialect was closer to Latin than French and the parish priest had to grow his own vegetables like everybody else. He joined the Christian Brothers, who taught in the Catholic schools; saw the slums of Paris with his own eyes; fled to Canada after being drafted into the French army. There he founded a farming commune on the prairie with a male friend, but the farm failed and the friend died, leaving him alone, whereupon he crossed the border into upstate New York and worked his way around the Midwest, laying railroad ties and breaking rocks—and in his free time, or so the story goes, he devised a philosophy, a personal synthesis of workaday poverty and Franco-Russian anarchism and the writings of the recent popes, in which the robber baron and the needy immigrant were said to have a basic equality before God.

He settled in Chicago, where he taught other people French to pay for his room in a flophouse. There in the city where Day had first seen the cruelty of poverty, he was appalled by what he saw—a daily ritual in which "man fed himself into the machine" of industrial capitalism. Day paraphrased his view as follows:

Man was placed here with his talents, to play his part, and on every side he saw the children of this world wiser in their generation than the children of light. They built enormous industrial plants, bridges, pipe lines, skyscrapers, with imagination and vision they made their blue prints, and with reckless and daredevil financing made them actual in steel and concrete. Wheels turned and engines throbbed and the great pulse of the mechanical and physical world beat strong and steady while men's pulses sickened and grew weaker and died.

It was not unlike the diagnosis of social problems offered by the Fugitives and their successors, the Agrarians, or by Forster Batterham. But Peter Maurin saw a solution to those problems in the literal imitation of Christ and the saints, especially Francis, who had made Lady Poverty his bride.

In 1925, his forty-ninth year, Maurin left Chicago for New York, sleeping in boxcars, a St. Francis of the railyards.

He made it as far as the Catskills, north of New York City. There a priest had established a Catholic boys' camp in a clearing on a mountainside and enlisted some immigrant artisans to erect an A-frame structure of fieldstone and carved wood. The building, which still stands, is a matchless example of a church as the hub of a small, set-apart, semirural community, its plan drawing on the communal craft of faithful artisans—a combination church and religious compound.

Maurin spent the Depression there, sleeping in a barn. By day he swept and mopped and fixed things and sat in the priest's library reading philosophy and theology: Augustine, Aquinas, the papal encyclicals, the Catholic syntheses preceding his own.

From time to time he went down to the hamlet at the foot of the mountain, took the bus to the city, and made his way to Union Square, site of soapbox orators and self-anointed evangelists. He wore a tattered suit whose pockets were stuffed with books and papers. To make himself heard, he spoke in rhyme, calling out his verses to all nearby.

In this manner a rural French troubadour of God became a modern American Catholic agitator, at once a freak and a prophet.

"It was a long time before I really knew what Peter was talking about that first day," Day recalled. "But he did make three points I thought I understood: founding a newspaper for clarification of thought, starting houses of hospitality, and organizing farming communes."

A newspaper: in retrospect, it is so obvious an idea that one wonders why Day didn't come up with it herself. Every group of radicals had its own paper, and she knew how to write and edit a paper as well as anybody.

There were obstacles. She was a woman, and laywomen weren't encouraged to take the initiative in the Catholic Church or in the newspaper world, either. She had a daughter to raise, and the writing she did for magazines was her only means of support. There was a Depression on: she didn't have any money, and neither did anybody else.

Those obstacles were real, and would remain so even after the first issue of the newspaper was printed, folded, and bundled. But the best explanations for Day's hesitancy in her early years as a Catholic, and then for her sudden leap into action, go deeper than that. They have to do with her approach to life in general, the pattern of her pilgrimage.

She struggled in those years, first of all, because she lacked a literary model. In becoming a Catholic she sought to imitate Christ and the saints, such as St. Teresa of Avila. But she hadn't glimpsed a way to imitate them in Depression-era America until she read the life of Rose Hawthorne Lathrop, Nathaniel Hawthorne's daughter. "Rose, with her husband, had become a convert in 1891. She had started a cancer hospital for the poor and homeless—such institutions were a rarity in those days—in three dark, airless rooms down on the East Side," a tenement apartment "such as the one I was living in," Day explained in *The Long Loneliness*, and one only a mile away from her own place on East Fifteenth Street. Married to a dissolute man at age twenty, separated soon after, a New Yorker with a literary pedigree, Rose Hawthorne was a holy woman whom Day could identify with wholeheartedly.

She also struggled because she was alone. The fact that after five years as a Catholic Day knew no living Catholics is one of the real mysteries of her story. She was gregarious, charismatic, striking to the eye, and it is unimaginable that this single mother coming to Mass with her daughter every morning didn't elicit other believers' curiosity.

It is likely that she shied away from the other believers in the fear that she would be thought too heterodox for them—that her recent conversion and her despair over the social order meant that she was not as authentically Catholic as a working-class immigrant. She believed, yes. She belonged, at least theologically. But a great distance lies between the outward expressions of believing and belonging and the inward embrace of religious belief as one's own, not only to be learned but to be professed in one's own voice.

Now Peter Maurin took care of that. He was a real-life ideal, but more than that he was the first Catholic to take Day's faith for granted. A shrewd evangelist, he grasped that the way to reach this particular believer was to treat her as a full believer like himself. Unlike the priests Day knew, he asked no questions about her background or her conversion or her odd way of life. He spoke to her as one Catholic to another. In later years, telling their story, she would always stress all that he taught her; but what he really did, this ancient Catholic, was make her feel, at last, that she held the Catholic faith firsthand—that the faith he professed was her faith as well.

The paper they put together is usually described as a counterpart to the Communist Party's *Daily Worker*: an attempt to present the Catholic point of view in the marketplace of ideas that was Union Square; a publication about "work and men and the problems of poverty and destitution—and man's relationship to his brothers and to God." Starting out, Day saw it more modestly. The paper would be eight pages, folded tabloid style, written and published to reach the proverbial man in the street—in the shelters, on park benches, on the sidewalks in search of work—and call to his attention the fact that "the Catholic church has a social program" which would take account of his everyday problems, not just eternal life and the salvation of his soul.

Day had already perceived the extent of her differences from Maurin—a man twenty years older than she was, who seldom bathed and never stopped talking, who saw the worker as the peasant working with his hands in the fields, whereas she thought of "factories, the machine, and man the proletariat and slum dweller, and so often the unemployed." But it was on the question of the man in the street that they differed most fundamentally. Maurin, a soapbox veteran, sought to instill his ideas in all those who had ears to hear—"Communists, radicals, priests, and laity." He envisioned a paper called the *Catholic Radical*, which would counter all the other radical sheets, tracing anarchocommunist principles to their roots in Christian love.

Day proposed calling it the *Catholic Worker* instead. She did so, no doubt, in order to reach the common people and not just the radical vanguard; not just the masses, but the *Catholic* masses. She had become a Catholic, in part, to be joined to them, bound together in community by the Holy Ghost. Now she wanted to put out a newspaper in order to be bound to them not only in spirit but in fact.

The first issue was planned for May Day, the Communist workers' holiday, when tens of thousands of jobless workers, as well as radicals, college students, and the like, would congregate in Union Square. Day's brother John, apparently, transcribed several of Maurin's rhymed orations, dubbing them "Easy Essays."* A church printer was engaged. Contributions were accepted. It was decided that the paper would be sold for a penny—to cover expenses and, it seems, to make clear that it aspired to be a legitimate newspaper, not a Catholic propaganda sheet.

Day wrote several pieces: the opening address "to our readers," a waspish essay deriding the government directive urging the poor to dine by candlelight, and a chronicle of a day in a poor mother's life, probably taken from her abandoned novel and recast as present-tense documentary fact.

Meanwhile, Maurin continued her "indoctrination." Though his preferred form was the spoken word, he wrote prose eloquently, and a piece he wrote (it ran in the second issue) suggests his program: in his view, a "Utopian, Christian communism" with three aspects. Clarification of thought would be brought about through open meetings at which everybody and anybody was encouraged "to set forth his views." Houses of hospitality for the poor would revive the medieval tradition of showing hospitality to pilgrims and wayfarers. And farming communes—"agronomic universities," he called them—would enable people to "get back to the land." The goal: "a society where it is easier for people to be good"—a society rooted in Christian ideas of the "personal responsibility" to express one's love for one's neighbor through acts of love undertaken "at a personal sacrifice."

Maurin reiterated his program to Day tirelessly. But as the first issue of

---

*Here is one, entire: "The world would be better off / if people tried to become better. / And people would become better / if they stopped trying to become / better off. / For when everybody tries to / become better off, / nobody is better off. / But when everybody tries to / become better, everybody is better off. / Everybody would be rich / if nobody tried to become richer. / And nobody would be poor / if everybody tried to be poorest. / And everybody would be / what he ought to be / if everybody tried to be / what he wants the other fellow to be."

their newspaper went to press he left town, displeased with the miscellany of articles that had nothing to do with his program. For all his poverty and simplicity he was, in the end, an old-fashioned European Catholic intellectual, unnerved by professions of faith that didn't fit into a synthesis.

The papers—twenty-five hundred copies—arrived on East Fifteenth Street in neat bundles. The morning of May 1, 1933, when Day and three young male volunteers set out, walking west, to sell the *Catholic Worker* on Union Square, the troubadour of God was not with them.

Nothing so aptly captures the unworldliness of the first Catholic Workers, their holy indifference to all but the task at hand, as the surviving photographs of their early adventures on Union Square. Although Day—tall, dark-haired, and ardent, typically clad in a dress suit and cloche hat—must have looked especially striking selling a radical Catholic newspaper for a penny a copy, evidently no one in her group thought to photograph her. Nor are there any pictures of the Catholic Workers distributing the paper in a sea of Communist banners and placards. Whoever had the camera focused it on the paper's first readers instead. There are two photographs, taken that May Day or perhaps the next. In one, some men have withdrawn from the crowd to sit on a flight of steps and peruse the paper, and a church lady stands judgmentally appraising the front page; in the other, half a dozen men in topcoats huddle around a bundle of papers, some selling, others buying. The pictures are blurry and indistinct, and the strongest impression they leave is that the unemployed were awfully well dressed in those days: in suit jackets and neckties and snap-brimmed hats, these men, far from the usual documentary image of indigent jobless men, could be factory workers, or butchers, or radical agitators, or students, or seminarians, or businessmen awaiting a train.

Thomas Merton is somewhere in that crowd. Union Square is where, the summer before he went up to Cambridge, the New York leg of his pilgrimage began; and the way of life he found there, the blend of lofty philosophical ideals and lust for life, of revolution and burlesque, shaped forever his idea of the city, and indeed the whole fallen world that he entered a contemplative monastery to escape. His hell was Cambridge, but his Sodom is New York. For him as for Day, Manhattan will be, first of all, a rebel's paradise, a place of sin and temptation, against which he will rebel in turn by becoming religious. And yet for him, as for her, the firsthand experience of

New York, of its legendary excesses and waywardness, will lend authority to his renunciation of it. Because he seems to relish the lost life as he describes it, his conversion seems authentic.

He spent that first summer in the company of Reginald Marsh, the artist, a friend of his father's. Marsh, then thirty-five years old, was notorious for his cartoonish images of working-class New York, such as his 1932 scratchboard etching of a scene from the Bowery—a group of shadowy figures lurking under the el, outside a barbershop, a tattoo counter, and an ALL NIGHT MISSION —and his work now defines the place and time as distinctly as any WPA production.

Marsh had a studio on Fourteenth Street, and in the summer of 1933 Merton visited there, then began to show up regularly, tagging along as Marsh made the rounds of the city in search of idle pleasures and subjects to depict. For the first time since his father's death Merton was seeing the world in the company of an older artist, and Marsh was an ideal guide. "We got along very well together," he wrote in *The Seven Storey Mountain*, "because of the harmony of our views, I worshipping life as such, and he worshipping it especially in the loud, wild bedlam of the crowded, crazy city that he loved." He went on: "His favorite places of devotion were Union Square and the Irving Place burlesque, stinking of sweat and cheap cigars and ready to burn down or collapse at any minute."

Back from Cambridge the next summer, newly worldly, he saw Marsh again, bringing his brother along, and their main diversion was the movies. Another of Marsh's best-known etchings depicts a movie house, but for Merton the movies were everything life with Marsh was not—unreal, phony, contrived. "My ears are still ringing with the false, gay music that used to announce the Fox movietone and the Paramount newsreels with the turning camera that slowly veered its aim right at your face," he recalled. They were, he declared, a hell of sorts, but he "could not keep away from them."

In 1934, he was nineteen years old, still boyishly drawing cartoons like Marsh's. By the spring of 1935 he was, by his own account, a young man in thrall to Communism.

Although there is no doubt that Merton came to think Communism simplistic and misguided, it is hard to judge his experience of it through the anti-Communist passage in his autobiography. For him as for Day and other converts of their era, strident anti-Communism was the price of admission to the Catholic Church. At the time, his chief complaint was that Communist "cell" meetings were boring. It appears the Party attracted him in the first place as one more college club to join.

He had transferred to Columbia in midyear, arriving dressed in a vested suit, a felt hat, and a pocket watch. He joined half the clubs on campus: the student newspaper, the yearbook, the literary magazine, the humor magazine, the cross-country team, a fraternity. In his free time he worked as a tour guide at Rockefeller Center for pocket money, drew advertising cartoons for an agency downtown, and tutored high school students in Latin. In the evenings, he and his friends "would go flying down the black and roaring subway to 52nd Street, where we would crawl around the tiny, noisy and expensive nightclubs . . . shoulder to shoulder with a lot of surly strangers and their girls, while the whole place rocked and surged with storms of jazz."

Recalling his student days in his autobiography, Merton means to depict himself as a dissipated young man in rebellion against his true nature. But the effect is the opposite. He seems exceptional, and his life, far from seeming sinful, sounds exotic and exciting.

There are some truly disturbing passages. A fraternity brother's disappearance led Merton and the other pledges to joke about the missing student's whereabouts—until his body turned up in the Gowanus Canal. A class assignment required him to visit the morgue at Bellevue, where he saw "rows and rows of iceboxes containing the blue, swollen corpses of drowned men along with all the other human refuse of the big, evil city"—addicts, paupers, murder victims, suicides. Although he doesn't say so, Bellevue was where his mother died.

One day on the train he met death directly. His grandfather had just died, and his grandmother had forced him to take a long look at the stiff body; during a cross-country meet he had collapsed on the grass after his race, breathless and exhausted. Now, as he rode the Long Island railroad into the city for classes and a date, he recalled, "My head suddenly began to swim. It was not that I was afraid of vomiting, but it was as if some center of balance within me had unexpectedly been removed, and as if I were about to plunge into a blind abyss of emptiness without end."

He wobbled in the aisle until the train reached New York, then went to see the doctor at the hotel opposite Penn Station, who told him to lie down, then go home and rest. "So next I found myself in a room in the Pennsylvania Hotel, lying on a bed, trying to go to sleep. But I could not." He lay there, with eyes clenched shut, listening to the wash of traffic from the street below—"afraid that if I even looked at the window, the strange spinning in my head would begin again." The window was giant and animate. It seemed to want to suck him out of it. "And far, far away in my mind was a little, dry, mocking voice that said: 'What if you threw yourself out that window . . . ?'"

There, high above Penn Station, Merton hit bottom. A European, he found New York literally disorienting: chaotic, when he craved order and discipline; unreal, in its spectacles and diversions, compared to the simple life he recalled from rural France. And yet—this was the problem—it was attractive nonetheless.

"I had come very far, to find myself in this blind alley," he recalled. "But the very anguish and helplessness of my position was something to which I rapidly succumbed. And it was my defeat that was to be the occasion of my rescue."

The passage ends the first part of his autobiography. From there on Merton set the events of his life against the scheme of Dante's *Purgatorio*, in which the dead prepare to enter the kingdom of heaven by climbing the terraces of a mountain, on each of which a characteristic sin is on view. The title, *The Seven Storey Mountain*, which has mystified many, is meant to call the reader's attention to the scheme. But Dante's account of purgatory is not especially vital to Merton's life or his recounting of it; Dante's account of pilgrimage is. Dante is the great artist of pilgrimage, making the journey to firsthand experience an ideal in art and life alike, and inspiring countless artists and pilgrims to imitate him. In the *Divine Comedy*—patterned, in a double act of imitation, on the classical epics and on the historic events of Christendom—he visits the hereafter to see the world he has read about. He goes with a guide—a writer like himself—whose path he follows and behavior he imitates. But for the journey to be fruitful he must leave Virgil behind and see with his own eyes.

The pattern of pilgrimage, more than any purgatorial scheme, will be the pattern of Merton's life leading up to the monastery. Like Dante, he will set out to see for himself and to tell his own story, not anybody else's. Like Dante, he will follow a series of guides; and one after another they will reveal religion to him, persuading him, each in his own way, that life lived in search of God is real life, the only life worth living.

At the University of North Carolina, meanwhile, Walker Percy was skipping classes to go to the movies. That is the impression left by a candid photograph in the college yearbook, at least. Percy, rakishly stepping out of the line for tickets outside a Chapel Hill movie house, resembles a young Fred Astaire—dressed in coat and tie, his thick hair slicked back, his complexion clear, his eyes fixed on the camera as they would fix on the screen inside.

It is an apt image of the future author of *The Moviegoer*. But the people who knew Percy in Chapel Hill offer a very different image of him: sitting silently, present but indifferent, transfixed by a book. "He could sit right in the middle of a crowded room in the SAE house and read a novel or a chemistry book and never miss a beat," his brother Roy recalled.

Somewhere between those two images lies the story of Percy's college years. An intellectual and an idler; a scientist and a moviegoer; a popular figure and a loner—it seems that Percy was comfortable in both roles and took no trouble to try to reconcile them.

Like Merton and Day, Percy is a distinct religious type. If Day is a reformer and Merton a rebel, Percy is a seeker—a searcher, one might say, taking the term he used himself.

The searcher is driven toward the object of the search, not by achievement or rightness of life. Looking for something, the searcher is indifferent to much else; having few conventional expectations and no regrets, he often seems to wander or drift. The searcher is equally at home by himself and with others. The passage of time is of no great importance. Neither is the logic of a life's progress. The searcher will look here, there, elsewhere. Finding, or failing to find, what he is looking for, the searcher will keep looking for something. There is no deadline for the inquiry, no finish line.

To this point in the pilgrimage the reformer and the rebel have had much to say to each other; but from here it is the rebel and the searcher who will go forth side by side.

A year apart in age, orphans both, Merton and Percy are temperamental opposites. Where Merton is excitable and prone to anxiety, Percy is passive and underwhelmed by life. Where Merton rages against the contradictions in himself, Percy shrugs them off as inevitable.

For both Merton and Percy the motive for pilgrimage is the quandary of the self. There the similarity between them ends. Merton is on pilgrimage in order to lose himself, Percy in order to find himself.

Merton's sense of self is so strong that he is moved to rebel against it, to cast it off and start over. He will conclude that a false, modern self stands in the way of his true self, rooted in the old French Catholic tradition to which he is heir. To recover his true self, he must recover the lost world of the Catholic past—and then eventually renounce this, too, believing that it has begotten a false self which stands between him and the experience of God.

Percy, for his part, believes that tradition stands in the way of the self. As he becomes an adult his sense of self is still vague and fugitive. To find his true self he must shake off the lost world of the Old South and the burden of being a Percy. He will search for himself fitfully and find himself by slow degrees. But once he does find his true self he will not lose it or feel compelled to change it. With the search for the self more or less concluded, the search for the real can begin in earnest.

As a student, Percy was in no great hurry. The week he arrived at college, for example, he was asked to provide a "diagnostic" writing sample. He wrote a description of the Mississippi River in "a single long paragraph without punctuation"—an imitation of *The Sound and the Fury*, which he had read that summer. He was diagnosed as language-deficient and placed in the remedial writing class. His reaction—his lack of reaction—is telling. Although he was a reader of Faulkner and Dostoevsky, a renowned poet's adopted son, he didn't protest the decision or cleverly explain what he had done. He took the class, and learned from it.

His college experience was a miscellany of activities. He rushed a fraternity, joined two secret societies, conducted experiments in the laboratory, wrote some articles for the student magazine. He studied German intensively and went on a class trip to Germany, where he walked through the Ruhr Valley and irreverently smoked a cigar in Cologne cathedral (the Hitler youth impressed him with their discipline). He went to dances with a girl from Greenville and took a bus to New York to root for the football team. He read Shakespeare and Goethe and the big novels—*The Magic Mountain*, Santayana's *The Last Puritan*, *Gone with the Wind*—and a four-volume life of Robert E. Lee. He went to the movies.

His admirers often relish his moviegoing as a sign of his easygoing nature. But for Percy himself the movies were a complex escape. Afternoons, when he generally went to the movies, were for him times of anomie and even despair—times "which ought to be the best of times," he later explained, "but are, often as not, times when places, people, things, green leaves seem to be strangely diminished and devalued." The movies served as an ideal contrast. Percy found them more intense, more real, than everyday life, and full of searchers like himself. "For a lot of people," he remarked some years later, the movies "provide important moments, maybe the only point in the day, or even the week, when someone (a cowboy, a detective, a crook) is heard asking what life is all about, asking what is worth fighting for—or asking if anything is worth fighting for."

Percy himself singled out a different activity as the heart of his college life. He recalled that he spent college "rocking on the porch of the SAE house and going to the movies in the afternoon"; he reported that he "sat on the porch for four years, drinking and observing the scene." The porch suited his search and his developing sense of himself. It was like the pantry in Uncle Will's house, where Harry Stack Sullivan had situated himself—an in-between place, with heavy traffic but no single purpose, where one was free to watch and listen and think. There on the porch, Percy found that (as the hero of *Lancelot* remarks) "the narrower the view, the more you can see." There, he found that he could take in real life in concentrated form, as if it were a movie.

Thomas Merton wandered into Mark Van Doren's class by accident. Van Doren was a poet as well as a college professor. The class was on Shakespeare. Merton sat in, liked what he heard, and decided to enroll.

Through Van Doren, Merton found a new set of friends. From then on his real friends at Columbia would be Van Doren's students: Robert Lax, Ed Rice, Sy Freedgood, Bob Gibney, Bob Gerdy, Robert Giroux. Like the bohemians in the Village, they congregated in the offices of the college journal, the yearbook, and the satirical magazine, and discussed literature; and for Merton, an orphan after all, they became a surrogate family, joined by books.

To them all Van Doren was at once a friend and a guide. He—young, handsome, accomplished, soon to be famous as an expositor of Great Books—is cast as the Virgil in *The Seven Storey Mountain*, and Merton's sketch of him is an outline of his own ideal literary figure. Such a figure "talks about writing and books and poems and plays: does not get off on a tangent about the biographies of the poets or novelists: does not read into their poems a lot of subjective messages that were never there." He doesn't preach; rather, he educates his audience by "educing" their own ideas. He shows them how to tell good writing from bad, the genuine from the phony. Above all he draws on "the gift of communicating to them something of his own vital interest in things, something of his manner of approach."

Van Doren sponsored a way of reading grounded in the conviction that genuine literature is a kind of wisdom literature, in which readers would find the deepest account of the way life actually is. "Mark said everyone is prepared to read Shakespeare by the time they are 18," Merton recalled many years later. "They have been born, they have had Fathers, Mothers; they have loved, feared, hated, been jealous, etc." Van Doren, that is, expected his students to bring their life experience to Shakespeare, whose works would enable them to make greater sense of their experience than they could otherwise.

More than he introduced Merton to particular books or writers, Van Doren emboldened Merton to read the way he read already: with his whole self, his whole life. That was hardly necessary. He was taking literature classes of all kinds: English, Latin, Spanish, French. And yet the writers most formative to him, those who showed him a way or led him further on, he encountered on his own.

He saw *The Spirit of Medieval Philosophy* in the window of the Scribner's bookshop on Fifth Avenue while browsing after classes with "ten or twenty dollars burning a hole in my pocket." On a whim, he bought it. Though it was in English, the author, Etienne Gilson, the dust jacket reported, was a professor from the Sorbonne.

On the train back to Long Island he opened the book and spied some odd text on an early page: black cross, a Latin inscription—*Nihil Obstat. Imprimatur*—and, below it, a bishop's name, printed like a signature.

He knew what the Latin meant: Nothing stands in the way; officially stamped. "I felt as if I had been cheated! They should have warned me that it was a Catholic book! Then I would never have bought it. As it was, I was tempted to throw the thing out the window at the houses of Woodside—to get rid of it as dangerous and unclean."

The problem wasn't that the book was about a Catholic subject. Merton hardly could have expected otherwise. The problem was that it was an official Catholic book; if it was official philosophy, he reasoned, it was not philosophy. One has no trouble imagining him—young, headstrong, anxious, violent in his passions—throwing the book out the window, and his life going in a different direction altogether. He didn't throw *The Spirit of Medieval Philosophy* out the window, however. He started to read it. When the train reached his stop he took the book with him.

He read the book (most of it; he never got to the end) in the next few weeks, and was changed by the experience. In that book, by his own account, he found a conception of God that he thought plausible and appealing. This God was not a Jehovah or a divine lawgiver, not a plague-sending potentate or a scourge of prophets, not the heavenly Father of Jesus Christ or the stern Judge waiting just past the gate at the end of time, but the vital animating principle of reality—"pure act," being itself or per se, existence in perfection, outside of space and time, transcending all human imagery, calmly, steadily, eternally being. "What a relief it was for me, now," he recalled, "to discover not only that no idea of ours, let alone any image, could adequately represent God, but also that we *should not* allow ourselves to be satisfied with any such knowledge of Him."

He got more out of the book than a felicitous idea of God, however. He got a sense of God as a living reality, existing beyond all human approximations, and also of the claim to realism at the heart of the Catholic intellectual enterprise. This effect was no accident. It was by design. *The Spirit of Medieval Philosophy* collected Gilson's Gifford lectures—the same lecture series that had produced William James's *Varieties of Religious Experience* thirty years earlier. The Gifford lecturers were enjoined to discuss "natural theology" and to treat it as a "natural science . . . just as astronomy or chemistry is." As James had done with religious experience, Gilson did with medieval philosophy. He sought to establish it as "real" philosophy, valid apart from any act of faith; at the same time, he spoke of the medieval Christian worldview, God and all, with the confident exactitude of a scientist.

God as being itself, to be known and contemplated: this was just the god for the anxious young man on the train. When his grandfather died Merton had tried to pray, but he had had trouble conceiving the object of his prayer. Now he had come upon a conception of God that he could respect, and it was in this discovery, by his own account, that his religious life really began.

On the Fifth Avenue bus one day Robert Lax told Merton about a book he was reading, Aldous Huxley's *Ends and Means*—"told me about it in a way that made me want to read it too."

At first Merton was attracted as much to Huxley's persona as to his argument: scion of a family of great scientists, popular novelist who had given up writing fiction and begun "preaching mysticism." In the past few years Huxley "had read widely and deeply and intelligently in all kinds of Christian and Oriental mystical literature," and had reached the conclusion that religious experience is real and worth seeking. Merton's recollection of *Ends and Means* conveys his sudden excitement in this line of thought. "Not only was there such a thing as a supernatural order, but as a matter of concrete experience, it was accessible, very close at hand, and extremely near, an immediate and most necessary source of moral vitality, and one which could be reached most simply, most readily by prayer, faith, detachment, love."

Huxley called for asceticism, the attainment of detachment from all worldly things through self-discipline. To Merton, the word "asceticism" was seductive, prompting "a complete revolution in my mind." He put the book aside, yearning for ascetic detachment as the prelude to religious experience.

In *The Seven Storey Mountain* Merton makes his yearning comic, recalling the nights he lay in bed in his grandparents' house and tried to shut down his overactive senses by declaring, one by one, that the parts of his body did not exist. But his desire for asceticism took root through a more common form of self-denial. As he finished college, in the fall of 1937, he set aside his worldly ambitions—his plan to go downtown and find a job as a journalist—and enrolled at Columbia for a master's degree in English. He would be a graduate student.

Walker Percy had gone up north for medical school that August, driven there by a black employee of his uncle's.

He had hoped to study medicine at Harvard, where his father, his uncle, and Quentin Compson in *The Sound and the Fury* had studied at one time or another, but Harvard had rejected his application. So had the University of Virginia. The medical school that had accepted him was the College of Physicians and Surgeons at Columbia. More than Harvard (his biographers report), Columbia had a reputation as a center for "scientific medicine": it emphasized the study of the nature of illness and the "mechanism of disease" rather than the care of sick people. Its new campus and teaching hospital in upper Manhattan, fifty blocks up Broadway from the Columbia campus, in effect quarantined the students, sequestering them from the distractions of the buzzing, blooming cultural life to be found downtown.

Early on, however, Percy established an independent life in downtown Manhattan—a life so strong that it might be said to be his real life. Uptown was the world of scientific medicine; downtown was the world of literature and culture, of romance and society. His Columbia classmates recall him as easeful and indifferent, even lackadaisical, but it seems that he was genuinely conflicted, though so matter-of-fact about it that they hardly noticed.

Before classes began he lived for several weeks at a YMCA on the West

Side of Manhattan, near Central Park. Although he had a car of his own, whose Mississippi license plates attracted attention, he traveled by subway instead, choosing remote destinations on the city map—New Lots Avenue, Forest Hills, Fordham Road—and taking the train there to see what he found.

Once school began he fell into the student regimen: classes in anatomy, physiology, and the like; lab work on a cadaver; evenings spent drinking beer with classmates at a bar-and-grill on Broadway or playing squash in the dormitory basement. At the same time he carried on downtown, following a social schedule Will Percy had helped arrange for him. He met women under the clock at the Biltmore Hotel and squired them to debutante balls; he went to the opera and the symphony with a male friend of Will's—and with Will himself when he came to town.

He wrote a short story describing his double life. It isn't much of a story, but the fact that he wrote it at all suggests that, far from renouncing art while he sought to be a doctor, he simply made fiction a kind of hobby.

The story, called "Young Nuclear Physicist," tells of a Student (physics, not medicine) who is new to New York and already disillusioned. The Student has come north hoping to put off the old man and put on the new, but "life in New York had not fulfilled all expectations." His mentor in the South has described the city as part Los Alamos, part bohemia, with "much good talk about philosophy, art, mysticism, and a thousand other subjects." But the Student finds the city lonely and alienating. Two other students have killed themselves in the first semester. Himself, he feels "a certain permanent sense of strangeness."

A woman he knew in the South lives in a residential hotel downtown. The Student takes her on a few dates. He haunts the lobby of the hotel until a doorman tells him to stop lingering unless he wants to find himself "in Bellevue with the pansies and the peepers." Finally, he places a personal ad and arranges a blind date with a stranger, but when she shows up he flees, his search ended: she is thinner than he likes a woman to be.

Percy spent the summer after that first year at Will Percy's mountain "cottage" in Tennessee, called Brinkwood, in flight from medicine and the city grind. He dated a poet named Barbara Howe and had dinner with Allen Tate and Caroline Gordon, who had a cottage nearby. With Shelby Foote, he built a small stone house on Uncle Will's property and went on a pilgrimage to Rowan Oak, William Faulkner's whitewashed house near Oxford, Mississippi, but stayed in the car while Foote spoke with Faulkner.

In New York the next fall, he began to see a psychoanalyst. He went for drinks with Harry Stack Sullivan, and shortly afterward started treatment with a disciple of Sullivan's named Janet Rioch.

Their sessions went on through the end of medical school, and the schedule he kept is remarkable: a fifty-minute hour, five days a week, plus a half-hour commute each way.

Percy's biographers discuss the treatment at length, conjecturing that Percy sought to explore the abandonment represented by his parents' deaths and the transference of his feelings onto Uncle Will but failed to transfer his feelings for his dead parents onto the psychiatrist, a striking woman in her early thirties who (it was later said) looked like Ingrid Bergman.

Rioch also evidently invited Percy to examine his love-hate relationship with the South—its code of conduct, its stoic bearing of loss and failure and misfortune, its twisted way of requiring its sons to distinguish themselves *and* at the same time to revere and honor their fathers.

Percy himself, recollecting the experience, concluded ruefully that after three years neither he nor Rioch knew what ailed him. His biggest problem, it seemed, was that he didn't want to be a doctor—that he didn't want to be anything in particular. He had said so in a tormented letter to Uncle Will, who had replied that "glory and accomplishment are of far less importance than the creation of character and the individual good life."

But in another sense, the outcome of Percy's analysis was clear. A further set of contraries was defined in him. Against the scientific approach of the College of Physicians and Surgeons, with its treatment of disease as such, was set the individual approach of psychiatry, which sought to discover what ailed one person at a time.

Thomas Merton chose to focus his graduate work on the literature of the eighteenth century, and as the topic of his thesis he chose an English novel called *The Spiritual Quixote*. But he changed midway, and in the end he wrote on a subject that, as he told it, chose him. He recalled running out of the library full of excitement: "I had just had in my hands the small, neatly printed Nonesuch edition of the *Poems of William Blake*, and I now knew what my thesis would probably be. It would take in his poems and some aspect of his religious ideas."

He had read Blake's poems in school in England. But now he embraced Blake anew as "the one poet who had least to do with his age, and was most in opposition to everything it stood for." Solitary, religiously obsessed, in protest against his age, Blake was a model for Merton's mounting rebellion against his own age and its idea of success. "More than once," Merton explained, "smug and inferior minds conceived it to be their duty to take this man Blake in hand and direct and form him, to try and canalize what they recognized as 'talent' in some kind of a conventional channel. And always this meant the cold and heartless disparagement of all that was vital and real to him in art and in faith."

Merton spent the summer of 1938 in a rented apartment on West 114th Street "in contact with the genius and the holiness of William Blake." In his thesis he argued that Blake was no fantasist, but rather a poet whose religiosity was evidence of a fierce and profound inner experience. For Blake, unlike his contemporaries, was an authentic "religious artist": there was a real and undeniable relationship between what he wrote and what he believed.

Merton stressed the fact that Blake, in his visual art, did not—could not—work from life or by looking at a sitting model; rather, Blake worked in reference to an ideal that had lodged in his head through his reading and his tireless copying of the works of other artists—first Gothic architecture and sculpture, then the works of Michelangelo and Rembrandt.

Merton saw this approach as an expression of Blake's religious ideas. Blake "does not love nature for and in herself, but looks at natural objects *sub specie aeternitatis*, as they are in God." He seeks "to 'copy' a 'vision'; not natural objects but mental images."

Described thus, Blake seems the most otherworldly of artists. But Merton took the contrary position, proposing that Blake's method, while grounded in his religiosity, also grew out of his training as an engraver rather than a fine artist—as a craftsman who made work with qualities of line and form and color which he had learned through imitation, and which were esteemed by all who practiced his craft. Odd as he was, Merton's Blake was a faithful copyist, whose work was an imitation of life itself—of the supernatural life, not the natural one.

The religious artist as the realist par excellence: that is a difficult and paradoxical argument, running against conventional ideas of realism and religion alike. To support it, Merton turned to a philosopher who, just then, was exploring the intersection of religion and art—a philosopher whose art of preference was the Gothic, his religion the Catholic, and his philosophy the *Summa* of St. Thomas Aquinas.

Jacques Maritain had published *Art and Scholasticism* in France in

1927, and an English translation came out in 1930. Among intellectuals his life story was already well known: born in France, raised a Protestant, educated agnostically at the Sorbonne, he had converted to Catholicism in 1906 in company with an émigré Russian Jewish poet, Raïssa Oumensoff. Like Etienne Gilson, he saw in the *Summa* a philosophy that would serve the Church and the modern university alike. His field of interest was aesthetics, and in *Art and Scholasticism* he took up Aquinas's idea of the "habit of art," arguing that artists rely on a faculty of intelligence called the "practical intellect," not the "speculative intellect" of philosophers, and that the confusion of the two had led artists astray—with Romanticism as the consequence.

For Merton, Maritain's account of "the habit of art" was as life-altering as Gilson's concept of God. In his thesis on Blake, he explained it this way:

As distinguished from intellectual activity of the speculative order, the practical intellect operates in two spheres: first, in that of action, where human ends are concerned, and where the means to those ends are selected on a moral basis. Secondly, in the sphere of "making." This is the sphere of productive action, considered not in relation to the *use to which we put our freedom* but in relation to *the thing produced*. The ends are here extrahuman. The artist does not have to consider our needs or desires but only the perfection of the work of art itself.

Maritain had distilled this point into a dictum: "Art is a virtue of the practical intellect." Merton quoted it approvingly, then made a further point: "The presence of virtue in the workman is necessary to the goodness of the work. As a man is, so are his works. The tree is known by its fruits."

On the face of it, that seems obvious, and it is true to the letter of Aquinas, who says that the true artist must possess virtue. But it is actually a conclusion Maritain had written *Art and Scholasticism* to refute. For Maritain's conclusion (following Aquinas) is that the artist must possess the virtue *proper to his activity.* That is, the person who would be a good artist need not be virtuous in manners or behavior, so long as he possesses the virtues necessary for his art: those of line and form and color, or those of meter and rhyme, or those of plot and character and motivation.

By a strange and telling misreading, Merton grasped Maritain's argument inside out; and as a result, it seems clear, he came to believe that if he wanted to be a good artist—which is all he had ever wanted to be—he would have to be a good man, even a holy one.

"It is the mark of the true mystic that, after his initiation into the mysteries of the unitive life, he is impelled, in some way, to serve his fellow men." That sentence, an aside in a scholarly book about Blake, intrigued Merton when he read it, and he underlined it with a pencil. In it his strange misunderstanding of Maritain is given a further explanation. For that summer, while he communed with the spirit of Blake, Merton also met a genuine mystic and holy man.

The story of Bramachari, as he was called, is a set piece in every Merton biography. A Hindu monk sets out on pilgrimage from India to the Congress of Religions at the Chicago World's Fair, only to find the Congress finished when he arrives; takes a doctorate virtually overnight from the University of Chicago and becomes notorious on campus in his turban and brown overcoat; travels to New York, hand to mouth, to see Merton's friend Sy Freedgood, who has a picture of a big-eyed cross-legged incarnation of Vishnu tacked to his dormitory wall, which his friends throw darts at to amuse themselves; arrives at Grand Central Terminal, where Freedgood and Merton await him—"It was a long time before we found him in the crowd, although you would think that a Hindu in a turban and a white robe and a pair of Keds would have been a rather memorable sight"; and goes with them to the Columbia campus, where his peace and happiness are obvious to everyone he meets.

Bramachari stayed with them all that summer, apparently. The conclusion invariably drawn from his presence, beginning with Merton's own account in *The Seven Storey Mountain*, is that this Hindu monk pointed Merton toward Roman Catholicism; rather than proselytizing Merton and his friends, Bramachari urged them to explore the religious traditions of the West. So he did, but there is another, simpler point to the story. Poverty and simplicity of life made Bramachari happy as well as holy, a holy man whose holiness actually let him enjoy life.

Bramachari was the true mystic Merton had read about in his study of Blake, who had known nirvana and now was called to serve others. He served them, first of all, by urging them to look into religion; but like Peter Maurin, whose path from Chicago to New York he followed, Bramachari served chiefly by being himself, the holy man being living proof, a walking, talking piece of philosophy.

The *Catholic Worker* was thriving. The first issue had drawn letters, subscriptions, donations of cash and supplies. Several dozen volunteers came to Dorothy Day's apartment, eager to pitch in. She rented a disused barbershop in the basement as the newspaper's first office. A second issue was produced, then a new issue each month. Pastors around the city ordered whole bundles, which they set out in the vestibules of their churches alongside the holy cards and pious pamphlets. The bundles of papers were delivered by a volunteer named Dan Orr, who had a horse and wagon; whenever they clopped past St. Patrick's Cathedral, he claimed, the horse genuflected.

Within a year they were printing a hundred thousand copies of each issue and mailing them to people all over the country.

In many ways, the paper's editorial mix—articles of local interest, first-person narratives of the hard life, polemics against the powers that be, and provocative illustrations, as well as Day's own column, called "Day by Day"— was not remarkable among the progressive papers of the era. What was remarkable was the movement that, seemingly from the start, emerged around the paper, a movement which the paper seemed not just to address but to embody. Soon the paper's volunteers were known as Catholic Workers. The name of the paper, meant to refer to its readers, had affixed itself to them.

From East Fifteenth Street they moved to East Seventh Street, then west to a cluster of apartments on Charles Street, then down to a whole building on Mott Street, which was lent to them rent-free in a prodigal act of hospitality.

The building's storefront space became their headquarters. They christened it St. Joseph's House, placing a plaster statue of the saint in the window and painting the name in gold leaf on the glass. This was an invocation of St. Joseph the Worker, the earthly father ("foster father," it was said then) of Jesus, and the carpenter whom the Church, cognizant of Communism, had declared the patron saint of workers, making May 1 his feast day. But it also may have been a reference to the palatial St. Joseph's House that Day had walked past every day on Staten Island. This St. Joseph's House would be the poor's own place.

The work, like the newspaper, had spread beyond Manhattan, and within a few years there were thirty-three Catholic Worker "houses of hospitality" in cities across America, many of them founded by Catholic college graduates who had no job prospects. It was a movement such as Peter Maurin had envisioned.

Maurin's program notwithstanding, Day, recalling the early years several decades later, suggested that the *Catholic Worker* was transformed from newspaper to social movement not programmatically but by accident:

What do *I* do? That's how our houses of hospitality started during the Depression. A girl came in. She had read a letter we sent to the bishops about the Church's tradition. She had been evicted from her furnished room. She had a couple of shopping bags and was sleeping in the subway. We didn't have any room, we were all filled up. We didn't know of any place that could take her. The girl looks at us and says: "Why do you write about things like that when you can't do anything about it?" It shamed us, you know? We went and rented us another apartment. Then we got a whole house. We were pushed into it. Everything we've done, we've been pushed into.

We never started a bread line. We didn't intend to have a bread line or a soup line come to the door. During the Seamen's Strike of 1937, six of them showed up. They said: "We're on strike, we have no place to stay, we have no food. We're sleeping in a loft on the waterfront." We took in about ten seamen. We rented a storefront, while the strike lasted for three months. We had big tubs of cottage cheese and peanut butter, and bread by the ton brought in. They could make sandwiches all day and there was coffee on the stove.

While we were doing that for the seamen, one of the fellows on the Bowery said, "What the hell are you doing down there feeding the seamen? What about the men on the Bowery? Nobody's feeding them." So when the men would come in for clothes or a pair of shoes or socks or a coat and we didn't have any left, we'd say, "Sit down anyway and have a cup of coffee. And a sandwich." We kept making more and more coffee. We brought out everything we had in the house to eat. That's how the first bread line started. Pretty soon we had a thousand men coming in a day, during the Depression. It started simply because that Bowery guy got mad.

Bramachari had urged Merton to read two books from the Western Christian tradition: *The Imitation of Christ* and the *Confessions* of St. Augustine.

But Merton didn't read them, not yet. He read—reread—*A Portrait of the Artist as a Young Man.*

Joyce was then the Church's most notorious apostate, and the best evidence of his defection was the *Portrait*, with its depiction of Stephen Dedalus's apostasy as an act of courage. Merton, however, was undeterred. In his autobiography (perhaps for the sake of his readers) he alludes to the strangeness of his being led toward the Church by Joyce, but at the time he was struck by the respect Joyce retained for the Catholic tradition and the care he took in presenting it believably in fiction—so believably that it could convince the reader in its own right.

He was struck especially by the celebrated hellfire sermon—a spectacularly eloquent Jesuit dramatizing hell for Stephen Dedalus and his classmates and inviting them to imagine being in hell literally forever. Because the sermon is presented verbatim (and without quotation marks) from beginning to end, it is as if the priest is addressing the reader directly.

The effect of the sermon on Stephen Dedalus is to convince him that hell is real and to make him feel that he is going there—"that he had already died, that his soul had been wrenched forth of the sheath of his body, that he was plunging headlong through space." But the effect on Thomas Merton was to make him feel that he was there with Stephen and his classmates in the chapel of a Catholic church in Dublin. Etienne Gilson had led him into the Catholic milieu, William Blake into the realm of religious experience; now he was brought through the doors and into the church proper by the power of realistic fiction. "What impressed me was not the fear of hell, but the expertness of the sermon," he recalled. "Now, instead of being repelled by the thought of such preaching—which was perhaps the author's intention—I was stimulated and edified by it. The style in which the priest in the book talked, pleased me by its efficiency and solidity and drive: and once again there was something eminently satisfying in the thought that these Catholics knew what they believed, and knew what to teach, and all taught the same thing, and taught it with coordination and purpose and great effect."

Seven years earlier, he had read *Ulysses* while visiting churches in Rome; now, reading *A Portrait of the Artist* sent him to a church as a genuine pilgrim, who sought to have for himself the experience he had read about.

He went to Sunday Mass at Corpus Christi, a small, bright church off upper Broadway past the Columbia campus. Arriving early, he took a seat in a pew in the rear and looked around. He was surprised by what he saw. The church was full of people, which amazed him. A few pews ahead, a beautiful girl knelt and prayed, oblivious of all else, and her beauty and piety put together amazed him, too. Never hesitant to generalize, he concluded that these were people whose minds were on God, not on each other: they had come to worship, nothing else. "Soon we all stood up. I did not know what it was for. The priest was at the other end of the altar, and, as I afterwards learned, he was reading the Gospel. And the next thing I knew there was someone in the pulpit"—a priest, slim and wearing horn-rimmed glasses, a man not much older, it appeared, than Merton himself.

He could hardly believe what happened next. The priest gave the sermon, and it was convincing. It sounded like the word of God. "For behind those words you felt the full force not only of Scripture but of centuries of a unified and continuous and consistent tradition. And above all, it was a vital tradition: there was nothing studied or antique about it. These words, this terminology, this doctrine, and these convictions fell from the lips of the young priest as something that were most intimately part of his own life."

It was a sermon as convincing as the one in Joyce. The priest, like Blake, seemed to live by what he preached. His words, words to live by, made Merton long to live by them.

He knocked on the church door and told the priest that he wanted to be a Catholic. It was September 1938. That fall he took instruction (as it was said), read the catechism, and was baptized.

Like Dorothy Day, Merton in retrospect saw baptism as the moment in which his life changed once and for all. But again, the differences between their two stories are significant. Where Day was vague about the details of her daughter's baptism and the events leading up to it, Merton gives a moment-to-moment account, seeing every detail as significant in a larger pattern. And where Day was nudged toward the baptismal font by *The Imitation of Christ*, Merton was impelled there by the life of Gerard Manley Hopkins.

Today Hopkins is known as a poet who shook off Victorian conventions through diction and syntax meant to imitate the quiddity of things; he is "of realty the rarest-veinèd unraveller," as he wrote of Duns Scotus, the mystical theologian who was perhaps his greatest influence. But the outlines of Hopkins's life are still unfamiliar: his studies at Oxford, and adventures in an aesthetic brotherhood like the pre-Raphaelites; his deep Anglican piety and ardor for the Oxford Movement reformers and their leader, John Henry Newman, who had "gone over" to Rome; his determination to become a Roman Catholic and a Jesuit priest, culminating in a desperate letter of entreaty to Newman, who received him into the Church of Rome in 1866.

Merton had checked a life of Hopkins out of the library, a book written by a priest. Time and space fell away as he read it, the outlines of the life supplanted by the desire to imitate its protagonist. The book, or a voice coming out of it, spoke to him:

> "What are you waiting for? Why are you sitting here? Why do you still hesitate? You know what you ought to do! Why don't you do it?"
>
> I stirred in the chair, I lit a cigarette, looked out the window at the rain, tried to shut the voice up. "Don't act on impulses," I thought. "This is crazy. This is not rational. Read your book."

Read your book. But there was the voice. *Live your life.* What was he waiting for?

> I got up and walked restlessly around the room. "It's absurd," I thought. "Anyway, Father Ford would not be there at this time of day. I would only be wasting time."

He read the book.

> Hopkins had written to Newman, and Newman had replied to him, telling him to come and see him at Birmingham.
>
> Suddenly, I could bear it no longer. I put down the book, and got into my raincoat, and started down the stairs. . . .
>
> And then everything inside me began to sing—to sing with peace, to sing with strength and to sing with conviction.

In retrospect the scene seems overdone, until one realizes how skillfully written it is—written with classical rhetorical skill, a thorough fitting of the language to the need. Merton tells no more about Hopkins than is necessary to his own story, and he conveys his own native skepticism so naturally that you hardly realize that a mysterious voice is telling him to change his life and he is listening to it.

He also casts the scene as a kind of annunciation, setting up a contrast with the scene of his baptism, which comes a few pages later. Whereas he went to ask for baptism at night and alone, he goes to the baptism itself on a bright morning, bringing four friends along. Whereas the voice calling him to baptism took him by surprise, the baptism itself fills him with anticipation and worry, as he frets that he will not be able to fast overnight (as was required) and that he has broken the fast by brushing his teeth. And whereas the voice's questions, which came in a set of three, were slangy and cajoling, the voice of the Church in the baptismal rite is unshakably solemn, as "in a triple vow I renounced Satan and his pomps and his works":

"Dost thou believe in God, the Father almighty, Creator of heaven and earth?"
"*Credo!*"
"Dost thou believe in Jesus Christ His only son, Who was born and suffered?"
"*Credo!*"
"Dost thou believe in the Holy Spirit, in the Holy Catholic Church, the Communion of Saints, the remission of sins, the resurrection of the body and eternal life?"
"*Credo!*"

The baptism scene, with the First Communion scene that follows it, makes clear that *The Seven Storey Mountain* is not an autobiography per se but a conversion story, written to explain why Merton has embraced religious faith and to persuade the reader to go and do likewise. As it happens, however, of all the scenes in the book these are the least convincing, especially in comparison to the real and affecting drama of the night the resolve to be baptized took hold of him. Here the imagery is taken whole from the baptismal rite and the customs attached to it. Mountains tumble from his shoulders; scales fall away; devils depart as the priest, performing the ritual exorcism, blows into his face. Receiving the Eucharist, he observes, he is at last a "Temple of God," a person "incorporated into his Incarnation"—but at this moment of firsthand experience the words for the experience are not his own, not yet.

FOUR

Another World

Growing up in Milledgeville, Mary Flannery O'Connor drew cartoons. They were not the doodles of a bored child in the margins of a notebook. They were small works of a young woman who was already determined to be an artist, works conceived to delight others and to inflict her point of view on the world. Some were printed in the high school newspaper. Others she sent to the *New Yorker* (they were returned). A few were presented to her father, who would fold them and tuck them into his wallet, so as to show the people he met on his travels what kind of girl his daughter was.

In one of her cartoons, two fish are swimming side by side. One fish says to the other, "You can go jump out of the lake." That, as Robert Fitzgerald remarked, is "the authentic O'Connor humor," at once homely and surreal. On one level the cartoon is a rural expression turned upside down, a low joke overturned; on another it is an image of two worlds, this one and another, a place distinct from ordinary life but no less real.

For the O'Connors, Milledgeville in the late 1930s was doubtless such a place: another world, a place set apart. The pillared white house with the slave-brick wall surrounding it was a refuge from the poverty and strife of the Depression, and after working all week for the Federal Housing Administration Edward Francis O'Connor was doubtless happy to rejoin his wife and daughter there.

Regina Cline O'Connor was one of sixteen children, and the Cline house was often full of people: cousins, aunts, and uncles, mostly on the

Cline side, since Mr. O'Connor had only a sister, who also married a Cline.

After eight years of parochial schooling O'Connor was enrolled in Peabody High, a public school. In a sketch called "Biography," probably written for a class, she introduced herself as a "pidgeon-toed, only-child with a receding chin and a you-leave-me-alone-or-I'll-bite-you complex." The new kid in town, an only child in a household of adults, she sought a refuge of her own. She went up to the attic, a vast space with gabled windows facing the main street and the cemetery, and set up an artist's workspace there. When she wanted to draw, to write, to think, to be alone, she would climb the stairs to the attic and shut out the world below.

In 1939, when she was fourteen years old, her father returned from Atlanta and didn't go back. Though he was in his early forties, his limbs and joints ached in such a way that he'd had to resign his job with the government. The diagnosis was arthritis.

Her own life was now divided between upstairs and downstairs, home and school, the world she imagined and the one she found set out for her. Peabody High was "a progressive high school where one did not read if one did not wish to," she recalled. "I did not wish to." After school, however, her creations issued from the attic in a steady flow: cartoons, poems, nonsense verse, homemade books—three of them—which she saw as "too old for children and too young for grown-ups."

Downstairs her father's arthritis had gotten worse. His ailment was now diagnosed as something else, a rare disease of the blood, known by its Latin name, meaning "red wolf." "This is something called lupus," O'Connor later recalled. "At the time he had it there was nothing for it but the undertaker." Edward Francis O'Connor, a native of Savannah like his daughter, had come to Milledgeville for good.

In 1937, the Metropolitan Museum of Art opened a museum of medieval art. The Cloisters, as it is called, was like no other museum in America: an odd and remote outpost compounded from the ruins of several disused European monasteries—chapels, cloisters, stained-glass windows—which had been taken apart stone by stone, shipped across the ocean, and put together on a bluff in uptown Manhattan as a New World meta-monastery.

Thomas Merton went to the Cloisters on a date one Sunday the summer after it opened, then returned by himself later in the year. Looking back, he described those visits as the happiest days he spent in New York—happier, it seems, than the days he spent in actual churches.

At the museum he learned that one of the cloisters had been brought from Prades, the French village where he had been born. The old stones had been uprooted from his birthplace and situated in Manhattan, just as he had been. "Synthetic as it is," he wrote, "it still preserves enough of its own reality to be a reproach to everything else around it, except the trees and the Palisades."

Better than any symbol he himself chose, the Cloisters, a blend of the medieval and the modern, of church and museum, of religion and art and worldly striving, embodies his religious life in the time after his baptism.

In becoming a Catholic, Merton sought to leave 1930s Manhattan behind and enter the world he had read about in Gilson and Hopkins and Joyce—a world oriented around the Church and shot through with divine purpose.

Whereas Walker Percy was in search of a life outside the vexed history of his family and his region, Merton sought a lost world he had lived in once and, in a sense, had fallen from, then had glimpsed again in literature and philosophy. He yearned for an ideal he could live in, in which he could immerse himself and be surrounded.

The story of his life during the next few years is the story of his search for that ideal. A rebel, he will stop rebelling against himself and rebel instead against the modern world, which stands between him and the ideal. He will try to find an ideal medieval world but will wind up incorporating medieval elements into a modern structure, the way his father did when he bought an old chapel for its arches.

The impulse to find and inhabit an "other" world over and against the present one is perhaps the most common form the religious pilgrimage takes. God, the pilgrim suspects, is other and elsewhere. There must be another world where God is. The pilgrim yearns to see God face to face, so earthly life becomes a pilgrimage toward that other place; sometimes it displaces the religious yearning and becomes a religion unto itself. Its source, often enough, is the imagination of the artist, which seeks expression in religion, the only world as vivid as the starlit world within. But sometimes the human person is seen as the image of God, and earthly society as the fallen analogue of the heavenly one.

In the 1930s, as world war came to seem inevitable, the artists and writers of Europe sought an otherworldly ideal. There, the other world of religious aspiration had been embodied most vividly in the Middle Ages—the great upthrust of the cathedrals, the self-denial of the saints, the two-tiered universe schematized by Aquinas, in which the revealed truths of Christianity were laid atop Aristotle, as Dante's epic was laid over Virgil's. So successful were the medievals in their efforts that their creations have come to stand in imaginatively for that other world: Dante's hell *is* hell, and the cathedral at Chartres is a kind of heaven.

In the 1930s the retromedieval impulse, as the historian Norman Cantor has called it, was especially strong in England, as a group of Christian writers called the Inklings sought to evoke the Middle Ages as "a larger, brighter, bitterer, more dangerous world than ours." J.R.R. Tolkien brought out *The Hobbit*, whose colorful and modernly playful surface concealed a story of struggle between pagan and Christian civilization. C. S. Lewis, a scholar of medieval literature, began to champion the medieval outlook to the general public: on the radio, in book-length blasts of polemic, and eventually, too, in mythic fiction.

The Lord of the Rings and *The Chronicles of Narnia* would make them beloved authors. In 1939, however, they were little known. The best-known representative of the retromedieval worldview was T. S. Eliot, the most famous, and most modern, of modern poets.

Eliot, as Michael Schmidt has written, was "an expatriate twice over" whose movements "from Unitarian St. Louis to agnostic Boston, from New England to England" were thought to reflect "his hunger for a natural home." His conversion to Anglican Christianity in 1927 was seen as an expression of his Englishness, a costume for his verse akin to the tailored English suit and bowler hat he wore around London. But in truth his conversion was a third expatriation. The Anglo-Catholic movement he joined stressed the Church of England's roots in pre-Reformation English Christianity—medieval Catholicism, that is. Although he glorified the English seventeenth century above all as an era of sublime liturgy, firm doctrine, and exquisite English prose, his hero was the "pure," "medieval" seventeenth-century divine Lancelot Andrewes, who had helped fashion the Authorised Version of the Bible.

Among Anglo-Catholics Eliot was taken to be a saint in the making, and the ironic epigraph to an early poem—"Only the divine stands firm; the rest is smoke"—seemed an earnest precept for his life and his poetry. The verse he wrote after becoming a Christian is shot through with the distinction between the fallen world and the perfect other world of eternity: a poem spoken by a penitent on Ash Wednesday; a verse history of the Church in England; verse meditations on the Virgin Mary and the Magi; a pageant written for performance in Canterbury Cathedral, setting Thomas à Becket against a band of functionaries and making the conflict an allegory for the conflict between the broad medieval Christian worldview and the narrow pagan one.

In the eyes of the retromedievalists, such a conflict was taking shape in modern Europe. As Hitler claimed Czechoslovakia, annexed Poland, sought France, and ordered the bombing of London, the other world of medieval Christendom looked at once attractive and under threat, and Eliot's poetry especially seemed to speak to the situation. The long poem consolidating the insights he had gained as a Christian—*Four Quartets*—would be a war poem whether he intended it to be or not. Already "Burnt Norton," published in 1936, had counseled: "Descend lower, descend only / Into the world of perpetual solitude, / World not world, but that which is not world . . . while the world moves / In appentency, on its metalled ways / Of time past and time future."

There matters stood in January 1939 when Merton, newly baptized, a freshly minted Master of Arts, moved to Perry Street in Greenwich Village.

Perry Street is two streets down from Bank Street, where the Cowleys' literary-social circle had met, and one street down from Charles Street, where the Catholic Workers had been headquartered until the need for more space sent them east again. Merton rented an apartment at No. 35 and, he says in *The Seven Storey Mountain*, began work on his Ph.D. At the same time, he began a regimen of round-the-clock religious devotion: Sunday Mass at St. Joseph's on Sixth Avenue, weekday Mass at St. Francis of Assisi near Penn Station or Our Lady of Guadalupe on Fourteenth Street, a few hours' reading in the *Summa* in the Columbia library, followed by the Stations of the Cross at Corpus Christi Church or the Church of Notre Dame on Morningside Drive, after which he would ride the subway downtown, where a shiny new black telephone sat on a table, awaiting him.

No sooner had he rented the Perry Street place than he wanted to leave it. In *The Seven Storey Mountain*, he explains that it was too expensive, but there was doubtless another reason for his yearning to escape. The West Village, a neighborhood of brownstones and brick townhouses with wrought-iron railings, was no place for a person who longed to be back in the Middle Ages. It was early America through and through.

When summer came he sublet the apartment and traveled upstate, where he hoped to live simply, even monastically, in a cottage with his college friends.

The cottage, owned by Robert Lax's family, was located west of Buffalo, on top of a mountain overlooking the Erie Valley, which was full of oil wells and logging camps. Down the mountain was St. Bonaventure's, a college run by Franciscan friars. A sanatorium for tuberculosis patients was set atop a mountain a mile away.

The cottage was at different times a fraternity house, a writers' colony, and a homestead for Merton and his friends, who set themselves up as a kind of extended family. But it was no hermitage, and life there was not solitary. It was a chaste communal life. In the summer several of them made the garage into a literary clubhouse. They set up their typewriters in the garage. They ate hamburgers and discussed modern fiction in the driveway while dishes lay unwashed in the sink. They played bongo drums, swung gaily on a trapeze. They grew beards. They tried to write novels. They piled into an old car and went down the mountain into town to drink beer or see a movie or play nickel-and-dime games at a carnival. "I think we all had a sort of feeling that we could be hermits up on that hill," Merton recalled, "but the trouble was that none of us really knew how."

It was doubtless a hard place in which to be a new and ardent Catholic convert. Merton's friends were either Jewish or impious. There was no place where he could be alone. If he wanted to pray he went for a walk in the woods. To go to Mass he had to hitchhike down the mountain.

In August, then, he returned to Manhattan and reclaimed the apartment on Perry Street. The Village had emptied out. The holy/worldly scheme was reversed. The upstate countryside was crowded, busy, worldly. The city would be a retreat. There, all alone, he was free to be religious.

The Catholic Workers, meanwhile, were on the move from city to country. They rented a farm on Staten Island to use as a "halfway house," then bought a farm in Pennsylvania, half a day's drive from New York, where, Dorothy Day announced in the paper, they would establish "a true farming commune," enacting the third point in Peter Maurin's program for Catholic alternative living.

In the annals of the Catholic Worker the move "to Christ—to the land!" is recalled as the occasion of the movement's first great conflict. The lofty notion of "agronomic universities" is contrasted with the shabby actuality of the farms, the theoretical and absentminded Maurin is opposed to the practical and hardheaded Day, and the scene is set for the divide in the movement between the "workers" and the "scholars," between the life of poverty and the concept of it. But it is clear that the conflict between the theoretical and the practical, between the ideal world and the fallen one, was felt most keenly within Day herself, and that the farms were part of her own program to narrow the gap between the life she lived and the life she wrote about. "We are making this move because we do not feel that we can talk about something we are not practicing," she declared. "We believe that our words will have more weight, our writings will carry more conviction, if we ourselves are engaged in making a better life on the land."

As communes the farms were failures. The Staten Island farm came to seem a "household of sad afflicted creatures," as Day put it, not workers so much as wounded denizens of the city. The Pennsylvania farm was riven by worker-scholar conflict, and as a result the soil was not tilled, the gardens were not weeded, the house was not repaired; the farm never became communal or self-sustaining, and Day never moved there to live as she had planned.

Rather, she remained in the city, where the second point of Peter Maurin's program—"roundtable discussions"—was being realized. On Friday evenings workers and scholars and interested others would meet at St. Joseph's House to join guest speakers in discussions on labor, poverty, papal encyclicals, the lives of the saints. Like those of countless other radical groups of the period, these meetings were meant to reconcile theory and practice, to bring about clarification of action as well as thought.

In the middle 1930s two concerns joined the regular agenda for the meetings. One was anti-Semitism, both in Germany and in the Catholic Church. Day and the Catholic Workers, it is often pointed out, were among the first people in the Church in America to denounce the Nazis and stand up for European Jews. They went to the Hudson River pier to protest the arrival of the German ship *Bremen* in 1935. They picketed the German embassy as the Nazis annexed Europe. They invited Jacques Maritain, who was teaching at Princeton, to speak about Christian anti-Semitism at a Friday-night meeting. Peter Maurin set up a stall on the sidewalk on the Lower East Side, from which he sought to engage Jewish passersby in dialogue.

The other concern was the Spanish Civil War, which began in July

1936. Like the execution of Sacco and Vanzetti, this war, as Eric Hobsbawm has written, "now seems to belong to a prehistoric past, even in Spain," and the terms used to describe it—Popular Front, Comintern, Falange, pronunciamento—are now as remote as those of the Baltimore Catechism. But the war, as Hobsbawm puts it, "raised the fundamental political issues of the time: on the one side, democracy and social revolution, Spain being the only country in Europe where it was ready to erupt; on the other, a uniquely uncompromising camp of counter-revolution or reaction, inspired by a Catholic Church which rejected everything that had happened in the world since Martin Luther." And it did so in a way that appealed especially to artists and writers, inviting their direct involvement, and leading several thousand to go to Spain to take part in a "people's war." The Russian Revolution, stirring as it was, had taken place in a country as real and yet as distant as a nineteenth-century novel. The elected Popular Front's battle to withstand a Fascist overthrow was taking place in present-day Europe. Marxism had taken root in the soil of Catholic Europe; on the "arid square" of Spain, W. H. Auden wrote, "our thoughts have bodies; the menacing shapes of our fever / Are precise and alive."

To that point the Church's anti-Communist rhetoric had been directed largely against Soviet Russia, a distant country with no Catholic populace; if the conflict was real, the battlefield was otherworldly, imaginary. Now Communists or those backed by them were desecrating churches and torturing clergy in a country as indubitably Catholic as Italy itself, on the grounds that the Church, as much as the Nazis and the Italian Fascists, was the source of Falange power.

The war in Spain was the first challenge to Day's instinctive blend of Catholicism and radicalism. As priests denounced the Popular Front from the pulpits and radicals decried the "Fascist Church" on the streetcorners, she chose to remain neutral. It was not an uncommon position. The governments of the United States, Britain, and France called themselves neutral. Day's reason, however, was spiritual, not tactical. She had become a pacifist.

She had been against war categorically ever since her childhood, but had supported so-called people's wars in Russia, Mexico, and Nicaragua. Her conversion to Catholicism turned her against war once and for all. In a sense, her pacifism was an outgrowth of her emerging philosophy. With Peter Maurin as guide, she and her movement had embraced personalism, the view that the human person is the basic unit of society, and that all forms of social organization—family, nation, church, state—are sound only insofar as they uphold the dignity of each and every person and prompt every person into direct encounters with others. But in another sense her pacifism—and her personalism—was grounded uncomplicatedly in the imitation of Christ. Christ was a man of peace; therefore the Christian should be one as well. "Today the whole world has turned to the use of force," she remarked, but the Christian faith and its "counsels of perfection" urged the believer to seek change by other means: prayer, the sacraments, personal striving for sanctity.

She wrote a long letter to a priest to explain her stance, and published it in the *Catholic Worker*. The letter—one of many she would address to a symbolic interlocutor—is more complex than her other writing thus far.

Then as now the complaint against pacifism was that it was unrealistic, indeed escapist—an attempt to opt out of the messy process whereby power is gained and exercised. So Day sought to establish that pacifism was practical. "Yes, wars will go on," she acknowledged. "We are living in a world where even 'Nature itself travaileth and groaneth' due to the Fall. But we cannot sit back and say 'human nature being what it is, you cannot get a man to overcome his adversary by love.'" Rather, Christians had to love their neighbors, even their enemies, with all their might. "Love and prayer," she insisted, were "not passive, but an active glowing force." Was Christian love impractical? There was no way of knowing. It had never really been tried. And the difficulty of practicing such love made it vital for Christians to practice it sooner rather than later. "We must prepare now," she declared. "There must be disarmament of the heart."

So she and her movement would not pray for General Franco and the Falangists. Nor would they pray for the elected socialist government. "We are praying for the Spanish people—all of them our brothers in Christ—all of them Temples of the Holy Ghost, all of them members or potential members of the Mystical Body of Christ."

Pacifism cost the Catholic Worker popular support. Parish priests canceled their bulk orders for the newspaper. Subscriptions dropped by two-thirds. Catholic Workers left the houses of hospitality or, in other Catholic Worker papers, such as the one in Chicago, began to defend the theory of the just war.

Pacifism also complicated the movement's response to other events in Europe. In March 1939 the Spanish Civil War ended: the Fascists had won. But another war was under way, and one less susceptible to appeals to the

Mystical Body of Christ, for already it was clear that, whatever else it might become, this war would be a war against the Jews of Europe.

"The book said the room should be darkened"—Merton read the instructions carefully—"and I pulled down the blinds so that there was just enough light left for me to see the pages, and to look at the Crucifix on the wall over my bed. And the book also invited me to consider what kind of a position I should take for my meditation. . . .

"So I thought and prayed a while over this momentous problem, and finally decided to make my meditations sitting cross-legged on the floor. I think the Jesuits would have had a nasty shock if they had walked in and seen me doing their *Spiritual Exercises* sitting there like Mahatma Gandhi."

The *Spiritual Exercises* of St. Ignatius were not recommended for home use. Ignatius of Loyola and his first companions had performed them in their lodgings in sixteenth-century Paris, but Ignatian meditation was soon formalized for Jesuits, who were introduced to the technique in a month-long silent retreat supervised by a spiritual director. The order had invested the *Exercises* with otherworldly mystery, making them seem to Merton less a text than a strange intoxicant that might "plunge you headfirst into mysticism."

Merton, once again, was undeterred. A Ph.D. candidate, fluent in languages, self-directed in his reading, confident in his ability to grasp difficult texts on his own, he undertook the *Spiritual Exercises* alone in his apartment, communing with the text directly. His spiritual director would be the saint himself.

He spent an hour a day on the meditations. They were not meditations in the sense in which the word is used today, a disciplined shutting down of the senses. Rather, they invited him to envision the supernatural world in all its vividness, to imagine himself present at the great events of sacred history, and to identify with the people there, the better to grasp the religious significance of what had taken place.

Such an approach was akin to Merton's own approach to religious experience. Ever since his boyhood in France he had practiced the technique Ignatius called the "composition of place," obsessively recollecting a setting from the past so as to inhabit it imaginatively; more recently, he had meditated on the texts of Joyce and Blake and Hopkins, putting himself imaginatively in the religiously tormented protagonist's place.

Even as the *Exercises* enjoined him to meditate on sacred history, he was meditating on personal history as well—recollecting an episode, pondering, and drawing a moral conclusion much as the saint suggested.

His apartment had a wrought-iron balcony overlooking the street. In the late summer of 1939, as Nazi Germany made an alliance with the Soviets, prompting England and France to declare war, he sat on the balcony—"sitting on the good boards and letting my feet dangle through the place where the boards had broken"—and wrote obsessively in his journal. A self-portrait he sketched on a blank page shows him in the window, ready to climb out—dressed in a T-shirt, notebook in hand, light hair thinning, one eye cocked at the world below.

There on the balcony (and in the window later in the year) he performed a series of *literary* exercises, training himself to write about his life in a new way.

In graduate school he had roughed out several novels, each a bildungsroman about a young man thrust uneasily into modern life. The last of these, *The Labyrinth*, he wrote at the cottage upstate, and as soon as he got back to Perry Street in August he deposited the manuscript in the mailbox on the corner, then went to Our Lady of Guadalupe to light a candle and say a prayer that it might be published.

The manuscript came right back, rejected as dull and "an unresolved narrative."

Merton took it as a sign. Upstate, Robert Lax had urged him to cease imitating Joyce. Now he himself surmised his talent was not for autobiographical fiction so much as for "straight" autobiography.

On the balcony above Perry Street, above the world and apart from it, he began to discipline his meditations. With war approaching, he sought to depart the charged historical present in two ways at once, through an exploration of the self and through an excursion into the world of Catholic philosophy.

The balcony was his outpost, his observation deck, his open-air hermitage. There, his journal, a series of exercises in observing and recalling, thinking and writing, became a religious devotion.

The journal Merton kept on Perry Street is a laboratory in autobiographical writing, in which he sharpens his powers of observation, recollection, and discernment. He reviews the 1939 World's Fair at length. He makes lists: of odd words, Spanish words, "words of our century," things he hasn't thought of lately, "unimportant things," the different ways to describe something. He records things he has seen and heard in ordinary life—a girl outside a church discovering that some carnations for sale are fake, a lady at an El Greco show remarking that all El Greco's people look as if they have tuberculosis.

Now and then he pushes past pure documentation to plumb his impressions for their significance. He admits to liking the film version of *Gone with the Wind* and tries to figure out why. He recalls the WPA "woikers' " art of the Depression—"pictures of bums sleeping on newspapers" and the like—and opines that "the whole 1930s are already dated although the decade isn't even over."

In these exercises he is still taking after Joyce, who had shown in *Ulysses* that everybody's life is prospectively of literary interest. Although disillusioned with fiction, Merton has not abandoned the Joycean notion that every moment of every life is somehow significant. He merely seeks to apply it to his own experience.

The holiness of the ordinary is a Catholic position as well, and his discovery of the parallel makes his writing come alive. Much of the religious writing in the journal consists of straight transcription of Thomistic philosophy, in which he explains what it might be to see things—a tree, say—"as they are in God." "Everything was important to St. Francis," Merton observed.

Such an analysis of the essences of things seems at first to be remote from the events of 1939: the war in Europe, the changing of the seasons on Perry Street. But the aim of seeing things "as they are in God" has become Merton's motive for autobiography. His own journey is at once religious and literary. He invokes the Holy Ghost as a kind of muse, for "although He is right with us and in and out of us and all through us we have to go on journeys to find him." If in literary terms he is moving toward a more subjective truth, from thinly disguised fiction to the frank recitation of the facts of his own life, in religious terms he is going the other way, toward a quality of personal insight that will have "objective" solidity and authority.

It is not self-knowledge he yearns for, but religious peace, which "is not in knowing ourselves but in knowing God." On Perry Street he feels, and describes, such peace:

> The air outside my window is quiet, and light hangs among the leaves and is soft and blue and warm. In one of the next houses I can hear pots in a kitchen, and water running from a tap, and I can hear the voices of kids.

... This sunlight, this warm air, the sounds of kitchens, speak of God's goodness and His mercy. I can sit here all day, now, and think of that, and ask God to show me everywhere more and more signs of His mercy, and His goodness, and to help me regain my liberty. Peace.

I know they are hearing confessions now at St. Francis' Church. Everywhere, tomorrow morning, Masses.

Here on my shelves, Pascal, St. Augustine, Thomas à Kempis, Loyola, The Bible, Saint John of the Cross (no, Lax has that).

Here is liberty, all I have to do is to be quiet, sit still.

There, perhaps for the first time, is the authentic voice of Merton's writing: clear, direct, eternally present, describing the world about him in such a way as to reveal his inner life to himself and his reader. From 1939 on his voice will be an unabashed *I*, and his approach that of spiritual autobiography.

For Walker Percy the year 1939 was decisive as well. The third year of medical school was the year when he finally became serious about medicine. It was the year when he commenced work with live patients. In a sense, it was the year when, for the first time, he left the South behind.

He returned to New York from Mississippi in September, shortly after war was declared in Europe. The city was on tenterhooks, but he went about his business—strolling through the World's Fair in Queens, taking the commuter train to Princeton to visit Caroline Gordon and Allen Tate (who were now teaching there), attending *Der Rosenkavalier* at the Metropolitan Opera with his uncle's friend. But his real life was in the laboratory, where after two years of halfhearted effort he was suddenly obsessed with the science of pathology.

In Greenville for the summer, he had found his Uncle Will transformed by a new project: an autobiography. In Will's view the new war was a recapitulation, tragic but necessary, of the Great War, in which he had fought, and in the autobiography he would valorize war as the experience that best tested a man's honor. The book, already under contract to Knopf in New York, would relate his life story as an illustration of his personal philosophy, and it would be a primer and object lesson about modern war.

Percy's response to this endeavor was to throw himself into his medical work. Despite his experience of psychoanalysis, he struggled through the course in psychiatry (his final grade was a C). On the ward, however, he thrived. Pathology, the study of disease as such, was the specialty of the Columbia medical program. It was the particular field of a professor who became Percy's mentor—a Southerner, a bachelor, uncommonly well-read. And it was the field most congenial to Percy as a man whose parents were dead and whose uncle was a poet of decline and fall. In 1939–1940, examining patients and conducting tests in the laboratory, he grew fascinated with the question of how illness and disease come about.

Percy's biographers find the appeal of pathology for him in its impersonality, its distance from the messy business of the individual patient. Percy suggested as much some years later, recalling his lack of enthusiasm for the "arts and crafts of the bedside manner." But in describing pathology and its effects on him he was not cold or impersonal. He was animated and ardent. "It was the elegance and order and, yes, the beauty of science that attracted me," he recalled, its "constant movement . . . in the direction of ordering the endless variety and the seeming haphazardness of ordinary life." He went on, practically rhapsodizing about disease: "Under the microscope, in the test tube, in the colorimeter, one could actually see the beautiful theater of disease and even measure the effect of treatment on the disease process." One could watch "these elegant agents of disease," such as the "scarlet tubercle bacillus . . . lying crisscrossed like Chinese characters in the sputum and lymphoid tissue" of TB patients.

Perhaps he disdained the "art" of medicine in favor of the science of it, but he described it with the ardor of a poet or a mystic.

His attraction to the science of pathology was not an aversion to life: it was an attraction to another life, a world apart, one different from the world in which he had been raised. In the "beautiful theater of disease" he could forget his personal history. There, his parents were not dead. There, world war did not threaten. There, his uncle, the great man, was not writing an autobiography—was not putting his philosophy of life into a book so that his nephews could not forget it. In the "beautiful theater of disease," Percy felt unique and alive.

Merton made a plan to go to Cuba on pilgrimage during Holy Week. Then he learned that he had appendicitis and would have to undergo surgery.

He left the doctor's office and went home to get a toothbrush and a copy of Dante's *Paradiso*. The hospital performing the surgery was a Catholic hospital, with nuns acting as nurses, and he envisioned it as a kind of paradise.

The hospital episode, more than any other in *The Seven Storey Mountain*, is written in emulation of Dante: a pilgrimage in miniature, a gradual ascent from depths to heights. Merton gently slides a drunk away from the subway turnstile; he rides the train far uptown; he ascends "the scores of monumental steps to the top of the bluff where St. Elizabeth's Hospital was"; finally, atop the bluff—it is night now, and icy—"I climbed the steps of the hospital, and entered the clean shiny hall and saw a crucifix and a Franciscan nun, all in white, and a statue of the Sacred Heart."

The operation was uneventful, but the hospital, where he stayed ten days, was all he had hoped for. As he recalled it, it was a place of peace and virtue, where, recovering, he was treated as a newborn in the life of faith. A priest brought him Communion in bed every morning. He prayed the Rosary, concealing the beads under the bedclothes. He read Dante: there was plenty of time, in this paradise, to read about paradise, and the brightly lit ward on a hilltop suited the book just right.

But the appeal of the hospital was more basic than that. Like Dorothy Day ten years earlier, Merton scarcely knew any Catholics; his pilgrimage, like hers, was still solitary and largely imaginative. But whereas she longed to be incorporated into the body of other Catholics, he sought an apt setting for his new faith, an outward sign of his inward journey. He was happy at St. Elizabeth's Hospital because it was a Catholic place.

Likewise Cuba, where he went as soon as he had recovered, in time for Holy Week. There he, like Day in Mexico, had a whole country as the correlative for the religious ardor he felt.

At the time Cuba was as Catholic as any country in the Americas. In *The Seven Storey Mountain* Merton prefaces the story of his pilgrimage—to the shrine of Our Lady of Cobre, where the Virgin Mary was said to have appeared—by calling it "one of those medieval pilgrimages that was nine-tenths vacation and one-tenth pilgrimage." But the account that follows suggests that the trip, no matter how easeful or enjoyable, was religiously intense. He went to early Mass and received Communion, then went to hear another Mass at a different church (and sometimes a third and a fourth). He said the Rosary and walked through the Stations of the Cross. He gave alms to beggars on the street. He was reading *Poet in New York* by Federico García Lorca, who had been murdered the previous year, but he had brought his Catholic books with him, too, and "when I was sated with prayers, I could go back into the streets, walking among the lights and shadows, stopping to drink huge glasses of iced fruit juices in the little bars, until I came home again and read Maritain or St. Teresa until it was time for lunch."

The books he was reading described not merely a Catholic faith but a whole Catholic society, held together by common assumptions about the purpose of life. Born in France, he believed that he was a native of such a society, and ever since his baptism he had imagined such a society or sought to create one in his journal. In Cuba, for the first time since he had left Rome at the age of eighteen, he was in an actual Catholic society again, and he felt like "a spiritual millionaire."

His pilgrimage to the shrine of Our Lady of Cobre was uneventful; but in Havana the next morning the unmistakable physical presence of Catholicism aroused him to mystical insight.

He had been to Mass at one church and was now at a second. He stood at the back, listening. As one priest consecrated the Eucharist, another led a First Communion class, and to the priest's question the children replied— "*Creo en Diós!*"—as Merton had the day of his own baptism and First Communion eighteen months earlier:

> That cry, "*Creo en Diós!*" It was loud, and bright, and sudden and glad and triumphant. Then, as sudden as the shout and as definite, and a thousand times more bright, there formed in my mind an awareness, an understanding, a realization of what had just taken place on the altar, at the Consecration: a realization of God made present by the words of Consecration in a way that made Him belong to me. . . .
>
> And the first articulate thought that came to mind was:
> "Heaven is right here in front of me: Heaven, Heaven!"

That, Merton wrote, was his first genuine mystical experience, and from it he dated his yearning for the experience of God in contemplative prayer. It is telling that it took place in Havana, whose very name hinted at heaven. To that point Merton had encountered the Catholic faith secondhand, in libraries and churches, a solitary stranger. Suddenly to be in a Catholic city, and to hear a group of Catholic schoolchildren uninhibitedly proclaim their faith—his faith—was to feel as never before that the Catholic religion was real, as real as an earthly city, and that he belonged there.

At a village called Matanza one evening, he spoke aloud while the locals strolled in the square, and as he spoke a crowd gathered: "And I heard someone who had just arrived in the crowd say: '¿Es católico, ese Americano?' 'Man,' said the other, 'he is a Catholic and a very good Catholic,' and the tone in which he said this made me so happy that, when I went to bed, I could not sleep."

For as long as he had been a Catholic Merton had thought of becoming a priest. On Perry Street, he filled his journal with counsels of the Church Fathers, such as St. Gregory, who had felt called to "leave the world" but had been held back by "anxiety of mind." After hearing Jacques Maritain speak at Columbia, he was full of excitement, and a professor who was with him asked him if he had a "vocation" to the priesthood.

At the time he yearned to be a priest mainly because the priesthood would mark him as oriented toward the other world of Catholic belief. A year and a half after his baptism, there were few outward signs of his religiosity, except that he was trying to give up cigarettes, alcohol, and red meat—no great sacrifice, since "I rarely smoke or drink and I have stopped eating meat because I don't particularly like it." He was struck by how little conversion seemed to change a person. Supposing his friend Ad Reinhardt—modern artist and Communist—quit Communism and became a Christian, he wrote in his journal, Reinhardt would "still be the same guy, the same artist, etc." He went on, "In what way does it change you and in what way does it not change you? Why do you have to travel so far to change, outwardly, so little?"

One evening in the fall of 1939 he had gone with some friends to hear jazz at a nightclub in the Village. Afterward his friends came to spend the night at his place on Perry Street, and Merton, sleeping on the floor, had a taste of the austerity he imagined was a fact of life in a monastery. The next day he announced that he wanted to be a priest. His friends were not as surprised as he thought they would be.

Once they had left—it was evening again—he went to a Catholic bookstore, then to the church of St. Francis Xavier a few blocks away. He hastened down the steps to the basement chapel. There, Benediction was under way—the priest kneeling before the big gold monstrance, the people ("workmen, poor women, students, clerks") singing the Tantum Ergo. He knelt and began to pray. As he pondered the Eucharist he perceived that he was at a "moment of crisis." Did he really want to be a priest? If so, why was he hesitating? "During that moment my whole life remained suspended on the edge of an abyss," he recalled in *The Seven Storey Mountain*. "But this time, the abyss was an abyss of love and peace, the abyss was God. . . .

"I looked straight at the Host, and I knew, now, Who it was that I was looking at, and I said, 'Yes, I want to be a priest, with all my heart I want it. If it is Your will, make me a priest—make me a priest.'"

This, the climax of the second part of the book, is what Flannery O'Connor would call a "moment of grace," and one akin to the moment in O'Connor's story "A Temple of the Holy Ghost." As in the story, the Benediction service gives dramatic emphasis to the belief that Christ is present in the consecrated Communion bread; and the encounter with Christ in the Eucharist—the firsthand experience of God, so to speak— effects a change of heart.

In Merton's life, however, the scene settled nothing. He still had great "anxiety of mind." Now that he had resolved that he should be a priest, he grew anxious about what kind of priest he should be.

The search for the *right* priesthood was his search for an otherworldly ideal, and he explored every aspect of the ideal in his journal: if he was going to leave "the world" for another, holier one, which one would it be?

The question was complicated by a lack of firsthand knowledge. For all his ducking into churches, his weekday afternoon devotions, he knew hardly any priests to speak to. What he knew about the priesthood he knew from books. Aquinas had been a Dominican, Hopkins a Jesuit; the Jesuits were everywhere in Joyce's fiction. But the Catholic writers Merton most admired—Dante, Gilson, Maritain—were laypeople, who lived "in the world" as he did.

Here and there in his reading he had encountered descriptions of the "charisms" of the different religious orders, and Merton imagined himself a member of each: a black-clad Jesuit moving through the city with military precision, eager to defend the faith from heresy; a white-robed Dominican meditating on Scripture in a big country abbey surrounded by tilled fields and vineyards, as in a medieval altarpiece; a dour Trappist subsisting on milk and cheese and sleeping in his coffin; a Franciscan, barefoot and in brown, begging alms on doorsteps, footloose in the simplicity of the order's founder, who (Merton writes in *The Seven Storey Mountain*) "invested [such a life] with a kind of simple thirteenth century lyricism."

His decision was complicated further by the fact that it was not really his to make. For the rhetoric of religious vocation turned his search for an otherworldly ideal inside out. To have a "vocation," in the sense in which the Church uses the word, means to be called by God to a specific role; in the 1930s it meant vocation to the consecrated life as a priest, a nun, or a lay brother. In this sense, it was not up to Merton to choose a priestly ideal for himself. If he had a vocation, there was a priestly ideal marked out as his, a place in that other world set aside for him, and it fell to him to simply search for the signs and traces of his calling.

In this search his own aspirations were no guide, for Catholics in general and prospective priests in particular were trained to distrust their natural desires: the more attractive something was, the more suspect.

In Merton's case, the impasse was broken by an older and wiser figure, a spiritual adviser of sorts.

Dan Walsh had taught Merton philosophy at Columbia and helped prepare him for baptism. It was he who broached the topic of vocation after Jacques Maritain's talk. Crucially, he introduced Merton to the distinction between a "Thomist" and an "Augustinian"—a distinction between two ideals, which, like the ideals of the different religious orders, were basic to Catholic philosophy. Thomas, the systematic theologian, explored revelation as it might be comprehended intellectually by every rational being. Augustine, preacher, bishop, and autobiographer, emphasized the encounter with faith in the experience of the individual, and the struggle between the grace of God and the sinful, rebellious, independent human will.

Walsh told Merton that by temperament he was an Augustinian. It was Walsh's way of saying that Merton was the kind of person who didn't want to spend his life merely thinking about Christianity in the dispassionate service of an ideal. For him the life of faith would be grounded in firsthand experience.

With all this in mind, Merton decided to become a Franciscan, for the order, he thought, was a kind of school in the life of poverty. He chose a new name for himself: Frater John Spaniard.

For the better part of a year, as he worked toward his Ph.D. and the Nazis occupied Paris, he prepared to enter the Franciscan life at a friary in New Jersey. Then one day at the friary near Penn Station he was told that he did not have a vocation to the order; an hour later, in the confessional at a Franciscan church nearby, he was told that he did not have a vocation to the priesthood, period.

It was, he recalled, a shattering blow. It was as if God had spoken to him through the Franciscan order—not to call him, however, but to reject him, condemning him to remain in the modern world as in a kind of prison.

In *The Seven Storey Mountain*, however, it feels less like an end than a beginning. Because the reason for his rejection—the child he had fathered—was struck from the text by the Trappist censors, it is as if Merton was rejecting the Franciscans. More than he yearned for poverty or simplicity, he yearned for a religious life as vivid as those he had read about, an ideal he could live in. But in America, as he tells it, the Franciscans were college professors, not beggars and tramps; except for the brown habits they wore the friars were scarcely distinguishable from men of the world.

Rejected, he strove to embody the Franciscan ideal in his own self and his own life. He had been told that he had no vocation to "the cloister." Yet he believed that he had a God-given "vocation to live the kind of a life that people lived in cloisters. If I could not be a religious, a priest—that was His affair. But nevertheless He still wanted me to lead something of the life of a priest or a religious." So he resolved to live *as if* he were a monk in a cloister. He had the prospect of a job teaching English at St. Bonaventure, the Franciscan college outside Buffalo. He went to Penn Station to catch a train upstate for an interview. First, however, he went to a religious bookshop and bought a set of breviaries—"the set of four books, bound in black leather, marked in gold," with "red and green markers."

On the train that day he prayed, for the first time, the Divine Office, reading the biblical texts and prayers as directed by the complex rubrics found in the front of each book. On the train to Long Island in 1937 he had nearly thrown *The Spirit of Medieval Philosophy* out the window; now, in late summer 1940, "as the train was well started on its journey, and was climbing into the hills towards Suffern, I opened up the book and began right away with Matins." It is a fine image of the next stage of Merton's pilgrimage, in which he will enter a monastery of his own making and live according to the monastic ideals as they exist in his imagination.

"Never before have I had such a complete sense of failure, of utter misery," Dorothy Day wrote. ". . . In Boston for three days. Spoke to large group and they collected forty dollars. Nothing in the bank and two checks bouncing. Free-for-all fight on personalism and Fascism. Took boat at five for New York. Still low and dragged out. Feeling nothing accomplished."

She was keeping a journal for *House of Hospitality*, a book about the rise of the Catholic Worker movement. To the three "points" of Peter Maurin's program (papers, meetings, farms) she had added a point of her own—

pilgrimages to Catholic Worker communities around the country—and the journal was in large part a chronicle of her own movements and the conflicts that they sparked. The Catholic Workers on Mott Street thought she was away too often. Those elsewhere thought she didn't come often enough. Her daughter was left in the care of others. Her father mocked her as a "Catholic crusader" who "skyhoots all over the country, delivering lectures." Herself, she felt at once "hard and rigid," "ready to sit like a soft fool and weep," and so "completely alone" that she felt tempted by the devil to find a new mate (despite the Church teaching against remarriage).

House of Hospitality was published in 1938. A year later Preservation of the Faith Press published *From Union Square to Rome*, billing it as a former Communist's account of the "incidents and people who helped her along the path to God." The publisher thought up the title and, possibly, the device used to frame the story: a letter from Day to her younger brother, John, in which she shows Catholicism to be more human than Communism, the supernatural life superior to the natural one.

Her biographers say she was loath to discuss the book, even the year it came out. She disliked the title, with its simplistic opposition of New York and Rome. She thought the book too personal, too much concerned with sordid affairs she wished to forget about.

Her columns of the period suggest a further reason. As the Nazis conquered Europe, the conflict between Catholicism and Communism had given way to a more immediate conflict. With her sharp sense of timing she perceived that it was no time to try to refute Communism or to proselytize. It was time to urge Catholics to be faithful to the Gospel as she saw it—to oppose anti-Semitism, to denounce the Nazis, but also to reject violence.

All through the 1930s she had addressed her articles to "the workers": urging them to resist the appeals of capitalism and Communism alike, imploring them to strike rather than work on military production lines, which would create thousands of jobs. Now she turned her rhetorical emphasis to Catholics, and to Catholic Workers first of all.

In 1940 she drafted a statement of the Catholic Worker's "Aims and Purposes," and printed it in the paper. But she said nothing of current events. Instead she set out to " 'give reason for the faith that is in us.' " With collective ideology leading to disaster in Europe, she sought to bind the movement together through her powers of persuasion as a writer.

Day located the roots of her movement, and of "the faith that is in us," in the individual conscience. At the same time she found the basis of community in the observable fact of human interdependence. "We cannot live alone," she remarked. "We cannot go to Heaven alone. Otherwise, as Péguy said, God will say to us, 'Where are the others?' "

The first-person plural pronoun is not just a rhetorical device. It is the heart of Day's message: the Catholic Worker, singular, is made up of Catholic Workers, plural. What are they working for? A new heaven and a new earth, "wherein justice dwelleth." Why must they strive for justice on earth, and not just in heaven? Because the human race is one race, one people, who share a basic equality. "We believe in the brotherhood of man and the Fatherhood of God," she explains, and goes on:

> This teaching, the doctrine of the Mystical Body of Christ, involves today the issue of unions (where men call each other brothers); it involves the racial question; it involves cooperatives, credit unions, crafts; it involves Houses of Hospitality and Farming Communes. It is with all these means that we can live as though we believed indeed that we are all members of one another, knowing that "when the health of one member suffers, the health of the whole body is lowered."

Although she hungered for earthly justice, Day upheld the "primacy of the spiritual" and the practice of spiritual disciplines such as Mass, private prayer, and spiritual reading. Mainly she urged her readers to "practice the presence of God" by seeing God in one another. "He said that when two or three are gathered together, there He is in the midst of them. He is with us in our kitchens, at our tables, on our breadlines, with our visitors, on our farms." God himself, she believed, had called believers to come together in community, as if community were a precondition for His presence in the world. But religion should not be reduced to "pressure groups" or "mass action" of any kind. "We are addressing each individual reader of *The Catholic Worker*," she declared. "Essentially the work depends on each one of us, on our way of life, the little works we do."

The statement of "Aims and Purposes" was as eloquently, hardheadedly persuasive as anything Day had written, and in the months that followed she sought to apply its message. The need was urgent. The movement was dissolving over the commitment to pacifism in the face of world war. Once conscription began, male Catholic Workers were likely to be drafted, sent to work camps for conscientious objectors, or jailed for noncompliance. Many

Catholic Workers were eager to go to war against Nazism—a just war if there ever was one—and thought Day's pacifism an immoderate position.

In June 1940, then, Day published a "Peace Edition" of the paper with an editorial setting forth "Our Stand," now investing the plural pronoun with her singular claim to authority. Following the Sermon on the Mount, she declared, the Catholic Worker stood for peace and against violence for any cause or of any kind. "Members of other 'Catholic Worker' groups who do not stand with us in this issue" could remain Catholic Workers—as long as they did not suppress the paper. Those who did should "disassociate themselves." Some halved their orders of the paper. Some sent letters accusing her of inflexibility or naivete. Some cut ties altogether.

In August, as Nazi warplanes blitzed London, she called a retreat for the entire Catholic Worker movement. All the communities were asked to send representatives.

She had gone on organized retreats for some years. She once fled a silent retreat at a convent in Manhattan after two days: "I felt that I had been in jail in solitary confinement," she recalled, and "could not wait" to "get out on the streets" again. But when a French Canadian retreat master named Pacifique Roy came to St. Joseph's House she warmed to him, and became a regular at his "conferences." These were not like the retreats of Joyce's Jesuits—metaphorical affairs in which the retreatants were enjoined to imagine themselves in hell or out with Christ in the desert. Rather, they were sustained statements of what came to be called "applied Christianity"—religion made so literal and direct as to be revolutionary. The priest emphasized the distinction between the natural and the supernatural, the worldly and the otherworldly, but sought to shatter the distinction between this world and the next. The other world was the life of holiness here on earth. "Those who wish to enter heaven must be saints. Sanctity must be achieved in our lifetime. We are here for no other reason," Day wrote in her notes on one conference. "Heaven is not a place [but] a condition of soul—the vision of God, union of God. . . . It can begin here."

The first Catholic Worker retreat took place over Labor Day weekend at the farm in Pennsylvania. A hundred Workers came, as well as five priests. There was Mass and Benediction in the chapel fashioned in a barn. Silence was kept. Only Father Roy spoke. Yet the sense of community, Day recalled, was such that "there seemed no reason for discussion. When we separated, it was with pain; we hated to leave each other, we loved each other more truly than ever before, and felt that sense of comradeship, that sense of Christian solidarity which will strengthen us for the work."

When the weekend was over the Catholic Workers set out for their own communities, a caravan of cars and trucks snaking away from the farm much the way, at the other end of the decade, before the movement began, one had snaked toward Washington. Day later remembered that retreat fondly. "It was the last great get-together the Catholic Workers had before we were separated by war, our workers dispersed to the far ends of the earth, in the service, in jails and conscientious objector camps." For the next few years they would be a movement in spirit only.

Shortly afterward she returned to the city, where she began a retreat of another sort, this one solitary and of her own devising. In her journal she made a note: "Turn off your radio, put away your daily paper. Read one review of events a week and spend time reading." Life would go on; other people would continue to "eat, sleep, love, worship, marry, have children, and somehow live in the midst of war, in the midst of anguish." Herself, she would pray, work, and read novels.

It is no wonder that Day felt the movement to be so fragile. At the time there were fewer pacifists in the Catholic Church in America than there were poor men in line for coffee at the Catholic Worker house on Mott Street on a weekday morning.

Thomas Merton was one of them. It is unclear precisely how he became a pacifist—or rather, a person committed to nonviolence, for unlike Day he believed there were situations in which, as a means of self-defense, violence would be justified. Day, the reformer, sought through pacifism to change the Church and the world; Merton, the rebel, shunned violence as an aspect of his rebellion, a refusal to employ the ways and means of the modern world, which, as the Blitz of London suggested to him, had managed to make even war impersonal—"just a vile combat of bombs against bricks."

Like Day, Merton reached his position more or less independently, as an aspect of his imitation of Christ: Christ was nonviolent; he was a follower of Christ; he would be nonviolent. But his position (as he stated it at the time) had a further dimension—grounded in the notion that all of human life, no matter how depraved, is an imitation of the divine. Every human being, even a Nazi, he reasoned, is created in the image and likeness of God. Christ had said, "Whatsoever you have done to the least of these my brethren, you did it to me." To use violence would be to do violence to Christ.

He had gotten the teaching job, and classes began in September 1940.

On the face of it, St. Bonaventure was the kind of college—eager to usher the children of Catholic immigrants into the American middle class—that made him disdain the Franciscan life as insufficiently ideal. But it turned out to be an ideal place for a program of strenuous imitation, where he could live as if he were a monk in a monastery. There, he dwelled "under the same roof as the Blessed Sacrament," just like a novice. There, he taught *The Canterbury Tales* and *Piers Plowman*, and "was back again in the atmosphere that had enthralled me as a child, the serene and simple and humorous Middle Ages." There, reading and writing, walking in the fields and woods, he felt as if he were back in "the twelfth and thirteenth and fourteenth centuries, full of fresh air and simplicity, as solid as wheat bread and grape wine and water-mills and ox-drawn wagons: the age of Cistercian monasteries and the first Franciscans."

Given a room in a dormitory, he made it into a would-be monk's cell, a chamber dedicated to his self-chosen vocation. His description of it suggests how bound up together religion and art were for him: "Tacked on the door are pictures of Saint Dominic, Saint Francis receiving the stigmata, two of the Blessed Mother and Child, and one, a Dürer, of the Virgin of the Annunciation. Raphael, Fra Angelico, Dürer, Guido da Siena, The School of Giotto. On my desk, Kierkegaard, *The Biographia Literaria*, Metaphysical Poetry—Donne to Butler, Saint Bonaventure, Saint Teresa of Avila, Hopkins, Lorca, Aristotle, The Pearl, Little Flowers of Saint Francis, Saint John of the Cross."

Most of the books were old favorites or teaching texts, which he was rereading for his classes. The exception was Kierkegaard, whose work he was reading closely for the first time. In *Fear and Trembling* he found a deep motive for his secret vocation. Kierkegaard presents the life of holy silence as a primordial act of religious honesty, a recognition that God is not easily described; he speaks (Merton wrote in his journal) "of those who carry with them the terrible secret of faith: a faith which has seen God directly and therefore can no longer be put into words."

At St. Bonaventure, Merton also wrote poems—the first, in his estimation, that were any good. In his journal, meanwhile, he strove to lose himself in the objective other world of Catholic thought: to his usual plans, recollections, regrets, and conjectures, he added long Latin quotations from St. Thomas and St. Bonaventure and the other Fathers of the Church. The ideal voice of the Church was overtaking his own.

He was now proficient in the Divine Office, which he said from the black leather breviaries he had bought. Just as his image-adorned room placed him in the company of the religious people of the past, the breviaries put him among the religious of the present. The significance of the Liturgy of the Hours, as it is called, lay not only in the texts and prayers but in the unity they gave him with actual priests and monks and nuns and brothers, who said the Hours at more or less the same time, Vespers, Compline, Matins, Lauds, Prime, Terce, Sext, and None. It was as if, eight times a day, the whole church read aloud together.

But even with his door closed, his breviary open, Merton could not ignore the sound of the radios that played constantly in the dormitory, carrying news of the war. "Radios are forcing men into the desert. The world is full of the terrible howling engines of destruction, and I think those who preserve their sanity or do not become mad or become beasts will become Trappists in secret and private—Trappists so secretly that no one will suspect they have taken a vow of silence."

To counter them, he went on the radio himself. At a local AM station in town, as in the town square in Havana, he found himself "saying everybody should pray for peace," he wrote in his journal the next day. "It doesn't seem so much, to have asked over a small unheard of radio station for some people to pray for peace. What I wonder is, did anybody pray for peace? Maybe to wonder that is a sacrilege. All I had to do was give the message."

The more real the war became, the more Merton needed to realize his religious aspirations in the world—all the more so because a military draft was being instituted and he, as a resident alien, was eligible. In February 1941, then, he enrolled in the Franciscan "third order," a group of religious people living ordinary lives in the secular world, and to mark his vocation he wore a scapular round his neck, two pieces of brown cloth on a thin cord.

The next month, he arranged to go to Kentucky for Holy Week to make a retreat at a Cistercian monastery.

Upon receiving a notice from the draft board, he registered as an objector noncombatant, which meant that he would willingly carry stretchers or change bandages, like a medieval hospitaller, as long as "I would not have to kill men made in the image and likeness of God."

One day during Lent he went to the college library. He found the *Catholic Encyclopaedia* on a shelf, took it down, and turned the pages to the entry for CISTERCIANS.

There in a few English sentences was an account of the order: the foundation in 1098 by Benedictines who sought to obey the Rule of St. Benedict to the letter; the ideal of a "school of charity," a blend of work and prayer, community and solitude; the coarse woolen habits, the plain white churches, the admission of "bearded laymen" as brothers; the monastery of La Trappe in France, which gave rise to the nickname "Trappists."

He sat in the library and read. There is nothing about the episode in his journal, but in his autobiography he recalls that "the thought of those monasteries, those remote choirs, those hermitages, those cloisters, those men in their cowls, the poor monks, who had become nothing, shattered my heart."

It was as if he had discovered that the other world of his imaginings lay only a train ride away. As he read, he was already a monk in a monastery, such was the vision of Trappist life the book stirred in his imagination:

> Day after day the round of the canonical hours brought them to-gether and the love that was in them became songs as austere as gran-ite and as sweet as wine. And they stood and they bowed in their long, solemn psalmody. Their prayer flexed its strong sinews and re-laxed again into silence, and suddenly flared up again in a hymn, the color of flame, and died into silence: and you could barely hear the weak, ancient voice singing the final prayer. The whisper of the *amens* ran around the stones like sighs, and the monks broke up their ranks and half emptied the choir, some remaining to pray.

No doubt the very plainness of the *Encyclopaedia*'s account of Cistercian life was what made it so powerful. There an otherworldly ideal was reported as real; and as if to dispel all doubt, there was a photograph of a monastery, one little different from those he had considered in books in his boyhood. The images on his walls were works of art. This one was taken directly from life. "What wonderful happiness there was, then, in the world! There were still men on this miserable, noisy, cruel earth, who tasted the marvelous joy of silence and solitude, who dwelt in forgotten mountain cells, in secluded monasteries, where the news and desires and appetites and conflicts of the world no longer reached them."

The monastery, in a sense, was a conclusion to the story that had been taking form in Merton's reading and writing. Etienne Gilson had declared in *The Spirit of Medieval Philosophy* that the goal of life on earth is the con-templation of the divine essence, and that some people should devote them-selves to it wholeheartedly. Now Merton had found a report of the existence of people who still lived for God alone, in a place where life was still lived the way it was lived in the books he had read. Alone, away, outside modernity, detached from the world and its cares, the Trappist monks knew God firsthand. "They were in Him," he concluded. "They tasted the sweet exultancy of the fear of God, which is the first intimate touch of the reality of God, known and experienced on earth, the beginning of heaven. . . . And all day long, God spoke to them: the clean voice of God, in his tremendous peacefulness, spending truth within them as simply and directly as water wells up in a spring."

The passage, from *The Seven Storey Mountain*, is one of the most thoroughly composed passages Merton ever wrote. The poetic packedness of the language, the biblical rise and fall of the sentences, the description of the Trappists in the past tense and from a great distance: with these effects he means to capture the Cistercian way of life and its attractions—its aims and purposes—so that the passage will strike the reader the way that the encyclopedia entry struck him. Skillful as it is, though, the passage takes its authority from life itself—from the fact that, as he writes, he is present there among the Cistercians, living within the four walls of his own description.

And then it was Holy Week, and he was on his way there. The journey was spread out over two days: a morning train from Olean; an overnight stay in Cincinnati; a layover in Louisville, awaiting a night train, which would pass by the monastery en route to Atlanta. Merton's two accounts of it—in his journal and in his autobiography—are a contrast between the ideal and the real, the archetypal and the everyday.

As he describes it in *The Seven Storey Mountain*, it was a Whitmanesque venture into "an American landscape, big, generous, fertile, and leading beyond itself into limitless expanses." Most train rides left him feeling "cut off entirely" from the surrounding terrain; this ride had the opposite effect. As the train reached Cincinnati—freight yards, lit houses, tall buildings, neon signs—"I felt as if I owned the world. And yet that was not because of all these things, but because of Gethsemani, where I was going. It was the fact that I was passing through all this, and did not desire it, and wanted no part in it, and did not seek to grasp or hold any of it, that I could exult in it, and it all cried out to me: God! God!"

The suspense of his story, at this point, has as much to do with the monastery as with his yearning to be there. What is a cloistered monastery

? What will be expected of him there? In his autobiography he renders the suspense perfectly, imagining himself back to the time when, like most of his readers, he had never been to a monastery. The monasteries of his boyhood in France had been piles of mute, figured stone; the abbey at Trefontane outside Rome was more museum than monastery. But the Abbey of Our Lady of Gethsemani was a functioning religious community, where the rule of silence was not an aspiration but a round-the-clock fact.

The journal he kept during the trip is very different from the autobiography. In retrospect, it seems a last spasm of Merton's worldly writing, a last shout from the young man fluent in modern literature and the ways of the world. In a hotel in Cincinnati, he conducted a comic colloquy, part self-interview, part Joycean mock catechism:

Q: What public building, or buildings, impress you in Cincinnati?
A: The Station. The housing project on the way from the Station—not in itself, but as a symptom of Cincinnati's good will, in making a nice clean new avenue, through a slum, to the station.
Q: Others?
A: The Cincinnati Club. Saint Francis Xavier's Church. The other, newer church, on 8th St. just beyond Vine, where I hope to go to Mass tomorrow morning (Palm Sunday).
Q: What else pops into your head, concerning Cincinnati?
A: Count Cincinnati, in E. Waugh's *Vile Bodies* . . .

During a layover in Louisville, he went to the public library and read another Evelyn Waugh book. *Remote People*, an account of the extravagant coronation of Haile Selassie as emperor of Ethiopia, includes accounts of other "remote people"—a pious American pilgrim to a nearby monastery, and Arthur Rimbaud, who fled France to live as a poor and simple pagan in Ethiopia, only to be reconciled to the Church by a Capuchin friar shortly before his death. The story of those remote people, in flight from the world, was an awful lot like Merton's own. Put off by Waugh's caustic humor ("If the Capuchins there are Saints," he observed, "Waugh doesn't seem to know, or want to"), he turned to Graham Greene, then to Blake and Hopkins.

After Louisville the journal goes silent, the autobiography goes dark. The landscape out the window is obscure and barren, the towns desolate. All Merton hears are thick rural accents. The clearest indication of Kentucky is that the Negro passengers are now in a separate car—a telling moment of documentary realism, in which the separation of monks from the men of the modern world stands in contrast to the separation of blacks from whites in the American South.

Then, as the train approaches Gethsemane Junction, the language lights up again. It is as though the train has pulled up to the junction of modernity and the Middle Ages. The ideal and the real are suddenly in phase, and the description, though realistic, seems to echo the literature and lore of a pilgrim approaching a medieval fastness on a moonlit night: the land barren and knobby, the station dark and unpeopled, the driver awaiting him like a messenger or ferryman, the road unfurling like a ribbon below the sky:

> Then suddenly I saw a steeple that shone like silver in the moonlight, growing into sight from behind a rounded knoll. The tires sang on the empty road and, breathless, I looked at the monastery that was revealed before me as we came over the rise. At the end of an avenue of trees was a big rectangular block of buildings, all dark, with a church crowned by a tower and a steeple and a cross: and the steeple was as bright as platinum and the whole place was as quiet as midnight and lost in the all-absorbing silence and solitude of the fields. Behind the monastery was a dark curtain of woods, and over to the west was a wooded valley, and beyond that a rampart of wooded hills, a barrier and a defence against the world.

He describes his final approach as a series of strong impressions: the gate, the Gothic arch, the bearded lay brother showing him in and asking if he will be staying for good; the motto carved into the wall: GOD ALONE; the flights of stairs, four of them, and the footfalls as the lay brother goes away, leaving him—for the first time in his life, he believes—alone with God.

"I should tear out all the other pages of this book and all the other pages of everything else I ever wrote, and begin here."

He sat in his room in the monastery guesthouse, writing in his journal.

"This is the center of America. I had wondered what was holding this country together, what has been keeping the universe from cracking to pieces and falling apart. It is this monastery . . ."

He had arrived at two a.m., gone to sleep, and risen at four to find the monks already down in the church praying the Divine Office. As a layperson, he was restricted to the visitors' gallery in the rear of the church, and from there he watched the long, slow ritual of monastic worship—the sea of white woolen cowls, the chant seeming to rise toward the stained glass.

"This is the only real city in America—in a desert. It is the axle around which the whole country blindly turns . . ."

The monks had scattered to the separate aspects of the monastic day: private prayer, study in theology, work in the barns and fields surrounding the monastery, a meal of bread and cheese taken in silence at long tables, and at last the night office, followed by lights out.

Now, with the monks asleep, Merton sat awake, writing.

"What *right* have I to be here?"

He was there exactly a week, arriving one Monday and leaving for New York the next. In *The Seven Storey Mountain*, that week among the Trappists is a set piece: the long Masses and shorter offices, the guest house filling up with other retreatants, the mood growing more and more austere as Holy Thursday approached. "It was a tremendous thing to hear the terrible cries of Jeremias resounding along the walls of that dark church buried in the country," he wrote, and in them "to detect the voice of Christ, in the liturgy of His Church, crying out in the sorrows of His Passion."

The journal is different. There is almost nothing in it about the particulars of the monastery. The omission was deliberate. "I have not written what a paradise this place is, on purpose," Merton explained.

The reason seems clear: for Merton, the monastery—and this was what made it so "overpowering"—lay beyond description. A pilgrim by nature, he had known the goal of his pilgrimage practically since he read *The Spirit of Medieval Philosophy*, indeed had known it since childhood: a world ordered toward God both inwardly and outwardly, medieval in character and French in accent. But he hadn't expected ever to arrive there, or to find it intact when he did. Now here he was at the Abbey of Gethsemani, a place to rival his vividest imaginings. There was no need to describe it, to evoke it imaginatively. To do so, in fact, would maintain the distances he was trying to collapse—between himself and God, between the retreatants in the visitors' gallery and the cowled monks in the choir below, between his ordinary life as a college teacher with a pending draft notice and the solemn and profound life of the monastery.

So he did not describe the place. Rather, he defined it in terms of the ideals it represented. It was a literal Gethsemani, where monks sacrificed themselves for Christ as He had been sacrificed for them; a purgatory, where "you have nothing to do but lament your separation from Him, and pray to Him"; a place of retreat, where the world was left behind so that God might be glimpsed. It was an earthly paradise—all order and harmony, silence and peace—and an unearthly one, a mirror of God's purposes, a foretaste of heaven.

Meanwhile, he read hundreds of pages of religious writing. The monastery was a kind of living library, where the saintly authors of the Christian past were as real as the wool-clad monks chanting in the church. So he consulted the spiritual masters, as if they were there: St. Luke, St. John the Evangelist, St. Bernard, Thomas à Kempis. Write His words on your heart, *The Imitation of Christ* urges, and that is what Merton was doing.

Finally, he imitated them in prose of his own. On Wednesday of Holy Week he tried to describe the experience of "sudden intuition." The passage is a cross between a Joycean epiphany and a landscape painting:

> Sometimes we see a kind of truth all at once, in a flash, as a whole. We grasp this truth at once, in its wholeness, as a block, but not in all its details. We see the whole pleasing perspective of its meaning at once, and easily. We get a vast, large, pleasing, happy, general view of some truth that's near to us.
>
> We contemplate it awhile from this standpoint, as long as the truth stands vividly before us: we hold this new, luminous whole figure of truth in our minds—we do not understand it thoroughly by any means, but anyway we possess it to some extent. . . .
>
> But once this general figure has become our property and, we think, part of us in this first easy-seeming intuition—then by a series of minute, difficult, toilsome steps . . . through a long desert of difficulties, we come upon little scraps of intuition and dialectic with great labor, and all these are only part of the same old idea.

The intuition, as he sees it, gives "a kind of *image* of completeness. But it is not real completeness. We have to make it up, afterwards, in our own rag-picking way, grubbing around in our own rubbish, like a man whose house has been burned down scraping around in the ashes for something that might have survived." As we do so "we are really living that idea, working it out in our lives."

The passage is an account of the process of pilgrimage—of the way secondhand knowledge becomes firsthand experience, of the way one comes to see with one's own eyes. Written in haste in a monastery guest room, the passage defines his calling as a monk and his career as a writer; those cool, hard, smooth, objective words describe Merton's pilgrimage, on which he was now wholly embarked.

When the retreat was over, Merton was thrust back into the world. In Louisville, where he went to board a train for New York, the things of the everyday life assaulted him: billboards, traffic, hurried businessmen shrouded in their newspapers.

In Manhattan he went to see his college friend Robert Gerdy, an editor at the *New Yorker*, and then to the Scribner's bookstore on Fifth Avenue. There, unexpectedly, he met another college friend, Robert Giroux, who had edited the Columbia literary magazine. He told Giroux that he had just returned from a Trappist monastery and that Gerdy had asked him to write about the experience. Giroux was surprised—at Columbia, Merton had not seemed monkish; he told Merton that an article about a Trappist monastery in the *New Yorker* would be something truly remarkable. "Oh no," Merton told him. "I would *never* think of writing about it."

A month later—May 1941—Walker Percy graduated from the College of Physicians and Surgeons at Columbia. As a fourth-year student he had gone on "rotations" at Bellevue Hospital and qualified for an internship in the pathology department there, under his mentor, a Dr. von Glahn. But in 1940 and 1941 the College of Physicians and Surgeons had been transformed into a school for wartime medicine ("war neuroses, aviation medicine, military sanitation, and submarine medicine," Patrick Samway's biography reports).

The expectation of war was everywhere. Shelby Foote had joined the National Guard. Will Percy, upon finishing his autobiography, had sought to enlist in the Canadian army, although he was fifty-six years old. (He was rejected.) Walker Percy, upon receiving a draft notice, wrote to the draft board saying he would be ready to serve as soon as his internship (which exempted him) was over. The internship would not even begin until the first of the year. A doctor, with twenty years of education behind him, Percy found himself without any urgent purpose.

The previous year Uncle Will had gone out west to finish his book. Now Percy, accompanied by a medical school friend, went west, too, to Yellowstone and Jackson Hole, then up to South Dakota, Iowa, and Illinois, driving mile after mile on the open road. There was no motive for the trip, save the motive of his search, which he had not yet articulated, namely, to figure out who he was and what he ought to do with his life.

In August he returned to Greenville and went to work for a local doctor who specialized in pathology, taking urine samples and the like. Mornings, he saw patients at the white hospital; afternoons, he saw patients at the "colored" one.

The real patient, however, was his Uncle Will. One night at the family cottage in Tennessee, Will felt weak, and Percy drove him down the mountain and back to Greenville, where he was diagnosed as exhausted and hypertense. Will had had a stroke, and in the fall he had several more, which weakened him further and left his speech slurred. He spent his days wrapped in a black kimono in bed in the house in Greenville, organizing his affairs, making a will. Doctors said that no course of treatment would improve him. Modern medicine, to which Walker Percy had devoted four years, could do nothing for the man who had devoted half a life to raising him.

At St. Bonaventure Merton resumed his extramonastic routine: classes, Masses, journal, breviary. He wrote poems (one was published in the *New Yorker*). He made notes for a collection of "Poems Religious or nearly Religious." Blake and Hopkins would be included, but not "The Hound of Heaven": "I sure don't want Francis Thompson in my anthology."

The friars sponsored two diversions from the daily news of the war: Hollywood movies and talks by prominent Catholics, both held in the auditorium. One week there was a speaker who led a group of lay street preachers. Another it was "one from *The Catholic Worker*." That night Merton stayed in his room and worked on his poetry.

The night Catherine de Hueck spoke he decided to attend. He already knew something of her story: a Catholic upbringing in czarist Russia, marriage into the aristocracy, flight from the Communist revolution to America, and time spent working in a department store and a laundromat; time spent telling her adventures on the lecture circuit, which made her wealthy, and then a sudden intuition that she should give away all she had and live among the poor. She had founded the Friendship House in Toronto, in 1930, taking advice in hospitality from Dorothy Day, and then established

Friendship House in Harlem, the epicenter of poverty, home to the poorest of the poor.

The Baroness, as she was called, was a large woman dressed in castoff clothing. She spoke without a lectern or a microphone. To her audience that night at St. Bonaventure—chiefly priests and nuns—she declared that it was the Communists who did the things Christians were always promising to do: feed the poor, care for the sick, visit the imprisoned, and cry out for justice. Nowhere was this more true than Harlem, and the lack of Catholics in Harlem revealed the decadence of the Church. For (as Merton paraphrased her remarks)

> if Catholics were able to see Harlem, as they ought to see it, with the eyes of faith, they would not be able to stay away from such a place. Hundreds of priests and lay people would give up everything to go there and try to do something to relieve the tremendous misery, the poverty, sickness, degradation and dereliction of a race that was being crushed and perverted, morally and physically, under the burden of a colossal economic injustice. Instead of seeing Christ suffering in His members, and instead of going to help Him, Who said: "Whatsoever you did to the least of these my brethren, you did it to Me," we preferred our own comfort: we averted our eyes from such a spectacle, because it made us feel uneasy: the thought of so much dirt nauseated us—and we never stopped to think that we, perhaps, might be partly responsible for it.

Merton went home that night wanting to join her in her work, and later that summer he went to New York to volunteer at Friendship House.

He was there, in the evenings, for two weeks. He folded secondhand clothes in the Friendship House thrift shop. He played piano and supervised children. And he watched the children put on a one-act play, parroting the lines from a comedy—it was the story of King Arthur, set in a modern country club—while their parents proudly looked on. This imitation of white middle-class life, itself an imitation of the medieval court, captured all the phoniness of the life to which he and the black people in Harlem alike were supposed to aspire:

> Let me tell you, this piece of wit practically gave me gray hairs, watching its presentation by little Negro children in the midst of that slum. The nameless author, speaking in the name of twentieth-

century middle-class culture, said: "Here is something very jolly." God, replying through the mouths and eyes of these little Negro children, and through their complete incomprehension of what the jokes and the scene and the situations could possibly be about, said: "This is what I think of your wit. It is an abomination in my sight. I do not know you, I do not know your society: you are as dead to me as hell itself. These little Negro children, I know and love, but you I know not. You are anathema."

He returned to St. Bonaventure, having told his friends that he was going to live in Harlem for good.

It was an announcement as surprising to them as the announcement that he had gone on retreat to a monastery. It is certainly the most surprising twist in *The Seven Storey Mountain*. After two hundred pages of medieval Catholicism, grounded in the distinctions of scholastic philosophy, suddenly Merton is asking blunt questions: Shouldn't the imitation of Christ consist in living the way Christ lived, nothing less, nothing more? Why don't Christians love their neighbors as themselves, as the Gospel instructs? Where are the saints, not to minister to the poor, but to do away with poverty?

In Harlem, the world made its final appeal. "Harlem is, in a sense, what God thinks of Hollywood," he wrote, "and Hollywood is all Harlem has, in its despair, to grasp at, by way of a surrogate heaven." Harlem, no less than the monastery, was another world, which held the modern world under judgment. Yet it was a world more real and more concrete than a monastery, in which the imitation of Christ was literal and actual.

That September the Baroness came to St. Bonaventure to give another talk. She and Merton had been exchanging letters, and now she asked him, "Well, Tom, when are you coming to Harlem for good?"

He told her he needed time to write: Would he be free to write at Friendship House?

She answered with another question: Was he actually thinking of becoming a priest?

He told her what he thought—that he did not have a vocation to the priesthood.

He was asked the same question twice more in the next few days, however. First one of the friars asked it. Then his old teacher Mark Van Doren, after lunch in New York, asked it and, when Merton told him, went on:

" 'You know,' he said, 'I talked about that to someone who knows what it is about, and he said the fact that you had let it all drop, when you were told you had no vocation, might really be a sign that you had none.' "

Merton thought otherwise: that Van Doren's question, coming after those of the others, made it clear that God was searching him out.

He made a vow. He would become a monk of Gethsemani, if the Trappists accepted him—accepted him before the draft board did.

In the end, the Axis powers decided for him, the big events coming one after another: a notice from the draft board, then the Japanese raid on Pearl Harbor and the U.S. entry into the war on the side of the Allies.

All at once Merton was burning the pages of his unpublished novels in a barrel; packing up his poems and journals to send to Van Doren, his clothes for Friendship House; writing letters of farewell; importuning a colleague to teach his classes; closing his account at the bank in Olean; kneeling to pray in haste at the Church of Our Lady of Angels; climbing aboard the evening train and falling asleep right away; fingering his beads in the dark outside Galion, Ohio, where he had asked God to wake him to say the Rosary in the middle of the night.

He was going to Gethsemani to make an Advent retreat, hoping that once he was inside the walls they—He—would let him stay.

He had been called on two occasions to become a Trappist: on the retreat in April, and at the college in December. The repetition was significant. On retreat, he believed, it was his own will calling him, telling him that he wanted to stay. The second time the call had come from outside himself: this time, he believed it was God calling, leading him back to the monastery.

This idea follows the pattern of pilgrimage, the journey to firsthand experience. The first time, Merton was called at second hand: the surroundings, the Masses and offices, the long quotations from religious texts all spoke of the monastic life, but did not speak directly to him. The second time, he was called by people who knew him personally—firsthand—on the ordinary college campus where he followed a monastic life of his own making. The Lord, so to speak, had found him where he lived.

From Louisville he took a bus to Bardstown, stepping off right on the edge of the abbey grounds. The lay brother who greeted him told him he'd been praying for his return.

He went through the gate, and his worldly self was lost to him. On retreat, he had seen a postulant disappear one day into the sea of woolen cowls; now it was happening to him. "Suddenly we saw him no more. . . . The waters had closed over his head, and he was submerged in the community. He was lost. The world would hear of him no more. He had drowned to our society and become a Cistercian."

One afternoon in December Dorothy Day walked uptown from St. Joseph's House to Old St. Patrick's, the antebellum cathedral on Mott Street. Inside, it was cool and dark, the stained-glass windows like icicles. She settled in a pew in the back. She thought. She prayed. She said the Rosary. Then she took out paper and pen and wrote an editorial for the *Catholic Worker*. The title she gave it captured its message: OUR COUNTRY PASSES FROM UN-DECLARED WAR TO DECLARED WAR; WE CONTINUE OUR CHRISTIAN PACIFIST STAND.

FIVE

Independents

W e of my generation have lost one line of fortifications after another, the old South, the old ideals, the old strengths," William
Alexander Percy declared. "We are now watching the followers
of Jesus and Buddha and Socrates being driven from the face of the earth.
But there's time ahead, thousands of years: there is but one good life and
men yearn for it and will again practice it, though of my contemporaries
only the stars will see. Love and compassion, beauty and innocence will return. It is better to have breathed them an instant than to have supported in-
iquity a millennium. Perhaps only flames can rouse a man from his apathy
to his destiny."

Will Percy died in Greenville on January 21, 1942. Walker Percy was not
with him. He was in New York, three weeks into his internship at Bellevue.
He returned to Mississippi. The burial rites for Uncle Will, led by a
Catholic priest, began at the big house and proceeded to the cemetery in
the center of town, where the earth stood open not far from the stone knight
Will had had erected to mark his own father's place of burial.

Walker Percy was twenty-six years old, tall, spare, bright-eyed, already
balding. He had no unanswered questions about who his uncle had been.
His uncle had made sure of that. *Lanterns on the Levee*, published the previous year and praised in the *New York Times* for "the candor and completeness of the revelation of the Southern aristocrat's point of view," was Will
Percy's memorial to himself and his philosophy of life. The book, subtitled
Recollections of a Planter's Son, was presented as a tribute to ancestors and
companions "who have gone on the long journey," and whom the author ex-

pected soon to join. But it was dedicated to Walker Percy and his brothers, and was written for them, *at* them: it was "a pilgrim's script, a man's field notes of a land not far but quite unknown," written to ensure that his ideals would outlast him in prose.

The book is fashioned after Marcus Aurelius's *Meditations*—a catalog of maxims, strong assertions, and admonitions about life in the South. Will Percy believes that the South is bound together by its cooking, its hospitality, its history of disasters, and its recognition that "manners are essential and are essentially morals." He believes that democracy, no political ideal, is "a poor makeshift, but the best devised by man for keeping the peace and at the same time permitting personal liberty." He believes that "calling to mind with gratitude those to whom we are indebted on our journey is not only a sort of piety, but one of the few pleasures that endure without loss of luster to the end"; that a mint julep should be made with good bourbon, crushed ice, and two sprigs of mint, and to add anything else is "sacrilege"; that beneath the nominal Christianity of the region there lay a stoic code of nobility and honor.

It is a philosophical book; but the strongest impression it leaves is not so much of a philosophy as of the man who holds it—an independent, who stands alone, thinks for himself, and speaks with personal authority. He is sharp-witted, moody, artistic, quarrelsome; lively, lonely, sad; humble, prone to self-examination, but finally convinced—whether about the Negroes, the demagogues, or the "damyankees," that they are inferior and he superior, that they are wrong and he is right.

For Walker Percy the book was doubtless full of surprises. It is likely that, reading the book, he came to know Will Percy fully for the first time. The book showed him that Will had once been a directionless young man like himself, who had finished school with no idea of what to do with his life and who had found his calling—as soldier, planter, poet, civic leader, foster father—only when circumstances led him to it.

The book also revealed the unexpected intensity of Will's religious feeling. Percy had known his uncle to be a wistful unbeliever, who spoke fondly of the Catholic past but saw the Church "as a purely human institution with a noble history and a great store of wisdom." The autobiography made clear that Will felt religious yearning right up to the end, and the chapter written "For the Younger Generation" is a peroration about the hazards of life without religion, in which, having raised three boys without religion, he worried about "their bewilderment, their craving, in a world without faith, among a people without gods." In the twentieth century, as ever, Will asserted, "without faith the people perish, and they are perishing before our eyes." In his view science had not unseated religion, for the scientific study of nature suggested the presence of a Master Schemer behind it all. Rather, religion had undone itself by offering people palliatives and stock phrases when it should have told them the meaning of life—that "there is no unity except the unity of brotherhood, no brotherhood without a common father."

That is no Stoic speaking. That is a Southern revivalist preaching a religion of his own devising—a blend of medieval chivalry, aristocratic noblesse oblige, and a Victorian confidence in the best that has been thought and said in the world.

"Death, Heaven or Hell, Rewards or Punishments, Extinction or Survival, these are epic troubles for the epic Mind," Will Percy concluded. "Our cares are fitted to our powers. Our concern is here, and with the day so overcast and short, there's quite enough to do. So I counsel the poor children. But I long for the seer or saint who sees what I surmise—and he will come, even if he must walk through the ruins."

Walker Percy returned to New York and went back to work at Bellevue. To his uncle's exemplary life he now compared his own life as an intern performing autopsies on the ward. To his uncle's death he now contrasted the deaths of the alcoholics, street people, murder victims, and suicides who were the indigent poor of New York. The vital individual was subsumed by the dying crowd, in which death was a mere outcome, a subject of study for the pathologist.

He got sick almost immediately. The hours were irregular, the work exhausting. He began to cough constantly. He thought he might be dying. He had contracted tuberculosis; so had three of the dozen other interns, twice as many as usual. Then, as now, there was no cure.

The only remedy was a regimen of rest and clear, cold air. One night in August 1942 Percy boarded a specially quarantined train bound from Grand Central Station to Saranac Lake, a village in the Adirondacks dotted with cure cottages and sanatoria. In five months at Bellevue he had performed autopsies on 125 corpses and had treated many "live patients" with tuberculosis. "Now," he reflected, "I was one of them."

Edward O'Connor had died of lupus the previous February. He left no autobiography, no statement of principles, no memorial to himself, just a sheaf of patriotic speeches he had delivered to audiences of Legionnaires. "I really only knew him by a kind of instinct," Flannery O'Connor recalled.

Upon his death, shortly before she turned sixteen, she became an independent. The term is one she applied some years later to Mason Tarwater, the fierce old backwoods preacher in her second novel. Old Man Tarwater was an "independent, a prophet in the true sense"—a character shaped by his native region, by his religion, by his instincts, by the guidance of the Holy Ghost, but "true to his own nature" above all. Her father had been such a character,* and so would she be: alone in her judgments if not in fact, supremely confident of her sense of the world, which she appraised as if from afar.

Independence will be the main theme of O'Connor's pilgrimage, in her life and in her fiction. For her, as for Walker Percy, the pilgrim is nothing if not an independent, striving to God without obvious means of support. But she and Percy come to independence in strikingly different ways. For Percy independence—a whole and distinct self—is the goal or destination of a search, hard won and long in coming, the result of a strenuous effort to set himself apart from his ancestry. For O'Connor independence is instinctive and effortless, a point of departure. She is a prodigy, born fully formed, or so it seems, and determined to leave her mark on whatever she touches, so that nothing she will write—stories, novels, essays, letters—could have been written by anybody else. Like Bunyan's pilgrim, resisting the lures and snares of the world, she will cherish her independence and struggle to maintain it. Her aim will be to find its fullest expression—to develop it from an attitude to a habit of art to a vision of life on earth, even as she recognizes that she is dependent on others after all.

Her father had been her best friend; she had his disposition as well as his surname. The year after his death, she distracted herself with typical small-town pursuits, as Sally Fitzgerald's laconic chronology in the Library of America edition suggests: music lessons, the school paper, arts and crafts, home economics.

Peabody High left her with disdain for progressive education and "grim memories of days and months of just 'hanging out.' " Classes, called "activities," were integrated with one another until the subject was "integrated out of existence." Literature was taught as a probing of the topical or a case study of the psychology of the author.

---

*The novel about Tarwater, *The Violent Bear It Away*, carried the dedication "For Edward Francis O'Connor, 1896–1941."

The Georgia State College for Women was little better. The redbrick campus was a ten-minute walk from the Cline house. Classes were dull, all the more so because of the war, on account of which the college had been colonized by the Women's Auxiliary of a nearby navy outpost. "All the tra-la-la is about to begin at the institution of higher larning across the road, folderol and poopoopadoo . . . ," she wrote to a college friend a few years later, recalling the place. "The spirit of Progress, advancement, and progressive education in the pursuit of happiness and holding the joint open as long as possible without funds."

She majored in sociology, and discovered that she loathed it. Bored, she threw herself into student clubs—the yearbook, the newspaper, and the literary journal, the *Corinthian*. A photograph shows her and another editor, in skirts and saddle shoes, admiring a fresh issue of the *Corinthian*. As Mary F. O'Connor, she wrote stories ("just a little, for my own amusement") and drew cartoons. In the yearbook she gave her hobby as "collecting rejection slips." A cartoon she drew shows a girl in big glasses looking on as couples dance: "Oh well," she reflects, "I can always be a Ph.D."

There were soldiers stationed in town, and she got a crush on one of them, a story Sally Fitzgerald later told. He was a U.S. Marine named John Sullivan, an Irish Catholic from Ohio, "handsome" and "resplendent in his dress blues." He came to dinner at the mansion in Milledgeville, invited there by one of O'Connor's aunts. He and O'Connor saw movies together, took walks, and lingered around the house. Then his unit was transferred to the Pacific theater, and he went away. She wrote long letters to him, drafting and revising them in a notebook beforehand. He wrote back. In one letter he told her that he would be leaving the marines and entering the priesthood.

She wrote to tell him that she was going away, too. In her third and last year at the Georgia State College for Women she had gotten a scholarship for graduate work at the University of Iowa, a thousand miles from Milledgeville, Georgia.

In Saranac Lake, Percy was kept to a strict schedule of meals, naps, and prolonged rest out on a sleeping porch, where he lay wrapped in blankets even when the temperature dropped below zero. No family came to visit—only Shelby Foote. The only diversion, at first, was the radio: classical music and reports of the world war, in which his two brothers, and Foote as well, were

136

taking part. To entertain himself, he learned to play piano, practicing on a keyboard drawn on a piece of wood.

In a letter he told Foote that he had become resigned to the "life of a hermit." The Percy melancholy had caught up with him. Alone, idle, weak, without purpose, he was in despair.

The image of the doctor as patient is irresistible, and Percy's biographers situate the prone patient within the history of the sanatorium movement and of tuberculosis itself, a disease depicted copiously in literature. The most insightful account, in Bertram Wyatt-Brown's history *The House of Percy*, shows Percy left to "ruminate on his misfortune and the vagaries of fate," and also on "what it meant to be a Percy in a war-torn world that seemed headed for the apocalyptic ruin that his guardian had predicted."

"I was in bed so much, alone so much, I had nothing to do but read and think. I began to question everything I had once believed," he recalled. His workmen's compensation checks piled up uncashed in a desk drawer. Meanwhile, books surrounded the bed.

Sickness was a firsthand experience, a direct encounter with the phenomena he had read about and then diagnosed in others. At the same time, it was an opening to another kind of experience. The course of self-directed reading he followed in bed was his first direct experience of the intellectual life: away from his uncle, his teachers, and his omnivorous best friend, he was free to think for himself.

Strictly speaking, he was alone; but the room, and his interior life, was full of companionship. Like Merton in the monastery, he found himself in the company of writers and thinkers of the past. They played, each of them, the role his Uncle Will had played—that of conscience and dialogue partner, mentor and interlocutor, example and model for imitation.

Each writer was doubly suggestive, at once offering an insight into the human predicament and representing a way of writing about it.

Sartre convinced Percy that the novel can be an instrument of diagnosis. *Nausea*, about the "bad faith" of the French bourgeoisie, spoke directly to him as a doctor, because it turned conventional notions of sickness and health upside down. In it "the apparently well are sick and the sick are on to the truth," Percy later explained, and the symptoms of their sickness—"anxiety, solitariness, loss of meaning"—are the very signs that they are onto something, "appropriate responses to a revelation of the way things are and the way people really are."

Dostoevsky showed Percy how to make an antihero come alive. A Dostoevsky novel was not a story so much as a dramatized crisis—a book about "characters who're obsessed with some idea or something, or find themselves in a certain situation, a terrible predicament, and behave accordingly." Reading Notes from Underground, Percy found the first great modern example of the literary form of Nausea—the philosophical monologue delivered by an outsider who has an especially keen grasp of the human situation; and when he reread The Brothers Karamazov, he recognized Ivan Karamazov as a character something like himself, pinioned between science and literature, between doubt and affirmation, between his weakness and his sense of intellectual superiority.

Thomas Mann brought fiction to bear on Percy's own life. The parallels between The Magic Mountain and Percy's own circumstances—the mountain, the sanatorium, and tuberculosis itself as symbols of decadent society—gave him a sense of fiction's explanatory power. It was as if the novel had anticipated his predicament and he was imitating it, walking in its shadow.

Together—Percy later recalled—these writers challenged his scientific outlook. "The whole modern novel is a novel of alienation, is about man as dislocated, disoriented, uprooted, homeless, not at home—which seemed absolutely the exact opposite of the thrust of the education that I had," he later recalled, "where the whole burden of point-of-view was to fit man into a body of phenomena." The novels, as he explained it, didn't turn him against science all at once. "The effect was rather a shift of ground, a broadening of perspective, a change of focus. What began to interest me was not so much a different question as a larger question, not the physiological and pathological processes within man's body but the problem of man himself, the nature and destiny of man: specifically and more immediately, the predicament of man in a modern technological society."

He had been moved from a cottage to a large sanatorium, called Trudeau, in the center of town. With two hundred patients, Trudeau was a combination college, clinic, cloister, and plantation house.

There, his tuberculosis began to recede. He gained weight and became ambulatory. Like the patients on Mann's mountain, he was free to eat sumptuous meals and talk endlessly, to walk into town, to go on dates (a ritual called "cousining"). He went motorboating on Lake Placid, bird-watching in the woods; he went to restaurants and saw movies.

He was still a doctor, and in the spring of 1943 he moved to a cottage inhabited by a dozen or so doctors, all recovering TB carriers themselves, who tended to patients at Trudeau. He was struck by their love of medicine, a love he realized he had lost, or perhaps had never had in the first place.

Because there is no cure for tuberculosis, a relapse is always possible; thus it was seen less as a disease than as a condition of existence. As Percy got better he considered his career prospects. The most obvious, for the time being, was to stay in the world of tuberculosis, to serve as a doctor to other people of his type. But his program of self-directed reading had made him feel that the other people on the mountain, though they shared his condition, were not his type after all. He felt more akin to the writers he was reading. Better than any pathologist, they had devised a term, clinical in tone, for the acute separateness he felt: they had diagnosed his alienation.

Dorothy Day spent five months of 1943 away from the House of Hospitality on Mott Street. Constant travel, which she had undertaken to build up the movement, then to support it through her talks, then to shore up its pacifism, was now a habit, a discipline, a way of life, a context for her aloneness. The photographs of her testify to this development. Those from the movement's early years are group portraits: the Catholic Workers gathered in front of a storefront or farmhouse, with Day typically standing in the back row and Peter Maurin set in a chair in front. Beginning in the 1940s, the photographs show Day alone and on the go. She invariably has on a large wool overcoat. Her hair had gone gray in her early forties, and, pulled back, it gives an eagleish cast to her eyes and jaw. Her look is that of great concentration amid great exhaustion.

"Our Lord walked the highways and byways, dusty and tired, to teach his brothers 'whom God so loved,' " she wrote, and yet she observed that she was "so weary that I could almost say with Odysseus: 'Than roaming naught else is more evil for mortals.' " She roamed even so. She went to Georgia, Alabama, and Arkansas; she took a long trip to the West, where she saw "a bit of Germany" in the camps where Japanese-Americans were held on suspicion of treason; she visited the sixteen Houses of Hospitality, six farms, and two camps for Catholic conscientious objectors. She made a weeklong retreat at a farm outside Pittsburgh and spent a month at the Grail Folk School in Canada, a school in applied arts and crafts—baking, weaving, spinning—where she had enrolled Tamar, now seventeen years old.

She traveled by bus, and her columns are full of on-the-road accounts of a people unsettled by war. "Bus stations these days, crowded with soldiers, their wives and children, whole families on the move following the lure of jobs, are anything but comfortable. The bus is an inn itself, everyone sleeping on everyone else's shoulder, a mad confusion of feet and legs in the aisles."

The deep motive for her travels, it seems, was the restlessness and alone-ness she felt. Travel was a kind of counterpoint to the absolute fixity of her pacifism—a stand she was committed to maintaining "in season and out of season." In her columns she delighted in the direct application of gospel truths about war and peace and the straightforward imitation of Christ that absolute pacifism made possible. In wartime, she suggested, the claim of Christianity to be a religion of love, and its betrayal by so many Christians, could be seen especially starkly. "Love is not the starving of whole popula-tions. Love is not the bombardment of open cities. Love is not killing, it is the *laying down of one's life for one's friend.*"

Before Pearl Harbor she had written in the first-person plural, enjoining Catholic Workers to stand fast against all wars. With the war under way she writes as a Catholic radical who must obey the dictates of her own con-science, and she relishes the independence of her position. In a column against the proposed conscription of women, for example, she speaks for herself only. She will not register for conscription, she says, because "I be-lieve modern war to be murder, incompatible with a religion of love." She will not register, even though Mary and Joseph went to Bethlehem to regis-ter in the Roman census, since they did not register "so that St. Joseph could be drafted into the Roman Army, and so that the Blessed Mother could put the Holy Child into a day nursery and go to work in an ammunition plant." She will not register even for a noncombatant role, because the war is a "to-tal war" in which "housewives are urged to save fat for explosive and school children are urged to buy bonds for bombers, and to bring scrap for shrapnel to disfigure, maim and kill their brothers in Christ, but with love."

Among Catholic Workers, Day's pacifism is perhaps the most cherished of her convictions, and the loneliness and scorn she suffered on its account are often described as a spiritual discipline which she courageously shoul-dered. Pacifism alienated her from the great majority of Catholics and work-ers alike; at a time when the American people, rich and poor, religious and not, were united in pursuit of a just cause, she stood apart, cut off from the main body.

A column from 1944 suggests the estrangement she felt. The human body, she wrote, is "our dear companion on this pilgrimage . . . through which we receive our greatest joys of body and spirit." Her knowledge of the body was a woman's knowledge. "A woman contemplates her body, 'that earthen vessel,' that temple of the Holy Spirit, and young or old it is always holy . . . If a woman is wife and mother she rejoices that her flesh is used and worn. If she is virgin, a single woman, if she has willingly cast herself into the arms of the Lord, then blessed are those who have not seen but believed in this love, this terrible, overwhelming, demanding love of the living God."

She had seen Forster Batterham recently, and she doubtless had in mind the sacrifice she had made in declining to seek another mate. But she was also thinking of her daughter. While she was away, Tamar had fallen in love with a man at the Catholic Worker farm in Pennsylvania. They wished to marry. Day discouraged them strongly. They persisted, and in her column for the May 1944 issue of the paper, Day announced the marriage of her daughter to "David Hennessy, bibliophile, roofer, and farmer." The marriage, and the family it produced—eight children in the next dozen years— would require more of her than raising Tamar had done. But for the time being, with her daughter gone, she was on her own once more.

Walker Percy was discharged from the sanatorium in August 1944, pronounced well enough to resume ordinary life. He came down from the mountains and went here, there, and everywhere—to New York to see Will's friend Huger Jervey; to Atlantic City, where he lived for two months with his brother Phin, on leave from the navy; back to New York to teach a course in pathology at Columbia; to a sanatorium in Connecticut because his tuberculosis had flared up.* In Greenville, where he lived in a room over the garage behind Uncle Will's big house, he asked a woman to marry him and was refused. Finally, he went to Santa Fe with Shelby Foote, partly as a road trip and a postwar reunion of best friends, partly to reconnoiter a sanatorium there.

Those episodes, which took up nearly two years of his life, hardly figure in the story he later told about himself. He said almost nothing about them in interviews or his published work; instead he evoked the period in general terms as a time of searching and discovery, a *Wanderjahr* like the one his uncle had spent in Europe after college. "I wanted to go home, but I had no home," he told one interviewer. To another he recalled that "I just kind of washed up on shore—no home, hadn't fought in the war like others my age, no profession, but had the scars of a mysterious illness I never suffered from." Looking back, he likened himself to a pilgrim and wanderer.

---

*The staff, identifying him as a literary type, assigned him to the bed Eugene O'Neill had slept in.

Physically, he was adrift; intellectually, he was gaining clarity in his efforts to grasp the significance of his life. His illness and lack of a clear direction actually brought this about. Like Dostoevsky's underground man, he came to see his sickness as a sort of health, his wandering as a general condition, and himself as a representative man, a rootless modern. Like a spiritual autobiographer, he saw himself as the protagonist of his own life story.

Søren Kierkegaard spurred him on. In later years he was surprisingly hazy about when and how he has discovered Kierkegaard, the only intellectual influence to rival Uncle Will. But he always conveyed how decisive this encounter had been: a "great bombshell," a "tremendous breakthrough," a "staggering" experience.

The breakthrough, as he described it, was "the famous passage of Kierkegaard's describing Hegel as the philosopher who lived in a shanty outside the palace of his own system and saying that Hegel knew everything and said everything, except what it is to be born and to live and to die." Kierkegaard, writing a generation after Hegel, had concluded that Hegel's philosophy, and the nineteenth-century comprehensive confidence it represented, left out the one thing worth knowing, the significance of the individual life. Percy concluded that his medical education had failed him in the same way—that "after you learn everything you can at Columbia about what it is to be a human being, there is something awfully important left over."

Kierkegaard had obsessively posed the question of what it means to be born, to live, and to die. His approach—both an answer and a way of posing the question—was essentially religious. For Kierkegaard the question of the significance of life was the question of the salvation of the individual, and the only way to be an individual was to be oneself "transparently before God."

Kierkegaard left Percy with two distinctions he would employ for the rest of his life. One was the distinction between two modes of knowledge: that of science, which deals with types and generalities, and that of religious faith, which deals with the individual whose salvation is at stake.

The other distinction was a broader one between ways of knowing, which Kierkegaard defined most memorably in an essay called "Of the Difference Between a Genius and an Apostle." Percy summarized the argument: "Kierkegaard says that a genius is a man who arrives at truth like a scientist or a philosopher or a thinker. . . . He can arrive at a truth anywhere, anytime, anyplace, whereas an apostle has heard the news of something that has happened, and he has the authority to tell somebody who hasn't heard the news what the news is."

The news, in Kierkegaard's view, is the Christian message; for him, the genius is inferior to the apostle, whose knowledge bears most strongly on the individual life.

In the long term Kierkegaard's essay made Percy want to be a Christian and an apostle. In the short term it made him want to be a Kierkegaardian. For Kierkegaard's work seemed a precise distillation of all the diagnostic fiction Percy had encountered in the mountains. The novelists and the philosopher were so alike that a single term ("existentialism") had been devised to describe them, "for both approaches—say, Kierkegaard's in philosophy and Dostoevsky's in fiction—share a view in common, that of man, not of mankind, but of a particular man who finds himself in some fashion isolated from the world and society around him . . . alienated from his culture, not as an abstraction, not as specimen Homo sapiens alienatus pinned like a dogfish to a dissecting board, but rather as an individual set down in a time and a place and a predicament."

The philosophy there is Kierkegaard crossed with Dostoevsky, but the individual being described is Walker Percy. As the world war moved toward its end, recovery gave way to discovery. Restored to life and yet alienated from it, Percy embraced his existence outside of system and society. He had a new personal ideal, akin to his uncle but apart from him. He would be an existentialist, not a systematizer; a believer, not a knower; an individual, not a type.

Upon entering a Trappist monastery a man was said to die to the world, consecrating himself to God alone. Many of the things of the world were forbidden in the monastery, lest he come back to life. The list of proscriptions at the Abbey of Gethsemani in the 1940s is legendary: no meat, no fish, no eggs; no heat, no baths, no hair on the top of the head; no talking (only sign language), no music except sacred chant; no leaving the grounds, no "particular friendships," no privacy—Merton explained in his autobiography—except for "the box that was to represent all the privacy I had left: one small box, in which I would keep a couple of notebooks full of poems and reflections, and a volume of St. John of the Cross and Gilson's *Mystical Theology of St. Bernard*, and the letters I would receive from John Paul at his R.A.F. camp in Ontario, and from Mark Van Doren and Bob Lax."

That he saw the box as a stronghold for his "privacy" (not his possessions) is telling. From the beginning, his only cherished possession was his literary independence. The outside of the box was marked with his name in the religious life: FRATER MARIA LUDOVICUS, or Brother Louis, after the saintly Louis IX, king of France. The inside was a dwelling for his inmost self: an artist and the son of artists, consecrated to God but not to the monastery.

Mail was allowed four times a year. In April 1942—evidently his first opportunity—he wrote Van Doren a report on the Cistercian life. "And what a life! It is tremendous. Not because of any acts we perform, any penance, any single feature of the liturgy or the chant, not because we sleep on boards & straw mattresses & fast & work & sweat & sing & keep silence." It was "because the life *is* a real unity, because the foundation of its unity is God's unity . . . the simplicity & the purity of God."

From the beginning his enthusiasm for monastic life was extreme and his sense of God overconfident. But now it was an earned enthusiasm, rooted in experience. Finally he was writing from within his ideal, not toward it.

"The monastery is a school," he declared in *The Seven Storey Mountain*, and he was a novice with a lot to learn—"all the apparently meaningless little rules and observances and fasts and obediences and penances and humiliations and labors that go to make up the routine of existence in a contemplative monastery." He learned how to wax floors and wash dishes; how to say the offices; when to read Scripture via the commentaries and when to read it directly; that the most devout monks had the worst tempers; that mystical experience was expected to be *secundum quid*—secondhand—and contemplation in prayer would not be "acquired" by the monk but "vouchsafed" to him. "That word 'vouchsafe'!" he wrote with exasperation. "The idea you are supposed to get is this: 'infused contemplation is all right for the saints, but as for *you*: hands off!'" He learned to hide his longing for the experience of God, confiding it to his journal.

In time, he learned "that the interval after the night office, in the great silence, between four and five-thirty on the mornings of feast days, was a wonderful time to write verse." At Gethsemani, the poems came more naturally and more artfully than they had ever come in the world. He wrote poems about the monastery cemetery and the monastery barn, poems about the night office—and a poem about his brother, John Paul, a bomber pilot whose plane, he learned in a telegram handed to him by the abbot, had gone down in the North Sea, with no survivors.

While Merton was on pilgrimage toward the monastery, his brother had wandered: to college at Cornell, then into the Royal Canadian Air Force.

Visiting the monastery before he went on active duty, John Paul had asked to become a Catholic. Over four days Brother Louis catechized him, until he professed faith and was baptized. He was Brother Louis's first convert, and the first person to hear his conversion story—"all that I myself had found out by experience, and all that I sensed that he most wanted to know."

Then Sergeant J. P. Merton was dead, buried in the sea. Alone in the world, without immediate family, Brother Louis wrote an elegy "For My Brother, Reported Missing in Action, 1943."

He gave Robert Lax, who came to visit, a sheaf of poems to pass to a publisher in New York, because he had learned in the monastery that he was still a writer—"that I was born one and will most probably die one."

James Laughlin, publisher of New Directions, decided to bring out *Thirty Poems*. The abbot made a few stipulations before granting his permission. Brother Louis would not be pictured on the jacket of the book. He would be described in the publicity copy as a monk in an enclosed monastery. His name, in the literary life, would be Thomas Merton.

O'Connor left Georgia for Iowa City in August 1945, taking a muskrat fur coat and a new moniker. Mary F. O'Connor, she had concluded, sounded like an Irish washwoman, not a writer.

The story of her arrival at the Iowa Writers' Workshop, situated at the beginning of the *Complete Stories*, is many readers' first image of the eccentrically named author: a woman, plainspoken, charming, shy and yet sure of herself, and with good reason, the story suggests, for she had been exceptional all along.

Her scholarship was in journalism, but she called on the director of the Writers' Workshop, named Paul Engle, and made a special request in her best Deep South voice. He asked her to say it again. She did so. He looked at her as if she had spoken in tongues. Then he gave her pad and pencil and asked her to write it down. In her schoolteacherly script, she explained herself: *My name is Flannery O'Connor. I am not a journalist. Can I come to the Writers' Workshop?*

She was a twenty-year-old graduate of a distant women's college, but charming behind the big glasses and "barbarous Georgia accent." He let her in and made her his protegée. In his recollection she is a model student: self-possessed yet open to criticism, "adamant" but humble, a "presence" in the classroom in spite of her silence, or because of it. "The dreary chair she sat in glowed."

She spent three years at the Writers' Workshop, the longest time she spent anywhere outside of Georgia, and when she emerged it was with the ardor of a recent convert. She was doubtless precocious and confident from the beginning. But the story of her time there is not the story of a prodigy amazing the teachers and taking the top prizes. It is the story of a conversion to fiction, and then to a certain kind of fiction that was recognizably hers and no one else's.

The city itself she found "naturally blank," a city of "sooty tubercular-looking houses." She lived, with a roommate, in a dormitory on East Bloomington Street. On weekends, the roommate would go away, leaving her by herself.

She took courses in drawing, political cartooning, advertising, and magazine writing, along with the courses in the Writers' Workshop. She went to daily Mass and paid regular visits to the zoo, which had a collection of game bantams, as well as "two indifferent bears in it and a sign over them that said: These lions donated by the Iowa City Elks Club."

She wrote a letter to her mother every day, without fail, remarking tartly on the affairs described in the Georgia newspapers, which her mother rolled and sent to her.

She read and read, making up for her supposedly spotty education. She later remarked that the beginning writer is inspired less by life than by books, and in Iowa she read hungrily as if (to borrow an image from a story) she could eat all the loaves and fishes, after they had been multiplied:

> I read all the Catholic novelists, Mauriac, Bernanos, Bloy, Green[e], Waugh. I read all the nuts like Djuna Barnes and Dorothy Richardson and Va. Woolfe (unfair to the dear lady of course); I read the best Southern writers like Faulkner and the Tates, K. A. Porter, Eudora Welty and Peter Taylor; read the Russians, not Tolstoi so much but Dostoievski, Turgenev, Checkov and Gogol. I became a great admirer of Conrad and have read almost all his fiction. I have totally skipped such people as Dreiser, Anderson (except for a few stories) and Thomas Woolf. I have learned something from Hawthorne, Flaubert, Balzac and something from Kafka, though I have never been able to finish one of his novels.

As she recalled, she read "everything at once, so much that I didn't have time I suppose to be influenced by any one writer." But there was one book that influenced her directly. Brooks and Warren's *Understanding Fiction* was the standard textbook in the fiction courses. O'Connor read it carefully, and later urged it on another writer, describing it as "a book that has been of invaluable help to me."

Today Cleanth Brooks and Robert Penn Warren seem as distant as Old Testament prophets, and it is hard to recall that their approach—the New Criticism—was once considered revolutionary. In truth, it was highly traditional. But it was a direct refutation of the social-science approach to literature that O'Connor had endured in Milledgeville. Brooks and Warren drily recommended "the close analytical and interpretative reading of specific examples" and called for an "emphasis on formal considerations" rather than social ones. But they were writers more than pedagogues, and their counsel is directed to the writer as much as to the reader. Even as they sketch the rules of literary realism, they allow that fiction is "a process of exploration and experiment" and stress that there is "no fixed and sanctified way of handling things." The folksy accent in the prose underscores the point, grounding their approach in the regional wisdom of the Agrarians. There is an outsider's perspective in the observation that every writer must find the form "specially adapted to the kind of effect which he is trying to give. He has his own view of the world; certain kinds of persons interest him, and certain problems and issues."

Brooks and Warren were what O'Connor aspired to be: Southern independents, who had transplanted themselves to the North and gained their independence without losing their native accents. She read their book and accepted their authority. She would later claim that she was "congenitally innocent of theory," but her own authority in the essays in *Mystery and Manners*, her offhand certitude about the nature and aim of fiction, is rooted, it seems clear, in the "Brooks and Warren" understanding of fiction. From their notion that "a piece of fiction is a tissue of significances" came her sense of the "total effect" of a story. From the recognition that "there is no sanctified way of handling things" is derived her remark that "you can do whatever you can get away with, but nobody has ever gotten away with much." From them she learned that "formal considerations" such as symbolism and point of view are the means by which the writer finds the approach that is distinctively his—or her—own.

All the while she was reading, she was also writing fiction, but poorly and conventionally. There is no high comedy in her early work, no artful dramatic structure, no stern and judgmental narrator, no extravagantly barbed metaphor and symbolism. Her knowledge of the problems of the beginning writer, pinpointed in her talks, came from firsthand experience.

The earliest story, "The Coat," is a story fashioned after Maupassant's "The Necklace," which was printed in *Understanding Fiction*. When a black man comes home drunk and flush and wearing a new coat, his wife knows he murdered the white man she saw splayed cruciform-like and coatless on the roadside. One thing leads to another, and he is shot by a posse of angry whites. She has told him that "you ain't worth all this wearyment," but it turns out he was innocent, and she is left with "a little core of something light buried in the dark weight her head was."

Her six thesis stories are student work, nothing more. They take place in settings only vaguely described. They don't begin so much as join action already in progress. They are (to quote one of them) "sunk in the self" of their protagonists, whose thoughts smother the action. "The Turkey," for example, cuts back and forth between a boy's chase of a turkey, his fantasy that he is a Wild West cowboy, and his odd notion that his capture of the turkey means he ought to be a priest.

The stories are also deformed by an obsession with "niggers." The word appears dozens of times in the six stories, given every possible meaning, stress, twist, slant, connotation, and emphasis. And this is not just because the author is being faithful to the way people talk. The stories are directly concerned with the word and what it means. "The Geranium": an old white man in New York wants to go back to the South to die, for there a white man doesn't have to live next door to a "nigger." "Wildcat": a blind old black man lives in fear of a wildcat that has a special knack for sniffing out "niggers." "The Barber": a lily-livered liberal can't bear to tell the men at the barbershop that he plans to vote for the politician who likes "niggers."

Of the fiction writer, Brooks and Warren had said that "certain kinds of persons interest him, and certain problems and issues." O'Connor may have meant to write about what she later called "manners under stress," and the stories do dramatize the stress of the races in conflict. The old white Southerner in New York is helped up some stairs by a black neighbor, then hassled by a white one. A blind (and, by implication, color-blind) black man is afraid of a wildcat because, with its ability to sniff out "niggers," it is like a white posse. But O'Connor's interest in "niggers" seems not so much an aesthetic curiosity or a social concern as a verbal tic, one that reduces the stories to a crude and unintended simplicity.

She would find a solution to her race problem. But there is a more basic trouble with the Iowa fiction, one seen plainly in the story called "The Crop," which depicts a Miss Willerton, a writer of potboilers who lacks material and doesn't know what to write. Evidently that was O'Connor's problem as well. Something vital is missing in these stories. They are all manners and no mystery. They are now published alongside her other work, but she deemed them unreadable or unpublishable, and her judgment seems well-formed.

During the war Dorothy Day had taken an interest in the Desert Fathers of the late Roman Empire. Faced with conscription, religiously opposed to war, "they retreated by the tens of thousands to the desert wastes to pray, to work, and God knows what the world would have been without them." In their lives of silence and self-denial, of radical apartness, the first Christian monasteries were formed.

She had spent the war in the desert, so to speak. She took a long sabbatical from the newspaper to go on a self-directed retreat at a convent school on Long Island. She ordered the communal farm in Pennsylvania disbanded and turned into a retreat house. She walked down Mott Street to visit the sick at the cancer hospice Rose Hawthorne had founded. Feeling more like an abbess than an activist, she wrote to the abbot of Our Lady of Gethsemani in Kentucky, whom she knew at second hand, asking for advice on how to manage an unruly community whose only rule was the Gospel.

The dropping of atomic bombs on Hiroshima and Nagasaki in 1945 brought her back in full and furious voice. With atomic weapons, she exclaimed, there surely could be no more just wars: the killing of large numbers of civilians was simply immoral; the "colossal slaughter of the innocents" far outweighed any conceivable benefits. In her column for September 1945 she scorned President Truman, the "True Man" who had called for the bombs to be dropped and now boasted of their effectiveness; she derided all those who were taking a wait-and-see position about the "new era." These people were eager to know what the pope thought—"but Our Lord Himself has already pronounced judgment on the atomic bomb. When James and John (John the beloved) wished to call down fire from heaven on their enemies, Jesus said: 'You know not of what Spirit you are. The Son of Man came not to destroy souls but to save.'"

By the next month, she was writing with the righteous anger of a Jeremiah: "The great and glorious cities of the past have fallen: Ur of the

Chaldees, Babylon, the cities of the Egyptians, Jerusalem the Golden. Now destruction hangs over New York and London, Moscow and Shanghai." Human extinction was imminent; the day of judgment was at hand.

Emboldened, the Catholic Workers began a new round of protests: against union busting in coal country, against the peacetime draft, against the production of more and bigger bombs. Their independence was now based on opposition to manifest evil, and their practice of works of mercy, Day proposed, was a form of protest against atomic weapons, perhaps the only one. "In the face of the approaching atom bomb test," she wrote in June 1946, ". . . we face the situation that there is nothing we can do for people except to love them."

To love and to do what she was doing: writing, traveling, speaking out. In the postwar years, as Catholic Workers returned from abroad, her column oscillated between prophetic utterances and diary-like recitations of people seen, books read, things done and left undone. She had given the column a new name: "On Pilgrimage." She explained why: "When things get tough, I like to recall St. Teresa's 'Life is a night spent in an uncomfortable inn.' And from the gay way she wrote about her adventures, she agreed also with St. Catherine of Siena, who said: 'All the Way to Heaven is Heaven, for He said, I am the Way.' "

"Reverend Father just O.K.ed a new project," Thomas Merton wrote to James Laughlin in the winter of 1946. "Creative, more or less poetic prose, autobiographical in its essence, but not pure autobiography. Something, as I see it now, like a cross between Dante's *Purgatory*, and Kafka, and a medieval miracle play, called 'The Seven Storey Mountain.' It has been brewing for a long time . . ."

Six months later *The Seven Storey Mountain* was finished: a "straight biography, with a lot of comment and reflection." Merton was permitted to write two hours a day but probably wrote more, typing on scrap paper, waste paper, the backs of business letters, and the insides of envelopes, which he slit open and unfolded, since nothing was wasted at the monastery. The typescript swelled to 650 pages. Nights, he could not sleep, so charged up was he with his own story.

The Seven Storey Mountain is the best evidence, perhaps the only evidence necessary, that Merton was meant to be both a monk and a writer. His confidence in his religious calling has given his life "wholeness, harmony, and radiance," the Scholastic formula for an achieved work of art. It has given his life a story, one that imitates, which is to say participates in, the larger Christian story, that of the individual soul's peregrination to God. Through this story, he understood his life for the first time.

Merton hoped to have it published; the abbot approved, thinking it would inspire further vocations to the monastery.

Merton sent the manuscript to Naomi Burton, his literary agent from the start. At his suggestion, she sent the manuscript to Robert Giroux from Columbia, now editor-in-chief of Harcourt, Brace and Company, who had rejected his early novels. Giroux had thought of Merton as missing in action once he entered the monastery. He was surprised that his friend had already written an autobiography—Merton was only thirty years old—and more surprised that it was as good as it was. Giroux took Burton to lunch. One night in late December Brother Louis was handed a telegram in the refectory. "My heart sank into my dinner," he wrote in his journal—ever since his father's last illness, telegrams had brought bad news. He waited until the meal was over to open it. "It was from Bob Giroux. And it said: 'Manuscript accepted. Happy New Year.' "

After receiving her MFA degree from Iowa in 1947 Flannery O'Connor went south to Milledgeville, where she kept writing through the summer in the Cline mansion in town. Her uncle Bernard had died, and in his will he had left her mother and another uncle the farm outside of town, known as Grey Quail Farm: five hundred acres of pasture and a thousand acres of woods, with a white farmhouse out front.

She was now at work on a novel, which she had started writing in her last semester at the Writers' Workshop, using an early episode to round out her thesis. She had gotten two postgraduate fellowships, one of which involved a publisher's pledge to bring out the novel if she finished it. In September she returned to Iowa City, took a room in a boardinghouse, and got to work in earnest.

There, independent of relatives and teachers for the first time, she was transformed into a novelist. She was twenty-two years old, pretty, funny, healthy, ambitious. Her work, so far skillful but unremarkable, suddenly became original both in style and in what she was trying to accomplish; her desire to be a writer turned into an urgent sense of calling.

There is no telling just how it happened. But it seems that for her, as for Thomas Merton, Jacques Maritain's *Art and Scholasticism* was instrumental.

Reading the book in Iowa City, she was struck, as Thomas Merton had been, by Maritain's emphasis on art as a virtue of the practical intellect, concerned not with speculative knowledge or virtuous behavior but with "reason in making"—a proper application of the "habit of art" to the materials at hand. Here was a Catholic counterpart to Brooks and Warren, shifting the emphasis away from the artist and toward the work of art. An artist (Maritain proposes) does not need to be holy, only to be a good artist; the artistic calling is no less a calling than, say, the priesthood or the life of poverty, which means that the artist serves God most faithfully by being a good artist.

O'Connor would paraphrase those ideas for the rest of her life. But she was evidently struck just as powerfully by Maritain's chapter on "Christian Art," which offers a powerful and unexpected conception of the religious artist.

As a French Catholic and an exponent of medieval philosophy Maritain might be expected to champion the manifestly Christian art of cathedrals and chant. But he declares that there is no Christian art per se. Subject matter—biblical themes, candles and incense, nuns and priests—does not Christianize a work of art. Nor do virtuous characters, happy endings, or sermons from the artist. Christian art is simply art made by a Christian believer. In the act of making, Maritain insists, the artist's faith operates behind and around the work of art, which will be Christian to the degree that religious faith shapes artistic vision.

For O'Connor, the distinction between subject matter and artistic vision was eye-opening. In Nathanael West's *Miss Lonelyhearts*, which she read at the Writers' Workshop, a character named Shrike brandishes a newspaper clipping—ADDING MACHINE USED IN RITUAL OF WESTERN SECT, the headline says—and declares that stories like that one, and not obscure points of neo-Scholastic philosophy, warrant pondering. O'Connor's early work had lacked a religious perspective. She had not known how to write religiously about people who were religiously unlike herself. Now Jacques Maritain showed her how—showed her her territory, akin to that farm on the edge of town, and invited her to cultivate it however she thought appropriate. She was a Catholic, yet she was drawn to write about country people who were not. Maritain's book suggested to her that she should write about them in her own way, making them protagonists, in spite of themselves, in works of religious art.

Her breakthrough in the novel came in the form of Hazel Motes—the first real character to appear in her fiction, the first of the "large and startling figures" who would dominate her work from then on.

"The Train"—the section of her novel submitted with her thesis—has the weaknesses of the thesis stories, and in it Hazel Wickers is an indistinct figure, inexplicably obsessed with his dead mother's ancestry and fixated on a Negro porter on a train, who looks like a "gulch nigger" from back home in Eastrod.

But as O'Connor wrote and rewrote in the boardinghouse in Iowa City, Hazel Motes emerged: a war-scarred veteran in a shiny suit and black hat, going from the country to the city to preach the Church Without Christ, a new religion numbering precisely one member.

Hazel Motes is a fully imagined character, but his abrupt appearance in O'Connor's work makes it worthwhile to ponder his origins. Some say he came from Dixie—but O'Connor insisted that he was not typical of the preachers found there. Some say he came from Kafka—but of Kafka's influence on her she would allow only that he made her bolder as a writer. Some say he came from philosophy—but O'Connor seems to have read the existentialists only later on.

There is no telling, but it seems plausible that this "admirable nihilist" is kin to the agonized figures in the Catholic fiction she read in Iowa. Her time there coincided with a spate of Catholic novels from France and England, some of them new, some freshly issued in translation after the war—enough of them for there to be talk of a "Catholic renascence." Reading everything at once, O'Connor took note.

On the face of it, the Catholic novelists of France and England were radically unlike one another. France was forever Catholic, and its Catholic novelists seemed to have their religion bred in the bone. England, Catholic once upon a time, was now a defiant holdout from Rome, and its Catholic novelists, converts all, saw the church as an empire larger and profounder than the king's but freshly planted on English soil—a church they could claim firsthand and make their own.

Those differences are significant. But the Catholic novelists of England and France were alike in depicting religious faith as a source of fixity and independence in a world of shifting alliances, and focusing on characters who, far from representing the faith, are set apart by it. The tubercular hero of Georges Bernanos's Diary of a Country Priest is isolated from church, parish, village, and French society, at home only in his diary.* The heroine of François Mauriac's Thérèse is straight out of Dostoevsky—a woman

---

*Robert Bresson's 1950 film version stylized the priest's solitude into existentialist alienation.

scorned by the pharisees of her village after she tries to poison her husband, but revealed, over time, to be holier than they. As a Catholic, an unapologetic realist, and a native of Bordeaux, Mauriac was triply distinct from Paris literary society; alongside Sartre and de Beauvoir, Malraux and Camus, he was indeed a writer from another country.

Among English writers of midcentury it was thought to be modish to "go over" to Rome, but the two great English Catholic novelists of the era, though no strangers to society, cast their Catholic heroes as lonely and defiant outsiders. Graham Greene was drawn to the figure "on the edge of things." A gang member in Brighton, a hunted priest in Mexico, a scrupled police officer in colonial Africa: these, the heroes of his "Catholic novels," all stood as examples of his ideal—"the man on the run [said one critic] from God himself."

Evelyn Waugh was seen as a wicked satirist of London society who then joined that society; but in fact he remained, as the late Noel Annan pointed out, a "true deviant" from that society, and his deviancy was of a piece with his Catholicism, which made him disdainful of the false optimism and sham community of London and Oxbridge. *Brideshead Revisited*, published in 1945, is often seen as a love letter to another, older English society—the "Household of Faith" represented by the old Catholic Marchmain family. But the novel, Waugh suggested, is not so much about society as about "the operation of divine grace on a group of diverse and closely connected characters"; and as Charles Ryder becomes a fixture at Brideshead Castle he observes that the Marchmains are, each of them, Catholics who are alone in their faith, even in their own family. They are representative figures, but not types: Teresa, a woman whose piety has driven Lord Marchmain to exile in Italy, where he will return to the fold on his deathbed but not before; Bridey, a bachelor heir who misses his calling to the priesthood; Celia, a pious charmer who becomes a nun to escape the cynical believers who share her blood; Julia, a beautiful woman who places herself outside the Church through divorce; Ryder, who is most himself when alone in an empty room, painting murals on the walls; and Sebastian Flyte, once the bright young thing of Oxford, who ends the novel as a lay brother on a lonely pilgrimage—lost to his family, broken by alcoholism, faithful to God alone, which, Waugh suggests, is faith enough.

These characters are the unlikely forerunners of Hazel Motes, whose eccentric faith is bound up with his independence from society.

They are also the ancestors of the author herself. In school, she had struggled with the conflict of faith and doubt, especially the question of Christianity's relation to other religions. She later described the experience to a doubt-ridden student: "You are bombarded with new ideas, or rather pieces of ideas, new frames of reference, and activation of the intellectual life which is only beginning, but which is already running ahead of your lived experience. After a year of this, you think you cannot believe," she told him, but in fact, she went on, "you are just beginning to realize how difficult it is to have faith and the measure of a commitment to it."

This struggle would be at the center of her work as an adult. Belief, she liked to say, was the engine that made perception operate, but the conflict between belief and unbelief, often in a single character, was the conflict that made the work worth doing at all. She explained:

I don't think you should write something as long as a novel around anything that is not of the gravest concern to you and everybody else, and for me this is always the conflict between an attraction for the Holy and the disbelief in it that we breathe in with the air of our times. It's hard to believe always but more so in the world we live in now. There are some of us who have to pay for our faith every step of the way and who have to work out dramatically what it would be like without it and if being without it would be ultimately possible or not.

The passage, written in 1959, is practically a summary of *Wise Blood and Simple*, as she was calling her novel. Her calling was to work out her quandaries imaginatively, through the stories of characters apparently very unlike herself.

In 1948, she was just starting out. She would be "at" the novel three years, and would come to see Hazel Motes and his disciple, Enoch Emery, as her companions in solitude. The believer Enoch came easily to her; the skeptic Haze she struggled with. What she and Haze and Enoch had in common was "wise blood, which is something that enables you to go in the right direction after what you want." Like them, she was trying to make out her calling, to figure out how to do what she believed she was called to do.

She booked a sleeper compartment on the overnight train going east from Iowa City. Her destination was Saratoga Springs, in upstate New York. She had gotten a fellowship at Yaddo, the artists' colony there.

With its old wooden race course, its pillared mansions and gabled Victorian houses, its strict sense of class, Saratoga is perhaps the southernest town north of the actual South. Yaddo is a Gothic Revival manse on the outskirts of town, surrounded by woods and gardens. There, in the last week of May 1948, O'Connor went on retreat with her two wise-blooded companions, writing and rewriting their story. In one scene, she had Haze plunk Enoch on the head with a rock, drawing blood—wise blood; and when Enoch recovered his senses, she observed, "he knew that whatever was expected of him was only just beginning."

Later the same week Walker Percy bought a house in Covington, Louisiana, a hundred-mile drive around Lake Ponchartrain from New Orleans. The house and the place represented a decision to live in a certain way, a kind of existential commitment to the ordinary.

Six years had passed since Percy had gotten sick and been sent away to the sanatorium. In that time he had been converted in multiple aspects. The scientist had become an artist. The bachelor had become a husband, the Southern legatee a member of the swelling postwar middle class. The habitual skeptic had become a person of religious faith. The aimless medical intern had become, by his own reckoning, a searcher and a pilgrim.

Topologically, Covington—flat, low-lying, with pine trees everywhere— is a cross between the Delta and the Adirondacks, and quite pretty in its own right. But Percy later explained his decision to settle there in abstract terms, calling it a "pleasant nonplace" where he could "avoid the horrors of total placement or total nonplacement or total misplacement." There was nothing particularly attractive about it, and that was what made it attractive. There, more than in the storied places of the South, he would be free to live the next chapter of his own story.

Percy's religious conversion had come jumbled together with his other conversions, and on the surface it seems only incidentally religious. There is no moment of grace, no mystical experience, no sense of the divinity of creation. Percy himself later described it as an instance of what Kierkegaard called the "will to one thing," and it also echoed William James, whose own religious experience culminated in an existential decision, a "will to believe."

In the summer of 1946, Percy and Shelby Foote set out on another cross-country road trip. Foote, who had been married and divorced, had sold a short story to the *Saturday Evening Post* and was full of confidence about his writing. His only problem was that he was short of cash. Percy was still a bachelor, still tubercular, with an inheritance but without prospects.

As they drove west on Route 66 and then through the desert, Percy spoke of becoming a writer himself. Foote was encouraging. So were the surroundings. The long horizon, the high sky, the towns innocent of history: for Percy, as for Will Barrett in *The Last Gentleman,* the Southwest was "the locus of pure possibility," a place where "what a man can be the next minute bears no relation to what he is or what he was the minute before."

Santa Fe was different. They took a room in a hotel in the center of town. At the top of a hill stood the Catholic cathedral, built by Juan Bautista Lamy, the legendary missionary bishop who was Willa Cather's model for Latour in *Death Comes for the Archbishop.* "From the end of the street," Cather had written, "the tawny church seemed to start directly out of those rose-coloured hills—with a purpose so strong that it was like action."

There, out of nowhere, Percy told Foote that he was thinking of becoming a Catholic. Foote was alarmed. He believed the writer's most vital resource is his freedom to see the world in his own way, as Faulkner, Proust, and Dostoevsky did. He had found marriage a threat to his own freedom, and he warned Percy that religion would surely threaten his. Some years later, he explained why: "The best novelists have all been doubters. Their only firm conviction, the one that is never shaken, is that absolute devotion and belief in the sanctity of art which results in further seeking, not a sense of having found."

Foote left Santa Fe and drove back east. Percy stayed on. He took a room at a local dude ranch. The clear air of the Southwest was said to be good for TB patients. He stayed there all summer, pondering his next move. He had turned thirty in May. Alone, without plans or prospects, he told himself: "I've got to have a life."

In *The Moviegoer* Binx Bolling's thirtieth birthday prompts a long monologue about mortality, a rant against self and world alike. "Now is the thirty-first year of my dark pilgrimage on this earth," Bolling says, and all he knows, as far as he can tell, is how to spot the "merde" in the modern world, a "great shithouse of scientific humanism" in which "men are dead, dead, dead; and the malaise has settled like a fallout and what people really fear is not that the bomb will fall but that the bomb will not fall."

Happy is the man who no longer thinks all possibilities are open to him, Kierkegaard had written. Now Percy aimed to rule out possibilities and be a particular man living a particular life. He didn't crave freedom. He sought independence, which is something different. Like his uncle, he wished to stand somewhere and to understand why he did. In New Mexico he made a resolution, or rather a series of resolutions: "I'm going to be a writer. I am going to live in New Orleans. And I am going to marry Bunt."

Mary Bernice "Bunt" Townsend was an apprentice doctor's aide in New Orleans. Percy had met her in Greenville the summer after medical school—she was a nurse in the clinic where he was a doctor—and courted her on and off ever since. He had courted other women as well, inevitably pursuing hard for a few weeks and then backing off. His manner of courtship was strangely ungentlemanly. The first time he broached the idea of marriage to Townsend, it was in a telegram.

From Sante Fe, he called Bunt; he wrote her a letter suggesting that she come out to Santa Fe and drive back to Louisiana with him. He had rented an apartment in New Orleans, he told her, but he wasn't sure how long he'd keep it.

She declined to go west. He went to New Orleans by plane and took up residence there, and they started dating again. One night, while they were sitting on a park bench, he proposed marriage.

Then, joined by Foote, he went back out west, to retrieve his car, leaving Townsend to plan the wedding.

They were married November 7, 1946, in a Baptist church in New Orleans, with Foote as the best man; then they drove to Brinkwood, Uncle Will's old "cottage" in the mountains near Sewanee. They meant to stay there through the winter, part honeymoon, part retreat. They would live in the cottage and Percy would try to be a writer: he started to write a novel he had schemed up, which he was calling *The Charterhouse.*

It can't have seemed much like a new beginning. The cottage was damp and drafty. Percy had another flare-up of TB, and had to be nursed by his new wife. He also had trouble concentrating on his writing. Family and friends came to visit, among them Caroline Gordon and Allen Tate, who were teaching at Sewanee.

The Percys stuck it out a year, then moved to New Orleans, where they rented a house in the Garden District, not far from the church where they had been married—and not far from Loyola University, which was crucial, for they had returned to New Orleans because Percy, joined by his wife, had decided to become a Catholic.

He had written a letter to the Reverend Fulton J. Sheen, the celebrity "radio priest," asking him how to go about taking instruction (as it was said) in the faith. He was told to contact the Society for the Divine Word in New Orleans. He did so, and was told that the society ministered specifically to Negroes. So he went to Loyola and arranged to meet with a Jesuit priest instead.

They took instruction on the campus in the fall of 1947, joined by Mrs. Percy's best friend, who was engaged to a Catholic. The priest drilled them in the catechism. At the end of the process, Patrick Samway reports, Percy had a final question. Where did the Church stand on evolution? The Church, at the time, thought evolution a pernicious idea, and the priest's answer cannot have been encouraging.

They were baptized anyway and confirmed the next April, striding up to the altar rail behind a group of freshly catechized schoolchildren. The next month they moved to Covington, and there, in a house screened from the road by pine trees, Percy finally bore down on his novel.

Why Covington, Louisiana? He thought the question pertinent enough to write a little essay, years later, explaining "Why I Live Where I Live." There are plenty of reasons: Covington was near New Orleans, but apart from it. It was in the South, but outside the sphere of Percy reputation and influence. For a Catholic church the town had St. Joseph's Abbey, a Benedictine monastery set among the pine trees, and it generally had the air of a place of solitude and retreat. "The serious writer, or any other artist for that matter, is a peculiar bird who has to find his way in his own time and who had better be left alone to do so," Percy explained.

It hardly matters, however, why Percy chose to live where he lived. The pertinent question is why he chose to believe what he believed. Although he insisted that the experience happened without emotion, he later called religious conversion, along with marriage, mortal illness, and his father's suicide, to be one of the few important things to happen to him.

Why did he become a Catholic? Various impressions are said to have attracted him to Catholicism: the quiet discipline of a college fraternity brother, rising for Mass at dawn without saying a word to anybody; the skill in disputation of a Catholic convalescent at the sanatorium; the esteem enjoyed by the Scholastic philosophers; the prospect of religion as an alternative to science or as a beacon of order and stability in a chaotic world.

Percy himself, later in life, generally answered the question by saying, "I

believe that what the Catholic Church proposes is true." It was a clever rejoinder to interviewers who anticipated a searching retrospect of his religious development. At the same time, it was honest: he did believe in the
truth of the Church's claims about existence. The question, then, is how he
saw them as truthful, and what led him to do so.

The best answer is to be found in a series of paradoxes which, for Percy,
Catholicism embodied. It offered him a community and set him apart. It
had a philosophy but was not a philosophy. It was not about writing but
would be good for his writing.

He hadn't gotten very far in writing *The Charterhouse*, but he had already conceived of the kind of novel he wished to write. It would be an
amalgam of all the influences that had meant the most to him. It would feature a representative man like his uncle, who took it upon himself to ponder
the human predicament in his own place and time. It would make this man
an outsider, like Dostoevsky's underground man, whose sickness gives him
special insight into the ills of society, and also a diagnostician like Harry
Stack Sullivan. It would be "an instrument of exploration and discovery: in
short, of sciencing." It would be a "diagnostic novel," the kind of novel that
only he could write.

There was only one thing lacking. As a diagnostic novelist Percy needed
a measure of man, a standard to use in making his diagnosis. This was all the
more so because, in a sense, he was his own patient, whose ailments would
provide the subject matter of the novel. Novelist, protagonist, and diagnostician would be one and the same man, and it would be fruitlessly circular to
diagnose himself in his own book by his own lights. Though he had rejected
any scientific synthesis, he needed an objective standard that lay outside
himself.

This is what he claimed he found in Catholicism, and specifically in
what he called the Christian anthropology. Catholicism, as he put it, considers the human person part angel, part beast. It locates the divided human
nature at the center of its scheme and asks the right questions: Why are so
many of us so unhappy? Why is there such cruelty in the world? It also gives
a powerfully suggestive answer. The human person—as Percy understood
it—is a creature suspended between two infinities, a pilgrim and wayfarer.
We don't know quite where we came from or where we are going. Man is
born to trouble "as the sparks fly up."

For the rest of his life, Percy would set this anthropology against the scientific view of the human person as a mere "organism in an environment."

But in retrospect his conversion to Catholicism seems the fulfillment of his scientific temperament, not a repudiation of it. Paradoxically, he became a Catholic out of fidelity to the scientific method, in search of an objective measure with which to measure the human person.

It is a further paradox that Catholicism, far from threatening his independence, seemed to guarantee it—to protect him from the claims of the Percy past. There were three suicides among his forebears. He had survived mortal illness. He had lost his uncle, whose memoir told of a sadness that had persisted "even though he lived in as good an environment as man can devise, indeed had the best of all possible worlds in literature, music, and art." In becoming a novelist and a Catholic, Percy sought not only to diagnose his own unhappiness but to remedy it. He had his uncle's life as an example, a path marked before him, lights trailing off into the darkness. Like his uncle, he would devise a philosophy and test it with his life. Like his uncle's Stoicism, his philosophy would diagnose the modern malaise and suggest a remedy for it. But in a crucial way his life and his rule of life would be his own. Whereas Will Percy's adulthood—and his unhappiness—had begun with the rejection of religion, Walker Percy's would begin with the acceptance of it, in which he found, in his own fashion, the faith that Will had lost on his way down the mountain.

SIX

The School of the Holy Ghost

I n 1947 Peter Maurin disappeared from Mott Street. He was in his room
at the back of St. Joseph's House; then he was gone. "For three days we
searched the streets of the Bowery, the hospitals, for him; for three days
and nights we listened for his slow step on the stair, the sound of his cough
or the door opening," Dorothy Day recalled. He had gone out for a walk,
and had gotten lost. "And we wondered with a dreadful constriction of the
heart, whether this was the way Peter Maurin was going to end. Was he, the
poor man, going to wander out on the streets and disappear, lost and forgotten, perhaps put in as dead storage in a vast mental hospital such as we have
in New York state, where fifteen thousand inmates sit around in wards all
day every day of the year . . . ? And, would we never find him?"

He had been ill since 1944: senility, loss of memory, asthma, a hernia,
and a perpetual cough. The year before, he'd been so sick that they had
called a priest to give him the last rites, but he recovered and resumed his
usual pattern of life: Mass at Transfiguration Church or in the chapel at the
house; breakfast in a cafeteria; long days spent sitting by the woodstove or in
a chair on the sidewalk.

All through the 1940s Dorothy Day had been trying to write a book
about him. Now, as his health declined, she sought to define what he had
meant to her. He was "a St. Francis of modern times . . . used to poverty as a
peasant is used to rough living, poor food, hard bed, or no bed at all, dirt, fa-
tigue, and hard and unrespected work." He was Prince Myshkin, the "holy
fool" out of Dostoevsky. He was a Frenchman, a European, a man of the
nineteenth century, the century of her favorite novels. He was a "cradle

Catholic," a life member of the church she had joined, a man for whom Catholicism was bred in the bone. Through his enthusiasm, his powers of "indoctrination," and his sense of her as an equal, even as a modern Teresa of Avila, he had bound her to the Body of Christ, the Communion of Saints, and the great mass of Catholic working people, to which, until she met him, she had not in everyday fact belonged. With him the Catholic Worker was the movement it claimed to be. Without him it would be perceived as *her* movement, an aggregation of so-called Catholic anarchists, but with her as the Anarch.

He returned after three days, confused but cheerful, complaining that the house was inconveniently hard to find. He had gone away, he explained, because he had wanted to take a trip on a bus. Thereafter they pinned a name tag to his coat.

Maurin's whole philosophy was meant to express his instinctive sense of the Body of Christ. He urged people to be self-sufficient, independent of industry and government, not for the sake of independence, but the better to recognize and act upon the truth that the human race is one, and we are all dependent on one another. Now he himself was literally a dependent, kept alive by hospitality like so many of the men on the bread line.

Day bought another farm, in Newburgh, in upstate New York. Maurin was taken there and made to feel at home. Each day he was bathed, shaved, dressed in secondhand clothes, and led from his bedroom to a chair set out in the sun.

He began to mumble his words; then for long stretches he stopped talking altogether. He'd had a stroke. God "took from him his mind, the one thing perhaps he took delight in," Day observed. "He could no longer discuss with others, give others in a brilliant overflow of talk his keen analysis of what was going on in the world."

The Catholic Workers decided to tape-record him reading some of his "Easy Essays" before it was too late. They gathered around his bed, set the reels going, and held the microphone close. "His voice strangely enough was louder and clearer as it came over the wire than it had been for a long time . . . ," Day recalled. "Then, after we had triumphantly made a fifteen-minute spool, someone else tried to work the machine and erased it all."

Robert Giroux sent proofs of *The Seven Storey Mountain* to Graham Greene, Evelyn Waugh, Fulton J. Sheen, and Clare Boothe Luce (playwright, Catholic, and wife of the founder of Time-Life), with a letter inviting their comments. Waugh was the first to reply. "This book," he wrote, "may well prove to be of permanent interest in the history of religious experience."

Waugh was now a Catholic celebrity. In England, *Brideshead Revisited* had been read as a panegyric for Christendom; in the United States, selected by the Book-of-the-Month Club, a pillar of the Luce empire, it had become a best-seller. Hollywood sought the author. So did *Life*. Tired of postwar rationing, eager to avoid British income tax by making money abroad, Waugh traveled to America. In his starched collar and bowler hat on the MGM lot, he, like Dorothy Day, found that there was no work for him to do, so he decided to explore California. A cemetery in Los Angeles captured his fancy. "I am entirely obsessed by Forest Lawns," he wrote to his London literary agent. He had been writing a novel about St. Helena, the mother of Constantine, and the Catholic epoch of the third century, before the sack of Rome and the Dark Ages; on the ship back to England he started writing a different novel—a satire—about Forest Lawn and the society it represented. America, in his view, was "Substitute Land"—a place of secondhand experience, phony culture, "debased" language, and "counterfeit" art. But the pet cemetery at Forest Lawn was "an entirely unique place—the *only* thing in California that is not a copy of something else."

The proofs of *The Seven Storey Mountain* reached him the month before *The Loved One* was published. He read them at once, transfixed by Merton's story. After sending a comment to Robert Giroux he sent a letter suggesting improvements to the text. He urged a publisher friend to obtain British rights to the book, volunteering to edit it himself. And he told his agent to find an American magazine that would publish an essay he was writing. Graham Greene's new novel, *The Heart of the Matter*, had been chosen by the Book-of-the-Month Club, which, Waugh knowingly remarked, "will bring it to a much larger public than can profitably read it." In a rare nod to a peer and a rival, Waugh drafted a review, one meant to show readers—especially American readers—how to read the new Catholic writing.

By 1948 Waugh and Greene, like Tolstoy and Dostoevsky, were permanently paired. They were exact contemporaries (born in 1903) who had taken the same path—public school, Oxford, schoolteaching, journalism; light novels, travel books; conversion, and a new seriousness—in different directions, the one becoming an ardent defender of Christian civilization, the other searching the margins for traces of authentic faith.

In retrospect, however, the similarities between them are more clear. In their work the Church is a permanent ideal, which does not change and which needs no explanation. And in their work the conflict turns on an encounter with an aspect of the Church that now seems remote and arcane: in Waugh, the manners of the Catholic upper classes; in Greene, questions of sin drawn directly from the catechism.

The Heart of the Matter is about a religious type familiar in the lore of midcentury Catholicism: the scrupulous believer who keeps a scorecard of his sins. Scobie is a British official in West Africa. He cheats at the office to gain money to please his wife. When she has an affair he takes a mistress, whom he keeps out of trouble with another man. He has a small part to play in the murder of his servant. Then, tortured by his faith, which tells him that theft, adultery, and murder are mortal sins, he commits suicide, the mortal sin to top all mortal sins.

Is Scobie damned to hell forever? It seems a scholastic question; but Greene—this was Waugh's point—had dramatized the prospect of eternal damnation in such a way that the reader (if only for a few hours) could imagine it. Greene had prefaced the novel with a quotation from Charles Péguy, the French Catholic writer, to the effect that the sinner is more of a Christian than anybody except the saint—that a grave sinner has a better grasp of guilt and forgiveness than a pious Christian does. Waugh praised Greene for recasting a point of theology in the "brilliantly plain human terms" of modern fiction—and for depicting a character purified by his religious anguish, a character who, in effect, had sinned his way to God.

To support the point, Waugh drew on the American Trappist conversion story he had just read. He worried that the typical Catholic saw not only sins and damnation but religious experience generally as remote and exotic. Paraphrasing Thomas Merton, he went on: "I ask in all humility whether nowadays logical rule-of-thumb Catholics are not a little too humble towards the mystics. We are inclined to say: 'Ah, that is mysticism. I'm quite out of my depth there,' as though the subject were higher mathematics, while in fact our whole Faith is essentially mystical. We may well fight shy of discussing ecstatic states of prayer with which we have no acquaintance, but sacrilege and suicide are acts of which we are perfectly capable."

After the piece ran in *Commonweal* in July, Waugh turned to editing *The Seven Storey Mountain*. He cut a third of the text, wrote a foreword, and proposed a new title: *Elected Silence*, from a poem by Hopkins.

As he worked, making Merton's chatty style more like his own, he gained an altogether new perspective on the future of Catholicism. In England the real-life model for Brideshead Castle, which Waugh had made a symbol of Christendom (the "Household of Faith"), had become a place of pilgrimage for devotees of "the cult of the English country house." In America, the Catholic Church struck Waugh as suddenly formidable—not a shallow imitation but something original and vigorous. The leaders of the Catholic Church in America, Waugh surmised, were the "future leaders" of the Church worldwide.

He contacted Clare Boothe Luce and proposed to write an article for *Life* about the Catholic Church in America. He explained, "It seems to me likely that American monasticism may help to save the world."

Dorothy Day wrote: "Today the *Commonweal* came with a chapter from Thomas Merton's book in it about his entrance into the Trappist monastery in Gethsemane, Kentucky. He mentions the need we have in our religious life for a formal observance of prayer, the need for ritual."

She was keeping a journal of the year 1948 and planned to publish it. In bringing out *On Pilgrimage*, as she called it, from Catholic Worker Books, she hoped to earn some money for the movement, and probably wished to give David Hennessy a book to sell through the mail from the Distributist Bookstall he had started after marrying her daughter. But she was doubtless motivated by literary ambition as well. Ten years had passed since *From Union Square to Rome* had come out. She was better known as an organizer and a pacifist than as an editor and a writer.

The excerpt from *The Seven Storey Mountain* spoke to her main concern that year: the struggle to cultivate the interior life amid the life of poverty. Although the abbot of Gethsemani had told her the Catholic Worker was "a companion order in the world," the Catholic Worker life as she found it was far from contemplative, and Merton's account of Trappist life in *Commonweal* surely made it seem even less so by comparison. Merton described Trappist poverty as a means to detachment, which would free the monks for the interior life. Day had the same idea of "holy poverty," but in 1948 poverty seemed to her to get in the way of interiority. Everywhere she looked she saw obstacles. Banks and insurance companies "dispossessed the poor man." Advertisers stirred "his useless desires. . . . Loan and finance companies have further defrauded him. Movies, radio have enslaved him. So that he has no time nor thought to give to his life, either of soul or of body."

The clearest instance of the trials of poverty was the life of her daughter,

Tamar. Whereas Day, the Tolstoyan, had chosen the life of poverty as a religious discipline, Tamar was simply poor, like a peasant wife out of Dostoevsky. She and her husband had bought a farm in Stotler's Crossroads, West Virginia—the money had come from the sale of Day's cottage on Staten Island—and Day spent much of 1948 there, helping them out after the birth of their third child. The farm had no electricity or running water. The porch was collapsing. The cellar was flooded. The firewood had to be chopped and the pipes kept warm in winter, lest they freeze. "What kind of an interior life can a mother of three children have," Day asked, "who is doing all her own work, on a farm with wood fires to tend and water to pump? Or the grandmother either?"

At the farm, surrounded by poverty, with the nearest church along a country road and far away, Day found ritual observance in the journal she was keeping, a deep sounding of her interior life. "How to lift the heart to God, our first beginning and last end, except to say with the soldier about to go into battle—'Lord I'll have no time to think of Thee but do Thou think of me?'" she asked. The answer, she found, was to sit down and write.

While in West Virginia Day received an odd message from St. Joseph's House. Evelyn Waugh was in New York for *Life* magazine and wished to take her to lunch. He could be reached at the Plaza Hotel on Fifth Avenue.

She had not read any of Waugh's novels. She was no admirer of *Life*. Even so, she returned to New York, where a telegram awaited her, proposing lunch at the Chambord. The Catholic Workers were amused and horrified. "The Chambord! It's one of the most expensive restaurants in town. People like the Duke and Duchess of Windsor eat there," a Catholic Worker named Jack English explained. "If you go there *Life* might very well carry a picture of the breadline next to one of you and Evelyn Waugh feasting, with the caption 'No soup for her.'" Day sent a cable to the Plaza: FORGIVE MY CLASS CONSCIOUSNESS BUT THE CHAMBORD APPALLS ME AS MOTT STREET DOES YOU, whereupon Waugh phoned St. Joseph's House to say he would meet her anywhere she chose.

A Cadillac arrived on Mott Street at noon the next day with the famous author inside. Half a dozen Catholic Workers piled in, Dorothy Day among them, and the car proceeded one block to Mulberry Street and a red-sauce place called Angelo's.

"I gave a great party of them luncheon in an Italian restaurant," Waugh wrote to his wife that evening, describing the outing. "Mrs. Day didn't at all approve of their having cocktails or wine but they had them and we talked till four o'clock."

Over food and drink, they discussed wealth and poverty. Tom Sullivan, a stalwart of St. Joseph's House, questioned whether the poverty of a Yeats in a "vine-clad cottage" in Ireland could really be called poverty. Another Catholic Worker pointed out that most rich people were miserable—as Waugh's novels made obvious. In the end, Day recalled, they all wound up "debating whether the poor or the rich had the worst of it in this world."

Waugh had already spent a week in New York as *Life*'s "honorary correspondent," meeting Catholics for his article. From there, he went to Baltimore to receive an honorary degree from a Jesuit college, and afterward sought out descendants of pre-Revolutionary Catholic families such as the Baltimores—the fictional Marchmains' American counterparts. Then he went by train to Kentucky and the Abbey of Gethsemani, to meet Thomas Merton.

They had corresponded about *The Seven Storey Mountain*. Merton was grateful for Waugh's editing, and for the dialogue with another writer it brought about. "I need criticism the way a man dying of thirst needs water," he explained in a letter. ". . . Because this business of writing has become intimately tied up with the whole process of my sanctification." In reply Waugh had urged Merton to devote himself to literary work and "leave mass-production alone."

Waugh reached Gethsemani on a Saturday night. Merton greeted him in the guest house and found him grumpy and unimpressed with America: the trains did not run on time; the monastery was too warm; the new religious art was terrible, a lot of "saints fixed up 'like motor mascots.' "

He left after Mass the next morning, bound for New Orleans. He would return to America the next spring on a lecture tour of Catholic colleges, speaking on three Catholic writers* who revealed the "great diversity" within the Church's "essential uniformity." The tour was a further stage of research for his *Life* article, whose theme would be the workings of the Holy Ghost. Always Christianity is somewhere in decline, he proposed, and "always Providence has another people quietly maturing to relieve the decadent of their burden." The Church was led by the Holy Ghost, and the Holy

---

*G. K. Chesterton, Ronald Knox, and Graham Greene.

Ghost had alighted on America, where, he now believed, "Providence is schooling and strengthening a people for the historic destiny long borne by Europe."

The Seven Storey Mountain was published October 4, 1948. The occasion passed without acknowledgment in Merton's journal, as it did in the outside world. Three book clubs had opted to offer the book to their members; celebrity Catholics had sent words of praise—Fulton J. Sheen calling it a modern *Confessions*, Graham Greene "a book one reads with a pencil so as to make it one's own"—but the book did not begin to sell until Christmastime. Then it began to sell strongly: 31,000 copies in December, 60,000 in January, with 10,000 sold on one singularly lively day. *The Seven Storey Mountain* was a best-seller, but the *New York Times* refused to list it as one, on the grounds that it was a religious book, like the Bible.

Why was the book such a best-seller? Most explanations are variations on the idea that Merton was the right man at the right time. One view is that twentieth-century America was ready for a searching spiritual autobiography, and Merton, in this account, anticipated the craving for order and stability that would characterize the 1950s; his disgust for the American century gave voice to public doubts about the nation's ideals, prosperity, optimism, and military might, and his flight to a Trappist monastery, a world where order prevailed and life made sense, proposed a striking alternative.

Another view is that the book captured a "Catholic moment." American Catholics had escaped the confines of parish and ghetto and entered the middle class and the wilds of postwar America. They were going to college and reading for pleasure. The war had confirmed them as patriotic Americans. To them Merton's book suggested that the Catholicism they had grown up with and taken for granted was not to be despised. A European, an Ivy Leaguer, a convert, a poet, Merton was a Catholic they could boast of and expect Jews and Protestants to admire.

There is doubtless some truth to these conjectures. The Jesuit scholar Mark Massa comes closest in identifying Merton as a "great individual" whose struggles represented those of countless people of his generation in a time of drastic change. As Merton described his entry into a monastery, a place where few readers, even Catholics, had gone, the reader identified with him, all the more so because of the book's chatty and deprecatory style, through which Merton confided in the reader as a person like himself.

But even this view misses the essential spirit of *The Seven Storey Mountain*. The book became a best-seller because it was a religious book, not in spite of the fact. It is an account of religious experience, the first book to speak with authority about American Catholicism, which Merton seems to know inside and out. At the same time, it is a firsthand account of one person's religious experience, the aspect of religious life so many books about American Catholicism left out of the story. Not only does Merton tell about what life is like behind the walls of a cloistered monastery; he tells what it feels like to be in the grip of God. And he does so in such a way as to make the reader feel not only that such an experience is real and possible, but that it is necessary, vital, and attractive, the center of life, just as the Catholic tradition insists it is. The Latin motto he uses to close the book—SIT FINIS LIBRI, NON FINIS QUAERENDI—makes his point clear. *Let this be the end of the book, not the end of the search.* Merton's search will go on—and so, it is hoped, will the reader's, as the reader takes the book's insights beyond the book and into his or her own life.

The spirit of the age; the nature of the Church; postwar anxiety; divine providence—these abstractions pale in light of the personal challenge Merton makes to the reader of his autobiography. God exists, he insists. The way to seek God is firsthand, through religious experience. So I have done. Here is the story. Now go and do likewise.

Flannery O'Connor worked "ALL the time" at Yaddo, and in January 1949 she sent out nine freshly typed chapters of her novel, hoping to get a contract with Rinehart, which held an option on it. She had found a literary agent, Elizabeth McKee, who was sympathetic to her work and her working habits, which she explained: "Like the old lady, I don't know so well what I think until I see what I say; then I have to say it over again." She had no doubt that the novel was strengthened by her constant rewriting, but she could not stay at Yaddo forever.

Looking back, she depicted her time at Yaddo, in a series of strong images, as the sojourn of an exile in the East, a stranger among the Freud-addled "interleckshuls" of the New York literary establishment. She went to a few parties with the other guests "but always left before they began to break things." From behind her typewriter she observed their dalliances, which in the Yaddo ethos were "not sin but Experience." Sunday mornings she went to Mass in Saratoga Springs with the Irish Catholic couple who were the caretakers of the colony.

"You survive in this atmosphere by minding your own business and having plenty of your own business to mind; and by not being afraid to be different from the rest of them," she told a friend a few years later, by way of advice. At Yaddo she cultivated apartness, and so adamantly that it seems her real companions there were the creatures she pondered in her studio each day: a squirrel, a "chipmonk and a large important-looking woodchuck," as well as Hazel Motes, Enoch Emery, Onnie Jay Holy, and Hoover Shoats.

Surely she behaved better, and wrote more, than the other guests. Yet she was no hermit. In her six months at Yaddo she made a lifelong friend in Elizabeth Fenwick; got to know Malcolm Cowley and Alfred Kazin, each an important critic; had her stay extended twice by the director of the colony; and obtained letters of recommendation from three of the most prominent literary figures in America—Robert Penn Warren, Philip Rahv of the *Partisan Review*, and Robert Lowell, a guest at Yaddo who became her companion and coreligionist.

Lowell later reverted so thoroughly to type as a square-jawed New England sage that his Catholic phase has been largely forgotten, but it coincided with the most intensely creative years of his life. He had won the Pulitzer Prize with *Lord Weary's Castle*, his first full-length book, and *Life* magazine had told his story in the manner of an emergent American legend, one so strong even Thomas Merton in the cloister heard about it: a Boston Brahmin upbringing leading straight to St. Mark's School and Harvard; flight from Boston to Nashville, where he sought refuge with Allen Tate and Caroline Gordon, living in a tent in their backyard; college at the Kenyon School of Letters in Ohio; marriage to Jean Stafford, a novelist from Colorado who, for reasons of her own, had already converted—*was* converted, as was said then—to Catholicism, and whose first novel had become a best-seller.

In 1940 Lowell, who had thought of Catholicism as "a religion for Irish servant girls," was converted himself after reading Maritain, Gilson, and Hopkins. It is hard to tell precisely what in Catholicism he accepted or for what reason. But it is clear that, in his life and his poetry, he claimed Catholic rhetoric and symbolism, which set him apart from his ancestry and the literary world alike. He was especially drawn to the Church's ancient image of community. Protestants were the Elect, Jews the Chosen, but Catholics were members of the Mystical Body of Christ, initiates into the mysteries of its priestcraft, as into a secret society.

The next ten years for Lowell were a series of episodes in a search for God. After a sojourn in Louisiana he and Stafford moved to New York, where they went to work for Sheed and Ward, a Catholic press. At lunchtime, while he stayed at his desk, she would leave the office, at his instigation, and walk "through the kind of slums you do not believe exist when you see them in the movies" to pitch in at the Catholic Worker house on Mott Street.

When the United States entered the war Lowell held out as a conscientious objector, writing letters of protest to President Roosevelt, and in 1943 he was sent to prison for draft evasion. After his release a year later he and Stafford went to live in Maine, where he began to follow a penitential regimen of Mass, Benediction, the Rosary, spiritual exercises, a vow of celibacy, and retreats at a Trappist monastery in Rhode Island. Stafford, who had become an alcoholic, found it all unbearable, and they split up. "I fell in love with Caligula," she complained, "and am living with Calvin."

Now Flannery O'Connor fell for him. Before coming to Yaddo he had left the Church, moved to New York, had several affairs, and started drinking wine by the gallon jug. But at Yaddo, living a "monk's life" with O'Connor and two other guests, he became a Catholic again. "To make a long story short, I watched him that winter come back into the Church," she recalled. "I had nothing to do with it but of course it was a great joy to me."

He was on the verge of psychosis, but he was handsome, charismatic, brilliant, and a fellow member of the Mystical Body of Christ. Is it any wonder she fell in love with him? Like the handsome preacher who ranted and raved in her studio every day, he was an odd species of prophet—oracular, puritanical, self-possessed, walking the line between holiness and madness with great poise and eloquence.

On March 1, 1949, Lowell, O'Connor, and Elizabeth Hardwick, another novelist, left Yaddo abruptly. The press had fingered a Yaddo guest as a Soviet spy, and FBI agents came to investigate the place, which they claimed was a colony of Communists, not artists. Lowell, in high dudgeon, accused the director of harboring a well-known and self-acknowledged Communist, Agnes Smedley, as a longtime guest. The Yaddo community was a "body," he asserted, and the director was a "diseased organ, chronically poisoning the whole system." When she stood her ground (joined, in time, by a long list of writers who stood by her and accused Lowell of "Red-baiting"), he left in protest against "the great evil of the world."

The way the story is usually told, Lowell got O'Connor to go with him, prevailing on a lovestruck young woman to join his crusade. But the evidence suggests that it was he who tagged along with her. Nearly a month before the conflict at Yaddo O'Connor had made plans to go to New York to resolve a graver conflict, which was about her novel.

This conflict, readers of *The Habit of Being* know, was played out in an exchange of letters between O'Connor; her agent, Elizabeth McKee; and John Selby, an editor with Rinehart. O'Connor presents her own position so colorfully in her letters that the reader assumes she is in the right. The letters, however, suggest that she was as headstrong in behalf of her cause as Lowell was in his, and for similar motives.

Even before she sent the chapters, she hoped Rinehart wouldn't exercise its option. Once she sent them she grew impatient for a reply. When a week had passed, she asked: "How long is it supposed to take the Brothers Rinehart to decide if they want to risk their money on me?"

She'd had lunch with Selby once and found him empty and evasive. But it seems likely that she'd also heard bad things about Rinehart from the people at Yaddo—people who already had another publisher in mind for her. One was Alfred Kazin, whose first book, *On Native Grounds*, had been a great success in 1942, and who was now being paid to recommend writers to Harcourt, Brace and vice versa. He told O'Connor that Harcourt would be interested in her novel. Another was Lowell, whose book had sold well for Harcourt, and who liked the place and felt at home there. His editor, Robert Giroux, he told her, was also T. S. Eliot's editor. Giroux was Jesuit-educated and looked like a priest. He too was a member of the Mystical Body of Christ.

She communicated her findings to her agent, who confirmed Giroux's interest, and even discussed a price. O'Connor was "very much pleased."

Then came Selby's letter. It was, O'Connor told Paul Engle, "a long time coming"—twenty-nine days, including the time it took for chapters and letter to travel in the mail. Past impatient, she was petulant.

The letter is best known through Robert Giroux's paraphrase in *The Complete Stories*. Selby "said he thought she was a pretty straight shooter, that she had an astonishing gift, but that some aspects of the book were obscured by her habit of rewriting over and over again. To be honest, he added, he sensed a kind of aloneness in the book, as if she were writing out of her own experience, and consciously limiting this experience. He wished she would sit down and tell him what was what."

In retrospect, that seems a fair appraisal of the novel O'Connor was writing. But she was enraged. She showed the letter to Lowell, who sympathized with her. She wrote to her agent, "Please tell me what is behind this Sears Roebuck Straight Shooter approach." Would the Rinehart people be willing to publish the novel "as it will be if left to my fiendish care"? Or did they want to "rescue it at this point and turn it into a conventional novel"?

> The criticism is vague and really tells me nothing except that they don't like it. I feel the objections they raise are connected with its virtues, and the thought of working with them to correct these lacks they mention is repulsive to me. The letter is addressed to a slightly dim-witted Camp Fire Girl, and I cannot look with composure on getting a lifetime of others like them.

It is hard to side with the editor after that. In the reader's mind, O'Connor has won the argument. And yet only six months earlier she had called the early chapters of the novel "formless stuff." At the age of twenty-three she was (as she herself admitted) "prematurely arrogant."

The question is what made her that way. What so enraged her? What made the prospect of working with this editor so repulsive?

Her reply to Selby provides a further suggestion. She explained that the novel was not a conventional novel but one whose virtues were connected with its limitations—"the peculiarity or aloneness, if you will, of the experience I write from." It was an odd book but would be even odder if she had her way. She did not care to work with him in the usual manner. "In short, I am open to criticism but only within the sphere of what I am trying to do; I will not be persuaded to do otherwise."

The published exchange ends there. But O'Connor made sure to have the last word. In an "Author's Note" ten years later, she recalled: "*Wise Blood* was written by an author congenitally innocent of theory, but one with certain preoccupations. That belief in Christ is to some a matter of life and death has been a stumbling block for readers who would prefer to think it a matter of no great consequence."

It seems clear that she detested Selby because he thought her Christian preoccupations "of no great consequence." In patronizing her religion, he had patronized her. In rejecting his advances she wasn't defending her odd prose style or her habit of rewriting. She was defending "the experience I write from"—that of a true believer.

She and Lowell left Yaddo. First they went to Mass in Saratoga Springs. There Lowell, by his own account, "returned to the Church . . . in an incredible outpouring of Grace."

Then they went by train to New York, along with Elizabeth Hardwick, who had an apartment on East Tenth Street.

O'Connor was to stay with Hardwick. While in New York she would meet her agent and have appointments with editors from Rinehart and Harcourt, Brace. Lowell had other ideas for her. He took her to meet his friends Robert and Sally Fitzgerald. They were Catholics and literary people; Robert Fitzgerald was translating the *Oedipus* plays for Harcourt, Brace.

The Fitzgeralds later recalled the day vividly: O'Connor in a peacoat and brown corduroys and speaking with a strong accent; Lowell's eyes shining—he was "shooting sparks in every direction," Sally Fitzgerald remembered—as he told them what had happened to him at the church, then looking to O'Connor to corroborate it; she "frowning and struggling softly in her drawl to put whatever it was exactly the way it was."

He also took her to see Robert Giroux at the Harcourt, Brace offices on Madison Avenue. Giroux later remembered being struck at once by her talent and originality. "Behind her soft-spoken speech, clear-eyed gaze and shy manner, I sensed a tremendous strength. This was the rarest kind of young writer, one who was prepared to work her utmost and knew exactly what she must do with her talent. I rather regretted, as a publisher, meeting such an interesting writer at the start of a career in which I could play no part. She told me she was committed elsewhere, and if I knew anything it was that she would honor her commitment."

She would honor her commitment to Rinehart; she would also tell her agent to show her novel to this man as soon as possible. He was as impressive as Lowell had said he was, and as sympathetic to her point of view. The books on his shelves said as much. "She asked me about a new writer I had recently published—Thomas Merton," Giroux recalled, "and I gave her a copy of *The Seven Storey Mountain* to take with her."

A good editor is hard to find, and in Robert Giroux, O'Connor had found hers. She strode along Madison Avenue, carrying the book he had given her, a book that was American, Catholic, and literary all at once.

Lowell had become manic, and by the time he returned from a retreat at the Trappist monastery of Our Lady of the Valley the next week, his reconversion had turned grotesque. He phoned the Fitzgeralds at dawn to dictate the revelations vouchsafed to him: that he was a prophet, like Sacco and Vanzetti, and that O'Connor was a saint. "Today is the day of Flannery O'Connor, whose patron saint is Therese of Lisieux," he announced March 4, the feast of the Little Flower, saying he had spent the morning in the bath-tub, prostrate in prayer.

Robert Fitzgerald was alarmed. He wrote a letter to the Tates, and later an open letter to the literary community, explaining Lowell's troubles. He saw in Lowell the symptoms of mania and schizophrenia; at the same time, as "a Catholic made alive by grace to some realities," he believed Lowell was laboring "under the strain and exaltation of religious experience." He con-jectured that the spirit of God had borne down on Lowell, as it had on St. Teresa of Avila and St. John of the Cross, leaving him shaken and over-whelmed. "I do believe," Fitzgerald wrote, ". . . that God sometimes inter-venes directly and unmistakably in our lives and that one effect of this, of the sense of God's power and other perfections, is to unbalance the person acted upon. Why should it not? It is a power with which our own are in-commensurable."

O'Connor moved out of Hardwick's apartment and into a YWCA on Lex-ington Avenue, where the room she rented "smelled like an unopened Bible." Shortly thereafter, she was invited to join Lowell and Hardwick for dinner with Mary McCarthy and her husband, Bowden Broadwater.

McCarthy had undergone a religious conversion in reverse, progressing in turn from a stereotypical "Catholic girlhood" to Vassar College, the apart-ment of Edmund Wilson, and the pages of the *Partisan Review*. "A Big Intellectual," as O'Connor dubbed her, McCarthy was the nearest thing to O'Connor's opposite. Later, in a letter, O'Connor recalled the eve-ning:

> We went at eight and at one, I hadn't opened my mouth once, there being nothing in such company for me to say. . . . Having me there was like having a dog present who had been trained to say a few words but overcome with inadequacy had forgotten them. Well, to-ward morning the conversation turned on the Eucharist, which I, be-ing the Catholic, was obviously supposed to defend. Mrs. Broadwater said when she was a child and received the Host, she thought of it as the Holy Ghost, He being the "most portable" person of the Trinity; now she thought of it as a symbol and implied that it was a pretty good one. I then said, in a very shaky voice, "Well, if it's a symbol, to hell with it." That was all the defense I was capable of.

The closing remark is the most famous of all O'Connor's remarks, an economical swipe at the reductive, liberalizing view of religion.

In the light of Lowell's situation, however, the whole episode seems more complicated than is usually thought. It is no wonder O'Connor couldn't get a word in over dinner: Lowell was ranting, and all of literary New York was abuzz with his exploits. It is no wonder the talk turned to the Eucharist: in those weeks Lowell, aflame with religiosity, poured out doctrine and symbolism and imagery and "mixed it all in with his wild humor," O'Connor recalled. One day he had announced to Hardwick, "It's no good telling you these things that have to be experienced; but Christ is present in the Eucharist and love is at the heart of the altar, and this is something perfectly real, just like getting your hand wet. This you must be told."

It is no wonder O'Connor defended the Eucharist so bluntly. She was defending the sacrament that the Catholic faith holds to be the central religious experience, the communion with God in the Eucharist. At the same time, she was doubtless sticking up for her maladjusted friend and fellow member of the Mystical Body, affirming her belief that his religious ardor, however twisted, was rooted in something genuine.

Lowell wound up in Indiana "raving against devils and homosexuals" in the streets of Bloomington, a city whose name, he thought, came from *Ulysses*. Police bulletins had gone out, and when he knocked on the front door of a house and was recognized, he thought it was divine intervention.

O'Connor, in her room at the Y, was "distressed" by his ordeal. The dramatic religious experiences she had read about in books were suddenly taking place in life, happening to a person she loved. Yet the torments visited upon Lowell were less like religious experience than like insanity, and the respect she and his other Catholic friends had accorded them may have made them worse.

She made plans to go to Milledgeville and put some distance between herself and the episode. "I was only 23 and didn't have much sense," she later said. Lowell's vision she called a delusion — "the delusion that he had been called on some kind of mission of purification." His declaration of her as a saint she dismissed as "revolting," and pointed out that he had been canonizing all and sundry.

Lowell himself returned to New York, married Elizabeth Hardwick, and shortly afterward was checked into a mental hospital, where he was given electroshock treatments.

When the ordeal was over, his faith was gone. "I guess the shock table took care of it," O'Connor ruefully remarked. "It was a grief for me as if he had died."

She went home to Georgia, then returned to the city and her novel. Her fellowship application had been rejected ("I didn't get any Guggenheim," she lamented). A literary quarterly called *Tomorrow* had bought an excerpt from the novel. *Partisan Review* couldn't run its excerpt for six months. Contractually, the novel was in limbo. Artistically, however, the novel was sound. The end was in sight. She wrote toward it.

Like Hazel Motes, she was living in a rooming house: an apartment hotel on West 108th Street, in a nameless, charmless, in-between neighborhood, neither uptown nor downtown. "I did well to get out and get a meal or two a day," she recalled. Usually she walked a few blocks up Broadway to the Columbia University student cafeteria—"one of the few places I suspected the food of being clean."

Some years later she wrote "The Enduring Chill," a short story about a writer who leaves the South to live in New York. In the city Asbury Fox lives in "two damp rooms and a closet with a toilet in it." Asbury stays four months and feels "the end coming" all the while like a chill in the air. "Alone in his freezing flat, huddled under his two blankets and his overcoat and with three thicknesses of the *New York Times* between, he had had a chill one night, followed by a violent sweat that left the sheets soaking and removed any doubt about his true condition." But Asbury is a man, not a woman, a playwright, not a novelist, and his season of misery in New York—winter, not summer—is the least autobiographical aspect of the story.

O'Connor herself professed to like living in New York: going to Mass at the Church of the Ascension on West 107th Street, riding the subways and buses, and finding, in the crowds, a certain advantage: "Although you see several people you wish you didn't know, you see thousands you're glad you don't know."

One day she went on an excursion to the Cloisters. She lingered in the light of the stained-glass windows, strode through the corridors of imported stone. She was "greatly taken" with a wooden statue on display in one of the chapels. "It was the Virgin holding the Christ child and both were laughing; not smiling, laughing." It was a piece to emulate as well as admire; like her own work, it was religious and comic at the same time.

She had stayed in touch with Robert and Sally Fitzgerald. That summer, following the pattern of literary pilgrimage Malcolm Cowley had described, they had bought a house in the country—in Ridgefield, Connecticut, two hours' drive from New York. It was expensive, and they sought a boarder to rent a room over the garage. O'Connor had no great yearning to leave the city, but her savings were low. The Fitzgeralds wanted sixty-five dollars a month. She decided to join them. "Me & my novel are going to move to the rural parts of Connecticut," she told a friend—to "a house on top of a ridge, miles from anything you could name." There, she would be an exile in the East once more.

"It is always a terrible thing to come back to Mott Street," Dorothy Day observed. "To come back in a driving rain, to men crouched in stairs, huddled in doorways, without overcoats because they sold them perhaps the week before when it was warm, to satisfy hunger or thirst, who knows. Those without love would say, 'It serves them right, drinking up their clothes.' God help us if we got just what we deserved!"

In 1949 she came back to one problem after another. *On Pilgrimage* had been shoddily bound, and the money from its sale (it was selling "slowly and steadily") was "immediately misappropriated for running expenses of the house" instead of the printing costs. In New York that winter there was a battle in "that most awful of all wars, the war between the clergy and the laity." Gravediggers at the vast Catholic cemetery in Queens, Catholics themselves, went on strike for higher wages. Cardinal Spellman vowed to break their union. He ordered seminarians to dig the graves in their stead and refused to negotiate, calling the workers Communists in the press. A picket line appeared outside the archbishop's residence—a mansion on Madison Avenue behind St. Patrick's Cathedral known as the Powerhouse—and the Catholic Workers joined them, carrying placards quoting papal texts on the dignity of labor and the right to organize. In the end the union yielded, and Cardinal Spellman called the victory his greatest achievement as archbishop. But first there came an intimation from the Powerhouse that the Cardinal might have the Catholic Worker shut down.

For Day the dispute was a rending of the Mystical Body of Christ, one not unlike the rending taking place in Eastern Europe as the Soviet Union extended its empire. "At one end of the world Cardinal Mindszenty and Archbishop Stepinac are lying in jail suffering at the hands of the masses, and here in our at present peaceful New York, a Cardinal, ill-advised, exercised so overwhelming a show of force against a handful of poor working men." Where was Christ, the Gospel ideal of the leader of all as the servant of all, who washed the feet of his followers? Far, far off, Day concluded. The only consolation was that while the strike went on, the striking workers "spent as much time in church as they did on the picket line."

Then Peter Maurin died. Day was traveling. She hastened back to the city, where he was buried out of Transfiguration Church on Mott Street, after a wake at St. Joseph's House, where the body was placed for viewing on one of the work tables where the newspapers were folded.

Maurin's death was reported in *Time* and the Vatican newspaper *L'Osservatore Romano*, as well as the *Catholic Worker*. Day herself wrote several obituaries, and recollections of Maurin filled her column for some months. By September, with letters of condolence still arriving, some Catholic Workers criticized the funeral as a waste of money. Day rose in its defense. The undertakers had charged too much, she allowed, "exploiting grief" and taking advantage of Catholic reverence for the body, an image of Christ that would someday be glorified. Even so, the funeral of Peter Maurin, a St. Francis of modern times, had been as simple as possible; and lest there be any doubt, Day, like Thoreau tallying the costs of his pondside cottage, gave her readers an itemized account:

> Embalming, $35; casket, $190; outside box, $50; personal service (Newburgh), $25; removal to New York City, $50; suit, $12. For the New York services and "equipment" which consisted of one stand for the coffin when Peter was laid out in the office, $147. Opening the grave, $40. Hearse to the cemetery and three limousines, $80; the death notice in the paper, $3. The total is $632.

She made "gratitude" a theme of her column that month, thanking the readers who had sent donations to pay for the funeral, and her columns of 1949 are a running account of gratitude offered and withheld. The gravediggers of this world, in her account, get no thanks for their thankless work. Neither do the Peter Maurins. Their holy poverty, she seems to say, is held against them, and they are begrudged even the least portion of glory.

"The American Epoch in the Catholic Church" ran in *Life* in September, a lesson in how to read history as if with Catholic eyes. As the divide between capitalism and Communism hardened into ideology, Waugh reiterated the ancient division of history into the times before and after Christ. Before Christ, "man lived in the mists"; after Christ, all history, "the migrations of peoples and the rise and fall of empires," has been "merely a succession of moods and phases" in the life of the Church, the supernatural society Christ founded.

The Church was "she" and "her" to the faithful of the era, and Waugh, using the dominant image of the period, described the Church as a living body, an organism, whose history is best understood as a life, active and purposive, led by the Holy Ghost. The article was a supernatural account of what he had seen in America. "It seems that in every age some one branch of the Church, racial, cultural or national, bears peculiar responsibilities towards the whole," he explained, and in the present age that branch was the American one. Youthful, optimistic, democratic, America seemed ill-fitted for Catholicism, but the Church had taken root in unlikely places repeatedly in its pilgrimage through time, and would do so again.

Waugh, taking stock of the Church in America, was impressed by her variety, her energy, her schools and colleges, her magazines, her convents and monasteries. He was struck especially by the experience of Ash Wednesday in New Orleans, where, across the street from his hotel, which was full of Mardi Gras revelers, "the Jesuit church was teeming with life all day long; a continuous, dense crowd of all colors and conditions moving up to the altar rails and returning with their foreheads signed with ash. . . . All that day, all over that light-hearted city, one encountered the little black smudge on the forehead which sealed us members of a great brotherhood who can both rejoice and recognize the limits of rejoicing."

He found the Church in America lacking in two respects: She lacked saints, and she lacked writers. The writers he had met at *Life*'s expense rated no serious introduction to the magazine's readers. Thomas Merton he depicted as a cloistered monk, not a writer—"merely one, unusually articulate, representative of a wide and healthy movement." Dorothy Day and her cohorts he left out altogether. "Without doubt lives of deep unobtrusive sanctity are being lived in all parts of the United States," he allowed, but "the American Church up to the present time has produced few illustrious heroes or heroines." This he found worrisome, but the lack of writers he dismissed as no cause for concern. "The Church and the world need monks more than they need writers. These merely decorate. The Church can get along very well without them. If they appear, it is a natural growth. They are not much in evidence in America at the moment."

At age forty-five, Waugh, his biographer Martin Stannard reports, was becoming an old man: afraid of death, losing his hearing, convinced that he was finished as a writer, intolerant of change, which he saw bringing only decline and fall. But America, as he pointed out, was another country, and the American Catholic writers—no matter what he thought—were just getting started. If they were not much in evidence just then it was because they were busy writing, making ready for the next stage of the pilgrimage in the solitude they required.

"Me and Enoch are living in the woods in Connecticut with the Robert Fitzgeralds," O'Connor told a friend in a letter. "Enoch didn't care so much for New York. He said there wasn't no privetcy there."

She had developed a daily routine as regular as that in a monastery: Mass; egg; novel; lunch; walk; mail; baby-sitting for an infant Fitzgerald. Then a pitcher of martinis was prepared, and husband, wife, and boarder (he, she, and the other) talked about books and authors well into the night, pausing only to say a long Latin grace over supper. These conversations, Sally Fitzgerald recalled, were "our movies, our concerts, and our theatre." O'Connor urged the Fitzgeralds to read Miss Lonelyhearts, Faulkner's As I Lay Dying, and Art and Scholasticism; they opened their library to her. They all discussed Catholic writers: Lord Acton, the historian; John Henry Newman ("If Newman is a saint," O'Connor said, "his saintliness didn't destroy his scrupulous intellect or his finickiness and you'll have to accept him as a finicky saint"); and a Father Philip Hughes, whose history of the Reformation in England made her feel "like I was at it."

Away from the South, she was finally among people of her own kind. Robert Giroux of Harcourt, Brace had offered a contract for Wise Blood. Robert Lowell, diagnosed manic-depressive and restored to health, sent the manuscript of the long poem The Mills of the Kavanaghs (she claimed she couldn't get past the epigraph). Robert Fitzgerald passed her the drafts of his translation of *Oedipus Rex*, and she read them: "I did a lot of thinking about Oedipus."

Hazel Motes was almost to the end of his pilgrimage. The question was what he would find there. O'Connor had spent three years writing the novel, and it was no longer than *As I Lay Dying*, which legend said Faulkner had written in six weeks. At Yaddo she had yearned "to go about my business to the end." At the Fitzgeralds', in contrast, she had settled in. Their stone house on a ridge in Connecticut was the nearest thing to a Catholic writer's colony that existed in America, and she seemed ready to stay there indefinitely. It was as though she were loath to finish her book, not knowing what was next.

Walker Percy lay on a daybed in the house in Covington, writing in longhand on a legal pad. He worked slowly, discarding hundreds of pages at one point. In time he finished a draft and gave it to his younger brother, Phinizy, who read fifty pages and gave it back, finding it unreadable.

The Charterhouse was "a sort of Southern *bildungsroman*" made up of elements drawn from his life and his reading, especially *The Magic Mountain*. The main characters were a wealthy Southern orphan, Ben Cleburne, who was prone to strange illnesses, and a Catholic, Ignatius, or Ignatz, who had entered and then left the priesthood. The settings were a country club known as the Charterhouse, in ironic evocation of the legendary Carthusian monastery, and an insane asylum called the Retreat—two sites for a running conversation about the meaning of life. As Ignatius tried to decide whether or not to be a priest, Ben Cleburne struggled to decide whether to marry and settle down or to go west and run a gas station in the Southwestern desert— the desert of postwar American civilization.

Percy later dismissed *The Charterhouse* as "a bad imitation of Thomas Mann," a novel he had had to write in order to write something else. At the time, however, writing it was a personal challenge. He and his wife had adopted a baby girl, and the novel, likewise, was a test of whether he could adopt the themes of other writers and make them his own.

He was trying to be a writer because it offered the best prospect of his being happy and being happy in his own way. Pascal, in the *Pensées*, which he was reading, found the root of human unhappiness in the average man's inability to sit alone in a room contentedly for any length of time, and the effort of writing *The Charterhouse*, a man alone in a room, was a test of whether he could be happy as a writer.

As far as he knew, he was the only writer in Covington, but he kept up a correspondence with Shelby Foote, whose first novel (he had written two more) was soon to be published. In the usual account of their correspondence, each saw to the needs of the other. Percy sent Foote money and chapters of *The Charterhouse*. Foote sent Percy advice: lists of books to read, exhortations about prose style, and spirited commentary on his own work, all offered with a wise man's authority, although Foote, like Percy, was still in his early thirties. "It's really a compliment to your strength of character," he declared, "that I'm willing to risk telling you of the heartaches and sweats ahead."

In Foote's published letters to Percy there is no letter about the draft of *The Charterhouse*, and Jay Tolson suggests that Percy did not show Foote the whole manuscript. For Foote, eager to help as he was, was a less than ideal reader: hectoring, expert, certain that all the problems of fiction would eventually succumb to the will of the author. He saw fiction as a secular priestcraft. Percy, in contrast, saw it as an act of reconnaissance, less about the known than about the unknown. His ideal reader was someone still unknown to him, someone with an appreciation of mystery.

Merton was in the monastery's "book vault," writing in his journal. "What do you think, you dope, after having been a Trappist for seven years?" he wrote on December 13, 1949, the eighth anniversary of his entry into the monastery. "I think—where did the time go? I caught myself thinking: have I changed? Not that it matters. I have and I haven't. I'm balder. Somehow I have more of an interior life, but I'd have a hard time trying to say how."

Inwardly, he still sought God in the same way that had led him to the monastery: through prayer, ritual, and self-denial in a place silent, austere, medieval, and essentially out of this world. Outwardly, he was in circumstances that by his own account made it even harder for him to grow in the experience of God. He was thirty-four years old, a priest, a writer, and a celebrity whose earnings were suddenly the monastery's largest source of income. Dozens of strangers wrote to him each week, asking for his prayers or advice or just trying to establish a direct connection between reader and writer. Many men had come to the monastery gate, inspired by *The Seven Storey Mountain*, and announced their desire to leave the world. The author who had modeled himself on Joyce and Blake and Hopkins was now a model for others. A monastic revival was under way, and he was said to be responsible.

He was under orders to keep writing. The abbot had given him the key to the book vault, a chamber full of rare books and manuscripts, to use as a workspace. He wore the giant key on a cord around his waist, a token of his secret life.

In the vault he answered his mail, writing ten letters a day, as did several other monks, who crafted their replies to suggest that Thomas Merton had written them himself.

He worked on a book about the "School of the Spirit," in which the voices of St. John of the Cross and other Catholic contemplatives conversed about the experience of God, with Merton serving as the reader's surrogate. But he found that "the theology of contemplation does not mix well with fan mail."

Like the book vault, his journal was a place in between: between poetry and expository prose, between the literary writing Waugh had stressed and the "obedience writing" the abbot required of him, between the religious experiences of others and those vouchsafed to him directly. In his journal (which he wrote "under obedience") he described his life as that of a writer with too many readers and "a contemplative who is ready to collapse from overwork"—for he had fainted at the altar during Mass one morning.

Merton generally diagnosed his problems as a conflict between two aspects of himself: the writer and the monk, the public figure and the Trappist "hidden in God." Likewise his biographers. But Merton's most telling conflict in those years was actually between two places, the world and the monastery, each of which loomed in spiritually charged form in his mind.

He had left the world for the monastery. Now he could see that the monastery was far from ideal; with its emphasis on work, on rules, on results, on belonging, on the subjugation of the self to the group, it was all too much like the world he had left behind.

At the same time the world seemed less detestable than he had thought it to be. The proof (though he was loath to acknowledge it) was the success of his autobiography. The American public, supposedly so oblivious of real religion, so contemptuous of the life of the spirit, had bought half a million copies of a book which was explicitly "the odyssey of a soul"—*his* soul. Clearly, many people shared his otherworldly yearnings. Through his big book, he had discovered the essence of the Mystical Body of Christ: that the human race is "a body of broken bones," as he put it, and yet a single body. "God does not give us graces or talents or virtues for ourselves alone," he had written in *Seeds of Contemplation*, which was read aloud to all the monks during meals that summer. "We are members of one another and everything that is given for one member is given for the whole body."

He was still inclined to denounce the world and to curse the complications fame had brought him. His ordination as a priest—on May 26, 1949, after seven years' preparation—attracted the national press, and Michael Mott tells the story of a reporter who asked Merton to mug for the camera during the ceremony: the new Father Louis told him to go jump in a lake nearby.

The writing of his autobiography enabled him to bring his two selves, his two lives, into phase. Then the success of the autobiography set the two at odds once more. Suddenly he was unhappy again; and his instinct was to blame his writing—to rebel against his autobiography and the false self it had created. But in truth his writing was a refuge from his predicament, not a cause of it. In his published work, he surreptitiously described his problems as those of "religious men," as in this passage from *Seeds of Contemplation*:

> Many poets are not poets for the same reason that many religious men are not saints: they never succeed in being themselves. . . .
>
> They wear out their minds and bodies in a hopeless endeavor to have somebody else's experiences or write somebody else's poems or possess somebody else's sanctity. . . .
>
> They waste their years in vain efforts to be some other poet, some other saint. For many absurd reasons, they are convinced that they are obliged to become somebody else who died two hundred years ago and who lived in circumstances utterly alien to their own.

In his journal, meanwhile, he identified with other monks in other monasteries, whose lives he imagined to be religiously more sublime than his own. Surely the monks being sent to new foundations in Georgia and South Carolina—monks his book had attracted, foundations his book would help pay for—would find greater purity and simplicity than he had in Kentucky. Surely the Carthusians, who lived in private cells around a common foundation, had more perfect solitude than he did. An American charterhouse would be a great thing, if only one were chartered. The land over on the other side of the knobs (as the low hills of Kentucky are called) was ideal for "a one-man hermitage . . . where one could go for a month at a time or even more and get in some real and solid contemplation"—if only he were given a chance to build one.

He would not find out. He was forbidden to go. In the abbot's view, the departure of Thomas Merton from Gethsemani, the place he had described as an earthly paradise in his autobiography, would scandalize his public; so the abbot kept him right where he was, assigning him to tutor the new monks in theology. If he wished to go elsewhere, it would have to be inwardly, through his prayer, his reading, and his writing.

One afternoon late in 1949 Dorothy Day took the ferry to Staten Island. "It is a fine sight to see the skyscrapers of Manhattan slip away astern; with them fade the cares and clangor of the city. The salt spray is fresh; the ships we pass speak to us of far places . . . ," she wrote in *Loaves and Fishes*, evoking the ferry ride, which, on this particular day, was at once a retreat and a pilgrimage.

She was fifty-two years old. Her step had slowed. Her appearance had changed. "The figure is deplorable—farinaceous food does spread one out so—but her head and shoulders are magnificent," an old friend from Greenwich Village observed. "And the clothes she gets out of the 'clothes room' look wonderful on her. It is particularly interesting to us to observe her because we remember so well what she looked like in the old days: the same features but transformed because they have been put to such a different use."

The old friend was Caroline Gordon, who had sought out Day after becoming a Catholic in 1947. Gordon came to St. Joseph's House on Mott Street, where she was astonished to find signed first editions of books kept on open shelves where just anybody could take them. She went on retreat at Maryfarm in upstate New York and concluded that the place, at once rural and Catholic, would be a good place to retire to someday (Day was "fixing up cells in the barn," she told a friend, "any one of which would suit me to a T"). She invited Day to spend a weekend in Princeton, where she and Allen Tate were teaching, and Day accepted the invitation. A habitual matchmaker, Gordon arranged a small party for people of like mind: Robert Giroux from Harcourt, Brace; the Maritains, who were instructing Tate in the Catholic faith; Malcolm Cowley, who was a visiting professor. Cowley was planning a revised edition of *Exile's Return*, his memoir of the 1920s; Day and the Tates figured in it, and that weekend, seeing Day for the first time in years, he called forth her recollections.

Now, on the ferry, Day was returning to the scene of their twenties adventures—the dinners, the parties, the long walks on the beach.

She had a present purpose as well. No matter what Gordon thought of Maryfarm, Day was disenchanted with the place. The Catholic Worker community there had descended into drunkenness and scholastic squabbling. The farm itself had fallen into decay. During retreats, aircraft from a nearby military base roared overhead, shattering the silence. When Day learned of a farm for sale on Staten Island, not far from the beach, she went at once to see the place.

She liked it immediately. In *Loaves and Fishes*, she described it this way: "The buildings themselves are not impressive in appearance: a brown-shingled farmhouse, sagging somewhat and falling apart at the seams; a barn with the cross on the side that is now our little chapel; a row of little rooms made from a carriage shed; carpenter shops; a chicken coop; and, at the foot of the hill, a duck pond which is claimed right now by a flock of geese."

A farm in the city, near the open sea, was her idea of paradise. The price was sixteen thousand dollars. A thousand dollars down would hold the place.

Twenty-five years earlier she had bought a cottage on the beach. The cottage had changed her life. There she had become a Catholic. There she had taught herself to write. There she had learned of her own need to get away on retreat, and had satisfied it.

This farm offered her a similar opportunity. Without it, she had no real getaway. With it, she, and the rest of the community, would have a place of retreat just a ferry ride from Mott Street.

A way to pay for the farm presented itself. Malcolm Cowley was updating his memoir of their younger days. Her own memoir, which was out of print, stood in need of drastic revision. It had been hastily written and was incomplete; it concluded with her conversion, saying nothing of Peter Maurin, the Catholic Worker, hospitality, round-table discussions, communal farms, pacifism, World War II, the atomic bomb, the newspaper, or "On Pilgrimage"—saying nothing of the state of the world or of her life since she became a Catholic.

Although she had not finished her book about Maurin, she had written several hundred pieces for the *Catholic Worker*, and her yearlong journal had sold respectably. Yet Evelyn Waugh in *Life* had claimed that Catholic writers were not much in evidence in America, and neither were heroes or heroines.

Meanwhile, among Catholic Workers, as in the rest of America, Thomas Merton's autobiography had been an astonishing success. The Catholic

Workers on Mott Street cited the book chapter and verse around the house. Jack English had been moved to leave St. Joseph's House and enter a monastery. English was now "clothed" in the Trappist habit, and Day was praying for his vocation. She hoped to read the book herself when she got a chance.

She prayed on the matter, then acted quickly. Back in Manhattan, she met with an editor from Harper & Brothers and signed a contract for an autobiography. The advance was a thousand dollars, which she promptly used to make a down payment on the cost of the farm while she set about raising the rest.

The new farm would be called Peter Maurin Farm. It would settle an old debt, reconcile her present and her past. She had bought the cottage on the beach with Hollywood's reward for telling her story provocatively. Now she would buy a farm a short distance away with money she would make by telling her story in frankly religious terms—as a confession of her sins, an account of herself, and an explanation of the faith that was in her.

The new book would be called *The Long Loneliness*. The expression came from the memoirs of an English nun of Shakespeare's day, but the feeling was distinctively Day's. "We have all known the long loneliness," she believed, "and we have learned that the only solution is love and that love comes with community."

The community to which she now belonged was a more definite community than the bohemian crowd of her youth. They were united in work, in poverty, in resistance to what they called Holy Mother the State. They were united, too, she was confident, by religious faith, which joined friends and strangers, neighbors and distant correspondents, the living and the dead, and bound them all together.

Flannery O'Connor climbed the stairs to the room over the Fitzgerald garage, eyes bright with inspiration. She sat down at the typewriter, turned her gaze upon her fictive hero, and blinded him—swiftly, in a few bold strokes, using quicklime, which left whitish streaks around his eyes.

Once it was done, it seemed inevitable, the foreordained end of Hazel Motes, whose name had always hinted at spoiled sight. But once it was done, Robert Fitzgerald recalled, O'Connor returned to the body of the book, rewriting Hazel Motes's story to prepare him for blindness. Thus far his sight had been that of a self-styled prophet. As the founder of the Church

Without Christ he proclaimed that there was nothing to see beyond the world before his eyes: no god, no heaven, no supernatural life, just a blank horizon. He was a "realist of distances" (as she later defined the prophet), who saw the Gospel profaned by ordinary believers, who could see the outlines of a world without Christ. And yet he could not rid his sight of "the ragged figure that moves from tree to tree in the back of his mind."

Now, blinded, Hazel Motes ceased to be a prophet and became a kind of saint, like Greene's whiskey priest or Waugh's broken lay brother Sebastian Flyte. The stern judge of others looked to his own experience, with its harsh and unexpected mortification, and recognized it as a point of departure, a kind of second sight. The man of vision looked inward, where that ragged figure still stalked him, and saw the image of God there. The preacher on the hood of a secondhand car became a pilgrim walking alone and in darkness toward a "pin point of light."

All that came clear much later, as O'Connor sought the significance of what she had done. For the moment, she worked by instinct. Like Hazel Motes with his wooden cane, she was walking in the dark.

She typed the whole text once more, revising it throughout. When she was done—the fall of 1950—her arms ached, no great surprise. But the ache did not subside. She went to see a doctor in the next town. He told her the ache was probably arthritis and advised her to get it checked down south during the holidays.

Advent came. She boarded a train bound for Georgia, wearing a peacoat and a beret, a writer, age twenty-five, returning home on the verge of success in the wider world.

The trip from Connecticut to Georgia was a long day's journey. One of her uncles met the train. He found Mary Flannery looking "like a shriveled old woman."

They went directly to the hospital in Milledgeville. She had been overwhelmed by fever on the train. She had something more than arthritis. She was dying of lupus.

Her mother told her it was arthritis even so, saving the truth for a time when she was strong enough to bear it. But she had seen her father die of lupus, and she doubtless feared the worst. "I will be in Milledgeville Ga. a birdsanctuary for a few months, waiting to see how much of an invalid I get to be," she wrote to a college friend. "At Christmas the horsepital is full of old rain crows & tree frogs only—& accident victims—& me, but I don't believe in time no more so it's all one to me."

The lupus got worse. She was moved to a hospital in Atlanta. She was given cortisone and put on a no-salt diet. Her cheeks grew puffy. Her hair fell out.

She was in the hospital for eight months, on and off, longer than she had spent at Yaddo. Piedmont Hospital was no retreat or writer's colony. Dorothy Day had felt joined to all humanity as a new mother in Bellevue Hospital; Thomas Merton had thought St. Elizabeth's Hospital a Dantean paradise; Walker Percy had found the Trudeau sanatorium hospitable to his calling as a writer. For O'Connor a hospital was a place where death roamed the halls.

As she lay dying, she revised her novel one more time. Later, she would downplay the autobiographical aspects of her fiction—except when describing the draft of Wise Blood that she rewrote by hand in the hospital. "I was five years writing that book and up to the last I was convinced that it was a failure and didn't work," she told a friend, recalling the experience. "When it was almost finished I came down with my energy-depriving ailment and began to take cortesone in large doses and cortesone makes you think night and day until I suppose the mind dies of exhaustion if you are not rescued. I was, but during this time I was living my life and H. Mote's too and as my disease affected the joints, I conceived the notion that I would eventually become paralyzed and was going blind and that in the book I had spelled out my own course, or that in the illness I had spelled out the book."

The ordeal she had put Hazel Motes through was akin to the one that had come upon her; Wise Blood and the blood disease she had gotten were mysteriously joined.

Between hospital stays she sent her novel to Robert Fitzgerald, then to her agent and to Robert Giroux at Harcourt, Brace. Again she was impatient for a reply. This time she was wholly justified. Aching all over, unsure what ailed her, she had reason to believe that she would die before the novel was published.

Recovering, she went to live with her mother's family in the house in Milledgeville. A broad staircase led up to the house. A staircase led to the upper floors and the attic. Her bones ached coming and going.

In the spring of 1951, shortly after her twenty-sixth birthday, she and her mother moved to the Grey Quail Farm outside town. The white farmhouse, built in 1800, had two storeys, but the drive sloped gently from the road right up to the house, and the screened porch was only four steps off the ground.

In Savannah she had worked in a room overlooking the backyard; in Milledgeville she had worked in the attic, away from the family tumult below. Now in the farmhouse she made a room off the hall on the ground floor into a combination bedroom and studio. Robert Fitzgerald's description of its furnishings suggests a cross between a hospital room and a monk's cell—narrow bed, desk, wardrobe, bookshelves, typewriter, bedside table bearing holy books—but it might as well have been a room in a boardinghouse.

In this manner, the story goes, Flannery O'Connor came home. Reduced by disease, but guided by "an unusually strong sense of active destiny" (as Sally Fitzgerald put it), she discovered her true country.

There is no question that the South was O'Connor's true country. But her discovery of it was more complex than any confident pronouncements about destiny will allow. For just as the South was a place, she later said, sickness was a place as well, and while she came to embrace these two places as her setting and her calling, it is doubtful that she embraced them readily or at once. While in Connecticut, Robert Fitzgerald remarked, she "was out to be a writer on her own and had no plans to go back to live in Georgia." And her depiction of Asbury in "The Enduring Chill"—a writer brought back from New York to the South kicking and screaming, vexed by his misfortune, afflicted with the chills and sweats of a disease thought to be tuberculosis but later shown to be something else—is too bitter, too charged, to be merely a setup for his rescue through the ingenious power of the Holy Ghost. It is a portrait of the artist.

Coming home for O'Connor was a crucifixion, with all the term implies. In her illness, and the loneliness it brought, she saw the suffering of Christ, whose suffering was the model for the suffering of Hazel Motes.

The farm was five miles outside Milledgeville on the main road into town. It was a hundred percent Georgia. There was nothing foreign about it. But she decided to call it Andalusia, a name it had borne long before. The farm would be what she made of it. She would claim it as her own.

There her own religious experience commenced in earnest. Unlike Day, Merton, and Percy, O'Connor was a "cradle Catholic," brought up in the Mystical Body of Christ. They, as converts, had come to religious faith from somewhere else, constantly measuring their own experience against the testimony of others. O'Connor, in contrast, had professed her faith before life put it to the test.

She was no Tolstoyan, choosing the strenuous life for the experience it afforded; she was a Dostoevskian, who had affliction thrust upon her. Now, in her sickness, and in her response to it, she began to know the Catholic faith firsthand. As she injected herself with ACTH and learned to walk on her fragile bones, she was converted to the religion she already believed in, and her imitation of Christ began.

Out of O'Connor's hands, *Wise Blood* had begun to make its way in the world. John Selby relinquished Rinehart's claim upon the novel. Robert Giroux accepted the novel for Harcourt, Brace. Robert Fitzgerald told O'Connor it was good.

Fitzgerald also sent it to Caroline Gordon, who was teaching in Minnesota. No sooner had Gordon become a Catholic than she began calling for new Catholic fiction. Having served as Ford Madox Ford's secretary in Paris, Gordon traced a line of literary ancestry from herself directly back to Flaubert. Even before her conversion she was the most doctrinaire of critics, regarding fiction as a discipline with rules, standards, and a distinct tradition. She spoke of Flaubert, Turgenev, and the like as "classical" writers whose work every writer should know chapter and verse. She was a disciple of Henry James and believed that his prefaces held answers to all the quandaries of fiction. Now she, with Allen Tate, who had just been baptized Catholic (with the Maritains as his godparents) sought to recast fictional orthodoxy in Catholic terms.

Gordon received *Wise Blood* in the mail, read it, and wrote a letter to Fitzgerald. She was an excitable reader—a reader of violent enthusiasms, O'Connor later said—and the novel left her particularly excited. "This girl is a real novelist," she announced, ". . . already a rare phenomenon: a Catholic novelist with a real dramatic sense, one who relies more on her technique than her piety."

She declared that O'Connor had a better grasp of her subject than she herself had had at that age. "She is, of course, writing the kind of stuff people like to read nowadays: about freaks," even if they were real folks who'd become freaks on account of original sin.

Inevitably, she had suggestions to make. She thought O'Connor had "muffed" two scenes and saw "certain technical imperfections" here and there. She made a list of them. Fitzgerald passed the list along to O'Connor, who was in and out of the hospital in Georgia all summer, and O'Connor "inked in corrections" on the manuscript.

In September 1951 O'Connor wrote a series of letters to the Fitzgeralds concerning the novel. In the first she warned them to "steel yourselfs to read the changed parts of that manuscript again." It is the first of her country letters, a sketch of the life of "Me & Maw" on the farm: her ducks, her drugs, her reading, which included a stack of back issues of the *Saturday Review* ("The face of Malcolm Cowley shines out in every issue"). Sally Fitzgerald was pregnant with a fifth child, which prompted her to say, "I hope this one will be a girl & have a fierce Old Testament name and cut off a lot of heads."

She wrote another letter later in the month. "Enclosed is Opus Nauseous No. 1. I had to read it over after it came from the typist's and that was like spending the day eating a horse blanket," she reported. Robert Giroux had promised to review the changes, "but I doubt if the poor man puts himself to reading it again. Do you think Mrs. Tate would? All the changes are efforts after what she suggested in that letter and I am much obliged to her."

The Fitzgeralds got in touch with Gordon, and Gordon wrote to O'Connor directly to say she was eager to read the novel again: "As you know, I was much impressed by the manuscript in its original form. There are so few Catholic novelists who seem possessed of a literary conscience—not to mention skill—that I feel that your novel is very important."

She went on, "I had a letter yesterday from Will Percy's nephew, Walker Percy, who lives at Covington, Louisiana. He says that he has written a novel which he guesses is 'a Catholic novel, though it has no conversion or priests in it.' I don't know that your paths are likely to cross, but if they ever should I imagine that you'd find it interesting to know each other."

Percy had written to Gordon to ask whether she would read *The Charterhouse*. As a Southerner, a Catholic, and an old friend of his Uncle Will's, she was on paper an ideal reader. But he later suggested that it was simpler than that: apart from Shelby Foote she was the only literary person he knew.

In reply, Gordon told Percy that she would be glad to read the novel, for a fee of a hundred dollars, which she would apply to "a Catholic project." From their times together at Brinkwood, she recalled him as a serious writer, and one who understood the importance of literary technique. "A Catholic novelist who relies more on his technique than his piety is what is badly needed right now," she told him. "I wouldn't want to pass up the chance of discovering one."

The Charterhouse arrived first. It was eight pounds and nearly five hundred pages. "My heart sank when I saw it," Gordon told a friend. She recognized it as a Southern bildungsroman, à la *Of Time and the River*, and "feared a wolfe had gotten into the fold."

She turned instead to *Wise Blood*. She read it one day and wrote O'Connor a letter the next. Instead of putting the date at the top, she typed in the Catholic feast: St. Didacus's Day.

"Your manuscript has come!" she began. "I think it is terrific! I know a good many young writers who think they are like Kafka. You are the only one I know who succeeds in doing a certain thing that he does. . . . I do not mean that it is in any way derivative of Kafka. In fact, this book seems to me the most original book I have read in a long time."

Enthused, she went on for several pages, typing single-spaced. Much of what she had to say was the sort of fictional maxims she delivered to her classes: E. M. Forster's notion that there should be more than one plane of action, Chekhov's remark that "he and she are the engine that makes fiction move."

But much of it was criticism specific to *Wise Blood*, and in this letter O'Connor's work, perhaps for the first time, was read in frankly religious terms. Gordon overstated her case, but her commentary lit up the novel. "In geometry a straight line is the shortest distance between two points. Theology takes cognizance of a soul only in its relation to God; its relation to its fellow-men, in the end, helps to constitute its relations with God. It seems that it is the same way in fiction. You have to imitate the Almighty and create a whole world—or an illusion of a whole world, if the simplest tale is to have any verisimilitude."

A soul's relation to God and only secondarily to other people is an apt description of *Wise Blood*. But Gordon was convinced that this intensity of focus made the novel wearying and observed that "the scene itself is too meagre for my taste."

So she suggested ways to make the scene vivid and vary the intensity, drawing again from her bag of pedagogical tricks: Flaubert's technique of "going outside" the scene to make it more vivid, Yeats's way of setting off every "tense line" with a "numb line" for greater effect, James's conviction that a "stout stake" must be driven into the beginning of a book for the action to swirl against. She related a Negro preacher's "formula for a perfect sermon": "First I tells 'em I'm going to tell 'em, then I tells 'em, then I tell 'em I done told them."

"You won't, of course, pay too much attention to anything I've said in this long letter," she remarked. "After all, it's just one novelist talking about the way she thinks things ought to be done."

O'Connor received the letter in Milledgeville in mid-November. She wrote to the Fitzgeralds, thanking them again for sending Gordon the manuscript: "She sent it back to me with nine pages of comments and certainly increased my education thereby." She wrote to Robert Giroux to say she hoped to make further revisions, apologizing "for all this shilly-shallying."

Finally, she sat down at the typewriter and wrote a letter to Gordon, thanking her for all her advice. But there is no evidence that she ever sent the letter, or that she finished writing it. All that survives are two draft passages, and these suggest why O'Connor may not have sent them: they are as vulnerable, as exposed, as anything she wrote.

The two passages are very different, tellingly so. In the one, O'Connor comes across as a lonely writer, exiled from New York and Yaddo to a small town, eagerly awaiting commentary in the mail. "There is no one around here who knows anything at all about fiction (every story is 'your article,' or 'your cute piece'?) or much about any kind of writing for that matter. . . . So it means a great deal to me to get these comments." She explains her problems in the humblest terms. Her work is awkward on account of "laziness," which keeps her from getting things right. And the natural world is meagerly described in the book because she is loath to describe it—"afraid to try my hand at being lyrical for fear I would only be funny and not know it."

That is a very different writer from the one who found work with an editor "repulsive." Her illness and the loneliness it imposed upon her had brought about the change. So had Gordon's careful attention to the manuscript. And so, especially, it seems clear, had their common calling as religious artists, which is the subject of the other passage. This time, writing as an artist on her own terms, she told Gordon:

> Thank you so much for your letter and for wanting to help. I am afraid it will need all the help it can get. I never have, fortunately, expected to make any money out of it, but one thing that has concerned me is that it might be recognized by Catholics as an effort proper to a Catholic; not that I expect any sizable number of them who arn't kin to me to read it—reading is not necessary to salvation which may be why they don't do it—but I have enough trouble with the ones who are kin to me to know what could be expected. You can't shut them up before a thing comes out but you can look forward to a long mortified silence afterwards.

She turned to the question of the Catholic novel. "When I first started my book," she explained, "I was right young and very ignorant and I thought what I was doing was mighty powerful (it wasn't even intelligible at that point) and liable to currupt anybody that read it and me too, so I visited a priest in Iowa City and very carefully explained the problem to him. He gave me one of those ten cent pamphlets that they are never without and said I didn't have to write for fifteen year old girls." Now she professed to be "no longer concerned with writing a 'Catholic novel' ":

> I think now I was only occupying myself with fancy problems. If you are a Catholic you know so well what you believe, that you can forget about it and get on with the business of making the novel work. This is harder to do, knowing what you believe, but Catholic writers ought to be freer to concentrate on good writing than anybody else. They don't, and I wouldn't know why.

It is a moving confession, one in which O'Connor insisted on her independence, even in a moment of need, even with a coreligionist. At precisely the moment when Gordon was obsessed with the nature of Catholic fiction, O'Connor claimed not to care about the nature of Catholic fiction. And she observed offhandedly that Catholics know exactly what they believe when the other novel on Gordon's desk suggested otherwise—in fact, was intimately bound up with a Catholic's struggle to figure out what he believed.

Caroline Gordon liked *The Charterhouse* even better than *Wise Blood.* When she reached the end of the long manuscript she thought it "the best first novel that I have ever read." Before she told Walker Percy, she wrote to a friend, Brainard Cheney, to announce the discovery of the Catholic writer she had sought—and had found within her own social set, the last place she would have looked. Walker Percy "had sort of disappeared from Sewanee after stirring up a lot of commotion in the dove cotes there and all we'd heard about him since was that he'd got married and joined the Church. It is evident now that in the five or six years he's been lying doggo that he's done a lot of reading and thinking and writing."

The Charterhouse, she was certain, was "a sample of what the next development in the novel will be": Catholic fiction, written by "people consciously rooted and grounded in the faith."

She sent Percy himself a telegram of congratulations. Then she wrote him one of her pedagogical letters. It ran to thirty pages and bore the heading "St. Damasus's Day."

The letter, as Percy's biographers have summarized it, is a reprise of the letter to O'Connor: the same concern with the pace of the story (too brisk) and with the tendency to "muff" crucial scenes, the same urging to build up the physical world of the novel more thoroughly, the same preacher's formula for an ideal sermon.

As with Wise Blood, Gordon saw The Charterhouse in frankly religious terms; commenting on a passage about Ben Cleburne's yearning to run a gas station in the desert, for example, she remarked: "The human life is an analogue of the Divine Life. The desert figures in the life of anybody who makes any progress from the human toward the divine. It was no whim but the same kind of necessity that is governing your hero that drove the early fathers out into the desert, that drove Mary Magdalen to wander in the desert for thirty years." But with Percy, a recent convert and an obvious apprentice, she was more frank and insistent about her "fancy theories" of the Catholic writer. As she explained, the modern writer—whether Protestant or Communist—felt obliged to "set the universe up fresh for every performance." There was hubris in this: it was akin to "setting up a new heaven and a new earth as one goes." But the Catholic "knows that God has already created the universe and that his job is to find his proper place in it." Confident of "what moral order prevails in the universe," he was free to write fiction. She ended with an exhortation. "You have an enormous—an incalculable—advantage over most people writing today," she told Percy. "You know what it is all about."

Percy received the letter shortly before Christmas 1951. He sent Gordon two hundred dollars and got to work revising.

Gordon could not contain her excitement about her new discoveries. She wrote to Brainard Cheney again about them. She had "put my money on a good many horses in my time," she allowed, but this time she had found the real thing. "Walker's novel and Flannery's novel are IT. They are both so damned good!"

In Gordon's estimation, the two novels were not simply good in themselves; they were proof of her theory that religious orthodoxy was useful, even vital, for great fiction. In her view the "Protestant mystique" was "sucked-dry, beginning to rot, to stink." The Mystical Body of Christ, by contrast, was fresh and lively. "Everybody has suspected it for some time but the fact is now being brought out into the open," she declared. "Flannery's novel—as grim a picture of the Protestant world as you can find—and Walker's novel, which is the story of a man's desperate effort to stay alive spiritually, will be sensations when they come out."

Gordon had told Robert Giroux that she would help *Wise Blood* any way she could, and when he asked her to give a comment for the jacket of the book, she obliged: "I was more impressed by *Wise Blood* than any novel I have read for a long time. Her picture of the modern world is literally terrifying. Kafka is almost the only one of our contemporaries who has achieved such effects. I have a tremendous admiration for the work of this young writer."

That February she also wrote twice to Percy, two in a series of letters tracking the progress of *The Charterhouse*. She was eager to tell him more about Flannery O'Connor. With one letter she sent Percy a book that O'Connor had sent her—in all likelihood the proofs of *Wise Blood*. In the next she told him her reservations about O'Connor's novel: that it was too stripped down and barren, too much like Kafka. "Everything in it stands for something and you only find out what it stands for after you've left the book and the events sort of explode in your mind."

Percy himself later praised *Wise Blood* as a book that made *The Charterhouse* seem "a very bad novel" in comparison. Because the manuscript of *The Charterhouse* no longer exists, there is no telling how good or bad it was, but it is clear that Gordon favored the well-born and affable Percy to the independent and outspoken O'Connor, whose work she criticized out of the side of her mouth.

When she read a revision of *The Charterhouse* several months later, she was delighted. She told Percy that she'd never had a student who so richly repaid her efforts, adding, "You are in the position to receive help from the Holy Ghost, which none of my other students has been in. I really feel that in this novel he is using you as his agent."

And she confided in him an idea that had been taking shape in her mind. Over the summer she had gone on a retreat at Maryfarm, and she considered it "the finest experience I ever had." Now she envisioned its literary counterpart: a school or workshop for Catholic writers, held at Maryfarm or some place like it. There writers would attend Mass, pray the Divine Office, and read and comment on one another's work. The older writers would instruct the younger ones, the experts teaching the novices. "But the real teaching," she explained, "will be done by the Holy Ghost."

There is no telling how serious Gordon was. But it does not matter, and in truth it is a good thing that she never acted on the idea. For a school or movement was taking shape already, and it was more complex and mysterious than her fancy theories would allow. Four like-minded writers had become aware of one another, as in Greenwich Village in the twenties or in Nashville ten years later. Already they were skeletally joined, as members of a body are joined. They will have no headquarters, no neighborhood, no university fiefdom or corner bar. They will write no manifesto, pose for no group portrait. Their unity, rather, will be that of pilgrims who are taking different routes to the same destination, conversing at long distance from time to time. Its roots are artistic and religious, grounded in their belief that their writing and their religious faith, each informing the other, presents them with a predicament shared in common.

SEVEN

The Stranger

*W*ise *Blood* was published May 15, 1952. The ladies of Milledgeville gave a party at the college library in honor of the author. She had on a shiny blue-black dress with a corsage affixed to it; she sat in a straight-backed chair and inscribed copies of the novel, a hardback with a white dust jacket featuring a photograph of her and a text saying she hailed from Savannah. "Cocktails were not served but I lived through it anyway," she told a friend in a letter. "It was very funny to see relics like Miss N. toting home a copy and to imagine it going on inside particular minds, etc."

Robert Giroux had sent an early copy of the book to Evelyn Waugh, who replied, "If this is really the unaided work of a young lady, it is indeed a remarkable product."* Chauvinistic as it is, the comment suggests that Waugh knew from his own experience the problem *Wise Blood* would face: that readers, not knowing who the author was—a man or a woman, a believer or an unbeliever, a comic writer or a serious artist—would not know what to make of the book, whose strangeness consisted in its "unaided" quality, its lack of obvious antecedents or a clear social purpose.

Reviewers were perplexed, and legend says that one of those Milledgeville ladies burned her copy, but the notion that *Wise Blood* was shocking has little to support it. In many ways it was akin to the other great novels

---

*Hearing this, Regina O'Connor asked her daughter, "Who is this Evalin Wow?"

published that year, a year as rich in new fiction as any in American literary history. *The Catcher in the Rye, Go Tell It on the Mountain, Invisible Man, The Adventures of Augie March*: these novels (published between mid-1951 and mid-1953) were the first works of distinctly postwar American fiction, in that they push past the standard theme of lost illusions and make disillusionment a starting point and a reason for being. Salinger's Holden Caulfield mocking phonies and creeps, Bellow's Augie March picaresquing around Chicago, Baldwin's young black preacher finally leaving his father's house, Ellison's invisible man finding the North no less than the South a place without promise: these characters are all variants on the stranger or outsider, whom Albert Camus had made the postwar era's representative figure. "In a universe suddenly divested of illusions and lights, man feels an alien, a stranger," Camus had written. "His exile is without remedy since he is deprived of the memory of a lost home or the hope of a promised land."

As *Wise Blood* opens, on the train from the country to the city, Motes seems to be a representative American stranger: displaced, orphaned, his people all dead; just back from the war, survivor-slim, his eyes "the color of pecan shells and set in deep sockets," his face "ashen and set in a grimace, as if he were in some sort of permanent pain."

But he is distinctly different from the other strangers of postwar fiction. His problems are the opposite of theirs. He is neither secular nor especially modern. He is not rootless; rather, his roots go deeper than he would like, and he remembers his lost home in Eastrod, Tennessee, all too vividly. No dangling man, he has a distinct calling: to be an evangelist like his grandfather, who, preaching from atop the hood of a car, pointed him out to strangers as the boy Christ died to redeem. As he sets out for the city, he is dogged by faith, not doubt: although he is determined not to believe, indeed to preach a gospel of disbelief, he is haunted by Jesus, a "wild ragged figure" moving from tree to tree in the back of his mind.

In his glare-blue suit and heavy black hat, Hazel Motes is the postwar American pilgrim, the age's representative religious figure. He is a person who is trapped between belief and unbelief, torn between the promised land of religious faith and the fallen world of his own religious experience, in which God is profaned in absentia, so to speak, by the very people who call themselves believers. He is estranged from believers and unbelievers alike, but takes satisfaction in this position, for it sets him over and against all that is false in the world around him.

In Hazel Motes the reformer and the rebel, the searcher and the independent, come together in a single obsessed figure. Odd as he is, he is utterly recognizable, for his predicament is that of what might be called the Christian diaspora in postwar American society, a whole people caught between belief and unbelief. As a child he was brought up to believe that Jesus was his Lord and Savior. Now he yearns to know whether that is true and what it might mean. To come of age he must come to terms with Jesus. Only firsthand experience will do. Unless he sees the evidence of his redemption for himself, he will not believe.

His arrival in neon-lit Taulkinham is medievally grim and gray, like a scene from an allegory in which a Lost Soul trudges onstage: "He walked very slowly, carrying his duffel bag by the neck. His head turned to one side and then the other, first toward one sign and then another. He walked the length of the station and then he walked back as if he might be going to get on the train again. His face was stern and determined under the heavy hat. No one observing him would have known that he had no place to go."

He visits a prostitute, rents a room, buys a car, climbs up on top of it, and preaches to a crowd coming out of a movie theater. These are distinct moments, not episodes in a story; as Caroline Gordon observed, each is staged in its own pinpoint spotlight, a miniature drama set in contrast to the dramas flickering on the screen inside the darkened theater.

In the same way, the gospel of his Church Without Christ is a catchall of maxims of unbelief, which float like supertitles above the action. Put together in one long peroration, they go like this:

The Church Without Christ is that church where the blind don't see and the lame don't walk and what's dead stays that way. There was no Fall because there was nothing to fall from and no Redemption because there was no Fall and no Judgment because there wasn't the first two. There are all kinds of truth, your truth and somebody else's, but behind all of them, there's only one truth and that is that there's no truth. You needn't to look at the sky because it's not going to open up and show no place behind it. You needn't search for any hole in the ground to look through into somewhere else. You can't go neither forwards nor backwards into your daddy's time nor your children's if you have them. In yourself right now is the only place you've got. Jesus was a liar—that's all that matters—and what the world needs is a new jesus, whose blood isn't fouled with redemption, who nobody has to believe in.

Motes chose to become a preacher in order to keep himself pure, so as to make it unnecessary for any Lord or Savior to redeem him. But while he claims to hold back from religious experience, in truth he craves it. When he stands on the hood of his car and challenges a crowd at his feet, he demands evidence: " 'Where in your time and your body has Jesus redeemed you?' he cried. 'Show me where because I don't see the place. If there was a place where Jesus had redeemed you that would be the place for you to be, but which of you can find it?' "

On the face of it, Motes is a blasphemer who believes that the only way to the truth is through blasphemy. But his ministry consists of lashing out at other blasphemers, accusing each of bad faith, in which religious belief is divorced from religious experience. There is Mrs. Flood, his landlady, who superstitiously "thanked her stars" that she was not "religious or morbid." There is Hoover Shoats, aka Onnie Jay Holy, an "artist-type" who recognizes the Church Without Christ as a catchy idea and wants to take it over and make some money from it. There is Solace Layfield, Onnie Jay's hired accomplice and prophet, who claims not to believe in Jesus but really does.

And there is Asa Hawks, the city's established sidewalk preacher, a fixture in black hat and dark glasses. Although Hawks doesn't believe in Jesus, he says he does in order to collect change from passersby, telling them about the night he blinded himself before a crowd of people on the street to prove his faith in Jesus.

Motes suspects that Hawks isn't really blind, but he has to know for sure: he has to see the other man's blindness for himself. First he steals a newspaper clipping describing Hawks's exploit—the nearest thing to proof that Hawks possesses. Then he breaks into Hawks's room in the middle of the night so as to catch the sleeping Hawks unawares. "Haze squatted down by him and struck a match close to his face and he opened his eyes. The two sets of eyes looked at each other as long as the match lasted; Haze's expression seemed to open onto a deeper blankness and reflect something and then close again."

This is the first great moment in O'Connor's fiction: a flash of clarity, a night vision which confirms the state of things that the hero—and the reader—has suspected from the beginning.

Against the agonized unbeliever who must must see and know is set Enoch Emery, a lonely boy, eighteen years old, with a cold sore on his lip, who works at the zoo in the park in the center of the city. When they meet, Haze mocks Enoch as naive and lacking in experience. But Enoch, innocent that he is, is the only person who takes Haze altogether seriously, and he becomes the preacher's only disciple. And it emerges that Enoch, too, is a type of believer: he has "wise blood," a "knowing," a "sudden intuition" akin to faith.

Like Ivan and Alyosha Karamazov, like the two priests Latour and Vaillancourt in *Death Comes for the Archbishop*, Haze and Enoch are a pair defined by their differences. Whereas Haze has been called to the city, Enoch was forced by an uncle to go there. Whereas Haze seeks converts, Enoch wants a friend. Haze is nasty, Enoch kindly; Haze is blasphemous, Enoch reverent, spending his lunch hours in the city museum gazing at a shrunken mummy in a glass case, which he considers Haze's "new jesus" (and which looks as diminished as the name does without a capital *J*). While Haze is always on his way to another new place, Enoch ritually treads the path back and forth from zoo to museum to diner to rented room, reading the daily comic strips "like an office" and turning a cupboard into a shrine to the new jesus. And while Haze knows exactly what he believes and does not believe, Enoch feels his way intuitively, one step at a time.

They are—in terms Iris Murdoch applied to fiction—the existentialist and the mystic, the one "an anxious man trying to impose or assert or find himself" and the other "an anxious man trying to discipline or purge or diminish himself."

In the course of the novel, they trade places, and the conversion of existentialist to mystic, and vice versa, is the action of the book. Stirred by his wise blood, Enoch decides that he must do something dramatic. He smashes the glass case in the museum and brings the mummy to Haze in a paper bag, giving him, in the "new jesus," the evidence that his redeemer lives.

Hazel Motes, meanwhile, is driven inward by experience, which thwarts his ambitions. He exchanges his black hat for a white one. He seduces Hawks's daughter, Sabbath Lily, who teases him mercilessly. After the hired pseudo-preacher Solace Layfield imitates him—the scene, of two tall-hatted men standing like chess pieces on the town square, suggests a cartoon encounter of good and evil—Motes drives his car over Layfield in a murderous rage. A patrolman pushes the car off a cliff, putting an end to Motes's ministry. It is then that Motes goes back to the boardinghouse, climbs the stairs, and blinds himself with quicklime. His pilgrimage, from this day forward, will be an interior one.

The reviewers "recognized her power but missed her point," as Robert Giroux put it. *Time*'s critic called Hazel Motes "one of the most unlikely dullards ever to grumble through an American novel." The *New Republic*'s critic (O'Connor ruefully told the Fitzgeralds) "found it completely bogus, at length." Yet half a century later *Wise Blood* is less dated, and more powerful, than the other Great American Novels of 1952. Why is this? It is not a "great book" in the conventional sense. It is narrow, not broad. It has only one character of any depth. It has almost nothing to say about the way life is lived in America today; the world it depicts, a world of three-dollar-a-week rooming houses and hearselike automobiles and black-hatted evangelists, was disappearing even when the novel was written. Its action is hard to make out and hard to recollect once the last page is turned.

Wise Blood's power consists in the combination of strength and strangeness that Harold Bloom sees as the mark of truly great literature. Its strangeness has withstood fifty years because it is no mere stylistic effect. O'Connor later said she tried to leave "skips and gaps" in her prose to suggest the mystery at the heart of things, but the jagged style seems a surprise even to her, a brave new biblical surrealism discovered by an author working delightedly out of her depth.

The story, likewise, is irreducibly strange. To depict a character whose defiance of God is so great that it suggests an underlying faith is the approach of Dostoevsky, but Ivan Karamazov's defiance is representative of a whole tradition of Enlightenment rationalism, and is supported by the grave style of the novel he figures in. *Wise Blood* is different. Its parts seem not to fit together. For a book about the defiance of God it is strangely sportive, at once seedy and shiny-bright; the characters are light on their feet as they blaspheme and curse to high heaven, like tap dancers, or shadow puppets, or inmates at the asylum. And where Ivan Karamazov invites the reader to identify with him through his brilliance and eloquence—and, in the Grand Inquisitor episode, by telling the story to the reader directly—Hazel Motes elicits the reader's identification in spite of himself, as his rejection of Jesus, at first so forceful as to be repellent, comes to seem, as O'Connor observed, a kind of integrity, and then, by a reversal as strange as any in modern fiction, so does his underlying religious faith.

In the last chapter of the novel, the reader's identification with Hazel Motes suddenly clicks into place, as the point of view shifts away from Motes and toward Mrs. Flood, who is the first instance of a type of character that will show up again and again in O'Connor's fiction: the middle-aged busybody who knows exactly what she thinks, who sees all and understands nothing. Mrs. Flood is fascinated with Hazel Motes. As they pass time together on the porch, as she climbs the stairs to take him his meals, as she watches him set out in the morning with his cane tapping the road, as she discovers glass in his shoes and sees barbed wire wrapped round his chest, she ponders him as if from the inside, trying to imagine "the whole black world in his head and his head bigger than the world, his head big enough to include the sky and planets and whatever had been or would be."

In this way O'Connor suggests the essential mystery of religious experience—by pointing toward it rather than trying to describe it from the inside. The landlady's imaginings suggest what is going on in Motes's head: he is like a monk of old, an ancient fanatic; the pinpoint of light in his head is like a star over Bethlehem on a Christmas card. At the same time, her simplicity suggests that what he is is more than she says, that his inner life is more complicated than she, or the reader, can imagine.

She asks him to marry her, but he turns her down, already feeling for the first porch step with his cane. He is leaving for good.

"Maybe you were planning to go to some other city!"
"That's not where I'm going," he said. "There's no other house nor no other city."

She watches him go, standing at the top of the steps as he finds his way down and goes out into the street.

Where is he going? What does he see? About this, the journey of the postwar pilgrim, the novel has little to say. The circumstances of his demise are enigmatic. That he is found in a ditch—a stranger awaiting a good Samaritan—is a strained bit of symbolism. That he dies in a squad car—a criminal—is better, more vivid. But as he dies, he might be either holy or crazy.

O'Connor's admirers have always seen Motes as a saint in the making, a witness against the blindness of modern society. But the book—and this is the key to its power—is more equivocal than that. At the end of it Hazel Motes is not a prophet or a saint or a wise man or even a religious believer—

not yet. He is a person walking in darkness, a blind man stabbing the ground with his cane. Walking in darkness *is* his religious experience, not merely the context for it. All we know is that he feels he has something to atone for and no longer knows what he doesn't believe. Faith (in the catechetical formulation of the period) is the substance of things hoped for, the evidence of things not seen, and Motes's blindness, at best, is a recognition that the proof of Jesus' divinity that he yearns for cannot be seen with the eyes only, and that nothing he might see, no miracle or act of blasphemy, can tell him whether or not to believe.

Each night at Gethsemani, while all the other monks were asleep, a lone monk would make the rounds of the dark and silent monastery. He would put on tennis shoes; arm himself with a flashlight, a ring of keys, and a clock; and set out in search of fire or threat of fire.

The task was rotated among the monks, and on the night of July 4, 1952, it fell to Thomas Merton. That summer he was busy: teaching, preaching, celebrating Mass, advising the younger monks, and, in the time left over, writing. He had spent the past few weeks typing up his handwritten journals from the previous six years, editing them here and there (his longing to leave Gethsemani, out; his devotion to the Virgin Mary, in) so as to form a spiritual journal, which Harcourt, Brace would publish as a sequel to *The Seven Storey Mountain*. No sooner had he sent the text to Robert Giroux than he got an idea for an epilogue. That night, as he set out, he resolved to "watch" himself making the rounds of the monastery, and the next morning he described the experience on the typewriter, dating the entry the Fourth of July.

"Fire Watch," one of Merton's most famous pieces, is perhaps the purest expression of his spirituality of places and spaces. In it he is monologuist, secret sharer, investigator, and tour guide, and the fire watch is a stage of his pilgrimage, one described in the second person, in the present tense, in such a way that the reader might be at his elbow, accompanying him—in such a way that the reader might *be* him, trying to see how he and the Abbey of Gethsemani have changed since *The Seven Storey Mountain* made them famous. "Alone, silent, wandering on your appointed rounds through the corridors of a huge, sleeping monastery," he declares, "you come around the corner and find yourself face to face with your monastic past and with the mystery of your vocation. The fire watch is an examination of conscience in which your task as watchman suddenly appears in its true light: a pretext devised by God to isolate you and to search your soul with lamps and questions, in the heart of darkness."

He goes in stages, each more private and hidden than the one before: to the "catacomb," the scullery, the cloister, the tailor shop; the furnace room, where some woolen habits (shades of Dante or Blake) hang drying in the heat; the choir and novitiate chapel, "where You are all alone, the windows closed upon You, the windows closed all upon You, shutting You up with the heat of the afternoon"—where you is "You" and it is God that Merton is addressing.

By the time he reaches the abbey church he has left the reader behind and is, by his own reckoning, alone with God. Yet the writing hardly changes: as he shines the flashlight on the altar, on some relics in a glass case, he speaks to God in the same voice with which he speaks to the reader—now chatty, now arch, now confidential, now hushed with significance. "This nearness to You in the darkness is too simple and too close for excitement," he says. "It is commonplace for all things to live an unexpected life in the night: but their life is illusory and unreal. The illusion of sound only intensifies the substance of Your silence."

He passes through the cloister, through a hallway in which stands a table set for guests; through a big door into the guest wing, which is vacant for the first time since his book was published; through the sweltering library, known as Hell; through the scriptorium and the dormitory where the new monks sleep; through organ loft and infirmary. He clambers around the dome above the high altar, beaming the flashlight down onto the seat in choir where he prays each morning. At last he climbs up into the bell tower—"and now my whole being breathes the wind which blows through the belfry, and my hand is on the door through which I see the heavens."

The monastery has a metal roof, and it gleams in the moonlight. He steps out into the "shining air." Beyond the sleeping abbey, the state of Kentucky is spread out before him.

There on the roof, alone and in darkness, looking out at nature and "the frozen distance of the stars," he poses a litany of questions to his maker. "Lord God of this great night: do you see the woods? Do you hear the rumor of their loneliness? Do you behold their secrecy? Do you see that my soul is beginning to dissolve like wax within me?"

Does God reply? Merton would say yes. For him, God's reply is the reply given by religious faith: whether God knows those woods, the woods speak of Him; all the earth sings the praises of Him, and so forth. But here as ever the Merton who is confident in his knowledge of God is at war with the Merton who believes that God is past all knowing and can be met in the experience of contemplative prayer only; and the real drama here—it will be the drama of his next few years—is the struggle between the monk who finds God in consecrated brick-and-mortar places and the pure contemplative who finds God only in a realm of selfless attention, an indescribable inner darkness. "There is greater comfort in the substance of silence than in the answer to a question," he says, and goes on: "The things of time are in connivance with eternity. All things change and die and disappear. Questions arise, assume their actuality, and also disappear. In this hour I shall cease to ask them, and silence shall be my answer."

It is appropriate that "Fire Watch" is an epilogue, because in it Merton's romance with the monastery comes to an end. For ten years at Gethsemani he has been resident in a symbolic country set apart from modern life. From this point forward he will strive to be simply a monk in a monastery. Although he will remain faithful to his calling as a Trappist, he will no longer write about Gethsemani as an ideal place, a world unto itself. Rather, he will see it as a place of imaginative possibility.

Two developments, each reported in *The Sign of Jonas*, suggest the change in his point of view. On June 22, 1951, he had become an American citizen, a commitment that would lead him to engage directly with the world he had supposedly left forever. At the same time, his prolonged encounter with the Catholic mystics had sent him deeper inward, to the place of solitary prayer he describes in the book's closing pages: "the darkness of my empty mind, this sea that opens within me as soon as I close my eyes." There, like Jonas in the biblical tale—like Hazel Motes at the end of *Wise Blood*—he finds that "everything is charged with intelligence, though all is night."

He has spent the past ten years knowing all the answers. Now he begins to walk in darkness, an authentic postwar pilgrim. He will seek a place outside the monastery or apart from it, in the world, in his surroundings, in the depths of his being or in flights of fantasy; from here on his places and spaces will be longed for, self-made, envisioned, imaginary.

"Many people think that Dorothy Day is a saint and that she will someday be canonized." Thus opened the *New Yorker*'s profile of Day, published in two issues in October 1952.

The Long Loneliness, published in January, had sold nearly ten thousand copies on the strength of "good reviews. *Newsweek, NY Times,* and *Herald Tribune,*" Day reported in her journal, and the *Catholic Worker* published a "valentine" of a review. But she had hoped for more, and there was little recognition that the book summed up a life's work. In her columns she said nothing about the book, and she twice canceled a speaking tour after Tamar and her children came down with pneumonia.

In the *New Yorker* profile, likewise, Dwight Macdonald said very little about her work as a writer and editor. Although an old-time radical himself, he made her into a curiosity. The war resister and jail veteran is nowhere to be found. Neither is the imitator of Christ and devotee of the saints. Instead, Day is likened to "an elderly schoolteacher or librarian" and a "fond and watchful mother"; and the Catholic Worker emerges as a charming aggregation only tenuously connected with the church of Irish cops and washerwomen. The movement is "a leaven on the American Catholic community," and its sacrament is hot coffee, which "serves the same function among the Workers that a dry Martini does in many other circles."

Beneath the affected urbanity, however, is a crucial insight: the Catholic Worker, for all its principles, its lofty aims and purposes, its complex relation to Catholic doctrine, is a movement with the character of its foundress, "in whom lightheartedness and spiritual fervor are strangely and effectively intermingled." Tom Sullivan at St. Joseph's House had warned Day that the *New Yorker* would distort her ideas; but they are not distorted so much as placed in a new context, in which social activists are looked upon admiringly, benignly, and from afar.

This is precisely what Day had tried to do with her autobiography. She had written it for the general reader, not just the Catholic reader, and everything about it suggests her desire to reach beyond the small circle of her admirers. *The Long Loneliness* opens in a church, during confession on a Saturday evening, but the church is evoked sensually, not historically or doctrinally—"a warm, dimly lit vastness, with the smell of wax and incense in the air"—and the confessional rite is described as to an outsider. Like Merton's fire watch, the whole scene is presented in the second person, as though to place the reader in the midst of it. "Going to confession is hard— hard when you have sins to confess, hard when you haven't," Day explains, and as much as this opening is meant to set the book in the tradition of confessional spiritual autobiography that begins with Augustine, it is meant to make her readers, whatever their backgrounds, identify with her in the adventures to follow.

Together, *The Long Loneliness* and the *New Yorker* profile set going a new stage of Day's pilgrimage, in which she would reckon constantly with the image she presented to the world, striving at once to fulfill and to dispel other people's expectations for her. In becoming a Catholic she had joined the Catholic masses, and ever since she had always made her appeal first to other Catholics, calling them to live up to their baptismal promises. Now she began to turn her energy toward the secular masses as well. There are a number of likely reasons why. Perhaps her clash with Cardinal Spellman over the gravediggers' strike had made her despair of bringing about change within the Church. With Peter Maurin's death her movement had lost a vital connection to working-class Catholics. Moreover, those Catholics were moving up in the world—moving out of the Catholic ghettos and into the suburbs. In such a world the person of faith was called to appeal to believer and unbeliever alike. "Péguy said that the race of heroes and the race of saints stand in contradiction, the contradiction of the eternal and the temporal," she wrote shortly after the *New Yorker* profile was published, but ideally saint and hero were joined in a single person, whether Gandhi or Joan of Arc. "With the Bishops of the United States pointing out that the greatest danger of our age is secularism," Day declared, "it would seem that it is a time when we must beg God to raise up for our time men in whom saint and hero meet to solve the problems of the day." Although she didn't presume to name herself as such a figure, clearly a blend of sanctity and heroism was her personal ideal.

The book and the profile made her the object of other people's pilgrimages. Strangers would arrive at St. Joseph's House expecting her to greet them at the door, and be disappointed to find that she was not there. She was traveling more than ever, confident that her calling was "not to settle down, take roots, enjoy a home, but in the words of the hymn of John Wesley, 'to be a pilgrim.' "

Once her grandchildren were well she undertook the speaking tour she had postponed, going by bus "from New York to Vancouver, down the coast to San Diego, across the South through Phoenix and New Orleans, down to Tampa and West Palm Beach and up through Atlanta to New York," with "a bit of zigzagging through the middle west, too." She stayed at Houses of Hospitality or in monasteries and convents, where she "felt a piercing in my heart, and wondered why more people did not enter." She might have found an explanation in her own restlessness.

In Georgia she went to Holy Ghost Monastery, an hour's ride from Atlanta. The monastery had been founded during World War II as a "daughter foundation" of the Abbey of Gethsemani, with some monks erecting a chapel and cloister in an old hay barn in rural Rockdale County. The community had grown with the end of the war, then grown considerably after the publication of *The Seven Storey Mountain*; men who went on pilgrimage to Gethsemani to become monks in Thomas Merton's company were sent to Georgia, where a proper church and cloister were being built, in effect, with the book's royalties.

One was Jack English from St. Joseph's House, now a novice called Brother Charles. Day found him full of enthusiasm for the Trappist life. " 'You are always conscious of being held up by others,' he said. 'You are never alone, never idle, never have quite enough food or quite enough sleep.' "

During a stay at St. John's Abbey in Minnesota she visited Caroline Gordon and Allen Tate, who were teaching in St. Paul. She gave Gordon a reliquary in the hope that it would help Tate finish a long poem he was writing. Gordon described her scheme for a School of the Holy Ghost. Day, Gordon's biographer Ann Waldron reports, "thought it was a wonderful idea and said, 'One thing we must not worry about is money. That will be provided. Leave that to St. Joseph.' "

Gordon had a special reason to be glad for Dorothy Day's visit. In 1951, after reading Flannery O'Connor's and Walker Percy's novels, she had begun a new novel of her own, her first as a Catholic writer; and *The Malefactors*, as she was calling her book, would have a good deal in common with theirs. Like *The Charterhouse*, it would be a conversion story—"a story of one man's journey of faith, the old story that is or ought to be the story of every human being."* Like *Wise Blood*, it would be set in the rural South and would feature the imagery of blood, the substance that bound country life, violence, and Catholic ritual all together. What was more, it would also feature a character very much like Dorothy Day, a bohemian who had renounced her wayward past to devote herself to God and perform charitable works on the Bowery.

Once Day was gone, Gordon resumed reading a revised version of *The Charterhouse*, which Walker Percy had sent to her. Halfway through, she

---

*The protagonist of *The Charterhouse* is named Cleburne, that of *The Malefactors* Claiborne.

wrote Percy an approving letter. When she had read it all, she sent the manuscript to her editor at Scribner's, saying that she and Allen Tate considered Percy "the most important talent to come out of the South since Faulkner."

Shelby Foote had warned Percy against getting too involved with Gordon and Tate. He thought they had "smothered their talent" with dogma and would smother Percy's as well: "These articulate people who can put their finger on the trouble, and tell why, are archfiends incarnate." Percy himself had told Gordon that he was dubious about the School of the Holy Ghost, fearing that the writer who "cleaves too close to the liturgy" is "liable to breed something quaint and cultish." But he entrusted his novel to her and her associates.

The novel was turned down. First John Hall Wheelock of Scribner's rejected it; then Denver Lindley of Harcourt, Brace; then Malcolm Cowley of Viking. A year earlier, Gordon had urged Percy to make the novel longer than it was; now Henry Regnery, Tate's publisher, offered to publish it if Percy would make it shorter.

Instead, Percy started over. He bought a new car, a black four-door Lincoln Town Car. He began writing a new novel, one modeled even more closely on *The Magic Mountain*, about a man who is converted to a new view of life while recovering from tuberculosis at a sanatorium in the woods. Through a friend of Gordon's, named Sue Brown Jenkins, he sought a literary agent, and he began, this time in earnest, to read existentialist philosophy.

He had been reading existentialist writers on and off for ten years. At first he had read Dostoevsky and Kierkegaard. Now he read the French existentialists: Camus, Sartre, and especially Gabriel Marcel, whose situation resembled his own and Will Percy's together. An orphan, a Jewish convert to Catholicism, a veteran of World War I, Marcel was a "Christian existentialist," who sought to reconcile the nihilism of Camus and Sartre with the theism of Kierkegaard and the Church. Marcel grounded his thought in a conception of *homo viator*—of the human person as a traveler, a wayfarer and pilgrim, whose existence depends on his or her fidelity to the belief that death is not an end but a portal to a further destination.

Conceived during the Vichy occupation, Christian existentialism was a wartime philosophy, stressing the individual as an antidote to the collectivist philosophies of Fascism and Nazism, taking the historical present as the extreme of absurdity and human cruelty, defying death through "a metaphysic of hope"—a notion akin to Pascal's wager and William James's will to believe. By the time Marcel's books were published in English translation in the early fifties his position seemed validated, not undermined, by the collective crimes of the Holocaust and the atomic bombardment of Hiroshima and Nagasaki.

Marcel would be a major influence on Percy. He introduced a number of points that Percy would make keystones of his own thought: the notion of philosophy as a form of anthropology, meant to seek an answer to the basic human question "What am I?"; the emphasis on "the concrete examination of the individual and the transcendent, as opposed to all idealism based on the impersonal and the immanent"; the striving for "a calm in some way supernatural."

For the moment, Marcel was an influence on Percy's sense of himself as a pilgrim and wayfarer. All his life Percy had been tutored by others: his uncle, his teachers, Shelby Foote, Caroline Gordon. Philosophy would be different. In philosophy he would teach himself; an existentialist already, he would go it alone.

Flannery O'Connor learned that she had lupus in the summer of 1952. She had gone to visit the Fitzgeralds in Connecticut. It was her first trip since her illness and her first airplane flight, and she undertook it with gusto. Arriving, she presented the Fitzgerald children with ducklings which she had snuck onto the plane in her coat. She went to Manhattan for a day to have lunch with Caroline Gordon. In Ridgefield she observed the tense interactions of two other guests—a white "displaced person" from Croatia and a black Fresh Air child from New York—whom the Fitzgeralds had taken in out of charity. She helped Sally Fitzgerald, who was pregnant once more, to look after the children; after one child drove the family car into a pile of rocks O'Connor gave him a whipping, which he received (so she claimed) "as if it were a great honor."

Then she was struck with a fever. She returned to Georgia, where she was bedridden for six weeks. She asked the Fitzgeralds to return a suitcase full of clothes she had left behind, as well as her marked copy of *Art and Scholasticism*. Sally Fitzgerald had told her what her mother would not. What ailed her was not arthritis. It was the Red Wolf.

She reconciled herself to existence as a semi-invalid living in a house in the woods. In time, she would become the very type of the rural artist; but at first rural life was as alien to her as terminal illness. The girl who had grown up in a townhouse on a grand city square had to make herself at home in a place which her uncle had rented to tenant farmers. The finicky eater had to follow a salt-free diet and a daily regimen of pills and shots. The writer who had worked "ALL the time" on *Wise Blood* had to conserve her strength, writing only in the mornings, between Mass and lunch. The independent young woman who had christened herself Flannery O'Connor had to answer to "Mary Flannery" or "Miss Regina's daughter" and to get used to the malaprop-ridden repartee of life with Mother. The prodigy who had kept company with Robert Lowell at Yaddo and discussed Sophocles over cocktails with the Fitzgeralds would have to find conversation partners close to home.

Life in the woods was a new life in another sense, too. In Iowa and Saratoga, in New York and Connecticut, O'Connor had had Hazel Motes and Enoch Emery to keep her transfixed and amused. For now, she had no novel to preoccupy her.

Like Haze at the end of *Wise Blood*, she was walking in darkness. Sally Fitzgerald saw "active destiny" at work in O'Connor's new life at Andalusia, but O'Connor herself did not know what was next for her or where she was going.

She ordered books by mail (*Moby-Dick*, *The Idiot*) and subscribed to learned journals: the *Partisan Review*, *Kenyon Review*, *Thought*. She took up painting, thinking of it as an aid to writing, for it would help her to learn to look. Although her writer friends were either abroad or going abroad, she gained admirers nearby: the critic Brainard Cheney, who was invited to Andalusia after praising *Wise Blood* in *Shenandoah*; a young professor named Ashley Brown, who wrote her a letter in praise of the book. "It is always good to get some reaction to what you've written," she told him, "and I don't get much."

In time she conceived a new novel. Like *Wise Blood*, it would feature a country preacher; but he would be an old man, not a young man, and he would die at the beginning of the novel, not the end. He would live mainly in the memory of his young nephew, who would spend the novel quarreling with the old man's spirit—and with an invisible stranger who whispered in his ear as he tried to bury the old man's body.

A conflict between two invisible presences that takes place in a young man's mind: it is a shaky premise for a novel, and the fact that O'Connor undertook it, despite the lessons of Caroline Gordon and the Iowa Writers' Workshop, suggests the depths of her isolation at Andalusia and the nature

216

of the predicament she faced there. She was stuck spending her days in her own mind making conversation with characters of her own devising. She would have to get them out of her mind and into real life, where they could encounter one another directly.

She set the novel aside and started something else. She had promised Caroline Gordon that her next book would be about folks, not freaks. Now she told Gordon, "I am just writing a story to see if I can get away from the freaks for a while."

The story was set on a farm like Andalusia. It featured a mother, a daughter, and a stranger who came to visit them. The solution to her problem lay in the farm itself. Isolated at Andalusia, she would people the place imaginatively; she would invite folks to visit her and see what happened next.

"The old woman and her daughter were sitting on their porch when Mr. Shiftlet came up the road for the first time. The old woman slid to the edge of her chair and leaned forward, shading her eyes from the piercing sunset with her hand. The daughter could not see far in front of her and continued to play with her fingers. Although the old woman lived in this desolate spot with only her daughter and she had never seen Mr. Shiftlet before, she could tell, even from a distance, that he was a tramp and no one to be afraid of. His left coat sleeve was folded up to show there was only half an arm in it and his gaunt figure listed slightly to the side as if the breeze were pushing him. He had on a black town hat that was turned up in the front and down in the back and he carried a tin tool box by a handle. He came on, at an amble, up her road, his face turned toward the sun which appeared to be balancing itself on the peak of a small mountain."

With that opening passage, O'Connor started over again. A whole story is suggested in it. So is the manner that she would employ again and again in her short fiction, in which the stranger (seen departing at the end of *Wise Blood*) is seen approaching. The situation is established with a few strong strokes. Life is grasped whole and seen objectively. The drama is taken out of the author's mind and into the world. The setting is fixed. The action is joined in progress. The pace is as slow as a sunset in midsummer; the point of view is indicated with a cupped hand. The story, once in progress, seems to tell itself, with the author following the characters, not controlling them—knowing where they are going but not how they will get there.

She followed Mr. Shiftlet as he reached the house, as he tipped his hat and set his toolbox on the porch step, as he introduced himself to the old woman and her daughter. As the old woman introduced herself—her name was Lucynell Crater and so was her daughter's—and he told her that "the world is almost rotten." As he boasted of his handyman's skills and she boasted of her daughter's charms. As the daughter, an idiot it turned out, writhed and whimpered. As he rolled a cigarette and struck a match on his shoe and held it up "as if he were studying the mystery of flame" and asked her, "Lady, what is a man?" As she inquired whether he was married and he replied that he was not because all he saw was trash and he hadn't been raised to marry trash. As she told him that he was free to stay on the farm if he didn't mind sleeping "in that car yonder."

Mr. Shiftlet did stay. He repaired a roof, kept company with the daughter, and even taught her to stay a few words. Meantime, Mrs. Crater told him that her well never ran dry and enumerated the rewards of living in a permanent place with the sweetest girl in the world.

One evening Mr. Shiftlet told Mrs. Crater that the car in the yard was almost ready to run, because he had taken a personal interest in it. That was what was wrong with this rotten world—"that nobody cared, or stopped and took any trouble."

He finished fixing the car the next day. "With a volley of blasts it emerged from the shed, moving in a fierce and stately way," the driver bearing "an expression of serious modesty on his face as if he had just raised the dead."

That evening Mr. Shiftlet and Mrs. Crater spoke on the porch. She told him there was no place in the world for "a poor disabled friendless drifting man." In reply, he turned philosophical. "He rolled himself a cigarette and lit it and then he said in an even voice, 'Lady, a man is divided into two parts, body and spirit. . . . The body, lady, is like a house: it don't go anywhere; but the spirit, lady, is like an automobile: always on the move . . .'"

Saturday morning Tom T. Shiftlet and the two Lucynell Craters drove to town in the old car. Flannery O'Connor followed them, led by the story, which she made up as she went along.

When the story was done—"The World Is Almost Rotten," she called it—she sent it to the Fitzgeralds. In the following months she would write another story, then a third, and then three more. She had found her fictional approach, in which the characters are both freaks and folks, the action is at once brutally realistic and wildly imagined, and the territory is archetypally broad and deep and yet recognizably her part of Georgia.

Her strength had begun to return, and she was able to roam the property surrounding the farmhouse. She had seen a certain advertisement in the newspaper too often to ignore it. She placed an order for a pair of peafowl and four peachicks. One day she met the birds at the railroad station, where they awaited her in a wooden crate by the tracks. Soon Andalusia was aswarm with peafowl, which screeched and yelled like characters in one of her stories.

She rewrote "The World Is Almost Rotten," giving it a title the Fitzgeralds had suggested to her. It came from a sign seen periodically at the roadside at the end of the story. As he drives off into a gathering storm, Mr. Shiftlet passes the sign more than once. It warns: DRIVE CAREFULLY. THE LIFE YOU SAVE MAY BE YOUR OWN.

"Evening. St. Anne's. I got permission to stay out here till collation," Merton wrote in his journal.* "It is a tremendous thing no longer to have to debate in my mind about 'being a hermit,' even though I am not one. At least now solitude is something concrete—it is 'St. Anne's'—the long view of hills, the empty cornfields in the bottoms, the crows in the trees, and the cedars bunched together on the hillside. And when I am here there is always lots of sky and lots of peace and I don't have distractions and everything is serene— except for the rats in the wall. . . . Here there seems to be less and less need even of books."

He had discovered an old toolshed abandoned in the woods surrounding the monastery, and had made it into a place of retreat: brought in a small desk, painted a cross on the door with two strokes of red paint, stuck up a print of a medieval Christ from a French village near his birthplace. He dubbed the shed St. Anne's, after the mother of the Virgin Mary, and went there to pray and read and write in his journal as often as the monastic schedule and the abbot allowed. "St. Anne's is like a rampart between two existences," he declared. "On one side is the community to which I must return. . . . On the other side is the great wilderness of silence in which, perhaps, I might never speak to anyone but God again, as long as I live."

The shed was the solution to his so-called stability crisis. Trappist monasticism was in full revival; the more crowded the monastery got, the more

---

*February 9, 1953.

Merton wanted to leave, and the more vigorously the abbot upheld his decision that Merton should stay where we was.

When Merton's wanderlust threatened to overwhelm him, the abbot (having read "Fire Watch") proposed that he go and live as a hermit in a fire watchman's tower that had been erected on the edge of the monastery property. As a symbol the fire tower was apt, but as a place to live it was less than ideal, being too far from the monastery for Merton to go back and forth regularly. He claimed the toolshed in the woods instead. Forbidden to go to the Carthusian enclave at Frascati in Italy or to the new Trappist foundation in Vermont, called Sky Farm, he set about becoming a hermit in Nelson County, Kentucky. The shed would be his hermitage. There, he would be a stranger to both the world and the monastery. There, he could imagine that he was somewhere else.

For the time being, he exulted in the place and the freedom and solitude he felt there. As he had felt about the monastery, he now felt about this "fixed-up shanty" in the woods: that it was the destination of his pilgrimage, the place where, alone with God, he might be the person God intended him to be. "All the countries of the world are under this sky: I no longer need to travel. Half a mile away is the monastery with the landscape of hills which haunted me for 11 years with uncertainty. I knew I had come to stay but never really believed it, and the hills seemed to speak, at all times, of some other country.

"The quiet landscape of St. Anne's speaks of no other country."

One afternoon Mr. Erik Langkjaer came to lunch at Andalusia. He worked as a traveling sales rep for Harcourt, Brace, in the Deep South, and his boss had suggested that he call on Flannery O'Connor the next time he was near Milledgeville, Georgia. He wrote the author a letter and she wrote back to extend an invitation. It was the first week of May, 1953.

She went partway down the drive to greet him, leaning on a wooden cane. That winter she had been "practically bald-headed on top," with a face like a watermelon. She called herself Grimrack. Now her face was returning to normal and her hair was coming in. Lest he ask about the cane she carried, she told him that she had lupus.

He was a handsome man of her generation. They strolled up the drive. He spoke with an accent as strong as her own. He was from Copenhagen, Denmark, it turned out, but he had studied at Princeton and taught at Fordham, the Jesuit university in New York, where an "aunt" of his—in fact, an old family friend—ran an institute for the study of Russian Christianity and put out a journal called *The Third Hour.* Her name was Helene Iswolsky, and she was a regular speaker at the Catholic Worker and places like it. Although he came from the most reformed of Protestant countries, through her and his job at Fordham he knew a good deal about American Catholicism.

They went inside the farmhouse, where her mother awaited them, and sat down to eat. Over lunch, they discussed Dorothy Day and the Catholic Worker. Mr. Langkjaer described Caroline Gordon's idea for a School of the Holy Ghost headquartered at the Catholic Worker farm on the Hudson. Gordon was now calling it "Conversations at Newburgh" after a similar enterprise in France. O'Connor didn't know a thing about it: "Is it some more philosophers and bums and priests conversing at a retreat at one of those farms or what?"

She paraphrased their conversation in a letter to the Fitzgeralds a few days later. Mr. Langkjaer, she reported, was "much interested in Dorothy Day, only he couldn't see he said why she fed endless lines of bums for whom there was no hope, she'd never see any results from that, said he. The only conclusion we came to about this, was that Charity is not understandable." She added, "Strange people turn up."

Over lunch, she had grown fond of Mr. Langkjaer. Once he was gone (her letters suggest) she ordered some back issues of *The Third Hour* and took out a subscription to the *Catholic Worker,* so as to resume the conversation when he returned.

The question of charity and the "undeserving poor" was one that Dorothy Day heard often, and the current issue of the *Catholic Worker*—April 1953—featured an essay in which she answered it by explaining the movement's understanding of charity, or Christian love. In its revised version, called "The Faces of Poverty," it is so apt a reply to O'Connor and Langkjaer that Day might have been sitting there at lunch with them.

"Poverty is a strange and elusive thing," she begins. "I have tried to write about it, its joys and its sorrows, for thirty years now; and I could probably write about it for another thirty without conveying what I feel about it as well as I would like. I condemn poverty and I advocate it; poverty is simple and complex at once; it is a social phenomenon and a personal matter. Poverty is an elusive thing; and a paradoxical one."

People who are not poor, she knows, find poverty easy to overlook, and one paradox of poverty is that the people who are hardest on the poor are the people who were once poor themselves. The Catholic Church is full of such people. They escaped poverty through education, sacrifice, and hard work. Many of them became priests and nuns, pledged symbolically to the life of poverty, but like efficient merchants they wonder why everybody else can't climb out of poverty the way they did.

"Good souls" though they are, Day sighs, "these people don't know about the poor." So she will describe some of "the faces of poverty." There is the poverty of the person who has no space, no light, no fresh air. The poverty of slum-dwellers, who lack food, clothing, and decent housing. The poverty of people "on the installment plan," living from one debt payment to the next. The poverty of the migrant workers she has seen in Georgia, who live in fear of illness and "a sudden plunge into destitution."

Why offer charity to people who evidently don't deserve it, for whom there is no hope? Day's answer is that the believer is enjoined to do so. Plenty of poor people are weak of will—but then, all people are weak-willed, are they not? And the poor person's weakness has been aggravated by newspapers, radio, television, and advertising, which "instill in him paltry desires so compulsive that he is willing to sell his liberty and his honor to satisfy them."

Her conclusion is blunt: "Charity is only as warm as those who administer it." Charity, she suggests, is a form of the imitation of Christ; it is very well for people to support government aid to the poor, or denounce the social forces that aggravate poverty, but the act of charity must finally be "a personal one. The message we have been given comes from the Cross."

That was very well for the believer. Erik Langkjaer's beliefs were still a matter of speculation at Andalusia. As he became a regular visitor, O'Connor set about winning him over, converting him to the true believer's point of view.

That spring she had painted "a self-portrait with a pheasant cock that is really a cutter." It is a portrait of the artist the way she might have appeared on a Russian icon, with big staring eyes and a halo. Now she put on some lipstick and stood in front of it and had a photograph taken, as if to capture proof of her beauty before it was banished by lupus.

She went to Connecticut to see the Fitzgeralds, who were moving to Italy. When she got back to Andalusia in early September, a family of displaced persons from Poland had arrived to work on the farm, welcomed by her mother as an act of charity.

She felt displaced herself. Her writer friends were getting grants and going abroad. "Since I can't take the continental tour on Mr. Rockefeller," she quipped, "I am buying books." To the Fitzgeralds she remarked, "I had a letter from Caroline in Paris & from Ashley [Brown] in Dublin & feel like the world is moving off and leaving me in the United States alone."

Except for Erik Langkjaer. He came on weekends, driving a hundred miles or more. She had fallen in love with him. He and she were going together, in her view. Weekends they sat on the porch, admiring her peacocks. During the week, in her room, she courted him imaginatively, trying to capture the mystery of charity, or Christian love, in fiction.

"The Displaced Person" is another story in which a stranger comes to visit. But this stranger has come all the way from Europe, arriving at the farm at the end of a procession led by a peacock and a priest. When the lady of the house extends a hand in greeting, "he bobbed down from the waist and kissed it."

His presence forces all the others on the farm to consider who he is. For Astor and Sulk, longtime black farm workers, this Mr. Guizac is just another worker passing through. For Mrs. McIntyre, who owns the place, "that man is my salvation," a loyal worker who does not smoke, knows how to operate complex machinery, and dutifully reports on other workers' thieving. For Mrs. Shortley, the wife of a white farm worker, he is a rival, a latecomer from the Old World. He embodies the European decadence that led to the world war. He is from Poland, "the devil's experiment station," "where all them bodies were stacked up at"; from Poland, "where the religion had not been reformed—with this kind of people, you had to be on the lookout every minute."

The Displaced Person is the first Catholic character in O'Connor's fiction. He is also the first plainly admirable character. As he settles on the farm, he remains aloof from the others; because he does not speak English, he is talked about more than heard from. More than any other O'Connor character, he is an allegorical figure, who stands for something, or someone, else.

She wrote the story all that fall, dividing it into two parts, another first in her short fiction. In December, during a visit to Tennessee, she read a draft aloud for the Cheneys and some friends. She had received a holiday card in the mail from the *Catholic Worker*, with a linoleum-block print of St. Raphael the Archangel on one side and a prayer to the saint on the other. "The prayer had some imagery in it that I took over and put in 'The Displaced Person,' " she later recalled. From the prayer came the image of eternal life as another country, across the border; as she read the end of part one, in which the Shortleys, displaced by the Displaced Person, leave the farm after dark rather than be fired outright, the imagery of migrant poverty and suffering might have come straight from the *Catholic Worker*. The Shortleys pile into a black car loaded "like some overfreighted leaking ark" with iron bedsteads and rocking chairs and bedrolls and crated chickens. Mr. Shortley, who is driving, asks, "Where we goin'?" while Mrs. Shortley, abruptly felled by a stroke, "her huge body rolled back against the seat and her eyes like blue-painted glass, seemed to contemplate for the first time the tremendous frontiers of her true country."

Early in 1954 Langkjaer told O'Connor that he was going to return to Denmark to live. She was "distressed," as Sally Fitzgerald put it, and she doubtless would have been more distressed had she known that he was leaving the country in part in order to dispel any misapprehensions about their relationship.

Once he was gone, she wrote a letter to him in Copenhagen, then another. Meanwhile, she resumed "The Displaced Person" and its account of the hired man's departure. With the Shortleys gone, Mrs. McIntyre delights in Mr. Guizac, who seems to her "a kind of miracle" until she learns his ideas of marriage. He has arranged for Sulk, the young black worker, to marry his teenage niece, who is in a camp in Europe, thus making her an American citizen. Mrs. McIntyre declares such a marriage impossible: on her farm, a mixed marriage she will not stand.

The question of charity is now heard in Mrs. McIntyre's mouth. She resolves to get rid of the Displaced Person. First, though, she talks it over with the priest: she is not responsible for the world's misery, is she? The priest doesn't reply, at least not directly. A peacock has wandered toward them as they speak, and the priest, watching it preen, speaks of the Transfiguration, which the peacock's plumage puts him in mind of. "He came to redeem us," the priest declares.

Meanwhile Mr. Shortley has returned to get his revenge. He spreads the word against Mrs. McIntyre in town, resenting that he "fought and bled and died and come back on over here and find out who's got my job—just exactly who I been fighting."

Mrs. McIntyre has to get rid of the Displaced Person. The longer she waits, the angrier Mr. Shortley gets. At last she is ready to act. But she doesn't have to. As she watches from a distance there is an accident with a tractor the Displaced Person is trying to fix. It is a grisly scene, rendered in close-up: the tractor slipping; a Negro jumping; Mrs. Shortley making to cry out and then stopping; Mrs. Shortley fainting as she hears a man's back break; Mrs. McIntyre perceiving "her eyes and Mr. Shortley's eyes and the Negro's eyes come together in a look that froze them in collusion forever."

Who is the Displaced Person? Whom does he represent? Innocent, misunderstood, persecuted, put to death, he is, it seems obvious, a Christ figure, akin to Melville's Billy Budd, or Dostoevsky's Idiot, or the Lord Jim of Joseph Conrad, a native of Poland and one of O'Connor's favorite writers.

All the symbolism of the story tends that way. But as O'Connor rewrote the story she packed in the symbolism until the mystery of charity is shown to be complex and paradoxical.

The basis for charity, in the view Dorothy Day espoused, is simple: the stranger is Christ, and is to be treated the way the believer would treat Christ. "We do it by seeing Christ and serving Christ in friends and strangers, in everyone we come in contact with," she explained. "All this can be proved, if proof is needed, by the doctrines of the Church. We can prove it by Christ's Mystical Body, about the vine and the branches, about the Communion of Saints. But Christ himself has proved it for us, and no one has to go further than that. For He said that a glass of water given to a beggar was given to Him. He made heaven hinge on the way we act toward Him in His disguise of commonplace, frail, ordinary humanity."

So it is in the story. The Displaced Person is a stranger, an *alter Christus*. At the same time, the Displaced Person is simply a particularly striking example of the displaced people near at hand. And at the end of the story, it is Mrs. McIntyre who is the stranger, alone and friendless on her land, a displaced person in her own country. Justice has been done: the rough equality of people, white and black, moneyed and poor, has been revealed through charity and its absence.

In February 1954 Percy sent his second novel to Caroline Gordon in Minnesota, who read it, praised it, and sent it to her friend Sue Brown Jenkins in Connecticut, who sent it to a literary agent named Elizabeth Otis in New York, who sent it to publishers around town, who turned it down one after another. The whole business was over in a year.

No one regretted the demise of *The Gramercy Winner*, not even Percy himself. His biographers describe it as a novel struggling to get out from beneath several literary conceits at once—a philosophical novel, another veiled autobiography (with Uncle Will's house transplanted to Gramercy Park in New York), a novel of baptism à la *Brideshead Revisited,* and a novel modeled, fop for fop, twist for twist, portent for portent, on *The Magic Mountain.*

The setup is recognizable. Well-born Will Grey gets TB during the war. He goes to an Adirondack sanatorium, meets a dark seductress, makes a Catholic doctor friend. He slides toward death and the prospect of nothingness, whereupon the doctor friend, following the Catholic doctrine which says a layperson may administer the sacraments in times of grave need, baptizes him.

The novel was meant to be an examination of Will Grey as a whole, a young man whose malady is his inability to figure out who he is and what he ought to do with his life. It featured a set piece about the limits of science and the secular worldview. As a secular doctor examines Will Grey for TB, the Catholic doctor scolds him: "You look at everything but Willy! Look at Willy here! . . . Here's the mystery right under your nose, man! Not Willy's lung but Willy himself."

Why didn't the novel come off? The answer lay right under Percy's nose, in the philosophy he was reading. For all his commitment to the individual rather than to a type, to the concrete predicament of a particular person, he was still writing about character types familiar to him chiefly from other novels. Although he was telling his own story, that of a religious conversion through an encounter with ideas at a TB sanatorium, he was still imitating Dostoevsky and Thomas Mann, the way he had imitated Uncle Will.

A comparison with O'Connor is revealing here. Whereas O'Connor, an independent, set out from the beginning to tell the story in her own distinctive way, Percy searched for his own story within the stories of his predecessors. Whereas she transposed her own displacement imaginatively onto fictional characters like the Displaced Person, he sought models for his alienation in alienated antiheroes created by other writers. Whereas she embedded her symbolism within the manners of life on a Georgia dairy farm, he put his symbols in plain sight. Whereas she was instinctively drawn to making even the least character colorful and distinctive of speech, he was drawn to depicting blank slates, the Will Greys of the world, which put him at a disadvantage. He had not figured out how to create a character, to tell a story, to dramatize the inward back-and-forth of ideas that his conversion had brought about.

He was nearly forty years old. He looked the way he would look for the rest of his life—lean, bald, tanned, somewhat skeletal inside his plain clothes. His adopted daughter had started parochial school. His wife was pregnant with their first natural child. His best friend had completed five books and was gaining a reputation as a fiction writer. Himself, he had money, a family, a house, a religion, a regular spiritual life at the abbey nearby, but no publisher for his book and no next move.

He read *Feeling and Form,* by Susanne K. Langer, the best-known younger philosopher in America. He had read Langer's previous book, *Philosophy in a New Key,* and now, lying on the bed with a legal pad in his lap, he made some notes about her work.

After publication in hardcover by Harvard University Press, *Philosophy in a New Key* had been published in a "drugstore edition" as a work of so-called popular philosophy. The subtitle was *A Study in the Symbolism of Reason, Rite, and Art,* but the cover proclaimed "A Major Contribution to Modern Thought" and hinted at a grand tour of the big ideas: a Gothic cathedral, a Renaissance Madonna, a Rodin *Thinker* floating among the pastel clouds.

The book is hard going. It begins with Langer's proposition that after many centuries of disputation scientists and philosophers can finally agree about what makes humans human. This is the act of "symbolic transformation," which is the way the human person takes raw experience and makes it into symbols, and especially into language. The human person, Langer argues, is a symbol-maker with an innate need to "convert" experience into symbolism.

In postwar philosophy this argument had radical implications. It "saved" language and symbolism from the modern philosophers who denied any causal relationship between experience and what is thought and said about it. It proposed that symbols are not imposed on experience but spring forth as a vital part of it; and thus that the great human symbol-systems—ritual, myth, literature, art, religion—are not obstacles to science, but still-vital expressions of the human need to claim experience through language and symbol.

As he read Langer, he later recalled, Percy was at once thrilled and annoyed. Her synthesis of science and humanism was what he had sought in his reading. But her invocation of "need" made him suspicious, for the scientists who had trained him held that there are finally only two human needs: survival and propagation of the species. Why does humanity "need" symbols? What are they the "key" to? "She picked up the key and dropped it," he later explained. "She didn't do anything with it, she didn't use the key to unlock anything."

Emboldened, he roughed out an essay, following Langer's argument step by step. She had conveyed "all the power and contagious excitement of a first-class mind exercising a valuable new insight." Working from the assumptions of the naturalistic philosophers, who denied the existence of a God or an ultimate purpose behind human ideas, she had reached a view of art akin to the "theistic realism" of St. Thomas Aquinas. But when she hit the question of *why* humans symbolized, Percy said, she was stuck. Instead of answering the question, she merely defined the symbol—and defined it the way Aquinas and Maritain defined it, as a kind of knowledge consisting of the identification "of knower and the object known," in the sense that one person comes to "know" another person, so that, even though there is always more to learn, they are strangers no more.

Was Langer becoming a Catholic in spite of herself? In the essay, Percy doesn't say so. Rather, he tells a story—a conversion story—and as he leads the reader along a path he has already taken to a place he has already reached, he speaks in the first person: "Is it not possible that this startling semantic insight, that by the word I *have* the thing, fix it and rescue it from the flux of Becoming around me, might not confirm and illuminate the mysterious Thomist notion of the interior word, of knowing something by becoming something? That the 'basic need of symbolization' is nothing more or less than the first ascent in the hierarchy of knowledge," which stops at "nothing short of Truth itself?"

The questions are rhetorical ones. What Percy suggests is what he himself believes. The first proposition of philosophy—he cites Marcel—is not "I think," but "we are." Knowledge is intersubjective. We know, in the end, by knowing one another. The goal of this kind of knowing is the knowledge of the truth, which, in Catholic terms, is the knowledge of God. The story Percy has just told, of the movement from symbolism to theism, from *I* to *we*, is his own story.

He sent the essay to *Thought*, a journal of Catholic philosophy published at Fordham, with a conclusion suggesting that the consequences of the idea of symbolic transformation might surprise even "its gifted delineator."

Thought's editor accepted the essay, and in September 1954 twenty-five offprints arrived, as though to suggest the twenty-five strangers who might read what Percy had written. The person most surprised by this outcome was Percy himself. Sloughing off the conceits of fiction, he had gone at ideas directly, and had wound up telling a story. Writing a philosophical essay had produced the effect of authentic discovery, and had made him a published writer at last.

By 1953 Thomas Merton was the best-known Catholic writer in America. The *Atlantic* had run a reverent appraisal of him. His books were eagerly sought, by publishers and readers alike, as long as they were about Catholicism or life as a monk. But he had begun to wonder whether he was a serious writer or a propagandist for the contemplative life—whether in becoming a religious writer he had given up his true calling, which was to be an artist like his father.

Each book of his was slightly less literary than the last. His poetry was reviewed chiefly in the Catholic press, and there as the work of the "literary Trappist." The abbot gave him one writing job after another: a history of the order, a pamphlet about contemplation, a short book on St. Bernard of Clairvaux, which he considered "an impertinence and a waste of time." Even the books he had chosen to write left him unsatisfied. Rereading his early work, he found it brittle and cocksure, the kind of work "that might have been written by some wiseguy outside the monastery." He worried that he was serving up "professional spirituality" instead of describing what the experience of God was like.

He had no model, no other writer to imitate, no school, as far as he knew, to join. No one had ever been in his position, a cloistered monk with a large audience of ordinary people. What did he aspire to? What was his ideal for the religious art of his time?

Bread in the Wilderness gives the best idea. The book, about the Psalms, was published in 1953 as an oversize objet d'art, full of large photographs of a carved wooden Christ, gaunt and agonized as a Giacometti sculpture. Here, he explained, was the Christ anticipated by the Psalms, and also "the Christ of our own time—the Christ of the bombed city and of the concentration camp. We have seen Him and we know Him well."

Against this image Merton set a series of texts about the nature of religious art. In one, he made a distinction that was in the front of his mind. Devotional poetry involves the manipulation of religious symbols to produce a certain effect in the reader; religious poetry "springs from a true religious experience," which the poet aims to convey in words. To underscore the point, he discusses the Psalms. The Psalms are religious art par excellence, the "bread, miraculously provided by Christ, to feed those who have followed him into the wilderness." They are poems to live by, a script or template for monastic life. "Monks get up to chant Psalms in the middle of the night. They find phrases from the Psalter on their lips at Mass. They interrupt their work in the fields or the workshops of the monastery to sing the Psalms of the day hours. They recite Psalms after their meals and practically the last words on their lips at night are verses written hundreds of years ago by one of the Psalmists."

This is Merton's brief for contemplative prayer recast in aesthetic terms—in the same terms Susanne Langer and Walker Percy were using to account for religious symbolism. Scripture is bread in the wilderness and secular modern humanity is starving. The symbolism of the Bible has been "submerged under a tidal wave of trademarks, political party buttons, advertising and propaganda slogans," and the like. Because they need such symbolism, artists and writers are especially deprived, and Western civilization lacks authentic religious art. "And that is why some of the best poets of our time are running wild among the tombs in the moonlit cemeteries of surrealism," Merton declared. "Faithful to the instincts of the true poet, they are unable to seek their symbols anywhere save in the depths of the spirit where these symbols are found."

It may be that he was himself the poet he had in mind. In any case, he acted according to the implications of his own argument and sought to purify the source of his writing. The books of reflection kept coming: *The Last of the Fathers*, about St. Bernard; *The Living Bread*, about the Eucharist; *The Silent Life*, about solitude; *Existential Communion*, which would be "an attempt to show that whatever is good about existentialism is and has been for a long time part of the Christian mystical tradition." He kept writing articles and letters. But he set his journal aside. For the first time in his life, about himself he would be silent.

O'Connor was still exchanging letters with Erik Langkjaer, and in one letter, pondering what was next in his life, he told her that he was thinking of spending the summer doing charity work at a Catholic communal farm in France.

Each time she wrote to him, she awaited his intercontinental reply. Her mother warned her against carrying on a lopsided one-way correspondence.

Early in 1955 she started writing a new story. The story—"Good Country People"—was finished before she knew it. She was shocked. "I wrote GCP in about four days, the shortest I have ever written anything in, just sat down and wrote it," she recalled.

She was just as shocked by the way "Good Country People" turned out. "I merely found myself one morning writing a description of two women that I knew something about, and before I realized it, I had equipped one of them with a daughter with a wooden leg. As the story progressed, I brought in the Bible salesman, but I had no idea what I was going to do with him. I didn't know he was going to steal that wooden leg until ten or twelve lines before he did it, but when I found out that this was what was going to happen, I realized that it was inevitable."

She described the story as "a low joke," but it is another attempt to made sense of the predicament of the mysterious stranger, with which—with whom—she was now obsessed.

This time the stranger is a "tall gaunt hatless youth" who shows up at the farm selling Bibles door to door, carrying a black suitcase so heavy that he lists to one side as he walks. Instead of working his way through college like a lot of boys, he mumbles, he is devoting himself to "Chrustian service." The woman of the house invites him to stay for dinner. In her world, there is trash and there are good country people, and he is clearly "good country people." The implication is clear: she knows who he is, and who she herself is.

Her daughter thinks otherwise. She finds her mother sadly lacking in self-knowledge. "Woman! do you ever look inside? Do you ever look inside and see what you are *not*? God!"

After Hazel Motes, she is O'Connor's most familiar character. She is thirty-two years old and has a wooden leg. She is trained as a philosopher and has a Ph.D.; she has a heart condition and believes she has not long to live. Although her given name is Joy, she has a different name, Hulga, which she has chosen for herself, a perverse declaration of independence; and she resolves to seduce the Bible salesman, to show her mother how different, how independent, she is.

He returns, carrying his black suitcase, and they walk toward the barn on the far reaches of the property. He asks her about her wooden leg, venturing to say that God takes care of her in her affliction. She tells him that she is an atheist. "That's very unusual for a girl," he says.

It is a shock when he kisses her, for she has never been kissed before. "The kiss, which had more pressure than feeling behind it, produced that extra surge of adrenalin in the girl that enables one to carry a packed trunk out of a burning house, but in her, the power went at once to the brain. Even before he released her, her mind, clear and detached and ironic anyway, was regarding him from a great distance, with amusement but with pity."

They climb a ladder to the hayloft over the barn. He hoists his black suitcase. She drags her wooden leg behind her.

Their courtship consists of an exchange about the differences between people. "Don't you think some people was meant to meet on account of what they all got in common and all?" he asks. She disagrees: she doesn't believe in God, for one thing. But when he tells her that her wooden leg is what makes her different, she agrees to let him see it. "She decided that for the first time in her life she was face to face with real innocence. This boy, with an instinct that came from beyond wisdom, had touched the truth about her. When after a minute, she said in a hoarse high voice, 'All right,' it was like surrendering to him completely. It was like losing her own life and finding it again, miraculously, in his." And as he unhooks the leg, and insists that she leave it off while they get to know each other, "she felt entirely dependent on him."

An atheist with "a number of degrees" could not be less like a devout Catholic. O'Connor was writing stories about mysterious strangers well before Erik Langkjaer came to visit. The role that this Danish textbook salesman played in her life was brought to light only long afterward and then obliquely. Yet readers have always supposed that "Good Country People" is personal and autobiographical. The urgency of the telling, the pitiless way in which the self's surrender to another turns into its undoing: here, it seems, is a story grounded in firsthand experience.

O'Connor insisted otherwise. Joy-Hulga, she allowed, was *like* her; Joy-Hulga had some aspects of her character, but no more than Hazel Motes or Enoch Emery did. Art, she believed, is finally a mystery, and she never found this to be so true as in "Good Country People," in which she exercised "less conscious technical control" than at any time in her life as a writer.

The story became her favorite example of the use of symbolism in fiction, and she explained its symbols with all the subtlety of a preacher expounding on Scripture at a revival meeting. "Early in the story," she declared, "we're presented with the fact that the Ph.D. is spiritually as well as physically crippled. She believes in nothing but her own belief in nothing, and we perceive that there is a wooden part of her soul that corresponds to her wooden leg."

Symbolically, the black suitcase is to him as the wooden leg is to her. Now he opens it. Inside is a pair of Bibles, one a dummy containing a flask of whiskey, a deck of cards, and a box of prophylactics. These appurtenances, in O'Connor's terms, are meant to suggest the nature of *his* affliction; and as he adds Hulga's leg to them and goes on his way, a reversal has taken place. For all her learning, she is foolish; for all his simple ways, he is cunning. There are no good country people.

Why does the Bible salesman steal Hulga's leg? He is a crook, a swindler, a seducer, the end of the story makes clear. But there is more to the story. He turns on her when she cannot say she loves him; and right up to the end, she considers herself his superior.

Here ends a line of imaginative inquiry O'Connor had followed for two years. Failure to love the stranger has disastrous consequences. She who condescends to the stranger will be brought low. She who manipulates the stranger will be manipulated. And what about the young woman who does love the stranger? That story O'Connor left untold, instead taking an instance of love's failure and transmuting it into fiction.

She wrote another letter to Erik Langkjaer, adding a postscript in her loopy hand: "I think that if you were here, we could talk for about a million years."

This letter, according to Sally Fitzgerald, crossed in the mail with a letter from Langkjaer. In it he announced that he was engaged to be married, in Copenhagen, to a Danish woman. After the wedding, he planned to bring his bride to America and resume his work there. He hoped that O'Connor would have a chance to meet the new Mrs. Langkjaer some day.

In the two years they had known each other, she had reinvented herself as a writer of short fiction, publishing her stories in the journals that came in the mail. Four of the stories had been nominated for O. Henry awards. Two had won. A collection of them, *A Good Man Is Hard to Find and Other Stories*, had just gone to press.

She wrote to him once more. "When I told my mother this time what you were now going to do, she said, 'I told you that boy wouldn't enjoy being a ragpicker.' Moral: you can't get ahead of mother. In any case you know you have my best wishes, affection and prayers in this new venture and I hope it will be the beginning for you of always finding what you want."

Then, switching to the plural pronoun, and the promises of hospitality to the stranger for which her part of the world was known, she concluded: "We are glad that you plan to return South and we want you to let us help you make your wife at home in this part of the country. Consider us your people here because that is what we consider ourselves."

When *A Good Man Is Hard to Find* was published—May 1955—she traveled to New York. She had been invited to be a guest on a television talk show. She and the host would discuss her work and watch some actors perform a scene from one of the stories. "Do you reckon this is going to corrupt me?" she asked her Iowa friend Robie Macaulay in a letter. "I already feel like a combination of Msgr. Sheen and Gorgeous George. Everybody who reads *Wise Blood* thinks I'm a hillbilly nihilist, whereas I would like to create the impression over the television that I'm a hillbilly Thomist, but I will probably not be able to think of anything to say to Mr. Harvey Breit but 'Huh?' and 'Ah dunno.'"

Galley Proof was broadcast live over WRCA at one-thirty in the afternoon. The voice-over is the confident voice of postwar America. The host, Harvey Breit, a book editor from the *New York Times*, wears a sack suit and brandishes a lighted cigarette. O'Connor walks onto the set unaided, wearing a black dress, and peers off to one side as Breit speaks. She is thirty years old, but she replies to his questions in the voice of an older woman, thin and formal, shy and strong:

". . . I understand you are living on a farm."

"Yes. I only live on one, though. I don't see much of it. I'm a writer, and I farm from the rocking chair."

"Do you have a fixed pattern of work?"

"Yes, I work every morning."

". . . and you don't miss a day?"

"No. Not even Sunday."

The camera swivels to a makeshift front porch, where two actresses are waiting, dressed as good country people. A stranger approaches, an archetypal hobo with big ears and wearing a too-large coat, one sleeve of it knotted at the elbow. Together they behold an invisible sunset and ponder the question of what a man is, while the author looks on.

"We'll go back to it in a few minutes," Breit says. ". . . What about some of those fascinating characters? Do you know them at all? Have you seen people like that?"

"Well, no, not really. I've seen many people like that, I think, and I've seen myself, I think. Putting all that together you get these people."

It is becoming clear that Breit will do most of the talking. As he speaks of the Southern literary renaissance, and compares the postwar South to nineteenth-century Russia, and suggests that fiction allows one to transcend one's environment, she quietly asserts her own point of view.

"I think that to overcome regionalism, you must have a great deal of self-knowledge," she says. "I think that to know yourself is to know your region, and that it's also to know the world, and in a sense, paradoxically, it's to be in exile from that world. So that you have a great deal of detachment."

"We're going to exile you right now and take you back to *Galley Proof* and to the show. Shall we? Can we call it a show?"

The camera swivels again, and Mrs. Crater tells Mr. Shiftlet the advantages of marrying her daughter.

"It isn't over," Breit says, as the actors shamble offstage. "What we're seeing now is only part of the story 'The Life You Save May Be Your Own.' Flannery, would you like to tell our audience what happens in that story?"

"No, I certainly would not," she declares. "I don't think you can paraphrase a story like that. I think there's only one way to tell it and that's the way it is told in the story."

She remained in the city three days, staying in a hotel near Grand Central Station. She saw the Broadway production of *Cat on a Hot Tin Roof.* "I thought I could do that good myself," she told her agent. "However, on reflection I guess it is unwise to reflect that."

On the weekend she went up to Connecticut, where Sue Brown Jenkins, a neighbor of the Fitzgeralds, was having a party for local literary folk; Caroline Gordon would be there.

When she arrived, she discovered that the party was a party for her. Gordon had arranged it, inviting people who (Gordon thought) might understand her work: Van Wyck Brooks, who had written a biography of Mark Twain; Malcolm Cowley, who had led the Faulkner revival.

As they chatted, Cowley asked her whether she had a wooden leg. Then (she told the Fitzgeralds), "Dear old Van Wyke insisted that I read a story, at which horror-stricken looks appeared on the faces of both Caroline and Sue. 'Read the shortest one!' they both screamed."

Gordon's biographer Ann Waldron tells the story differently. Asked to read aloud, O'Connor announced that she would read "Good Country People." Gordon urged her not to, insisting that these sophisticated Yankees wouldn't believe a seduction in a hayloft.

Gordon thought "Good Country People" the best thing O'Connor had written. Was she protecting O'Connor from having the story interpreted as autobiography? Or did she honestly think it was too long? In any case, she prevailed, and O'Connor read the title story of her book, the one about an escaped convict who shoots an old lady on a highway because once upon a time Jesus came and turned everything upside down. With her thin voice and thick accent, she later said, she sounded "pretty much like the old lady." Already "A Good Man Is Hard to Find," a story as bold as a comic strip, as objective as a myth, was being canonized as her greatest story, and her transformation from literary prodigy to ageless rural artist was in progress.

A few weeks later—June 15, 1955—thirty peace activists were arrested outside City Hall in Manhattan. Dorothy Day, who was one of them, described their aggregation: "seven from the Catholic Worker group, Eileen Fantino and her two companions from East Harlem, and members of the War Resisters League and the Fellowship of Reconciliation, and finally one lone bootblack named Rocco Parilli who was arrested because he wanted a drink of water just as the warning sounded."

The "warning" was the high point of a civil-defense drill, in which all citizens were required to take shelter in designated areas or else face arrest. As the signal wailed, traffic stopped and lower Broadway emptied. The thirty pacifists remained. They had printed a pamphlet and notified the media and the police. Now, as they were led to a paddy wagon, a news crew trained cameras on them, and Day read a statement:

> We make this demonstration, not only to voice our opposition to war, not only to refuse to participate in psychological warfare, which this air raid drill is, but also as an act of public penance for having been the first people in the world to drop the atomic bomb, to make the hydrogen bomb. We are engaging only ourselves in this action, not the Church. We are acting as individual Catholics.

That morning she had received a copy of Jacques Maritain's book *True Humanism* in the mail—her own signed copy, from 1938, returned anonymously by someone who had taken it from the shelves of St. Joseph's House. A passage she had marked then suggested answers to the questions facing her now: "Why did we do it? What did the Chancery office think of it all? Of these ten Catholics making a spectacle of themselves, 'a spectacle to the world, to angels and to men'?" Now she read from it:

We are turning towards men, to speak and act among them, on the temporal plane, because, by our faith, by our baptism, by our confirmation, tiny as we are, we have the vocation of infusing into the world, wheresoever we are, the sap and savor of Christianity.

The thirty pacifists were jailed and released at midnight. On trial six months later, they were found guilty and given suspended sentences.

The "shelter action" was Day's first act of civil disobedience, or direct action, a tactic that became the first new point in the Catholic Worker program since pacifism itself.

It is apparent that direct action suited the era. Whereas the Great Depression and World War II were actual circumstances, with tangible effects, the Cold War was a symbolic standoff, a war waged in laboratories, at summit meetings, and in the cultural imagination; it called for a symbolic reaction. So did television, which invited the swift and vivid public gesture more than the unspectacular work of showing poor people hospitality. So did Day's desire to make an impression on the stranger, the ordinary God-fearing patriotic American.

So did Ammon Hennacy, who had a calling to direct action as Day had a calling to poverty. A war resister from the Southwest, slight and bristle-haired as a Beckett character, he moved to New York in 1951 to live at St. Joseph's House. Shortly afterward he became a Catholic. But his real religion was his devotion to Dorothy Day. He bought her flowers on the street. He declared his love. He imagined their life together. All through 1953 and 1954, while Flannery O'Connor was courting Erik Langkjaer, Day was resisting Hennacy, who wrote her love letters twice a day.

The chief inspiration for direct action, however, came from outside the movement. Eight years after his death, the memory of Gandhi was still fresh. The Supreme Court had just outlawed segregated public schooling in the two *Brown* cases, and in the coming years black students would enroll peaceably again and again in the face of "massive resistance."

Six months after the City Hall demonstration, down in Alabama Rosa Parks refused to yield a seat on a city bus to a white passenger, and the

Montgomery bus boycott began, led by the Reverend Martin Luther King, Jr., whose approach was strikingly similar to Dorothy Day's: a blend of traditional Christian doctrine and radical practice, grounded in biblical ideas that ordinary believers accepted—the regard for the stranger, the life of a people as an ongoing pilgrimage.

That spring, traveling in the Midwest, Day had visited Caroline Gordon in St. Paul. The two women spent a day sitting side by side, knitting and talking.* Gordon was now corresponding with Jack English, Day's old cohort, at Holy Ghost Monastery in Georgia, showing him some of the tricks of the literary trade.

In the fall Day received the manuscript of Gordon's new novel in the mail, sent by Sue Brown Jenkins. She read it with gathering astonishment: Gordon had put her into the novel—put her in as a holy seductress with a blasphemous past. Her character was called Catherine Pollard, and Peter Maurin's was called Joseph Tadieu, but she and the movement were clearly recognizable. There were Houses of Hospitality on Mott Street and the Bowery. Maryfarm was named Mary Farm. Her life had been altered in only one aspect: Gordon had made Catherine Pollard a *failed* writer, whose failure in the literary life had led her to turn to God.

Day was angry and aggrieved. Gordon had told her nothing about her role in the novel during their visits of the past five years. When proofs arrived from the publisher, Harcourt, Brace, it became clear why. Gordon wished to dedicate the novel to her. She had already done so. There it was: "To Dorothy Day." The book was considered a tribute, an act of devotion.

Some people would read *The Malefactors* as a novel about Gordon's troubled marriage to Allen Tate. As the novel opens a literary couple are living on a farm they have inherited from a relative. In middle age, the wife is full of bustle and raises prize bulls. The husband, once a great poet, has lost his inspiration and his sexual vigor besides, until a friend of his youth comes to visit. Catherine Pollard is "awfully big and awfully calm," but he recalls her as she was—"a tall handsome girl, with remarkable eyes, who had a habit of backing you into a corner and asking you questions that, as he had once told her, 'only God can answer.' " Now she is a Catholic and runs a charity in the slums, "like a medieval abbess, with her own chapel and her

---

*Recounting the visit, Gordon (her biographer Ann Waldron reports) claimed that Day, holy woman that she was, "knitted bandages for lepers."

own priest and her own butcher and baker." She has already made a convert of his best friend's daughter. Maybe she will try to convert him, too.

Day wrote forceful letters to Gordon and to Denver Lindley at Harcourt, Brace, insisting that the novel be rewritten: she could not bear the depiction of poor Peter Maurin, who was made out to be a senile halfwit; and she was horrified by a set piece, told in flashback, in which the bohemian characters celebrate a pagan "Black Mass," with Catherine Pollard taking part.

She was told that it was too late: the novel was set in type. She insisted that at the very least, the dedication should be removed and the Black Mass scene eliminated. This was done: Gordon replaced the Black Mass with a rite in which the bohemians perform tests on a cruet of consecrated altar wine, seeking evidence of God's "real presence."

Revised proofs were sent to Day. She read them, then wrote a letter to Denver Lindley. "The alchemical experiment with 'consecrated wine obtained from some friendly priest' is to my mind so fantastic as to be unbelievable," she told him, and "Peter Maurin, presented as he is, in all his darkness, with no contrast of the light of his earlier days, also hurts. But it is all too late now."

Flannery O'Connor also got a set of proofs in the mail. Gordon had praised *Wise Blood* and raved about *A Good Man Is Hard to Find* in the Sunday *Times* book section. Now she and her editor were hoping that O'Connor might return the favor.

O'Connor evidently admired the novel more than liked it, and her discharging of her obligation is a masterpiece of literary tact. She wrote Denver Lindley to say she had read Gordon's novel "with my usual admiration for everything she writes," and added, "It would be impertinent for me to comment on the book, simply because I have too much to learn from it."

If she could not support the book wholeheartedly, at least she could rise to the defense of the author. Upon hearing of Day's objections, she wrote Lindley another letter, suggesting that Day was being oversensitive: "I wish Caroline had dedicated the book to 'My dog, Spot,' or anybody." To the Fitzgeralds, in Italy, she reported, "Caroline's book was to be dedicated to Dorothy Day, but Miss Day on inspecting the page proofs declared she would burn every copy she could get her hands on if she had her way. So the dedication has been withdrawn . . . and now, with that tree off the road, Miss D. begins to like the book better."

The novel, published in the spring, was reviewed unfavorably in *Time*.

O'Connor was "disgusted" by the review and dismissed *Time* as a "stupid" magazine that "could not be expected to like" a book like *The Malefactors*. "I don't think it is entirely successful as she is trying to do something impossible, but I think it is a good deal better than most of what they will recommend during the year."

The Malefactors was an example of the kind of Catholic novel O'Connor would never write, one in which good and thoughtful people discuss the quandaries of religious faith in an earnest and intelligent way. Good people, she believed, are especially hard to write about, and so it was with Caroline Gordon and Dorothy Day. "She certainly had a hard time making those CW people believable," O'Connor observed. "The one who is Dorothy Day is a little *bodiless*. . . . She keeps emphasizing that this is a large woman but the effect is different."

She wrote her own review of the novel for the *Bulletin*, the diocesan newspaper of middle Georgia. "A novel dealing with a conversion is the most difficult the writer can assign himself," she declared. "Miss Gordon brings a sure knowledge of the craft to bear upon a task that most novelists today would have neither the desire nor the courage to attempt." She had chosen her words carefully; although they seem approving, they say nothing of the novel itself. Concluding, she buried her single word of praise in midsentence and qualified it beforehand, saying that "*The Malefactors* is undoubtedly the most serious and successful fictional treatment of a conversion by an American writer to date."

Another civil-defense drill was held in June 1956. Catholic Workers and other pacifists resisted again, standing their ground in Washington Square Park until they were arrested. In the paper, Day addressed the charge that they were mere publicity seekers. "I don't think any of us, not even Ammon Hennacy, enjoys these demonstrations, this 'going to the man in the street,'" she wrote. "It is so much easier to sit behind a typewriter, to sit in an office or a meeting house and talk about these actions and these ideas." So why were they demonstrating? To bear witness, she explained—"to show our willingness to go to jail, to be deprived of our freedom, to suffer disgrace in the eyes of those who cannot understand our position." Offered a choice of punishment—pay a fine, or serve a brief jail sentence—they elected to go to jail.

All through 1956 the Montgomery bus boycott continued. Today its episodes—the King home bombed; the boycott's leaders jailed; black citizens forbidden to use their cars in carpools; burning crosses left on lawns in black neighborhoods by the Ku Klux Klan; Reverend King's invocations of the "weapon of love"—are familiar markers on the time line of the civil-rights movement. At the time, though, the South, and the United States, had seen nothing like it. In the bus boycott the black people of Montgomery had pioneered a new form of nonviolent civil disobedience, one grounded in the same principles as the shelter actions but on a much larger scale, demanding a good deal more effort, inconvenience, and self-restraint.

The months passed with no word of the boycott in "On Pilgrimage," an absence that is surprising in retrospect. Not until her October 1956 column, written late that summer, did Day mention it—announcing that she would be going on pilgrimage to Montgomery, "where the notion of non-violent resistance to oppression is slowly taking hold."

The absence of any remarks about the boycott in Flannery O'Connor's letters is even more surprising. For Martin Luther King was a Georgian, four years younger than O'Connor, and he was taking a path strikingly similar to hers: raised and educated in Georgia, he had gone up north for graduate school, absorbed the lessons of the moderns, and then, at age twenty-six, returned to the South, there to carry out a life's work, as it turned out, in a dozen years.

In O'Connor's letters of 1955 and 1956 the news of race comes from even closer to home than Alabama. The state of Georgia had banned two textbooks as too progressive—"one that said Negroes learned as fast as white folks and another, a song book, that changed the word 'darkies' to the word 'brothers' in one of Stephen Foster's songs."* Two black farm workers akin to those in "The Displaced Person" had come to Andalusia, prompting O'Connor to say that she wouldn't dare "go inside their heads" in a story: "I can only see them from the outside."

Is that all she had to say on the subject? It may also be that O'Connor already felt, as she remarked later, that she had said what she had to say about race relations in the South in a short story—"it being my vocation to say it that way."

The story is "The Artificial Nigger," from 1954. On the surface it is the least topical of all O'Connor's stories. Like the "artificial nigger" of the title—a Negro minstrel figure modeled in plaster and paint—the story

---

*In the latter case she declared herself "wholly in sympathy," lamenting that before long the rural staple "Ol Black Joe" would be changed to "Old Neutral-colored Joe."

is heightened and artificial in style. The grandfather who opens the story is likened to the great literary pilgrims of old—"Vergil summoned in the middle of the night to go to Dante, or better, Raphael, awakened by a blast of God's light to fly to the side of Tobias." His grandson, in a new gray suit and hat, is his faithful companion. In the sky above their shack, at dawn, hangs an archetypally bright moon, which "rolled forward and cast a dignifying light on everything," giving their story the aspect of a fairy tale.

Like *Wise Blood*, it is a story of a pilgrimage to firsthand experience, in which poor rural whites go from country to city to see some "niggers"— strangers par excellence.

As they set out, boarding a train at a desolate crossing, each boasts of his knowledge of city life. Mr. Head has been to the city twice before and means to show his grandson all its menace, the better to keep the boy from becoming proud. The grandson, Nelson, was born in the city, and this, he feels, gives him a native familiarity:

> "How you know I never saw a nigger when I lived there before?" Nelson asked. "I probably saw a lot of niggers."
>
> "If you seen one you didn't know what he was," Mr. Head said, completely exasperated. "A six-month-old child don't know a nigger from anybody else."

Once there, they wander, having no real destination, only the objective of seeing "niggers" for themselves. Strangers in the city, they soon become estranged from each other. They quarrel outside the railroad station and get lost in a black neighborhood.

In his innocence, Nelson doesn't know he is supposed to think of Negroes as strangers, and his grandfather decides to play upon the feeling for Nelson's own good—letting him wander off alone, and then, after the boy accidentally upends a white woman's groceries, denying that he knows him. As they search for the railroad station, Nelson, in turn, registers his grandfather's betrayal by ignoring him—his mind "frozen around his grandfather's treachery as if he were trying to preserve it intact to present at the final judgment." The sun is setting. The time of their train's departure is growing near. Together yet estranged, they wander the city in silence, hungry, thirsty, tired, fearful, altogether lost, each of them alone in the world.

They have stumbled into a white suburb when they come upon a Negro "about Nelson's size" and "pitched forward at an unsteady angle because the putty that held him to the wall was cracked. One of his eyes was entirely white and he held a piece of brown watermelon."

The artificial Negro astonishes them; they ponder it in silence, like two pilgrims at a shrine. They are described as if they, too, are made of plaster— "with their necks forward at the same angle and their shoulders curved in almost exactly the same way and their hands trembling identically in their pockets. Mr. Head looked like an ancient child and Nelson like a miniature old man. They stood gazing at the artificial Negro as if they were faced with some great mystery, some monument to another's victory that brought them together in their common defeat. They could both feel it dissolving their differences like an action of mercy."

O'Connor rewrote the story twice in the autumn of 1954, each time elevating the ending, giving it greater significance. When it was done, she was delighted. She would read the story to herself over and over, laughing at the funny parts. She pronounced it "probably the best thing I'll ever write," a story whose significance was greater than anything she had put into it.

"The Artificial Nigger" really is a profound work, and the O'Connor story that comes closest to achieving the "moment of grace" she considered the key to her short fiction. Here the moment of grace, often obscure or overblown, is prepared for, dramatized, earned, justified: there is no doubting that the encounter with the painted plaster statue has brought the grandfather and grandson together and sent them home reconciled.

O'Connor later tried to explain the title and its significance. "Nigger statuary," she explained, screamed out the tragedy of the South; and the "artificial nigger" in the story was meant to suggest "the redemptive quality of the Negro's suffering for us all." Having seen it, Mr. Head feels at once judged and cleansed, at once fallen and redeemed.

Ingenious as it is, the ending is disconcerting. The suffering of blacks is seen to bring about the reconciliation, indeed the redemption, of whites. The "redemptive quality" of blacks' suffering is made to depend on laws and social mores—"manners"—that are oppressive. While an "artificial nigger" reconciles grandfather and grandson, the actual Negroes remain strangers, and if they are redeemed by their particular sufferings the story doesn't say so.

In the next few years several thousand whites from the North would come on pilgrimage to the cities of the South—to see the Negroes, to be with them, to join them in struggle, and to be reconciled by the experience. O'Connor would scorn them as self-righteous outsiders, and in "The Artificial Nigger" she had envisioned the form their reconciliation with blacks might take. The reconciliation of blacks to whites, it happened, would be left to her fellow Georgian Martin Luther King to dramatize.

In Memphis, Dorothy Day saw a friend who ran a nursery in a slum where the Catholic schools, refusing to integrate, stood nearly empty: "The buildings are there, but there is no room for the Negro . . . no room at the inn." In Mississippi, she had lunch with Bayard Rustin and met with a group of black college graduates; although blacks outnumbered whites five to one in the state, the whites sought to drive the blacks out, and the return of these students to fight segregation in their hometowns was a reason to hope. Then, in Montgomery, she visited the offices of the Southern Christian Leadership Conference.

The Catholic Worker had been out in front in race matters, and there was a reminder on page one of the newspaper, where a black worker and a white one shook hands in front of a cross. But the movement's solidarity with Southern blacks was largely symbolic. Their own poverty was voluntary. Their jail terms were chosen. They had not suffered the way the blacks of the South had. This Day sought to remedy with her pilgrimage to Montgomery. For all her traveling, she lacked firsthand knowledge of the plight of blacks in the South. Now she was making up for lost time—visiting black priests and nuns, meeting with black leaders, staying in black parishioners' homes, and reporting it all in the *Catholic Worker*.

"The white man in the south likes to emphasize that the northerner does not understand the Negro," she wrote. "But how can it be said that he does, either?" Segregation, in her view, was not a tragedy; it was an evil. The manners of the South were not revelatory of mystery; they were evidence of injustice. The suffering of the Negro was not socially redemptive; it had been redemptive for many Negroes, insofar as suffering brought one closer to God, but no one would dare argue that such suffering was worth perpetuating through an unjust social system.

What was to be done? White Southerners insisted that the undoing of segregation would do more harm than good. But Day saw the consequences as of no account. "In the beginnings of Christianity, when his troubled listeners asked St. John the Baptist what they were to do, he told them simply, 'Let him who has two coats give to him who has none,'" she wrote. "The answer is always the same: Love is an exchange of gifts. To show our love for

God, we must show our love for our brother." Whites and blacks were brothers. Now blacks were being asked to forgive their white oppressors, an act so great that only God could ask it of them. Whites had it easy. They should treat the stranger—the Negro—as Christ. All the rest would follow.

In April 1957 Day boarded a Greyhound bus for the thirty-six-hour ride to Georgia. The weather, bright and mild, was at odds with her purpose: "It was as though I were on a vacation instead of on the rather gruesome mission of spending the last two weeks of Lent, passion week and holy week, with the beleaguered community, Koinonia."

She had visited the community once before: an interracial farming cooperative founded by a Baptist minister named Clarence Jordan. The farm (named after the Greek word for communion, fellowship, brotherhood) lay on a thousand acres in Americus, a hundred miles from Atlanta; the community consisted of five thousand chickens and sixty people, black and white. After fifteen years of fitful peace, segregationists were trying to put the farm out of business. They boycotted its produce, dynamited a roadside stand, cut barbed-wire fences, set fire to a barn, shot at the houses drive-by style, speeding up and then speeding off.

"The moon is shining brightly over the fields and I pray that there will be no 'deeds of darkness' this night," Day wrote shortly after her arrival. "I will not be afraid for the terror by night nor for the arrow that flieth by day. The only arrows around here are those of the children who practice after school at a big target. But I have seen the marks of gunshot in the houses," she remarked, and the farm families had vacated the houses that faced the road, "which is only a few paces away."

She stayed a week, writing a series of letters to the Catholic Worker community. Together, these are a vivid, tense, and dramatic report in which Day's talents as documentarist and homilist are sharpened to a single point. The writing is full of simple foreshadowing and telling contrasts: the placid daily life versus the threats of violence that come each night in every sweep of a car's headlights; Day's matter-of-fact remarks about chain gangs and organic gardening versus her lurking fear that she will be shot.

The third night, she and another woman volunteered for the night watch. They sat in a station wagon under a floodlight beneath an oak tree at the roadside. The other woman sang hymns and played an accordion. Day prayed from her breviary and thought of the Trappist monks at Holy Ghost

Monastery, across the state, who would be rising at 2 a.m. to sing the night office. Abruptly a car approached. Shots rang out. The car drove off. Bullets had peppered the station wagon, barely missing the two women, who were huddled in their seats. Others from the farm came to see whether they were all right, but they insisted on finishing the watch, although Day was shaking with fright. "It is what I came for—to share in fear and suffering," she wrote.

She stayed three more days, then went on to the monastery, where she rewrote her letters for publication. Naturally, she compared Clarence Jordan's community to her own. The Catholic Worker farms were places of symbolic witness to an alternative way of life. The Koinonia farm was a functioning cooperative in an agricultural state, where such farms could actually bring about a different way of life. "If others followed the example of Clarence Jordan—if priests and ministers throughout the country set out with their flocks, to build up a new society within the shell of the old by the hard labor of their hands"; if whites and blacks would see each other as brothers, not as strangers, "the problems of tenant farming, sharecropping, day labor, peonage, destitution, debt, and so on, would be solved."

"Whether or not Koinonia succeeds or fails, whether or not the families here move elsewhere, shaking the dust from their feet of this hostile town of Americus, this hostile county of Sumpter, integration of the races will continue," Day concluded. " 'What we want to do,' Clarence Jordan says, 'is simply the will of God.' "

The letters appeared in the *Catholic Worker* the next month. Flannery O'Connor read them and felt violated. Here was an outsider pronouncing judgment on life in Georgia; here was news of her own country being delivered by way of the Lower East Side. "I wish somebody would write something sensible about Koinonia—as you say it is something regressive which is getting all the benefit of martyrdom," she griped in a letter to a friend. "I think they should be allowed to live in peace but that they deserve all this exaltation I highly doubt. D.D. wrote up her trip there in the CW, which I duly enclose. It would have been all right if she hadn't had to stick in her plug for Their Way of Life for Everybody." She remarked that although she admired Day very much, "all my thoughts on the subject are ugly and uncharitable—such as: that's a mighty long way to come to get shot at, etc."

The conflict between the gradualist and the activist was taking place within Walker Percy as well. The Supreme Court's rulings on school desegregation had forced white Southerners into two camps—"for" and "against." Percy, however, was of several minds; he saw himself as a Southern moderate, caught in the middle of a war being fought "on the battleground of enlightened liberal North versus depraved reactionary South."

Will Percy—a segregationist—had considered himself a moderate, too. Now Percy was being asked to condemn his uncle and all he had stood for. This he refused to do. Yet he also refused to simply defend the South. In his view, the question for a white Southerner like himself was "how to oppose segregation and at the same time cherish his heritage," especially its "incredible triumph of manners," which had enabled the races to live side by side and survive a civil war together.

The conflict might have brought out Percy's Southern loyalties. Instead it called upon his Catholic bona fides. In the ten years since his conversion he had never written anything for the Catholic magazines. Suddenly in 1956 and 1957 he wrote several articles about race for *Commonweal*, as well as a long letter printed in the Jesuit magazine *America*.

The first and best of the articles, "Stoicism in the South," compares the Stoic viewpoint and the Christian one—the point of view Percy had been brought up with and the one he had come to espouse. It is an inward dialogue between Percy and his Uncle Will, in which Percy defines himself against his uncle once and for all.

Still a pathologist, he begins by diagnosing the most striking, to him, of all the South's problems. The problem is that the Stoic upper-class white Southerner is no longer the champion of blacks and their rights.

Instead the Stoic says nothing or else organizes to protect the South and "our way of life." For centuries he treated his neighbor well not out of love but because it reflected well on himself and gave him chances to act nobly. He relished decline and fall "because social decay confirmed one in his original choice of the wintry kingdom of self" as a place of noble resistance to an ignoble society. But the forced federal integration of the schools in Little Rock in 1957 was the final blow: with the ending of segregation, Stoic culture—its hierarchies and manners, its unlikely alliance between the white gentry and the poor blacks against the poor whites—has been ended once and for all.

The Stoic is a stranger in this new world. The lord of the manor is now homeless. Even his religious faith is no refuge, because it is no faith at all. For centuries, Percy explains, "the Southern gentleman did live in a Christian edifice, but he lived there in the strange fashion Chesterton spoke of, that of a man who will neither go inside nor put it entirely behind him but stands forever grumbling on the front porch."

The Christian, meanwhile, has entered public life as never before, agitating for black civil rights or supporting the cause. For the Christian, desegregation and the collapse of manners it brings are reasons for hope, not despair. The Christian, as Percy puts it, sees the black man insisting on his natural equality—his brotherhood—with the white man under God, which doesn't depend on manners or good behavior. It is only right for the Church to work for racial equality. The Stoic doesn't like it—"It is as if a gentleman's agreement has been broken"—but the Church is right and will prevail.

"The good pagan's view is no longer good enough for the South," Percy concludes. "We in the South can no longer afford the luxury of maintaining the Stoa beside the Christian edifice. In the past we managed the remarkable feat of keeping both, one for living in, the other for dying in. But the Church is no longer content to perform rites of passage; she has entered the arena of the living and must be reckoned with. The white Southerner, Catholic and Protestant, has been invited to either go inside the edifice he has created or to consider what he is doing on the porch at all."

Percy's position, here, is very close to the Catholic Worker's, an ideal position asserted in full knowledge of the raw racism of so many actual Christians. Black and white are brothers, shaking hands under the cross. In a divided society, the Church sees all humanity as one. Instead of seeing blacks as strangers, then, the white Christian should identify with blacks as neighbors, as kin, and also as the suffering outcasts of society.

But Percy goes on to say that the segregationist white Southerner must be seen as kin as well. Asked what to do about the "stubborn segregationist," he replies, "I would presume that if one is a Catholic, one does not 'do' anything with him. One follows St. Paul and, instead of despising him as an enemy, corrects him as a brother, all the while in fear and trembling for one's own salvation."

In "The Southern Moderate," published in December 1957, Percy pondered what would happen as desegregation was brought about. "No white southerner," he had written elsewhere, "can write a *j'accuse* without making a *mea culpa*," and if "Stoicism in the South" was grounded in his identification with the black Southerner, "The Southern Moderate" is an embrace of ordinary people, faults and all.

He makes his case in secular, commonsensical terms, tracing the effects of segregation on the ordinary white person. Blacks will go north, escaping de jure segregation, only to find de facto segregation in housing and social life. White Southerners will waste their creative energy defending an untenable (and suddenly illegal) way of life, as they did during Reconstruction. Blacks and whites alike will see coexistence replaced by phony friendship. When they wish to socialize, blacks and whites will retreat to their separate neighborhoods, their homes and their friends. Southern life will be more just, but more impersonal; there will be a narrowing of the zone of social encounter.

"Yet the growing depersonalization of Southern life may not be such a bad thing, after all," Percy concludes. "God writes straight with crooked lines. If the shrinkage of social intercourse to patio and barbecue pit serves no other purpose, it might yet provide a truly public zone outside where people are free to move about in a kind of secure anonymity until the time comes when they might wish to be friends."

Percy's affinity with the ordinary white Southerner was more than loyalty to his own tribe. It was a consequence of his philosophy. As the conflicts over desegregation turned on the definition of "public" accommodations, and indeed of "society" generally, Percy was writing about the function of the symbol as the means of identification between the individual and reality, between one person and another.

His position on segregation, and on race generally, reflected this theory of the symbol. In the South, as he saw it, the symbols were abruptly changing. Integration was just and desirable. Yet in his view genuine identification between strangers was something like miraculous and couldn't be legislated or preached into being. For blacks and whites alike it would have the side effect of the loss of common symbols: alienation.

Percy had changed. Faith had led him away from the plantation. Philosophy had given faith an intellectual basis and a practical rationale. Far from turning him abstract, as Shelby Foote had warned him it would do, philosophy had coaxed him down off the magic mountain and onto level ground to consider the mortal struggle of everydayness. It emancipated him from his Uncle Will and the scheme of Stoic noblesse oblige. It helped him to solve his own problems and ponder the affairs of the day. It made him, finally, an ordinary man.

"The Man on the Train" is about the ordinary man in his alienation; it is about the "literature of alienation" and its effects on the reader who is alienated. In it, Percy again looked to philosophy to bridge the gap between thought and experience, between life and what is made of it, by placing an ordinary person on a train and watching to see what would happen.

The essay (published in the *Partisan Review*) was Percy's most literary piece thus far, and the strain of his striving shows here and there. It is crammed with arch asides ("One is tempted to contrast Marquand's Book-of-the-Month-Club disenchantment with Kafka's Mittleuropa alienation . . ."). Terms from philosophy appear out of nowhere, then trail off unexplained. There is too much going on—a riff on amnesia as a soap-opera plot twist, an offhand critique of *Huckleberry Finn*. But it is a real essay—something is being essayed—and it crackles with discovery. The voice is all Percy, now formal, now wisecracking. The footprints tracked through the text are his.

The man on the train is a commuter, going the same way he goes every day. Unmoored from his surroundings, his fellow commuters, his own body, he is alienation incarnate—literally "both in the world he is traveling through and not in it." Percy explains, "Beyond all doubt he is in Metuchen, New Jersey, during the few seconds the train stops there, yet in what a strange sense is he there—he passes through without leaving so much as his breath behind. Even if this is the one thousandth time he has stopped there, even if he knows a certain concrete pillar better than anything else in the world, yet he remains as total a stranger to Metuchen as if he had never been there."

The essay has the subtitle "Three Existential Modes," and the man on the train, like the protagonist of Chekhov's "Man in a Shell," is a walking piece of philosophy—a figure of "extraordinary interest" because he embodies "the existential placement of all three modes, alienation, rotation, and repetition."

These categories are from Kierkegaard, but Percy adapts them for his own purposes, finding his examples in fiction and the movies. What is the alienated commuter to do to unalienate himself? There are several possibilities. The commuter can overcome alienation through a "zone crossing"—by stepping off the train onto trackside and into the yellow house he has glimpsed for a thousand mornings. He can accidentally stumble into the mode of repetition like Charles Ryder in *Brideshead Revisited*, who steps off the army train and sees Brideshead Castle again. Or he can stage a repetition deliberately, going home again on the train like Thomas Wolfe's overwrought protagonists. He can attempt a rotation, a sudden departure from the grid of everyday plans and expectations, like Huck Finn rafting down the

Mississippi. He can wait for the Bomb to drop and the End Times to come, which will break down the boundaries that alienate him from other people, who are alienated as well; or he can remain unaware of his alienation, a condition akin to despair.

Put a novel in the commuter's hand and things get more complicated. The train rounds a bend. Sunlight glints off the glass. There is a pretty girl waiting to board on the platform up ahead. Still, the novel is absorbing. This is what art does: it lets us escape our alienation temporarily. But some works of art do this better than others. Some banish our alienation; others distract us from it; some show it to us without offering any consolation. Whether they do so is a matter not only of quality, but of kind.

Making these distinctions, Percy is oddly assured: he seems to be writing from experience, even though he has never completed a novel to his satisfaction. Repetition, he declares, is usually diminished in a work of art; as the hero goes home again his passionate quest for the meaning of his life will strike the reader as interesting at best, because the reader wasn't there the first time. Alienation, in a novel, becomes something else: the novel of alienation, like a symbol, re-presents alienation, and so will dispel it in the reader, and as the alienated reader recognizes his condition in the text, the book "heals the very wound it re-presents."

This achievement, Percy says, "is an aesthetic victory of comradeliness, a recognition of plight in common. Its motto is not 'I despair and do not know that I despair' but 'At least we know that we are lost to ourselves'—which is very great knowledge indeed." Whereas "the nonreading commuter exists in true alienation, which is unspeakable," Percy goes on to explain, "the reading commuter rejoices in the speakability of his alienation and in the new triple alliance of himself, the alienated character, and the author. His mood is affirmatory and glad: Yes! That's how it is!"

That is ecstatically said, and for a moment the insight banishes alienation in just the way Percy claims it does. It also suggests that Percy is celebrating the novel of alienation. After all, he says the reversal of alienation is "the supreme intersubjective achievement of art," which is to "set forth the truth of it: how it stands with both of us."

A noble aim: but the man writing the essay is not the man riding the commuter train. Like Hazel Motes on the train to Taulkinham, Percy comes from a particular somewhere and is on his way somewhere else. He is in life, not a train ride, and wants to live fully, as himself, to see what further adventures await him.

"The road is better than the inn, said Cervantes—and by this he meant that rotation is better than the alienation of everydayness," Percy says. Like-wise, the road novel is better than the novel of home and family; and the novel of rotation, as Percy calls it, is the best hope for "deliverance from everydayness." Why? It takes place in a "privileged zone of possibility," where the hero is free to be a "stranger" in other people's everydayness. And it promises a complex escape. In Hemingway's A *Farewell to Arms*, for ex-ample, the hero, Frederic Henry, "rotates" in four different ways, escaping bourgeois America, expatriate Paris, the Italian army, and finally the nurse Catherine and their child—and "walks back to the hotel in the rain" a free man.

Rotation is better than alienation for another reason. The act of rotation, in which we plunge into the unknown and see what awaits us, is similar to the act of reading, in which we sit in a room and suspensefully turn the pages. The reader of *Huckleberry Finn*, in a sense, becomes Huckleberry Finn. "Reading about Huck going down the river or Tenente Frederic Henry escaping from the *caribinieri* in A *Farewell to Arms* is somewhat like going down the river and escaping," Percy explains. "It is by virtue of the fact that rotation is the quest for the new, as the new, the reposing of all hope in what may lie around the bend, a mode of experiencing which is much the same in the reading as in the experiencing."

The novel of rotation, then, Percy concludes, conveys an experience from writer to reader essentially intact; whereas the novel of repetition, if it is going to be more than a pastime for the alienated—here he speaks from experience—requires "a more radical identification."

Reading "The Man on the Train," you think: "No wonder the poor guy couldn't write a decent novel, with all that philosophy stuffed into his head!" There is something to this. Percy *was* burdened with self-consciousness (es-caping it is the theme of his later essays). But "The Man on the Train" is part of the solution, not the problem. However philosophy may have clogged his fiction, his experience of writing fiction was the source of the es-say; and underneath its surface clatter and partisan jousting is a clear running stream of self-knowledge, as Percy diagnoses why his two novels did not succeed.

"To leave the fixed right-of-way at a random point and enter the trackless woods is a superb rotation," he declares, and so it had been in his own life to that point. He had left the fixed path once in quitting medicine, a second time in becoming a Catholic, a third in becoming a writer. Each rotation had worked—had sprung him into a "zone of possibility" while providing a tradition, a different path with limits to define himself against.

Now he needed to achieve in his writing the kind of rotation he had achieved in his life. In switching from fiction to philosophy he had made a partial rotation. But the ideas in his essays were still repetitions of Kierkegaard and Marcel, the way his novels had been repetitions of Thomas Wolfe and Thomas Mann. The best parts of the essays, the freshest, were the parts that were the least philosophical—the most like fiction, that is.

He began to write a piece of fiction, akin to *The Stranger* of Camus, about an ordinary man who, in the ordinariness of his despair, is a living, breathing piece of philosophy.

His return to fiction, seen in his own terms, was not a repetition but a rotation. He was not going home again so much as breaking fresh ground, following the implications of his ideas. His philosophy led him toward a novel. Novels communicated: they reached ordinary men and women, who could be seen reading on commuter trains and streetcars, wholly absorbed. Essays in philosophy did not. Nobody read them, Percy had discovered. They lacked intersubjectivity. Writing one was like putting a message in a bottle.

Moreover, the essay form lacked the key to a successful rotation: narrative suspense, in which writer, character, and reader together wait to see what happens next.

EIGHT

Counterparts

One morning in 1958 Thomas Merton put on a black suit, left the monastery, and set out for the city. There, outside an old hotel on a crowded street, he had a religious experience:

In Louisville, at the corner of 4th and Walnut, suddenly realized that I loved all the people and that none of them were, or could be, totally alien to me. As if waking from a dream—the dream of my separateness, of the "special" vocation to be different . . . I am still a member of the human race—and what more glorious destiny is there for man, since the Word was made flesh and became, too, a member of the Human Race!

Thank God! Thank God! I am only another member of the human race like all the rest of them. I have the immense joy of being a man!

He stood there watching, like Dorothy Day during the San Francisco earthquake, and felt the wall between himself and others collapse. The unity of the human race, suggested in Scripture, professed in faith, was shown to him and put into perspective—"as if the sorrows of our condition could really matter, once we begin to realize who and what we are—as if we could ever begin to realize it on earth."

This episode is known as the "vision in Louisville," but it might better be called a street-corner epiphany, for it was not a glimpse of God so much as a recognition of other people. And although it has been seen as the beginning of Merton's "turning toward the world," it was the defining moment of a process that was spread out over several years.

Merton had gone outside the monastery on day trips ever since the 1940s—to perform a baptism in the nearby hamlet of New Haven, to scout a site for a new Trappist foundation across the Ohio River, to become a U.S. citizen at the federal office building in Louisville, and especially to receive medical care at the Catholic hospital there. In the same years, he had become a lively and fluent letter writer, often putting into letters the personal reflections he had once saved for his journal.

In his fifteenth year as a Trappist, he had gone on his first overnight trip, to a conference on monasticism and psychiatry in Minnesota. There, a popular psychiatrist diagnosed him as a narcissist who would set up "a hermitage in Times Square with a large sign over it saying HERMIT." Then, over dinner at the home of J. F. Powers, the *New Yorker* writer and the only American Catholic writer as respected as he was, he glimpsed the life he might have led had he not become a Trappist. Living in a house in the woods, writing fiction all day and then sitting down for dinner with his wife and adoring daughters, Powers was "forlorn and desperate"—unable to pray and unmoved, Merton thought, by the "prophetic vocation" of the religious artist.

Merton returned to Gethsemani chastened. His worldly counterparts were a depressed writer and a glib twentieth-century soul doctor. He was glad to be a monk in a monastery.

Still, he craved counterparts. Out in the toolshed in the woods, he sought God; at the same time, he sought human company—others, companions, partners in dialogue.

He found them, as ever, through his reading and writing. He requested books on all things Russian from libraries throughout the order. He filled his journal with quotations from Koestler and Orwell, Stalin and Marx (who "is, in some strange way, an heir of Ezechiel and Jeremias"). He read Bulgakov and Berdyaev, Russian Christian writers who had been stigmatized by the Soviets, and pondered the counterpoint between Roman Catholicism and Eastern Orthodoxy. Where Catholicism, in his account, stressed truth, dogma, and authority, Orthodoxy was "sapiential," emphasizing religious experience in pursuit of the divine wisdom, typified by the female figure of Sophia.

Over a period of weeks, Sophia became an obsession. He had a dream of a Russian ballet featuring "a dark-haired woman with her hair cut close like a boy's." He dreamed that he was being embraced by a Jewish girl on the sofa on the porch in Douglaston: "She clings to me and will not let go, and I begin to like the idea. . . . I ask her her name and she says her name is Proverb. I tell her that is a beautiful and significant name, but she does not appear to like it."

He told himself that *Sophia* sounded like *sofa*, that his unconscious had been teasing him. A week later, though, he wrote Proverb a letter—a love letter, in which he praised her "virginal solitude" and thanked her "for loving in me something which I thought I had entirely lost."

That was March 4, 1958. Two weeks later, he glimpsed the unity of the human race at Fourth and Walnut. "I have the immense joy of being a man!" he wrote in his journal, and went on:

> It is not a question of proving to myself that I either dislike or like the women one sees in the street. . . . It is as though by chastity I had come to be married to what is most pure in all the women of the world and to taste and sense the secret beauty of their girl's hearts as they walked in the sunlight—each one secret and good and lovely in the sight of God—never touched by anyone, nor by me, nor by anyone, as good as and even more beautiful than the light itself. For the woman-ness that is in each of them is at once original and inexhaustibly fruitful bringing the image of God into the world. In this each one is Wisdom and Sophia and Our Lady.

In his journal, he wrote another letter to Proverb. "I shall never forget our meeting yesterday," he told her. "The touch of your hand makes me a different person."

His "vision in Louisville," then, was, on the face of it, a commonplace experience: the sense of mystical union with another person brought on by sexual yearning. But there was more to it than that. He had followed the path of absolute solitude as far as he could go. His need for counterparts, strong even when unacknowledged, was now as strong as his longing to be elsewhere.

When, a month later, he read Martin Buber's *I and Thou*, he saw the feeling explained in the notion of "dialogic personalism," which made the relation between self and other an analogue for the relation between self and God.

By 1958 *I and Thou* (published in Germany in 1937) had gathered unto it thinkers of all sorts, calling forth a dialogue between Christianity and Judaism, philosophy and theology, existentialism and rabbinic midrash, thought and the life that lies outside of thought. "All real living is meeting," Buber proposed, and "all relation is mutual." All real religion is dialogic, an encounter with the Other. Most human relationships—and those of most human beings with God—are "I-It" relationships, in which one partner in the dialogue seeks to dominate the other. Authentic religion, in contrast, is an "I-Thou" relationship, an encounter with the Other as whole, personal, alive, and Other.

In some ways Buber's thought echoed that of the Catholic mystics, who conceived of God as radically unlike any human conception of God. In other ways it posed a direct challenge to the mystical life as Catholics understood it. If God is to be sought in relation to the Other, then the mystic, seeking God alone, is going about it all wrong—is making God into an idol.

Merton took up the challenge, judging *I and Thou* as a book "in which I am confronted by the hollowness and falsity of my own life." As an Orthodox Jew, Buber was the Other par excellence. Did his insights run against the grain of Catholic theology? Merton was unperturbed. "They are words drawn from experience. They can certainly be controlled by theology. That control is not my business. My business is to verify Buber's with my own."

Out in the toolshed, he made a kind of vow. For a long time he had sought God alone. Now, in midlife, he would seek to meet God in relation.

He would begin with his writing. His journal, he thought, was authentic "I-Thou writing," but his published work was not: too often he had set himself over against the reader, and so shut out the reader and God alike. From this point forward he would strive to make all his writing a dialogue, an encounter with the Other.

Walker Percy's essay "The Man on the Train" explained Thomas Merton's experience at Fourth and Walnut with uncanny precision. "One man's everydayness is another man's rotation," Percy had observed, and in his terms Merton's experience was a "splendid rotation," a pure "zone crossing." At Gethsemani Merton was known to all, and the once-otherworldly Trappist life had become the everyday, from which he was alienated and yearned to escape. In Louisville, out of his monastic dress, he was an ordinary man, "who walks through the town a stranger and keeps his own counsel." At the intersection of Fourth and Walnut he "rotated" out of his own everydayness and into that of others; at the intersection of Self and Other, he saw Self and Other clearly, and as he identified with the Other, his alienation gave way to "comradeliness" and a recognition of "plight in common."

Percy, for his part, had returned to New Orleans. At the end of 1957, as his articles about integration appeared, he had bought a "Louisiana cottage" in the Uptown district. The cottage, on Milan Street, was a Southern manor house reduced to essentials: four walls, white pillars, shuttered windows, sloping roof; in front, a porch just deep enough for a rocking chair; out back, a sunroom—a glassed-in porch—where he would write. At the end of the street was the St. Charles Avenue streetcar, which led downtown to the French Quarter or uptown to Loyola University.

He later said that he had returned to the city for family reasons: his second daughter, it had emerged, was deaf, and a hearing specialist he had engaged to tutor her kept an office there. But the move was in accord with his thought as well. Having banished alienation with an essay, he sought to do so in his everyday life. In his articles on segregation he envisioned a "public zone" of "secure anonymity" where the Southerner, white or black, was free to move unnoticed among others; and in his philosophical essays he had centered on the modern person's need to make "crossings" from one "zone" to another— to escape the "everydayness" of one's life without leaving it altogether.

Small, white, cloistral Covington was a separate place, New Orleans a mixed and relatively integrated one. This was the significance of his return to the city. Still, Percy didn't move there altogether. The Percys lived in New Orleans during the week only, returning to Covington on weekends. And the Uptown district, though well within the city, stood at some distance from the French Quarter of legend. The cottage on Milan Street was an in-between place, a site of pure possibility, where he could make a zone crossing whenever he wished.

In Louisville that day Merton had bought a literary magazine—*Encounter*— featuring an interview with Boris Pasternak. He knew of the Russian novelist already, through a *Partisan Review* he had "clandestinely acquired." Now he read the interview and wrote Pasternak a letter in care of his publisher.

> Although we are separated by great distances and even greater barri-
> ers, it gives me pleasure to speak to you as to one whom I feel to be a
> kindred mind.

It may surprise you when I say, in all sincerity, that I feel much more kinship with you, in your writing, than with most of the great modern writers in the West. . . .

When you write of your youth in the Urals, in Marburg, in Moscow, I feel as if it were my own experience, as if I were you. With other writers I can share ideas, but you seem to communicate something deeper. It is as if we met on a deeper level of life on which individuals are not separate beings. In the language familiar to me as a Catholic monk, it is as if we were known to one another in God.

This, not the letter to Proverb, is Merton's first real love letter. Addressing "my dear Pasternak," he promised to learn Russian and hoped they would have "the chance to enter upon a dialogue that will really lead to peace and to a fruitful age for man and his world."

At the time *Dr. Zhivago*, Pasternak's only novel, was soon to appear in English. Although he was nearly seventy years old and had been an eminence in Russia since the twenties, his life story was just becoming known in the West, told in such a way that he seemed to be Merton's perfect double: a solitary writer set against a repressive state, a mystic in a secular society, a religious artist whose embattled Judeo-Christian faith was vital to his work, a wise man whose dacha, an artists' retreat on the outskirts of Moscow, was a place of pilgrimage for writers from Russia and the West alike.

It would seem obvious that Merton, in his letter, was projecting onto Pasternak his own ardor—except that Pasternak was equally ardent. Through an English friend, he replied that Merton's letter had struck him as so "wonderfully filled with kindred thoughts as having been written half by himself."

Merton was euphoric. He had written to a stranger as an Other, a Thou, and the stranger had responded in kind. "*Everything* hangs on the possibility of such understanding which forms our interior bond," he wrote in his journal. ". . . This simple and human dialogue with Pasternak and a few others like him . . . is to me the true Kingdom of God, which is still so clearly, and evidently, 'in the midst of us.'"

He wrote to Pasternak again after reading *Dr. Zhivago*. "The great business of our time," he declared, "is this: for one man to find himself in another one who is on the other side of the world." The novel was full of sentences he might have written and characters he felt he knew. In fact, he confided, Dr. Zhivago's faithful companion, Lara, was a woman he had already met—and went on to share "the scandalous secret of a monk who is in love with a girl, and a Jew at that!"

It was October 23, 1958. That day, in Stockholm, Pasternak was announced as the recipient of the Nobel Prize in Literature. In the monastery, where news of the world was announced only briefly on Sundays, Merton had trouble keeping up with the events that followed. Pasternak was expelled from the official Soviet writers' union and ordered to decline the prize; at the same time he was invited to escape to the West. He declined the prize and the invitation to freedom, saying he preferred to live out his life in Moscow. At his dacha, he was beseiged by reporters and deluged with mail, even as Western writers—Eliot, Camus, and the like—decried the Soviets' handling of him.

Then he disappeared. The Soviets claimed he had gone to London; the Western writers, smelling a lie, feared he had been sent to Siberia, never to return. Merton was heartsick. Pasternak had told a friend that Merton's prayers had "saved his life." Now his life was in peril.

To his prayers Merton added an essay on the Pasternak affair, which he would revise repeatedly in light of events. He opened it by complaining that Pasternak's genius had been obscured by other people's definitions—"Christian, Communist; anti-Christian, anti-Communist; liberal, reactionary; personalist, romantic, etc."—then proceeded to define Pasternak in precisely the terms in which he would have defined himself, as a kind of dialogic personalist, whose "spiritual genius is essentially and powerfully solitary," but whose solitude made him "capable of extraordinarily intimate and understanding contacts with men all over the face of the earth."

By the time Pasternak turned up in London, alive and well, he was every Western writer's Other, the artist on the run from repressive society.

Merton's next letter, on December 15, was aggrieved and possessive, as if their intimacy had been violated. He likened Pasternak to Job, "surrounded not by three or four misguided comforters, but by a whole world of madmen," who had not "understood one word of what you have written." He warned him about the perils of fame and told him to be wary of Hollywood.

Was Merton obsessed, or admirably open and unguarded? From his letters it is hard to tell. The mawkish emotionalism of them suggests how unschooled Merton's feelings for other people were; at the same time, it suggests how unreservedly committed Merton was to treating the Other as a Thou. If he felt mystically bonded to the Other, he would say so. If he felt grandiose, convinced that such bonds were that of the Mystical Body of Christ, he would not hide it. He had nothing to lose but his pride.

It was Pasternak who lowered the flame of the correspondence. To a belated, fond, weary, overburdened reply, he added a postscript: "Don't write me, don't abash me with your boundless bounty. The next turn to renew the correspondence will be mine."

And then he was dead, of natural causes. In his journal, Merton wrote: "Pasternak died Monday. His story is finished. It now remains to be understood."

Merton's program of Russian reading had led him to *The Captive Mind*, Czeslaw Milosz's account of life under Soviet Communism. Out in the tool-shed, Merton wrote Milosz a letter, praising *The Captive Mind* as a statement of a "third position" akin to his own—"a position of integrity, which refuses subjection to the pressures of the two massive groups ranged against each other in the world."

Milosz, a Lithuanian living in Paris, replied by return mail. He was as lonesome in Paris as Merton was in the monastery. The "warm and brotherly letter," he told Merton, "created already a tie between us."

Like Merton, Milosz presented himself as a representative figure whose struggles were those of his generation; and Merton read his story as a distant commentary on his own experience, a report by a man whose sentimental education had been a good deal less sentimental than his own. Milosz, too, had traveled as a boy and come of age intending to make a life in poetry. Then war broke out. Merton had entered the cloister in Kentucky; Milosz had joined the underground resistance in Warsaw. "Had I then chosen immigration, my life would certainly have followed a very different course," he wrote. "But my knowledge of the crimes which Europe has witnessed in the twentieth century would be less direct, less concrete than it is."

Merton had taken a vow of poverty; Milosz had had poverty thrust upon him, until "the shabby worker's overall which I was wearing was all I possessed in the world." Merton had embraced "elected silence," a purposeful exile from the world; Milosz saw exile as "the worst of all misfortunes," a circumstance that enforced his otherness, barred him from firsthand experience of the life of his country, and estranged him from the Polish language, in which he continued to write poetry.

Merton had written a coming-of-age story, Milosz an anatomy of a whole society. And while Merton sought to close the gap between literature and life, so that he lived the life he had read about, Milosz saw this as the approach of totalitarianism, recalling the awful moment when the people of

Eastern Europe realized "that their fate could be influenced directly by intricate and abstruse books of philosophy [and when] their bread, their work, their private lives began to depend on this or that decision in disputes on principles to which, until then, they had never paid any attention."

The Captive Mind was Milosz's explanation of how this "New Faith" had captured the minds of Eastern Europe; and in his account, it had been embraced for the same reasons, and with the same rebellious ardor, with which Merton had embraced church and cloister. The New Faith spoke to the modern person's yearning for order, unity, harmony, and a superintending design. It offered the lonely self a sense of meaning in life. It appealed to the spirit of noble self-sacrifice and obedience to a higher authority. It did so by affirming that, for all its restrictions, its privations, its arbitrary rules and rites, it offered a life superior to the life lived in modern capitalist societies, which was vulgar, escapist, foolishly full of optimism.

Milosz illustrated the power of the New Faith by telling the stories of four writers, representative figures—Alpha, Beta, Gamma, Delta—who had embraced it in different ways. In the story of the one called Alpha—a Polish novelist named Jerzy Andrzjewski—Merton saw parallels with his own life: early success with a novel about a priest, shame over its popularity, a deep yearning to be a moralist rather than an artist, and yet a shrillness in his moralizing, which was shallowly rooted. "What he knew about man was based on his own subjective experiences within the four walls of his room," Milosz coolly observed. "His Catholicism was no more than a cover; he toyed with it as did many twentieth-century Catholics, trying to clothe his nudity in an esteemed, Old World cloak."

Against these four writers Milosz set himself, the independent writer. He had no obvious creed or dogma. His position was one he had found on his own through hard experience and embodied in absolute personal integrity. He thought for himself and stood alone.

For Merton, Milosz was a living reproach, and in their first letters Merton seemed almost ashamed to identify himself as a monk. But as he learned that Milosz was "crypto-religious," Catholic in temperament and respectful of the Church in Poland, he sought to enlarge their common ground, and their exchange became a dialogue between a crypto-religious man and an overtly religious one. Milosz, writing in English with a primitive eloquence, grounded his position in a suspicion of "today's longing for any, even the most illusory, certainty." In his view the real religious person lives in uncertainty, thrives on it, as the handmaid of mystery. "It is not so that I would like to understand what is mystery," he explained. "But one thing is to trace the limits of mystery and state clearly where the unsolvable contradiction of existence starts, another thing is to swim in the vague, as, I suspect, the theologians mostly do."

They exchanged work. Milosz sent novels, Merton a miscellany of published books. Milosz withheld his judgment. Finally, he commented on *The Sign of Jonas* in such a way as to appraise Merton's work as a whole. The book, he told Merton, had given him an impression of life in a monastery and had shown that monastic life need not be dull. "But the usefulness of your book is limited for somebody who is seriously interested in 'anatomy of faith' "—and had little to say to someone crypto-religious like himself. "The question tortures today many people: how one believes, what are the contents of faith, in any case those translatable into notions and images . . . ," he explained. "Your diary describes your internal country in its results," but not its causes.

The reader—Milosz summed up—"is eager to learn (gradually) what is the image of the world in Thomas Merton. In a period when the image accepted by majority is clear: Sky, no pity, stone wasteland, life ended by death. I imagine a reader who says: he possessed a secret, he succeeded in solving the puzzle, his world is harmonious, yet in his diary he tells already about sequences when we would be ready to follow him in 5 volumes through a very vision of the world redeemed by Christ." The problem with Merton's work was that he described the life of faith, not how one came to believe in the first place—which was what the modern person truly needed to know.

It was the most precise critique Merton had ever received, a dialogue with a writer who was at once Other and counterpart, and it forced him to clarify his understanding of religious faith for himself as well. In an earlier letter, he had stated his position in the terms of existentialist philosophy. "The only thing to be regretted without qualification is for a man to be perfectly adapted to totalitarian society," he wrote. "Then he is indeed beyond hope. Hence we should all be sick in some way. We should all feel near to despair in some sense because this semi-despair is the normal form taken by hope in a time like ours. Hope without any tangible evidence on which to rest. Hope in spite of the sickness that fills us. Hope married to a firm refusal to accept any palliatives or anything that cheats hope by pretending to relieve apparent despair."

To strengthen the point, he stated it again, this time in a biblical idiom, using the plural pronoun, the better to capture the plight he and Milosz had in common. "In the end, it comes down to the old story that we are sinners, but that this is our hope because sinners are the ones who attract to themselves the infinite compassion of God," he wrote. "To be a sinner, to want to be pure, to remain in patient expectation of the divine mercy and above all to forgive and love others, as best we can, this is what makes us Christians."

After the publication of A Good Man Is Hard to Find Flannery O'Connor had returned to her second novel, and an early chapter appeared in a quarterly in the fall of 1955. She was not pleased with the way it was going, however, and the title she gave the chapter—"You Can't Be Any Poorer Than Dead"—suggests the exasperation she felt about it. "My novel is at an impasse," she reported early the next year. "In fact it has been at one for as long as I can remember."

She turned to other writing. She started writing a short story ("It was like escaping from the penitentiary"). She wrote some book reviews for the *Bulletin*. She had been asked to give a lecture on "The Significance of the Short Story," and she worked up a "yammer" about "The Freak in Modern Fiction" instead. Like her novel, her stories had attracted freakish admirers, whose letters she delightedly answered: several patients in insane asylums, a truck driver who insisted that a good man really wasn't so hard to find, and a woman who read "A Temple of the Holy Ghost" as a lesbian allegory, prompting a letter which even O'Connor later acknowledged "surpassed my usual rudeness and achieved an air of superiority all out of proportion to my character."

A Good Man Is Hard to Find found congenial admirers as well—youngish male college professors, mainly—and O'Connor answered their letters at once graciously and bitterly, taking their understanding as an occasion to say how misunderstood she was. She thanked Andrew Lytle of the *Sewanee Review* for recognizing the "religious element" in her stories, which "nobody who reviews them cares to see." To Ben Griffith of Bessie Tift Women's College in Georgia she griped about the "stupid" and "terrible" reviews of her book, and added, "My editor wrote me that the book was selling better than anything on their list except Thomas Merton—which doesn't say much for their list, I guess."

Proud, confident, self-deprecating, offhandedly comic, at once traditional and independent, eager to hear other people's thoughts about her work but determined that her own thoughts should prevail: O'Connor's manner in her correspondence, as distinctive as that in her fiction, was already in place, and already being preserved in a sheaf of carbon copies next to her typewriter, when a letter came from Elizabeth Hester, a reader in Atlanta, who proposed that the stories in *A Good Man Is Hard to Find* were stories about God.

In her farmhouse study, O'Connor crafted a long reply. "I am very pleased to have your letter," she began. "Perhaps it is even more startling to find someone who recognizes my work for what I try to make it than it is for you to find a God-conscious writer near at hand. The distance is 87 miles but I feel the spiritual distance is shorter."

She went on, the remarks coming forth fully formed; although she was addressing Miss Hester, her motivations were various—she was replying to her critics, thinking aloud, and answering the questions that Harvey Breit, on the air in New York, had failed to ask her:

I write the way I do because (not though) I am a Catholic. This is a fact and nothing covers it like a bald statement. However, I am a Catholic peculiarly possessed of the modern consciousness, that thing Jung describes as unhistorical, solitary, and guilty. To possess this *within* the Church is to bear a burden, and a necessary burden for the conscious Catholic. It's to feel the contemporary situation at the ultimate level.

I think that the Church is the only thing that is going to make the terrible world we are coming to endurable; the only thing that makes the Church endurable is that somehow she is the body of Christ and that on this we are fed. It seems to be a fact that you have to suffer as much from the Church as for it but if you believe in the divinity of Christ, you have to cherish the world at the same time that you struggle to endure it. This may explain the lack of bitterness in the stories.

The notice in *The New Yorker* was not only moronic, it was unsigned. It was a case in which it is easy to see that the moral sense has been bred out of certain sections of the population, like the wings have been bred off certain chickens to produce more white meat on them. This is a generation of wingless chickens, which I suppose is what Nietzsche meant when he said God was dead.

I am mighty tired of reading reviews that call *A Good Man Is Hard to Find* brutal and sarcastic. The stories are hard but they are hard because there is nothing harder or less sentimental than Christian realism. I believe that there are many rough beasts now slouching toward Bethlehem to be born and that I have reported on the progress of a few of them, and when I see these stories described as horror stories I am always amused because the reviewer always has hold of the wrong horror.

You were very kind to write to me and the measure of my appreciation must be to ask you to write me again. I would like to know who this is who understands my stories.

In Elizabeth Hester's letter, O'Connor envisioned a correspondence unlike any she had undertaken. She had been reading Hopkins's letters to Robert Bridges, in which the Jesuit poet explained work that no one but his friend had read; and in them she found, it appears, not only a seed of her theory of the grotesque,* but also an ideal of the religious artist's correspondence: a particular friendship, at once literary and religious, which was not an exchange between equals but a dialogue between writer and reader, with posterity always in sight.

Her letter naturally called forth a reply, in which Hester evidently introduced herself as a single woman, thirty-two years old, who lived with an aunt, worked as a clerk in an office, and spent her evenings reading fiction and philosophy. But O'Connor kept her ideal in mind. "My audience are the people who think God is dead. At least these are the people I am conscious of writing for," she told Hester, and proceeded to explain religious faith in existentially bleak terms. Jesus was no realist: he was either God or a liar. Dogma is an "instrument of freedom," a protector of mystery. Religion is not a "blueprint" but an act of faith: "When I ask myself how I know I believe, I have no satisfactory answer at all, no assurance at all, no feeling at all. I can only say with Peter, Lord I believe, help me in my unbelief . . ."

She worried that Hester might not care to keep writing, whereas she was "afflicted with time." But Hester wrote back, and their correspondence was begun, a dialogue between Milledgeville and Atlanta, country and city, writer and reader, Self and Other, I and Thou.

Their correspondence—O'Connor's side of it, that is—dominates *The*

---

*"It seems to me that the poetical language of an age shd. be the current language heightened," Hopkins wrote to Bridges, "to any degree heightened and unlike itself, but not (I mean normally: freaks and graces are another thing) an obsolete one."

Habit of Being, and it has shaped the interpretation of O'Connor's fiction more than anything else she wrote. That is just as she wanted it. In undertaking such a correspondence, she wrote for "public consumption," and she later made provisions in her will for the letters to be published. She remarked that she would trade a hundred readers in the present for ten readers ten years later or one reader a century further on, and she wrote to Elizabeth Hester as if to the reader of the future, so that that reader might know who she was and what she was about.

She called her new friend Miss Hester at first, dropping the title after a few months. In *The Habit of Being,* however (for she asked that her privacy be respected), Elizabeth Hester is called "A," and the letter A, and the anonymity it preserves, gives the correspondence, tender and profound in its own right, an added dimension of mystery and intimacy. It makes O'Connor's stalwart correspondent a figure of the imagination—a clerk out of Kafka, living a secret life of the mind, or a Hawthornean heroine, emblazoned like Hester Prynne, the dark lady of American letters.

Above all, the letter A makes this unseen correspondent a surrogate for the reader, allowing us to enter into the correspondence more fully than we otherwise might. It enables us to identify with her; it invites us to put ourselves in the Other's place and read O'Connor's letters as if they are addressed to each of us, which they are.

I am learning to walk on crutches and I feel like a large stiff anthropoid ape who has no cause to be thinking of St. Thomas or Aristotle; however, you are making me more of a Thomist than I ever was before and an Aristotelian where I never was before. I am one, of course, who believes that man is created in the image and likeness of God. I believe that all creation is good but that what has free choice is more completely God's image than what does not have it; also I define humility different from you. . . . I really don't think *folly* is a wise word to use in connection with these orthodox beliefs or that you should call Aristotle "foolish and self-idolizing." At least, not until you have coped with all the intricacies of his thought.

That is from a typical letter from O'Connor to Hester. Hester, it appears, has made a blunt point; O'Connor, only slightly less bluntly, seeks to set her right.

She would write twenty-five letters in the first year, apportioning out the details of her personal life so that the character who emerges is endearingly complicated, an intellectual in spite of herself—each overbearing aspect offset by one homely and charming, each hard saying of Catholic dogma softened with humor and modesty. Knowing that Hester was awed by her reputation, such as it was, she strove to show that she was Just Folks, and the tension between her brilliancy and her disavowal of it is the heart of the correspondence. She had gone to the Iowa Writers' Workshop and knew Robert Lowell and the Tates but claimed her biggest influence was "Slop with a capital S." She read the *Summa Theologica* before going to bed each night, like a bedtime story; and "if my mother were to come in during this process and say 'Turn off that light. It's late,' I with lifted finger and broad bland beatific expression, would reply, 'On the contrary, I answer that the light, being eternal and limitless, cannot be turned off. Shut your eyes.' " She already had an impressive library—fiction, philosophy, theology, the literature of the South—but her workspace was "a rat's nest of old papers, clippings, torn manuscripts, ancient quarterlies, etc. etc. etc."

Soon they were swapping books through the mail—O'Connor from her shelves, Hester from the public library—turning the brown packing paper inside out and using it over again.

In time, each told the other what she looked like. O'Connor had pictured Hester as "a lady 7 ft. tall, weighing 95 lbs."; now she had to picture her as a woman her own size—"five three and in the neighborhood of one thirty"—with "thick hornrimmed spectacles, a Roman nose, and ash-blonde hair," resembling "a ginger beer bottle with the head of Socrates. Being damned by a faint prettiness turned a mite sour, I wish I looked like that," O'Connor added, "but as I don't I'm at least glad I can write somebody who does." She sent Hester her iconish self-portrait with a pheasant cock, explaining that it was "not exactly the way I look but it's the way I feel. It's better looked at from a distance."

Mainly, they exchanged ideas, in a kind of lovers' quarrel of the mind. They would choose a topic—a book, a writer, a personal conviction, a point of theology—and engage in disputation about it until they wore each other out. Who wrote better about the poor, Céline or Nelson Algren? Did it matter that Céline was a Fascist? Wasn't O'Connor herself a Fascist in countenancing the use of force in the history of the Church? Wasn't it true that doctrines like the Incarnation were no longer "emotionally satisfying"? O'Connor's letters leave the impression that she always got the last word, rebutting Hester colorfully and absolutely. Algren was "a talent wasted by sentimentalism," to whom Céline was "superior" whatever his politics. The Church in principle was extremely wary of force: "I know her hair-raising history, of course, but principle must be separated from policy." Whether or not the Incarnation was emotionally satisfying to the modern person, "I must say that the thought of everyone lolling about in an emotionally satisfying faith is repugnant to me." She explained, "The truth does not change according to our ability to stomach it emotionally . . . there are long periods in the lives of all of us, and of the saints, when the truth revealed by faith is hideous, emotionally disturbing, downright repulsive."

The letters kept coming, one each week, full of brilliancies and generalizations. They are the kind of letters one writer generally sends to another writer, not to an admiring reader she has never met. They left Hester astonished, and made her suspect that this "celebrity" Catholic was writing to her as an act of charity. O'Connor sought to assure her otherwise. "I have no letter-writing duties," she insisted, except for the letter she was obliged to write each Tuesday to her elderly Cousin Kate in Savannah. ". . . Be it understood that my writing to you is a free act, unconnected with character, duty or compulsion."

So it was, but her motives in writing the letters were various and complex, and as the correspondence gained a life of its own, she suggested the ways in which it served her purposes more than she had anticipated, making her, at the age of thirty, a woman of letters at last.

Through this correspondence she clarified the nature of her work, instructing Hester in how it ought to be read. When Hester read "Good Country People" as autobiographical, for example, O'Connor rose to the defense of art as art: there was much of her in Hulga, yes, and the lack of sexuality in her work spoke to a lack in her own experience; but as for Hulga's lack of love, that was all made up. "That my stories scream to you that I have never consented to be in love with anybody is merely to prove that they are screaming an historical inaccuracy. I have God help me consented to this frequently."

Hester also prompted O'Connor "to clarify what I think on various subjects or at least to think on various subjects." O'Connor was a contrarian if ever there was one; whereas in fiction she had to write indirectly—dramatizing her concerns, taking the reader's preconceptions into account and subordinating her ideas, and her personality, to the good of the whole—in letters she was free to write as directly as she wished, and the letters to Hester are full of a delight in this new liberty, as the rules are relaxed and she speaks as herself and in her own voice.

In their exchange about the depiction of poverty in fiction, O'Connor told Hester that in writing of the poor one had to consider what one lacked oneself. Her stories, as Hester had pointed out, were stories about God, and yet she herself lacked the usual religious experiences. She was "not a mystic" and did not "lead a holy life." Her sins were those of the "garden variety"—pride, envy, gluttony, sloth—"and what is more to the point, my virtues are as timid as my vices." As a cradle Catholic, whose faith had never been sorely tried, she lacked even the experience of the archetypal modern believer, who found a way to faith through despair and doubt. "If you live today you breathe in nihilism. In or out of the Church, it's the gas you breathe," she told Hester. "If I hadn't had the Church to fight it with or to tell me the necessity of fighting it, I would be the stinkingest logical positivist you ever saw right now"—and that she wasn't was a result of her Catholic upbringing, which had made her ready for the experiences that put faith to the test. Religious conviction, for her, had come prior to experience, and she was "only slowly coming to experience things that I have all along accepted."

She was an odd kind of believer, one situated in modernity but not formed by it, indeed formed in opposition to modernity and determined to maintain her independence from it through her religion. In Elizabeth Hester she saw her opposite, the modern unbeliever, the kind of person she wrote about. "I will never have the experience of the convert, or of the one who fails to be converted, or even in all probability of the formidable sinner; but your effort not to be seduced by the Church moves me greatly," she told Hester. "God permits it for some reason though it is the devil's greatest work of hallucination."

In that sentence, with its confident proclamation of what God allows, can be heard the evangelical motive that runs all through the correspondence. "I can't climb down off the high powered defense reflex whateveritis . . . ," O'Connor confessed to Hester. "If you were Pius XII, my communications would still sound as if they came from a besieged defender of the faith." Like Hazel Motes or Mason Tarwater, the character who was taking shape in her second novel, she was wholly committed to her own point of view and determined to express it to others as vividly as possible. Her point of view was that of Christian orthodoxy, and whereas in fiction she was pledged to approach the reader indirectly, to embed her beliefs in the work itself, in her letters she could frankly seek to persuade Hester of the truth of the Catholic faith.

The wish to evangelize, for some readers the least attractive aspect of O'Connor's correspondence, is for others its essence. Although she claimed a lack of religious experience, the power of her letters comes from the sense that they *are* written from experience, with an authentic knowledge of the life of faith and a genuine desire to share it with another.

In *The Third Hour* she had read about Simone Weil, the wartime martyr to scrupulosity whose attraction to the Church was mixed with contempt for its role in the world, and early in the correspondence she asked whether Hester had read Weil's work: "I never have and doubt if I would understand her if I did: but from what I have read about her, I think she must have been a very great person."

French, Jewish, agnostic, a philosopher, fluent in Greek, politically engaged, Weil was for O'Connor an authentic Other. They were alike in their precocity, their concern with their stubborn independence.

But in their approach to religious faith they were opposites. For O'Connor, faith came first, and suffering arrived as a cross she had not chosen to bear; the doctrine of the Body of Christ explained the pain in her bones, making her confident that she was joined to others, and even to God. For Weil, faith was the end of the ordeal: she had sought experience, especially suffering, finally in starvation, in the hope that it might yield the experience of God.

Hester had indeed read Weil, and she sent O'Connor *Waiting for God*, the volume of *pensées* whose skeletal character was thought to suggest the spirit of the age. In reply O'Connor made Weil a running topic of dialogue with her real-life Other. She acknowledged receipt of the book, and went on: "The life of this remarkable woman still intrigues me while much of what she writes, naturally, is ridiculous to me. Her life is almost a perfect blending of the Comic and the Terrible, which two things may be opposite sides of the same coin. In my own experience, everything I have written is more terrible than it is funny, or only funny because it is terrible, or only terrible because it is funny. Well Simone Weil's life is the most comical life I have ever read about and the most truly tragic and terrible."

She added, "If I were to live long enough as an artist and develop to the proper extent, I would like to write a comic novel about a woman—and what is more comic and terrible than the angular proud intellectual woman approaching God inch by inch with ground teeth?"

Perhaps this remark made Hester think that O'Connor saw *her* religious struggle, too, as material for a novel. In any case, she bristled at O'Connor's image of Weil, and O'Connor, in her next letter, tried to clarify it. She thought Weil a woman of "great courage" who was "more intelligent and better than I am." She insisted that she wouldn't dare write about Weil because she could not dominate her the way she could her usual characters. In calling Weil's life both comic and terrible she was "paying her the highest tribute I can, short of calling her a saint, which I don't believe she was. . . . Of course, I can only say, as you point out, this is what I see, not, this is what she is—which only God knows."

O'Connor declared that Weil's pilgrimage toward the Catholic Church was remarkable, "considering where she started from." She felt the same way about Elizabeth Hester's. She was writing a new short story, about a proud farm woman who would be gored by a bull which showed up outside her window "like a patient god come to woo her"; but the real story in her life was that of Hester's fitful approach to the Church, which she had helped to bring about, and the strongest writing she did that fall was in her letters to Hester, which had become an odd correspondence course in Christian doctrine, with O'Connor as the witty and all-knowing teacher and Hester as the student with a crush on her instructor.

After six months of letters Hester sent O'Connor a photograph of herself, along with the news that she wished to be baptized a Catholic. "I'm never prepared for anything," O'Connor replied, impressed by the fact that while she had had baptism "thrust upon me" as an infant, Hester was choosing it for herself as an adult. The opposite of dumbstruck, she rattled on, "To my credit it can be said anyway that I never considered you unbaptized. There are three kinds, of water, blood, and desire, and with the last I thought you as baptized as I am."

Suddenly there was a new warmth in her letters, as the Other, the opposite, became a conspirator, a fellow member of the Mystical Body of Christ.

Hester would be baptized in Atlanta during Mass at Eastertime. O'Connor wanted to mark the occasion but wasn't sure how. She sent Hester a draft of "Greenleaf." She ordered Hester a breviary like her own. On Easter, she told Hester, she would go to Mass in Milledgeville with Hester in mind, "holding some kind of figurative candle and croaking the proper responses." She would receive Communion "for" Hester, "and since we will then share

Clockwise from top left: Dorothy Day at her cottage on Staten Island; Thomas Merton upon arrival at Columbia; Walker Percy in Germany; Flannery O'Connor on First Communion Day

From top: Day (in center row, third from left) with an early aggregation of Catholic Workers—Peter Maurin is to her left; a soup line outside St. Joseph's House; the absolute pacifist in wartime

Merton with editors of the *Jester* at Columbia; his sketch of himself in the window of the apartment on Perry Street; on the day of his ordination at Gethsemani

Percy (right) with his brother LeRoy (far left) and Shelby Foote in Greenville

Percy (with leg outstretched) outside the Carolina movie house in Chapel Hill

O'Connor (at right) reviewing
the college literary magazine

O'Connor wearing a muskrat
fur coat in Iowa City

Merton as the author of an unlikely best-seller (*left*), and as Master of the Scholastics, set up in the toolshed he called St. Anne's

Two images of Day: a Fritz Eichenberg print for
The Long Loneliness (*left*), and the sketch that
accompanied the *New Yorker*'s profile

Day protesting against civil-
defense drills in Washington
Square Park

O'Connor at a party given in Milledgeville upon the publication of *Wise Blood* (*left*), and with her portrait of herself and a pheasant cock, c. 1953

O'Connor with her
self-portrait, c. 1960 (*left*),
and on the grounds at
Andalusia

THE CATHOLIC WORKER

Vol. XXVIII No. 4 November, 1961 Subscription: 25c Per Year Price 1c

The Shelter Ethic

By THOMAS MERTON

The October issue of **The Catholic Worker** carried an article by me entitled "The Root of War," an excerpt from a book to be published in December, **New Seeds of Contemplation.** This article did not intend to enter directly into the current controversy about the legitimacy of defending one's safety in a fallout shelter by keeping others out at the point of a gun. However, discussion of the article has involved me implicitly in the controversy and therefore an explicit statement of my position has become necessary. I feel this is something much more than a simple "moral case." It is a symptom of the confusion and pervasive madness of our society.

What precisely is the question? A great deal of discussion was aroused in October by an article of an associate editor of **America,** Fr. L. C. McHugh, S.J. Rather, to speak more accurately, a great deal of discussion was raised by the confusing and one-sided presentation of that article in the national press. The article itself is perfectly reasonable, and it contains nothing with which a professor of ethics would disagree. It states clearly that the natural law guarantees everyone a right to defend his life and the safety of his dependents, and that he may even defend his life with violence, risking the death of the unjust aggressor, **if violence is clearly the last available recourse.** It also makes quite clear that the violence may only be used at the actual moment of assault, and **when the assault has been initiated with evident intent to kill.** Lethal violence may never be used merely to forestall the possibility of assault. Finally, the violence must be limited to what is strictly necessary, and if possible the death of the unjust aggressor must be avoided.

These are purely and simply the principles laid down by Catholic moral philosophy, and it might be pertinent to observe, at this point, that they are definitely applicable in the case of what our missile

people now refer to as "first strike" in nuclear war: by such principles as these, one wonders how the idea of a surprise attack on an enemy who is only feared as a **potential** aggressor could be accepted and blessed by any Christian moralist. Quite apart from the frightful injustice of the death and maiming of millions of innocent people, the mere fact of a surprise "first strike" on an all-out destructive scale, when no aggression has been initiated by the enemy, is clearly unjust and utterly unacceptable to a Christian moralist.

Most of the reports in the national press evidently failed to draw any attention to the most important paragraph in Father McHugh's article. I quote:

"To say that one has a right to employ violence in defense of life is not to say that one has the duty to do so. Indeed, in the Christian view, there is a great merit in turning the other cheek and bearing evils patiently out of the love of God." Fr. McHugh hastens to add that this is "heroism" and a "dedication to a full Christian ethic that is far above what God requires under pain of eternal loss."

He then points out that an "unattached individual" may well resign his place in the shelter in favor of someone else. This is excellent.

I have no intention whatever of criticizing Father McHugh, and I have absolutely no complaint about his principles. My intention is to speak about the whole situation that makes such discussion inevitable, and which dictated certain assumptions which to my mind completely falsify the Christian moral perspective in this problem. What is disturbing today is the widespread and unreserved acceptance of these assumptions.

What are they?

First of all that a shallow backyard shelter itself makes any sense. That one can surely save his life by taking refuge in one. That it is really worth the trouble having such a shelter, and that it is even so important to get into it that one can go to the lengths of killing another person in order to keep him out. This whole mentality is deeply disturbing. It seems to me to be equivalent to saying that if the only food left in the

(Continued on page 5)

Cuba and the Christian

By Dianne Gannon

We are saved not because we are worthy, but only in God's love and the grace He gives us in the knowledge of our weakness. With this in mind, we can never become self-righteous, for we recognize thus that what we see in the other may well be a reflection of ourselves. We are told that if we see a beam in the other's eye, we should look to our own eye first. St. Paul instructs us: "Brethren, even if a person is caught doing something wrong, you who are spiritual instruct such a one in a spirit of meekness, considering thyself, lest thou also be tempted. Bear one another's burdens, and so you will fulfill the law of Christ. For if anyone thinks himself to be something, whereas he is nothing, he deceives himself."

Essentially the Christian vocation is to bear witness to Christ's love. But with so many evils and abuses in our society, which is one where only those "lucky" enough survive, a society maintained by forcing the weak to remain weak, sometimes it is difficult to know how to speak. In this impure world, a world which has not yet come to fulfillment in Him, how can one learn without rejecting, and in turn, instruct?

The complexity of the Cuban situation makes an evaluation of Cuba and our attitude toward the revolution all the more difficult, but if we allow ourselves to "circumcise our hearts," to keep ourselves unhardened, as the prophet Jeremia calls out for us to do, perhaps it would then be possible to seek out the Christian vision. We must continually call to mind the fact that our life should be a straining after the Kingdom of God. It is for this alone that we must work.

Perhaps I may recall an incident which is repeated more than daily at Siloe House, for one learns best from children: they have not yet learned to dress up their motives in logical patterns. And quite often they get into squabbles about the most minute differences. The fight begins. But none can stop because he must have the last word, the last punch. How many times I must have said, "What difference who started it right now, you've got to be the one to stop it!" They know so well what our attitude toward this finger-pointing is that Miguel will sometimes say, after my latest pronouncement, looking up at me with his mischevious

(Continued on page 4)

A. de Bethune

Mississippi and "MOM"

By Terry Sullivan

I first saw the sovereign state of Mississippi on June 6th, 1961, when I came up by bus from New Orleans to Jackson, one of a group of seven Freedom Riders. We were arrested and tried the same day, sentenced to 4½ months including fine time, and joined 65 others arrested before us. The older man in my party, Newell Weber from East Orange, New Jersey, and I served our full time, accompanied by six others from later groups with 6½ months to serve, all of them still being held at Hinds County Jail in Jackson.

From the experience of the Freedom Rides two things stand out in my mind. One is the stubbornness of the state of Mississippi. The other is the militancy of a small group of Negro students from Nashville, who have entrenched themselves in Jackson and McComb, Mississippi, as the first phase of "MOM," a "Move on Mississippi."

Mississippi

Mississippi is said to be the most economically backward of the states. It still preserves much of the plantation tradition, 3 out of 4 people in Mississippi live on farms, and its largest city, Jackson, has a little over 100,000 population. That partly accounts for Mississippi's position as the deepest of the deep South states and the bulwark of Southern segregation. That reputation, Mississippi audacity to arrest the first group of Freedom Riders. In succeeding weeks, that became the pattern. On the long route from Washington, D.C., to New Orleans, La., through Maryland, Virginia, North Carolina, South Carolina, Georgia, Alabama, Mississippi and Louisiana, the road block was Jackson. The riders from the east passed unmolested, under heavy police protection now, through Alabama until they were stopped in Jackson. The riders from the west and south, such as my group from New Orleans, knew in advance that we would get to Jackson and no farther.

What was more surprising was that Mississippi held the ground all summer long against approximately 300 Freedom Riders, crowding the jails, an act which was ccompanied by national publicity. Not only did it continue to arrest 11 who breached the segregation in the public terminals, but it fought back with legal stratagems —for instance, the judicial ruling in late summer that Freedom Riders out on appeal could not return to jail without standing trial and the psychological pressure to discourage the prisoners, depriving them of all normal prison comforts except for the Bible and a pair of shorts. Mississippi was successful in that only a handful of Freedom Riders stayed in prison to serve their sentences,

Letters From California

Here is a picture I thought you would like to have. It is "God made the sun, the moon and the stars." It is one of the many pictures made for me by Linda Smith —age 8. Linda is a migrant child who stayed a few days in the camp here in Corning where we are for the olive harvest. The camp is on the property on which a highway is to be built—so many of the migrant families are camping here during the harvest. Of course, there is no water or electricity but the police have not bothered us as yet. Linda was sick all the time she was here as she had run into an orchard which had just been sprayed. She and her brother and sister and parents live in an old trailer so tiny that they cannot all get in it at once. She and Rachel (my daughter) stayed in my bed all day bundled under the covers because it is almost freezing and neither our trailer nor theirs had windows or heat.

This morning Linda's family moved to Imperial Valley to work in the vegetables during the go South for the winter too when Benny finishes his job. He is working in a packing shed this year and I have been in camp all day with the children. Every afternoon I read a few stories and Rachel has been loaning her books to all her little friends here.

It is a terrible year for union organizing because the people are convinced that the AFL-CIO sold them out to the farmers when they abandoned the organizing drive and that their situation is hopeless. Some of them had believed that President Kennedy was going to help them but Public Law 78 passed again and this year there are more Mexicans than ever and almost no one else can get a job. Only here and there in a few areas the people are organizing themselves and trying to fight for better conditions. In Santa Cruz the Filipinos who work in the brussel-sprout harvest organized to ask for $1.25 an hour instead of a $1.00 an hour, which they have been getting.

Your issue which carried so

Center though many books still remain to be indexed. Mrs. Brickey has been ill this summer which makes everyone sad but nevertheless there have been some splendid fiestas at the Center this summer, and in the town to the South of Tracy, Paterson, the ladies' auxiliary of the AWOC gave a big fiesta for the benefit of the union strike fund. All the Tracy people wish you well and want me to thank you for writing about them in your paper. I forgot to tell you that Mrs. Brickey gave away over a thousand mason jars for canning this year, and many people canned food for the winter. I did a little canning myself but working and caring for baby Andy have kept me pretty busy, so I did less than I wanted to.

My best wishes to yourself and may the good work of the CATHOLIC WORKER prosper.

Liza Bowman

So much happens in a few months that it is hard to even

The November 1961 *Catholic Worker*—in which Merton and Day offered two different views on the use of violence in self-defense

Day looking out over the Lower East Side

Merton at a distance from the monastery he made famous (*above*), and returning to his hermitage

Merton reading
meditatively (*above*),
and celebrating Mass
at the hermitage
(Jacques Maritain is
at the right)

Percy at work, photographed by Jill Krementz, Covington, Louisiana

Dorothy Day, writer and editor (*left*); Dorothy Day, reformer and agitator

Percy with Lyn Hill's portrait of him, as photographed by Christopher R. Harris (*left*); Percy meeting John Paul II

the same actual food, you will know that your being where you are increases me and the other way around."

In Elizabeth Hester, O'Connor had found more than a close reader and a friend. She had won her first convert and disciple.

Dorothy Day sat in a pew in Old St. Patrick's on Mott Street, writing an open letter to the "Friends of the Catholic Worker." "In the light of our present difficulties it is necessary to restate our position and tell our readers again just what it is we are trying to do," she began, and asked rhetorically: What did it mean to perform the works of mercy? It meant to love God and try to do God's will. It meant to treat the least person as holy, since "Jesus told us that what we do to the least we do to Him." It meant to see others as one's brothers, since "St. Paul told us we are 'members of one another, and that when the health of one member suffers, the health of the whole body is lowered.' "

Over the years she had gained dozens of correspondents, to whom she wrote in spare moments on notecards which she always carried with her. But her most effective correspondence was conducted in the pages of the *Catholic Worker*, where, twice a year, she addressed the reader directly in open letters that, in appealing for donations, summed up what the movement was about and served to bind it together.

It was expensive to be poor, she liked to say, and it was especially expensive to practice voluntary poverty. No Catholic Worker received a salary, and no fees were paid for the articles in the paper. Yet the workers at St. Joseph's House were constantly in need of funds. The act of serving soup to several hundred people each day—112,500 meals in one six-month period, she estimated—required far more food than the communal farms had ever produced. As paper, printing, and postage costs rose, the price of the newspaper did not change, so that Flannery O'Connor could tell Elizabeth Hester the *Catholic Worker* had "the distinction of costing 25¢ a year—the ideal subscription rate." Volunteers were enlisted to fold and mail the paper, but the printer had to be paid.

The Catholic Workers' principles cut them off from the usual means of support. They refused to take out loans, incorporate, or register as a "charitable organization." Collecting interest would make currency, not labor, the measure of value; claiming nonprofit tax status would put them in league with Holy Mother the State; incorporation would smack of business, when

Christ urged his disciples to take no thought for the morrow. All would obscure their basic conviction that charity should be performed as a personal sacrifice.

"A great many of our friends tell us to put our paper on a businesslike basis," Day wrote early on. "But this isn't a business, it's a movement. And we don't know anything about business around here anyway. . . . So our friends may expect us to importune and to continue to ask, trusting that we shall receive."

So she asked of her readers, multiplying the loaves and fishes; and so the movement received—money for the purchase of the Houses of Hospitality and the communal farms; day-old bread, coffee, milk, and vegetables from local merchants; pots, tools, crockery, cutlery; shirts and pants and coats for the "clothes room" from neighbors and parishes; used cars to get from place to place.

The readers, too, received. Just as the Catholic Workers needed money to carry on, those who read the paper needed the sign of communal uprightness that the paper provided. Charity—*caritas*—would join the two together.

When Day sat down to write the Fall Appeal in 1955, the Catholic Workers were being evicted from their headquarters on Chrystie Street. The cause was fire-code violations, but their real violation, in her account, was their strict adherence to principle. Because they refused to be classed as a "religious group" or charitable organization, they were seen by the city as merely an aggregation of individuals, and their tenement building was subject to the exacting fire codes applied to personal residences, not those applied to businesses or churches or charities.

The city's quibbling over definitions prompted Day to define the movement with great and disdainful gusto. What was the Catholic Worker? The city had concluded that the Catholic Worker was not an institution—"not a multiple dwelling, a rest home, a convalescent home, a shelter or an asylum or a convent—and that, she argued, was a good thing. Institutions were ruining society. People were forfeiting their personal responsibilities to institutions like the government, which then had the arrogance to define the terms on which those responsibilities could be undertaken.

What, then, was the Catholic Worker? "We are a group of people living together under one roof," she declared. And yet they were not a group in any legal sense, since no contract bound them. They were individuals, volunteers—people who acted out of a sense of personal responsibility.

So they were being evicted because of the threat of fire? Well, they were there in the first place because of their experience of God, who was a "consuming fire."

It was an ingenious and effective piece of writing. The city's case against the Catholic Worker was dismissed in court, the episode was written up in the press, and dozens of people made the pilgrimage to Mott Street to offer donations—among them W. H. Auden, dressed as scruffily as a Bowery bum, who gave Day a check for $250.

Two years later Day began the fall appeal more tenderly, recalling the time an old woman, coming upon a man asleep on the sidewalk outside St. Joseph's House, had exclaimed that he was Jesus, her son. "He *was* Jesus Christ, shocking as it may seem, drunk as he was," Day explained, citing Seymour Glass from the Salinger stories in the *New Yorker*, who saw Jesus "in the bourgeois fat lady on the porch in the rocking chair."

Again she worked through definitions of the Catholic Worker: the Body of Christ, in which all are members of one another; a family, bound to one another by love. "Even those dread words, *pacifism* and *anarchism*, when you get down to it, mean that we try always to love, rather than coerce, 'to be what we want the other fellow to be,' to be the least, to have no authority over others, to begin with that microcosm *man*, or rather, with ourselves."

Concluding, she made an invitation to the reader, including each of them in the economy of love through her use of the plural pronoun. "We can each do so little physically. The best we can say is that it is very direct, very immediate. We keep passing on what we have as quickly as possible. We certainly can try to grow in love, and it is good practice, this giving what you've got, whether it is a cup of coffee or money to pay the grocery bill. We ask you in the name of St. Thérèse, on whose feast I write, and in the name of St. Francis, whose feast comes tomorrow. It is always a feast where love is, and where love is, God is."

It was an open letter, but a personal one as well. Where the statements of Aims and Purposes were left unsigned and addressed, in effect, to the world, each of the Appeals was written and signed by Day herself, a personal communiqué between author and Other.

And Walker Percy? He sat in the sunroom of the house in New Orleans, writing essays which served as his correspondence with the world.

The others had found counterparts through their letters—Merton through imaginative identification with distant writers, O'Connor by casting her partner as an adversary to be won over, Day in stirring epistles to the community that had gathered around her.

Percy was still exchanging letters with Shelby Foote, but his letters have not survived. In their stead, we have Percy's essays, each one odder and more roundabout than the last, as Percy sought to banish alienation the way he had described in "The Man on the Train"—to name the "predicament shared in common" in such a way that others would recognize it.

In "The Coming Crisis in Psychiatry" (published in *America*) he defined the terms of the predicament. "We all know perfectly well that the man who lives out his life as a consumer, a sexual partner, an 'other-directed' executive; who avoids boredom and anxiety by consuming tons of newsprint, miles of movie film, years of TV time; that such a man has somehow betrayed his destiny as a human being," he declared, appealing to the reader's sense of things. He went on to argue that psychiatry, by treating the human longing for transcendence as a symptom of illness, actually compounds such a person's alienation, leaving him estranged not only from himself and others but from his reason for being.

It was one thing for Percy to assert transcendence in a Catholic magazine, another to figure out for himself how transcendence should be approached.

"Metaphor as Mistake" (published in *Sewanee Review*) is a piece of literary criticism, an appraisal of several scholarly books. In philosophy and literary criticism, Percy begins, the typical metaphor is considered a mistake, a piece of illogic, since it calls one thing by the name of another—as in the biblical metaphor "flesh is grass," for example. But Percy, venturing into the "no-man's land" between the two disciplines, proposes that metaphor is a key to transcendence.

He does not reason his way to this proposition so much as wander toward it, hopscotching from point to point. A metaphor, he declares, does more than simply name a thing; it affirms the thing's existence or presence. It says, "This is how it is." The metaphor "flesh is grass" says that flesh is mortal, naming the human condition.

For a metaphor to work it must appeal to another person's unspoken sense of things—must validate "that which has already been privately apprehended but has gone unformulated for both of us."

This apprehended thing—"fugitive something"—is Being itself. Metaphor is a way to know Being. The structure of the world is metaphorical, and a metaphor bridges the gap between thing and Being—between Self and Other, between perception and reality, between the everyday and the transcendent—by naming it indirectly. "We can only *conceive* being, sidle up to it by laying something else alongside. We approach the thing not directly but by pairing, by apposing symbol and thing."

The argument is implicitly religious, but only in the last sentence of the essay does Percy invoke the Scholastic idea of the "analogy of being"—the idea that the natural world is the image of the supernatural one, and that we know "not as the angels know and not as dogs know but as men, who must know one thing through the mirror of another."

In the sunroom on Milan Street, he had reached a conclusion akin to those proposed by the others: Merton's call for a restoration of the metaphors for religious experience, O'Connor's notion of the artist's task as the "accurate naming of the things of God," Day's insistence that the Gospel is an instance of metaphor made real—that the poor stranger is not merely like Christ but *is* Christ, with all that this implies.[*]

In "Metaphor as Mistake," more than anywhere else, Percy seemed confident of a solution to the modern predicament. With "The Loss of the Creature," however, he resumed his search. It is an essay about the ways language stands between the self and reality. Although it is written in the third person, Percy's own self is oddly prominent here. Percy is not a doctor urging the reform of his discipline, not a humanist urging scientists and artists to communicate with one another. He is a person who finds the world he lives in shallow, fake, imitative, manipulative; when he speaks of the "radical loss of sovereignty" he wants us to feel his pain, and when he tells stories featuring typical characters the experience he is describing is his own.

He tells the story of a couple of tourists from Boston on a visit to the Grand Canyon. Seen with wonder by the Spanish explorer who first discovered it, the Grand Canyon is now the destination of the typical tour-bus sightseer, who cannot see the canyon as it really is, but only as it has "already been formulated—by picture postcard, geography book, tourist brochure, and the words *Grand Canyon*." The sightseer measures his experience

---

[*]Percy considered a passage of Shakespeare's in which Othello says he is "steep'd in poverty." A notorious critic had faulted the expression, saying that one cannot be steeped in an absence or a lack, can one? Percy—the argument would have delighted Dorothy Day—insisted otherwise, invoking the testimony of experience, which says that poverty is "a veritable something, very much a milieu with a smell and taste all its own, in which one is all too easily steep'd."

against a preformed idea. Instead of looking at the canyon—confronting it with his own experience—he photographs it. "There is no confrontation at all. At the end of forty years of preformulation and with the Grand Canyon yawning at his feet, what does he do? He waives his right of seeing and knowing and records symbols for the next forty years."

By 1958, when the essay was written, the argument about the premeditation of American life was a common one. But Percy pushes the point further, into the mind of the manipulated, arguing that even the best escapes from self-conscious calculation are doomed to failure.

He tells the story of an American couple on their honeymoon in Mexico. Having come so far, they find themselves in a tourist town among "a dozen other couples from the Midwest." Dismayed, they leave the town, get lost, and stumble on some natives performing a "corn dance" in a remote village. "The couple know at once that this is 'it.' They are entranced. They spend several days in the village, observing the Indians and being themselves observed with friendly curiosity." But have they really escaped the falsity of modern life? By no means. They announce the ritual's authenticity to each other, as if to verify it. They find they are eager for it to end—to end before its authenticity is somehow spoiled. Back home in America, they tell an ethnologist friend about it, eager to have an expert say that it is authentic; the next year, they return, bringing the ethnologist with them. He watches; they watch him. " 'Didn't we tell you?' they say at last. What they want from him is not ethnological explanations; all they want is his approval."

Percy's point—in the language of pilgrimage—is that the modern predicament makes pilgrimage impossible. In the modern world (now generally called postmodern), all experience is always secondhand, planned and described for one's consumption by others in advance. Even the rare authentically direct experience is spoiled by modern self-consciousness. The modern person is doomed to an imitation of life; the self cannot escape itself and know the world or the Other.

The self can try, however. That is Percy's real point. To the stories of hapless tourists he appends the story of a traveler, seen as he "carves his initials in a public place"—a museum, say. This traveler, Percy insists, has a good reason for doing so. "He is disinherited. He is deprived of his title over being. He knows very well that he is in a special sort of zone in which his only rights are the rights of a consumer. He moves like a ghost through the schoolroom, city streets, trains, parks, movies. He carves his initials as a last desperate measure to escape his ghostly role of consumer. He is saying in effect: I am not a ghost after all: I am a sovereign person. And he establishes his title [in] the only way remaining to him, by staking his claim over one square inch of wood or stone."

Percy concludes that the human person—the self—"is not something one can study and provide for; he is something one struggles for. But unless he also struggles for himself, unless he knows that there is a struggle, he is going to be just what the planners think he is." The remark (a paraphrase of a remark by Emmanuel Mounier, a French personalist) is the closest thing to a credo in all of Percy's work, and the image of the traveler carving his initials into the wood in the museum is his most vivid image of the religious artist, making his mark, in the end, for one Other only, writing in order to make clear that he exists.

The Catholic Workers' protest of the civil-defense drill had become an annual carnival of nonviolence: hundreds of sympathizers, a pack of reporters, a squadron of police. When Day, with numerous others, was arrested during the action in 1957 and sentenced to thirty days in jail, she became a spectacle to the world. The New York papers ran pictures of her being ushered toward a paddy wagon, wearing a prim black dress. Protestors massed outside the jail—the Women's House of Detention in Greenwich Village, on Sixth Avenue near St. Joseph's Church and the site of the old Hell Hole saloon—the way they had on behalf of Sacco and Vanzetti fifty years earlier.

Inside, Day meditated on the life of her favorite saint, Thérèse of Lisieux, the subject of a new book she was writing.

Jail was an unlikely site of devotion to the Little Flower, but Day was undeterred. In her sense of things, jail was an ideal place to practice Thérèse's Little Way, in which every bit of suffering endured, every illness and infirmity, every slight, small or large, was a "little way" to sacrifice oneself and grow closer to God. The reporter in her observed the indignities of the place—the rules, the searches, the idleness, the din, the regimen in which "every event seems calculated to intimidate and to render uncomfortable and ugly the life of the prisoner." The radical in her considered it a site of thwarted human freedom in its most elemental form. The Catholic in her saw a chance to "be on the other side for a change, for only by experiencing such things can one understand and have compassion for one's brother," and she was "glad to go to prison" in order to do so. "When I lay in jail thinking of these things, thinking of war and peace, and the problem of human freedom, of jails, drug addiction, prostitution, and the apathy of great masses of people who believe that nothing can be done—when I thought of these things, I was all the more confirmed in my faith in the little way of St. Thérèse," she wrote. "We do the minute things that come to hand, we pray our prayers, and beg also for an increase of faith—and God will do the rest."

Once out of jail she wrote a series of articles about the experience, and worked on the saint's life in her spare moments, writing in the midst of everyday life.

The book had been under contract since shortly after *The Long Loneliness* was published, but Day had struggled to get it started. In its particulars, Thérèse's life could hardly have been less like her own: devout parents who had raised nine children after taking a vow of chastity; a childhood spent reading about the Desert Fathers in the parlor; a spiritual life of scruples, headaches, neuroses, and effusions to God; a pilgrimage to Rome to ask the pope for permission to enter the cloister at the age of fifteen; an early death from tuberculosis—she was twenty-four—and a "shower" of miracles attributed to her, prompting her canonization in 1925. Moreover, Day had never liked Thérèse's writing, which had struck her, on her first encounter with it in 1925, as "colorless, monotonous, too small in fact for my notice." Nor was she especially drawn to Thérèse's own practice of the Little Way, which consisted in "eating what was put in front of her, in taking medicine, enduring cold and heat, enduring the society of mediocre souls, in following the strict regime of the convent."

With already half a dozen biographies available in English, there was no urgent need for another. Day's editor, after reading some pages, urged her to go to Normandy to "gather material" at the publisher's expense. "You write at your best when you write from the very soil of your daily experience," he told her. "You should revise the book . . . on the very soil of France."

Day declined. She didn't say why, but the reasons are complex. *Therese* would not be a personal book like her other books. Rather, it would be an act of self-denial, a determined effort to write about someone other than herself, and an account of her going to the Lisieux convent with a worn copy of *Story of a Soul* in hand would defeat her purpose.

The more celebrated Day became, the more determined she was, it seems, to efface herself in someone else. The shelter actions had shifted the movement's emphasis, at least in the public eye, from charity to agitprop, and had made her an icon of nonviolence. The jail term had made her a cause unto herself. She admired Thérèse for her embrace of ordinariness as a means to God, and the book would be an exercise in ordinariness. At the same time, as a work of piety, it would call attention to the movement's roots in traditional Catholicism at a time when, more than ever, they were held in doubt.

The writing went on for several more years. The book (finally published in 1960) is wobbly and prosaic, and Day's asides, despite her best efforts, disrupt the story. It comes alive only in the afterword, where Day explains how Thérèse's unusual pursuit of the imitation of Christ "speaks to our condition" as modern people and to her own condition as a woman of protest. "When the whole world seems given over to preparedness for war and the show of force, the message of Thérèse is quite a different one," she declares. "Is the atom a small thing? And yet what havoc it has wrought. Is her little way a small contribution to the life of the spirit? It has all the power of the spirit of Christianity behind it. It is an explosive force that can transform our lives and the life of the world."

Flannery O'Connor had been pondering the Little Flower in her own way. "I have just read a very funny book by a priest named Fr. Robo—on St. Theresa Lisieux," she wrote to a Jesuit priest who had paid her a visit at Andalusia. ". . . He has managed (by some not entirely crooked means) to get hold of a photograph of her that the Carmelites have not 'touched up' which shows her to be a round-faced, determined, rather comical-looking girl. He does away with all the roses, little flowers, and other icing. The book has greatly increased my devotion to her."

She reviewed the book for the *Bulletin* as if from a great distance: "Those of us who have been repulsed by popular portraits of the life of St. Thérèse and at the same time attracted by her iron will and heroism . . . will be cheered to learn from Father Robo's study that this reaction is not entirely perverse," she began, and went on to decry the pious retouching of the saint's photograph.

There was more to her interest in Thérèse than a fascination with the grotesqueries of Catholic devotion, however. A wise child prone to lofty pronouncements, a young woman racked by illness, a writer in whom humility was mixed with a powerful desire to leave her mark on the world—in all these aspects Thérèse's life was akin to O'Connor's own.

So was her attitude toward illness. In the years since her own diagnosis O'Connor, like the Little Flower, had come to see illness, and the early death it portended, as an aspect of her calling. To Elizabeth Hester she wrote, "You are wrong that it was long ago I gave up thinking anything could be worked out on the surface. I have found it out, like everybody else, the hard way and only in the last years, as a result of I think two things, sickness and success."

Hester had visited Andalusia one Sunday, and once they met face to face O'Connor's letters to her grew more candid. Soon she would reveal that she had lupus; for the moment she described it indirectly, through metaphor. "I have never been anywhere but sick," she wrote, and explained, "In a sense sickness is a place, more instructive than a long trip to Europe, and it's always a place where there's no company, where nobody can follow."

As her sickness became chronic, she resigned herself to it; then, in the manner of Thérèse and her Little Way, she fashioned a religious discipline out of its requirements, believing that "every opportunity for performing any kind of charity is something to be snatched at." She couldn't fast on account of her special diet. She couldn't visit the sick, such as her Cousin Kate in Savannah. "I can't even kneel down to say my prayers," she complained. So she sought to do good works through her writing. She kept up her reviewing for the diocesan paper as an act of "mortification," and she wrote a statement about the Church and fiction for the *Catholic Radio Hour*. In letters she counseled a young Catholic writer who was struggling at the Iowa Writers' Workshop.

At the same time, she sought companions in the lonely place that sickness was, identifying with other believers who knew the territory firsthand.

One was Baron Friedrich von Hügel, a turn-of-the-century theologian. Born in Italy, bred during the demise of the Austrian Empire, resident of England, censured by the Vatican during a purge of progressive theologians, he had been as displaced in London as she was in Milledgeville, but his sickness—he was deaf—gave him a mystical sense of the "creatureliness" of creation and the "costingness" of religious faith. The letters he wrote to a cherished niece late in his life became another model for O'Connor's letters to Hester—compact works of religious reflection and instruction addressed to a soul "as yet only hovering around the precincts of Christianity." The Baron writes to his niece as to an ideal interlocutor. He seems to spend all his religious passion in each letter, as if it might be his last chance to do so. "I wonder whether you realize a great, deep fact. That all souls—all human souls—are deeply interconnected? That, I mean, we cannot only pray for each other, but *suffer* for each other?" he asked his niece, declaring that the "interdependence of all the broken and the meek, all the self-oblivion, all the reaching out to God and souls" was the essence of Catholicism.

Another of O'Connor's discoveries was Walker Percy. Apparently she had read Percy's essays, for she had discussed them during Elizabeth Hester's visit to Andalusia. When, during a writers' "jamboree" in Athens, Georgia, she met a graduate student named Phinizy Spalding who had written a paper about her stories, she invited him to lunch at Andalusia ("Anybody with a name like that could not but be welcome"), and he arrived bearing a copy of *Lanterns on the Levee*, the subject of his Ph.D. thesis. Will Percy, he explained, had been his uncle; Walker Percy, it emerged, was his first cousin. "It turns out that our mutual admiration, Walker Percy, is one of two adopted sons of Wm. Alex. P.," O'Connor reported to Hester, then told his story: "Anyway Walker Percy early in his way in the world came down with TB and had to be confined for a period during which he and St. Thomas became friends and he became a Catholic. He wrote a novel which Mr. Phinizy Spalding said he put aside as it was not good and is now writing some kind of philosophical treatese (sp?). He is a doctor but has to take it easy on account of the TB which gets active if he does."

Incurable illness; confinement; the consolations of philosophy; a novel; a turn to other writing; a need to conserve energy lest the dread disease act up—in a few sentences, she made Percy's life story strikingly like her own. In fact, it was even more like hers than she knew. She wrote about sickness as a sign of human dependence and limitation, he as a sign of irreducible human nature, which defied the totalizing claims of science; but both of them saw sickness as a sign of the mystery of existence, a mystery borne in upon them when their fathers died. In telling his story, she recognized him as her countryman, stressing their shared predicament.

A Good Man Is Hard to Find was being published in Germany, *Wise Blood* in France. O'Connor herself had gone no farther than Iowa City. She yearned to broaden her experience, but was embarrassed by the opportunity when it came. In letters to Hester and the Fitzgeralds she reported on a recent "turn of events": "My 88 year old cousin has decided that my mother and I must go on a pilgrimage to Lourdes and Rome," and half a dozen other European cities as well. The person who had "never been anywhere but sick" would be going to the place of sickness par excellence.

Lourdes was to France in the nineteenth century as Milledgeville was to America in the twentieth, a place where O'Connor's favorite themes were found in such concentrated form that she might have invented it for a story—the story of a Southern village whose traditional way of life was upended by folk religion, a Marian apparition, a claim of miracle cures, and an invasion of the incurably ill, and then by the novelists, who saw the village as the setting of a conflict between science and Catholicism, urban life and rural life, rationalism and mysticism, the conventional and the grotesque.

From the beginning O'Connor mocked the "pilgrumidge" to Lourdes as a "comic nightmare," one that would feature "a planeload of fortress-footed female Catholics being pushed from shrine to shrine. . . . I guess the way to stand it will be to indulge temporarily in Quietism, cut my motor off so to speak and be towed." She claimed that she was going only as an act of kindness toward her cousin Kate, who would be paying, and as a way of seeing the Fitzgeralds in Italy.

Yet in the months leading up to the pilgrimage she gave her friends a blow-by-blow report, in which her anticipation is obvious:

November 16: Mother, reading Lourdes guidebook aloud, tells her that pilgrims in low-cut dresses aren't allowed in. Tells mother: "I ain't got any low-cut dress." *December 14*: Dreads seventeen days of "Holy Culture and Pious Exhaustion"; expects to see more airports than shrines; declares that what she'd really like to see is Matisse Chapel in Vence; doesn't want to miss geese hatching at home; thinks of trip as penance; will pray for change of attitude; wouldn't mind washing in another's blood but dreads washing in Lourdes waters on account of lack of privacy. Tells Hester, "I will not be taking any bath. I am one of those people who could die for his religion easier than take a bath for it." *January 17*: Plans to cock an ear to dialogue of other pilgrims "when I should be looking at the windows of Chartres." *February 11*: Doctor tells her the pilgrimage is too demanding and she cannot go. She tells Fitzgeralds that "I am bearing it with my usual magnificent fortitude. Ha." *February 26*: Sheepishly explains further change in plans: Cousin Kate will pay for less strenuous pilgrimage. Drily reports that "The Monsigneur God help him wants me to 'write up' the Lourdes part of the pilgrimage. I don't think he has thought this through." *March 11*: Asks farmhand to procure pocketknives for her to take to the Fitzgerald boys as gifts. Plans travel wardrobe, as mother "is afraid my poor white trash look will disgrace you." *March 21*: Promises Fitzgeralds "we will arrive with no lethal weapons." Arranges for cot for Sally Fitzgerald, who has decided to join her at Lourdes, to be placed in room at the Hôtel de la Grotte. *April 14*: Tells Fitzgeralds: "If you don't hear from me again and the Lord continues willing we will alight at 12:10 p.m. on Thursday Apr. 24." Recites the itinerary—Italy, Paris, Lourdes, Barcelona, Rome, Lisbon, New York— and (echoing Mr. Head in "The Artificial Nigger") declares that once she is back home "you'll probably never catch me out of the confines of the United States again."

Why did she protest so much? She was an authentic homebody, for one thing, and she could not pass up an opportunity to entertain her friends with her scornful humor. Yet her dread of the place and the trip seems far out of proportion to the circumstances.

It may be that she was embarrassed about Lourdes. Feminine, superstitious, sentimental, tacky, devoted to the figure of the Virgin Mary rather than the person of Jesus, it embodied all the stereotypes she strove to avoid in her writing. A modern artist, a Catholic woman of letters, she belonged at Vence, praying in the light of Matisse's sublime stained glass.

It may be that, as Sally Fitzgerald said, she "dreaded the possibility of a cure." In "The River," one of her strongest stories, she had dramatized a baptism by contrasting it with a spurious faith healing. At Yaddo, she had seen Robert Lowell go mad from what Robert Fitzgerald described as the direct intervention of God.

Whatever the explanations, her dread of Lourdes was genuine, and the real reason went to the heart of her sense of herself. For all her courage, her "magnificent fortitude," her embrace of sickness as her calling and her true country, she was loath to see herself as a sick person.

"I am going as a pilgrim not a patient," she told Hester, and adamantly explained why. To take a bath in the curative waters would suggest that her lupus was past healing and that only a miracle could save her.

Worst of all—this she didn't explain—it would make a cliché of her and her malady. She had always seen herself as unique, and her lupus, even as it made her literally dependent on others, had strengthened her figurative independence, her sense of herself as a person set apart both in Milledgeville and in literary society. At Lourdes, however, sickness would be a trait she shared with pious folk by the hundreds.

The artist's job is to contemplate experience, not to be merged with it, she liked to say. In Lourdes, her life and her art, which she had strived to keep separate and distinct, would be merged as if by force. In the healing waters, she would be immersed in the kind of experience she liked to write about.

The pilgrims set out the Thursday after Easter, 1958, a hundred years after the Virgin Mary appeared to Bernadette Soubirous. They went to Milan; to Levanto, the port city where the Fitzgeralds were living, and where O'Connor presented the Fitzgerald boys with a set of Uncle Remus tales in lieu of knives; to Paris overnight by train; and then to Lourdes, in the Pyrenees.

Then as now, the village of Lourdes was dotted with souvenir shops. At the entrance to the grotto, however, the holy commerce subsided and the culture of pious infirmity took over.

The baths at Lourdes are set amid a compound of churches and comfort stations. O'Connor went to them early in the morning, when the water was rumored to be least foul. She wore a dress and a long sweater and brandished a pair of aluminum crutches, which she had told Hester made her "a structure with flying buttresses."

Sally Fitzgerald, her old landlady, accompanied her, like Mrs. Flood following the movements of Hazel Motes; like Enoch Emery, William Sessions, a friend from Georgia who was in France on a fellowship, tagged along.

The *malades*, as they are called, waited in a line at the edge of the pool of healing waters and ventured in one at a time, each led by a volunteer. When O'Connor's turn came she discarded her crutches (like Hulga removing her leg) and exchanged her sweater and dress for the sacklike robe the patients wore—which was still wet, for it was the same robe worn by the patient before her.

She waded in, lingered a moment, praying perhaps, then stepped out, dried off, and dressed again, noting the "distinct body odor" of the crowd.

A Thermos jug of holy water was circulated and the *malades* drank from it one by one, like farm hands passing milk around in "The Enduring Chill"; the real miracle of the place, O'Connor heard some pilgrim remark, was that the people who came to be healed weren't *made* sick from drinking the water.

They trudged back to the grotto for Mass, O'Connor putting one crutch after the other. She clutched a bottle, which her Georgia friend, rolling up his "drip-dry pants" like the preacher-healer in "The River," had waded into the pool to fill so that she could take some Lourdes water back to Caroline Gordon, who was bent on becoming a lay member of the Carmelite order.

When Mass was ended they returned to the village. It was midmorning, the time of day when, in Georgia, she would have been sitting at her typewriter, working on her novel.

In Rome, the pilgrims went to the weekly papal audience; through the archbishop of Atlanta's intercession, O'Connor was seated in the front row, where the sick were often placed, the better to receive a particular blessing from the pope.

Pius XII, at age eighty, was a sick person himself, exceedingly thin and suffering from a chronic case of the hiccups. In her letters, O'Connor had never mentioned him except to make a joke. In his presence, however, she was overcome with devotion, a church lady after all. "There is a wonderful radiance and liveliness about the old man," she reported to Elizabeth Hester. "He fairly springs up and down the little steps to his chair. Whatever the special superaliveness that holiness is, it is very apparent in him."

Herself, she had a bad cold. She sought to return to America right away, but could not get a flight. So she stayed in a Rome hotel room, reading and writing letters home.

In the letters, she was already making the pilgrimage into a story, one which would grow funnier and less reverent each time she told it. She'd had "the best-looking crutches in Europe." Lourdes was like a "sickly child with smallpox." While immersed in the healing waters she had prayed "for my book, not my bones." She would write about the trip in earnest "only later, when the reality has somewhat faded. Experience," she declared, "is the greatest deterrent to fiction."

Upon her return to America, a writer once more, she paused in New York to meet her new publisher, Roger Straus; and once more she set herself to finishing her novel. "Lord I'm glad I'm a hermit novelist," she liked to say, and to Elizabeth Bishop, who had sent her a letter, she replied: "We went to Europe and I lived through it but my capacity for staying at home has now been perfected, sealed & is going to last me the rest of my life."

She set about learning to drive. Shortly before the trip to Lourdes, Regina O'Connor, feeling chest pains, had checked into a hospital overnight, and O'Connor was left alone at Andalusia for the first time. It was a bracing experience. She had feared that her mother might die before her; now she worried that her mother might need her care in a crisis. So she took the road test, passing on the second try, and bought a secondhand car—"black, hearse-like, dignified," she told a friend, "a rolling memento mori."

In the fall, she learned that her hip bone had healed somewhat, and she was free to walk around the house without crutches. She passed the news to her Cousin Kate, who died shortly thereafter—died with the hope that the pilgrimage had produced a miracle.

Finishing the book was harder. "From here on out my novel will have to be forced by will," she told Hester upon returning from Lourdes. "There is no pleasure left in it for me. How I would like to be writing something I could enjoy." Her estimation of the novel improved, but she was never exalted about it the way she had been about *Wise Blood*. Shortly before Christmas, in a letter to a priest, she said the novel was at a "critical point," and added, "I need your prayers about it. I would rather finish this novel right than be able to walk at all."

She was calling it *The Violent Bear It Away*, and the title suggested the struggle of writing it. She saw it as a book about a baptism, and thought the challenge was to get the reader to see baptism as a matter of life and death. She had to "bend the whole novel" so that the baptism carried "enough awe and mystery to jar the reader into some kind of emotional recognition of its significance."

So she bent the novel toward what she supposed were the modern reader's sympathies. It would be a novel of initiation, about a boy's entry into manhood, a motif the reader would recognize. It would begin and end with a religious ritual: in the beginning the ritual of death, the boy's burial of his grandfather, who is a prophet, and in the end the ritual of life, the baptism of his nephew, who is retarded. It would lead the reader to see these rituals in the way that she saw them herself—baptism as the initiation into the life of grace, and burial as the initiation into the life of eternity.

Thus described, her approach has a Jamesian elegance, but in practice it proved so unwieldy that simply keeping the story straight became her biggest challenge. The novel opens like a piece of student fiction, with a boy all alone in "the farthest part of the backwoods." His mother is long dead. His father is long gone. His grandfather, who raised him, gives up the ghost over breakfast on page one. His home, Powderhead, is a "gaunt two story shack" in a deserted clearing. Alone, he faces two adversaries: an invisible stranger who whispers in his ear, and his only relative, the schoolteacher Rayber, a dullard enlivened only by his interest in psychology, a field O'Connor disdained without knowing much about it. The action takes place in flashbacks; the point of view wanders from one character to another. There are two Tarwaters, two Raybers, two nephews, two loose women, and in each case one is easily confused with the other, so that the crucial parallel or correspondence—between old Tarwater and young Tarwater, between the prophet and the prophet in the making—appears and disappears like the trail to Powderhead.

She finished in January 1959, nearly seven years after she started. "I am more and more satisfied with the title and less and less satisfied with the rest of it," she told Hester. To the Fitzgeralds she wrote, "I cannot see it any longer and the only thing I can determine about it is that nobody else would have wanted to write it but me."

Although it is a novel of initiation, the sense of an ending in the book is strong. The style suggests the Old Testament. The setting is the oldest part of the Old South. The drift of the action is not forward but backward, and this fact, no doubt, made it even harder for O'Connor to reach the end of the novel, as did the slowly gathering suspicion that she would not write another.

At the house on Milan Street, Walker Percy had begun writing a novel. From the start, "Confessions of a Movie-Goer," as he was calling it, was a departure from his two previous novels and from his philosophical work. It was set in present-day New Orleans. It was told from the point of view of an ordinary man, a small-time stockbroker who was about to turn thirty. It was thick with the quotidian, the small details of a not unusual life. It was written in the first person and in the present tense—written directly at the reader, confided to the reader like a long-kept secret.

There were certain continuities with his previous work. Ever since college he had wanted to write about a moviegoer in one form or another, and all through the fifties he had been tempted to write about New Orleans: "It has everything," Shelby Foote had told him, "intellectuals, whores, priests, merchant seamen: you could make it boil and bubble." His philosophical essays, which tipped into the present tense, were about the quandaries of tourists, honeymooners, commuters—ordinary people.

Yet this work was enough of a departure that Percy felt that in beginning it he had started over again. At the house on Milan Street, Patrick Samway has pointed out, he was away from his library: for the first time in his life as a writer he sat down to work without his influences literally surrounding him, and the effect was to relieve him of the weight of the literary past generally. "One begins to write, not as one thinks he is supposed to write, and not even to write like the great novels one admires, but rather to write as if he were the first man on earth ever to set pencil to paper," he explained. ". . . All past efforts are thrown into the wastebasket; all advice forgotten."

He thought of himself as discarding conventional ideas about plot and character and beginning with the situation of a man unmoored from expectations, "*coming to himself* in somewhat the same sense as Robinson Crusoe came to himself on his island after his shipwreck, with the same wonder and curiosity." As with the character, so with the author, who "came to himself" as he finally felt the experience of artistic creation firsthand.

The first few pages of the novel consist of several different openings, as if Percy was searching for a way to begin writing fiction again. Together (in the published novel) they give the telling its sideways, happenstance quality, as Binx Bolling—a shifty character—commences his story again and again, taking a slightly different approach each time. He starts this way:

> This morning I got a note from my aunt asking me to come to lunch. I know what this means. Since I go there every Sunday for dinner and today is Wednesday, it can mean only one thing: she wants to have one of her serious talks. It will be extremely grave, either a piece of bad news about her stepdaughter Kate or else a serious talk about me, about the future and what I ought to do. It is enough to scare the wits out of anyone, yet I confess I do not find the prospect altogether unpleasant.

In those sentences Percy's admirers, and for good reason, see the influence of disaffected first-person narrators like Camus's Stranger and Dostoevsky's Underground Man, the great protagonists of secular confession.

But these sentences—the novel in miniature—look forward, not backward, not to literature but to life itself. They suggest that this novel will be a personal story, about family, relationships, communication, and the question of what a particular man ought to do with his life. The man in question is a certain kind of postwar man—a man who knows too much, who knows, or affects to know, the whole story.

Another opening, a few paragraphs later, introduces the man and the situation in more general terms:

> For the past four years now I have been living uneventfully in Gentilly, a middle-class suburb of New Orleans. Except for the banana plants in the patios and the curlicues of iron on the Walgreen drugstore one would never guess it was part of New Orleans. Most of the houses are either old-style California bungalows or new-style Daytona cottages. But this is what I like about it. I can't stand the old-world atmosphere of the French Quarter or the genteel charm of the Garden District. I lived in the Quarter for two years, but in the end I got

tired of Birmingham businessmen smirking around Bourbon Street and the homosexuals and patio connoisseurs on Royal Street. My uncle and aunt live in a gracious house in the Garden District and are very kind to me. But whenever I try to live there, I find myself first in a rage during which I develop strong opinions on a variety of subjects and write letters to editors, then in a depression during which I lie rigid as a stick for hours staring straight up at the plaster medallion in the ceiling of my bedroom.

If the first opening suggests what kind of story the novel will be, this one says what kind it will not be. The man is no Quentin Compson, a self-conscious representative of his region. The city where he lives is not a city of history and hidden charms. The novel is not a novel of the South like those by Faulkner or Foote. It is, or is meant to be, something else altogether, a kind of novel the author knows exists but has not yet found the name for.

On television in New York, Flannery O'Connor had described the writing of fiction as a process of self-knowledge, in which knowledge of one's region brings about self-knowledge and knowledge of the wider world, a knowledge that makes the writer an exile from that world, rendered an Other by detachment. That is what happened to Walker Percy in New Orleans as he wrote *The Moviegoer*. He later recalled the experience in an essay, and whereas O'Connor described the process of self-knowledge in philosophical terms, Percy—reversing their usual roles—echoed the Bible:

> And so it came to pass that he wrote a short novel in which he created a character, an amiable but slightly bemused young man of a certain upper-class Southern background, and set him down in Gentilly, a middle-class district of New Orleans, in order to see what would happen to him. . . .
>
> What happens to him is that in the very anxiety of his despair, cool as it is—indeed, as a very consequence of his despair—it occurs to him that a search is possible. . . .
>
> So the novel, almost by accident, became a narrative of the search, the quest. And so the novel, again almost by accident—or was it an accident?—landed squarely in the oldest tradition of Western letters: the pilgrim's search outside himself, rather than the guru's search within.

Percy's search for himself had the outlines of a biblical parable. In order to find himself, he had to lose himself; he had to look outside of himself, going on pilgrimage. The novel, as he later put it, would be the story of a "pilgrim's search outside himself," not an account of introspection.

To put it differently, in order to find himself he had to search for himself indirectly, revealing mystery through manners in the way that O'Connor recommended. As he wrote about Gentilly, a place with no personal significance for him, his sense of his region was suddenly unerring. As he wrote in the present tense, the past was vivid and accessible; as he wrote about Binx's Aunt Emily, his own Uncle Will came alive on the page. As he worked up precise descriptions of everyday life in New Orleans, his philosophical ideas fell into place. And as he wrote about an imagined character, there emerged a protagonist who was complex and fully alive, not a straitened version of himself. In depicting another person, identifying with him, inhabiting him, Walker Percy found his own voice and became his own person, telling the story of somebody else.

"I am really a monk when I can let go completely of 'being a monk' (self-consciously) and I think I have let go of that long ago," Merton wrote in his journal. "Now I face the same terror of being, by the same 'letting go,' a Christian. And a writer and myself."

At the age of forty-three, he had been a Catholic for twenty years and a Trappist monk for seventeen. He no longer saw the Abbey of Gethsemani as the center of his or anybody's existence. Set apart from the other monks by his background, his fame, his literary calling, and his yearning for solitude, he had come to see himself as an independent, a Trappist of Gethsemani whose real life was elsewhere. He no longer saw the outside world as a nest of vipers, but he didn't yearn to be out in the world making his way as a poet or a college professor, either. He had no desire to be anything but a monk. Rather, he felt called to be a monk on different terms—to be more intensely a monk than he was.

The toolshed in the woods was no longer simply a place of solitude. It had become the place where he was free to imagine that he was someplace else. There, in the late 1950s, he went back to first principles and reoriented his monastic calling along independent lines.

Once, he had sought to submerge himself in the Christian past, regarding the monastery as a place where the past was not past. Now, as Gethsemani was modernized and mechanized, he ransacked the past for precedents, searching for practitioners of a simple, improvisatory monastic life: the "idiorrhythmic monks" of Mount Athos, who supported themselves by their own labors; the monks of St. Catherine on Mount Sinai, who acted as Samaritans in their remote locale, showing hospitality to "the Moslem nomads of the desert"; the original "primitive" Carmelites—"simple laymen, living as solitaries in a loosely connected group, in caves and huts on the side of Mount Carmel"; the Renaissance hermit Paul Giustiniani, who—describing him, Merton employed the present tense—"seeks to rekindle the ancient fire in an age that has no love for ascetisicm, for contemplation or for solitude."

He made of these monks—some long dead, some far off—companions in his own monastic life. At the same time, he brainstormed about a new, ideal monastery, which he would leave Gethsemani in order to establish. "The hope of a monastery in Ecuador," he had written in his journal the previous year, ". . . a small, simple monastery like Toumliline in Morocco . . . as unlike Gethsemani as possible." He sketched the place in a few sentences: a site with "perhaps very few Americans in it . . . without too many machines." He prayed to a Mexican saint and scrutinized his motives. Why did he want such a thing? Not to please himself, he concluded, so much as to help the helpless and atone for the sins of the conquerors. Yet he wondered if this conclusion was "another one of my lies."

In the next few years he would revisit the notion of the ideal monastery again and again. He looked at maps and illustrated books about South America, searching for the perfect setting. He corresponded with religious superiors who offered him sites: an Indian reservation in Nevada, an old hacienda in Cuernavaca in Mexico, a rundown mission on an island in the Caribbean, a plot of land in Venezuela—near Caracas, perhaps, "or in the mountains overlooking the lake of Valencia. Or on the other slope looking at the sea. Or near Barquisimeto—a most fascinating name."

Again, he scrutinized his motives. What was driving him? At its most basic, it was a desire to live out the monastic life more literally, more strenuously, than it was being lived at Gethsemani. At its most ambitious, it was a mystical vision of the unity of the Americas. Religiously the Americas were fatally split. The Protestant North had become alienated from the Catholic South—Latin America—and American Catholics had become "more akin to those new Puritans, the Communists, than to our Catholic forefathers." Only the mystic could reconcile them, gathering into his life and his prayer "the orientation of the whole hemisphere."

Extracted from Merton's journals, such notions seem impractical and grandiose, and they were seen as such at the time by his superiors in the Cistercian order. Accordingly, the story told in the journals (and in many books about Merton) is the story of the conflict between a visionary and the authorities, between a monk of the future and the guardians of the past. But in retrospect the story of Merton's clash with Church officials over his notions of monasticism is less important than the notions themselves, which expressed the impulse at the heart of his religious life—the impulse to renew his monastic calling. He had imagined life at Gethsemani, and had found (for a while) that the reality lived up to the image. Then, having drawn a vivid picture of the place in his autobiography, he found that he was expected to live up to it, when his imagination was racing ahead to other monasteries, other ways of life, other aspects of faith. The monastery, once a place of rule and ritual, embraced for the limitations it imposed upon him, was now a place of pure possibility, not so much a medieval fastness, another world to lose himself in, as a place where he could imagine that he was someplace else.

Merton's stability crisis subsided for another, profounder reason as well. As long as Merton's counterparts were other Christians, he could see himself being transplanted to a monastery in Europe or founding one in Venezuela. At the end of the 1950s, however, he began to find counterparts outside Christianity altogether. Martin Luther King's practice of nonviolence led him to Gandhi's *satyagraha*. A reading of the *I Ching* led him to Daisetz T. Suzuki, the Japanese Zen master who wrote about Buddhism in such a way as to engage curious seekers in "the West."

These encounters with the Other, so to speak, actually strengthened Merton's sense of himself as a Catholic and as a Trappist. He did not see himself—not yet—leaving Gethsemani for a zendo or an ashram. Rather, he sought to incorporate the insights of other believers, indeed of other religions, into his own Christian faith, so as to seek points in common, such as those between the sayings of the Zen masters and the *verba* of the Desert Fathers.

All the while, he tried to maintain some detachment. Even as he sought "a mystical action . . . which may need a geographic change to make it really complete," he deprecated the search in his journal in the voice that had made him a popular author. It was "always the old story of 'something missing,' " he observed. "What? Is it something essential? Won't there always be 'something missing'? Yet always that urge to 'go forth,' to leave, to take off for a strange land and start another life. Perhaps this is inevitable, just a desire one is supposed to have without fulfilling it," he concluded, adding, "It was that kind of desire that brought me here."

Pius XII, ill for months, died on October 9, 1958. On October 28 Cardinal Roncalli of Venice was elected Pope, taking the name John. A few Sundays later he left the Vatican compound and boarded a train which took him to Assisi, then to the shrine of the Virgin Mary at Loreto on the Adriatic coast. The excursion was uncommon for a pope, and the symbolism was clear. He was a humble penitent like every other Catholic. His pontificate would be a pilgrimage.

Merton, who had had little to say in his journal upon the death of the old pope—"Interminable articles on the way a Pope is buried in 3 coffins are being read in refectory"—was effusive upon the election of the new one. "John XXIII seems to me to be a most wonderful Pope and I love him already very much . . . ," he remarked November 9, evidently after reading a magazine article about Roncalli. "I cannot help feeling right away that perhaps he is a saint. My kind of saint—who smokes a cigarette after dinner."

The next day he wrote the new pope a long and fraternal letter. He introduced himself as a humble monk in America, "master of novices and author of a few paltry books," yet one who had "a sympathy for the honest aspirations of so many intellectuals everywhere in the world and the terrible problems they have to face." He went on:

I have had the experience of seeing that this kind of understanding and friendly sympathy, on the part of a monk who really understands them, has produced striking effects among artists, writers, publishers, poets, etc., who have become my friends without my having to leave the cloister. . . . In short, with the approval of my Superiors, I have exercised an apostolate—small and limited though it be—within a circle of intellectuals from other parts of the world; and it has been quite simply an apostolate of friendship.

It was for a furthering of this apostolate of friendship, he explained, that he sought the Holy Father's blessing—for "a monastic foundation in which the members would be monks and contemplatives, but at the same time would receive special groups, such as writers, intellectuals, etc., into their house for retreats and discussions," perhaps in South America.

When the pope replied, the next year, he did so cryptically, sending, in lieu of a letter, a photograph of himself and a liturgical stole he had worn during Mass at St. Peter's. Even so, it was as if he had given his blessing indirectly. For in March 1959 he called an ecumenical council, which would consider the Church's mission in the modern world, seeking understanding through dialogue, the earnest and sustained encounter with the Other.

At Eastertime, when the ban on visitors at the monastery was lifted, the doors of the Gethsemani guest house were flung open, and the pilgrims began to come. Merton wrote to his college friend Robert Lax in the guise of St. Blarney (patron of Trappist talkers and walkers), extending a Joycean invitation: "Everybody come the door is wide open and the floor is flatter than usual and the beds have for the most part sheets on them. . . . So come, rabbits, and see Blarney's cell, builded of square stones all about the bluegrass bourbons." While he awaited permission to establish a place of retreat for writers and artists, he would make one where he was.

Lax was now a Catholic and an editor of *Jubilee*, a high-toned magazine of religion and the arts, and in a sense he had become the "natural contemplative" Merton still longed to be—poor, lean, little known, effortlessly laconic, happy for no particular reason, kindly disposed toward all. He came in April, bringing another old classmate, Ad Reinhardt, the painter. Reinhardt's abstract crucifixes, black on black, had just been shown at the Museum of Modern Art, and they all discussed the prospect of Reinhardt's illustrating Merton's essay "Art and Worship" for *Jubilee*.

Next Robert Giroux came to visit. He had left Harcourt, Brace and joined Farrar, Straus (bringing a passel of writers with him), and was visiting authors who lived in the South. Merton said nothing in his journal about their time together, but Giroux recalled it as relaxed and pleasurable. They walked in the woods; they worshipped in the abbey church. They played a recording of Dame Edith Sitwell reciting her verse, which Giroux had brought, and Sitwell's arch pronunciations left Merton "laughing so hard that tears ran down his cheeks."

Giroux remarked that he was going to Georgia to see Flannery O'Connor. At this, Merton grew intensely curious. Giroux explained that O'Connor lived on a farm and raised peacocks—collected them, really. "I could not tell Merton enough about them or about Flannery and her surroundings. What was Milledgeville like? Well, one of its sights was the beautiful ante-bellum Cline house, where Flannery's aunt served a formal midday dinner. He was surprised to learn that far from being 'backwoods' Milledgeville had once been the capital of Georgia."

Giroux left the monastery for Atlanta the next morning, and the abbot of Our Lady of the Resurrection in Cuernavaca arrived, begging Merton to leave Kentucky and make a new foundation in Mexico. Once the prospect of a new foundation was real, however, Merton backed away from it. "My feelings are not all on the side of going," he wrote in his journal. "On the contrary, it is so wonderful, so quiet in the straw of the woodshed and under these pines by St. Teresa's field—I [would] have to leave all that for the uncertain and the unknown."

On the way from Atlanta to Milledgeville, Giroux pondered the affinities between the two great Catholic writers he published. "Over the years I came to see how much the two had in common—a highly developed sense of comedy, deep faith, great intelligence," he later recalled. "The aura of aloneness surrounding each of them was not an accident. It was their métier, in which they refined and deepened their very different talents in a short span of time."

He reached Milledgeville in time for the midday meal at the Cline house, where he and Flannery O'Connor made amused faces at each other while a gloved black servant waited on them from behind. Then they went to Andalusia to talk of "litrachur." They discussed *The Violent Bear It Away*, which O'Connor had revised. He gave her some bad news about Robert Lowell: another manic break, which had forced him to be hospitalized. She asked about Pierre Teilhard de Chardin, the Jesuit writer, whose funeral Giroux had attended. He presented her with *Prometheus: A Meditation*, which Merton had inscribed to her.

O'Connor was as curious about Merton and "Gethseminie" as he had been about her and Andalusia. "Was Merton allowed to talk to me? Yes, without restriction. I described our walks in the woods and the monastic routine of the day: first office (Matins) at two a.m. and last office (Compline) at sunset, followed by bed." He told her about the pleasure he and Merton had taken in Edith Sitwell's recording, mocking the Dame's mannered recitations—"even my pallid approximation of Dame Edith's renderings of 'Daisy and Lily, lazy and silly,' 'Long Steel Grass' (pronounced 'Grawss'), 'Black Mrs. Behemoth' and the rest made her face light up with smiles."

Holy Ghost Monastery was only ninety minutes' drive from Andalusia, and, at O'Connor's suggestion, they went there together. The monks had replaced the barn chapel with a conventional one, and a large abbey church was going up slowly, Gothic in design but made of concrete rather than stone. Some outbuildings were unfinished and, despite her crutches, O'Connor clambered around them, with Giroux looking on. "He said it was much better looking than the one in Kentucky, or at least will be when they complete it," O'Connor told Caroline Gordon in a letter later in the week. "All the people in the outlying areas go to look at the monks—like going to the zoo."

As Jack English progressed through the novitiate and was ordained a priest—Father Charles, O.C.S.O.—Dorothy Day became a regular visitor to Holy Ghost Monastery, and she had gone there early in 1959 to be present when he said his first Mass in the chapel. It was her kind of pilgrimage—a long bus ride with a liturgy at the end—and she wrote a column about it.

"The Story of Jack English's First Mass" opens as a postcard from Conyers, with plenty of vivid description: the "cement block and plywood" chapel, the granite altar ("a magnificent place of sacrifice"), the monks' "work of prayer" and their work on the grounds, "pushing wheel barrows of cement and rocks and gravel up long inclines, making and setting in stained glass windows, the carpentry work, the cobbling, the baking and cooking, the farming."

Mainly, though, the column is the story of Day's freshly ordained comrade. He had founded a Catholic Worker house in Cleveland; flown bombers in the war; been shot down, been rescued by the Russian Army, survived the Blitz in London, and then come shell-shocked to St. Joseph's House, where he drank too much, filled the room with his "Niagara of talk," painted the kitchen chartreuse and coral, and cashed benefit checks for a disability he refused to discuss. "Who would ever have thought he would finally choose the Trappists, the order of silence and hard manual labor?"

Jack English's calling was mysterious, but the inspiration for it was obvious: he had read *The Seven Storey Mountain*. Before setting out Day read the book herself. Excited at first, she wound up disappointed, feeling that once Merton became a monk he "plunged himself so deeply in religion that his view of the world and its problems is superficial and scornful."

Even so, she entered into a correspondence with Merton, her only rival for the admiration of the Catholic Workers at St. Joseph's House. She had published a poem of his in the paper, and when an approving letter from a reader arrived, she sent it to "Fr. M. Louis," attaching a typed postcard:

I enclose a letter to cheer your heart and keep you writing. Your books are regarded as treasures around the CW and keep circulating. One of the editors even made a pilgrimage to your old home on Long Island. Do pray for him as he is in a sad state of indecision about everything, idleness and melancholy which are hard to combat. The sense of futility is the curse of our time among the young. God bless you always in your work which has done so much for us all.

It was the kind of note she wrote to dozens of people each month: gracious, appreciative, devotional, spiced with an aside about the perilous state of the postwar soul. But she added a confiding postscript, as though she and Merton already knew each other:

Did I tell you that Caroline Gordon said she spent all the royalties from her own books, buying yours to distribute to others. She needs prayers. Her husband has left her, and she has gotten to the point where she thinks he is possessed and she is reading up on the devil. A dangerous state to be in—getting too close to *him*.

Merton wrote back three weeks later. He opened lightheartedly, announcing that a donation of "sweet-smelling and -tasting toothpaste" meant for the monks was being sent on to the Catholic Worker instead, so as to preserve "Cistercian simplicity . . . what's left of it." He assured her that he would "keep praying" for the Catholic Workers, then turned to war and peace. This would be the heart of their correspondence, and he began by taking the long view, already laying out the principles beneath direct action. As he read the *Catholic Worker*, he told her, he was "touched" by the movement's "witness for peace" and against air-raid drills. The issues were complex, but it was vital to do something, and nonviolent protest akin to Gandhi's *satyagraha* seemed the best prospect. "Nowadays it is no longer a question of who is right, but who is at least not criminal," he declared (echoing Czeslaw Milosz), and went on, "So don't worry about whether or not in every point you are perfectly right according to everybody's books: you are right before God as far as you can go and you are fighting for a truth that is clear enough and important enough. What more can anybody do?"

In closing, he sought her support. The paper had run an article about a Hopi reservation, and it had left him thinking the Catholic Workers were "the only ones left awake, or among the few that still have an eye open. I am more and more convinced that the real people in this country are the Indians—and Negroes, etc.," he told her. He confided his plan to live among Indians "as a kind of hermit-missionary," and asked her to pray that he be allowed to go.

Day replied in early summer, this time using both sides of the postcard. About peace, or *satyagraha*, or Indian reservations, she said nothing. Instead, she thanked him for the "gifts" and asked him for *his* prayers—prayers for two Catholic Workers, one an ex-Trappist, who had been arrested and convicted in direct actions. She thanked him again for his writings, adding that "it delights me especially to see them in bus stations and drug stores as I travel about the country."

She wrote to him again in December from the Staten Island ferry. He had sent her a book and some news—probably the news that he might be allowed to make a new foundation on an Indian reservation or in Mexico. She told him that he was in her prayers. Her prayer for herself, she explained, was "for final perseverance—to go on as I am trusting always the Lord Himself will take me by the hair of the head like Habbakuk and put me where he wants me," and her prayer for him was like it: she prayed that he would be "faithful unto death."

She can't have known that the plans for a new foundation had been scuttled in the meantime, but her prayer, and the hair-raising biblical image, fit Merton's situation precisely. It is as if she knew that he was restless over where to go and what to do next, and assured him the way an old friend would: by telling him that she had faced down the same restlessness herself.

Thus began the friendship of Thomas Merton and Dorothy Day, which was carried on in letters that expressed their temperaments remarkably well. Merton's were extravagant and impetuous, full of his sudden enthusiasms, his brainstorms, his pronouncements, his blunt advice. Day's, in contrast, were appealingly prosaic. As with everyone else, she would say as much to Merton as she could fit onto a postcard and no more, no matter that he was a famous writer. He was a priest who didn't look down upon her as a woman or a layperson; she gave him the news of the world while treating him as an equal, not an idol, a person who needed prayers and reassurance and sound advice as much as anybody else.

In his next letter he took up the matter of perseverance and gave it his own emphasis. Perseverance, he said, wasn't "a matter of getting a bulldog grip on the faith and not letting the devil pry us loose from it—though many of the saints make it look that way." No, it was a matter of "letting go" rather than keeping hold. "I am coming to think that God (may He be praised in His great mystery) loves and helps best those who are so beat and have so much nothing when they come to die that it is almost as if they had persevered in nothing but had gradually lost everything, piece by piece, until there was nothing left but God." He went on, "It is a question of His hanging on to us, by the hair of the head, that is from on top and beyond, where we cannot see or reach. What man can see the top of his own head?"

It was February 4, 1960. In this letter, and not at the corner of Fourth and Walnut in Louisville, Merton's turn toward the world truly began. The spirituality of stripping and letting go, the practice of religious detachment, would be his way out of Gethsemani; it would be the key to his life in the 1960s, the root of his sympathy with religious people of all kinds. He closed the letter with a kind of hymn of praise, the length of one of Day's postcard missives:

O Dorothy, I think of you, and the beat people, and the poor in virtue, the very poor, the ones no one can respect. I am not worthy to say I love all of you. Intercede for me, a stuffed shirt in a place of stuffed shirts and a big dumb phony, who have tried to be respectable and have succeeded. What a deception! I know, of course, you are respected too, but you have a right to be, and you didn't jump into the most respectable possible situation and then tell everyone all about it. I am not worried about all this and am not beating myself over the head. I just think that for the love of God I should say it, and that for the love of God you should pray for me.

In this manner Thomas Merton prayed to Dorothy Day. Through her, the longing he had felt on the street for Proverb, for the wisdom of the Other, was fulfilled and proven genuine. For this woman was truly alive, and truly wise; and when he called out to her, she responded.

NINE

Convergences

I n "The Man on the Train," Walker Percy had made a claim for fiction's power to banish alienation through the "triple alliance" of character, reader, and author. With *The Moviegoer*, he proved the point. In the cottage on Milan Street he wrote the first work of what is now called contemporary American fiction, the first to throw off the double burden of modernism and world war.

William Faulkner, writing to Malcolm Cowley, once characterized his approach as "oratory out of solitude." Of this approach Percy made a new thing altogether. The solitude of *The Moviegoer* isn't the solitude of a rebel or an independent, but that of a man who is alone in a crowd—in a movie theater or on a sidewalk in the French Quarter. The oratory in the book isn't that of the Bible or Stoic philosophy or a Russian novel but of a voice-over— the present-tense monologue of the person who does not tell a story so much as offer a running commentary on life as it passes before his eyes.

The present tense has acted as a preservative in the novel. The manners and everyday details, so closely observed, are noticeably out of date. Businessmen no longer wear hats to the office. Black citizens are not confined to the back of the bus. Cinemas are no longer called movie houses, and their managers no longer stand under the marquee offering passersby a "sample look" on a slow night. The trim certainties of the Baltimore Catechism are now unknown to even the devoutest Catholic child. Yet *The Moviegoer* still seems to describe the way we live now, for it describes a society in which alienation is collective, whose every aspect seems mediated, contrived, statistically anticipated, manipulated in advance, so that the direct experience of life can seem as elusive as the experience of God.

It is a familiar story of quiet desperation, with a New Orleans twist. Mardi Gras is approaching. So is Jack Bolling's thirtieth birthday. The stern aunt who raised him thinks that he ought to know by now what he wants to do with his life. Himself, he is in no hurry to find out. His job as a stock-and-bond broker is one he could do in his sleep. His real life is lived at the movies. His favorite pastime is taking a spin to the Gulf Coast with his secretary in his red MG. His strongest feeling is a vague kinship with his pretty cousin Kate, who is as lacking in direction as he is.

"For years now I have had no friends," he confesses. "I spend my entire time working, making money, going to movies and seeking the company of women."

That is an account of what he does, but not of how he lives. Bolling spends his life watching other people. What he sees is phoniness and calculation, the gap between experience and what is said about it. He watches two honeymooners in the French Quarter, whose stroll is redeemed from cliché when a movie star in town for a shoot asks them for a light. He stands talking with a business associate named Eddie Lovell, and in close-up, so to speak, watches the man's mouth move "while a little web of saliva gathers in a corner like the clear oil of a good machine."

As he watches, he riffs philosophically on what he sees, working up definitions of the varieties of contrivance and artifice and the means of escape from them. These are drawn from Kierkegaard by way of Percy's essays: the rotation; the certification, in which a person lives somewhere sadly until "he sees a movie which shows his very neighborhood," whereupon his existence is temporarily validated; the repetition of a past event so that the time between can be savored "without the usual adulteration of events that clog time like peanuts in brittle"—say, "the thirty million deaths, the countless torturings, uprootings and wanderings to and fro."

Bolling is an unlikely philosopher, but this actually makes his pronouncements more credible. Instead of seeming like secondhand Kierkegaard, and the novel like a philosophical novel, they seem to be the home-grown theories of an enlightened amateur, a Poor Richard type. When to define "the malaise," for example, Bolling appeals to the reader directly—"What is the malaise? you ask. The malaise is the pain of loss. The world is lost to you, the world and the people in it, and there remains only you and the world and you no more able to be in the world than Banquo's ghost"—his citation of Shakespeare is less important than the sense that he knows this malaise firsthand.

Bolling's own malaise is all the worse because his awareness of the usual escapes makes them seem contrived and false. Carnival and Mardi Gras leave him cold. A fishing trip is spoiled when friends theatrically exult about what a good time they are having. The French Quarter is phony, and yet he dreads going to Chicago, where he will be (he says) "No One No Place."

Instead, he follows what he calls the "Little Way" of the suburban bachelor. This is a long way from the Little Way of Thérèse of Lisieux or Dorothy Day, but the essence is the same: a mystical embrace of "everydayness." He lives in "exile" in the new suburb Gentilly, rather than in the French Quarter or the Garden District, in an apartment as drab as a motel room. He watches television with his landlady, a bigot who has three dogs to ward off Negroes. Before going to sleep, he listens to a radio show called *This I Believe*, to which he once sent a tape recording of his own beliefs, to wit: "I believe in a good kick in the ass. This—I believe." As he drives back from a day at the beach with his secretary, he explains, "Life goes on and on we go, spinning along the coast in a violet light, past Howard Johnson's and the motels and the children's carnival. It is not such a bad thing to settle for the Little Way, not the big search for the big happiness but the sad little happiness of drinks and kisses, a good little car and a warm deep thigh."

Because the novel is prefaced with a quote from Kierkegaard's *The Sickness unto Death*, Bolling has been seen as a representative man and his outlook as a symptom of the sickness of American society. Some commentators, finding bits of Percy's philosophy in Bolling's mouth, see him as a spokesman for the author; others see him as a philosopher in his own right, an existentialist in a seersucker suit and snap-brim hat. Yet the epigraph— ". . . the specific character of despair is precisely this: it is unaware of being despair"—actually points the reader away from philosophy. For all his philosophizing, Bolling is finally unaware of what ails him, unable to name his despair as despair. He is a representative man, yes; but what he says is less important than what he fails to say.

Moreover, Bolling is not the novel's only representative of despair. The two people closest to him—the only two people he knows at all—are sunk in it; the three of them are sick unto death together.

Aunt Emily Cutrer is "an Episcopalian by emotion, a Greek by nature and a Buddhist by choice," but she is a Stoic in practice, sending Bolling maxims of Marcus Aurelius in the mail. She is so set in her philosophy that she seems born to it, but in fact she is a convert, in effect, who became stoical in response to disaster: the Great War, which killed her valiant brothers, whose photograph she keeps on the mantelpiece. Like Dorothy Day, whom she resembles—a "fiercely benevolent demoniac Yankee lady" who is "handsome and formidable" and "soldierly in both look and outlook . . . with her blue-white hair and keen face and terrible gray eyes"—she "embraced advanced political ideas" as a young woman, working at a settlement house in Chicago and serving as a Red Cross volunteer in the Spanish Civil War. But unlike Day she has found no hope or consolation in her philosophy, only a grim satisfaction in a way of life steadfastly maintained.

Her stepdaughter, Kate, is twenty-five, fragile, sensitive, a weak woman raised by a strong one. She yearns to have her suicidal despair overcome through raw experience. Storms make her feel wonderful. Sometimes, she tells Bolling, she stays up all night having "revelations." The happiest moment of her life, she claims, was when she was in a car crash on the Natchez Trace. Her fiancé was killed. She survived. "I went over and looked at Lyell and everybody thought I was an onlooker. He had gravel driven into his cheek. There were twenty or thirty cars stopped on the road and then a bus came along. I got on the bus and went into Natchez. There was some blood on my blouse, so when I got to a hotel, I sent it out to be cleaned, took a bath and ordered a big breakfast, ate every crumb and read the Sunday paper."

Now Kate is on medication, and Aunt Emily Cutrer has enlisted Bolling to look out for her. He thinks that if Kate "can just hit upon the right *place*, a shuttered place of brick and vine and flowing water, her very life can be lived." What she craves, he discovers, is authority, someone—or some One—who can tell her what she ought to do and assure her that all shall be well. On a train to Chicago with Bolling (he has been called away on business) she suddenly declares that she is "a religious person." Bolling asks her what she means, and she explains, and the concrete particularity of her explanation makes it convincing: "Don't you see? What I want is to believe in someone completely and then do what he wants me to do. If God were to tell me: Kate, here is what I want you to do: you get off this train right now and go over there to that corner by the Southern Life and Accident and Insurance Company and stand there for the rest of your life and speak kindly to people—you think I would not do it? You think I would not be the happiest girl in Jackson, Mississippi? I would."

The difference between Kate and Bolling, the novel suggests, is that she seeks a remedy in religion: she longs for something to believe in and he does not. Although his mother is a Catholic, and "this accounts for the fact that I am, nominally at least, also a Catholic," he claims that he is congenitally unable to believe. "Other people, so I have read, are pious as children and later become skeptical (or, as they say on This I Believe: 'in time I outgrew the creeds and dogmas of organized religion'). Not I. My unbelief was invincible from the beginning."

What does Binx Bolling believe? He is commonly described by critics as some sort of religious figure—a mystic, an anchorite in the "desert" of suburbia, a pilgrim and wayfarer—and his story, set during Holy Week, is read, on slender evidence, as a conversion story. But what Bolling believes is less important than what he does not believe. Like Hazel Motes in *Wise Blood*, he is an admirable nihilist, whose main virtue is integrity—a refusal to believe what others believe just because they believe it.

The Moviegoer invites comparison with John Updike's *Rabbit, Run* and Richard Yates's *Revolutionary Road*, two other novels of middle-class anguish published the same year. But a comparison with *Wise Blood* is more telling; it shows Hazel Motes and Binx Bolling as complementary figures, each professing what Flannery O'Connor called "a kind of sub-religion which expresses its ultimate concern in images that have not yet broken through to show any recognition of a God who has revealed himself."

Haze once believed; Binx never did. Haze was raised a strict Christian, Binx brought up on his aunt's Garden District blend of Catholic, Episcopal, Buddhist, and classical teachings. After the war, Haze fled his beliefs by going to the city; Binx left the city for Gentilly.

Haze preaches outside a movie theater; Binx worships in one, so to speak. Whereas Haze (his own disbelief notwithstanding) sees everybody else as dead to the radical challenge of Jesus, Binx sees people "dead, dead, dead" to the "mystery and wonder" of everyday existence.

If Hazel Motes is the postwar pilgrim, versed in the canon but contemptuous of it, Binx Bolling might be called the postmodern pilgrim. He is indifferent to his ancestry and tradition. His search is outside himself, not inward. His struggle is not with the promise of the past but with the emptiness of the present. All he knows is that his own experience of life is not enough. What might the mystery of existence be? It is impossible to say. He will know it when he sees it, and the best sign of its authenticity will be that he wasn't looking.

Meanwhile, he will keep watching and wondering what it all means. At the end of the novel, when he marries Kate and settles down in a shotgun cottage "with its saloon doors swinging into the kitchen, its charcoal-gray shutters and its lead St. Francis in the patio," the Little Way of this particular pilgrim is complete. "There is only one thing I can do: listen to people, see how they stick themselves into the world, hand them along a ways in their dark journey and be handed along, and for good and selfish reasons."

The story ends on Ash Wednesday, Bolling's thirtieth birthday. He and Kate sit in a car outside a church and watch as a middle-class black man goes inside.

The church is a mundane affair, attached to a parochial school and decorated with a "schematic dove" hovering over a jungle gym and an ocean wave. In a sense, this church is the sort of "pleasant nonplace" that Walker Percy, in his own search, always found congenial. But for the reader, and perhaps for Bolling as well, the functional plainness of the church deepens the mystery of its appeal. Why, Bolling asks himself, was the black man in the church, getting ashes daubed on his forehead, so light on his dark skin that it is impossible to say they are there? "Is it part and parcel of the complex business of coming up in the world? Or is it because he believes that God himself is present here at the corner of Elysian Fields and Bons Enfants? Or is he here for both reasons: through some dazzling trick of grace, coming for one and receiving the other as God's importunate bonus?" He concludes, "It is impossible to say." Like Hazel Motes at the end of *Wise Blood*, he is not yet a believer.

In the church, the Lenten pilgrimage has begun. In the car, Binx Bolling and Kate Cutrer have decided how they are going to live their lives. They will go forward together. They will hope to change but will not count on it; they will be faithful to each other if to nothing else.

"The man took about a million pictures—me feeding geese, looking at calves, looking at a book (*Familiar Reptiles*), looking at nothing—and looking like all the time the witch of Endor," Flannery O'Connor reported to Elizabeth Hester. "I sputtered out a lot of incoherencies, which I will really hate to see when they appear."

By 1960 Andalusia had become a place of literary pilgrimage, and as *The Violent Bear It Away* was published, feature writers came to Milledgeville to profile the author, bringing photographers to take her picture. She would show them around town in her black car; show them the farm, insisting that she knew nothing about farming; show off the peacocks, nearly three dozen of them; and show them the public side of herself, providing a typed page of answers to the questions she knew they would ask and the ones she feared they wouldn't if she didn't insist.

The *Atlanta Journal*'s two profiles were like the others: the farm, the peacocks, the author's mother, the author's work, and the author's "crippling disease," which forced her to use crutches but was "of no consequence to my writing, since for that I use my head and not my feet." The photographs, however, were extraordinary. One photographer took the portrait, now ubiquitous, of O'Connor on crutches descending the porch steps with a peacock as her escort. Another took a hundred or so shots, and to see them today, on a set of contact sheets, is to realize how inflexibly iconic the view of O'Connor has become. Here she is, fully alive, semi-elderly in a black dress, carrying her body around in response to the photographer's every request: narrowing her eyes in response to an impertinent question; squinting intently at a book on her lap; smiling slyly as if at one of her own remarks; propped on a picket fence with an old barn behind; shadowed by a big straw hat; splaying her crutches as if to imitate a peacock in full spread; gazing off toward the tree line at the edge of the property; standing at the foot of a staircase she could no longer climb.

The pain in her hips had returned. Cortisone relieved the pain, but led to bone decay, which had spread to her jaws, making it as hard to eat as it was to walk. In a profile for a Catholic magazine called *The Sign* Richard Gilman praised her lack of self-pity, but he later recalled her being so ravaged ("her face twisted to one side," etc.) that at first he could not bear to look at her.

The book was published February 8, 1960, shortly before her thirty-fifth birthday. The critics were less kind than the feature writers. Orville Prescott, in the *New York Times*, characterized her as a "literary white witch . . . who brews her concoctions with the most exalted intentions" but dismissed her characters as "caricatured types of human misery . . . one can't believe in them, or care about them." *Time*'s reviewer linked her novel with her disease: "Despite such relative immobility, O'Connor manages to visit remote and dreadful places of the human spirit." "Sickening . . . ," she called it. "A full medical report. Lupus makes the news."

She had expected the novel to be "pounced on and torn limb from limb" by godless reviewers, who would side with the rationalist Rayber, not the prophet Tarwater. But she hadn't expected to be called out for poor writing. Stung by the criticism, she played the martyr (to Hester: "I enclose the latest in idiot reviews"). She complained that "even the ones that report favorably don't seem to have read the book," and wished that some Catholics would write about it, telling Robert Giroux: "If Fr. Louis reads it, I'd like to know what he thinks."

To John Hawkes, who had just finished a novel, she wrote: "I wish they could be written and deposited in a slot for the next century myself." At the same time, she approached the criticism of her own novel tactically. After seven years, she was at loose ends again ("I never know where the next word is coming from," she told Hawkes, "and now I don't know where the next 60,000 are coming from"), and she took the opportunity, in three unusual essays, to clarify her work for herself and for others.

She finished only one short story that year, "The Comforts of Home." But in the essays, all written at the behest of others, she set out her idea of art and replied to her critics, explaining, better than any feature writer could, who she was and what she aspired to do.

Her literary agent, Elizabeth McKee, suggested that she write a magazine article about peacocks. "I hate articles but I like money so I am toying with it," she protested, claiming that "I find there ain't much you can say about a peachicken."

In fact, she had a great deal to say. "The King of the Birds" is a vivid picture of Andalusia: the birds are seen roosting on fence and shed and water tower as the author watches with awe and her mother fusses in the background. At the same time, it is a personal essay in which author and subject perfectly complement each other. Although she cites the medieval idea that the peacock is a symbol of the transfigured Christ, the peacock seems a symbol of the author herself: odd, comic, proud, vain in spite of itself, resplendent in short bursts, good for little except aesthetic delight. Like the author, the peacock "begins shortly after breakfast, struts for several hours, desists in the heat of the day, and begins again in the late afternoon." Like the author, the peacock disdains the opinions of others, showing his plumage because it pleases him to do so. "The spectator will usually begin to walk around him to get a front view, but the peacock will continue to turn so that no front view is possible. The thing to do is to stand still and wait until it pleases him to turn. When it suits him, the peacock will face you."

"A Memoir of Mary Ann" was a nun's idea. Like Dorothy Day, O'Connor had become a regular visitor to Holy Ghost Monastery, riding north on Sundays with her mother to go to Mass and visit with the monks, among them Father Paul Bourne, one of the Trappist censors of Thomas Merton's books.

The letter from Sister Evangelist, Superior of the Our Lady of Perpetual Help Free Cancer Home in Atlanta, came as a surprise, and in "A Memoir of Mary Ann" O'Connor makes it seem an unlikely chance encounter, but the abbot of Holy Ghost Monastery had put them in touch.

Sister Evangelist explained her purpose. A girl in the home had died at the age of twelve. She had been a remarkable child, holy, funny, spirited, charming, and the nuns who had cared for her—raised her, laughed with her, then watched her die—wished to have her story told.

O'Connor knew right away that her answer was no. Hagiography was not her line of work. But the enclosed snapshot of the child, as she tells it in the essay, made her think a moment. "It showed a little girl in her Communion dress and veil. She was sitting on a couch, holding something I could not make out. Her small face was straight and bright on one side. The other side was protuberant, the eye was bandaged, the nose and mouth looked crowded slightly out of place."

She wrote back to Sister Evangelist saying that the nuns themselves should write Mary Ann's story—she was sure they wouldn't—and promised to write a preface if they did so.

Meanwhile, she had perceived the literary aspect of the dead child's story. The nuns' religious order had been founded by Nathaniel Hawthorne's daughter, Rose. The dead child might have walked out of Hawthorne's story "The Birthmark," about a woman who has a facial blemish that her husband, a scientist, considers so grotesque that he tries to rid her of it once and for all; or the child might have walked out of the life of Hawthorne himself, who had once been importuned by a disfigured child at a Liverpool workhouse until he took the child into his arms.

That summer, while the nuns in Atlanta struggled to memorialize Mary Ann Long, O'Connor pondered Nathaniel Hawthorne. Ever since Iowa, she had thought Hawthorne "a very great writer indeed." She had even allowed that she might have "learned something from him." Now she felt her admiration strengthen into something like kinship, conceiving herself as one of his own children, so to speak.

She had been asked to give a talk at a women's college in Macon and then discuss it with a panel of experts the next morning. "Katherine Anne Porter, Caroline Gordon, Madison Jones and me are going to be paid (well) to swap clichés about Southern culture," she told John Hawkes.

310

The talk, which she drafted over the summer, is full of brilliant insights about the South. She speaks to the Southerner's fear "that he may have been formed in the image and likeness of God," and the Southern writer's fear that his mule and wagon will get stuck "on the same track the Dixie Limited is roaring down." She moodily considers the prospect that in twenty years Southern writers, like Northern ones, "may be writing about men in gray-flannel suits and may have lost their ability to see that these gentlemen are greater freaks than what we are writing about now."

The rich lady who funded that lecture series surely got her money's worth. But "Some Aspects of the Grotesque in Southern Fiction" was finally not a view of the grotesque or of the literature of the American South. It was a declaration of independence and a defense of O'Connor's poor maligned second novel. Ten years out of Iowa, with three books behind her, O'Connor was redefining realism in accord with her own experience as a writer, and enlisting the first great writer of the American North on her side to her cause.

"These are not times when writers in this country can very well speak for one another," she began. The Agrarians had put out their pamphlet; the Depression-era social realists had all thought alike — "but today there are no good writers, bound even loosely together, who would be so bold as to say that they speak for a generation or for each other. Today each writer speaks for himself, even though he may not be sure that his work is important enough to justify his doing so."

She went on, "I think that every writer, when he speaks of his own approach to fiction, hopes to show that, in some crucial and deep sense, he is a realist; and for some of us, for whom the ordinary aspects of daily life prove to be of no great fictional interest, this is very difficult."

Hawthorne, she proposed, was such a writer. His solution to the problems that realism posed for him was to call his works "romances" rather than novels, and his problems were of interest because they "anticipated ours." They had to do with the reader's application of "a kind of orthodoxy" — to fiction that was decidedly unorthodox. Readers generally sought "a realism of fact which may, in the end, limit rather than broaden the novel's scope." They judged a work unrealistic because it was not typical of the region, the nation, the era, or the behavior of "the average American delinquent." They looked for the "movement of social forces" or for a pioneering treatment of sexuality. Applying the standards of realist orthodoxy, they had trouble appreciating another, deeper, profounder kind of realism, which demanded to be grasped in its own terms.

Echoing Hawthorne, O'Connor called this kind of realism the "modern romance tradition." To describe it, however, she used terms of the "grotesque," which she often applied to her own work. This grotesque realism has "strange skips and gaps" on its surface; it leans "toward mystery and the unexpected." It features violence and exaggeration. It is often "wild and comic." Yet this kind of realism, she proposed, is more realistic than the conventional realism, for it goes deeper to the heart of things, beyond realism's usual subject—social forces and group movements—to the "experience of mystery itself."

The artist or romancer of the grotesque uses an extreme image to join an instance from everyday life with "a point not visible to the naked eye, but believed in by him firmly, just as real to him, really, as the one that everybody sees." This artist, O'Connor said, "will be interested in what we don't understand rather than in what we do. He will be interested in possibility rather than probability. He will be interested in characters who are forced out to meet evil and grace and who act on a trust beyond themselves." This artist works in the dark, finding the path one step at a time, pushing past psychology and sociology "toward the limits of mystery," where the usual standards do not apply.

"When Hawthorne said that he wrote romances," she declared, "he was attempting, in effect, to keep for fiction some of its freedom from social determinisms, and to steer it in the direction of poetry." A century later, she was trying to do likewise.*

Although she derided critics for inventing schools and then putting writers in them, in Macon O'Connor invented a school, put herself in it, and claimed Hawthorne as its founder. In so doing, she replied to her critics and set herself apart from the critic in the audience—Caroline Gordon, the most vigorous upholder of fictional orthodoxy; and she cleared the ground for new work, although even she didn't know what it would look like.

She had one more essay to write, however. The Dominican nuns of the Free Cancer Home, defying expectations, had written Mary Ann Long's story, and one afternoon in July 1960 O'Connor welcomed six of them to Andalusia: the Sister Superior, "two old sisters, one of whom was Mary Ann's nurse,

---

*In a letter to William Sessions, September 13, 1960, she declared: "Hawthorne said he didn't write novels, he wrote romances; I am one of his descendants."

and three younger sisters, one of whom draws (very badly) and two of whom write (very very badly)," she confided to Elizabeth Hester. "However, the Sister Superior is the one doing the writing on the book. . . . She don't write like Shakespeare but she does well enough for this."

Preparing for their visit, O'Connor read the life of their foundress, Rose Hawthorne. It was the story, in O'Connor's paraphrase, of "a woman of great force and energy," a Catholic convert who sought "the kind of occupation that would be a practical fulfillment of her own conversion" and so "moved into a tenement in the worst section of New York and began to take in incurable cancer patients," whereupon a movement was born. Rose Hawthorne considered her work with cancer patients the fruit of her father's encounter with the "wretched and rheumy" child in the Liverpool workhouse, when, as he wrote, "I never should have forgiven myself had I repelled its advances."

Thirty years earlier, Rose Hawthorne's life story had inspired Dorothy Day to found the Catholic Worker. Now, as Flannery O'Connor read what the nuns had written, she came to see Mary Ann as a wretched child whose advances she could not repel. The manuscript was poorly, piously written, but the child's charm and pluck had come through; and moreover, its obvious deformities, she perceived, were akin to those of the child whose story it told. "The story was as unfinished as the child's face. Both seemed to have been left, like creation on the seventh day, to be finished by others."

For the moment, it was up to her to finish the story. She did what editing she could—trying to "get the obnoxious pieties out of it"—and asked Robert Giroux for advice.

She doubted that it was publishable, and even bet the nuns a pair of peacocks that they wouldn't prove her wrong. Nevertheless, she set to writing an introduction, as she had promised. She began at the beginning, telling the story of Sister Evangelist's letter; Hawthorne's story "The Birthmark"; the life of Rose Hawthorne; her distaste for the project; and the doggedness of the nuns. Caroline Gordon (who read a draft of the essay) thought there was too much of Flannery O'Connor in it and not enough of Mary Ann Long, but O'Connor knew better. The objective was not to depict the dead girl but to win over the skeptical reader, who would doubt that such a girl's story was worth telling at all.

The essay she wrote was more than the fulfilment of a promise. It was another act of self-definition, in which she explained herself and her aims once more. In her lecture in Macon, she had defined her kind of realism in literary terms; now she defined it in Catholic terms, making clear that the roots of her unusual fiction lay in religious orthodoxy.

A child like Mary Ann, she observed, is obviously grotesque, and in the modern world such a child is thought to "discredit the goodness of God." How can a good God allow such a child to die? the Ivan Karamazovs of the world ask. How, moreover, can a good God allow such a child to be born? The modern unbeliever prides himself on his realism, his willingness to recognize suffering and to ponder the problem of evil directly. But in O'Connor's estimation such an outlook is not realistic; it is naive, sentimental, and even dangerous. It is the believer, not the unbeliever, who is the realist. In a child like Mary Ann the believer sees the likeness of every human person—deformed, limited, imperfect. In human deformity the believer sees "the raw material of good." In human suffering the believer sees the grounds of our common humanity, recognizing that it is through suffering, above all, that human beings are stirred to the love of one another, and to the love of God, who showed his love for humanity through his willingness to suffer as one of us.

"The creative action of the Christian's life is to prepare for his death in Christ," O'Connor declared. Mary Ann Long, by this reckoning, had died amply prepared. In just a few years, the Dominican nuns had shown Mary Ann the value of her life and the meaning of her death; and in so doing, they had expressed in life the meaning of Nathaniel Hawthorne's work, which turned the reader's attention away from schemes for the improvement of humanity and toward an embrace of human imperfection. "There is a direct line between the incident in the Liverpool workhouse, the work of Hawthorne's daughter, and Mary Ann," O'Connor wrote. "By reason of the fear, the search, and the charity that marked his life and influenced his daughter's, Mary Ann inherited, a century later, the wealth of Catholic wisdom that taught her what to make of her death. Hawthorne gave what he did not have himself."

She was describing the Communion of Saints, whose outlines, she declared, "entwining the living and the dead," are "the lines that join the most diverse lives and hold us fast in Christ." In her introduction to the nuns' ragged manuscript several such lines converged. The line from Nathaniel Hawthorne extended past Mary Ann Long to Mary Flannery O'Connor, who was kin to Hawthorne not only in matters of literary style but (she proposed) in faith and morals.

The essay—as she must have known—was the most emphatic thing she had ever written. When she was finished, she affixed it to the manuscript of Mary Ann's story and rapped out a letter to Robert Giroux ("The enclosed jolly treat is the Sisters' manuscript," etc.). Although she didn't usually festoon her correspondence with references to feast days and saints' days and the like, the date that day, which she typed on the essay and the letter alike, seems to underscore the moral of the story. It was December 8, 1960—the Feast of the Immaculate Conception, celebrating the Catholic belief that the Virgin Mary alone among mortals was conceived without original sin, which disfigures all the rest of us here below.

She went into the hospital later that month "for a general inspection of my bones." She learned that they were disintegrating slowly, a side effect of the treatments for lupus.

Upon emerging, she started a new story. On Christmas Eve she told Elizabeth Hester, "Me, I am working on that story I told you about and having the best time I have had in a spell of working. If I can work it out, I'll have something here." At first it was just a sketch of a no-good layabout's recollection of the night in his childhood when he saw a tattooed man at a fair. But the title she gave it—"Parker's Back"—makes clear that she already knew where she was going with it. This would be the new work, at once romance and grotesquerie, whose qualities she had sought to define for her audience in Macon—a story about a character going out to meet evil and grace, acting on a trust beyond himself. This would be her treatment of the human mystery head-on; this would be her "Birthmark"—her attempt to out-Hawthorne Hawthorne by finding a grotesque fictional image for the human body, however disfigured, as the image of God.

John F. Kennedy had been elected president, the first Catholic to win the office. His election, acknowledged ever since as a turning point—as the moment when American Catholics, claiming the country as their own, came of age—was seen at the time as an appealing outcome, little more. Walker Percy was pleased. Dorothy Day recalled the night before the war when two of the Kennedy brothers—she couldn't recall which two—dropped by St. Joseph's House. Flannery O'Connor observed that "now that we have elected him, we can begin to cuss him." At the Abbey of Gethsemani, a longtime beneficiary of Ethel Kennedy's charity, the reading during meals in refectory was "nothing but Kennedy for days," and Thomas Merton, who ventured out to a school gymnasium in a nearby hamlet to vote for him, observed, "He ought to make a reasonably good president—with the aid of his brothers, sisters, cousins, aunts, uncles etc."

For Merton, that fall, there was news altogether more dramatic. He had been granted permission to erect a hermitage on the monastery grounds. He had picked the site himself, a natural clearing on a low rise of land. Plans were drawn up for a conference center. Merton proposed a few changes, as did the abbot, and it became "no longer a shiny, smart little pavilion but just a plain cottage with two rooms and a porch." He took up a shovel and helped dig the foundation, singing from a psalm about the house of the Lord being founded on a rock.

Two months later, it was finished: a square house, built of cinder blocks, with a wide porch and a sloping roof, all surprisingly modern-looking. Inside, there was a sitting room with a stone hearth and another, smaller room, where, in time, he would sleep at night.

He lit a fire in the hearth. The scent of woodsmoke filled the sitting room. He opened his journal and marked the anniversary of his entry into the monastery. Thirty years earlier, as Michael Mott has pointed out, Merton and his father had designed a house from the ruins of an old chapel. Now Merton had fashioned a house of his own, and he began to orient his life around it. "It is true, places and situations are not supposed to matter," he wrote. But "this one makes a tremendous difference. Real silence. Real solitude.

"After having thought for ten years of building a hermitage, and thought of the ten places where one might be built, now *having built* one in the best place, I cannot believe it. It is nevertheless real—if anything is real. In it everything becomes unreal."

The day after Christmas he "lit candles at dusk" and kept a vigil there. Quoting a Latin maxim to the effect that *this is my resting place forever*, he wrote of a homecoming, "a journey ended." He recalled a Hindu saying about the point past which one leaves no tracks.

At the hermitage, Merton meant to dedicate himself to the experience of God in solitude. In his journal, he resolved: "For my own part, I have one task left. To pray, to meditate, to enter into truth, to sit before the abyss, to be educated in the word of Christ and thus to make my contribution to world peace. There is not much left to be said."

Solitude, in a sense, was lonely and otherworldly, and the hermitage was inescapably an escape, a place for "the passage out of this world to the Father, entry into the Kingdom." Yet the hermitage had originally been conceived as a place of "encounter" with representatives from other churches and other faiths. In the toolshed there had been room for a lone monk only, who faced the world in dialogue with a distant Other. At the hermitage there was room for company, and in time he peopled the place imaginatively, gathering a community around him.

He had become obsessed with the Desert Fathers and had translated their sayings from Latin into idiomatic English, telling their story. The Desert Fathers of the fourth century lived in a community or "skete" in Egypt, outside Alexandria. They dwelt in cells arranged in a loose confederation. Pilgrims came from the city to see how they lived. One pilgrim, Athanasias, wrote about them; his book, nominally a biography of St. Anthony, became the first work of monastic literature, and the Fathers' sayings, or *verba*, became axioms familiar to every monk, hermit, and contemplative.

Merton had been struck by the kinship between the *verba* and the sayings of the Buddhist tradition, and after translating them had invited the Zen master D. T. Suzuki to write an introduction. When this idea was scuttled by his superiors, however, he wrote an introduction of his own, stressing the importance of the *verba* in the Catholic tradition.

In its clarity, its directness, its answers to obvious questions, "The Wisdom of the Desert" is one of Merton's most appealing pieces. What is the experience of God? Why seek solitude in order to attain this experience? How does solitude fit with community? The questions are not answered so much as the answers are implied in an evocation of a community on pilgrimage. "What the Fathers sought most of all was their own true self, in Christ. And in order to do this they had to reject completely the false, formal self, fabricated under social compulsion in 'the world.' They sought a way to God that was uncharted and freely chosen, not inherited from others who had mapped it out beforehand."

The Desert Fathers were not rebels so much as "anarchists," in Merton's estimation. They "did not believe in letting themselves be passively guided by a decadent state," yet they "had no desire to rule over others themselves." Rather, they sought a society "where men were all truly equal, where the only authority under God was the charismatic authority of wisdom, experience, and love."

Described thus, the Desert Fathers are precursors of the Catholic Workers, and in his letters to Dorothy Day that year Merton made clear that he saw the movement as something like a modern communal ideal. She sought to disabuse him of the notion. He had praised the "beat people" as the ones

God chiefly loved; she told him what life with such people was really like. "Aside from a disturbed family for whom I beg your prayers, and two exseamen puttering around fixing screens, I am alone," she wrote from Staten Island, where she was recovering from the flu. "To be alone with eight people is to be alone at the CW." One seaman was an ex-Trappist and "disturbed or a saint, who can tell. Both, probably." The family was bitter and faithless, like a family in Dostoevsky, whose stories life at the Catholic Worker seemed to imitate.

Merton replied that he loved Dostoevsky. With Day, however, he was more eager to discuss life than literature, and he kept directing their exchange back toward the life of poverty. Her account of the poor family, he told her, had "moved me deeply." So had the sight of some poor old folks at a convent in Louisville. It was in these people "that Christ lives and works most. And in the hurt people who are bitter and say they have lost their faith." And yet at Gethsemani, there were no poor people—only some monks who had taken a vow of poverty cloaked in "the illusion of spirituality."

Merton felt for Day the mixture of admiration and envy that he felt for all the figures he truly identified with. She knew the poor. She was poor herself. She even had the prayers of the poor, who loved her as one of them. She had an experience he knew he lacked, one that, unlike that of an anchorite or a hermit, could not be entered readily through the imagination. "You are the richest woman in America spiritually, with such prayers behind you," he told her. "You cannot fail even if you try to."

She wrote back in October. The poor, and the voluntary poor, she made clear, are bitter, critical, rebellious, and prone to see their rage as righteous anger. She thought of the woman at St. Joseph's House who dosed herself with drugs and liquor, "crying out constantly against her fate"; she thought of the "angry young men" whose "bitterness and criticism" filled the house. She tried to tell herself that " 'they are prophets crying out in this time.' But there are too many of them.

"All this rebellion makes me long for obedience, hunger and thirst for it, as a woman does for a husband whom she can esteem and who will direct her," she confessed. "Women especially cry out against their terrible freedom. But trying to be obedient and also personally responsible, responsive to the daily calls made upon one, means we are overburdened." The admiring envy was mutual, in other words. So Father Louis, living out the Trappist vow of poverty, envied her direct and anarchistic encounter with the poor?

Well, she, the Anarch, who had to make and enforce the rules of "holy poverty," yearned to be told what to do.

He had asked for her prayers and for those of the poor. She assured him that he had them. But she did so in a way that gave him something more important. As believers, they belonged to the same community. More than he wanted the Catholic Workers' prayers, she perceived, he wanted to pray along with them—to belong to the community of the poor she had founded. So she described the motley crew at Peter Maurin Farm, including "a former teacher with one eye, a mother of an illegitimate child," and the like. "Every night," she told him, "we say the rosary and compline in our little chapel over the barn, heavy with the smell of the cow downstairs (one can hear her chewing her cud), and we have a bulletin board there with the names of those who ask prayers. Yours is there."

That the publisher of *The Moviegoer* was Alfred A. Knopf—publisher of William Alexander Percy's memoir—made publication complex enough, threatening to undo the work of emancipation that Percy had done in writing the novel. As it turned out, establishing his literary independence was the least of Percy's troubles. Stanley Kauffmann of Knopf asked him to work over the novel twice, then found the house's other editors unconvinced. Then Kauffmann was fired. Then Alfred Knopf himself turned against the novel. The process took two years, and when the book was published at last—May 1961—the reviews were favorable but not numerous. Only Flannery O'Connor's friend Brainard Cheney, in the *Southern Review*, saw the kinship with Dostoevsky and the existentialists that Percy thought made the novel what it was.

It is no wonder that reviewers did not see the novel as a text about the sickness of modern life and Percy as the American successor to Albert Camus, who had died in a car crash the previous year. The novel's insights are delivered sideways, offhandedly. It was only in the rewrites that Percy prefaced the novel with a snippet from Kierkegaard and dedicated it to his dead uncle. It was in the rewrites that the title—which had been *Carnival in Gentilly: Confessions of a Moviegoer*, a double-barreled combination suggested by Shelby Foote—was made *The Moviegoer*, which echoed *The Stranger* nicely and put the emphasis on the emblematic main character, not the story. And it was in a rewrite that Percy added an epilogue, which, though opaque, does the most to suggest a religious dimension to the novel.

The epilogue was the editor's idea. Kauffmann had asked Percy to add some material about Binx Bolling's father, and Percy did so, developing a chance encounter with Bolling's mother and her new family of six at their vacation cottage in Biloxi, Mississippi, on the Gulf Coast. The Smiths are Louisiana Catholics through and through: daughters named Thérèse, Mathilde, and Clare; a wheelchair-bound teenager, Lonnie, who "uses the peculiar idiom of the catechism in ordinary speech," referring to his need to "conquer an habitual disposition" and requesting Extreme Unction when he comes down with pneumonia.

In the epilogue, Bolling and Kate visit Lonnie in the hospital and see that he is going to die of hepatitis. Outside, Lonnie's brother Donice asks:

"When Our Lord raises us up on the last day, will Lonnie still be in a wheelchair or will he be like us?"

"He'll be like you."

"You mean he'll be able to ski?" The children cock their heads and listen like old men.

"Yes."

"Hurray!"

Percy would later explain this scene as a "salute" to *The Brothers Karamazov*, in which Alyosha, asked about the resurrection of the body, gives a similar answer. In Bolling's mouth, however, the answer seems facetious, a pacifier for the children. Does he believe it? It is impossible to say, and that, perhaps, is the point of the epilogue, as well as the novel. *The Moviegoer* is not *The Brothers Karamazov*; the hour is late, the ancient faith attenuated; and the epilogue of the novel, one might say, is an epilogue to the long story of that old-time religion, ethnically rooted, catechetically certain, which was vanishing in 1961, as the book was published and the Catholic bishops prepared for the Second Vatican Council. The churchgoer was giving way to the moviegoer, Percy seemed to say, and in the years to come the churchgoer and the moviegoer, although related, would be strangers to each other.

Through Mary Ann Long, Flannery O'Connor had gained "a new perspective on the grotesque." Now more than ever she saw a human life as "something under construction" and the grotesque not as a touch of evil but as a sign of the working of God's grace.

While she seemed to come to it effortlessly, her new perspective had a source outside herself in the writings of Pierre Teilhard de Chardin, which she was reading ardently. "I don't understand the scientific end of it or the philosophical but even when you don't know these things, the man comes through," she later said. "He was alive to everything there is to be alive to and in the right ways."

Before his death in 1955 Teilhard (as he is called) had lived several lives: Jesuit priest, chaplain in the Great War, paleontologist in China investigating the origins of the species, author of speculo-mystical works kept unpublished because they seemed to challenge the Catholic teaching that God created the world out of nothing in six days.

Now that he was dead his works were being published in English translation, and O'Connor was "much taken" with them. *The Phenomenon of Man*, Teilhard's account of evolution, was hard going but "stimulating to the imagination." *The Divine Milieu* was shorter and more congenial. Here was an account of how the world might be transformed—"divinized," Teilhard puts it—through worldly activity, which Catholics were taught to shun. Here was a priest whose synthesis of science and mysticism, of worldliness and detachment, was grounded in his own experience.

Teilhard's account of the believer's participation in creation has three parts: about human action, about experience suffered or "undergone," and about the "divine milieu" in which "all the elements of the universe *touch each other* by that which is most inward and ultimate in them."

O'Connor was struck especially by the second part—by the notion that believers who endure "passive diminishments" such as disease in a Christian spirit contribute to the great work of redemption "like soldiers who fall during the assault which leads to peace."

Surely there was more to Teilhard's influence on her, however, than a view of the redemptive value of suffering, which she had grasped from the beginning.

Teilhard was the first "progressive" Catholic theologian she had read. To that point in her life Christian faith had been an absolute, true at all times and places, and all progress was suspect, especially progress in society, as in the South. Now in Teilhard's work she encountered an argument for what might be called the progress of grace—for the participation of all creation, especially the Church, in an upward evolutionary spiral which "will be completed at the end of time in Christ." In a sense, this was fundamental Christian doctrine ("I believe in love to be efficacious in the loooong run,"

O'Connor told Elizabeth Hester in 1955). But Teilhard's work made it emphatic: the believer was on the side of progress whether she liked it or not.

Teilhard's literary approach reflected his confidence in progress. Rather than arguing for or against evolution, he sought to look forward in time and write for generations of readers who would accept evolution as self-evident. Rather than defending himself, he strove to balance the theoretical and the personal, the orthodox and the visionary, knowing that he would not be around to explain his work. "As long as he lived he was faithful to his Jesuit superiors but I think he must have figured that in death he would be a citizen of some other sphere and that the fate of his book with the Church would rest with the Lord," O'Connor told Hester. Although others, inevitably, would distort his work, it was sound in itself: "The second volume complements the first and makes you see that even if there were errors in his thought, there were none in his heart."

Unpublished in his lifetime, Teilhard was an example of the kind of writer O'Connor took herself to be, one more concerned with posterity than the present. Stimulated imaginatively by his work—and, no doubt, by her gathering sense that her own time was short—she looked forward in her own work as though for the first time, anticipating the progress of grace in the years to come.

As it happened, this turn toward the future suggested a way to write about the present-day South. She would have to anticipate further developments; she would have to stylize her work for posterity, writing with one eye on the end of time and the other on the state of Georgia, A.D. 1961.

She wrote a new story, finishing it in March. She gave it the title of one of Teilhard's essays—at once an act of homage and an acceptance of the challenge of his work—and she already saw a whole book in the theme it announced. "The story is called EVERYTHING THAT RISES MUST CONVERGE and this is the title I want to put on my next collection," she told Elizabeth McKee. To Roslyn Barnes, a Catholic writer studying at Iowa, she reported on "a story called 'Everything That Rises Must Converge,' which is a physical proposition that I found in Père Teilhard and am applying to a certain situation in the Southern states & indeed in all the world."

The Dominican sisters of Hawthorne had given her a TV, and it brought the nightly news, which, that year, was the news of the South. More and more, Martin Luther King, once thought an opportunist, was recognized as a leader and his Old Testament rhetoric as apt. Blacks were the Israelites. He was their Moses. Their movement toward equality was a pilgrimage, a journey to a place where justice dwelled, a place seen in a dream and told of by the prophets. They would no longer be consoled by the imagery of heavenly justice. They would strive toward the promised land and hope to see it with their own eyes.

Although O'Connor would not have said so, King's approach was strikingly akin to her own. He cast the situation of the "Christ-haunted" South in the shadow of Scripture and the light of all time. Through sit-ins and marches and boycotts and vigils he posed the same question—*Lady, what is a man?*—that Mr. Shiftlet had posed in "The Life You Save May Be Your Own."

As if in reply, O'Connor sought to dramatize the situation herself. Thus far she had addressed "the race problem" indirectly and in her own terms. Now she took up a situation that was familiar to the public at large, and made her themes converge with those of her time and place.

"Everything That Rises Must Converge" is unlike anything she had written. Missing are the signature aspects of her style—the cartoonish characterizations, the extravagant similes, the relentless likening of one thing to another. In their place is a laconic matter-of-factness. The characters are typical twentieth-century Southerners. The situation is familiar and widely discussed. The symbolism is "the coin of the realm, which has the face worn off of it." The story does not spring forth from the mind of the author. It is joined already in progress.

Julian and his mother are going to take a city bus downtown. She is upright, chattery, quick with a cliché, proud to be descended from people prosperous enough to own slaves, nostalgic about "the old darky who was my nurse" but loath to ride the integrated buses at night. He is young, superior, bitter, thwarted. He sees her ways as a trial and her heritage as a burden, now to be envied, now to be ashamed of. He harbors "an evil urge to break her spirit."

Beneath their obvious differences are subtler ones, carefully set in place by the author. She goes to exercise class at the Y to "reduce"; he wishes to broaden her. She has "fallen" socially; he has elevated himself by going to college. She knows who she is; he knows what he is not. She thinks he is naive, a young man trying to find his way. He thinks she is naive, judging her "sky-blue" eyes to be "as innocent and untouched by experience as they must have been when she was ten. Were it not that she was a widow who had struggled fiercely to feed and clothe and put him through school and who was supporting him still, 'until he got on his feet,' she might have been a little girl that he had to take to town."

The comparison of the two, which reveals their characters, also anticipates the comparison of whites and blacks which takes place once they board the bus. It happens so inevitably that Julian might have planned it beforehand. His mother remarks that they don't have the bus to themselves. He cringes. A black man sits next to him. He decides to teach her a lesson. Though he has no cigarettes—though he does not smoke—he asks the black man for a light. In his mind he and the black man are kin. He sees himself taking part in a sit-in. He envisions making friends with blacks and bringing one home to his mother as her future daughter-in-law. "Prepare yourself, he said. There is nothing you can do about it. This is the woman I've chosen. She's intelligent, dignified, even good, and she's suffered and she hasn't thought it fun. Now persecute us, go ahead and persecute us. Drive her out of here, but remember, you're driving me, too."

When a black woman, accompanied by her son, boards the bus wearing the same bizarre hat as Julian's mother, the likeness strikes him as prophetically apt. "He gave a loud chuckle so that she would look at him and see that he saw. She turned her eyes on him slowly. The blue in them seemed to have turned a bruised purple. For a moment he had an uncomfortable sense of her innocence, but it lasted only a second before principle rescued him. Justice entitled him to laugh. His grin hardened until it said to her as plainly as if he were saying aloud: Your punishment exactly fits your pettiness. This should teach you a permanent lesson."

It is this observation that prompts his downfall—"his entry into the world of guilt and sorrow." In his pride, his vision is narrowed, not broadened. In his regard for the other, he cannot see himself. In his vision of racial progress, there is no place for his mother.

Some years earlier, O'Connor had told the story of the day she heard a white bus driver urge all the "stove-pipe blondes" to get to the back of the bus, recalling that on that day she became an integrationist.

Over the years, however, she had many misgivings about integration. In her view it did away with the manners that blacks and whites had developed over time. It demanded that complex problems be resolved overnight. It was a merely legal solution, imposed on the South from the outside. Above all, it was an abstraction, rooted in a view of an ideal society—and in the abstract identification of Northern whites with Southern blacks—rather than in the actual life of the South.

"For the rest of the country, the problem is settled when the Negro has his rights, but for the Southerner, whether he's white or colored, that's only the beginning," she explained in 1963. Echoing the language of evolution found in Teilhard's work, she went on: "The South has to evolve a way of life in which the two races can live together with mutual forbearance. You don't form a committee to do this or pass a resolution; both races have to work it out the hard way."

In "Everything That Rises Must Converge," she took no position on integration or race relations generally. Rather, she looked past the immediate conflict over integration to dramatize one of the tense encounters through which racial progress would come about. The title suggests a number of convergences: of blacks and whites, of children and parents, of the present and the past, of laws and manners, of love and justice. Dr. King employed the lofty rhetoric of the Bible; O'Connor would use the plain speech of the heart. And that would be the moral of the story. Love comes before justice. Race relations are as nothing compared to blood relations. Before he feels for the Negro, Julian should feel for his mother, because she is his mother.

The lasting popularity of "Everything That Rises Must Converge" suggests how artfully it was stylized for posterity. O'Connor's casual remarks on race, however, have dated less well. Always distasteful, they grow more so in retrospect, making her seem, at times, a double agent, a traitor to her true country.

Racial quips are scattered through her published letters, often accompanied by amused paraphrases of the racial slurs of others. There is a proud announcement of her purchase of "colored rental property." An offhand remark that "As the niggers say, I have the misery." A cool observation, after one of the workers, maimed in an accident, received workers' compensation, that "this is a very demoralizing situation. A wealthy sitting Negro." A declaration that she would not meet James Baldwin during his travels in Georgia on the grounds that such a meeting "would cause the greatest trouble and disturbance and disunion" among the whites of Milledgeville. A blunt affirmation that "about the Negroes, the kind I don't like is the philosophizing prophesying pontificating kind, the James Baldwin kind. Very ignorant but never silent." An explanation that her rule of thumb in judging a Negro was to ask herself "would this person be endurable if white." And, in the unpublished letters, suggestions that she does not like Negroes and that they should all be sent back to Africa, where they came from.

Sally Fitzgerald, who oversaw the publication of the letters (and left a good many out), sought to ease the sting of her late friend's remarks through euphemism, citation of extenuating circumstances, and circumloquacious apology. Recalling O'Connor in the introduction to *The Habit of Being*, Fitzgerald referred to "an area of sensibility in her that seems to have remained imperfectly developed," allowed that her "tongue could take on an unsaintly edge," acknowledged her fondness for "the prevailing locution of the South," and emphasized that her nastiest remarks are to be found in a "misbegotten dialogue" with a woman of modest literary talent whom she addressed, and was so addressed herself, in letters that were invariably full of "name-calling, jeers, and mock derision."

This was Maryat Lee, sister of Robert E. Lee, president of Georgia College in Milledgeville, O'Connor's alma mater. While visiting her brother in Milledgeville in 1957, Lee paid a visit to O'Connor at Andalusia. They liked each other immediately. Leaving, Lee accepted a ride with a black farm worker. The act might have scandalized the people of Milledgeville; in any case, it seems to have scandalized O'Connor. "I find it hard to imagine any conversation that might have taken place in that car," she confessed in a letter shortly afterward. "When you left, my mother said to me, 'Don't you tell a soul that she is going in *Emmet's* car. Don't you even tell Sister. If that got out, it would ruin Dr. Lee.'"

"It is often so funny that you forget it is terrible," O'Connor went on. "It" is the life of the segregated, two-tier South; and the remark, and the situation it describes, is a running theme of their correspondence—more than 250 letters over seven years.

To readers of *The Habit of Being*, Maryat Lee is Elizabeth Hester's opposite. Where O'Connor's letters to Hester are severe, superior, hortatory, her letters to Lee are spontaneous and abandoned. She mocks Lee's decision to leave behind "dear old dirty Southland" and live in Manhattan, where she is a playwright, community organizer, and devoted reader of the *Village Voice*. Upon learning of Lee's plans to marry, she wonders whether Lee will be able to bear life with a man. She derides her friend's frenzied creativity: "Did I understand you right that you are writing from 5000 to 7000 words of bad prose a day? . . . Girl, it couldn't be anything else but bad. It must be automatic writing. Slow down for pity sake." She decorates the margins of the letters with skulls and crossbones. She signs off, each time, with a variation on Tarwater, her chosen nom de plume: Tarpot, Tarblender, O'authwarter, and so on. In these letters, written from one headstrong Southern daughter to another, the author who kept carbon copies of all her letters seems, for once, to be writing for the mutual pleasure of herself and her correspondent—to be writing as a woman, a friend, a conspirator, not as an artist.

Where did Flannery O'Connor stand in matters of race? The evidence tells two ways. The black characters in O'Connor's fiction are invariably admirable: the farmhands Astor and Sulk in "The Displaced Person," who knowingly observe the Polish farmworker's rise and fall; the dairy workers Randall and Morgan in "The Enduring Chill," who see a problem coming long before the white writer Asbury does; the good neighbor Buford Munson in *The Violent Bear It Away*, who (as Sally Fitzgerald stressed) upbraids Francis Tarwater for neglecting his dead grandfather: "It's owing to me he's resting there. I buried him while you were laid out drunk. It's owing to me his corn has been plowed. It's owing to me the sign of his Saviour is over his head." Yet at the same time there is the word "nigger" running through the correspondence. There are the quips about blacks, offered again and again as punch lines. There is, in the letters, a habit of bigotry that grows more pronounced as O'Connor's fiction, in matters of race, grows more complex and profound—a habit that seems to defy the pattern established by her art.

It is in this seeming contradiction, perhaps, that an insight into O'Connor's view of race is to be found. Oddly enough, her casual insensitivity about race matters is bound up inextricably with her most cherished ideas about art, and with her understanding of sacred history as an evolutionary progress toward the divine.

Teilhard de Chardin's work prompted O'Connor more than ever to stylize her own work for posterity, casting it forward toward the end of time. Beginning with "Everything That Rises Must Converge," then, she made her fiction especially sound on race matters, writing in anticipation of a time when blacks, the equals of whites in the eyes of God, would also be the equals of whites in society—and in the reader's eyes.

For all that, she remained an artist schooled in Jacques Maritain's notion of the "habit of art." Early in her career, the notion of the habit of art had inspired her in a double way. It affirmed that as a religious artist she should strive to depict religious subjects according to the standards of art, not those of piety. And it affirmed that, as an artist, she was called to be virtuous in her own sphere of activity above all—that she need not be a good person to make good art; she needed to be a good artist.

Alas, the very notion of the habit of art that called forth *Wise Blood* in 1948 gave license to the loose talk found in *The Habit of Being*, for it invited the artist to segregate her art from her everyday life. In her art O'Connor took the long view, envisioning the equality of the races at a further point in time. In her life—emboldened perhaps by her confidence that her art, by which she would be judged, was sound—she followed the crude and dehumanizing manners of the white South, and even delighted in them, as if the South's dramatic resistance to racial equality was a down-home regional comedy.

In 1959 and 1960 the *Catholic Worker* printed several pieces in support of the new people's government in Cuba, formed by Fidel Castro after the ouster of the Batista regime. The letters poured in, protesting that Castro was a socialist, a persecutor of Catholics, who had nationalized the churches and deported the clergy, and whose regime had been condemned by the bishops—and now by the Catholic in the White House. After the failed invasion of Cuba in April 1961 the paper came under closer scrutiny—from the FBI, which suspected the movement of sheltering subversives; from pacifists, who saw support for violent revolution as a betrayal of nonviolent principles; and from the Catholic press, which insinuated that Day and her "anarchic beatnikism" were not really Catholic.

Day rose to the defense of her quixotic position. Trying to write a column at such a time, she told her readers that spring, was "like sitting down to meditate in the middle of Times Square." On the radio, on television, on the streets, all the talk was of the Bay of Pigs invasion or the trial of Adolph Eichmann in Jerusalem. She felt "crushed, submerged by events."

She waited till summer before speaking to the issue directly in "On Pilgrimage." Because she had not been to Cuba, she began, she could not say for sure what the situation was there. But she had been involved in the class struggle for nearly fifty years, and in Mexico in the 1920s, where she had witnessed the persecution of the Church firsthand, she had met Communists who were not Marxist-Leninists and who were persecuted themselves for their independence.

That is how she saw Castro. Atheism was basic to Marxism, but Castro, she proposed, was a Catholic socialist, not a doctrinaire Marxist. He had won the support of the workers by cutting cane in the fields with them. He wouldn't have had to persecute the Church if the Church hadn't protected the Batista oligarchy. Now he was calling for the "peaceful coexistence" of Catholic Church and socialist state, and there was reason to believe that he was sincere. Moreover, those who opposed him might well be "catspaws"— "might be fighting the battle of the rich, of the American corporations," which regarded Cuba as their possession.

"One could weep with the tragedy of denying Christ in the poor," she declared. Christ had said that He was to be found among the poor, and that whatever was done to the poor was done to Him. So the Catholic Workers were on the side of the poor first of all. If they found themselves on the side of the persecutors of the Church, well, that was a "tragic fact"; and if Catholics in Cuba were persecuted, well, the Gospels make clear that the faithful should expect persecution, even welcome it. "If we are not being persecuted," she declared, "there is something wrong with us."

In the midst of it Day evidently wrote to Thomas Merton, asking for his advice and his prayers. The letter is lost, if and when it was written at all, but Merton's reply suggests that in it she confessed her discouragement over the Cuba controversy and the state of the movement.

She knew from reading *The Seven Storey Mountain* that he had visited Cuba on pilgrimage, and the island represented to her, in 1961, something like what it had represented to him in 1940—the prospect of an ideal society, at once Catholic and populist, which led her to exaggerate its good qualities just as he had done in the autobiography. Now that ideal was being challenged by Castro and the Kennedy administration.

Merton knew the feeling from experience. In his reply, he urged her to maintain her vision of a Christian society as an ideal, but not to identify it with any worldly society. The failure of "Christian civilization" to be truly Christian left him and her both "tempted to despair." The solution was to keep up their hope in "God as the One Reality."

In the meantime, he went on, a place like the Catholic Worker kept the ideal alive—as "a place where really sincere people come to the end of the line, that is, they seek there the last resort of truth and hope to be able to do something, and see how helpless they are." So did a contemplative monastery, "but with a whole lot more cushions. In a way it is nice to be able to think that one's prayers are invisibly effecting great things: you don't have to look then."

He was as discouraged as she was. When it came to war and peace, the

"Catholic position" espoused by the bishops seemed to contradict the Gospel, making them all part of a "general system of delusion" that "wants and intends to defend itself—and the glory of God—with bombs." He confided, "I find myself more and more drifting toward the derided and probably quite absurd and defeatist position of a sort of Christian anarchist."

It is a telling remark, for it suggests how scant Merton's knowledge of Day's writing was—suggests the degree to which his affinity with her was instinctive, not learned or acquired. Although she had been describing herself as a Christian anarchist since the thirties, he tried out the term as if he had just devised it.

In 1961 Merton was still cloistered in prayer nearly half the day and was allowed to read the daily papers only now and then. "I am still a 14th century man: the century of Eckhard, Ruysbroeck, Tauler, the English recluses, the author of the *Cloud*, Langland and Chaucer—more an independent and a hermit than a community man, interested in psychology, a lover of the dark cloud in which God is found by love," he wrote in his journal. "That is what I am: I cannot consent to be it and not be ashamed that I am not something more fashionable."

He was still learning about World War II. As the Eichmann trial continued, he read *The Rise and Fall of the Third Reich*, discovering things that he had come to know late or not at all in the monastery, where the bombing of Hiroshima had not been announced till the appointed time for news came around the following Sunday.

The more he read about the great silence surrounding the Holocaust, the more his own elected silence in the monastery seemed a lapse of conscience. He had been a conscientious objector. Now he felt like a guilty bystander. As a monk he was a marginal man and his life was a witness against the age. In the monastery, his witness for peace was unknown and had no symbolic value.

Out in the hermitage, he suddenly entered the great debate of his time, schooling himself in war and peace with the enthusiasm he had brought to mystical theology.

He wrote a prose poem called *Original Child Bomb*, named after the bomb—"Little Boy"—that had been dropped on Hiroshima. He wrote a didactic piece about the Holocaust, "Chant to Be Used in Processions Around a Site with Furnaces," and sent it to a few correspondents, Day among them, with a note: "Here is a gruesome poem."

It was published forthwith in the *Catholic Worker*, a declamation in the voice of an Auschwitz furnace operator from a "good Catholic family," concluding thus: "In my days we worked hard we saw what we did our self sacrifice was conscientious and complete our work was faultless and detailed. . . . Do not think yourself better because you burn up friends and enemies with long-range missiles without ever seeing what you have done. . . ."

He received the paper in the mail, saw his poem, and was alarmed. The poem hadn't been meant for publication: it hadn't even been seen by the order's censors. As a cloistered monk, he was not supposed to write about war and peace. There was going to be trouble.

On August 15 Day wrote to apologize. "I am terribly sorry about that poem," she told him, explaining that she had taken it to be a submission—and then had had it "snatched from my hands" by Merton's admirers, "and before I knew it, it was at the printers."

The *Catholic Worker* had a problem of its own. Catholic Workers were being stigmatized for their antiwar position; one had been forbidden to make a retreat at a Trappist monastery because he was a conscientious objector. "Our position is more unpopular than ever, with recurring crises," Day told Merton. The only consolation was that it was August 15, the feast of the Virgin Mary's assumption into heaven. "Our Lady, body and soul in Heaven; our Lord, body and soul in heaven,—it makes Heaven a reality for us earthbound creatures," she closed. "Hope I am not being incoherent."

Merton replied right away, offering to arrange retreats for the Catholic Worker conscientious objectors at Gethsemani. Then he confessed the difficulties that he was having with obedience to his superiors. "This, Dorothy, is a very great problem to me," he began. He felt obligated to obey the abbot, but also to "say whatever my conscience seems to dictate, provided of course it is not contrary to the faith and the teaching authority of the Church." The silence of the monastery was a good thing, but silence in the face of an evil like the arms race was itself an evil. The fact that no one else was speaking out—no one except her—made speaking out all the more important. "Why this awful silence and apathy on the part of Catholics, clergy, hierarchy, lay people," he asked, "on this terrible issue on which the continued existence of the human race depends?"

In September he sent her an excerpt from *Seeds of Contemplation*, freshly revised, which he thought she might wish to publish. He enclosed a "quick note":

I will write more later. I have some other things to say. In any case let us be united in prayer and trust and work for the abolition of war in any way that we can, even if there seems to be a slight hope of success. Our faith demands it, and you have been one of the few that have really responded to God. One shudders at the mentality of so many American Catholics, feeding their minds continually with hate propaganda in the name of religion. May God have mercy on us.

The note was the fruit of months of anguish, a prayerful back and forth. For the excerpt, called "The Root of War," would be Merton's first article about war and peace. With it he would cease to be a bystander and enter the debate—in the pages of the *Catholic Worker*.

"At the root of all war is fear: not so much the fear men have of one another as the fear they have of everything," Merton declared. "It is not merely that they do not trust one another; they do not trust even themselves. If they are not sure when someone else may turn around and kill them, they are still less sure when they may turn around and kill themselves. They cannot trust anything, because they have ceased to believe in God."

Just as the excerpt was published, there arose a controversy that put Merton's theory about fear to the test. Many Americans had had fallout shelters constructed in their backyards. Once these were built, questions of their use arose, as newspaper columnists concocted nightmare scenarios: bandits holding up people at gunpoint for the use of their shelters, neighbors cramming in on one another and fighting over canned food in a tiny underground world. In the summer of 1961 a Jesuit priest writing in *America* defended the ordinary citizen's right to keep others out of his shelter—with a loaded weapon if necessary.

From his hermitage, Merton wrote a fresh piece on "shelter ethics" and sent it to the *Catholic Worker*. He considered himself "nonviolent" rather than an absolute pacifist—he had always held out for the individual's right to defend his own self against a violent aggressor—and now he defended the believer's right and even duty to defend self and family against gun-toting neighbors. "No one questions that," he said. At the same time, he urged the paper's readers to strive to imitate Christ, not to think in "purely selfish and pragmatic terms."

The essay was accepted at the paper and cleared by the Trappist censors, among them Father Charles at the Holy Ghost Monastery in Georgia, but there was a hitch: as an absolute pacifist, Dorothy Day did question the believer's right to violent self-defense. When the December issue of the paper went to press, she put Merton's piece on the front page; but in her column, printed inside, she took a different view.

The column is an artful piece of indirection, in which she rebukes Merton without seeming to do so. She contrasts priests in the Congo, preaching the Gospel amidst a civil war, with priests living comfortably in the developed world. "On the one hand missionaries go forth ready to die. And on the other hand, we have now a priest defending the right of man to defend his life, to ward off intruders from his family air raid shelter by force of arms." She considers it possible that such an action might be judged morally acceptable after the fact—but insists that priests should be making such judgments individually and "in the confessional, not in the pulpit or the press." It is a reference to the priest who had written in *America*, but she seems to be addressing the Trappist monk whose article appeared in her paper as well.

Merton answered with his own stroke of indirection. While his articles were scrutinized by the Trappist censors, his letters were left alone. In October 1961, then, he had begun to write letters to people in the peace movement, each time asking the recipient, who was left unnamed, to mimeograph the letter and send it to others in the movement, thus making each "Cold War Letter" an encyclical or circular letter, which would bind distant people together.

He addressed Cold War Letter 11 to D.D. "I have read your latest 'On Pilgrimage' in the December *CW* and I want to say how good it is," he began. "In many ways it is about the best thing I have seen that came out of this whole sorry shelter business." Day had stressed the roots of her own pacifism in her experience of seeing violent men in jail converted to peace through the peace of other prisoners. She had underlined the word "experience." Merton took the hint and restated his argument in terms of her experience of hospitality, in which the stranger was seen as a neighbor, indeed as Christ.

"If I am in a fallout shelter and trying to save my life, I must see that the neighbor who wants to come into the shelter also wants to save his life as I do," he declared. "I must experience his need and his fear just as if it were my need and my fear . . . and if I am strong enough to act out of love, I will cede my place in the shelter to him. "It is when we love the other, the enemy, that we obtain from God the key to an understanding of who he is, and who we are."

This willingness to walk in the path of another, he proposed, is the very essence of Christianity (and of all the world religions); and in order to see what we have in common with our enemy, "and to respect his personal rights and his integrity, his worthiness of love," he went on, "we have to see ourselves as similarly accused along with him, condemned to death along with him, sinking to the abyss with him, and needing, with him, the ineffable gift of grace and mercy to be saved. Then, instead of pushing him down, trying to climb out by using his head as a stepping-stone for ourselves, we help ourselves to rise by helping him to rise. For when we extend our hand to the enemy who is sinking in the abyss, God reaches out to both of us."

From his hermitage, the champion of solitude was advocating the practice of hospitality. He closed by apologizing to Day for his article, but this Cold War Letter was more than an apology. In it he put himself in Day's circumstances and tried to see things her way, and in so doing called forth some of his best writing about the bonds of love that join people together.

Day was struggling with shelter ethics of another kind. There was unrest at St. Joseph's House. She called it the "war between young and old, the twenty year olds and our senior citizens, as they are euphemistically called by the press." The young people called it the "Dorothy Day Stomp."

The young Catholic Workers of the early 1960s were less scrupulous in their piety than those of previous generations. They were passionate about pacifism, casual about poverty, and indifferent to the teachings about chastity before marriage. They were "sharing apartments, girls and men," Day observed. They were "turning night into day." When they allowed some friends to print an alternative newspaper on the Catholic Worker's hand press—*Fuck You: A Magazine of Literature and the Arts*—she threw them out. Jim Forest, an editor of the *Catholic Worker* and a conscientious objector, resigned in protest. He had just returned from a retreat at the Abbey of Gethsemani.

Day explained in a column that she found these "beats" contemptuous of life—"not only of the square, of the bourgeoisie around them, but of the life force in man himself. Also they lived and moved among the poor as though they were not there, taking their meager housing space, crowding aside the guests at the CW to get their share of the food, and so living that they disregarded the affront they offered the simple, reticent, decent and modest men among whom they lived."

She received a letter from Thomas Merton, consoling her about the "usual interminable troubles with the well-meaning men that join the CW." To judge from those he had just met at Gethsemani, he told her, they were drawn to poetry, not to poverty, and the Catholic Worker life was probably a "temporary phase" with them. "But I do say this, I think it is fine that you are able to have such a flexible and wide open setup there. CW certainly seems to me to be a real sign of life and to be full of a certain truth that one looks for in vain in many other quarters."

She wrote back to tell her side of the story. Her letter is lost, but it probably resembled one she wrote to him a few months later. "I do assure you that we are not 'beats,' " she declared. "I am afraid I am uncharitable about the intellectual who shoulders his way in to eat before the men on the line who have done the hard work of the world, and who moves in on the few men in one of our apartments and tries to edge them out with their beer parties and women. They can sleep on park benches as far as I am concerned."

It was Holy Week when he wrote to her next, and the problems at the Catholic Worker reminded him of Christ on the cross, whose followers betrayed him through infighting and dissension. "Our Lord has certainly had to do it all by Himself. We have not been much help to him, ever."

In 1962, the Catholic peace movement was only brand-new, and already its two most illustrious members were worried for its future, concerned that it would not be able to withstand the pressure of social change, the convergence of the Church and the world, the old and the new, then being pondered at the Vatican council. "It is so small and helpless in itself, and now to find it eaten up from the inside . . . ," Merton told Day. "It is a good thing that we are able to put our hopes in God and not in movements."

The Moviegoer was cited in *Time* magazine as one of the ten best novels of 1961. Then it was nominated for the National Book Award in fiction. Then Walker Percy, in Covington, received a telegram congratulating him and telling him to call a 212 phone number. He got out his suit jacket and bought a plane ticket for New York.

As the story goes, *The Moviegoer* was a surprise winner, given the quality of the other nominees—*Franny and Zooey, Revolutionary Road, Catch-22,* Isaac Bashevis Singer's *The Spinoza of Market Street,* William Maxwell's *The Château*—and the publisher's lack of support for the novel, which hadn't been formally submitted for the prize. Only the initiative of the judges— Jean Stafford's husband, A. J. Liebling, liked the book—allowed it to be considered at all.

If Percy was surprised, however, he didn't let on. The speech he wrote between the telegram and the award ceremony is effortlessly assured, as if he had thought he might win all along and looked forward to the opportunity to explain what he had been up to.

He told the audience that he felt like Binx Bolling, whose Aunt Emily suspected that his problems were a hangover from a previous life—"because the last time I was in New York (not counting one weekend) was twenty years ago and the occasion was so different that it is hard to believe that it belongs to the same lifetime." Twenty years ago, he had been examining corpses at a morgue. Now he was standing on the dais, accepting a prize.

"Providence works in strange ways," he observed. Fiction was not pathology, and a novel was not a diagnosis—"only a story, and unlike pathology, a story is supposed first, last, and always to give pleasure to the reader." Yet there were obvious likenesses. Like the pathologist, for example, the novelist began with "the suspicion that something is wrong."

It was not the time or the place for him to attempt to answer the question of what was wrong with society. "There is time to say only this: that the pathology in this case has to do with the loss of individuality and the loss of identity at the very time when words like the 'dignity of the individual' and 'self-realization' are being heard more frequently than ever."

In five minutes, Percy set out the themes he had explored over a dozen years: the sickness of modern Western society, the loss of the sense of self, the role of the writer as diagnostician. Concluding, he made his main point indirectly, as an offhand non sequitur—the point that "in short, the book attempts a modest restatement of the Judeo-Christian notion that man is more than an organism in an environment, more than an integrated personality, more than a mature and creative individual, as the phrase goes. He is a wayfarer and a pilgrim."

On the *Today* show the next morning he gave a different explanation of his work. In his speech he had quipped that a "well-nourished rancor against Yankees" was the source of his creativity. Now he declared that the literature of the South was thriving because the South had lost the Civil War. Defeat, he explained, had given Southerners something to attack and something to defend. It had forced them to band together to maintain their common language and culture, which meant that the Southern writer could still write in the hope that his neighbors would understand him.

He returned to Covington to find his picture in the paper. In New York he had worried aloud that success might mean he would "go back home and not write another word for ten years." So he got to work right away, spending mornings on a new novel, which he was calling *Fall Out*, and afternoons on philosophy.

The attention would last for several months. Strangers pointed him out on the street in Covington. Moviegoers wrote him letters. Father Charles of Holy Ghost Monastery initiated a fitful correspondence.

There came a letter in the mail, as succinct as the telegram telling him he had won the prize:

Dear Mr. Percy,

I'm glad we lost the War and you won the Nat'l Book Award. I didn't think the judges would have that much sense but they surprized me.

Regards,
Flannery O'Connor

One way or another, O'Connor had learned of his televised remarks, and she would later gloss them with startling eloquence: "What he was saying was that we have had our Fall. We have gone into the modern world with an inburnt knowledge of human limitations and with a sense of mystery which could not have developed in our first state of innocence—as it has not developed sufficiently in the rest of our country."

In this letter, though, she left out all but the essential. She said nothing about Percy's work; nothing about her own; nothing about Catholicism; nothing about Phinizy Spalding or Caroline Gordon. All that would have gotten in the way of what she wished to say, which she wished to say in the common language of the South: familiar, colloquial, allusive of a shared history, suspicious of outsiders.

You have a counterpart in Georgia, she was telling him. We are in this thing together.

Her own novels had won no prizes. Ten years after publication, *Wise Blood* was out of print at Harcourt, Brace. Robert Giroux was eager to reprint it at Farrar, Straus, alongside *The Violent Bear It Away*, but in order to update the copyright he needed new material—a preface, say—which he asked O'Connor to provide.

She resisted. She had been taught that novels should stand or fall on their own merits. She was loath to violate *Wise Blood*'s independence. She felt she would be "wasting my time saying what I've written when I've already written it and I could be writing something else," she told John Hawkes. "I couldn't hope to convince anybody anyway."

Experience, however, had shown her the drawbacks of New Critical notions of artistic self-sufficiency. She was receiving letters from readers with whose interpretations she violently disagreed. She saw a need to point the reader of the future in the right direction.

She sent Giroux "as much as I can get out of myself." It is a paragraph of genius, in which, like Percy in his acceptance speech, she introduced her themes indirectly, concealing her seriousness behind self-deprecating modesty.

"*Wise Blood* has reached the age of ten and is still alive," she begins, with detached affection, as if for a child. Her own "critical powers" are "just sufficient" to determine this. She is "an author congenitally innocent of theory." But like her hero she has "certain preoccupations."

What are these? He is a "Christian malgré lui" — in spite of himself. The use of French is telling. It places the novel in the tradition of Teilhard, and of Mauriac, whose *Mémoires Intérieurs* she was reading. It also soft-pedals the novel's religious preoccupations, even as it makes them explicit.

The next few sentences work the same way. "That belief in Christ is to some a matter of life and death has been a stumbling block for readers who prefer to think it a matter of no great consequence. For them Hazel Motes's integrity lies in his trying with such vigor to get rid of the ragged figure who moves from tree to tree in the back of his mind. For the author Hazel's integrity lies in his not being able to." She does not say: If you don't think belief is the center of existence the way I do, you probably won't understand my book. Rather, she swaddles the matter of religious faith in passive sentences, blunting its sharp edge, and making the subject of the passage, and of the novel, not Hazel's belief but his integrity.

By now she has introduced "readers" as a collective adversary, like those book-prize judges in New York who "surprised" her by choosing *The Moviegoer*. These uncomprehending readers "prefer to think" belief unimportant. For them it is just a matter of preference. For her hero, however, it is a matter of ultimate concern. Their notion of free will is simple and abstract; his is vivid and complicated, a drama in which ragged figures haunt the mind's dark spaces, murmuring of life and death.

She has made it fairly difficult for the prospective reader to side with "them." Instead of dismissing them altogether, however, she backs off a bit, introducing her own firm belief in the form of a rhetorical question. "Does one's integrity ever lie in what he is not able to do?" she asks, and when she answers—"I think that usually it does"—the humble comic novelist explains why with the dispassionate certainty of a scientist or philosopher or scholastic theologian: "Freedom cannot be conceived simply. It is a mystery and one which a novel, even a comic novel, can only be asked to deepen."

She heard from Walker Percy that spring. He sent her a draft of an essay about her work written by Caroline Gordon, which Gordon had sent to him prior to its publication in *Jubilee*.

She wrote back to him conspiratorially. In public she was generally kind toward Gordon, mindful of how much Gordon's advice had improved her fiction. Now, writing for the first time to another writer who had met with Gordon's ministrations firsthand, she was catty. A friend had reported that Gordon was now a "lonesome old lady," and here was the proof of it:

> Thanks for sending the unexpurgated version. It presented something of a problem. . . . I discovered that she had got *Wise Blood* all mixed up in her mind and had things going on that didn't at all happen in the book. Very delicate matter to set her straight on anything. She has probably not read that book in ten years and read it at high speed then. Also I am afraid old age has something to do with it.
>
> The piece was much too long for *Jubilee*. Maybe *Thought* will take it, but I hope she clears out some of the swampy areas before she sends it.

The letter, again, is unusually familiar, more so than their slender friendship warranted, and she closed it with an uncommonly emphatic invitation. "If you all ever come to Georgia," she commanded, "come to see us."

Andalusia had become a place of general pilgrimage, the visitors coming in an unending procession and for myriad reasons. Cub Scouts came to behold the peacocks. Roslyn Barnes came to commune with nature in the pasture. Two of the Dominican nuns came with Mary Ann's parents. "The mother has huge black eyes and the father has an over-large elongated head, the face covered with warts. I was much impressed with them," O'Connor told Elizabeth Hester. "You hear of The Poor, but you seldom see them." The archbishop of Atlanta came. "He is a man after my own heart and would be after yours . . . ," she told Hester. "Usually I think the Church's motto is The Wrong Man For the Job, but not this time."

She had characterized the pilgrimage to Lourdes as her last outing. In 1962, however, she started traveling again. Her medical care was expensive. Her mother had given up dairy farming in despair. Suspended between books, between grants, between short-story prizes, O'Connor strapped on her crutches and went on two "bread-winning expeditions," reading and speaking at colleges.

"A little of this honored guest bidnis goes a long way—but it sure does help my finances," she declared. Surely her motives were more complex than that. On campus, she met her readers and her peers, such as Thomas Stritch, a Notre Dame professor (and archbishop's nephew) for whom she developed an "inordinate fondness." Through her talks, she propagated her ideas about her work and about "The Regional Writer" and "The Teaching of Literature." As the Vatican council approached, she swapped conjectures about the disposition of the Holy Ghost with nuns who had Ph.D.s. Away from her farm and her mother, she saw the world.

Five years after her confirmation, Elizabeth Hester had left the Church, unable to find in it anything like O'Connor's religious clarity and certainty. O'Connor assured her that apostasy would have no bearing on their friendship. Writing to others, however, she mocked Hester as a woman who had lost her mind—which, in a sense, she had, for it emerged that Hester, like Robert Lowell, was manic-depressive. "She's high as a kite and on pure air . . . ," O'Connor wrote. "Everything is in the eeek eeek eureka stage. The effect is pretty sick-making but I manage to keep my mouth shut." To Hester herself she was forthright, declaring that loss of faith—"a lessening of the desire for life"—was for her a kind of grief.

Now she sought to explain the believer's point of view to students instead. After a talk at Emory, a university with a Protestant seminary attached, she got a letter from a young man in religious anguish there, named Alfred Corn, and although she couldn't recall meeting him, she wrote him a letter, then another and another, each one quietly astonishing in its tenderness and generosity. "If what the Church teaches is not true, then the security and sense of purpose it gives you are of no value and you are right to reject it," she told him, and went on:

One of the effects of modern liberal Protestantism has been gradually to turn religion into poetry and therapy, to make truth vaguer and vaguer and more and more relative, to banish intellectual distinctions, to depend on feeling instead of thought, and gradually to come to believe that God has no power, that he cannot communicate with us, cannot reveal himself to us, indeed has not done so, and that religion is our own sweet invention. This seems to be about where you find yourself now.

Of course, I am a Catholic and I believe the opposite of all this. I believe what the Church teaches—that God has given us reason to use and that it can lead toward a knowledge of him, through analogy: that he has revealed himself to us in history and continues to do so through the Church, and that he is present (not just symbolically) in the Eucharist on our altars. To believe all this I don't take any leap into the absurd. I find it reasonable to believe, even though these beliefs are beyond reason.

Her talks finished, she returned to Notre Dame to receive an honorary degree. The trip was exhausting. She staggered through the airport, struggling to put one crutch in front of the other, like the patient-pilgrims she had seen at Lourdes. Upon her return to Atlanta her mother "was on hand to meet me with, I regret to say, a wheelchair, so I was rolled to the main concourse, feeling at least 102 years old."

"The Lame Shall Enter First," currently in print in the *Sewanee Review*, she found unsatisfactory for the reason *The Violent Bear It Away* was unsatisfactory—her own lack of sympathy with the rationalist character, called Sheppard in this instance.

She yearned to do nothing but sit in her room and make up a new story, but she felt that she had reached a threshold or outer limit as a writer. "I'm cheered you like 'Everything That Rises Must Converge,'" she told a priest she knew. "I'd like to write a whole bunch of stories like that, but once you've said it, you've said it, and that about expresses what I have to say on That Issue. But pray that the Lord will send me some more. I've been writing for sixteen years and I have the sense of having exhausted my original potentiality and being now in need of the kind of grace that deepens perception, a new shot of life or something."

She set out again in November, planning to speak at schools in east Texas, southwest Louisiana, New Orleans, and southeast Louisiana. "4 talks in 6 days and too much too much," she reported to Maryat Lee. "My bones are not up to it."

She had a friend in New Orleans, and arranged to see him while she was there. Richard Allen was a native of Milledgeville. When they were teenagers he and she had gone on a double date, and had remained friendly. Now he was the curator of a museum of jazz at Tulane University. They met in the city in the morning and he gave her a tour from the back seat of a taxi-cab: the French Quarter, the waterfront, the tawdry establishments of Canal Street, Jackson Square and the old stone cathedral, where she watched intently as he had his shoes shined by a black man. "In his charge I saw a lot of New Orleans that I wouldn't otherwise," she told John Hawkes in a letter a few days later. "We passed a Negro nightclub called 'Baby Green's Evening in Paris,' which I might some day like to investigate."

Dorothy Day had come to New Orleans forty years earlier to await the publication of her first novel. Now O'Connor sought inspiration for new work in the city; and as she made her way uptown to Loyola University, where she would speak that evening, she imagined what it might be like to live there. "If I had to live in a city," she told Hawkes, "I think I would prefer New Orleans to any other—both Southern and Catholic and with indications that the Devil's existence is freely recognized."

Walker Percy drove over the causeway from Covington with his elder daughter, Mary Pratt, now a teenager. He was looking forward to the talk, sponsored by the Newman Club, and to the social hour with the author afterward. A society lady he knew was coordinating it, and he and Mary Pratt pitched in. They set up tables and chairs in an upstairs room, then went down and found seats in the auditorium.

On this tour O'Connor was giving a talk about the Catholic novelist in the Protestant South. She had given it several times, and to good effect—setting the Catholic Church and the South at odds the way the Baptist preachers did, then showing all they had in common: the Bible, a religious heritage, an awareness of human limitation, a respect for the concrete and actual, a recognition that "good and evil in every culture tend to be joined at the spine." But her tour of New Orleans had underscored an exception to the rule—that Louisiana was both Southern and Catholic—and she recast her remarks accordingly. Abandoning her usual text, she spoke of "a batch of wild Southern Catholic novelists" who had led Southern literary folk to wonder "how these strange birds got hatched in our nest." Upon reaching the passage about the need for the novelist to descend within himself to find his material, she improvised, saying, "When the Southern Catholic writer descends within his imagination—*unless he happens to have the good fortune of being from southern Louisiana*—what he is apt to find is not often Catholic life but the life of a region in which he is both native and alien." And as she came to the end, she recalled what Walker Percy had said on TV after he won the National Book Award and put the point her own way, telling the audience of the benefits for the novelist in the South's "history of defeat and violation: a distrust of the abstract, a sense of human dependence on the grace of God, and a knowledge that evil is not simply a problem to be solved, but a mystery to be endured."

The talk was a long one, forty-five minutes or more, as much as she could stand. The day of sightseeing was the most activity she'd had all at once since her pilgrimage to Europe.

She left the stage slowly, one crutch after the other. As the crowd rose and scattered some members of the Newman Club hastened her out of the auditorium. There were refreshments all set out upstairs, they told her. They led the way, and she followed, going as fast as she could, then turned a corner. A staircase loomed up. She didn't climb stairs anymore.

Richard Allen was alongside her now, and he gave her his shoulder. He beckoned to a teenage girl and told her to do likewise. They bent low, joined hands, and slung the honored guest between them, and then bore her up the stairs, step by step, as others stood watching.

In the upstairs room they set her in a chair. Somebody had brought her crutches and set them alongside her. Somebody else brought her a glass of water.

A bald man in a dark sweater introduced himself. He was Walker Percy. He was very pleased to meet her. One of his kinfolks in Georgia had met her once—Phinizy Spalding.

She was exhausted. She proffered a hand, summoned as much strength as she could find, and said: "That was a good story you wrote. Why don't you make up another one?"

Dorothy Day turned sixty-five years old November 8, 1962. The victims of her "stomp" at St. Joseph's House had derided her as "the grand old lady of pacifism," and plenty of her admirers saw her that way as well. Herself, she felt suddenly invigorated, for she saw the time at hand as a time of social ferment like the thirties, when change was in the air and anything seemed possible.

In particular, she saw a "rediscovery of poverty," led by Michael Harrington, an alumnus of the movement. Harrington had come to St. Joseph's House right out of the College of the Holy Cross in 1951. He had written the paper's review of *The Long Loneliness*. He had lost his faith and become a democratic socialist, but he had never lost touch with the Catholic Worker.

After he described the lives of "Our Fifty Million Poor" in a two-part article in *Commentary*, he was invited to turn the article into a short book about "the other America," still a country of poverty. He opened the book with a tribute to "Dorothy Day and the Catholic Worker movement," through whom "I first came into contact with the terrible reality of involuntary poverty and the magnificent ideal of voluntary poverty."

Day had planned for years to make her next book a chronicle of her travels around the country. On the road, however, she was struck, over and over, by the changing nature of poverty. Unions now sought to organize civil servants, not immigrant laborers. Middle-class people were migrating to the suburbs, where poverty was out of sight. The poor had televisions and department-store clothing; the overall prosperity of postwar America disguised the culture of poverty, which persisted on failing farms, in hill towns and forsaken mining communities, in black and "Spanish" neighborhoods where people who were not poor generally did not go. Whereas poverty in the Depression had brought people together in a great convergence of need and will, poverty in postwar America divided them from one another.

Day decided to write a history of the movement she and Peter Maurin had founded. She would try "to bring the Catholic Worker story up to date, to let people know that we go on in spite of jail sentences, evictions, the comings and goings of people." She would state their aims and purposes for a new generation, evoking the ideal of poverty as a way of life.

It would be a book about "the faces of poverty," like the books she most admired: Dickens's novels, Orwell's *Down and Out in Paris and London*, Ignazio Silone's *Bread and Wine*, Carlo Levi's *Christ Stopped at Eboli*, the *Report from Palermo* of Danilo Dolci, the "Gandhi of Sicily," the great Russian novels. "Last week, stopping to browse as I passed a secondhand bookstore on Fourth Avenue, I came across a battered old copy of Dostoevski's *The Insulted and the Injured*, a story which I had not read for many years," she wrote. "It was only twenty-five cents. I got it, and started reading it that very evening. It is the story of a young author—it might be Dostoevski himself—of the success of his first book, and of how he read it aloud to his foster father. The father said, 'It's simply a little story, but it wrings your heart. What's happening all around you grows easier to understand and to remember, and you learn that the most downtrodden, humblest man is a man, too, and a brother.' I thought as I read those words, 'That is why I write.'"

In her summer 1962 column she announced that she was done with the new book. She was calling it *Loaves and Fishes*. The publisher wanted to call it *The Cost of Love*.

Her timing was apt. Michael Harrington's *The Other America*, published that year, would become a best-seller, the sales prompted by a long article by Dwight Macdonald in the *New Yorker*; in time, it would become a white paper for the federal government's antipoverty programs. Day's own book was full of warnings. Writing well before the beginning of the War on Poverty, she pointed out the limitations of such programs. Poverty could not be eliminated through money and bureaucracy. More radical measures were required: on the one hand, the practice of voluntary poverty, and on the other, a thoroughgoing reorganization of society. "Yes, the poor will always be with us—Our Lord told us that—and there will always be a need for sharing, for stripping ourselves to help others. It is—and always will be—a lifetime job. But I am sure that God did not intend that there be so many poor. The class struggle is of *our* making and by *our* consent, and we must do what we can to change it."

In September she finally went to Cuba. She devoted four columns to the trip, which was at once a pilgrimage and a fact-finding mission, in which she sought to see firsthand the new society she had read so much about. "I want to see the collective farms, the educational system, the conditions of religion," she told Thomas Merton in a letter. In her column, she declared: "I want to see a country where there is no unemployment, where a boy or a man can get a job at any age."

More than she would have admitted, she saw what she wanted to see. She noticed that the newsstands sold Spanish translations of Tolstoy and Melville as well as Marx and Engels. She saw Fidel Castro make a speech, ill-clad, awkward, tireless, and was reminded of Peter Maurin. At a *granja*, or collective farm, she found good roads, shade trees, beautiful gardens, tile floors, sturdy furniture, and a hand-drawn sign saying *Even Fidel Cannot Imagine My Joy!* The church was shuttered, the *granja* was "not truly a cooperative but a state farm," the work was "year-round work, not just for a few months a year," and "the private farm sold all its produce to the state. But there is private ownership in homes and 1/2-acre plots. It was as I had envisioned it, and I was not disappointed."

The day she left Cuba, the Vatican council opened. During her pilgrimage to Cuba the twenty-five hundred bishops of the Church had departed their dioceses to go to Rome, some of them for the first time, and on October 11 they processed into St. Peter's Basilica, which was too small for them.

She regarded the Catholic Workers as forerunners of the bishops, who, guided by the Holy Ghost, would be guiding the Church during the council. "Man and the state, war and peace—it is endless, the issues we have written over almost thirty years," she remarked in the paper. "One might say we were preparing the ground, pointing up the issues." Now she prayed that "at the Council, the word made flesh will be among them."

Thomas Merton, in his hermitage, prayed that the council would be the "supernatural event" it was meant to be, and hoped it wouldn't be ended by a "major war" the way the Vatican council of 1870 had been. At the same time, he prayed for a change in his own life. Two weeks earlier he had written, "I keep thinking I haven't got much more time! Wind up your affairs!" only to "realize I perhaps have no affairs to wind up." Now he felt he was at a "turning point. Getting ready to come out of Egypt and into my own country."

While the bishops pondered the schema of Church reform, world leaders trained their sights on Cuba. The discovery of Soviet missiles there, the president's demand for their removal, the U.S. naval blockade of the island, the threat of nuclear retaliation: suddenly the conjectures of the peace movement about nuclear Armageddon seemed possible, even likely.

Then it was over. "Already it is as if there had never been any trouble over Cuba," Merton wrote in his journal on October 27. A week later he wrote, "Only just beginning to realize what a grave shock the Cuba crisis was to the whole world, and how near it really came to nuclear war."

The story of how the crisis had been averted—that John XXIII had telephoned the Russian premier—was no better known out in the world than it was in the monastery. No one would have guessed it: the pope was ill, the Church dead set against Communism, the council preoccupied with liturgical reform.

The next year, the pope intervened openly. With *Pacem in Terris*, a letter addressed to "all men of good will," he set aside the circumspection of previous popes and the ancient Christian "just-war" theory, which judges wars by why they are fought and how they are conducted, rather than by their conformity to the example of Christ in the Gospels. The human race, this pope declared, is made for peace, not war. Among nuclear powers, there can be no just wars. The leaders of such powers should lay down their arms; men of goodwill—believers especially—should recognize that the work of peace is a duty, "a requirement of love."

Merton was elated. In Cold War Letter 86, sent to Dorothy Day in June 1962, he had argued that while he, unlike her, maintained that there could be a war fought for a just cause, most wars "are shot through and through with evil, falsity, injustice, and sin so much that one can only with difficulty extricate the truths that may be found here and there in the 'causes' for which the fighting is going on." Now the pope seemed to be saying so, and the distinction between his own "nonviolence" and Day's "absolute pacifism" seemed unimportant.

Day felt that *Pacem in Terris* vindicated her own position. In March she had told Merton of her plan to go to Rome in April "with a group from Women Strike for Peace who are foolishly expecting to get an audience. I told them it will probably be with 500 other people but a pilgrimage is a pilgrimage and if we can call attention to all the things the Pope has been saying about peace, that itself is a good." The plan was all set when *Pacem in Terris* was issued, and the pilgrims arrived in Rome hoping to present themselves to the pope as the "first fruit of his great encyclical"—and intending "to ask for a more radical condemnation of the instruments of modern warfare."

The pope was near death. The pilgrims didn't know this. They took the dismissive air of the Vatican priests to be customary. "It is no easier to receive a hearing with the Princes of the Church," Day observed, "than it is to receive one from the princes of this world."

They visited churches and saw the sights. On May 15, the day Peter Maurin had died, Day had a priest—a Trappist named Father Urban—say a Mass for him in the crypt of St. Peter's.

They crowded in alongside hundreds of other pilgrims for the weekly papal audience. After two hours, the pope emerged, carried aloft in a ceremonial chair, and as he was conveyed to his throne the name of each group of pilgrims was read over the public address system—each group but Women Strike for Peace. "But then the Pope began to speak," Day recounted, "and the words that fell from his lips seemed to be directed to us, to our group, speaking as he did about the 'Pilgrims for Peace' who came to him, and his gratitude for their encouragement." The pope—a peacemaker—was one of them. It felt like a miracle.

The last day of the pilgrimage, she was on her way to meet a Vatican priest when she saw people rushing toward the colonnades of St. Peter's:

> I hastened to a good position in the square and was there in time to see the curtains stir and the pope appear. I had not realized how tremendous that square was until I saw how tiny the pope's figure seemed, up at that window of the apartment under the roof.
>
> The voice of the Holy Father came through a loudspeaker, of course, and seemed strong. He said the Angelus (which we say before meals at Peter Maurin Farm), then the prayers to the guardian angels, and ended with a requiem prayer for the dead.

She left Italy that evening, traveling by sea. The pope was dead before she reached New York. "It was the last time the public saw his face," she observed.

In the woods, writing in his journal, Thomas Merton bemoaned the "interminable repetition of news stories about the pope's death" read to the monks in refectory. "Poor Pope John! None of this idiotic reporting can change his greatness or his glory. And for all that he died a noble and Christian death, a holy death, that was not a cliché, however much they tried to make it one."

Proofs of *Loaves and Fishes* had come in the mail that day, with a letter from the publisher asking him to make a comment about them.

Dorothy Day invariably told him how much his writing meant to the Catholic Workers—the ex-Trappist who was walking across Europe as a "peace pilgrim," the "lovely" girl at St. Joseph's House who exclaimed, "Thank God for Thomas Merton." For his part, Merton had praised Day's way of life more than her writing, and he had been celebrated for his own way of life often enough to know that what the religious writer truly yearns for is literary insight. In any case, he made his comment a tribute to her style:

> Poverty, for Dorothy Day, is more than a sociological problem: it is also a religious mystery. And that is what gives this book its extraordinary grace, and gentleness, and charm. It is a deeply touching and delightfully humorous record of experiences. . . .
>
> This is a serious book about matters of life and death, not only for a few people, or for a certain class of people, but for everybody. Yet Dorothy Day never preaches, never pounds the table: she remarks quietly on the things she has seen, she points out their awful, as well as their beautiful implications, and she passes on to something else.

With nuclear war withstood, Merton turned next to race matters. The Abbey of Gethsemani was perhaps the whitest place in the entire South: white monks, white walls, white robes not unlike those worn by the Ku Klux Klan. Merton, recognizing this, sought to enter into the situation imaginatively. He listened to recordings of speeches by Martin Luther King and Malcolm X. He met John Howard Griffin, a white man whose book about traveling the South in blackface was an effort to identify with the Negro. He read *The Fire Next Time*, by James Baldwin—"one of the few genuinely concerned Americans, one whose concern I can really believe"—but decided not to write about it, for doing so would imply that he believed he himself was on the right side.

Instead, he wrote the first of his "Letters to a White Liberal," four essayish missives written "during the early summer of 1963" and revised in the fall. In them, Merton proposed that his location in a monastery allowed him to be "free of the confusions and falsities of partisan dispute." In truth, it did the opposite: it enhanced the powers of radical identification on which his monastic calling depended. In the summer of 1963, more and more white liberals were identifying the cause of black civil rights as their own. Just as he identified strongly with people he admired through imaginative empathy, so he could identify strongly with people whose viewpoints he opposed.

The first letter is addressed not so much to a white liberal as to a Southern Catholic. American civil society, Merton began, now acknowledged that the Negro was equal to the white. "Our religion adds that what we do to him, we do to Christ . . . ," he added. How, then, "do we treat this other

Christ who happens to be black?" The Catholics of the South treated him as the devil—allowing him to receive Communion only after his white counterparts, beating up a priest who allowed the Negro to come to the altar alongside them, and refusing to let the Negro's children attend their parochial schools. It seemed that the civil-rights laws had been passed not to effect change, but to ease the consciences of whites. It was in recognition of this that the Negro protested—to "disturb the white man's precious 'peace of soul.'"

He went on to summarize the Southern Catholic's point of view with pinpoint accuracy, entering into it through the plural pronoun. "The Negro finally gets tired of this treatment and becomes quite rightly convinced that the only way he is ever going to get his rights is by fighting for them himself. But we deplore his demonstrations, we urge him to go slow, we warn him against the consequences of violence (when, at least so far, most of the organized violence has been on our side and not on his). At the same time we secretly desire violence, and even in some case *provoke* it, in the hope that the whole Negro movement for freedom can be repressed by force."

The last Sunday in August, Martin Luther King led the March on Washington. Two hundred fifty thousand people walked from the Lincoln Memorial to the Mall. King, in his speech, told them that what they had come to see—a promised land of racial equality—was still a way off.

Merton offered his Mass that morning for the success of the march. A week later, he read some news reports about it, and remarked in his journal that it had been "impressive, orderly, and successful. (Though it is hard to say precisely how.)"

The march was a religious pilgrimage such as America had never seen before, a great unified multitude of people walking peacefully for justice. But Merton had declined to identify with the marchers, for this would imply that he stood confidently on the right side. Instead, he had written as a guilty bystander, adopting a white Southern Catholic's point of view in order to show how grotesque it was.

Flannery O'Connor went to Washington in October to give a talk at Georgetown University. Georgetown—the first Catholic university in America—was celebrating its 175th anniversary, and she concluded her remarks about "The Catholic Novelist in the Protestant South" with an observation about the prospects for Catholic writing in America:

The poet is traditionally a blind man. But the Christian poet, and the storyteller as well, is like the blind man Christ touched, who looked then and saw men as if they were trees—but walking. Christ touched him again, and he saw clearly. We will not see clearly until Christ touches us in death, but this first touch is the beginning of vision, and it is an invitation to deeper and stranger visions that we shall have to accept if we want to realize a Catholic literature.

She returned to Georgia and started a new story, which she was "right enthusiastic about." With "The Artificial Nigger," and then with "Everything That Rises Must Converge," she had treated That Issue—the race issue—and each time she had wound up feeling that she had said all she had to say. With "Revelation," however, she outdid herself, responding through fiction to the public events of the summer of 1963.

It is an echo of "Everything That Rises Must Converge," a restatement in a higher key. The themes are the same—the last shall be first; pride goeth before a fall; judge not lest ye yourself be judged—but the approach is more comprehensive. One story concerns this world, the other the next; one, the rights of individuals, the other, the program of whole peoples. Whereas "Everything That Rises Must Converge" is "about" race relations, "Revelation" treats their basis in human personality, which, it suggests, is a mystery too complex for a "topical" story.

This time, the woman is the protagonist: stout, hardworking, churchgoing Ruby Turpin, who takes pride in her "good disposition" and has wrinkles around her eyes "from laughing too much." The story of Mrs. Turpin's point of view, and how it changes, is the whole story, and O'Connor, forcing a camel through a needle's eye, presents all the action through her "little bright black eyes," so that we see things the way Mrs. Turpin does, identifying with her in spite of ourselves.

The question, once again, is who may sit where. The waiting room where the story opens is a place of unspoken equality. Everybody is white, and everybody is waiting to see the doctor. A gospel radio station plays in the background. The conversation is of wall clocks and green stamps.

Mrs. Turpin's husband, Claud, got kicked in the shin by a cow. That is why she is here. Right away, she sizes up the others, beginning with their feet and working upward. There is the runny-nosed boy asprawl on the couch where she would like to sit herself; his mother, a "lank-faced woman" whose lips are stained brown by chewing tobacco; his "thin leathery old" grandmother, wearing a dress like a feed sack; a "lean stringy old fellow" with his eyes clamped shut; a "well-dressed gray-haired" lady; her daughter, a "fat girl of eighteen or nineteen" whose face is "blue with acne"; a nurse with "the highest stack of yellow hair Mrs. Turpin had ever seen."

Mrs. Turpin, in her way, is a hillbilly Thomist, who lies awake at night dividing and classifying people with medieval rigor, and once she has claimed a seat, she proceeds, in her head, to rearrange everybody else socially, according to her sense of the order of things:

> On the bottom of the heap were most colored people, not the kind she would have been if she had been one, but most of them; then next to them—not above, just away from—were the white-trash; then above them were the home-owners, and above them the home-and-land owners, to which she and Claud belonged. Above she and Claud were people with a lot of money and much bigger houses and much more land. But here the complexity of it would begin to bear in on her, for some of the people with a lot of money were common and ought to be below she and Claud and some of the people who had good blood had lost their money and had to rent and then there were colored people who owned their homes and land as well . . .

As for herself, she thanks Jesus for making her just who she is. She has nothing against Negroes. She would rather be a Negro than white-trash, "a neat clean respectable Negro woman, herself but black."

As the conversation turns to hog raising, the "topical" comes up, and because everyone in the room is white, That Issue is discussed openly. "Niggers don't want to pick cotton any more," Mrs. Turpin observes, explaining her own solution to the problem: that she is not above "buttering up" Negroes and even acting friendly toward them if that's what it takes to get them to work. Soon the white-trash woman is saying that the Negroes should be sent back to Africa, and Mrs. Turpin is saying, "They wouldn't want to go. They got it too good here."

Ruby Turpin—it has been revealed—is not merely narrow-minded; she is a bigot. Meanwhile the fat girl has fixed on her with eyes "lit all of a sudden with a peculiar light, an unnatural light like road signs give." Her name is Mary Grace. She is a student at a fancy women's college in the North. She is reading a book called *Human Development*. She glares, leers, groans in protest, and when Mrs. Turpin praises God for making her who she is—

"When I think who all I could have been besides myself and what all I got, a little of everything, and a good disposition besides, I just feel like shouting, 'Thank you, Jesus, for making everything the way it is!' "—the girl throws the book at her, then hurls an insult to accompany it.

The whole story flows toward this moment when Mary Grace calls Mrs. Turpin a wart hog and tells her to go back to hell where she came from—toward this moment, and then away from it. Mrs. Turpin wants to know what the girl's outburst means. So does the reader. Here, as nowhere else in O'Connor's work, the character and the reader are startled to precisely the same degree. What is revealed here has the force of a biblical revelation.

The girl has a fit and is taken away in an ambulance. Mrs. Turpin goes home and to bed. She turns to Claud to tell him what the fat girl said. She cannot wake him. Yet she cannot bear the knowledge all by herself.

So reduced is she, so wounded, that she goes, in spite of herself, to see the black workers on her farm. They are three women and a man, and in her weakness she speaks to them as equals, telling them what happened and inviting their sympathy. This they give, in their own fashion—it is a hilarious scene—but they refuse to treat her as an equal just because it would suit her needs. She cannot dispel the deference she has always expected of them.

Despised and rejected, she goes up to the concrete "pig parlor." She will commiserate with the pigs, which the girl in the waiting room has announced are her true kin.

There, standing on a rise of land, hose in hand, farm and woods and pasture and highway spread out before her, Ruby Turpin ponders her fate directly. " 'What do you send me a message like that for?' she said in a low fierce voice, barely above a whisper but with the force of a shout in its concentrated fury. 'How am I a hog and me both? How am I saved and from hell too?' "

She is "a country female Jacob" (O'Connor told Maryat Lee), a woman moved "to shout at the Lord across a hog pen." But she is recognizable to the reader who has never read a word of the Old Testament. O'Connor had been reading Shakespeare, buying the plays through the mail for a dollar each, and this is her version of a Shakespearean soliloquy.

" 'Why me?' she rumbled. 'It's no trash around here, black or white, that I haven't given to. And break my back to the bone every day working. And do for the church.' "

Revelation has led this hillbilly Thomist to question who she is. How, precisely, is she a wart hog? What do she and a wart hog have in common?

Why is she a wart hog, and not the lunatic girl in the waiting room? Why do the upright suffer and the white-trash go free? " 'If you like trash better, go get yourself some trash then,' she railed. 'You could have made me trash. Or a nigger. If trash is what you wanted why didn't you make me trash?' " She says to go right on ahead and call her a wart hog again—it wouldn't change things any. Some people are better than others. It is as simple as that:

> "Put that bottom rail on top. There'll still be a top and a bottom!"
> A garbled echo returned to her.
> A final surge of fury shook her and she roared, "Who do you think you are?"

Had it ended there—with Mrs. Turpin peering at the hogs "as if through the very heart of mystery"—"Revelation" would be a remarkable story. O'Connor's vividest characters are present: the obstinate farm woman, the grotesque young intellectual, the good country people, the black farm workers who seem to know the whole story. Stately biblical English rustles against the ragged idiom of the backwoods. Illness figures in. So does conjugal love, in the tender bedroom exchange between Ruby and Claud. There is great beauty in the descriptive writing, as of the fat's girl's eyes after she delivers her revelation, which "seemed a much lighter blue than before, as if a door that had been tightly closed behind them was now open to admit light and air." Everything works. It all adds up. It is very, very funny. And the so-called moment of grace—which in a number of O'Connor's stories seems forced or insisted upon by her own exegesis—is unmistakable, surprising, and wholly realistic, so much so that it is not diminished by the fat girl's name pointing the way to it. You don't have to be a believer to understand this story; you don't have to be a reader of Flannery O'Connor's fiction. You don't have to identify the moment of grace as a "moment of grace" or the revelation as a revelation to see that a self-righteous woman has been reduced to her proper stature—that she has been forced to recognize herself as a poor broken mortal like everybody else.

It doesn't end there, however. Ruby Turpin had been called a wart hog from hell and she wondered why. She demanded to know who she was and where she stood with her Maker.

O'Connor obliged. She kept writing into December, so as to show Mrs. Turpin her true country. She drew on the popular imagery of revelation, heard on gospel radio and seen in the protest marches on TV. "At last she lifted her head," O'Connor began, and only the whole passage, a great many images in stately procession, can communicate her vision:

> There was only a purple streak in the sky, cutting through a field of crimson and leading, like an extension of the highway, into the descending dusk. She raised her hands from the side of the pen in a gesture hieratic and profound. A visionary light settled in her eyes. She saw the streak as a vast swinging bridge extending upward from the earth through a field of living fire. Upon it a vast horde of souls were rumbling toward heaven. There were whole companies of whitetrash, clean for the first time in their lives, and bands of black niggers in white robes, and battalions of freaks and lunatics shouting and clapping and leaping like frogs. And bringing up the end of the procession was a tribe of people whom she recognized at once as those who, like herself and Claud, had always a little of everything and the God-given wit to use it right. She leaned forward to observe them closer. They were marching behind the others with great dignity, accountable as they had always been for good order and common sense and respectable behavior. They alone were on key. Yet she could see by their shocked and altered faces that even their virtues were being burned away. She lowered her hands and gripped the rail of the hog pen, her eyes small but fixed unblinkingly on what lay ahead.

Writing in the fall of 1963, O'Connor brought Ruby Turpin up to the mountaintop and vouchsafed her a vision of the promised land.

It is the ultimate image of Christian pilgrimage in her work, this procession of the saints in company toward heaven. It is set in emphatic contrast to Mrs. Turpin's vision of worldly society with its ranks and classes. Here God's justice dwelleth indeed. Here black and white, upright and trash, enjoy a rough equality. Here the last are first and the first are last. They are going the same way. Their virtues will be burned off, but not their individuality. Make no mistake, O'Connor says, our differences will remain. White will be white and black will be black, even in heaven.

It is also O'Connor's best effort at dramatizing her view of racial equality. Confident that progress toward equality on earth would be slow, halting, and fractious, she placed her hope in equality in heaven—in the belief that all men and women are created equal in the sight of God and meant for the same end, which is to know and love and serve God in this life and be happy with him in the next. Our pilgrim's progress is impeded by sin, which estranges us from God and each other. God willing, we shall all be happy together in heaven, but we will get there, she insisted, in our separate ways.

On November 23 Thomas Merton wrote in his journal, "There will be another solemn requiem today, this time for the President." There had been several deaths already that month: the South Vietnamese president; Jean Cocteau; the Cistercian abbot general ("King of all the censors"). Now there was a note on the bulletin board. Merton saw the assassination as a result of the "same blind, idiot destructiveness and hate that killed Medgar Evers in Jackson, the Negro children in Birmingham. . . . The country is full of madness and we are going to know this more and more."

Flannery O'Connor, at Andalusia, was sick with anemia and "too weak at the moment to care about hitting this typewriter much," she told Elizabeth Hester. She was "sad about the President. But I like the new one." To the Fitzgeralds, in Italy, she wrote: "The President's death has cut the country up pretty bad. All commercial television is stopped until after the funeral and even the football games called off, which is about the extremest sign of grief possible."

Dorothy Day, who heard about the killing at lunch with a friend in Chicago, "could only sit and weep at the senseless violence that had erupted again, this time striking down a young and vital leader of a state, a husband, son and father." The killing of Lee Harvey Oswald struck her as "even more horrible," coming in a police station, where one was presumed innocent. "To this we had come. To these low depths we had fallen." Rather than eulogizing the president in her column, she observed that the "violence in the rest of the world more or less accepted as a 'fact of life' " brought "shocked grief and bitter tears by our own people when it happens to us."

Walker Percy, beginning a three-day retreat in Louisiana, joined some priests in watching the early news reports on television, then went home, fearing further violence. A cryptic remark he incorporated into his new novel suggests that he had become sentimental about Kennedy. "The reason he was a great man was that his derisiveness kept pace with his brilliance and his beauty and his love of country. He is the only public man I have ever believed. This is because no man now is believable unless he is derisive."

Late that month Percy got an odd phone call. It was Father Charles from Holy Ghost Monastery. He was in Kentucky. He would be going to the

Abbey of Gethsemani. He asked if Percy could send a copy of *The Moviegoer* there, in care of Thomas Merton.

Father Charles had set out for Gethsemani before Thanksgiving, arranging to meet Merton, the man who had inspired him to become a monk. He had arrived and spoken in Chapter—"warmly," Merton wrote in his journal, "then had a heart attack afterwards. He is in Bardstown hospital."

Two weeks later, he was still there; and although Merton had not been allowed to leave the monastery to visit him, Dorothy Day had sent him a get-well note, saying she intended to visit.

Learning of her plan, Merton wrote to Day immediately, urging her to come to the monastery, where Father Charles would spend a few weeks recuperating. "You will certainly be most welcome to come down here," he wrote—alluding to the lack of hospitality shown to other pacifists—"and I earnestly hope that you will, because I have been wanting to see you if you were out this way." He added, "The events of recent days have been shocking enough to wake the dead. As though we were being bombarded with significant and terrible warnings."

Dorothy Day did not come to Gethsemani: "After I heard Fr. Charles was recovering, I gave up the idea . . . ," she told Merton in a letter. "I have done so much travelling this past year that I feel the need of a 'quiet' time at home—in the midst of the CW family."

The Moviegoer did reach the monastery, however, and once Father Charles was gone Thomas Merton read it. "Book full of emblems and patterns of life," he wrote in his journal; ". . . the whole book says in reality what the hero is *not* and expresses his awareness of what he is not."

Merton had been reading *Signs*, by Maurice Merleau-Ponty, the French philosopher. "The novelist converses with his reader in the language of initiates," Merleau-Ponty proposed, and Merton saw *The Moviegoer* as such a conversation. Here was a book that achieved the kind of dialogue to which he had aspired ever since reading *I and Thou*: not preformulated thought, but the "spontaneous elucidation of what we do not yet know"; not thought about what is already known, but "what will come to be known in our saying it to someone who will reply."

He wrote Percy a letter. "There is no easy way to thank you for your book," he began. "Not only are the good words about books all used up and ruined, but the honesty of *The Moviegoer* makes one more sensitive than usual about the usual nonsense."

He didn't introduce himself or allude to the things they had in common. He just spoke plainly as one initiate to another. "You are right all the time, not just sometimes. You are right all the time. You know just when to change and look at something else."

He went on, "The reason the book is true is that you always stop at the point where more talk would have been false, untrue, confusing, irrelevant. It is not that what you say is true. It is neither true nor false, it points in the right direction, where there is something that has not been said and you know enough not to try to say it."

This, from Merton, was a great compliment: he was praising the book in the terms of his own vocation, the struggle between speech and silence.

"All this says nothing about how I was stirred up at the book," he told Percy. He wanted to give the novel to the other monks as "a first lesson in humility" but thought they might be "bowled over" by the precise descriptions of Sharon Kincaid's rear end. He was glad "Fr. Charles came by here and got sick and told you to send the book.

"Now send me all your other books or things you write, please. Do you want anything of mine? I do artworks very abstract, maybe you would like one."

Percy was surprised and flattered by the letter. He had read many of Merton's books, and he thought of Merton as a person who was "coming from the same place" he had come from, a convert from "Columbia University agnosticism."

He wrote back, thanking Merton for his generosity. "I am a slow writer, easily discouraged, and depend on luck, grace, and a good word from others," he explained.

He was struggling with his new novel. The National Book Award had baptized him as a novelist. The Kennedy administration had seemed to augur a new age. So did the Vatican council, where the progressive bishops had begun to prevail. But Percy, like his uncle, was a natural catastrophist, and he felt that an era was ending. The civil-rights movement, fair as it was, banished the Old South of Uncle Will. The crisis in psychiatry he had predicted had come to pass. The pilgrimage of Western civilization was over. The present was an epilogue to the recent past.

With his career finally under way, his search fruitful, his literary approach achieved and acclaimed, he had returned to the story he had tried to tell in his two unpublished novels. The protagonist came from a short story he had written in medical school. The situation was that of *The Gramercy*

Winner, an Ivy League–educated "man without qualities" trying to find his way. He was writing in the third person, as if to renounce the device—the identification of himself with another through the first person—that had enabled him to find his own voice. The work was modeled on Dostoevsky's *The Idiot*, about a "knight of faith."

He had struggled for over a year when the president was assassinated. The killing seemed to confirm his sense of an ending. It was the catastrophe he had expected, the full stop at the end of the age. He decided to invigorate his novel by writing about it.

Merton sent him a drawing, a few raw, black brush strokes on a piece of heavy white paper. Although Percy wasn't sure what the drawing signified, he stuck it up over his desk. First Flannery O'Connor had written to him, then Thomas Merton. As he tried to recast his novel for a new age, he knew, at least, that he was not working in isolation. He had found a literary community at last.

"Me, I just got out of the hospital where I had my middle entered by the surgeons," Flannery O'Connor told Robert Fitzgerald in a letter. "It was a howling success from their point of view and one of them is going to write it up for a doctor magazine as you usually don't cut folks with lupus. But the trip in was necessary though nothing turned out malignant and I will soon be restored on green turnip potlicker."

She had gone in for the removal of a fibroid tumor, the cause of the anemia. There was a chance that the surgery would reactivate the lupus. She risked it, and by March 25, her thirty-ninth birthday, the lupus had returned. She took huge doses of steroids to slow its spread. The side effects were severe. Her face was puffy, her eyelids swollen nearly shut, her white blood cell count down to single digits. She returned to the hospital in Milledgeville.

In the hospital, she wrote "Parker's Back." After beginning the story in 1960 she had set it aside, then come back to it and kept at it, a few pages at a time, until she had a rough draft which told the story from beginning to end. Now, as she went in and out of the hospital, she worked on the story any way she was able: writing longhand in a notebook; revising pages in a shaky hand; and, when she was discharged from the hospital, typing at her desk at Andalusia. "I have worked one hour each day and my my I do like to work," she told Maryat Lee in May. "I et up that one hour like it was filet mignon."

The manuscripts (now in the college library in Milledgeville) tell the tale: the story of an artist working swiftly but not hastily, determined to give life to a story that already exists in her imagination.

She had begun with the moment in his teens when young man Parker was moved to rapture by the sight of a tattooed man at a country fair. She chronicled his exploits in the navy, then left off abruptly: "There were no designs on Parker's back. It remained bare, like a clean slate."

She sketched Parker and his wife; described their first meeting after his truck breaks down at the roadside; plopped them down on a couch to ponder "the problem of marriage," making it clear that this "plain" and "sour" Christian woman and the tattooed Parker don't belong together. She zoomed in on Parker, kept awake at night by the phrase "till death do you part." "He had always thought of death as a good thing because it rid the world of old people . . . but now death began to appear to him in a different guise—as the only way to escape being married."

So far, Parker and his wife were alive but not vivid. She filled them in. She gave Sarah Ruth eyes "like the points of two icepicks" and put her "on the front porch floor, snapping beans." She dressed Parker in a "grey felt hat" and "hightop workshoes" and turned his gaze "out toward the farthest ridge of trees miles and miles away where every morning the sun came up." She relocated the couple to a house "very close to the edge of an embankment overlooking the highway"—uprooting the story from the backwoods and setting it down in the New South.

Now the characters were running away with the story—away from what she had had in mind for Parker and the tattoo on his back. So she went with Parker to the tattoo parlor. She dubbed the tattooist Speeds and tattooed an owl on the top of his head; she set Parker rifling through the tattooist's stock book of religious images, his brainstorm on him like a fever: "The idea had hit him so quickly and the sheer brilliance of it had dazzled him so completely that it was an hour or more after the artist had set to work before Parker began to be suspicious that what he was doing might have some drawback to it."

Thus inspired, she wrote the story from beginning to end: the story of a man who tries to please his pious shrew of a wife by getting Jesus Christ tattooed on his back.

She finished this draft later that spring, and in those single hours at her desk at Andalusia she evidently filled in some blanks—sharpening the characters and sketching the scene. "It was getting on toward evening," she wrote one day. "The stores had closed and the empty streets had a shrouded look as if the sky were a purple pall flung over the city."

Her strength had not returned. In mid-May, she resigned herself to another hospital stay—as her own guest, she ruefully pointed out, since no insurer covered lupus patients. She signed a contract for a book of stories called *Everything That Rises Must Converge*, her signature slanting unnaturally across the page. Then she left Milledgeville for the hospital in Atlanta.

There, her real work began. As Caroline Gordon, who visited her, recalled, "She told me that the doctor had forbidden her to do any work. He said that it was all right to write a little fiction, though, she added with a grin and drew a notebook out from under her pillow."[*]

She had brought "Parker's Back" along with her, a batch of typescript. Atop the first page she wrote the title in block letters, as if carving it with a razor blade. Then, using a pen, she emblazoned the typed pages with fresh and vivid imagery, the way Parker had decorated his flesh with birds and beasts, filling in every available space until the total effect was that of an "intricate arabesque," alive and startling and altogether mysterious. Parker had a physical tic: she carefully put it "in the side of his face." As Parker began to get tattoos in great numbers she turned the page over and gave the reason: "When the pressure of dissatisfaction began to grow in Parker there was no containing it outside of a tatoo." When he crashed a tractor at the farm where he worked, then fled in despair, she added: "Parker did not allow himself to think on the way into the city. He only knew that there had been a great change in his life, a leap forward into a brazen unknown, and that there was nothing he could do about it. It was for all intents accomplished." By the time he got to the tattoo parlor he was physically diminished, and the tattooist—she now stressed—did not recognize "the barefooted hollow-eyed creature before him."

The "stout stake" of this story is the tattoo itself, and the passages describing it are heavily worked over, inked and re-inked in a shaky hand. It seems likely that O'Connor had in mind the great mosaic Christ of Santa Sophia in Istanbul, pictured in André Malraux's *The Voices of Silence*, a book she had read in her twenties and then received as a gift from Elizabeth Hester in 1962, and the reiteration of the word "silence" in the story seems

---

[*]"Caroline breezed in one weekend," O'Connor recounted. "She visited Fr. Charles at the monastery and they came out to see me. She has dyed her hair the color of funnytor polish. Startling effect."

to confirm it. Turning the pages of the tattooist's sample book, Parker is startled to see "the haloed head of a flat stern Byzantine Christ with all-demanding eyes" which speak to him "as plainly as if silence were a language itself." The tattooist tells Parker he wouldn't want "all those little blocks," but Parker insists and the tattooist obliges. At the end of the first day the tattooist sets up two mirrors and shows Parker his back, which is "almost completely covered with little red and blue and ivory and saffron squares; from them he makes out the lineaments of the face—a mouth, the beginning of heavy brows, a straight nose, but the face was empty; the eyes had not yet been put in."

At the end of the second day, Parker's back is finished. "Parker looked, turned white, and moved away. The eyes in the reflected face continued to look at him—still straight, all-demanding, enclosed in silence."

The description of Christ is the key to the descriptive method of the story, which is different from that of O'Connor's other stories. The language is more direct, less embroidered. The descriptions are less subtle, more pointed. Settings, each of them iconically familiar—a tree, a farm, a house—are introduced as needed. Whereas O'Connor's stories usually describe a country where the action takes place, this story exists only in the telling. In "Parker's Back," O'Connor was producing the grotesque modern romance she had promised in Macon, remaking her style anew at last.

This is especially clear in the climax of the story. At the hospital, she radically revised the scene in which Parker goes home to show his new tattoo to Sarah Ruth, replacing specific details with a bold outline. In the typescript, Parker got in his truck and

> drove clear of the city and out into the country night. Three or four mountains rose like the backs of sleeping animals against the black sky. There were no clouds but the moon was paltry and pale. Parker ran over a possum almost at the instant he saw its red glittering eyes, and drove on, cursing it soundly.

From her hospital bed, O'Connor rewrote the passage by hand as follows:

> He got in it and drove out of the city and into the country night. His head began to clear of liquor and he observed that his dissatisfaction was gone but he felt not quite like himself as if he were a stranger driving into a new countryside, though it was all familiar to him.

There is a theological point to the new style. Malraux in *The Voices of Silence* had described the Byzantine art of Santa Sophia as art which sought to overcome the conventional realism of antiquity, with its worldly drama, through a technique of "superb negation," a stripping away of all but the essential qualities so that the figures stood out starkly against a transcendent background. Now O'Connor, the transcendent realist par excellence, strove for a like starkness. She stripped away the sky, the moon, the clouds, and the mountains, leaving only the story of a stranger entering a new country as though at the end of a pilgrimage—a pilgrimage whose destination, she meant to make clear, is Jesus Christ himself.

She had been given blood transfusions. They hadn't helped. On June 20 she was discharged from the hospital and returned to Andalusia—"praise the Lord," she told a friend in a letter. "I'll have to stay in bed, even eat in bed for a while, but home is home."

She and her mother had come back home to find the farmhouse full of unwashed dishes and rotten food. In her notebook, she made Parker's homecoming more dramatic than her own. She sent him to a pool hall, where he got beat up on account of his new tattoo. She led him to the Good Haven Mission, where "the only light was from a phosphorescent cross glowing at the end of the room." She had him examine his soul—"a sooty spider web of facts and lies that was not at all important to him but that appeared to be to the authority beyond"—then crossed the self-examination out.

At last she left Parker with Sarah Ruth, knocking at the door, eager to show her what he had done to himself.

The conclusion of the story is notorious, but its meaning is less than absolute. Why does Sarah Ruth so loathe Parker's tattoo that she beats him "until she had nearly knocked him senseless and large welts had formed on the face of the tattooed Christ"?

Caroline Gordon claimed that O'Connor had "succeeded where the great Flaubert failed: in the dramatization of that particular heresy which denies our Lord corporeal substance." She meant that Sarah Ruth represents all those heretics who separate body and spirit, human and divine, denying that the Word became flesh and walked the earth.

There is no question that O'Connor cast Sarah Ruth as a puritan and set her against the sensualist Parker. But if "Parker's Back" is merely a dramatization of a heresy, it is worthless. It is a story, and more than any other

O'Connor story it suggests and sustains many different meanings at once, in a pattern as complex as the "perfect arabesque" of Parker's tattooed body.

Since the story was written, the interpretations have multiplied. It is a parable of the plight of Christ in the modern world, scorned and beaten senseless by those who purport to follow him; a work of "ecumenical fiction," contrasting a sacramental Christianity with one from which the body and blood of Christ have been removed; a work in the "school of Southern degeneracy," a story of domestic quarrels and bar fights. It is a conversion story, which ends with Parker crying like a baby under a pecan tree, answering at last to the Christian name given to him in baptism—Obadiah Elihu—which he has denied for so long. It is a final expression of O'Connor's art of the grotesque, in which she distorted the image of Christ himself so as to restore its power to shock.

In "Parker's Back," the question of love that had arisen the first time Erik Langkjaer came to visit—Why show love to people for whom there is no hope?—is answered once and for all through a story. The believer holds that we are called to love one another, neighbor and enemy alike—called to love the stranger because the stranger is an image of God. We carry God and God's story with us like a second skin. In bed, betrayed by her body, O'Connor made the human body the image of God, to be raised up and glorified.

Ten years earlier, in "A Temple of the Holy Ghost," she had used the biblical image of the body as a temple to dramatize the mystery of God's presence in the world. In "Parker's Back" she made the image literal. Each of us, she insisted, is an image of God. Our pilgrimages are images of his own.

"Prayers requested," she informed Sally Fitzgerald. "I am sick of being sick."

She wrote letters to Grace Bug, Marybat, Raycheek, and Raybat—to Maryat Lee—and signed them Mrs. Turpin, Tarbug, and Tarbutter. In a letter to Elizabeth Hester she remarked, "There's a right interesting review of Richard Hughes' Fox in the Attic by Walker Percy in the summer 64 Sewanee."

She spoke fondly of Hopkins's poem "Margaret, are you grieving / Over Goldengrove unleaving?"

To Janet McKane, who was also sick, she sent the Prayer to St. Raphael, which the Catholic Worker people had sent her on a postcard in 1953. She had said it daily for some years:

364

O Raphael, lead us toward those we are waiting for, those who are waiting for us: Raphael, angel of happy meeting, lead us by the hand toward those we are looking for. . . .

Lonely and tired, crushed by the separations and sorrows of life, we feel the need of calling you and of pleading for the protection of your wings, so that we may not be as strangers in the province of joy, all ignorant of the concerns of our country. Remember the weak, you who are strong, you whose home lies beyond the region of thunder, in a land that is always peaceful, always serene and bright with the resplendent glory of God.

She sent "Parker's Back" to Hester and to Catherine Carver, her agent. To Carver she wrote, "I have drug another out of myself and enclose it." To Hester she wrote, "This here instead of a letter." Caroline Gordon had already criticized the story as awkward and undramatic, she told Hester, "but I'm letting it lay. I did well to write it at all."

And then she was dead, age thirty-nine. Her kidneys had failed and she had been taken to the hospital one last time, and there, August 2, she went into a coma, never to emerge.

They buried her the next morning, alongside her father in the cemetery on the edge of town. The reluctant prophet Francis Marion Tarwater had tarried in burying his grandfather. The Catholics of Milledgeville made haste in putting their daughter into the ground.

By conventional standards, she was a little-known writer. She had written no best-seller, won no major prize. The *New York Times* obituary called her "one of the nation's most promising writers," adding that "in Miss O'Connor's writing were qualities that attract and annoy many critics." Caroline Gordon wondered publicly whether she was a major writer or merely a fine minor one.

Gradually the recollections came forth from the dozens of people who had met her in New York or had made the pilgrimage to Andalusia. The *New York Review of Books* published some of them. A Jesuit priest collected others for publication in a Catholic journal called *Esprit*.

The most affecting eulogies, however, came from writers she had never met. J. F. Powers declared her "one of those rare ones, among writers, whose work was not in vain." Elizabeth Bishop recalled sending her a religious miniature—"a cross in a bottle, like a ship in a bottle, crudely carved, with all the instruments of the Passion, ladder, pliers, dice, etc."—and receiving a delighted reply: " 'If I were mobile and limber and rich I would come to Brazil after one look at this bottle. . . . It's what I'm born to appreciate.' "

And Thomas Merton, in *Jubilee*, spoke of her as if she were the younger sister he had been too busy to get to know. "Now Flannery is dead and I will write her name with honor," he began, and focused his "prose elegy" around this, the honor he felt in writing the name of a counterpart who had written "as if she were the only one left who took this thing seriously." Where others referred to her as Miss O'Connor, he would call her simply Flannery. Quickly, deeply, he characterized her through her work, fixing on her un-yielding respect for people who "announced the gospel of contempt." Although he had never referred to her work before in his own writing, he spoke of it, and her, in essential terms, with the authority of a confidant, one who knows the whole story. "Flannery saw the contempt of primitives who admitted that they would hate to be saved, and the greater contempt of those other primitives whose salvation was an elaborately contrived possibility, always being brought back into question," he declared. And: "She respected all her people by searching for some sense in them, searching for truth, searching to the end and then suspending judgment." And: "She never said: 'Here is a terrible thing!' She just looked and said what they said and how they said it."

He concluded, "When I read Flannery I don't think of Hemingway, or Katherine Anne Porter, or Sartre, but rather of someone like Sophocles. What more can be said of a writer? I write her name with honor, for all the truth and all the craft with which she shows man's fall and his dishonor." It was praise as lofty as he ever gave another writer, but the praise is beside the point, which is in the familiarity, the intimacy, with which he spoke about her. They had never met, never corresponded, but Merton felt, and then put into words, the power that her work has over others—its ability to make us feel, as we read her, that we know her, that she is one of us.

TEN

Pilgrimage or Crusade?

No matter how overcrowded St. Joseph's House was, Dorothy Day always had a room of her own: bed, desk, typewriter, bookshelf, a crucifix on the wall, and a radio for the Saturday-afternoon broadcasts of the Metropolitan Opera, to which she was devoted.

Her room in 1964 overlooked the intersection of Mott and Kenmare streets on the Lower East Side. A corner room, it had two large windows, where she could sit and observe the life of the city below. One day that summer she sat gazing out on the street and wrote down what she saw. There were "trucks laden with furniture, lumber, animals, sacks of saw dust, potato chips, fruit and vegetables, gasoline, milk, cement, cane syrup, garments, lowing cattle," and even "an occasional horse and wagon, noisy on the cobblestones which pave the street." There were police cars, fire trucks, garbage trucks grinding up the trash "collected daily from all the battered ash cans which stand in rows in front of each tenement." And there were "people bringing down bundles of trash to push into these already crowded cans, old women marketing with their shopping bags, young women pushing baby carriages, still other women in stretch pants."

"We have lived long in this neighborhood," she observed. To judge from her description, the year might have been 1934, but in 1964 the Lower East Side was changing, the life of the poor giving way to a new, atomized, bureaucratized poverty. The city wanted to run a new expressway through the neighborhood. The federal government wanted to demolish hundreds of tenements and replace them with high-rise housing projects. Many Jews and

Italians had moved to the suburbs. The people who remained were at odds with each other, goaded on by news reports that made "whites fear Negroes and the rich the poor, and one neighborhood another. There is wild talk of people arming themselves, first tear gas pencils are suggested, and now guns!"

The Church was changing, too—for the better, it was hoped. The Mass would be in English come Advent. Opening the second session of the Vatican council in Rome, the new pope—Paul VI—had called on the Church to adjust its relations with the world: "not to conquer but to serve, not to despise but to appreciate, not to condemn but to comfort and to save." The assembled bishops had drafted a declaration on religious liberty and were debating one on Catholic-Jewish relations. Although the U.S. bishops championed the war in Vietnam, a number of American Catholics had declared themselves conscientious objectors, and a Catholic peace organization was being formed.

Day was uneasy even so. She had always sought to change society more than she had the Church, and while the Church was changing, the problem of poverty was getting worse. Catholics in California were now criticizing the bishops instead of working on behalf of the poor. In New York the proposed expressway would cost at least $100 million, and probably more. "If it only could be put into better housing for the poor of the East side!" she wrote. ". . . But no, there is money for arms and for traffic but not for the poor and unemployed—nothing for youth!"

She had been reading about Philip Neri, the Renaissance saint and founder of the Oratorians, who would kneel for hours in the window of the Oratory in Rome. This day, following the saint's example, she knelt in her room at Mott and Kenmare streets and, looking out, she prayed for the neighborhood.

Thomas Merton went to New York in June 1964, his first trip out of Kentucky on his own since he had entered the monastery.

It was a return as Walker Percy defined the term, a journey to an old place in radically altered circumstances. After exchanging a series of letters with D. T. Suzuki in 1959, Merton had invited Suzuki, who lived in Japan, to visit Gethsemani if he ever made a trip to America. In the spring of 1964 he was informed that Suzuki, who was ninety-four years old, would be traveling to America but was too frail to travel to Kentucky. Was Merton willing to come to New York? Merton was willing, and once he explained to the abbot that Suzuki would not live much longer, a three-day visit was approved.

Suzuki liked to say that "if anything new can come out of human values it is from the cup of tea taken by two monks," and this was doubtless the way Merton envisioned their meeting: two monks in conversation, as in a Chinese drawing he liked, facing away toward the beyond.

In New York he met Suzuki twice, and while he described the meetings as "extraordinary" they were clearly disappointing. He found Suzuki "bent, slow, deaf, but lively and very responsive." They sought to define the human person from their different perspectives, but got nowhere. Suzuki told Merton some Zen stories; he had already heard them. He quoted some poetry into Suzuki's ear trumpet; the old man didn't understand him.

Then he was out on Broadway, a monk on furlough. The abbot had made him promise not to call anybody. Alone, he roamed the rain-slick streets, at large the way he had been in the thirties. He visited the Metropolitan Museum, and found it smaller and more imitative of Europe than he remembered. At the Guggenheim, he was overwhelmed by the "wheels of fire" that were the van Goghs. He ate Chinese food one night, Japanese the next, relishing the mix of languages to be heard on the sidewalk.

He was staying in a hotel near the Columbia campus. Mornings, he rose early and went to Corpus Christi Church nearby. There, in the small Baroque church where he had been baptized, so unlike the vast abbey church at Gethsemani, he was something like alone with God. "Said Mass two mornings entirely by myself, without servers, deeply moved. . . . No one recognized me or discovered who I was." Evenings, he put on pajamas and prayed at the window, overlooking Harlem. There had been gang violence in the neighborhood, and before leaving the monastery he had imagined that he might be shot. Now, as he prayed, he heard revving engines, barking dogs, singing, drumming, and gunfire, his senses working overtime.

In August he began to live at the hermitage full time. At first the move stirred in him "the same mixture of anguish and certitude, the same sense of walking on water, as when I first came to the monastery." There, dressed in overalls and work boots, he followed his own ritual of formal prayer, contemplation, reading, and writing. There, independent of the other monks and the abbot, he was, he liked to think, dependent on God alone; there, away from the monastery he had made famous, he was beyond imitation, newly anonymous.

After twenty-three years as a monk, he still asked himself whether he had truly become a monk, and he was more determined than ever to fulfill his monastic vows of poverty, chastity, and obedience. "My fiftieth year is ending and if I am not ripe now I never will be," he wrote in his journal. The sky, the stars, the "sickle moon rising behind the dark tall cedar cross" told him that now was the *kairos*, the acceptable time, the day of salvation. He recalled what he had told the priest at St. Bonaventure the night he became sure that he was meant to be a monk: " 'I want to give God everything.' Until now I really have not, I think. Or perhaps in a way I have tried to."

By October, when he found a kerosene lantern left for him by the abbot as a housewarming gift, he felt as at home in the cinder-block house in the woods as he had ever felt anywhere. "Lamplight! It is good, quiet. Many years since I have had a lamp to read by! Not since St. Antonin, forty years ago!"

The hermitage was still a meeting house, and the meetings began to multiply. That fall Merton led a retreat of Catholic peace activists, including Daniel and Philip Berrigan, two of the mere handful of other priests in the movement. The Berrigans—one a Jesuit, one a Josephite—were only six and eight years younger than Merton was, but they looked to him as an elder, and he responded accordingly. In his letters to Daniel Berrigan he urged moderation, recognizing Berrigan's energy and restlessness and zeal as akin to his own. He warned him off "all forms of projects and statements and programs and explanations of anything" and encouraged him not to get too angry at "the Church or her representatives," since "God writes straight on crooked lines anyway, all the time, all the time." But as the retreat approached, he told Berrigan: "Let's make it purposeless and freewheeling and a vacation for all and let the Holy Spirit suggest anything that needs to be suggested."

There is no better evidence of the rightness of Merton's hermit life than the sudden clarity of his writing. The mystical jargon is gone, replaced with language of biblical strength. Solitude, so long defended or sought after, is no longer an end in itself, but a means to know God. God is suddenly, palpably present. So is death ("A flash of the 'not-thereness' of being dead," he recorded. "Without fear or grief, without anything. Just not there"). Prayer is joined to eschatology, the pondering of last things; and the contemplative life is one of prayer in the approach to death—the "experience" of being on the way to God, with God, and through God, who is "that Truth which is the end and by which we are already fully and eternally alive."

He was still writing on a wide range of topics, for tiny journals he had scarcely even heard of: *Charlatan, Motive, Eco Contemporaneo, Sponsa Regis.* Editors would write asking him for an essay, and he would take the opportunity to investigate a topic he was curious about—the English mystics, the Jesuit missionaries to China, the Shakers, the Andalusian mystic Ibn Abbad—in a few thousand words.

His most revealing piece of 1964 is one unlike any he had written. "From Pilgrimage to Crusade" is not a portrait or a meditation, an introduction or a polemic. It might be called a piece of religious typology, as objective as an encyclopedia entry, as if he had been asked to define the "sacred journey" for all times and places, describing the pilgrimage of Christianity in the West.

"Man instinctively regards himself as a wanderer and wayfarer, and it is second nature for him to go on pilgrimage in search of a privileged and holy place, a center and source of indefectible life," he began. "This hope is built into his psychology, and whether he acts it out or simply dreams it, his heart seeks to return to a mythical source, a place of 'origin,' the 'home' where the ancestors came from, the mountain where the ancient fathers were in direct communication, the place of the creation of the world, paradise itself, with its sacred tree of life."

From there he described the expansion of the Christian ideal of pilgrimage and its corruption into holy war, sketching representative pilgrims at each point: the early Christian pilgrims to Jerusalem, imitating Jewish pilgrims of the Bible; the Irish monks "who simply floated off to sea, abandoning themselves to wind and current, in the hope of being led to the place of solitude which God himself would pick for them"; the penitents of the Dark Ages, sent forth as outcasts; the brigands and murderers who, forced to go on pilgrimage as punishment, formed fearsome roving bands; the monks who, in response, made the pilgrimage "entirely spiritual," an inner journey undertaken from a cell and cloister; the first crusaders, who saw war on the infidel as their only hope of salvation outside a monastery; the explorers who saw the New World as a return to an earthly paradise that was theirs by right; the Protestant pilgrim fathers and the Catholic conquistadors, in whom "the mentality of the pilgrim and that of the crusader had fused together to create a singular form of alienation."

He wrote the piece straight through (adding seventy footnotes later on), and it has an odd, unsourced authority. It gives no sign of why he wrote it. There is no one book behind it, no charismatic figure, no obsession, no problem in need of solving. There is no "I" in it, no allusion to his Trappist life. As Merton tells of the believer's pilgrimage back to "the source and center of religion itself, the place of theophany, of cleansing, renewal, and salvation," he seems to be describing his own religious calling:

> The geographical pilgrimage is a symbolic acting out of an inner journey. The inner journey is the interpolation of the meanings and signs of the outer pilgrimage. One can have one without the other. It is best to have both. History would show the fatality and doom that would attend on the external pilgrimage with no interior spiritual integration, a divisive and disintegrated wandering.

The piece is the fulfillment of Merton's spirituality of place, a piece in which his cherished ideas of twenty years are profoundly upended. There is no earthly paradise to escape to, he now realizes, no desert island to find and claim as one's own. Rather, the human race, scattered to the four winds, is God's own archipelago, and we are the islands, "pieces of paradise isle."

The modern pilgrimage in our time, then, is a continual voyage out to the other—"to the stranger who is Christ and our fellow-pilgrim and our brother." Because the pilgrimage is the pattern and program of human existence, the pilgrimage must go on; but the modern pilgrim, Merton warned, must go forth in the knowledge that the pilgrimage has the seed of a crusade within it and inclines toward "a consecration of violence."

Better than anything that he wrote about the hermitage, "From Pilgrimage to Crusade" suggests the way Merton's thoughts tended in the woods. His journey, ever since he entered Gethsemani, had been almost wholly inward and metaphorical, enacted on a few acres of land. Now that he had reached its destination, a place of perfect fixity, he could not stay there.

Because she was deaf, every evening Walker Percy narrated the television news for his younger daughter, Ann, moving his lips carefully so that she could read them. The news in 1964 was excruciating to describe. Night after night the top story was from Mississippi: three young civil-rights workers murdered by the roadside in Philadelphia; James Meredith struggling to be the first black student admitted to the state university in Oxford, where he was mocked, threatened, spit upon; White Citizens' Councils contriving to keep black citizens from voting in the fall elections. A century after the Civil War, which was then being marked in the South with "pilgrimages" to the battlefields, the South was at war over race again, and Mississippi, the ancestral seat of the Percy clan, was the one place where the war was being won by the racists.

"What happened to this state?" Percy asked in an essay called "The Fallen Paradise." The editor of *Harper's*, Willie Morris, a Mississippi native, had invited him to contribute to a special issue marking the centenary of the battle of Appomattox, and Percy set aside his novel to do so. Like his uncle, he was now a public man, and like his uncle, he would use his position to fight the good fight, to speak out on the vital issues of the day.

The *Harper's* piece was a restatement of the points Percy had made in *Commonweal* in the fifties: the end of the "alliance" between planters and black sharecroppers, the rise of the parvenu white bigot, the decline of manners, the pain that came with racial honesty. Even so, it was his first essay for a national magazine, and he shaped the argument accordingly. He acknowledged that "no ex-Mississippian is entitled to write with any sense of moral superiority of the tragedy which has overtaken his former state. For he cannot be certain in the first place that if he had stayed he would not have kept silent—or worse." He also excised the religious dimension of the argument, about the decline of Stoic behavior and the emergence of Christianity as a political force.

He still believed that Christianity was being put to the test in the South, however, and he amplified this position the next year in *Katallagete*, the journal of the Committee of Southern Churchmen, an interracial, ecumenical group whose board he had been persuaded to join.

The role of the churches in the South gave the essay its title: "The Failure and the Hope." By the standards of their own religion, Percy declared, white Christians should have been ashamed of themselves. The failure of Christianity was that they were not—that they still saw the churches as "good" institutions. The hope was that they were still Christian enough to recognize their failure and change their ways. He thought such a change was possible—"because the South, more so than the rest of the country, is still Christ-haunted, to use an expression of Flannery O'Connor's."

In March 1965 the nightly news brought reports of the thwarted march from Selma to Montgomery, a pilgrimage on behalf of voting rights. The televised images told the story: white police officers brutalizing black marchers; blacks inviting whites to pray with them; white priests and nuns marching alongside Martin Luther King at the head of the line.

The *Harper's* piece makes clear that Percy felt himself to be a guilty bystander who had not done his part to foster civil rights, and one day he surprised Shelby Foote by suggesting that they should go to Selma and join the marchers. At the same time, he was skeptical of those " 'groups' or institutions which have a 'good' impact on society" but mainly salved the consciences of their members.

"The Failure and the Hope" was his attempt to play some part, however small. The journal of the Committee of Southern Churchmen was an in-between place, where he could update his uncle's legacy for the civil-rights era without disowning the South or being drawn away from his novel.

He had another motive for joining the board. Thomas Merton was also a member, and the other members spoke of visiting the Abbey of Gethsemani. Sooner or later, Percy was assured, they would have a board meeting at the monk's hermitage in the woods.

Percy's elder daughter, Mary Pratt, was a high school senior, and upon her graduation in June 1965 he took the whole family to Europe on the *Queen Mary*. It was a broadening experience for him as well as his daughters. Although he saw himself as an heir to Camus and Thomas Mann, he hadn't been to Europe since college; the self-styled pilgrim and wayfarer was actually a homebody, whose journeys had been to Florida and the Grand Canyon.

They went to London and Cambridge; to Scotland, redoubt of the Percy clan; and then to France—not to Paris, not to the Riviera, but to Lourdes and the shrine of Our Lady. They spent five days in Lourdes, longer than they'd spent in London. Over the years, Percy's faith, first embraced as a way out of the dead end of philosophy, had become a family affair, as he and Bunt raised their daughters Catholic and schooled them in the Church, like countless other American Catholic parents, with the hope that the faith would take hold in the next generation. Now they prevailed upon their deaf daughter to take the waters, hoping for a miracle.

There was a further dimension to the pilgrimage, however. Percy registered as *un médicin americain* and spent part of each day attending to pilgrim patients. Once upon a time, he had been a *malade* himself, awaiting his death in a cottage in the mountains. Now he was a husband, a father, a novelist, a diagnostician, a philosopher of the modern malady. Perhaps his own survival was miraculous; in any case, as he pushed the wheelchairs of others he was glad to be alive.

Everything That Rises Must Converge was published in May 1965, with an introduction by Robert Fitzgerald and a white jacket that set the author's name in Gothic type.

The introduction now seems mannered and overwrought, but it served many readers that year as the first portrait of the artist, and it left a range of vivid images for her new admirers to choose from: the gracious Southern lady who worshipped, wrote, went to town, then took the air among her fowl; the irreverent artist who inscribed *A Good Man Is Hard to Find* to the Fitzgeralds as "Nine stories about original sin, with my compliments"; the defender of the faith "hanging on her crutches at the lectern" and declaiming about "the Catholic sacramental view of life"; the perduring sick person, whose bedroom had a narrow and "severe" bed with missal, breviary, and Bible stacked beside it. No longer would Flannery O'Connor be mistaken for a gentleman or a rural primitive. She was a woman, and a literary saint.

The book included one story, "Judgement Day," that had not been published. Everything about it—the title, the topic, the placement at the end of the book—suggested that O'Connor had written it in anticipation of her death, putting herself into the description of the old Southern man Tanner: his body like "a great heavy bell whose clapper swung from side to side but made no noise"; his handwriting, "wavery but decipherable with patience"; his contempt for the Northern city where he was trapped in his daughter's apartment, "conserving all his strength for the trip home."

It later emerged that "Judgement Day" was a rewrite of O'Connor's first published story, "The Geranium," from 1946. Rewriting it, she had cleaned off her desk, making her work circle around from the end to the beginning.

As she revised the typescript by hand in the hospital, she had quietly nudged it toward profundity. Tanner does die at the end of the story, and his daughter has him buried in the city, not in the South, "but after she had done it she could not sleep well at night." From there the typescript goes on: Night after night she turned and tossed and very definite lines began to appear in her face, so she had him dug up and shipped the body to Corinth. Now she sleeps well at night." There is a conclusive note in that sentence, but O'Connor, in extremis, recast the sentence in the language of last things—"now she *rests* well at night"—so as to suggest eternal or heavenly rest. Then, in a wavery hand, she added: ". . . and her good looks have mostly returned." In the final line of her published work, like a medieval scribe sketching in the margin, she introduced an image of the resurrection of the body, an image of herself, but glorified.

The Second Vatican Council was the Old World's reckoning with the New: to read the coverage in *Time*, or the periodic "Letter from Vatican City" in the *New Yorker*, was to feel that Pope John had thrown open the Vatican windows to American-style practicality and optimism. The fourth and last session of the council, that fall of 1965, would be devoted to the role of the Church in the modern world. Redefining the Church's role in the modern world meant redefining the Church. Already, the notion of the Church as the Mystical Body of Christ was being supplanted by the "Pilgrim Church," the People of God on pilgrimage through time.

That summer, the modern world asserted itself. The assassination of Malcolm X, the fires and riots and lootings in Los Angeles, the escalation of the war in Vietnam: any simple optimism on the part of the People of God ought to have been banished in advance. The next stage of the pilgrimage would be far from peaceable.

In 1964, James Forest of St. Joseph's House had organized the Catholic Peace Fellowship, setting up a little office in Greenwich Village to counsel prospective war resisters and enlisting prominent peace activists—Daniel Berrigan, Thomas Merton, Dorothy Day—as an advisory board.

One item on the council agenda—Schema 13—dealt with war and peace in the modern world. The CPF members hoped Paul VI and the bishops would build on John XXIII's letter on war and peace and incorporate a condemnation of nuclear war into the council documents, which would be, in effect, the new constitution of the Church.

In September, Day set out, by ship, for Rome, to join a group of twenty Catholic women there. On her previous visit to Rome she had had meetings with Vatican officials and rubbernecked at the pope like any other pilgrim. This time she would act more directly. She went to a Roman restaurant and ate a sumptuous meal. Then she, and the others, began a fast.

The fast was ten days, water only. The twenty women passed the time in a convent, reading, knitting, talking, laughing, praying, attending Mass in the chapel, speaking with visitors—bishops from the council, members of the press—and sending cards to their correspondents around the world, such as Father Louis of the Abbey of Gethsemani, U.S.A.

Why fast for peace? What was the objective? Day was asked the question often. In a sense, the fast itself was the answer. Through the fast, the women sought to call attention to the cause of peace. They also sought to feel, in their bodies, their connection to others, their belief that the human race is one body, and the Church the Mystical Body of Christ. For her own part, Day sought to ponder the connection between war and world poverty. "I had offered my fast in part for the victims of famine," she wrote in her column, and the hunger pangs seemed to her "an intimation of the hunger of the world."

Schema 13 was adopted—the bishops condemned nuclear war and the targeting of civilians—and Day returned to America. She was sitting on her suitcase at the New York pier, waiting to clear customs, when reporters found her. A Catholic Worker had burned his draft card at the Selective Service office, defying a new federal law against the destruction of one's draft card, government property after all. Did she have any comment? "Our boys and our priests have been tearing up their draft cards for years," she told them.

A few days later several activists—including Thomas Cornell, a Catholic Worker—burned their draft cards in Union Square. This time Day was with them. She spoke in their defense, pointing out that by doing so she was aiding and abetting them. She was heckled as Moscow Mary. The activists were told to burn themselves, not their draft cards.

At St. Joseph's House, the Catholic Workers had debated the merits of the action for years. Burning one's draft card made plain one's refusal to register in the simplest possible way. It also called to mind the sufferings of Vietnamese civilians, whom the U.S. military was targeting with burning napalm—precisely the kind of warfare the Vatican council had just condemned as "a crime against God and humanity." And yet burning one's draft card widened the gap between witness and charity, between the dramatic gesture and the little way. More than a refusal to comply with an unjust law, it was an aggressive defiance of the law. It invited others to imitate the gesture, not the principled resistance to war. Moreover, it was the destruction of property, a kind of violence.

The next day the issue flared up and took the shape of a man. Roger La-Porte set himself on fire at dawn outside United Nations headquarters, which was deserted except for passing taxicabs. As he was taken by ambulance to Bellevue Hospital, he muttered that he was a Catholic Worker and was "against war—all wars"; and as he lay dying, with burns over 90 percent of his body, the Catholic Workers at St. Joseph's House tried to put together the pieces of his story. He was twenty-two years old, a cradle Catholic, an honor student, a teacher in training, a former novice in a Cistercian monastery. He shared an apartment with some other Catholic Workers; he had spent some time "on the line" the past two years, serving soup and bread and coffee. Speaking to the press, they called him Roger, but clearly they had not known him very well.

He died November 10. Daniel Berrigan led a memorial service for him at St. Joseph's House. In his eulogy, he described LaPorte in Christlike terms, as one whose "death was offered that others may live."

In retrospect it seems an obvious inference; Berrigan and the Catholic Workers may not have realized that it would be seen at Cardinal Spellman's office as a defiant rejection of the church teaching that suicides, having refused the gift of life and imperiled the soul, should be refused the funeral rites.

Once again the Catholic Workers were set against the Cardinal and the Catholic populace. Day's biographers grimly record the consequences— death threats phoned in to St. Joseph's House, an uprising near the stage as Day gave a talk at New York University, an inquisition led by the tabloid reporters, who hectored her and her cohorts as murderers, not pacifists who condemned violence. And a telegram from Thomas Merton:

JUST HEARD ABOUT SUICIDE OF ROGER LA PORTE. WHILE I DO NOT HOLD CATHOLIC PEACE FELLOWSHIP RESPONSIBLE FOR THIS TRAGEDY, CURRENT DEVELOPMENTS IN PEACE MOVEMENT MAKE IT IMPOSSIBLE FOR ME TO CONTINUE AS SPONSOR OF FELLOWSHIP.

In his hermitage, Merton saw a disturbing pattern developing. Already that year Buddhist monks had immolated themselves in Vietnam while their brother monks looked on. A Quaker had set herself alight in Milwaukee; another had lit himself on fire outside the Pentagon, holding his infant daughter. Now a Catholic—a Catholic Worker—had done so, and the Catholic peace movement seemed to be consecrating the violence.

Merton wrote letters to Jim Forest and Daniel Berrigan, declaring that the peace movement was becoming "un-Christian" and "a little pathological." Just when the Vatican council had recognized the believer's right to object to war as a matter of conscience, there came "this business of burning oneself alive." He concluded, "This suicide business is surely demonic. God help us."

The Catholic peace activists were upset. Some saw Merton's telegram as a betrayal, others as proof that the hermit of Gethsemani was sheltered from the struggle between good and evil on the streets of America.

Dorothy Day saw it as an occasion for clarification of thought. In an article she was writing about the episode, she answered Merton indirectly. Was suicide sinful? Yes, the Church condemned suicide as a mortal sin, but the Church also maintained that "mercy and kindness dictated another judgment"—as she had learned shortly after becoming a Catholic, when a priest urged her to follow her instincts and pray for the souls of the people she knew (there were ten of them) who had killed themselves.

With this in mind, she proposed that it was wrong to condemn Roger LaPorte. For one thing, he had made an act of contrition on his deathbed. For another—now she rose to her point—it was wrong to condemn one young man for killing himself in New York when in Vietnam "there were more killed on both sides last week than at any time since the war began." America was a country where war was considered a blessing, where the *Wall Street Journal* crowed that the war had given "extra zip" to the "peppy" economy. "There is something satanic about this kind of writing," she declared.

The peace movement wasn't "demonic." The war machine was. That was Day's point; and that, she insisted, was Roger LaPorte's point, too. In coming to the Catholic Worker he had sought to embrace the suffering of others, and surely that was what he had meant to do when he took his own life. "There is a tradition in the Church of what are called 'victim souls,'" she explained, and the "victim souls" in the headlines were "all trying to show their willingness to give their lives for others, to endure the sufferings that we as a nation are inflicting upon a small country and its people." The Church taught its people to judge an act by the intention behind it, and the Catholic Workers knew "Roger 'intended' to lay down his life for his brother in Vietnam."

Here was the meaning of Day's fast in Rome: it gave her insight into Roger LaPorte a few months later. Like him, she had felt the effects of war in her very bones. She felt his violent death the same way, and although he was a virtual stranger, in the hour of his death she identified with him.

On November 15 Day sent Merton a handwritten letter. "About your telegram—we are so glad you know about our tragedy, being assured you are praying for us," she told him. There, in a single sentence, she set him straight: LaPorte's death was a tragedy—their tragedy; and it called for prayer, not a telegrammed rebuke, especially from a man of prayer like himself.

She went on to tell him a little about "poor Roger." Although she had "actually never exchanged a word with him," she knew him to be one of a group of young Catholic Workers who were all " 'in love' with each other and with life," and "if anyone had ever dreamed he contemplated such an action, he would have been watched day and night."

She was trying to set LaPorte apart from the young nihilists she had described in her previous letters, perhaps fearing that Merton's telegram was a reaction to a stereotype of the young Catholic Workers that she had given him herself. "I am only hoping that your reaction, as evidenced by your telegram, is not general," she told him, "but I am afraid that it may be."

In any case, she made clear that the tragedy was not going to change her position on the war. In Vietnam, things were getting worse and worse: villagers had been targeted, U.S. troops napalmed by their own forces. "In view of the terrible things that are happening . . . there are bound to be increased protests," she observed, adding, "I am glad that there are so many now. The Catholic Worker has borne the burden for 33 years—protesting wars Chinese-Japanese, Ethiopian, Spanish, World War II, Korean, Algerian, and now this."

Merton got the letter at Gethsemani—a "warm, wise letter," he thought—and replied two days later. "You are well experienced in this kind of upset," he told Day, "and I was grateful to hear your human voice simply stating what you know, and not magnifying it any further."

He was already apologizing far and wide for the telegram he had sent, suggesting that it was (as he told Day) "a rather ill-considered and immediate reaction." He had decided to remain a member of the Catholic Peace Fellowship and had promised to write a pamphlet for the group on the roots of Christian nonviolence.

But his position would not change, either. While he could be restless, even faddish, in his reading, his writing, and his sense of himself, in moral matters he was as unbudgeable as Day. He still saw draft-card burning as wrong, as were all "provocative" actions whose main objective was to attract attention to a cause. He felt that the Catholic peace movement risked becoming too radical and that it should try instead to persuade "the people who are honestly bothered by the war in Vietnam and cannot see it as a just war, yet cannot identify themselves with a specifically pacifist protest." And while he thought the death of Roger LaPorte had turned out to be a genuine trial for the movement, he still considered the act itself objectively wrong. In a letter to his old mentor Catherine de Hueck the next January, he wrote: "Some tried to make out that Roger was a martyr, but in fact I think he was a kind of sign of judgment, in his well-intentioned confusion, something to teach the Catholic peace movement that there is something far more important than just getting coverage in the press and on TV."

In the aftermath of LaPorte's death, Daniel Berrigan had stepped into the spotlight fully formed: forty-six years old, equal parts poet and agitator, dressed in a beret and black turtleneck like a man in a Godard movie. Now his Jesuit superiors, under pressure from Cardinal Spellman, ordered him to leave the country—first to Mexico, then to South America—and discouraged him from taking part in any more political activities.

Some of the Catholic peace activists denounced this order as a fascistic abuse of Church power. Dorothy Day, however, thought Berrigan would be strengthened by obedience. "My feeling is that he is in some ways young and inexperienced—if you will consider my effrontery in making such a judgment—and that being sent off on such a tour is to his advantage," she told Merton in a letter in December. For one thing, he had become "too excited, in his actions—emotional, overwrought." For another, in his inexperience he had been disdainful of "the man of the street—the kind of people who read the Daily News." She explained, "These are the masses we will have to reach if we are trying to change men's attitudes. That is the distinctive thing about the Catholic Worker—that in all the houses the majority of these men [are those] the world calls derelicts and who really are men who have done much of the hard work of the country. We are not just talking to each other as so many in the pacifist movement do."

Merton saw the situation similarly, and tapped out an approving reply, telling Day, "I guess you and I are a bit old-fashioned." He had written the Jesuits a letter in Berrigan's support, and he thought that religious superiors would have to be more flexible in the future; but his own experience told him that "one never loses anything by obeying, quite the contrary, and sometimes God reserves special gifts and an extra fruitfulness for us, something we could not have gained without this sacrifice."

"As you say, his silence will say much," he told Day, "and probably a great deal more than a lot of noise by his friends."

The affair strengthened Merton's sense of the need for obedience to one's own calling. His calling to solitude, just then, demanded obedience to the specific aspects of solitude that were possible in the hermitage—silence, apartness, detachment from current affairs—and he had made a mistake in departing from these too readily with his telegram. And yet he understood that Dorothy Day was bound to see things differently, and to act differently, for civil disobedience was her form of obedience to her own calling.

In his journal he wrote, "Letter from Dorothy Day today. We agree." And in a fresh letter to her at year's end he offered a lyrical tribute to her and her movement, as if to dispel any doubts about his support for her calling, which was superficially so unlike his own. "To me the *Catholic Worker* stands for something absolutely unique and alive in the American Church," he told her, addressing her as Dorothy. "It would be hard for me to put into words how much it means to me, for so many personal reasons: it stands for my own youth and for the kinds of influences that shaped my own life thirty years ago. . . . If there were no *Catholic Worker* and such forms of witness, I would never have joined the Catholic Church."

The first Friday of March 1966 Walker Percy went on retreat at Holy Ghost Monastery. His motive was partly literary. Caroline Gordon was teaching at Emory University, and he arranged to meet her in Atlanta and drive to the monastery, bringing proofs of his new novel.

The Cistercian Abbey of Our Lady of the Holy Ghost had been renamed Holy Spirit Monastery, and it was no longer an outpost in the wilderness. The surrounding fields were being developed as a suburb of Atlanta. The poured-concrete arches and abstract stained glass were now standard in sub-urban Catholic parishes. Its most distinctive aspect, perhaps, was its con-gregation of peacocks, which Flannery O'Connor had bequeathed to the Trappists.

The weekend Percy and Gordon spent at the monastery was akin to the scheme for a School of the Holy Ghost that Gordon had once envisioned: part retreat and part editorial conference, a writers' workshop in a conse-crated setting. They followed the monastic hours, rising at dawn and retiring at sundown. They prayed the Divine Office, freshly translated into English. They met with Father Charles, whom Gordon was instructing by correspon-dence in the art of fiction; he struck Percy as "nutty as a fruitcake." And they discussed *The Last Gentleman* during a long walk on the monastery grounds.

After finishing a draft in the spring of 1965 Percy had spent the fall revis-ing it. He had labored under the concern that the "threadbareness of reli-gious words" was the challenge facing the religious novelist, a concern he had set out in an anguished letter to Gordon. "When the holy has disappeared, how in blazes can the novelist expect to make use of it?" he asked, and answered by citing O'Connor's remark that the religious novelist had to learn "how to shout in silence." For his part, Percy now thought of himself as a moralist more than a novelist, a descendant of Kierkegaard and Pascal. He wanted to call people's attention to the "deep human truths" they needed to know in order to live fulfilling lives. *The Moviegoer*, he complained, had been read as a novel of despair rather than one about the escape from despair. With the new book, he would state his themes directly.

The Last Gentleman would ingeniously take the themes of *The Moviegoer* to the next stage. Whereas Binx Bolling was an ironic searcher, Will Barrett would be one in earnest, a young man urgently in need of a purpose in life. And whereas Bolling's pilgrimage was metaphorical, a search for meaning in a featureless suburb, Barrett's would be an actual journey from a YMCA in Manhattan to the South and then the Southwest. The novel would reverse the usual movement from innocence to experience, from country to city, suggesting that the modern seeker needed to get back to the experience of a particular place; it would diagnose the restlessness of the middle sixties, and make the traditional picaresque or road novel into a story of contemporary pilgrimage.

Gordon read *The Last Gentleman* that weekend, then wrote Percy a long letter upon her return to Atlanta. She thought the novel impressively rich, but she had strong reservations about it. The novel, she told him, wasn't properly dramatic. The action began vaguely and fell off from there, depending far too much on the thoughts of the abstracted protagonist, Will Barrett. The problem was evident in the opening pages, where Barrett lies on his back daydreaming in Central Park. "*A young man, alone, thinking!*" she exclaimed. "It takes genius to triumph over a start like that."

Percy decided to disregard her, just as Flannery O'Connor had done, and he, too, drew on Nathaniel Hawthorne's vocabulary: he meant his novel to be an "existential romance," not a conventional novel. In a letter to Gordon he explained that Will Barrett's abstracted character was part of the plan for the book, which was to send a solipsistic man on a journey and gradually "break him out of the solipsism." And in a précis of the book written for his new publisher—Farrar, Straus and Giroux, publisher of O'Connor as well— he explained that the novel turned on a "fancy" which could be understood either scientifically or religiously as a sign of the times. Will Barrett, he declared, was a man who acted as if a catastrophe had already happened, and his disjointed behavior was either a "symptom of illness" or the "prophetic glimmering" of a postmodern pilgrim.

This time, Caroline Gordon was right. *The Last Gentleman* is a book with all the problems of its protagonist. Of Will Barrett, his counterpart Sutter Vaught observes: "His trouble is he wants to know what his trouble is," and this kind of circularity pervades the novel. Its theme is the modern person's need for the rootedness and particularity that society is eradicating, but its characters are sketchy and insubstantial. Its setting is the New South, but the sly and complex prose of *The Moviegoer* devolves into a blustery Old South idiom. Its title is *The Last Gentleman*, but its hero is not only not a gentleman, he is hardly a man: he is the callow youth of stereotype, trying to find his way, and the novel, for all its appurtenances, is Percy's bildungsroman all over again.

Percy later said he modeled Barrett on the saintly hero of Dostoevsky's *The Idiot*, and he spoke of the difficulty of making a good character come to life in fiction. His awareness of the problem, however, did not enable him to solve it, and Will Barrett's failure to come to life—or even to seem especially good—led Percy to assign to him all sorts of quasi-allegorical attributes. He is a "very sick boy" with a "nervous condition"; an amnesiac who is prone to mental "fugues"; hard of hearing, for he is deaf in one ear. He is an "engineer" who spends all his spare change on his telescope and is in thrall to the scientific worldview, and an "Anglo-Saxon sleuth" with extraordinary powers of intuition; he is a lapsed Episcopalian who has never given any thought to religion. And he is, for all this, an ordinary lusty American fellow who wants nothing more than to marry, settle down, have children, love his wife, and hold "her charms in his arms."

The other characters are scarcely more vivid. Will's fiancée, Kitty, is a mere shell of Kate from *The Moviegoer*: a young woman said to be all "noble matutinal curves" and nervous anxieties. Her brother, Jamie, is an echo of wheelchair-bound Lonnie Smith: a ghostly boy who lies in a hospital bed reading a book called the *Theory of Large Sets*. Their pilgrimage, meant to be an excursion into the "actual" and "realized" life of the South, does not feel like a journey. There is no sense of time passing or distance traveled, no sense of one place as distinct from another. The South is said to be an "intersubjective paradise," where "the air fairly crackled with kinship radiations"; but during the annual Georgia-Tennessee football game—the epitome of Southern rivalry and sociability—Barrett and Kitty meet no one: setting out for their rendezvous, Barrett finds all the streets in town deserted, for everybody is at the stadium or watching the game on TV.

Percy may have meant the novel to spring to life when the "exotic pair" of Sutter and Val Vaught appear. Sutter, a doctor, has devised his own philosophy; Val, who fled her country-club girlhood to become a Catholic and a nun, has established "a little foundation in the pines" of Alabama, where she works with poor blacks and waits for a sign from the hereafter.

Sutter and Val, brother and sister, are the two interesting characters in the novel, until they are enlisted to represent Percy's philosophy. Val explains that she became a nun even though God is dead because with God dead the sky is clear and it is time to start all over again; then she declaims about the modern person's yearning for authority. Sutter is an admirable nihilist, seeking transcendence through homemade pornography; but he sets out his philosophy tendentiously in *pensées* in a notebook and describes his sexual exploits in Latinate medical terminology.

For Walker Percy, the burden of accomplishment—namely, the expectation that he should write a "Catholic novel"—was the undoing of all he had accomplished with *The Moviegoer*. He thought he had to learn how to shout in silence the way Flannery O'Connor had done. From his own experience, however, he should have known otherwise: the truth—in his own work, at least—is best approached indirectly, through cunning and guile.

The most authentic religious image in *The Last Gentleman* is also the most worldly, and the most concretely described. It is the deluxe campertrailer in which Barrett and Jamie Vaught travel cross-country. Built by the Travel-Aire company of Sheboygan, Wisconsin, a cabin kitted out with a sink, a stove, a shower, and a refrigerator on the bed of a GMC pickup truck, the vehicle is at once primitive and postmodern, and so is the itinerant life it sponsors, the pilgrimage that it makes possible. "Now here surely is a good way to live nowadays," Barrett says to himself, "mobile yet at home, compacted and not linked up with the crumby carnival linkage of a trailer, in the world yet not of the world, sampling the particularities of place yet cabined off from the sadness of place." It is the missionary wagon of Father Vaillant in *Death Comes for the Archbishop* updated for the Vatican II era, the age of the split-level homestead and the interstate highway.

As the Abbey of Gethsemani expanded, the threat of fire remained, and in 1965 the abbot commissioned a renovation of the monastery, both to fireproof the buildings and to update them in accordance with the reforms of the Vatican council. An architect produced a plan of Cistercian-Kentuckian simplicity. The cloister would be laid out like a town square, with streetlights at the corners. The abbey church would be shorn of its Gothic aspect, reduced to whitewashed walls, wooden beams, a stone altar, and clear windows to let in the light.

Thomas Merton had gone into the hospital in Louisville for back surgery, and when he returned, the work was in progress. He sat outside the hermitage, watching. "I can hear the demolishers shouting from the top of the steeple. They are now stripping it. A momentous change: the steeple has been so much a sign of the place—the thing one looks for when one is getting close—the expression of the abbey's identity—the sign that it is *there!* . . . More shouting from the steeple. Slowly the plates of lead come off and the old brown lumber appears."

As he watched, he felt his life changing. At age fifty-one, he had fallen in love, with a woman, a young nurse at the hospital, and the "raided and ruined" abbey church suggested the state of his monastic calling. "Margie wants to see me," he wrote in his journal. "And I—want to see her. I tell myself it is because I want to help her. And so on."

After the operation he had spent two weeks recuperating. He still found hospital visits a foretaste of heaven, and so it was this time in Lourdes Hall of Louisville's Catholic hospital. He read and prayed and received Communion each morning. He underwent a daily sponge bath. The nurse was in her early twenties, dark-haired, pretty, a Catholic, a "talker." She told him she had read *The Sign of Jonas.*

She looked in on him regularly, declaring herself his nurse. She flirted with him, and he with her. When she was not working, he missed her, and as his discharge approached he wrote her a love letter. In it he explained that, by writing CONSCIENCE MATTER on the envelope, she could write to him privately.

She did so. It was a love letter. She was engaged to be married, but her fiancé lived out of town. Monk and nurse would carry on.

Back at the monastery, Merton pondered his situation. "One grey day after another," he wrote, "continued struggle in my heart."

As the monastery had been a refuge from the falsity of the world, the hermitage was a refuge from the falsity of the monastery. But suddenly the hermitage—and the life of solitude—seemed false. "The question of love: I have to face the fact that I have simply sidestepped it," he wrote in his journal, and "now it must be faced squarely. I cannot live without giving back to a world that has given me so much. And of course it has to be the love of a man dedicated to God—and selfless, detached, free, completely open love. And I have not attained to such a level, hence the risk."

All his life his imagination had run out ahead of his experience. He read about a way of being, then claimed it imaginatively in his writing. He had written exhaustively about love: the love of one's enemy, the love of one's neighbor, the love of God alone. Now it was time to know love first-hand—to place himself in love—even if, in worldly terms, it would come to nothing.

He had a doctor's appointment scheduled in Louisville. From the monastery, he called Margie and asked her to lunch.

"There is no question that I am in deep," he wrote in his journal three days later. "Tuesday (yesterday) Margie met me at the doctor's. Appeared in the hall, small, shy, almost defiant, with her long black hair, her grey eyes, her white trench coat. (She kept saying she was scared.)"

They had arranged to meet at a bar and grill in Louisville; they ate sand-wiches, flirted, kissed across the table, and felt right away that they had gone too far. "It is just that Margie is terribly inflammable, and beautiful, and is no nun, and so tragically full of passion and so wide open," he wrote. "My response has been too total and too forthright, we have admitted too much, communicated all the fire to each other and now we are caught.

"I am not as smart or as stable as I imagined," he added. And yet he still imagined that there could be such a thing as a "chaste marriage" in which he would keep his monastic vows.

During a rainstorm, he welcomed Margie into the hermitage imagina-tively: there, he felt "not lonely *for* Margie but in some strange way lonely *with* her, as if she had somehow peacefully become part of my loneliness and of my life that tries to be in God, tries to dwell at the point where life and grace well up out of the unknown." Meanwhile, he prayed to God for the strength to renounce her.

They began to meet on every available pretext, with Merton's worldly friends ferrying him to and from each rendezvous—at a pub in Louisville, at the Louisville airport, at a Derby Day picnic on a lake not far from the monastery. Because of his back injury, he was still spending nights in the monastery infirmary rather than the hermitage, and this made his comings and goings less obvious. Monastic life went on: the vigils, the chants, the

Masses; the guests, the conferences, the peace work, the dialogue. But Merton's chronicle of the everyday life of the place, of his inner life as a reader and writer and lover of God, ceased altogether as he filled his journal with poems and reveries about Margie. In them, he is not a monk, or a writer, but an ordinary person, overwhelmed by the experience of love.

One day in May she came to Gethsemani, where female visitors were still discouraged. She met him on the far reaches of the monastery grounds and they took a long walk, drank a bottle of wine she had brought, and "made love and love and love." Strictly speaking, there was no sex yet; they were going that way gradually, a movement Merton compared to the ripening of apples in the sun.

Yet when he tried to imagine himself as something other than a monk, he could not. He had no desire to wind up a college professor or an ex-priest on the lecture circuit. Even as he acknowledged the peace and wholeness he felt with Margie, he considered the "enormous, unthinkable problem of my vow," and reached the conclusion that "it had to stop."

There was a telephone outside the infirmary. He decided to call Margie after the night office. It was a call that he dreaded making. Only thirty-six hours had passed since their long walk in the woods, with all it had augured.

"To get away from it, began reading Walker Percy's new novel," he reported in his journal. Proofs had arrived in the mail that morning with a letter asking him to make an advance comment. The novel had already been praised by Caroline Gordon, who called it "the Odyssey of a Southern Prince Myshkin through regions as strange as Odysseus ever visited."

At eight o'clock, once the other monks had retired, he "finally called her from the Cellarer's office." As it happened, Margie was writing him a letter. They talked—it was a "healing" conversation, he wrote in his journal—and promised each other that their romance would remain unconsummated. "Life and death are at stake," he explained, "our salvation itself is involved, and immense suffering may come to be part of it."

He resumed reading *The Last Gentleman*. Like Gordon, he found the novel something other than realistic. More than her, however, he was in sympathy with the abrupt and overwrought style.

He must have read the novel quickly, for he sent a comment to New York two days later. "Walker Percy is one of the few novelists whose books I am able to finish," he began, and went on to describe the novel in terms that might have described the affair he was having—"a haunting, disturbing, funny and fantastic anti-novel structured like a long dream and relentlessly insisting that most of reality is unconscious.

"It ends up by being one of the most intelligent and sophisticated statements about the South and about America," he declared, "but one which too many people will probably find so baffling that they will not know what to make of it." Those who persisted in reading it, however, "cannot help being affected by the profoundly wacky wisdom of the book. Precisely because of the wackiness I would call it one of the sanest books I have read in a long time."

The affair had gone on for nearly five weeks—"a wearying, delightful, endless involvement that spurs on and on and onwards." Merton resolved to "drop her," but "gently and lovingly and not with pride." In a letter to Margie, he joshed that she was two-timing him. He filled pages of his journal with an account of the shame he felt. In his prayers, he begged God for forgiveness, and at the same time begged God "not to take away the gift of love He gave us." He began reading again: the Sufis, Camus's *Myth of Sisyphus*—"just what I need, suits me perfectly, for I see my vocation to be an absurd man if ever there was one! Or at least to *try* to think in some such honest terms."

A number of Merton's appointments in Louisville, that year, were with a psychologist. Now the psychologist arranged for Merton to have the use of the office when he was out. There, one afternoon in early summer, Merton and Margie met once more; there, they drank champagne and made love.

Afterward, they discussed their future. Should they get married? Should he stay a hermit and she marry her fiancé? Should they stay in touch, or break things off altogether?

They weighed their options in several telephone conversations. One night, they were overheard by a monk working the monastery's switchboard, who told the abbot, who heard Merton's confession in his office the next day. Asked about the affair, Merton admitted it. Asked if he was considering marriage, he denied it. The abbot, so often so strict, responded pastorally. As long as Merton made "a complete break" right away he could remain a monk in good standing—a monk allowed to live by himself in a hermitage.

As he celebrated Mass in the abbey church one Sunday, one of a group of priests vested and stoled at the altar, Merton had "stood there with all the others, soberly aware of myself as a priest who has a woman." And as he lay in bed one night thinking of his lover—"and asking myself a lot of questions"—he reflected that "so many priests are doing the same tonight—everywhere! It is a strange crisis in the whole Church."

By 1966 dozens of American priests had been laicized, leaving the ministry to get married or know the experience of sexual love outside of marriage. The Cistercian rule had already been relaxed considerably, and within a few years mail would no longer be opened by a censor, phone calls would be commonplace, and the grounds would be dotted with hermitages.

Yet Merton had been determined to end his affair with Margie even before he was found out by the abbot—even though had he left the monastery to get married, he would have been a representative figure to a generation of Catholic men, just as he had become one when he left the world in order to enter the monastery.

In effect, the affair was already ended: Merton would remain a priest, a monk, a man of solitude; Margie would follow her engagement through to marriage. It is obvious that Merton ended the affair because he believed he was called to do so. In a sense, it had been an existential test of his solitude, whereby he proved to himself that his solitary life was deeply rooted and freely chosen.

In the end, however, he was prompted to break off the affair not by his vow of chastity, or his zeal for solitude, or his meeting with the abbot, but by his encounter with a stern and reproachful secular agnostic who was then being canonized as a "saint without God."

He had read Camus before, but with a struggle; now he was reading Camus with a sense of discovery and likeness—the radical identification with another that was at the heart of his imaginative life. He was a monk, Camus a novelist and a veteran of the wartime Resistance, but they were both men "in revolt" against the absurdity of modern life and the coercive force of modern mass society, and their lives had uncanny similarities, which Merton half-consciously singled out. Camus had grown up in the ruins of the Roman empire in Algeria while Merton was growing up among the ruins of Norman France. He, too, was French and not French—a "cosmopolitan twentieth-century man" who saw himself as "to some extent a stranger and an exile." He had become a representative figure after the war by writing a book that gave voice to his own generation's alienation. He was a lover of ideas who was not a philosopher, a writer whose work was "essentially meditative, imaginative, and symbolic," a master of the "lyrical essay" in which he dramatized the play of ideas on the stage of his own anguished conscience.

Camus had had nothing to do with Christianity or any other religion. In his view, religion distracted the human person from the "lucid love of his condition" that he made the basis of his philosophy—every man's recognition of himself as a creature sentenced to death and doomed never to know whether his life had any significance.

Yet Camus had identified emotionally with the medieval monks at Fiesole, outside of Florence. "Sitting on the ground I think of the Franciscans whose cells I have just visited and whose sources of inspiration I can now see," he had written. "I feel clearly that if they are right then it is in the same way that I am. . . . Ah, I should become a convert to this if it were not already my religion."

As he struggled with Margie, Merton now redefined his monastic calling in Camus's terms. Faith was "the fundamental revolt"—a refusal to succumb to either utopianism or nihilism. The monk was the rebel par excellence, embracing limitation, living one day to the next, declining to go the way of society.

The question remained: What had kept Camus from believing? It was a question that Merton would explore for much of the next year in his writing. He would identify many reasons, but they all came down to this: Camus was not a believer because he had never found a believer he could identify with, one on whose faith he could stake his own. He had insisted that Christianity's "solidarity in revolt" depended on the existence of authentic Christians, and the lack of these was evident in his own refusal to believe.

Camus had rejected religion in the name of the human person's "fidelity to his limits, lucid love of his condition." Merton had accepted religion on the same basis. Now he would have to live out that fidelity as if the future of faith depended on it, to try to be the authentic Christian Camus had longed to meet. As many in the Church pushed past limits, he would remain faithful to them. He would cease to be a priest who had a woman.

He met Margie twice more, and spoke with her repeatedly on the phone. She told him that she was moving back to Cincinnati. He gave her a copy of a "Midsummer Diary" he had written as a memento of their romance. Sometimes musing to himself, sometimes addressing her directly, in the diary he explained his calling to solitude as "the struggle for lucidity, out of which compassion can at last arise." Why solitude? As a revolt against shallow ideas of belief; as a way of being open to others, exclusive to none; as a way of living for God alone; as a way, finally, of playing his role in the process of salvation. "I am here for one thing only," he wrote, ". . . to be open to God's will and freedom, to His love which comes to save me from all in myself that resists Him and says no to Him."

He wrote the first of his essays on Camus. A précis of Camus's revolt against a church which seemed to require the believer to "love a system, an explanation, a scheme of things," it was also a précis of Merton's revolt and an argument against those of others. He granted that "life as a priest in these times of questioning and renewal is neither simple nor easy," but warned priests against setting themselves up apart from the Church. Instead, he held out for Camus's dream of " 'a great conquering clergy, but magnificent in its poverty and audacity.' Poverty and audacity," he pointed out, "were two qualities that appealed more and more to Camus. He looked for them, as we shall see, in the Catholic Church but did not always find them."

It was the rare Merton piece written wholly on his own initiative—to explain himself to himself, and only then to others. He sent it to the *Catholic Worker*, with a letter to Dorothy Day. "You mentioned the fact that in the zeal for new things, many are losing all sense of proportion. I agree with you, and this will certainly cause a great deal of confusion and even do harm before we are through: yet the Holy Spirit remains with us and I have no doubt that through it all we will learn much—maybe even become more humble by our mistakes. I hope so."

The Last Gentleman got good reviews, feature articles, and reviews that judged it in precisely the existential-diagnostic terms Percy set out in interviews. And yet Percy was depressed as he tried to begin "Novel No. 3." He wrote a piece for the *Washington Post* about how he had come to write *The Moviegoer*, as if to remind himself how the process worked. And when he sat down to write one morning early in 1967, he wrote a letter to Shelby Foote instead.

After twenty years of correspondence, it is the first of Percy's letters that has survived for posterity, and it is a striking piece of artistic self-diagnosis.

"I am in low estate," Percy told Foote. "I have in mind a futuristic novel dealing with the decline and fall of the U.S., the country rent almost hopelessly between the rural knotheaded right and the godless alienated left, worse than the civil war." That was one aspect of the novel; the other was the "merriness" of suburban life: cookouts, bowling, Mass "at the usual silo-and-barn-style modern church," TV in the living room with one's wife and one's bottle of bourbon at one's side. "But it won't go, I am hung up, alas oh hopelessly hung up, sitting in front of my paper at 9:05 AM and growing sleepier by the minute. Fresh out of malice, piss, the love of God, hatred of things as they are, or whatever it takes, which I don't have."

He had come to suspect that art took malice—"a strong desire to attack one's enemies or at least those in the culture one considers to be wrongheaded and injurious"—but he was feeling melancholy, not angry. "The head of steam is too low. Or my sights are too high. I keep thinking that it is always possible to do the BIG ONE, bigger than Don Quixote, Moby Dick et al.—which is the shortest path to melancholy and perdition, since as St. Theresa of the Little Flower used to say, the only road is the Little Way, viz., the only way to do great things is to choose to treat of little things well."

Foote was no help; he had just learned that his mother was dying of cancer, and "right now everything else seems more or less irrelevant." In any case, Percy had always solved his own artistic problems. He began to solve the problem of Novel No. 3 the way he had solved the problem of *The Moviegoer* (but not *The Last Gentleman*, alas): by writing an essay about it.

That spring he received in the mail *The Added Dimension*, the first book of critical essays about Flannery O'Connor's work. It was sent to him by one of the editors, an English professor named Lewis Lawson, who had also made a mimeographed collection of all of Percy's published essays and planned to write a critical essay about Percy's work like those about O'Connor.

It is hard to imagine, now that O'Connor's essays and letters are widely available, how valuable a book like *The Added Dimension* was at the time. Here were testimonies by people who had known her; quotes from her letters; passages from talks she had given at tiny Catholic colleges; learned discussions of "The Realist of Distances" and "The Novelist as Prophet." And here was her essay on the grotesque, shaping the interpretation of her work the way she'd hoped.

With the O'Connor book in hand and the prospect of scholarly inquiry into his own work on his mind, Percy undertook to explain—for himself first of all—what he was trying to do.

"A serious novel about the destruction of the United States and the end of the world should perform the function of prophecy in reverse," he began, and went on:

> The novelist writes about the coming end in order to warn about present ills and so avert the end. Not being called by God to be a prophet, he nevertheless pretends to a certain prescience. If he did not think he saw something other people didn't see or at least didn't pay much attention to, he would be wasting his time writing and they reading. This does not mean that he is wiser than they. Rather it might testify to a species of affliction which sets him apart and gives him an odd point of view.

There in a few sentences he identified the approach he would take in Novel No. 3. In all his work thus far, he had proceeded from the existentialists' assumption that the person deemed sick by society is actually well, and sees truths the healthy person does not. Now he inverted this idea, proposing that the person to whom society looks for explanations—the doctor, the novelist, the diagnostician—might be the sick person. This sickness might give such a person a diagnostic sense akin to prophecy; but it might not. In the present age, Percy implied, the question was always open: Is the novelist crazy, or is everybody else?

It was a question only the novel could answer. Percy kept writing. The new book would be an emphatic reversal of *The Last Gentleman*, as *The Last Gentleman* had been an undoing of *The Moviegoer*. This time the doctor character would be the protagonist. The doctor would tell the story in the first person. Instead of a notebook full of *pensées*, he would make use of an actual diagnostic tool called a "lapsometer," a "stethoscope of the human soul." He would be "a Bad Catholic at a Time Near the End of the World," and the novel would be an adventure, a confession, and a diagnosis all in one.

Percy worked into the summer, turning down invitations and commitments. When the Committee of Southern Churchmen called, however, he answered. The next meeting of the *Katallagete* advisory board was scheduled for the first Saturday in July 1967, at the Abbey of Gethsemani.

Six Southern churchmen met in Louisville that morning and drove the hour to Bardstown, passing the distilleries and whiskey barns. As they came over a hill, the monastery stood before them. They went past a gatehouse, onto a dirt road, and uphill to the hermitage.

Percy knew the nature of Trappist life from his visit to Holy Ghost Monastery, but he didn't know what to expect of the most famous Trappist of all. "I'd heard the strangest things about Merton," he later recalled. "One that he was schizophrenic, and another that he had left the Church or he had broken his vows or he was living with a couple of women. I was amazed at the number of intellectuals who admired Merton and who could not tolerate the idea that he could be an observing Trappist monk for twenty years."

Merton was sitting on the porch of the hermitage when they arrived. He rose and greeted them, and Percy introduced himself, calling Merton Father Louis. Percy had envisioned a lean man in a white robe. Merton was robust, dressed in jeans and a T-shirt—"a sturdy, well-met fellow," Percy recalled. ". . . If you met him in a crowd or on the street you wouldn't pick him out as extraordinary looking."

Merton had a camera and an open bottle of bourbon at his side. He poured the churchmen a round of drinks, and the conversation began: race, peace, the war in Vietnam, nonviolence—which, he declared, was hard to define. Even the Trappists were violent, he said, pointing toward the monastery, and gave a roundabout explanation. Once upon a time the Trappists ate the food they grew themselves. Now they made "Trappist cheese" for the Catholic holiday market. Work for God had turned into capitalist exploitation, a kind of violence. "Look at the way they exploit these brothers, these monks—they got to break their asses carrying all this cheese around."

Percy was surprised by Merton's lack of reverence. He didn't necessarily go along with the idea that manual labor was a form of violence, but he didn't object aloud.

The group hiked down the hill and ate lunch in the monastery refectory, then returned to the hermitage, whereupon the others abruptly set out for a walk in the woods, leaving Percy alone with Merton on the porch. The two men sat looking out across the meadow in front of the hermitage. There was a long silence. "I was a little uneasy about what to do, and I think he was uneasy with me," Percy recalled. "You know, what do two writers say to each other?"

He started asking questions—obvious questions: What was life like at the monastery? What was it like to live under obedience? To write under it, the way Merton had done in the fifties? "I wasn't particularly, really interested in that," he recalled. "I wanted to ask him about himself."

Finally, he asked Merton what he thought about the future of monastic life in America. Merton said that as far as he could tell there was no future for big rural abbeys like the one down the hill. The future of monasticism, he thought, lay in small urban communities—say, a few men living in a house in Louisville.

This reminded Percy of his new novel, in which black guerrillas would take over a Christian suburb called the Paradise Estates, and he told Merton he was curious. Merton, in turn, described a book on African religion that he had checked out of the library—the sort of book Percy might want to take a look at sometime.

They sat on the porch gazing down the hill at the monastery. The sun hung high in the sky. After a while the others returned from their walk, and shortly thereafter the whole delegation departed, leaving the hermit on the porch with his books and his bourbon.

"It's amazing how little we found to talk about," Percy recalled. "I had the feeling that if I could have spent the weekend with him or maybe had six drinks or something I think I would have been able to say a lot more and ask him a lot more. But there was a sense of a great deal left unsaid and a great deal that I would have liked to ask him about."

Back in Covington, Percy wrote Merton a thank-you note. "I must admit I felt somewhat diffident putting myself in your shoes and imagining how it would have put me out having that somewhat diverse crew straggling about your hillside," he said. The idea was that "somehow some great ecumenical sparks would fly and *Katallagete* would be jump-started by many noble ecumenical ideas. When the truth is I haven't had an idea for months." He asked for further details about the African book Merton had mentioned, explaining, "It suddenly fits into a novel I am trying to conceive."

Merton wrote back right away, joking about the "ecumenical sparks that did not spark. All movements fill me with suspicion or lassitude," he declared. "But I enjoy talking to people (except about movements). I think the best thing is to belong to a universal anti-movement underground." He suggested that the problem Percy was having with his novel was the problem the whole country was having: the race problem. His solution: "Just keep a diary, maybe."

A month later Merton sent Percy an odd letter. Another book on African religion—describing tribal miracle cures—had put Percy in mind. Recalling Percy's idea for a new novel, he made a few suggestions: "You could probably distinguish a high Church sort of set with very decorous unctions of the infirm, and a low Church set with more rollings, beatings, vomitings etc. . . . There is by the way an African Castor Oil Dead Church in which new life is acquired by laxatives. Interesting possibility of description of a mass revival meeting of a church of this type."

The Percy-Merton meeting is seen as a failed meeting of the minds. Merton said nothing of it in his journal; when asked about it many years later, Percy had trouble recalling the specifics. Yet the pilgrimage to Gethsemani evidently fecundated Percy's difficult third novel. In Merton, Percy found the kind of character he was trying to write about—an irreverent Catholic whose oddness makes him seem either prophetic or a little crazy— and after their meeting *Love in the Ruins* burst to life. Its protagonist, now called Thomas More, was a descendant of the saint and also of a colonial-era American Catholic who had "removed to Bardstown, Kentucky, where he and his sons founded a whiskey distillery—and failed at that." It opened on July 4 with Thomas More sitting against a tree, looking down a hill at the ruins of the "yellow brick barn-and-silo of St. Michael's" Church, and drinking from a bottle of Early Times.

Merton had entertained several dozen pilgrims that year, each coming for his or her own reasons. Jacques Maritain came, bringing John Howard Griffin. Joan Baez came to recruit Merton for her institute for peace studies in California and "sat on the rug eating goat-milk cheese and bread and honey and drinking tea in front of the fire." Ralph Eugene Meatyard came to take photographs, bringing two poet friends, and the next day Merton joked that he had received "three kings from Lexington" at the hermitage.

Thich Nhat Hanh came on a peace mission. A Vietnamese, a Buddhist monk, an apostle of nonviolence, Nhat Hanh was in the United States urging an end to the war, and right away Merton declared him his Vietnamese "brother" the way he had seen Pasternak as his Russian one. A photograph of the two of them suggests that the sense of kinship was more than rhetorical: standing side by side, clad in monk's robes, staring into the heart of things, they do look like brothers, or like father and son. Merton asked his readers to recognize the two as counterparts, urging them to "do for Nhat Hanh whatever you would do for me if I were in his position. In many ways I wish I were."

Merton still had not met Dorothy Day. Like the monastery, St. Joseph's House had become a center of the Catholic peace movement, a site of pilgrimage for members of what was now being called the Catholic left. The more sought after she became, the more Day went on pilgrimages herself, visiting Catholic Worker houses around the country, as if to say that unsung Catholic Workers, not celebrity priests, were her natural counterparts.

As their interests converged, their friendship deepened through correspondence. Day wrote to Merton to report the "wide repercussions" from his Camus essay, even though she herself had thought it too long and belletristic for a workers' paper.

With her letter she enclosed an article she had written about the "grief" she felt over Cardinal Spellman's support for the war in Vietnam. During a visit to U.S. troops Spellman had exhorted them to pursue "victory, total victory." For Day, these words in themselves were un-Christian. Instead of criticizing Spellman directly, however, she did so indirectly, insisting that love of one's enemy was the way of Christ—and that Christian leaders had lost sight of this from the Church's very beginnings, as the New Testament reported. "When the Apostles wanted to call down fire from heaven on the inhospitable Samaritans, the 'enemies' of the Jews, Jesus said to them, 'You know not of what Spirit you are.' When Peter told Our Lord not to accept the way of the Cross and his own death, He said, 'Get behind me, Satan. For you are not on the side of God but of men.'" Spellman was no devil; he was merely betraying his Lord as followers were wont to do—but that was enough. "Deliver us, O Lord, from the fear of our enemies," she concluded, "which makes cowards of us all."

Merton was moved by the article, and wrote to say so. "It is beautifully done, soft-toned and restrained, and speaks of love more than of reproof," he told her. "It is the way a Christian should speak up." He went on in such a way as to suggest the nature of their callings:

> It *has* to be done. The moral insensitivity of those in authority, on certain points so utterly crucial for man and for the Church, has to be pointed out and if possible dispelled. It does not imply that we ourselves are perfect or infallible. But what is a Church after all but a community in which truth is shared, not a monopoly that dispenses it from the top down. Light travels on a two-way street in our Church; or I hope it does.

In itself Merton's notion of truth seems obvious and the letter one writer's tribute to another. But in 1967 the questions of how religious faith is gained and communicated to others were threatening to undo the Catholic peace movement just as it was gaining prominence. There had emerged a cadre of antiwar Catholics, a movement within the movement. They were bred-in-the-bone Catholics, not converts (Daniel Berrigan, for example, had entered a seminary at age eighteen in 1939). Though progressive in theory, they were intolerant in fact—triumphalists in desert boots, who saw the Catholic faith as self-evident and the world as a nest of vipers; and for them the truth about Vietnam, and about American life in general, was not to be found but to be asserted in confrontation, in actions that, like Cardinal Spellman's, left no place for another point of view.

Day and Merton had seen the problem coming. Their own experience told them that truth was to be found on a pilgrimage through time, in the search for God and in the encounter with others. As converts, as writers, as members of a community of believers, as representatives (whether they liked it or not) of the Catholic point of view, they never lost sight of the need to respect the point of view of the other, indeed to try to enter into that point of view imaginatively as fully as possible, until this imaginative empathy became their life's work, the injunction to love thine enemy made an aesthetic and an ethic at once. In their autobiographies they had engaged that other point of view explicitly, for it had been their own view once. Now, opposing an unjust war, they kept in mind all the well-meaning people who supported the war wholeheartedly. The tobacco farmers whose land surrounded the Abbey of Gethsemani were flag-waving patriots. Several older men at St. Joseph's House were proud veterans of World War II. One of Day's grandsons was an Army Ranger, a volunteer in Vietnam.

In her columns of 1967 Day chronicled the ongoing protest against the war: a march of half a million antiwar activists from Central Park to the United Nations, led by Martin Luther King; a sit-in in Washington that made the front page of the big daily papers—David Miller "obstructing the entrance while a handsome young woman in the usual short skirt, and carrying flowers and a large white handbag, attempted to step over him"; a "Mass Protest" at St. Patrick's Cathedral, where young people strode up the center aisle carrying placards saying THOU SHALT NOT KILL. Although Day herself would not have staged a protest during a Mass, she supported those who did—"because it was the nationalist attitude of Cardinal Spellman," not the Mass itself, "which the young people are protesting."

When Daniel Berrigan took liberties with the Mass itself, however, she drew a line. He had returned from South America emboldened, a victim and presumptive martyr, shuttling back and forth between Cornell University and New York; in the city, the Catholic Worker was his home away from home, and he became nearly as closely associated with the place as Day herself.

Celebrating a Mass at St. Joseph's House, he substituted a coffee cup for a chalice, consecrating the Communion bread in it. Day was disturbed. She told the Catholic Workers to bury the cup in the yard behind the house, where the trash was kept. Then she rebuked Father Berrigan sideways in a column, while continuing to stand beside him at protests. She was all for liturgical renewal: the Catholic Worker had invited priests to face the congregants and speak in English in Masses at their farmhouse chapels long before Vatican II. She knew very well that Christians in poor countries celebrated Mass with whatever was at hand, and that their doing so made clear that "the power of God did not rest on all these appurtenances with which we surround it." Yet in Berrigan's hands she found the symbolism contrived. In matters of liturgy, she explained, she was "a traditionalist" and even a romantic, who sought the beauty of Arthurian legend and the simple piety of *The Imitation of Christ*. To support the point she quoted *Seasons of Celebration*, Merton's new book of reflections on the liturgy, in which he urged Catholic people to retain "the discretion, the sobriety, and the modesty" of the liturgy so that each worshipper might find God there.

She drew another line when the sanctity of marriage was at issue. That year Jim Forest, the head of the Catholic Peace Fellowship, was separated from his wife and began a relationship with another woman. She, too, was a peace activist, and once Forest had divorced his wife, they were married by a Presbyterian minister active in the movement. Day disapproved. Having given up the prospect of marriage (or remarriage) when she became a Catholic, Day thought others should do the same, if only to earn the respect of "anti-Catholics." She told Forest that he was dishonoring the Church and compromising the peace movement; she asked him to take her name off the group's stationery, because "I do not think that while you are the head of the CPF it can be considered a Catholic Peace Fellowship."

Forest disagreed. Instead of challenging Day directly, however, he sent her letter to Merton for a second opinion. He probably didn't know that Merton, too, had banished thoughts of marriage in order to stay true to his calling, and Merton didn't tell him. In a long and nuanced letter, Merton found a way to disagree with Day while standing with her in principle and making clear that he was "no underground priest." "Dorothy is a person of great integrity and consistency and this hits one between the eyes in the way she sums it up," he declared. Strictly speaking he thought she was "quite right in demanding a like consistency from others who act as 'Catholics' formally and explicitly in the eyes of the world." She was also right to urge Forest to make the sacrifice, for sacrifice, he could say from experience, was a good thing. "*Nevertheless*"—he underlined—he urged Forest to follow his own conscience, even if it went against Day's judgment. If she had to withdraw her name from the CPF to follow her own conscience, it would be a "grave blow," but one that could not be avoided. The important thing was to follow one's own conscience.

Forest remained married and the head of the CPF. After several months of keeping her own counsel, Day quietly agreed to continue as a sponsor. In four letters to Merton, she did not mention the controversy.

She did not mention the war, either. She and Merton were alike in seeing the work for peace as only one aspect of the life of the believer, and as the antiwar protests grew more strident her letters to him remained chatty and miscellaneous, thick with everyday piety. She asked him to pray for Father Charles, whose alcoholism had forced him to leave Holy Ghost Monastery, and for "a young girl named Barbara" whose charity had led her to take in a heroin addict prone to violence. She had come to know some followers of Charles de Foucauld, the desert hermit, and she told Merton about their placid spirituality, so unlike the mood of the hour. And after thirty-five years as a voice for Catholic laypeople, she announced that she had had "the wonderful good fortune" to be invited to a Congress of the Laity led by the pope. "A dear friend who says she owes her conversion to the Catholic Worker is paying my fare both ways and my upkeep in Rome," she told Merton, and she would be sailing on September 30—or, as she put it in her column, "pilgrimaging again."

Merton had received an invitation from Rome as well. The Congress of the Laity would be followed by a synod of bishops, and the pope, through two Italian Trappists, asked Merton to contribute to a statement on the contemplative life.

The pope's request arrived August 21, 1967. Down at the monastery the day before, Merton had seen the renovated church. It struck him as a pagan place. "It is monstrous. A perfect Aztec altar for the sacrifice of the heart. Or a block for Druidical immolations. Black, squat, large, 'tragic,' grim, black.

No unbloody sacrificial meals here! This is for the real thing!" He had written, "Tonight I find myself half voluntarily wondering—and very uneasily—if perhaps I should not take thought in case—just in case—it might become suddenly necessary for me to leave here in a big hurry one of these days! . . . There is a strange kind of madness in the air . . . or is it only my madness? Somehow I feel more lucid than usual, but that may be the ultimate deception."

He put a piece of paper in the typewriter, rapped out the date, and begged off the task. A big statement about contemplation, he explained, would alienate the honest searcher the bishops were hoping to reach. Besides, he was no expert in contemplation. He could not speak for the order. All he could do was write in his own words, one sinner to another.

He wrote all this; and as he wrote, the letter, addressed to the Trappist superior in Rome, became a letter addressed to "my brother who is in the world and who more and more often comes to me with his wounds which turn out to be also my own."

Twenty years earlier Merton had concluded *The Seven Storey Mountain* with a poem addressed to his brother, the dead soldier, and in a sense all his work since then had been directed toward his brother in the world, a person distinct from him, unlike him, yet joined to him beneath it all. This time he began by apologizing for the one-sidedness of the dialogue—for speaking without being asked, and from behind the high wall of a monastery. The wall, he thought, was a problem to them both, yet he still believed that he belonged there. Why was he a monk?

> Can I tell you that I have found answers to the questions that torment the man of our time? I do not know if I have found answers. When I first became a monk, yes, I was more sure of "answers." But as I grow old in the monastic life I become aware that I have only begun to seek the questions. And what are the questions? Can a man make sense of his existence? Can a man honestly give his life meaning merely by adopting a certain set of explanations which pretend to tell him why the world began and where it will end, why there is evil and what is necessary for a good life? My brother, perhaps in my solitude I have become as it were an explorer for you, a searcher in realms which you are not able to visit—except perhaps in the company of your psychiatrist. I have been summoned to explore a desert area of man's heart in which explanations no longer suffice, and in which one learns that only experience counts.

It is a beautiful and powerful answer, rooted in the sense of place that is basic to Merton's spirituality, cast forward for the age of the space program and transcendental meditation. Still, the question remains: Why be a monk? Why be a believer at all? Merton's answer is blunt. Because the desert place in each of us—"an arid, rocky, dark land of the soul"—is the place Christ came to earth to save. After two thousand years, he acknowledges, the language of faith engenders such distrust that "you do not know whether or not behind the word 'cross' there stands the experience of mercy and salvation, or only the threat of punishment." But he can vouch for the cross with his own experience—"can say to you that I have experienced the cross to mean mystery and not cruelty, truth and not deception."

He speaks with the authority of the holy; but in the present age, when, he allows, the holy is found as often outside of the churches as inside, why should his brother seek God through religion at all? He answers again with his own experience, which is that God is a being to be known, not a problem to be solved, "and we who live the contemplative life have learned by experience that one cannot know God as long as one seeks to solve 'the problem of God.' To seek to solve the problem of God is to seek to see one's own eyes." God yearns to be known; human sadness is God's sadness at not being known; and the contemplative is a person who recognizes that he or she is a temple of the Holy Ghost, and that the desert is a place where God is to be found.

"Indeed we exist solely for this, to be the place he had chosen for his Presence," he declares. "If once we began to recognize, humbly but truly, the real value of our own self, we would see that this value was the sign of God in our being, the signature of God upon our being." In the lives of most of us, God's signature is shown to us in the love of others. The monk, seemingly in flight from love, aims behind his wall to remain open to God wholly and directly.

"The message the contemplative offers you, then, brother," Merton declares, "is not that you need to find your way through the jungle of language and problems that today surround God; but that whether you understand or not, God loves you, is present to you, lives in you, dwells in you, calls you, saves you, and offers you an understanding and light which are like nothing you ever found in books or heard in sermons": a radiant understanding like the union of self and other in love. In closing, he tells his brother that he loves him.

The letter—"written in haste"—has the lucidity that his encounter with Camus had led him to strive for, that of a man who understands and loves his condition, with all its limits and complications. It was not what Rome had asked for, however. Rome had asked for a statement to the Church's bishops, explaining the contemplative life in expressly Catholic terms.

The deadline was approaching. He was depressed and lonely. He had the flu. He spent the weekend in bed in the hermitage, reading Faulkner's *As I Lay Dying*—"the central part, the crossing of the river, and the chapter on Addie, and was simply floored by it."

Then he put a fresh sheet of paper in the typewriter and started over. The first letter had been addressed to a skeptic. This one would be written for the believer. It would be in the first-person plural, in the temperate voice he admired in Dorothy Day's pieces. It would be a "Message to Contemplatives," the title stressing the message—that every believer is a prospective contemplative, "called to taste God."

The question is the same: Is it possible for modern people to believe? Modern man, as Merton calls him, is beset with religious difficulties so acute that they "call into question the possibility of attaining to knowledge of the transcendent God who has revealed himself to men."

Such difficulties, he proposes, cannot be solved, only encountered; and the contemplative, he suggests, knows them intimately through experience. For although the contemplative life is "a sort of specialization in relationship with God," it is finally a religious life like any other, except that it is "lived in conditions which favor 'the experience of God.' " The cloister is a figure of the desert or dark night that every religious pilgrimage must pass through. The trials the contemplative faces there are "the trials and temptations which many of his fellow-Christians are undergoing." Alone, silent, hidden away in the monastery, the contemplative "feels that he is living at the very heart of the church."

Written for the bishops, the "Message to Contemplatives" might be a message to Merton's critics, the would-be revolutionaries and street-fighting men of the Catholic left. For it makes clear why he sees the contemplative life as crucial to any program for peace and justice. In Merton's view, the "experience of God," obedience to the Gospel or the affirmation of human solidarity, must be the basis of the believer's actions in the world. The contemplative life, in his account, is at once the opposite of worldly life and a concentration of it; it is religious experience exaggerated, grotesequely at times, so as to bring a truth to light—to describe the desert in the heart of every would-be believer, and to see in this desert the springs of religious experience. And it is in such experience that those who call themselves believers strive to "unite ourselves to the suffering of the world, carrying on before God a silent dialogue even with those of our brothers who keep themselves apart from us."

Merton dedicated the longest of his essays on Camus to Daniel Berrigan—a reading of *The Plague* "not simply as a drama or as a psychological study, but as a myth of good and evil, of freedom and historical determinism, of love against what Hopkins called 'the death dance in our blood.' "

In October 1967 he got a letter from Father Berrigan, whose brother, Philip Berrigan, having come to believe that protests were not enough, felt called to take events to a next stage and was urging Daniel to join him. Asked for advice, Merton wrote a long reply, taking care—mindful of the fallout from his condemnation of Roger LaPorte's self-immolation—to offer his views as "just my own way as it more or less appears to me at the moment."

The letter was a stern one. Merton suggested that the "new revolutionism" was a "fake revolution," which risked being "irresponsible, capricious, idiotic, pointless, haphazard and inviting disaster." Revolution involving priests meant one thing in Latin America, another in the United States. In fact, the peace movement's obsession with being "with it"—"now nonviolent, now flower-power, now burn-baby, all sweetness on Tuesday and all hell-fire on Wednesday"—was the sort of thing that invited Fascism rather than dispelled it. Violence, even against property, tended to turn to violence against people. "In my opinion the job of the Christian is to try to give an example of sanity, independence, human integrity, against all establishments and all mass movements and all current fashions which are merely mindless and hysterical." He thought the Catholic peace movement should "close ranks" with other Christian nonviolent activists, such as Martin Luther King, and should act in a way that "*stays with* a clearly recognizable Christian and gospel position."

He put the letter in the mail. Two weeks later Father Philip Berrigan and three other Catholics burst into the draft office in Baltimore and poured a blend of animal and human blood on draft records there. The action was kept secret from all except a group of reporters, who were invited along and given a manifesto, which explained the bloodshed as "a sacrificial and constructive act," invited those in sympathy "to continue moving with us from dissent to resistance," and asked God "to be merciful and patient with us and with all men. We hope he will use our witness for his blessed designs."

They were arrested and jailed; they fasted, and were released on bail. By then their nickname—the Baltimore Four—was all over the papers, just as they'd intended. The *New Yorker* initiated a profile.

As 1968 began, current events, always hard for Merton to follow in the monastery, now became hard even for people out in the world to follow. The commander of the U.S. war operation requested 200,000 additional troops for service in Vietnam. A teenage boy upset over the war burned himself alive in Syracuse, New York, and Daniel Berrigan, who had grown up there, visited him as he lay unconscious. Eugene McCarthy, an antiwar Catholic, nearly won the Democratic presidential primary in New Hampshire. Philip Berrigan was dismissed as pastor of an inner-city parish in Baltimore and forbidden to preach, hear confessions, or say Mass in public, although, once he was sentenced—six years for mutilating government property and interfering with the draft—he was permitted to say Mass in jail.

On April 4 Martin Luther King was murdered in Memphis. Merton, returning to the monastery after a visit to a Shaker settlement, heard the news on the car radio. In the previous months there had been a prospect of King's coming to Gethsemani on retreat with Thich Nhat Hanh to discuss nonviolence with Merton and to get out of the public eye. The assassination, Merton wrote in his journal, "finally confirmed all the apprehensions—the feeling that 1968 is a beast of a year. That things are finally, inexorably, spelling themselves out."

Dorothy Day "was sitting in the kitchen of one of the women's apartments on Kenmare Street when the news came." In her view, the manner of King's death—during a speech in support of striking garbage collectors—made clear that the work for peace, civil rights, and the rights of the worker were all bound up together in a single movement toward recognition of the God-given dignity of the human person.

Her eulogy, written three weeks later, is a study in grim realism:

> Cynics may say that he used nonviolence as a tactic. Many may scoff
> at the outcry raised over his death, saying that this is an election year
> and all candidates had to show honor to a fallen Black hero. But love

and grief were surely in the air those days of mourning, and all that was best in the country—in the labor movement, the civil rights movement, and the peace movement—cast aside all their worldly cares and occupations to go to Memphis to march with the sanitation union men, on whose behalf, during whose strike, Martin Luther King had given himself; and to Atlanta, where half a million people gathered to walk in the funeral procession, to follow the farm cart and the two mules which drew the coffin of the dead leader.

Now Merton left Gethsemani on a trip, one without precedent in his quarter century as a Trappist. The abbot of Gethsemani had resigned the previous fall in order to live as a hermit—in a stone house on a grand site, with air-conditioning. The new abbot, though also a hermit—a mobile home was his hermitage—thought it appropriate for Trappists to travel. When Merton was invited to attend a conference on monastic life in Bangkok six months hence, in December, the new abbot encouraged him to accept the invitation, and to plan a journey around the trip. For the moment, Merton and the abbott plotted out a short trip in which Merton would scout locations for a new hermitage, one set apart from any monastery and remote enough to discourage all but the most determined pilgrims.

In early May, then, Merton set out for New Mexico and California as Walker Percy had done twenty years earlier. The journal he kept—"Woods, Shore, Desert," he called it—tells of a series of intense encounters: a retreat at Our Lady of the Redwoods, an abbey for female Trappists; an afternoon spent reconnoitering prospective sites on the Pacific Coast—an abandoned house at a place called Needle Rock, and one at Bear Harbor, "more isolated, more sheltered," with "a hollow where one could comfortably put a small trailer"; an overnight spent at City Lights Books in San Francisco—in "a bedroom with a mattress on the floor, a guitar and a tape recorder and a window opening upon a fire escape." At last he reached Christ of the Desert in New Mexico. In 1948, working from photographs and his imagination, he had described the conversion of the place "from a dude ranch into a Trappist monastery." Now, arriving there, he saw, for the first time in his life, a "real desert" akin to the symbolic deserts of the monastery and his imagination—"marvelous long line of snowless, arid mountains, clean long shapes stretching for miles under pure light. Mesas, full rivers, cotton woods, sage brush, high red cliffs, piñon pines . . . miles of emptiness." It reminded him of the view from his hermitage.

He was back at Gethsemani four days later. There, he began at once to write about the trip, seeking "to establish the shape of an experience, a pilgrimage, memories of which keep coming back in recurrent flashes and impressions." The significance of the trip was already clear: it had aroused, and not dispelled, his deep yearning for "change and transformation."

While he was gone the Berrigans and seven others had forced their way into a Selective Service office in Catonsville, Maryland, and shredded draft files into a wastebasket filled with homemade napalm while a TV crew looked on. A photograph of the two priests seeming to consecrate the flames made the big-city papers.

In his journal, however, Merton passed from desert to Albuquerque to Memphis to Kentucky to hermitage without mentioning the incident. News of the world was reaching him: of the Poor People's March on Washington, the general strike in Paris, the student uprising at Columbia University, which amused him—the "long-haired students" smoking cigars in the president's office "as if they liked cigars." The Catonsville action called forth, after five days, only an offhand, dismissive entry:

Somewhere, when I was in some plane or some canyon, Dan and Phil Berrigan and some others took A-1 draft files from a draft center in a Baltimore suburb and burned them in a parking lot. Somewhere I heard they were arrested but I've seen no paper and don't know anything, but an envelope came from Dan . . . saying he was going to do this. It was mailed from Baltimore, May 17, and had scrawled on it, "Wish us luck."

The activists would liken the action to the fire of Pentecost and the descent of the Holy Ghost, a birth and a baptism, a cleansing and a dawning, a reformation and an exorcism in which they "removed an abomination from the Earth." The press, writing the first draft of history, depicted it as a turning point—the moment when the Catholic left merged with history and came of age. It was indeed a turning point. It was an ending, not a beginning, a separating rather than a convergence, the moment when a pilgrimage became a crusade.

Walker Percy sent a letter denouncing the Catonsville action to *Commonweal*, which had just published a missive by Daniel Berrigan. In Percy's view, the Catonsville Nine were a left-wing Ku Klux Klan, right down to their weapon of choice, fire. "As it happens, I stand a good deal closer to the Berrigans than to the Klan," he wrote. "The point is, however: God save us all from the moral zealot who places himself above the law and is willing to burn my house down, and yours, providing he feels he is sufficiently right and I sufficiently wrong."

"These actions are not ours," Dorothy Day declared. In the days after the incident she was continually sought out for comment by the press. She spoke of the destruction of draft files as an act of violence, a failure to do unto others, even to one's enemies, as one would want others to do to oneself. She described the conspirational nature of the action as contrary to the openness and directness the witness for peace required. Even as she denounced their actions, however, she steadfastly supported the Berrigans and their cohorts, who brought their own tactics to a cause that she and they had in common — Christian witness against an unjust war, and indeed all wars; practical as ever, she entered in sympathy into a position that was not her own.

Merton was less sympathetic. In a circular letter to friends that summer he made clear that he considered the Berrigans "my good friends" and their action "in essence non-violent," a "provocation" meant more to shock than to harm. He went on: "It may be too shocking. All I'd like to say is this: I noticed very little, if any, shock at all when a Catholic bishop had the droll effrontery to speak of the Vietnam war as an act of Christian love. CHRISTIAN LOVE! It seems to me that this fantastic concept of what the New Testament is all about ought to have shocked a few more people than it did."

In a letter to an admiring reader he was succinct and emphatic: "They are friends of mine. I don't agree with their methods of action, but I can understand the desperation which prompts them. They believe they have to witness *in jail* to the injustice of the war. That is their business. It is certainly not a necessary teaching of the Church."

In his journal he sketched Daniel Berrigan in words that suggest how estranged from his "good friend" he felt. "He's a bit theatrical these days, now he's a malefactor — with a quasi-episcopal disarmament emblem strung around his neck like a pectoral cross. He wants me in N.Y. agitating for and with him in October or November, whenever the trial is. I definitely want to keep out of anything that savors of a public 'appearance' or semi-public or *anything*, especially in America."

In retrospect Merton is invariably described as a friend, mentor, and precursor of the Berrigans. He was all of those things, but he did not lend his support to the Catonsville action. Although he remarked that he could envision himself someday breaking a law he thought unjust, and basically agreed with the Berrigans' claim that the United States was "becoming a totalitarian society," he sent no letter of solidarity to the embattled activists, filed no declaration of approval in his journal for the sake of posterity.

The closest he came to a direct statement about the incident is a short piece he wrote in response to a request from *Ave Maria* magazine. *Ave Maria* was read by the sort of Catholics Merton thought of as caught in the middle—Sunday churchgoers, people of good conscience, who were open to fresh thoughts on the war but who felt alienated from the Catholic left in general and the Berrigans in particular—and Merton wrote as if addressing them directly. "What were the Berrigans and the others trying to do?" he asked rhetorically, and in answering the question—the question in the mind of the Catholic caught in the middle—he neither defended nor scolded the Berrigans, nor even acknowledged that he knew them. Rather, he made clear that he, too, was caught in the middle, open to both points of view. He stressed that he didn't think the Catonsville activists had crossed the line to real violence, at least not yet, for their action was "an attempt at nonviolent provocation. It bordered on violence and was violent to the extent that it meant pushing some good ladies around and destroying some government property." Yet he rejected the usual defense of such provocations: the notion that Gandhi-style nonviolence had been tried and found wanting, making a more intense form of protest a necessity. On the contrary, he insisted (like Dorothy Day in the thirties) that nonviolence hadn't really been tried—and that even if it had been tried, nonviolent protest should not be judged by its results but by its fidelity to the Gospel.

The Catonsville action, by this measure, was bold and prophetic "in the classic nonviolent fashion," insofar as the participants accepted the punishment brought on by their breaking the law so as emphasize the injustice of the law itself. He explained: "The standard doctrine of nonviolence says that you can disobey a law you consider unjust but you have to accept the punishment." Then, having slipped into the second person, he seized the opportunity it offered; having addressed the *Ave Maria* reader, he faced the other way, in effect, and addressed the Berrigans, now speaking to them as *you*, rather than of them as *they*. "In this way you are distinguished from the mere revolutionary," he declared. "You protest the purity of your witness. You undergo redemptive suffering for religious—or anyway ethical—motives. You are 'doing penance' for the sin and injustice against which you have protested."

So ran the classic nonviolent approach. But the Catonsville provocation was something else. It had "frightened more than it has edified," Merton observed, as if he in the monastery, and not they out in the world, was in the best position to judge the mood of the Catholic populace. "The country is in a very edgy psychological state. Americans feel terribly threatened, on grounds which are partly rational, partly irrational, but in any case very real." Precisely because the country was edgy, it was necessary for protestors to be clear, precise, and unambiguous in their witness, exposing unjust laws through nonviolent civil disobedience. That was not the case in Catonsville and nor was it the case with other, similar, provocations. "It seems to me that the protest and resistance against the Selective Service Law is all oriented toward the affirmation of the rightness, the determination and the conviction of the protesters, and not to the injustice of the law itself," he declared. Then, as if speaking to the Berrigans on retreat at his hermitage, he put the point idiomatically: ". . . if nonviolence merely says in a very loud voice '*I don't like this damn law*,' it does not do much to make the adversary admit that the law is wrong. On the contrary, what he sees is an apparently arbitrary attack on law and order, dictated by emotion or caprice—or fanaticism of some sort." Merton went on: "And he will send you to jail with a firm and righteous conviction that the law is just. He will not even for a moment have occasion to question its justice. He will be too busy responding to what he feels to be aggressive and indignant in your near-violent protest."

What was to be done? Concluding the piece, Merton counseled realism and political moderation, which would begin with an effort to "study, practice, and use nonviolence in its classic form, with all that this implies of religious and ethical grounds." And he gave the Berrigans the fatherly advice they sought from him, saying: "Violence is useless if it is merely pragmatic. The whole point of nonviolence is that it rises above pragmatism and does not consider whether it pays off politically . . . I admit that may sound odd. Someone once said, did he not, 'What is truth?' And the One to whom he said it also mentioned, somewhere: 'The truth shall make you free.' It seems to me that this is what really matters."

He evidently passed over their mutual friends in a letter to Dorothy Day, too, simply praising her and the Catholic Worker for housing the families of activists who were in jail for draft resistance: "Another of the quietly eloquent things so typical of you. I have to get busy and write to some of those in jail." And it may be that this silence was owing to overwork and distraction. His real life was elsewhere. "I have a big thing coming up," he told Day. "I am to go to Asia as peritus [adviser] for a regional meeting of abbots and also to attend a meeting of leaders from non-Christian religions. I hope this may mean a deepening of understanding and a chance to enter more deeply into the mind of some of the Asian monastic traditions. Prayer will be the most vital help."

At Maryfarm, Day told a group of Catholic Workers on retreat that Father Louis was leaving the monastery for the Far East. At Gethsemani, Merton made preparations like any tourist. He got inoculated against tropical diseases and applied for his first passport since the thirties. "What (very slowly) sinks into my mind is that soon I will really leave the place, to live for a long time out of a suitcase—everything I 'have' will be within the 44 lbs. a plane will take for you," he wrote in his journal. "Leaving my books, cottage, security, time to write, time to be alone, and going on where I don't know, with only a few plans ahead that can all be changed."

He wrote to a few friends, swearing them to secrecy. He tried to phone Margie, then burned her letters to him. "Incredible stupidity in 1966! I did not even glance at any one of them." A Trappist lay brother had begun to act as his secretary, and he arranged for the brother to live in the hermitage, lest it be commandeered for some other purpose. He reread *Ulysses*.

One Friday in August he went overnight to Washington, D.C., in order to meet the ambassador from Indonesia, which he hoped to visit. As it happened, that weekend a conference on liturgy, full of Catholic leaders, was being held in the city, and the program included a performance of four of Merton's poems set to gospel music sung by the choir of Ebenezer Baptist Church, King's own congregation in Atlanta. But Merton's return flight was booked and he returned to Gethsemani without attending the conference.

There his mail included a card from Dorothy Day, postmarked District of Columbia. "We have just listened to your poems, set to music by Alexander Peloquin. There were four of your eight 'Freedom Songs.' . . . The songs were enough to break down the walls of Jericho. People wept with joy. What beautiful music! Magnificent! . . . It is one a.m. and I had to write to you at once, I have been so entranced by the music and words."

It was a passionate outpouring, as if to evoke, in her own words, music that Merton might never hear. As he was humbled by her life, she was humbled by his writing; while she saw herself as a journalist—exposing injustice, keeping accounts, bearing witness—she saw Merton as an artist, whose writing had the power to move people in its own right.

"Thank you, thank you . . . ," she told him. "You have enriched our lives so many times.

"Love and gratitude—

"Dorothy"

He wrote a letter to be sent to all his correspondents, explaining where he was going. It is as if he sought to defend or justify the trip, to rebel once more against the notion that he was needed in America as the house priest of the antiwar movement. "The length of my stay in Asia is indeterminate," he declared. He would not be answering mail or signing letters of protest. He would not be going to Vietnam. "Our real journey in life is interior," he concluded, clearly choosing his words with care, ". . . a matter of growth, deepening, and an ever greater surrender to the creative action of love and grace in our hearts. Never was it more necessary for us to respond to that action. I pray that we all may do so generously."

He celebrated Mass in the hermitage, joined by three young monks. The Gospel reading that day—September 9—was the story of the Good Samaritan, and Merton told the other monks what good Samaritans the Trappists of Gethsemani had been to him. He said it was as though he had been found dying at the roadside and been brought to the monastery to recuperate, as though his time there—twenty-seven years—had been a long overnight.

Then he was gone, joining his inward journey to an outward one at last. He was fifty-three years old, husky and bald, with bright eyes and distinct eyebrows. He wore a priest's black suit and Roman collar and shiny black oxfords; he carried a notebook and a camera and toted two large suitcases. He had left his black-and-white wool Trappist habit behind.

The first few days were a reprise of the earlier trip west, a slow movement in which everything seemed significant. In Chicago he was shown a deconsecrated convent, and was struck by the "church with no adoration" and the "old empty rooms and corridors, with here and there an ancient statue lamenting the emptiness, the dark. One felt that it was a place where prayer had 'been valid.' " In New Mexico, he went to see Georgia O'Keeffe, who played a role in the art world something like his in religious life—a revered figure whose ranch was the destination of other people's pilgrimages. In Santa Barbara, at a conference on the contemplative life, he warned monks and nuns against the lure of the "revolutionary mystique" and declared that his own calling was to recover tradition, not shatter it.

In Alaska, he scouted sites for a hermitage, led a retreat, and gave a talk. His purpose, however, was the search for wisdom, and his ideal of wisdom came not from the monastic past but from the work of William Faulkner, which he had been reading ardently. For Merton saw Faulkner as something other than a Southern chronicler or a modernist pioneer. Like Eliot, Yeats, and William Carlos Williams, like Boris Pasternak and Flannery O'Connor, Faulkner in his view was a creator of "wisdom literature"—literature that "brings you into living participation with an experience of basic and universal human values on a level which words can *point* to but cannot fully attain.

"Wisdom is the highest form of cognition," he had written. It is not simply "knowledge *about* human values" but "an actual possession and awareness of these values as incorporated in one's own existence." Wisdom literature is literature of initiation, and through the "power of enactment" it can "initiate" the reader into the "ultimate causes of things." But it cannot make the reader wise. "For wisdom cannot be learned from a book. It is acquired only in a living formation. . . . It is 'lived.' And unless one 'lives' it, one cannot 'have' it."

Faulkner's work, seen this way, made an ideal prologue for Merton's pilgrimage. In the ensuing weeks he would give many reasons for his trip to Asia, some of them obscure or contradictory. But the reason behind the reasons is clear. He was going to Asia not as a teacher or writer, but as a learner and a listener, a seeker after *sapientia*, or wisdom, the knowledge gained and tested through direct experience.

A letter reached him from Philip Berrigan, who was in jail in Maryland, asking him to come to serve as a character witness at the trial of the Catonsville Nine. With a guilty verdict all but assured, and with this Father Berrigan already sentenced to six years in jail for the previous action, the activists hoped to put wartime American society on trial, the way the Yippies had done during the Democratic convention in Chicago. Merton wrote a tart reply, wishing the group luck but explaining that it was "impossible" for him to be there. "Hope you enjoy your new Trappist vocation," he remarked. "But don't get too much of it. Enough is enough."

He took a long flight to Bangkok October 15, traveling west to go east. He had two practical objectives: to gain firsthand experience of the monastic life of Buddhist Asia, and to spend time with "important people in the Buddhist monastic field." Accordingly, he had arranged a series of visits with lamas and holy men across Asia—Bangkok, Calcutta, Dharamsala, Madras, Ceylon—in the eight weeks before his speech in Bangkok in December.

He found Bangkok "wildly exciting": the traffic, the crowds, the noise, the commerce. The abbot of the Buddhist monastery there lectured him on the need to ascend to the "knowledge of freedom." "What is the 'knowledge of freedom'? I asked. 'When you are in Bangkok you know that you're there. Before that you only knew about Bangkok.' " Knowledge, for so long the knowledge of elsewhere, was now the knowledge of his surroundings.

Calcutta overwhelmed him with its blend of beauty and poverty, the opposite of the blend of abundance and ugliness he associated with the modern world. In the "fecal" city—he was there to attend a "Spiritual Summit Conference"—he was struck again and again by the beauty of the people he met. He closed the conference with a prayer, one that applied the language of direct action to the act of imaginative empathy. "O God," he prayed, "we are one with You. You have made us one with You. You have taught us that if we are open to one another, You dwell in us. Help us to preserve this openness and to fight for it with all our hearts."

All the while he was awaiting word from the Dalai Lama, via a young American man who had dropped out of college to seek wisdom in the East. When word came, they set out, the monk and the seeker, traveling by train and jeep through a setting that outdid Merton's imagination in its iconic vividness—"mountains, small villages, canyons, shrines, ruined forts, well cared for forest preserves. Then the climb to Dharamsala itself and the vast view over the plains from the village. It rained when we arrived and the thunder talked to itself all over and around the cloud-hidden peaks."

Dharamsala was the fulfillment of a dream: a working city full of monks, a place of literal exile, a world within a world. "Tibetans are established all over the mountain in huts, houses, tents, anything. Prayer flags flutter among the trees. Rock mandalas are along all the pathways. OM MANI PADME HUM ('Hail to the jewel in the lotus') is carved on every boulder. It is moving to see so many Tibetans going about silently praying—almost all of them are constantly carrying rosaries."

The Dalai Lama was thirty-three years old and still in training. Even so, an audience with him was uncommon, and Merton, in the midst of the "people looking for a freak religion" in Dharamsala and the Dalai Lama's "noncontemplative aides," felt like a member of a spiritual elite, an honorary lama from the West.

They met for a whole morning and "spoke almost entirely about the life of meditation, about *samadhi* (concentration)," and about "the higher forms of prayer." Merton found the Dalai Lama placid in spite of the "enormous problems" he and his people were facing.

The Dalai Lama doubtless understood Merton's renown as a man of prayer and his role in popularizing Buddhism in the West. Whatever the reason, Merton was invited to come back a second day, then a third. Now the Dalai Lama drilled him with questions about the conceptual framework of Western monasticism. What did a Christian monk's vows signify? In what sense were they an initiation? What were the stages or degrees of illumination in the mystical life? "And lots of incidental questions: What were the motives for the monks not eating meat? Did they drink alcoholic beverages? Did they have movies? And so on."

Merton identified strongly with the Dalai Lama, and "felt we had become very good friends and were somehow quite close to one another." A photograph of the two of them brings out their likenesses: round faces, big smiles, a soft intensity in the eyes. Like Merton at Gethsemani, the Dalai Lama in Dharamsala was compelled to imagine an ideal monastery, of which the present one was only an anticipation. And like Merton the Dalai Lama, given a notoriety he had not chosen, sought to make it an aspect of his calling. He told Merton that he understood the monk as a person "for the world," and Merton, in turn, defined the vocation of monks like themselves in public terms, as a calling to be "living examples of the freedom and transformation of consciousness which meditation can give."

Merton went next to Darjeeling, passing through Calcutta on the way. Traveling with a guide, he sought out Chantral Rimpoche, a Zen hermit who

416

lived in a hut on the mountainside. He found the rimpoche, or spiritual master (literally "precious one"), supervising the painting of frescoes in a dormitory. "Chantral looked like a vigorous old peasant in a Bhutanese jacket tied at the neck with thongs and a red woolen cap on his head." They settled in for a three-hour meeting. Merton asked "hermit questions"; Chantral asked questions about Christian doctrine, and they settled on "the ultimate perfect emptiness . . . beyond God."

At one point Chantral declared Merton a "natural Buddha," astonishing him. Merton, writing in his journal, declared Chantral "the greatest *rimpoche* I have met so far," and went on: "The unspoken or half-spoken message of our talk was our complete understanding of each other as people who were someone *on the edge* of great realization and knew it and were trying, somehow or other, to go out and get lost in it—and that it was a grace for us to meet one another."

A month into his Asian journey, Merton was intensely alive, obviously happy, an honored guest in a place of beauty, splendor, and holiness. In the journal he kept, the literary Merton has gone missing. Gone is the self-doubt, the relentless scrutiny of his motives. Gone is the self-deprecating wit that serves as a check on his enthusiasms. Gone is the clear and strong explication of difficult concepts. Gone, especially, is Merton's identification with the reader, a pilgrim like himself, whom he seeks to put in his place imaginatively through his writing. He is traveling for his own fulfillment, not the reader's, and for once the experience outstrips what he can think or write about it.

It is a relief when he comes down from the lamasery and explores Calcutta like a tourist, camera round his neck. Suddenly the writing is vigorous, dramatic. "Pushed further and further into town. Buildings. Crowds. Rags. Dirt, laughter, torpor, movement. Calcutta is overwhelming: the elemental city, with no room left for masks. Only the naked truth of overpopulation, underemployment, hunger, disease, a mixture of great vitality and permanent exhaustion—but an exhaustion in which the vitality renews itself."

In Darjeeling he spied a Catholic school near the hotel, sought out the Mother Superior, and said Mass "in the big, 19th-century English-type convent school chapel: a few nuns on one side, a few little girls in uniform, hastily rounded up, on the other. Then coffee and talk with the sisters, who are mostly old, all in the regular habit. No experimenting with other clothes here!"

He rented a room in a big, old-fashioned Western-style tourist hotel, among German expatriates from Pakistan and secretaries from "N'Orleans." It was not far from Mount Katchenjunga, one of the highest of the Himalayas—twenty-eight thousand feet—and he spent the week in a kind of dialogue with the mountain. The mountain is "incomparable. I need to go back for more." He photographed it over and over. A few days later, in a bungalow with a view, he was "tired" of the mountain, "its big crude blush in the sunrise, outside my bungalow at 5:45." It seemed to represent the "postcard" Asia he had been trying to avoid.

Then he went to the mountain. Once on it, he could not see it, and it sheltered him in its largeness. It was monastic in its fixity, the earth's own anchorite, and on it he abruptly saw his time in Dharamsala as a frenzied hunt for rimpoches, in which he had sought again and again to meet the master and be changed, the way so many people had sought to meet him. "All morning alone on the mountainside, in the warm sun, now overclouded. Plenty of time to think. Reassessment of this whole Indian experience in more critical terms. Too much movement. Too much 'looking for' something: an answer, a vision, 'something other.' "

He was due in Bangkok two weeks later. He spent the remaining time making two conventional pilgrimages.

The first was to Madras, in the south of India. Before he ascended into heaven, the New Testament reports, Jesus enjoined the apostles to spread the Gospel to the ends of the earth, and legend has it that Thomas went to India, settling in Madras, where he was martyred. This was "doubting Thomas," and the Christians there, formally Catholics, call themselves St. Thomas Christians.

Merton went first to the beach with a local Sanskrit professor, who hoped to show him the Southern Cross. Then he went to the Cathedral of San Thomé, a small Gothic cathedral with an inscription over the high arch: THOMAS, ONE OF THE TWELVE, CALLED DIDYMUS.

The next morning he went to St. Thomas Mount, eight miles away, where the saint was martyred, and climbed a long flight of steps to the church of Our Lady of the Expectation:

I entered the little church and found the high altar prepared. It was delightful, a perfect hermitage.

. . . I said the Mass of St. Thomas, looking at the ancient gray carved stone that was found on the site. The altar is a sort of folk-art baroque, with a folk-type icon of the saint in a quasi-Franciscan tunic, being pierced by a spear.

. . . The old pulpit was charming, too. A very lovely little church, so quiet, so isolated, so simple, so fresh. It stands on an abrupt hill overlooking an army camp and the airport. One of the nicest things I have ever found anywhere. I felt my pilgrimage to it was a great grace.

It is a measure of a certain repose Merton had found in his writing, a trust in his experience, that he did not grasp after the significance of the pilgrimage to Madras. Here was the shrine of his namesake, who had proved to be an auspicious patron: a man of the West who went east, an apostle who heard the news of the resurrection but insisted on knowing it firsthand, a doubter who is the twin or double or Other of every believer, torn between here and there, between doubt and faith, between the testimony of others and the test of experience. Yet Merton made it merely one more stop along the way. At Our Lady of the Expectation, he "signed the visitors' book and escaped before the sisters could read it." At San Thomé, he gazed up at the arch marked for the saint. "I find the inscription strangely touching. I kneel for a while looking up to the shadows of the sanctuary where all is still as it was before the Council. Then we depart."

He went to Polonnaruwa, in Ceylon, near the city of Kandy. Now it was December, and Advent, but "hardly like any December or Advent I have known! Clear, hot sky. Flowering trees. A hot day coming." He was the guest of the local bishop, who had read *The Seven Storey Mountain* and thought the exploits it described made Merton one of the "first hippies."

The bishop drove him to the ruined old city—a complex of temple buildings collapsed into heaps of stone, and a grouping of reclining statues. A guide led him into a cave. "The old man has two small candles. He holds them up. I discover that I am right up against an enormous reclining Buddha, somewhere around the knee."

Left on his own, he wandered among the statuary and the fallen stones the way he had wandered in the ruins of St. Antonin in France, except that the ruins of Polonnaruwa were giant and magnificent renderings of the human person: "The silence of the extraordinary faces. The great smiles. Huge and yet subtle. Filled with every possibility, questioning nothing, knowing everything, rejecting nothing."

He went on: "Looking at these figures I was suddenly, almost forcibly jerked clean out of the habitual, half-tied vision of things, and an inner clearness, clarity, as if exploding from the rocks themselves, became evident and obvious. . . .

"The thing about all this is that there is no puzzle, no problem, and really no 'mystery.' All is clear. The rock, all matter, all life, is charged with *dharmakaya*—everything is emptiness and everything is compassion. I don't know when in my life I have ever had such a sense of beauty and spiritual validity running together in one aesthetic illumination."

He had been abroad two months. He had come to Asia in search of something, at the same time mindful not to seek whatever it was too aggressively, but to await it, to discover himself in its midst. Now here it was—or rather, now here he was in the midst of it:

"Surely, with Mahabalipuram and Polonnaruwa my Asian pilgrimage has come clear and purified itself. I mean, I know and have seen what I was obscurely looking for. I don't know what else remains but I have now seen and pierced through the surface and have got beyond the shadow and the disguise."

He called it "Asia in its purity . . . clear, pure, complete." But the outward pilgrimage was the image of the inner one, a vision of the spirit in the immediate experience of a ruined Zen garden—"a span of bareness and openness and evidence, and the great figures, motionless, yet with the lines in full movement, a beautiful and holy vision."

"The rest of the 'city,' the old palace complex, I had no time for," he wrote. "We just drove around the roads and saw the ruined shapes, and started on the long drive home to Kandy."

On December 8 Merton returned to Bangkok. He would take part in the conference, then proceed to Jakarta, then to Trappist monasteries on Java and Hong Kong.

The conference was taking place at the International Red Cross compound—a group of cottages surrounding a meeting house—but to arrive there was to return, momentarily, to the world of the Church and Catholicism. Several dozen monks and nuns were present, most in traditional habits. A Trappist habit had been sent to Merton from America.

So had a letter from Daniel Berrigan, who was free on bail. Francine du Plessix Gray of the *New Yorker* was writing a profile of the two Berrigans and the rest of the Catonsville Nine. Was Merton willing to be interviewed? Gray was willing to fly to Bangkok overnight to spend some time with him.

Merton declined. To a friend he wrote, "*New Yorker* profile idea is a gas. I don't want to meet no NY ladies no place."

He would give his lecture in two parts, speaking from notes in the morning and leading a dialogue with the conferees in the afternoon.

He stood at the lectern in the Trappist habit and apologized for his limitations. He was no scholar and no expert on Marxism. He could speak only as a monk who was "trying to find where he stands, what his position is and how he identifies himself in a world of revolution." He could not speak to the experience of those in the audience whose encounter with Marxism had forced them to flee for their lives. "I don't see that there is much that can be said about this, except indirectly," he said. "You save your life by saving your life; you do what you can."

Speaking from a prepared text, he touched on a great deal. He told the monks and nuns about some student revolutionaries in California who described themselves as monks. He related his conversations with Tibetan lamas. He suggested that the real dialogue warranting further exploration, the division worth overcoming, was not between Marxism and monasticism, but between East and West, Asian and European, Buddhism and Christianity.

He evoked for those present an image of the monk who is concerned for society and yet is not a revolutionary. Marxism and monasticism, he proposed, are alike in their suspicion of social structures. Marxists look toward the eradication of such structures. Monks are confident that, though structures change, the monastic impulse will endure wherever people believe that at the root of ordinary experience, there is transcendence to be found. "Wherever you have somebody capable of giving some kind of direction and instruction to a small group attempting to do this thing, attempting to love God and serve him and reach union with him, you are bound to have some kind of monasticism. This kind of monasticism cannot be extinguished. It is imperishable. It represents an instinct of the human heart, and a charism given by God to man," he declared, ". . . and because we believe this, we have given ourselves to the kind of life we have adopted."

He had spoken for nearly an hour. It was lunchtime. He explained that he would take questions when they all returned. The group scattered, and Merton, like the others, went to his cottage, to be alone, to rest, to read, and to write in his journal.

A cry of pain came from his room shortly afterward. That he was killed instantly no one seems to doubt. He had taken a shower; coming out, he slipped on the floor and grasped a fan whirling on a stand. He cried out, but there was no immediate response.

Some time later the door was broken down and the monks and nuns gathered around him. A Trappistine nun gave him the last rites. A Red Cross official confirmed that he was dead. And then the monks and nuns, experts in the experience of God, began to pray together over the body.

In the weeks to follow, as the body was sent back to Kentucky, given the funeral rites, and buried behind the abbey church, people who knew Thomas Merton would seek the meaning of his death and of the grotesque fashion in which it came about. Some hinted at suicide. Others suggested that he had attained nirvana. A friend determined that after twenty-seven years in the world and twenty-seven in the monastery, he had just begun the third half of life. But there was no great significance to be found in Merton's sudden death. In that year of grandiose acts, of blood and fire, it was a spasm of direct and terrible experience, with no significance outside itself.

ELEVEN

The Holiness of the Ordinary

Early the next year, while a group of Catholic radicals was planning a raid on the headquarters of the Dow Chemical Company, one of their peers set out on an odd and lonely expedition. He withdrew some money from a bank in New Orleans, put on a white shirt and a black tie, and drove west in a car he had bought upon his discharge from the army. He drove all the way to California, where he visited the Hearst mansion and the grave of Marilyn Monroe. Then he returned to the South. Six years earlier he had written a novel in the spirit of the Southern Catholic fiction then being published. The setting was New Orleans. The hero was a fat, ill-mannered, oddly dressed grotesque who pondered life from the standpoint of medieval philosophy. The villain was his domineering mother. The love interest was a liberal female from New York who urged him to take part in sit-ins and the like. The novel's conscience was a Negro handyman, who was made out to be savvier and more honorable than anybody else. Its heart was its dialect, its local characters, its seedy locales—the Levy Pants factory, the Night of Joy cocktail lounge, the Paradise Vendors pushcart warehouse, and the Prytania cinema, where Ignatius Reilly, moviegoer and philosopher, found his only real pleasure in life.

Had it been published, *A Confederacy of Dunces* would have been recognized at once as a blend of Walker Percy and Flannery O'Connor, and John Kennedy Toole, age thirty, would have been seen as the first of a future generation of American Catholic writers. As it happened, the novel was turned down by a publisher and Toole was overcome by paranoia. He wound up in Biloxi, Mississippi, where he ran a garden hose from the car's tailpipe through a window while the engine was running, with a predictably grim outcome. In the days before he killed himself, the story goes, he had driven farther south, to Milledgeville, Georgia, to visit Andalusia, the home of his favorite writer.

Mystery and Manners was published that May. Flannery O'Connor had hoped to go to California someday "for about two minutes" to further her "sideline researches into the ways of the vulgar"; she described her stories as reports on terrible beasts slouching toward Bethlehem to be born. She never made it to California, did not live to see admirable nihilists converging on Haight-Ashbury and the Altamont Motor Speedway. Yet she spoke to the age sideways through her "occasional prose." Defining her approach at the conference in Macon, she had described the South as "Christ-haunted," and added that she would like to write a book on the subject, "but it would take me ten or twelve years to do it." That book is *Mystery and Manners*.

Surely no book published in 1969 seemed less occasional at the time. As priests grew beards and presided over Masses suggestive of Broadway musicals and the Top 40, as Catholic parents protested the renewed papal ban on birth control, as Catholic revolutionaries held forth in courtrooms, on street corners, in squares and parks, raiding draft offices and proclaiming a gospel of "militant nonviolence," *Mystery and Manners* offered remarks about "Catholic Novelists and Their Readers," "Writing Short Stories," "The Teaching of Literature," and "The Regional Writer." Yet the book is oddly apposite, as if the realist of distances had seen the age of Aquarius on the horizon. O'Connor describes the present as "an unbelieving age but one that is markedly and lopsidedly spiritual," at once "an age of searchers and discoverers" and "an age that has domesticated despair and learned to live with it happily." She describes the present's fanatics, "who seem to carry an invisible burden; their fanaticism is a reproach, not merely an eccentricity." She portrays the religious artist as a kind of radical, pushing past the surface of things to the "limits of mystery," portraying characters "who are forced out to meet evil and grace and who act on a trust beyond themselves—whether they know very clearly what it is they act upon or not." And she justifies the use of violence to make a religious point: "For the hard of hearing you shout, and for the almost-blind, you draw large and startling figures."

To say that O'Connor would have recognized the new Catholic militants—recognized them as her own children—is not to say that she would have thought them admirable. It was as though her standards of evaluation had been inverted. Now the religious grotesques were all Catholics and Catholicism was a "do-it-yourself religion." The believer was like Hazel Motes after the quicklime had been applied, tapping his cane in the darkness, hoping to find the way; the Church was like Mrs. Flood, his landlady, trying to guess what was going on in his mind.

American Catholics had long tolerated the gap between religion and experience on the grounds that being Catholic was an experience unto itself—a countercultural one—and that worldly experience was to be shunned or held under judgment. Inspired by the Vatican council, some Catholics thought the gap might be narrowed or closed altogether. Upon finding that it could not be—that religion and experience would always be somehow at odds—they sought to close it by force through a striking gesture. In this regard, the two Father Berrigans and their cohorts were not revolutionaries or prophets. They were typical Catholics of the period, trying to make belief believable through sheer effort. While they cited Gospel precedents, their religion seemed ad hoc and expressionist. While they claimed to obey the dictates of conscience, they seemed to be making things up as they went along. While they invoked the authority vested in them as people of God, they seemed more apart than ever, those alienated from Church and society alike.

In those circumstances *Mystery and Manners* was an arresting book, and it remains one. O'Connor usually suggested that her work's power to shock lay in the violence it dramatized or in the "strange skips and gaps" of its style. This may have been true in her lifetime. It is not true today. The violence in her work now makes it recognizably contemporary, makes it familiar and accessible. The prose style now seems as clear as a headline. Today it is the religious faith in the work that has the power to shock, especially in this book of her essays and talks, in which the religious challenge, implicit all through her work, is made explicit and pointed directly at the reader.

On the surface it is a book about fiction, not faith, but O'Connor's point of view is so bound up with her religion, and vice versa, that her remarks about the art of fiction are a defense of the faith. Theology falls from her lips effortlessly. A novelist like herself, she declares, is called to "observe our fierce and fading manners in the light of an ultimate concern." The proper subject of fiction is "the mystery of our position on earth"; the mystery of "the Divine life and our participation in it"; the mystery that life "has, for all its horror, been found by God to be worth dying for." Writing a novel is so hard that "if the novelist is not sustained by a hope of money, then he must be sustained by a hope of salvation, or he simply won't survive the ordeal."

Like *The Seven Storey Mountain* and *The Long Loneliness*, it is a book of firsthand testimony about the life of faith. Outside the two personal essays there is hardly an autobiographical moment in it. O'Connor says she is an orthodox believer, nothing more or less. Yet she speaks for nobody but herself, and the book is grounded in her personal authority. She believes what she says. She believes it not because somebody else says so, but because she has found it to be true in her own experience. Her experience, however, is that of a lifelong believer, who cannot see things any other way. And the tone of the book—that of friendly advice and wise counsel to people younger than herself—makes her religious statements seem less like preferences than recommendations. If you want to write a really good short story, she seems to say, you ought to look into the Catholic faith. For her the divinity of Christ, not the Vietnam War, is a matter of life and death.

It is this combination of objectivity and fierce personal conviction, of aloneness and absoluteness, that gives the book its staying power. Like Faulkner, like Walker Percy, like Dorothy Day and Thomas Merton, O'Connor spoke out of a profound aloneness, making oratory out of solitude. Her aloneness, that of a Catholic in the South, of a Southerner in the North, a believer in a disbelieving literary society, an artist in a church of philistines, is now the aloneness of the religious believer generally. In her case, it is not loneliness or alienation. It is the independence of a person who knows precisely what she believes. For her, there is no gap between experience and religion. The gap is filled with faith.

Mystery and Manners was published quietly. Meanwhile, the new Catholic radicals filled the gap with outsize actions. Due to present themselves to the authorities and begin serving their sentences, Philip Berrigan and a cohort in the Catonsville Nine disappeared for ten days, then went noisily to jail. Daniel Berrigan, a fugitive as well, set out on a path of radical apartness, remaining at large nearly four months before he was captured. The Holy Ghost had gone underground; pilgrimage had become flight.

"And now I pick up Thomas Merton's last book," Dorothy Day wrote in the *Catholic Worker* in 1970, in an article headlined "Adventures in Prayer."

Contemplative Prayer, a hundred-page manual for other monks, was published as "Thomas Merton's final testament to us." It was not his last book at all, though, merely his first posthumous one. Over the years he had assembled many books from scattered articles, and now his acolytes did likewise. A pacifist collected his writings on war and peace; a Hindu scholar introduced the "Asian journal," which came swaddled in reverential commentary. His friend Edward Rice from Columbia brought out *The Man in the Sycamore Tree*, in which memories of "a beatnik, peacenik, Trappist, Buddhist monk" are at war with sober portrait photographs in Trappist black and white.

There is little sense of loss in these productions, despite the editors' ritual protestations about the grief and shock they felt. In their accounts, Merton's death was tragic but somehow appropriate, a "fitting" end to 1968, the "year of blood and fire."

In the short term, his sudden death boosted Merton's reputation more than anything since *The Seven Storey Mountain*. It left him voluble and forward-looking, eternally bright-eyed in the abbey church or at the hermitage. It placed him in the pantheon alongside Martin Luther King and Malcolm X, the slain Kennedy brothers and Good Pope John. And it emboldened his correspondents—there were hundreds of them, it turned out—to speak with confidence about the meaning of his life. Douglas Steere likened Merton to a "spiritual masseur" who hoped "to free some of his monastic brothers and sisters from the serious adhesions that are holding them back." Gordon Zahn argued that he was a pacifist in spite of himself—yet a pacifist who would have come to accept violent protest and would have offered Daniel Berrigan "safe haven at his hermitage."

In the long term, sudden death set Merton in the realm of pure possibility that Walker Percy spoke about. Whereas Flannery O'Connor's power derives from her fixity, her stubborn refusal to be anyone but herself, Merton's lies in his fluidity, his ability to represent and call forth the aspirations of others. In his life and work he thrived on the radical identification of himself with another and called forth a like identification in his readers. Strong in life, this identification has become the key to his work in death, the current passing back and forth between him and his public. His friends, as they grew and changed, lined him up alongside them as an ally, a perpetual supporter of their causes. His readers have done the opposite, putting ourselves in his place, tagging along on his adventures, imagining that his outlook is ours.

It was otherwise for the living. As Merton and O'Connor were stylized for posterity Day and Percy carried on, negotiating between what they sought to do and what was expected of them, between the demands of eminence and what Percy called "the holiness of the ordinary."

Percy was finishing Novel No. 3, now called *How to Make Love in the Ruins: Adventures of a Bad Catholic at a Time Near the End of the World*. He sent a copy of *Mystery and Manners* to Shelby Foote, and Foote wrote back declaring that O'Connor had died a "minor-minor writer" because she "didnt have time to turn her back on Christ, which is something every great Catholic writer (that I know of, I mean) has done."

Foote urged Percy not to take offense—he didn't think of Percy as a Catholic writer—but when he brought up the subject again Percy was provoked to reply. "You were right the other day about me not being a Catholic writer as Flannery was," he told Foote in a letter. As evidence, he enclosed a draft of the new novel. "What's it about? Screwing and God (which all Catholic novels since Augustine have been about)."

There is hardly a novel less like O'Connor's fiction than *Love in the Ruins*. Chatty, skeptical, ribald, willfully undramatic, it seems flagrantly to defy the precepts set out in *Mystery and Manners*. Although set in the future, it is Percy's most topical book; its torrent of verbiage, its ceaseless commentary, is directed at a present that was already past by 1971, when it was published. "Just now, of course, the violence has abated," he explained at a publicity event in New York; it had been replaced by "a period of eerie tranquillity." He called the novel "an entertainment for people who are thinking things over."

The belatedness that hovers around the novel, it now became clear, was characteristic of Percy's outlook. O'Connor had regarded Christianity as a timeless truth, Merton as a quandary forever unfolding. Percy had come to see it as something akin to his Uncle Will's ideal of the Old South: ancient, noble, run-down, disrespected, clearly flawed and yet worth cherishing while it was still around.

Dorothy Day did not worry about Christianity's prospects. Rather, she feared the demise of the dream of a new social order, which had inspired her since her childhood, and for a few years she pointed her efforts toward the future, as if to be sure that the dream was not over.

She was the Anarch of the Catholic Worker and the movement's main fund-raiser as well, and a spell of difficulty breathing during a trip cross-country—her heart was enlarged—reminded her that she wouldn't live forever. She had already begun to consolidate the affairs of the movement somewhat, buying an old tenement on East First Street* to serve as a new St. Joseph's House and resolving a dispute with the Internal Revenue Service, whose agents didn't believe that people would do such hard work without receiving salaries or hidden benefits.

She became an ardent supporter of the United Farm Workers and their founder, Cesar Chavez, traveling to California several times to speak at their rallies. Reporting on a strike in Bakersfield in 1940, she had declared that the migrant workers needed a new St. Francis to lead them, and in Chavez she saw the closest thing to a saint to be found in California. A worker himself, ruggedly handsome, committed to nonviolence, traditionally Mexican in his devotion to Jesus and the Virgin of Guadalupe, Chavez was the anti-Berrigan—an unquestioned representative of oppressed people, committed to practical victories rather than agitprop. Day had written about him since 1967, and in a sense her support for the organization of migrant workers grew in parallel to the Catholic Worker's opposition to the war in Vietnam. The more strident the CW's antiwar witness became, the more she championed the UFW's calls for higher wages and better working conditions. The more the Catholic Workers were left to tend "the wounded in the class struggle," the more she looked to farm workers as the last hope for the reorganization of society. "We need communities of work, land for the landless, true farming communes, cooperatives and credit unions. There is much that is wild, prophetic, and holy about our work—it is that which attracts the young who come to help us. But the heart hungers for that new social order wherein justice dwelleth."

She also sought evidence of social change abroad. In 1970 she went, with a friend, a peace worker named Eileen Egan, on a trip around the world—to Australia, Hong Kong, India, Tanzania, Rome, and London. They had no agenda, no great work to accomplish, and Day was free to be a pilgrim pure and simple, venturing forth with a cane which could be converted into a compact stool.

In Tanzania, they sought out Julius Nyerere, the popular president, who, like her, Day declared proudly, was both a Catholic and a socialist. In India, they were met at the airport by Mother Teresa, and Day gave a talk to

---

*"Finally have *permit* to reconstruct our new headquarters in N.Y.," she had written to Thomas Merton. "Need $20,000 or more!! If you see any benefactors around, nudge them. Or tell St. Joseph to."

Teresa's nuns. Teresa was admired but not yet a living icon, and Day was struck by the sight of her "kneeling by the side of one of these starving old women who had been picked up from the streets, and with three fingers (they do not use spoons or forks), tucking rice and vegetables into the mouth of the patient who had come to life enough to open it like a bird being fed by its mother"—the gesture combining in a stroke Day's own care for the poor and Rose Hawthorne's care for the incurably ill.

Day herself had become a living icon, and she sought to put her iconicity to use. As a generation of Catholic women, nuns in particular, sought to direct their own religious lives as if for the first time, they looked to Day as an exemplar, a woman who was at once holy and modern—only to be confounded by her stress on the "women's work" of hospitality and her love for traditional devotions like the Rosary. Around St. Joseph's House, her position on sainthood was well known: "Don't call me a saint—I don't want to be dismissed that easily." The remark, often taken to express her humility, in fact expressed the opposite—her desire to be canonized on her own terms and in her own way—and as she grew older, she was more mindful of the image she presented. A personalist, she recognized that holiness inhered powerfully in a single individual. A lover of holiness, she understood how one holy person inspired another. A journalist, she knew the power of photographs. Although her movement was, in a sense, larger than ever— 300,000 people went on a "peace pilgrimage" to Washington, she noted with pleasure in a column—in photographs she was now invariably depicted alone. In Bob Fitch's photograph she is kneeling in an empty church, embarked on an adventure in prayer, her head in her hands, her cane hooked over the pew before her. In Richard Avedon's remarkable portrait she sits restlessly against a gray background, her mouth set, her white hair swept back, her shoulders broad in a checked overcoat, her eyes alert with an animal aliveness; she is ageless, intense, fierce in her understandings, leaning forward to answer a question the viewer has posed.

Love in the Ruins got good reviews and was nominated for a National Book Award. Even so, Percy worried that he was losing his powers as a novelist. He had never been a natural storyteller, and now the burden of telling a tale, inventing characters, and conducting research had begun to weigh on him, and at the same time to seem an effort not worthy of a self-taught philosopher. O'Connor's request that he "make up another one," he told Foote, had left him feeling slighted.

He was glad to be alive. His father had killed himself at forty. His Uncle Will had died at fifty-six, the age he was now. Soon he would be the oldest male Percy in memory. "With my family's history, I count even a sober old age as a windfall," he told Foote in 1971.

Later, in the same mood, he reported: "I have come to the damnedest watershed in my life — done what I wanted to do in the novel, with linguistics, children gone, sitting down here in the Louisiana autumn. Everything quiet. What now? It would be a good time to die, but on the other hand I'd as soon not." He went on, "My life breaks exactly in half: 1st half = growing up Southern and Medical; 2nd half = imposing art on 1st half. 3rd half? Sitting on Bayou and repeating over and over again like old Buddenbrooks: *Kurios!*"

A role for the third half of life was marked out for him, foreordained, not by Thomas Mann but by his own work. An escaped scion of the South, a refugee from medicine, a survivor of tuberculosis, a hobbyist in philosophy, an acclaimed novelist by surprise, he now found himself the last gentleman of American Catholic writing.

He began to act the part. Under doctor's orders, he gave up whiskey. (It didn't last.) He took up golf. He dandled his grandchildren. He taught a class, met with scholars, spoke at length in interviews, making oratory out of solitude.

And he started writing another novel. Once again he solved a problem in his life by devising a literary approach to it: an approach that would characterize the fiction of his "3rd half" of life. The belatedness he felt, the sense of last things, would be built into the very structure of the book, which would begin at the end of the story, with the crime already committed and the criminal arrested, convicted, sentenced, and locked away in an asylum, needing only to confess his sins. "Come into my cell," Lancelot Lamar would begin his confession. "Make yourself at home . . ."

That summer Day went to Eastern Europe and the Soviet Union, one of a delegation of fifty peace activists — "Quakers, Methodists, Episcopalians, and perhaps a number of 'unbelievers' whatever that all encompassing word means" — allowed to visit as a gesture of dialogue between people in America and those in the Soviet bloc. Although, again, there was no agenda, the trip, Day reported, was "not just a sightseeing trip, but was rich in associations for me." More than a peace mission, it was a pilgrimage to her past — to a place in her past which she knew intimately but had never visited. Sixty years after the great Russian writers had inspired her to become a writer and a radical, she would see the country for herself.

What she saw was restricted, despite her best efforts and her protestations to the contrary. Tolstoy's estate was off limits, as was Zagorsk, the monastery outside St. Petersburg where the model for Father Zosima in *The Brothers Karamazov* once lived. But she visited the grave of Dostoevsky, went to the Hermitage—where Rembrandt's depiction of the prodigal son reminded her of the men on the line at St. Joseph's House—and saw evidence of the Orthodox faith.

When she praised Aleksander Solzhenitsyn during a meeting with "state" writers in Moscow, one of them rose to denounce Solzhenitsyn for selling out to the West. Yet she was convinced that the Soviet propagandists had not gotten the best of her, even as she praised the clean streets, the vast and shiny subway, the well-trained guides, and the well-kept churches, many of which had been turned into museums. Russia, for her, was still a place of romance, and in the Russia of Leonid Brezhnev she saw the Russia of Trotsky and Kropotkin, of Tolstoy and Dostoevsky, such was its vividness in her mind's eye.

The National Book Award for 1971 went to Flannery O'Connor's *Complete Stories*, and January 16, 1972, was declared Flannery O'Connor Day in Georgia. Regina O'Connor presented some of her daughter's papers to the college library in Milledgeville; she shook hands with the governor of Georgia, Jimmy Carter, who smiled broadly over a wide necktie.

The Complete Stories was an instant classic, but it undid the careful selection and discrimination that O'Connor had brought to her short fiction. Here were the chapters of novels she had recast as short stories to make a little money. Here, placed right up front to deter the unwitting reader, were the stories she had written in graduate school and had deemed unreadable soon afterward. "A Good Man Is Hard to Find" was sandwiched between "Enoch and the Gorilla" and "A Late Encounter with the Enemy," between an excerpt and a trifle.

The collection could have diminished her reputation, but it did the opposite. Now, with all her work in print with one publisher, with the stories taken out of the realm of art and placed on the time line of a literary life, with Robert Giroux's introduction casually assuming her greatness and conveying her charm, the "minor-minor" writer looked like a writer of stature.

That year, Percy wrote an introduction to a new edition of Will Percy's *Lanterns on the Levee*. "For most of us, the communication of beauty takes two, the teacher and the hearer, the pointer and the looker. The rare soul, the Wolfe or Faulkner, can assault the entire body of literature single-handedly. I couldn't or wouldn't. I had a great teacher . . . ," he explained. "But he was more than a teacher. What he was to me was a fixed point in a confusing world."

He was now held in greater esteem than his uncle. Eminence ran in the Percy family; now it was stalking him. As awards and honors piled up—three honorary degrees, induction into the American Academy of Arts and Letters—he threw himself into local affairs. He signed up to teach a course at Louisiana State. He joined a book group made up of Covington worthies: a lawyer, a judge, a Catholic priest, an Episcopal one, a philosopher, a novelist. He took a hand in the ongoing process of integration in Covington—a pillar of the community after all.

November 8, 1972, was Day's seventy-fifth birthday. As if by decree, she ceased to be a radical in the public eye and was recognized as a holy person. The Catholic magazines published tributes to her. Mike Wallace interviewed her on *60 Minutes*. Bill Moyers visited St. Joseph's House to tape a documentary about her work. The University of Notre Dame gave her a medal reserved for exceptional laypeople. More rewarding than the medal was Theodore Hesburgh's summation of her life's work: he praised her for "comforting the afflicted and afflicting the comfortable."

Day didn't reject the honors, merely sought to complicate them. On *60 Minutes*, she called abortion a grave evil and stressed that, as a Christian pacifist, she was called to love any enemy, even Adolf Hitler. Around St. Joseph's House, she grumbled about the "women's lib" movement and the lack of traditional piety among young people.

She went to jail one more time. The United Farm Workers had gained higher wages and safer working conditions but were still forbidden to strike. When they struck anyway, cadres of activists and celebrities went to Fresno to be arrested in solidarity. "Ninety-nine women and fifty men" were arrested that day, "including thirty nuns and two priests," Day reported in a column. They spent nearly two weeks in a prison camp, doing makework.

The best-known photograph of the event (by Bob Fitch) tells a different story. Cesar Chavez is not there. Neither is Joan Baez or anybody else. Dorothy Day sits on her portable stool, wearing a plaid dress and a straw hat, and stares down two police officers, a great-grandmother defying the powers and principalities all by herself.

The fortieth anniversary of the Catholic Worker came in May 1973. As Day's leadership of the movement passed from actual to symbolic, she defined the movement over and over again. She stressed its basis in love. The Catholic Workers were "holy fools," like Prince Myshkin in *The Idiot* or the Berrigan brothers in jail, in that they were determined to share the sufferings of others. They were anarchists, insofar as Christianity was anarchic: " 'Love God and do as you will.' 'For such, there is no law.' 'If anyone asks for your cloak, give him your coat too.' " They were demonstrators of "the providence of God, how God loves us." They were writers and journalists who had put their words to the test with their lives: "This work came about because we started writing of the love of God we should have for each other, in order to show our love of God. It's the only way we can know we love God."

There were new young people, clearly committed to the movement. Unlike the young people of the sixties, they were not disdainful of the Church. Unlike those of previous decades, they hadn't grown up with traditional Catholic piety. The Catholic Worker was the beginning of their religious experience, not its fulfillment; they had come to St. Joseph's House to know poverty, community, political dissent, or authentic religious faith as if for the first time.

They went away, in any case, having known Dorothy Day, an experience they recounted later on. Robert Ellsberg was struck by her "intense, haunting beauty." Eric Brandt, who repainted her room, removed a crucifix from the wall to find a bright and clear-edged image of the cross beneath. Patrick Jordan went into her room unannounced one Saturday afternoon and came upon her absorbed in an opera on the radio like St. Teresa in ecstasy.

Robert Coles, visiting with a station wagon full of college students, found her "frail in body, but as feisty as ever in spirit." Coles had volunteered at St. Joseph's House briefly while a medical student in the fifties. As a young doctor he had worked in the South, and there had reckoned with Flannery O'Connor's stories; then he had come upon *The Moviegoer* while shuttling between psychiatry clinics in New Orleans and Biloxi. He read the novel "over and over again," going around New Orleans with the novel in hand as if it were a guidebook, written expressly for him and his journey.

Coles was the very archetype of the secular postmodern pilgrim—not a believer himself, but a person who is attracted to belief, prone to it, often covetous of it in others, and who is brought to the threshold of belief imaginatively through his reading.

He was also a Pulitzer Prize winner and Harvard professor, and he made a habit of bringing students from the elite university to the rundown "school" of poverty. When his wife was mortally ill he had asked Day for her prayers. Pray Day did; she also sent a postcard every day. "Now Jane was better," Coles recalled, "and I had come to say thank you."

He turned on his tape recorder and engaged Day in a discussion of "her great loves": Dickens and Dostoevsky, Silone and Chekhov, the Orwell of *Homage to Catalonia*. She envied those writers, she explained, wanted to meet them, to write the way they did. She thought of the books themselves as her friends, as her companions on the way. She considered them her only possessions. "When I've read a passage from *Bread and Wine*, or *Homage to Catalonia*, I think of so many people who can't read at all—what they've missed," she said. "I wish I could spend the rest of my life with those people, giving them the bread and wine that is *Bread and Wine*."

There was one writer Day and Coles disagreed about. "I had been trying to get her to enjoy Walker Percy's fiction, without success," he recalled. He sent her *The Moviegoer*; he imagined that she and Percy might meet. "She hadn't taken to it at all. She politely excused her lack of interest or response as 'generational,' but I thought then, and still do, that she favored writers whose gift and mission it was to render storytelling justice to the poor and to Christ as their one-time (and all-time) companion." She evidently found it hard to admire a philandering stockbroker like Binx Bolling. She was impatient with European philosophy, which hadn't stopped the Nazis, after all. She thought it too late in life to discover new writers. She was "too old."

Coles had spent several days in Covington interviewing Percy for a *New Yorker* profile. On the face of it, he was Percy's ideal interlocutor: a doctor-writer, skeptical of medicine, professionally curious about the South, who claimed that Percy's books made him feel "at home" with himself. Yet Percy, his biographers report, was made nervous by Coles's style as an interviewer.

Although he was a psychiatrist, Coles didn't ask Percy any questions about his father's suicide or his mother's fatal car accident. He didn't use a tape recorder or take notes, just tried to match Percy drink for drink during long conversations on the back porch.

Percy later explained his discomfort by saying he felt that Coles made him out to be more liberal and well-meaning than he actually was, casting him in the role of enlightened Southern sage. There was doubtless another, deeper, reason. With the *New Yorker* profile, the usual roles were reversed. All his life Percy had sought to diagnose other people. Now here he was explaining himself and the meaning of life to another diagnostician, who simply watched and listened.

Percy made his discomfort into philosophical dis-ease in the novel he was writing. *The Moviegoer* had been a confession to the reader. The new novel would be a confession to an unnamed authority figure: a psychiatrist-priest, roundaboutly described but never positively identified, whose chief attribute is his silence.

In 1974 a young black writer went on pilgrimage to Andalusia. The year she was seven, Alice Walker had lived on a farm outside Milledgeville. She'd toted buckets of water through the fields. She'd gone to segregated school in an old jail, been frightened by the electric chair. She'd lost her cat when the family, who were sharecroppers, had to pick up abruptly and move on.

Later, as a student and then as a writer, she had been drawn to Flannery O'Connor's work for the perfection of the prose and for the toughness, the vitality, the truth to life of the depictions of blacks and whites alike. Then she had renounced it, since in race matters, it seemed, O'Connor had been on the wrong side.

Now Walker returned to middle Georgia, accompanied by her mother. Before going to O'Connor's house they went to their own, trudging past fence and gate and NO TRESPASSING sign to the "typical abandoned share-farmer shack" where they had lived in 1952. They went for lunch at a new Holiday Inn, where ten years earlier they would not have been served.

Across the road was Andalusia. The farmhouse was as it had been described by others, white and noble and neatly kept. But in Walker's telling, published in 1975, her effortlessly confident voice—and her use of the present tense—suggests how much had changed since 1964. "Although an acquaintance of O'Connor's has told me no one lives there now—but that a caretaker looks after things—I go up to the porch and knock. It is not an entirely empty or symbolic gesture: I have come to this house to learn something about myself in relation to Flannery O'Connor, and will learn it whether anyone is home or not."

Standing before O'Connor's house while her own was "rotting into dust," Walker found that the racism she had known in childhood was still palpable and hurtful. Justice was still anything but swift; O'Connor had been on the other side, and Walker was still angry at her for it.

Like O'Connor, however, Walker sought, in art, the convergence of two sides of the story. Over lunch at the Holiday Inn, she'd told her mother about the time she gave a talk to a group of librarians in Mississippi, some black, some white. A white librarian declared that "she really *did* think Southerners wrote so well because 'we' lost the war," whereupon Walker set her straight: " 'We' didn't lose the war. '*You*' all lost the war. And you all's loss was our gain."

Hearing this, Walker's mother insisted there was no changing the minds of old white Southerners; they would have to die out. Walker herself was more hopeful, insisting that the conflict between opposing points of view was constructive, for "the truth about any subject only comes when all sides of the story are put together," and in a piece of writing "each writer writes the missing parts to the other's writer's story." But there was no convincing her mother: " 'Well, I doubt if you can ever get the true missing parts of anything from the white folks,' my mother says softly, so as not to offend the waitress who is mopping up at a nearby table; 'they've sat on the truth so long by now they've mashed the life out of it.' "

"Beyond the Peacock: Reconstructing Flannery O'Connor" is the most genuine of homages, an act of redress without reproach. In a few sentences Walker cast a cold eye on the basis of O'Connor's kinship with other Southern whites— the "inburnt knowledge" of limitations supposedly given them by the war—and replaced it with a knowledge of limitations given by racial injustice. Meanwhile, through a kindred style—the comic interplay of mother and daughter, the regional expressions, the granting of the last word to a black woman while a white woman labors underfoot—she made clear that she and O'Connor came from the same literary territory, whether anybody liked it or not.

"Buddhists teach that a man's life is divided into three parts: the first part for education and growing up; the second for continued learning, through marriage and raising a family, involvement with the life of the senses, the mind, and the spirit; and the third period, the time of withdrawal from responsibility, letting go of the things of this life, letting God take over," Dorothy Day wrote in her column for March 1975. The readers of the paper hardly would have known it, such was her indirection, but she was announcing her retirement from the Catholic Worker, forty-two years after its founding. There would be no farewell party, no ritual changing of the guard. She would simply leave the work of hospitality and newspapering to "the generous crowd of young people."

In *The Long Loneliness* she had written about the first part of her life. In this quietly valedictory column, and in the columns to follow, she sought to explain the second part:

> "What is it all about—the Catholic Worker movement?" It is, in a way, a school, a work camp, to which large-hearted, socially conscious young people come to find their vocations. After some months or years, they know most definitely what they want to do with their lives. Some go into medicine, nursing, law, teaching, farming, writing, and publishing. They learn not only to love, with compassion, but to overcome fear, that dangerous emotion that precipitates violence. They may go on feeling fear, but they know the means, they have grown in faith, to overcome it.

The Catholic Worker had been the site of her own schooling, the place where she had come to firsthand knowledge of the life of poverty she had read about—and of the life of religious faith as well. Now, at the age of seventy-seven, she was back where she started. The movement had bought two cottages in a colony on Staten Island, not far from the site of the cottage she had owned in the twenties, and the place, called Spanish Camp, was already a place of retirement. "Man works from sun to sun but a woman's work is never done," she liked to say, and in retirement she would not be idle. She would read, write, spend time with her grandchildren, and do the work of prayer, cultivating the "interior senses" Teresa Avila described.

In Manhattan, the "unprogrammed" work of the Catholic Worker went on as usual. "And here I am living on the beach, writing, answering some letters, and trying to grow in the life of the spirit. I feel that I am but a beginner."

"The royalties of the dead author will go to the monastery," Thomas Merton had declared upon taking his final vows, dying to the world as a Trappist. By the mid-1970s it seemed that he was even more prolific as a dead author than he had been as a live one.

The books kept coming: *Contemplation in a World of Action*; a journal from the middle sixties, called *A Vow of Conversation*; a boxy volume of his collected poems; a short biography, and then another, with two more ambitious books in progress.

A group of Catholic Workers put together a chapbook called *Ishi Means Man*. Merton's contributions to the newpaper had included five essays on Native Americans, the fruit of his fitful desire to be a priest on an Indian reservation. In 1975 a small press was engaged to publish them all together, with a cover featuring a wood-block print by a Catholic Worker artist. In the briefest of forewords, Dorothy Day wrote, "Reading these essays, which we are proud to have printed in *The Catholic Worker*, I could only cry out, as another staff member did, 'More, more!' "

She had been listening to cassette tapes of retreats Merton had given, and she recommended them in her column as the best available. "It was a joy to hear his voice," she remarked, so casually that her readers would not realize that she had never met Thomas Merton and that she, like most of his admirers, knew his voice only through his writing.

With St. Joseph's House overcrowded, the movement had bought a building on East Third Street for use as a residence for poor women. Two years passed while the building was renovated. Early in 1976 it was ready, and the women moved in: elderly women, recovering alcoholics and drug users, unwed mothers, and Dorothy Day. "Now at Maryhouse my windows on the second floor face the street with its teeming life and noise and the hot sun pouring in. If I leave my door open a breeze comes through. I have a rocking chair in front of my window and I never tire of sitting there and looking out at a sycamore tree, that tree Zaccheus made famous by climbing into its branches (he was a short man) so that he could see Jesus better as He passed by."

Maryhouse, in effect, was Day's response to the women's liberation movement. Maryhouse was a companion place to St. Joseph's House; it was a community of women; it was a reminder that "the flesh of Jesus was the flesh of Mary," and a reminder of "how great the dignity of woman" is, "how large a part she has played in the redemption of the world."

At the same time, it was Day's convent and cloister. For forty years she had been on pilgrimage from one place to another, a ceaseless to and fro. Now she was on an adventure in prayer. "With prayer, one can go on cheerfully and even happily," she liked to say, "while without prayer, how grim is the journey."

That summer American Catholic lay leaders held an elaborate conference on the liturgy in Philadelphia. Eight thousand people would attend, and the organizers persuaded Day to come and take part in a discussion on "Women and the Eucharist." Mother Teresa would be there, too.

It was the bicentennial year, and during the conference the archbishop of Philadelphia celebrated a Mass for the U.S. armed forces. Some Catholic Workers held a protest against the Mass outside the cathedral, their placards pointing out that the day—August 6—was the twenty-first anniversary of the day the United States dropped an atomic bomb on Hiroshima.

Day opened her own remarks by calling attention to the juxtaposition. For the most part, though, she spoke nostalgically and anecdotally. She emphasized the human need for ritual, recalling the Corpus Christi processions in Little Italy in the movement's early years—the streets "decorated as for a festa" with portable altars and bright bedspreads in lieu of banners, the sidewalks thronged with people, the pushcarts piled high with "an abundance of food for body and soul." As she explained it, "The Catholic Worker soup line is also a celebration (of a kind)." Many of the men found at the Catholic Worker houses actually ate and slept elsewhere: they came to the Worker in order to satisfy a hunger "for human warmth" that food could not satisfy.

Later that month Day had another heart attack. She spent a month recuperating at the Catholic Worker farm in upstate New York. Bedridden, she reread her favorite novels one more time: *Anna Karenina, David Copperfield,* the unending Russian epic of Solzhenitsyn, who was now a neighbor of her daughter's in Vermont. Novels, no less than the Eucharist, no less than the Catholic Worker, provided the "human warmth" she longed for, the opposite of the long loneliness.

Percy was calling his new novel *The Knight, Death, and the Devil,* after an engraving by Dürer. Writing it, he ran into trouble.

His biographers explain the trouble variously. He was depressed. He was drinking too much. He had an undiagnosed case of hepatitis. With his daughters grown and out of the house, he felt bereft. He was distant from his wife and their friends in town. He couldn't find the voice in which to tell his story. He was writing about sin and evil, about modern excess, and his firsthand experience of these suddenly seemed thin and antiquated.

Percy himself said he was in the "horse latitudes." More precisely, he was in flight from eminence, trying to escape the burden of representing a certain position to others—the Catholic writer, the Southern grandee, the philosopher who can speak to the questions of the meaning of life.

By his own estimation, his writing had just culminated with the publication, in 1975, of *The Message in the Bottle*, a book of his philosophical essays. One of the book's central insights is that, strictly speaking, there is no such thing as a literature of alienation. An authentic work actually dispels the reader's alienation. *The Message in the Bottle* would essay to dispel the alienation of a new generation of readers. This was no great consolation for Percy, however. The essays were twenty years old. He was alienated all over again and in a different way.

In a series of letters to Shelby Foote he hinted at troubles in his marriage. "Jesus, in a little more than a year, I'll be 60—and you, what, 61?" he wrote in April 1975. "So what now? It's a question of desire, what one wants to do—write something better or run off with two girls to the islands. Having just delivered the last word on the nature of man, I am in a quandary." The next month, upon receiving a scholarly journal full of essays on Southern writers, he remarked, "Yeah, Percy, O'Connor, and Foote. A fine trio. Two at least will never get to heaven." Upon learning that Foote, having finished his million-and-a-half-word Civil War trilogy after twenty years, was reading Romantic poetry: "I'm not sure I envy you. Shelley 5 hrs per day? Don't you ever want to (1) shoot your wife (2) burn your house (3) run off with 2 26-yr-old lovely Foote-admiring graduate N.C. students . . . (4) shoot your mother in law (5) move to Greece?"

He saw the third half of life as a life his ancestors hadn't survived to enjoy. As he neared sixty he was still healthy, trim, sharp-witted, charming, and ardent for fresh experience, all the more so because it would stimulate his creativity for the new novel.

At his wife's suggestion, he rented an artist's studio in town. Barren, simply furnished with a desk and a daybed and a refrigerator, it suggested the cell from which Lancelot Andrewes Lamar was telling his story. Lamar was in an asylum after murdering his wife. In the next cell was a young woman, a rape victim, and their communication, through crude tappings on the wall, is an antidote to the failure of communication that led Lancelot to kill his wife in the first place.

The artist in the studio next door was a painter named Lyn Hill, twenty-eight years old, the age of Percy's elder daughter. They began to kibitz in their studios between bursts of creativity. They would go out to lunch on the main street. They began to frequent a restaurant on Lake Ponchartrain. They had asked other artists to join them, and in time they became a community of sorts, calling themselves the Sons and Daughters of the Apocalypse.

Percy was still restless in Covington, however. In *The Message in the Bottle* he had given a precise account of how to escape the everydayness of one's life; and when it came, he seized the opportunity to make a "zone crossing," postwar American style: a flight to Las Vegas, a few days spent gallivanting around the Southwest, a lost weekend, to be regretted and not repeated.

Back in Covington, Lyn Hill painted Percy's portrait. When they were done, a photographer came to the studio and took a picture of Percy alongside it. The photograph shows two Walker Percys, one in the flesh and one in oil paint. The one is smiling and the other glaring; one is a writer in a studio and the other a sage in the midst of expressionistic apocalypses and barbed-wire bondage. Together, the photograph and the portrait suggest the divided man Percy was just then. One is a professor type, relaxed and affable in a crew-neck sweater. The other is a handsome devil.

Percy finished his novel and began teaching a writing workshop at Loyola University in New Orleans. He now read the manuscripts of several dozen unpublished novels every year, the way Caroline Gordon had once read his own unpublished novels. When a woman called him at Loyola and insisted that he read her son's novel, he refused. She called again. She sought him out on campus and produced the manuscript, demanding that he read it. Later, he recalled the scene: "Why would I want to do that? I asked her. Because it is a great novel, she said."

Percy's story of how *A Confederacy of Dunces* came to be published is legendary in New Orleans, as cherished as the story of how *The Moviegoer* came to win a National Book Award. The story is not original to Percy, however. Telling the story in an introduction to the book, he echoed the story

Flannery O'Connor had told in her introduction to A *Memoir of Mary Ann*—the story of a work that overcomes every obstacle, even the resistance of the professional author, such is its raw power:

> Over the years I have become very good at getting out of things I don't want to do. And if ever there was something I didn't want to do, this was surely it: to deal with the mother of a dead novelist and, worst of all, to have to read a manuscript that she said was *great*, and that, as it turned out, was a badly smeared, scarcely readable carbon. . . . There was no getting out of it; only one hope remained—that I could read a few pages and that they would be bad enough for me, in good conscience, to read no farther. Usually I can do just that. . . . In this case I read on. And on. . . . Surely it was not possible that it was so good.

Percy explained that the novel's reason for being was Ignatius Reilly, "who should repel the reader with his gargantuan bloats, his thunderous contempt and one-man war against everybody—Freud, homosexuals, heterosexuals, Protestants, and the assorted excesses of modern times." But the source of Percy's enthusiasm for the novel could also be found in his own life. In Reilly, Toole had created the kind of outsize character Percy had tried to create in Lancelot Lamar: a man at once repulsive and likable. Yet Toole had not survived to write a fourth novel. Hectored by his mother, thwarted by a publisher, he had killed himself. As Percy celebrated Ignatius Reilly, he doubtless pondered John Kennedy Toole, a literary prodigy who wound up a failure and a suicide, and thought to himself: There but for the grace of God go I.

Nineteen seventy-seven was the centenary of Peter Maurin's birth. Many of the "young people" to whom Dorothy Day had entrusted the Catholic Worker had not yet been born when he died in 1949. Still, they spoke of "Peter" as if they had known him. This was not due to his "Easy Essays," although they were reprinted regularly in the paper. It was due to the portrait of him that Day had created in her own words: a happy agitator, at once comic and grave, both foolish and wise, a disciple of Christ who seemed less like a figure out of the Gospels than one out of a Dickens novel.

Nineteen seventy-seven was also the fiftieth anniversary of Day's own conversion to Catholicism. She spent the summer in one of the beach cottages on Staten Island, attended to by two young Catholic Workers. She no longer roamed the beach from one end to the other, looking for driftwood. Instead, she gathered her thoughts in her diary:

> Stormy day. Woke at 5:30 a.m. Reading Scriptures—Genesis and Psalms. Today I will begin with the Ascension and read Acts. Mass at nine at Huguenot—Anne Marie and Kathleen and I (with Hannah).

> I need a Bible, large print. I read so much, my eyes tire. . . .

> Still reading Dr. Zhivago—his last days in Moscow. Remembering Claude McKay, Langston Hughes, Wally and Rose Carmen, and Mike Gold, all these friends of mine who spent time in Moscow at this same time Pasternak writes of. And Diego Rivera in Mexico City, and his telling me of the reprinting, in Russia, of my story from New Masses, "Having a Baby." "Go to the Soviet Union," he said. "You can collect royalties."

She spent the winter confined to her room at Maryhouse. In Union Square, on picket lines, editing the newspaper, in jail, she had inspired others to go and do likewise. Now she was a holy person, who inspired others to come to see her, to be in her presence, to enjoy the favor it bestowed, and to recall the encounter precisely.

Cesar Chavez came. So did Mother Teresa. So did dozens of the less celebrated people who had been her co-workers over the years.

Jim Forest was struck by the intensity of her prayerfulness: "She spent at least half an hour in preparation for receiving Communion, which Frank Donovan brought each day from the house chapel, and half an hour in thanksgiving afterward. The rest of the day was punctuated by reading the Psalms and other parts of the monastic office, times of silent prayer, reading, meals, radio and television. There were many for whom she prayed each day, among them various people who had committed suicide. She prayed that those who had taken their own lives would have the grace of final repentance. That her prayers occurred long after the deaths was of no matter, she said. "There is no time with God."

Patrick Jordan was struck by the depth of her religious faith, which was evident in every aspect of her life. "I suppose it is what attracted so many of us to her: in seeing her faith we experienced our own hoped-for faith being validated and strengthened."

Daniel Berrigan saw the debate between prayer and social action resolved in her person, the peace of a life well lived; at the same time, her achievement as a writer called forth, from him, the most eloquent words ever said about her—making him, as he portrayed her, once again a writer first of all. "At length, all was said and done; no more needed saying or doing. She stood there, or sat down, like Christ, like Buddha. This is the image of her last years. Her life passed over into the passive voice. Now she was served, reverenced, cherished, protected. Her flame was failing; her memory glimmered and guttered; 'On Pilgrimage' became a barely audible murmur of space and silences as she struggled to say her farewell to the world."

To promote *Lancelot*, a novel an interview had brought about, Percy sat for a series of interviews, answering the obvious questions. Lancelot Lamar (he explained) represented the "broad-sword tradition"; the confession device came from Camus's *The Fall*; the novel was an "upside-down religious novel," in which the protagonist must take the downward path to find the way out.

To conclude the process, Percy interviewed himself. In "Questions They Never Asked Me," which ran in *Esquire*, he contorted his usual answers, turning his public image upside down. Did he care to comment on his own writing? "I can't stand to think about it." How about the literature of the South? "I'm fed up with the subject of Southern writing. Northern writing, too, for that matter. I'm also fed up with questions about the state of the novel, alienation, the place of the artist in American society, race relations, the Old South." How about the longtime hospitability of the South to the serious writer? "Well, I've heard about that, the storytelling tradition, sense of identity, tragic dimension, community, history, and so forth. But I was never quite sure what it meant. In fact, I'm not sure that the opposite is not the case." It was a recanting of one of his most cherished positions. The literature of the South, he now averred, was not informed by a common legacy of defeat. In truth, the South had no literary community or tradition, and that was all to the good. "It is the very absence of a tradition that makes for great originals like Faulkner and O'Connor and Poe," he declared, and the less the writer shared with other writers the better. It left him alone like Robinson Crusoe on his island, able to make a fresh start.

He was trying to stay a step ahead of the scholars, the new Catholic exegetes. His faith, he insisted, was not about order or community or permanence. It was an act of desperation, made true by his stubbornness in maintaining it. Why believe? "What else is there?" Why not scientific humanism? "It's not good enough." Why isn't it? "This life is too much trouble, far too strange, to arrive at the end of it and have to answer, 'Scientific humanism.' That won't do. A poor show. Life is a mystery, love is a delight. Therefore I take it as axiomatic that one should settle for nothing less than the infinite mystery and the infinite delight, i.e., God. In fact I demand it. I refuse to settle for anything less."

It sounds like an existentialist answer, offered in defiance of a shallow and indifferent world; but it is the answer of an eminence, who considers it his due to have his life make sense.

Day struggled to walk across her room, which "feels like the Russian tenement in Dostoevsky's 'The Honest Thief,' where people lived in corners." Even at its most strenuous, her life had been a Tolstoyan adventure, a hard road but one that she had chosen to take. Now she was diminished, suffering against her will. Her limbs were tired. Her heart was weak.

She listened to opera on the radio and watched the nightly news. In the summer of 1978, Catholicism was all over the television: the announcement that Paul VI was dead; the cardinals going to Rome to assemble in conclave at the Sistine Chapel; the election of Albino Luciani, the first pope to come from the working class; his inauguration as John Paul I; the reports of his sudden death; the cardinals en route and in conclave again; another election, and another inauguration—of Karol Wojtyla, or John Paul II, the first non-Italian in half a millennium. All the news reports mentioned the new John Paul's youth—he was fifty-eight—and his athletic good health.

Day liked to quote a retreat master who told the people in his care that they should start stripping themselves of worldly cares as soon as possible, because, no matter who we are, in the end "we shall be stripped"—stripped of health, wealth, body, breath, and, finally, of life itself.

Robert Coles's profile of Percy ran in the New Yorker in October 1978, five years after it was written. Percy had spent those five years trying to shake his reputation as an earnest searcher after life's meaning. Now he saw his search recounted reverently and at great length: two parts, twenty-five thousand words, complete with charcoal sketch. "I am having the uncomfortable feeling of having been at last stuck in my slot—as a 'Christian existentialist,' " he told Shelby Foote. "I hear sighs of relief all over: now that they know what I am, they don't have to worry about me." He thought of writing "a mean nasty novel" to fix things.

His two ideas for fiction since completing *Lancelot* had been intriguing but odd. One was for a Swiftian science-fiction satire, the other for "a dreamlike novel exploring all the fuckups, options, and delights" of the New Age. But *Lancelot* had not sold well, and Percy thought he knew why: it was a dramatic monologue, whereas "the reader still likes a once-upon-a-time third-person-singular story and he may be right." He wound up taking one of Foote's suggestions and writing "a novel type novel" about "the doings of Will Barrett after he leaves Santa Fe," and he finished a first draft shortly after the *New Yorker* profile appeared.

No novel ever demanded a sequel less than the *The Last Gentleman*; it is doubtful that even Percy himself had wondered what had happened to Will Barrett and Kitty Vaught. Yet he set to finding out, plunking them down in North Carolina, epicenter of the New South. They had not married after all, and now, in middle age, they sidled up to each other romantically. Kitty had grown bold sexually and spoke like the secretary in *The Moviegoer*, calling Barrett "son" and "big buddy." Barrett had become a corporate lawyer but still suffered from "depression, fugues, certain delusions, sexual dysfunction alternating between impotence and satyriasis, hypertension," and "inappropriate longing." He pondered suicide like Sutter Vaught in *The Last Gentleman*; he huddled on the floor like Tom More in *Love in the Ruins*, having been shot at.

Percy was openly repeating himself. The question is why. He was just writing along, he told Foote, when a middle-aged character turned into Will Barrett. He may have found once again that he could not imagine new characters. He may have honestly seen a sequel as a way forward, a classic Kierkegaardian return, a visit to old territory as a different person and a different writer.

The exploits of Will and Kitty are scarcely more compelling in *The Second Coming* than they were the first time. Yet Percy really is a different—a better—writer than he was. The dialogue crackles. The action ticks forward relentlessly. The descriptive prose is sometimes precisely, sometimes spectacularly eloquent (a toothache is described as "such a pain in an upper canine that every heartbeat feels like a hot ice pick shoved straight up into the brain"). The text rolls along with a wave of purpose behind it, an unwarranted vigor, a life drive. The main characters are thin, the story slight, but in this, his fifth novel, Percy is writing wholly as a novelist.

Two set pieces in the text, unconnected with Will and Kitty's romance, make the novel worthwhile. Halfway through the novel Barrett decides to conduct a test, which he explains in an "outlandish" letter to Sutter Vaught, who is now working with paraplegics in a veterans' hospital in New Mexico. "For once in my life I know what is what, what I know, what I don't know, what needs to be done, and what I shall do," Barrett explains. "If you remember, it was your constant complaint that I was forever looking to you for 'all the answers.' . . . It should at least please you to know that I have at last understood you. One must arrive at one's own answers." His question is this: Is there a God? To get an answer, he will go down into a cave in the Great Smokies—a cave he used to explore as a boy—and live there for thirty days, without food or drink, waiting for a sign. If he lives, he declares, there must be a God. If he dies, "people will know why I died: because there is no sign. The cause of my death will be either his nonexistence or his refusal to manifest himself, which comes to the same thing as far as we are concerned."

The thirty pages that follow are some of the best Percy ever wrote, as Barrett follows a scarcely remembered path, finds a rocky chamber, lays out his supplies (sleeping pills and tin foil), waits upon the Lord, and then comes to his senses (that ice-pick toothache) and clambers out. He is clearly crazy, and yet so powerful is the writing, so vivid the obsession, so perfect the fit between a biblical desert and an old boyhood haunt, that the reader comes to believe that Barrett's test will actually give him the evidence he wants. "I've got you both, God-seekers and suicides," he says. "I've got you all, God, Jews, Christians, unbelievers, Romans, Jutes, Angles, Saxons, Yankees, rebs, blacks, tigers. . . . One of you has to cough it up. There is no way I cannot find out."

Barrett's sign comes in the form of a young woman who nurses him back to health. Allison Huger has "severe free-floating anxiety." When she arrives in town she has just had shock therapy, which has made her an amnesiac, and she is reconstructing her life from instructions she wrote out before the procedure. So she makes a new home in an abandoned greenhouse and follows the tasks of modern life with ritual precision, buying groceries and the like. Allie, it turns out, is Kitty Vaught's daughter, but the plot twist is superfluous. She is present in the novel as a New Age pilgrim, a witness to the strangeness of the everyday. Caught in the present, affectless, lacking direction, benignly alienated from her surroundings, living life secondhand from a list written with a ballpoint pen, she is a more convincing pilgrim than Percy's usual male philosopher-protagonists, a person who truly seems to be looking for something and finding her way one step at a time.

Like Simeon in the Gospel story, Day was prepared to die, having seen a sign of salvation. She ate, slept, prayed, worshipped, waited, and made notes in her journal:

> Woke up this morning with these lines haunting me: "Joyous, I lay waste the day." Let all those who seek Thee be glad in Thee, and let such as love Thy salvation, say always, the Lord be praised.

> Beautiful cards are sent in with donations. One came from an Eskimo cooperative in Canada. I have been keeping the card as a bookmark in my Bible. "The world will be saved by beauty," Dostoevsky wrote.

> There was a mini-earthquake in Brooklyn, Staten Island, and New Jersey. Why was not Manhattan Island affected? What a thought? Unimaginable to think of those two, fantastic World Trade Center towers swaying with a sudden jarring of what we have come to think of as solid earth beneath our feet.

> Yet I sat one day in a rocking chair, fifty years ago, nursing my tiny daughter in front of a large mirror which hung on the wall in my beach bungalow on Staten Island, and suddenly saw the mirror begin to quiver, as though a train or a truck (neither of which could have been within miles of us) had suddenly passed the little house, making it tremble.

Flannery O'Connor's last book was published in March 1979. *The Habit of Being*—617 pages—is also her longest book; coming out of nowhere, as it did, it astonished even those who had known her. No misanthrope, no recluse, no fanatic, O'Connor, it turned out, had corresponded widely and reasonably. Sally Fitzgerald's image of her as a phoenix rising from the ashes seems at first a friend's fond hyperbole, but by the end of the book it is apt. With the letters she carboned and set next to the typewriter O'Connor had painted a self-portrait akin to the one she had painted for Erik Langkjaer. Now through them she was brought to life again, as if for the first time.

Percy sent a copy of *The Habit of Being* to Shelby Foote: the "minor-minor writer" now had a book as formidable as any Foote had ever written. As with *Mystery and Manners,* sending it was Percy's way of asserting who he was and where he stood. This time, though, he would hear no remarks to the contrary. "I attach great importance to it—a truly remarkable lady, laconic, funny, tough, smart, hard-headed, no-nonsense, the very best of US, South and Catholicism," he told Foote, as if to have the last word in the argument before it even got started.

Himself, he was done with *The Second Coming* and unsure what to write next. "Strange, having finished this novel and having a free choice of what to do," he told Foote. "All I know is that I don't want to write another novel now, maybe ever. Writing a novel is an incredible ordeal, which gets worse and worse, requiring all manner of alternating despairs, piss-offs, deaths and rebirths, too much for an aging infirm novelist."

He hardly needed to tell Foote how hard writing a novel could be, and the echo of O'Connor—"Writing a novel is a terrible experience," she had said, "during which the hair often falls out and the teeth decay"—is obvious and gratuitous, as if he were speaking to posterity.

Early in 1980 he settled on a work of semiotics aimed at the television generation, and his plan for the book grew more and more ambitious. It would be a distillation of his life's work in the philosophy of language. It would be his diagnosis of the postmodern person, a creature condemned to ever-greater estrangement from itself. And it would be a compendium of his illiberal thoughts on "some of the familiar oddities and anomalies of modern times, e.g., the rise of boredom and suicide amid the good life, the longing of people for UFOs and trivial magic, the eroticization of society." It would be called *Novum Organum,* after Francis Bacon. To explain it, he sent Foote a preambular passage oddly akin to one of Peter Maurin's "Easy Essays":

NOVUM ORGANUM
or
Glimmerings of the New Science,
Especially that Branch of the Science which
Pertains to the Self, to Your Self, and most
Especially What to do with Yourself

Since Most Likely You do not Presently Know,
Since the Present-Day Science, the Old Science
Cannot tell You, has no Way of Knowing,
Cannot in Fact Utter a single Word about Yourself
Considered as an Individual Self,
Even Though It, the Old Science, can tell you a
Great Deal about everything else.

"It is strange: I feel as though I were just starting out," he told Foote. He predicted that it would be his most important book yet.

"Transit strike has ended," Day wrote in her journal that April. "It was very exciting to watch its coverage on television—the whole city moving to work on foot, through rain part of the time, moving over bridges from borough to borough."

She passed the summer rereading her favorite novels and watching reruns of old movies on TV. There had been three deaths in her family that year: her great-grandson, her sister, and her sister-in-law, who was staying with her at the apartment on East Fifteenth Street when Peter Maurin first presented himself there.

She wished she were not confined to her room, but traveling by bus again: "You feel you are really seeing the country, as you speed along the highway, over plain and mountain."

On November 8 she turned eighty-three. A foe of the New Deal because it forfeited the duty of charity to Holy Mother the State, she now saw Ronald Reagan elected president. Already Catholic Workers were protesting U.S. military policy in Central America.

Three weeks later, November 29, 1980, a Saturday evening, she died, after watching a television news report about an earthquake in Sicily. An earthquake, Ignazio Silone had written, "achieves what the law promises but does not in practice maintain—the equality of all men."

As her body was dressed and laid out in the chapel on the ground floor at Maryhouse, the pilgrimage to the Catholic Worker began.

By midnight Monday a multitude had come to Maryhouse to pay their respects, the way people had come to the Houses of Hospitality for soup and bread and coffee since the Depression: Catholic Workers, social workers, migrant workers, the unemployed; addicts, alcoholics, anarchists; Protestants, Jews, agnostics, and members of the press; the devout and the strident and the simply curious, there to see what a saint looked like.

The funeral was to be held at the Church of the Nativity on Second Avenue, a charmlessly functional postmodern church around the corner from Maryhouse.

On Tuesday morning, then, Dorothy Day set out one last time. The coffin, built by a friend, was shouldered down the stairs by six of her grandchildren. A crowd of people had gathered in the street, and they formed a ragged procession, spilling out into the avenue.

The archbishop stood waiting on the church steps. The coffin was borne past him, through the doorway, and up the aisle, and the funeral Mass began, said by a priest of the parish.

She was ushered gently into posterity, with remarks that now appear on her books like inscriptions on a monument. The *New York Times* described her as "a nonviolent social radical of luminous personality as well as a pious Roman Catholic." In *Commonweal* she was called "the most significant, interesting, and influential person in the history of American Catholicism."

She was buried on Staten Island, far enough from the city, it happened, to ensure that most of the people who sought to commune with her memory in the coming years would not visit her grave, but would go to St. Joseph's House instead.

During a visit to St. Joseph's House, one of Robert Coles's students had asked her: *What is the meaning of your life? How would you like to be remembered?* She had replied at length, apologizing for her "rambling, disconnected thinking." She said she had tried to treat the stranger as Christ: speaking kindly to the guests, making sure they were well fed, earning their respect. And she hoped she had lived a life worthy of the great books she had read. "I'd like people to say that 'she really did love those books!' You know, I'm always telling people to read Dickens or Tolstoi, or read Orwell, or read Silone. I could be one of your teachers—though I'm not a great one for analyzing those novels; I want to live by them! That's the 'meaning of my life'—to live up to the moral vision of the Church, and of some of my favorite writers . . . to take those artists and novelists to heart, and live up to their wisdom: a lot of it came from Jesus, as you probably know, because

Dickens and Dostoevski and Tolstoi kept thinking of Jesus themselves all through their lives."

Now Walker Percy was well and truly on his own, the last gentleman of Catholic writing in America, a school unto himself.

In a sense, he was less alone than ever. Scholars trod the path to his house in the woods and badgered him to appear at their conferences. Librarians at his alma mater appraised his papers for purchase (estimated value: thirty thousand dollars). Lewis Lawson, author of the first scholarly essay about his work, proposed to write his biography.

He had no real peers, however. The "brilliant crew" of Catholic novelists Garry Wills had anointed in the *New York Times* had failed to deliver on their promise. J. F. Powers had stopped writing. Caroline Gordon had died in 1977, so grotesque in her orthodoxy that she insisted wives, whom Our Lord after all had commanded to obey their husbands, ought not to be allowed to vote.

The exception was John Kennedy Toole. *A Confederacy of Dunces* had been published within months of *The Second Coming*. Early in 1981 both books were nominated for the PEN/Faulkner Award. Then, in April—in a first for a book by a dead author—*A Confederacy of Dunces* was awarded the Pulitzer Prize in fiction. (*The Second Coming* was a finalist.) The prize made the Toole book a major best-seller, with more than half a million copies in print.

Percy took note. A couple of years earlier he had told Foote he was "convinced that times were never worse for novelists in the sense that somehow the straight narrative form is in default and so one must resort to all manner of tricks, cons, blandishments, obfuscations, curses, lies, jokes, animadversions." Yet he still yearned to write the big book, and although he didn't say so, *A Confederacy of Dunces* was the proof that it was possible: a straightforward novel could still work as art, win a prize, and find a public.

For a while, aloneness suited Percy. It squared with his image of himself as a solitary artist at work. In a sense, it seems to have set him free of comparison with his predecessors. For the two books he wrote in the 1980s are his least traditional and conventionally "literary." They are light, prospective, indifferent to influence, defiant of posterity. They confront the present and the present-day reader directly. The problem with most contemporary philosophy, he liked to say, was that it just didn't apply—it didn't capture what it felt like to be alive in the United States in the twentieth century. Now he sought to put that feeling in words himself.

Lost in the Cosmos is a "thought experiment": a counterblast to the messages that he heard society putting out. It is a philosophical grab bag written as a multiple-choice test about the self. For twenty years he had embedded questions sideways in his work, posing them indirectly. Now the work *was* the questions. What is the self? Why is the self so unhappy? Why are so many creative types unhappy people? Why is self-knowledge so elusive in an age enslaved to the self?

To write the book as a series of test questions was an ingenious strategem, grounded in a mode of knowing that had become ubiquitous in American life and expressive of Percy's notion of the shrinking self. Ingenious, too, was the focus on the self, at once the obsession of the age and the point on which his views diverged from society's most sharply. The book itself is airless and wearying, however. As he poses questions about the "amnesiac self" and the "fearful self"—"Why the Self Wants to Get Rid of Itself"; "Why the Self Is So Afraid of Being Found Out"—Percy hectors the reader sarcastically until the book becomes not a test so much as a trap, a test only the all-knowing author can hope to pass.

Lost in the Cosmos—subtitled *The Last Self-Help Book*—is also a spoof of self-help books, and of *Cosmos*, the public television series about the universe. Like them it is willfully self-obsolescent, stuffed with references to fads and trends and now-forgotten celebrities. It sold well on publication and for some years thereafter, but it is not a popular book; it is a frontal assault on its audience. In his novels, and in the essays published as *The Message in the Bottle*, Percy had artfully sketched a recognizable postmodern self—fractious, confused, a pilgrim searching for a path and a destination alike—and had led the reader to identify with it. This time he reached out of the book and declared the reader bored, lonely, phony, and trapped in a meaningless existence. The reader winds up silently insisting otherwise.

In the 1970s Percy had come to identify strongly with Chekhov, like him a doctor and a "diagnostic" writer, a strange pathologist of the modern age. Now, however, as his seventh decade approached, he found that his interlocutor—once and for all—was Flannery O'Connor.

Two decades after her death, he still spoke of her as if she had just left the upper room in New Orleans where they had met. Her essays lurked behind his. She cropped up in his conversations, in which he made her out to be a "dear friend." His agon with her was over: much as he admired her, he recognized that she was a different kind of Catholic writer than he had become, and that this was all right.

A talk he had given in Georgia in 1978 was his update of O'Connor's essay on "The Regional Writer": Whereas she and her peers had cherished the South for being unlike the rest of the country—had "traded on the very exoticness, the uniqueness of the Southern phenomenon"—he recognized that the "so-called Southern renascence" was over; the South's problems were now America's problems. An interview with two scholars in 1981 turned into a long exchange about O'Connor's work, with Percy admitting that "I'm not sure I always understand that the Holy Spirit is working in the denouement of the story" and unwittingly putting his own theories about man as *homo viator* and the novel as "the Judeo-Christian form par excellence" into O'Connor's mouth.

The next year, he turned the first annual Eudora Welty Lecture into a Flannery O'Connor lecture, picking up their conversation where it had so abruptly been cut off. He saw the New South as paradoxical, a place where middle-class prosperity and conformity, far from pushing religion to the margins, had called forth a new breed of fundamentalists, who could be found on TV in every living room, dressed in the gray flannel suit of the Northern businessman and commuter—a state of affairs that presented complications for the Southern novelist.

"You have to envy a writer like Flannery O'Connor, who saw the enemy clearly, namely a certain sort of triumphant humanist, and who could discern the orthodox virtues of backwoods preachers and assorted nuts and murderers," he told the audience, and crisply added, "She knew where the devils were, but if she were beating the same devils now, she would find herself in some strange company, on the same side as Jerry Falwell and Jimmy Swaggart."

Against her timeless certainties he set his own more provisional ideals. His kind of novelist sought to dramatize his own uncertainty. This novelist directed the reader's attention to "fault lines in the terrain" and pointed out not "how awful the happenings are but how peculiar it is that people don't seem to notice how awful the happenings are." And this novelist took care never to be too confident that his alienation from society was a kind of prophecy. "Poets and novelists seem to be possessed by a whole separate coven of witches, demons, terrors, and premonitions, of which the general population seems by and large oblivious," he remarked. "Either one is crazy and the other sane, or the former has gone crazy for reasons which the latter has not caught on to. And, to tell you the truth, I am still not sure which is right."

While Percy's essays can be read as a series of glosses on O'Connor's, replies from posterity, it was with a novel that he turned her into a true conversation partner.

In the lecture in Georgia he had declared, "What engages the novelist's attention now is not the Snopeses or the denizens of Tobacco Road or Flannery O'Connor's half-made backwoods preachers or a black underclass. It is rather the very people who have overcome these particular predicaments and find themselves living happily ever after in their comfortable exurban houses and condominiums. Or is it happily ever after?" Now he sought to answer that question with a story.

He was sixty-seven years old when he began *The Thanatos Syndrome* and nearly seventy when he finished it, but you'd never know it from the writing. It is the most vigorous and ambitious of any of his novels, including *The Moviegoer*, and although it is not a perfect book, it gains its power from the sense that the author is onto something; it has what the protagonist calls "the heavy, secret, lidded, almost sexual excitement of the scientific hit."

Like *The Second Coming*, it brings back an old character, this time Dr. Tom More from *Love in the Ruins*. More is now a doctor working for the government. In the opening pages he pays a house call and offers a diagnosis, adding up his observations. Female patients acting funny (speaking in fragments, making bold come-ons); a nuclear power plant on the outskirts of town; too much sodium in the water supply; an old colleague who has argued for adding sodium to the water, like fluoride, because it affects the brain in such a way that it reduces violent crime: as More puts the different elements together, Percy's lifelong concerns—science, medicine, religion, morality, the Old South, the selfless future—converge in the story of a public-health quandary in the bogues and swamps of southern Louisiana. And as the doped-water crisis leads back to a school for deviant sexuality run by an ex-priest and a former nun, they fit together so obviously that one feels that this is the kind of book—it might be called a medico-philosophical thriller—that Percy should have been writing all along. Science, a rhetorical bogeyman in Percy's previous books, is now vital to the story. Morality, represented thus far as an Old World quality, a thing of the past, now bears strongly on the question of whether and why the water system is being poisoned. Dr. More, whose medical practice was purely symbolic in *Love in the Ruins*, is a real physician—seeing patients, sitting on review boards, in touch with the Centers for Disease Control. Movies are not merely a theme—they suggest the structure of the book, which owes less to Percy's other books than to movies like *The China Syndrome*. The prose is sober, akin to speech, and laconically wise, always serving the story. The picture of the New South is full of paradoxes: the old slave quarters More's wife has sold as condominiums, the nuclear reactor by the Mississippi—"Except for the cooling tower of Grand Mer looming directly opposite and flying its plume of steam like Mt. St. Helens," More observes, "it could be the same quaint lordly river of Mark Twain, its foul waters all gold and rose in the sunset. There's even a stern-wheeler, the new *Robert E. Lee*, huffing upstream, hauling tourists to the plantations."

The biggest breakthrough is Percy's discovery of plot, as significant a discovery as the discovery of the present tense in *The Moviegoer*. There is no telling whether he set out to write a thriller and supplied a plot or found plot inexorably leading him forward. Either way, one can feel a broad and felicitous territory opening up before him as he submits to the discipline of making the parts depend on one another.

The Thanatos Syndrome is also Percy's only explicitly Catholic novel— more so than the one said to be the adventures of a bad Catholic. More is still a bad Catholic. "I am only a Catholic in the remotest sense of the word—I haven't given religion two thoughts or been to Mass for years," Dr. More reports. Yet he *is* a Catholic, and the power of vestigial belief is Percy's point. In one episode, More's friend Father Rinaldo Smith confronts him about abortion: "You are a member of the first generation of doctors in the history of medicine to turn their backs on the oath of Hippocrates and kill millions of old useless people, unborn children, born malformed children, all for the good of mankind—and to do so without a single murmur from one of you." More sees the analogy the priest is drawing: that putting heavy sodium into the water is akin to abortion and euthanasia—an act of social engineering which might lead to genocide.

Percy made Father Smith a complex character, not to be taken without qualification. He is an alcoholic. He has an unseemly obsession with the "sign" represented by the Jews, and as it turns out he is spooked by the memory of his own behavior during a spell in Germany in the years before the world war, which, after forty years of secrecy, he describes to More in a long set piece—the priest confessing to the physician, not the other way around. Dissolute, he withdraws to a fire tower in the forest, where he drinks and prays and surveys the horizon.

Father Smith is Percy's most vivid character since Binx Bolling. It may be that Percy was thinking of Jack English, who drank too much and had a murky war history he didn't like to discuss. It may be that he was recalling Thomas Merton, who surveyed the world from his hermitage with a bottle of bourbon at his side. But in depicting this odd prophet, who can see long distances from the fire tower, Percy (Patrick Samway has pointed out) had one person uppermost in his mind. Father Smith argues that the problem of contemporary life is that morality is based on so-called tenderness, not on justice or a sound idea of the human person or the dignity due the least of us. In the tower, with a mysterious stranger looking on, he asks More:

"Do you know where tenderness always leads?"
"No, where?" I ask, watching the stranger with curiosity.
"To the gas chamber."

The remark—which is woven through the book—is a direct quote from Flannery O'Connor's essay about Mary Ann Long. In the absence of faith, O'Connor proposed, "we govern by tenderness. It is a tenderness which, long since cut off from the person of Christ, is wrapped in theory. When tenderness is detached from the source of tenderness, its logical outcome is terror. It ends in forced-labor camps and in the fumes of the gas chamber."

O'Connor had urged Percy to "make up another one." For years he had resisted, instead writing fables or dramatic monologues. At last he had obliged. The rewards were great. The publishing rights to *The Thanatos Syndrome* were placed in half a dozen countries. The publisher printed nearly sixty thousand copies of the book. After thirty years of philosophical novels and anecdotal philosophy, Percy had discovered that the best way to reach the reader—and the most direct—is to tell the reader a story.

There is one other direct way, and Percy's publisher urged it upon him. In the spring of 1987, after the book was published, Percy set out on a tour of bookstores, where the "intersubjectivity" of his fiction would come to life as he emerged from the woods to meet his public. But the tour was cut short when Percy came down with diverticulitis. He returned to Louisiana and began, once again, a summation of his philosophy.

In ten years as pope, while sponsoring solidarity in Poland, disciplining theologians in Latin America, rebuffing nuns who called for the ordination of women, John Paul II had done something of real religious importance: he had taken the image of the Church as a people on pilgrimage, the guiding metaphor of the Second Vatican Council, and had made it literal and actual, going on pilgrimage himself and so allowing countless people to go on pilgrimage along with him. Where once Catholics went to Rome to see the pope, now the pope ventured forth with them, in parks and stadiums and fields on the outskirts of town, encountering them at first hand, and vice versa, until it was unclear who had come to see whom.

In the fall of 1987 John Paul, touring America, went on pilgrimage to New Orleans. He would celebrate Mass for eighty thousand people in the Superdome, at a portable altar erected in one of the end zones.

As a prominent Catholic, Percy was given tickets, but he was ill and did not go. He wrote a piece for *America* setting out what he would say "If I Had Five Minutes with the Pope." With friendly candor, he told the pope not to worry about Catholicism in America—to lay off the Jesuits, lay off the bishops, lay off the theologians; lay off the doctors about abortion, lay off the young people, and "do what you've been doing; that is, visiting ordinary Catholics around the world, concentrating on the poor of the Third World."

It was a lark, and yet evidently it met with approval at the Vatican. At the year's end he received an invitation to become a member of the Pontifical Council for Culture, and in January 1988 he went to Rome to give a speech before a group of bishops and the pope.

This time he was altogether serious, arguing soberly that the very secularness and shallowness of America made it ready for re-evangelization. The chronicler of the adventures of a bad Catholic, the lover of bourbon and sass and slang, was giving advice to His Holiness. A photograph of the two of them makes them look like counterparts, one in white, one in black, both pale and bald.

Back in Covington, Percy was facing a long run of ordinary Wednesday afternoons, as he called them. He felt ill; a doctor diagnosed what ailed him as prostate cancer and treated it promptly, but the treatments left him feeling lousy.

He was calling his new book *Contra Gentiles*, after the polemic by Thomas Aquinas, and he worked on it halfheartedly. Mainly, though, he wrote short, pointed pieces. He thought of himself as a "cranky novelist," and now he was playing the role. He wrote a letter to the *New York Times* about abortion, then a second claiming they were "suppressing dissent" by failing to publish the first. He wrote a loopy answer to the question "Why Are You a Catholic?" in which he gave all the reasons why he didn't like to explain why he was a Catholic—the whole business reminded him of the "This I Believe" bit he had satirized in *The Moviegoer*.

And yet he did answer the question of why he was a Catholic, explaining his faith as clearly as he had ever done. A couple of years earlier, introducing a book of Catholic conversion stories called *The "New" Catholics*, he had confessed that he found it hard to write about religious conversion, since faith, after all, was believed to be a gift from God. "When it comes to grace, I get writer's block," he declared, and yet among these converts he felt "immediately at home," for they were "as motley (in the old, best sense of the world) as Chaucer's pilgrims."

Now, explaining his own conversion, he defined what the Catholics of the new age would have in common. Why was he a Catholic? Because he believed that the Church's teachings are true; and because the Church, in his view, stood above and apart from the present age, which he called the age of the "theorist-consumer." In his view, the present age has no use for anything that cannot be bought and sold or theorized about. So the present age has no use for Christian faith. But the believer, he thought, should count this as an advantage, and see the present age as preferable to "Christendom," when the churches prospered. "In the old Christendom," he explained, "everyone was a Christian and hardly anyone thought twice about it. But in the present age the survivor of theory and consumption becomes a wayfarer in the desert, like St. Anthony: which is to say, open to signs."

The cancer had come back. Percy sent Shelby Foote a terse self-diagnosis: "Colon was normal, but there were masses around the aorta and along spine. Don't yet know what it is, but presumably it's metastases from prostate carcinoma or pancreatic CA. Will keep you informed."

They had been reading Chekhov stories and discussing them by mail, and now Foote sent Percy "The Bishop," in which death comes for a Russian bishop as he celebrates the Palm Sunday liturgy. Percy read the story and wrote to Foote, pointing out that, because of the skill with which the story was written, it didn't matter whether or not Chekhov was a believer.

They both knew why it had been sent. "The Bishop is in poor shape, dying in fact," Percy told Foote. His death he would conceive of as an imitation of fiction, in which he imaginatively put himself in the place of a protagonist from the past.

The conclusion of "The Bishop"—driven home by Chekhov—is that posterity is merciless, as the bishop, an eminence in life, is forgotten as soon as he is dead and buried. In his letter to Foote about the story, Percy quoted a passage in which the bishop, on his deathbed, wishes he had been "a village priest or a deacon or just a simple monk" instead.

The Benedictine abbey in Covington—St. Joseph's—had been Percy's parish church for nearly forty years. He had once hoped to move into a house near the monastery. He had gone on retreat there often. In a commencement address one spring to the monks in the small college connected with the abbey, he had confessed that he envied them their sense of calling.

As his cancer became general, he entered the Benedictine "third order." This joined him to the community formally; and it would allow for him to be buried in the graveyard behind the abbey church.

He spent some months traveling back and forth to the Mayo Clinic, in Minnesota. He resented the travel, the bother, and the humiliation of sickness. Spiritually, he felt ready to die, prepared for death by religion, and he was surprised that irreligious people didn't kill themselves.

He kept writing. He wrote a piece about the Waffle House in town, and one about "the holiness of the ordinary." After reading an article about the "Catholic imagination" in Bruce Springsteen's songs, he wrote Springsteen a fan letter, asking him about his "spiritual journey." In particular, he wanted to know about "your admiration for Flannery O'Connor. She was a dear friend of mine," he told Springsteen, "though she was a more heroic Catholic than I."

He died on May 10, 1990. Family and friends and parish priest had been visiting him for weeks. He had been self-administering morphine from a pump at his bedside. He had received the last rites.

He was buried out of the abbey church two days later, with two archbishops presiding. As his Uncle Will had started life wanting to be a priest, Percy ended his life, in a sense, by becoming one in his own fashion—interred near the church but independent of it, his own man after all.

He had authorized a Jesuit priest to write his biography, and the priest, Patrick Samway, organized a public memorial service at the Jesuit church on Park Avenue in New York—that "gray warren" of a city where Percy had nearly died the first time.

It was held on a weekday in October 1990, nearly five months after Percy's death. The vast church was crowded as though for Mass on Easter Sunday. Robert Giroux, editor of Percy's books, opened the proceedings, saying, "We come here today to honor the memory and the work of Walker Percy, a superb novelist, a distinguished man of letters, a witty and searching critic, a great American." Then, although the congregation already knew it, he told Percy's story.

The Life You Save May Be Your Own

What is the meaning of their lives? It is a presumptuous question, and yet one that demands to be asked. The four of them spent their lives asking such a question of themselves and indirectly of their readers, inviting us to ponder the meaning of our lives through theirs. Their story, which is the story of this book, would not be complete without an attempt at an answer.

Not long ago, then, I went on pilgrimage to the places where these four writers lived and wrote, seeking further clarification of thought, or at least the opportunity to pose the question firsthand.

St. Joseph's House stands where Dorothy Day left it, at 36 East First Street in Manhattan. Maryhouse, the residence for women, is two blocks uptown. Except for the hand-painted signs over the doors, they appear to be tenement buildings like any other, dingy but dignified, encrusted in paint. Inside, the work of the movement continues. The newspaper still publishes a mix of articles about war and peace, hospitality and spirituality, and it still costs a penny a copy, though Catholic Workers can no longer be found selling it on the sidewalks. The house still looks the way it did when Day was in charge, furnished with beat-up chairs and a cast-iron stove out of a Grimm tale. A pot of coffee brews perpetually.

It is the surroundings that have changed. In the years since Day's death the neighborhood where she hoped to build "a new society within the shell of the old" has become one of the more attractive—and expensive—in downtown Manhattan. Art galleries and boutiques have replaced the junk shops and flophouses. One-bedroom apartments rent for several thousand dollars a month. Restaurants on East First Street serve four-dollar coffees and ten-dollar bowls of soup. The new East Village has been shoehorned into the old Lower East Side, and, inevitably, the poor of the neighborhood have been displaced. The Catholic Workers used to serve three hundred meals a day; they now serve half as many, and on Saturday, a day that once drew new volunteers, St. Joseph's House is often closed altogether.

The changes in the neighborhood, together with Day's foresight in purchasing the buildings, present the Catholic Workers at St. Joseph's House with a dilemma. Should they protest and organize in response to gentrification, establish a satellite house in the South Bronx or East New York, or stay where they are as a witness to poverty amid plenty? Should they stay or should they go? Although the two buildings are worth several million dollars in the real-estate market, the movement's refusal to sit on principal, amass working capital, or collect interest makes selling them unattractive, and their association with Day has made them sacred spaces, the "motherhouses" of the movement. It is unlikely that they could be sold without a process of "clarification of thought" that might tear the movement apart.

Some of the Catholic Workers have thrown themselves into direct action, leading peaceable campaigns against U.S. intervention in Central America and against the long economic sanctions on Iraq. Early in the war on terrorism, a group of them could be found Saturday mornings in Union Square, site of the movement's first outing, holding up a bedsheet painted with the words AN EYE FOR AN EYE MAKES THE WHOLE WORLD BLIND.

Meanwhile, a religious order in Chicago has called for Day's canonization as a saint. Their campaign began shortly after her death. Prayer cards were printed. Articles were published. A Catholic film company produced a movie about her early years, depicting her as "a Mother Teresa with a past."

The Catholic Worker movement reacted possessively. One of Day's granddaughters called the proposal "sick." Catholic Worker communities printed agitated articles in their newspapers. Father Daniel Berrigan wrote a letter, declaring that the money spent on canonization should be used to feed and house poor people instead. "Her spirit haunts us in the violated faces of the homeless in New York," he wrote. "Can you imagine her portrait, all gussied up, unfurled from above the high altar of St. Peter's?"

Many can. On the centenary of Day's birth—November 8, 1997—a Catholic Worker's recollections of Day were read into the *Congressional Record* as a tribute. The same week, the archbishop of New York, Cardinal John O'Connor, formally initiated the "cause" for Day's canonization. "If anybody in our time can be called a saint, she can," he said.

Most of the Catholic Workers support the canonization process. Those who don't are fearful that the Church's saint-making bureaucrats will stress her regret over her abortion, not her opposition to war of any kind; that they will evict her from the underworld of flophouses, rallies, and jails and recast her as the Patron Saint of Soup Kitchens, a kindhearted woman with a touch of anarchism on the side. Thus her sanctity will be wrested from those most committed to emulating it, leaving the Catholic Workers with St. Joseph's House but without their foundress, who would suddenly belong to everybody.

Unexpectedly, the Catholic Worker movement has grown since Day's death, and there are now several thousand Catholic Workers in 150 Houses of Hospitality. Some of the Catholic Workers are fervently Catholic, some grudgingly so, or by casual association. Some see Day as a saint, and make a practice of asking, "What would Dorothy do?" Others see her chiefly as a bred-in-the-bone American radical—a pacifist, a woman, a layperson, a journalist, a mother and grandmother—and look to her less as an exemplar than a worthy precursor. The Catholic Worker House in Houston (among others) combines the two, showing hospitality to illegal aliens on the one hand and publishing long-out-of-print "resources of the Catholic Worker" on the other.

Beyond the Catholic Worker, many people follow Day's example improvisationally. A laywoman ministers to prostitutes, helping them to reorient their lives. An activist attorney files lawsuits opposing predatory lending practices in poor neighborhoods. In parochial schools and Catholic Charities offices, older women keep her spirit alive at their desks. The members of a New York volunteer group, in a litany to the "saints of our city," pray for her intercession.

Now as ever, Dorothy Day is a person who inspires imitation, who makes others want to live the way she did. Many have changed their lives at her prompting. She, however, saw her own life as an imitation of Christ, and liked to say that the saint is a person whose life would not make sense if God did not exist. Something is lost when she is merely venerated, whether by Catholic Workers or by the sponsors of her sainthood. She meant for her life to point beyond herself—to God, and to the poor people among us; to ourselves and to the wider world, which alike always need reforming.

When Thomas Merton went to Gethsemani on retreat in 1941, the first thing he saw, arriving, was "a steeple that shone like silver in the moonlight, growing into sight from behind a rounded knoll." Today the first thing you see is the late-model floodlights over the parking lot, which is full of cars, like the lot outside a suburban high school on game night.

No doubt the monastery has changed considerably. It was already changing when Merton was alive. But the strongest impression you get, entering the place, is of how extraordinary his imagination must have been to see it the way he saw it—as the center of the universe, a stray shard of medieval France, a Kentucky equivalent of an outpost of prayer in the Himalayas. In winter, at least, the surroundings are nearly blank. The monastery itself is not a shining city on a hill or a fastness against the world outside, but a kind of industrial plant for religious practice. The arched gate of entry is gone, and the carved block that struck Merton so powerfully—GOD ALONE—is now embedded in a side wall, a monument rather than a command.

Inside the abbey church, Mass is beginning. The celebrant says, "Let us pray." The music is standard-issue Spirit of Vatican II. The brutalist architecture, now four decades old, no longer looks startling, just incomplete. The monks are arrayed in a horseshoe shape behind the stone altar; many—perhaps a third—are parked in wheelchairs or have aluminum walkers set before them. They are Merton's contemporaries. But the center of vitality during the Mass, once the rows of choir stalls where the monks chanted in synchrony, is now the separate visitors' area in the rear of the church, which is full of retreatants and worshippers from nearby towns.

Retreats are still crucial to the life of Gethsemani, as they were when Merton first visited the place. Today, however, far fewer of the retreatants come to stay. The retreatants, in many cases, are not Catholics, particularly since the Dalai Lama paid a visit in 1997, and the Trappist retreat is a discrete religious experience, intense and self-contained.

The monk who was Merton's secretary in his last months, Brother Patrick, has arranged an excursion to the hermitage, and after Mass he emerges in mufti—a cheerful Irish Catholic in plaid shirt and slacks—and expertly pilots a pickup truck up a snowy hill. The hermitage looks just as it does in the photographs: broad porch, sloping roof, miniature smokestack. A

Brother Placid emerges, a man in his early thirties, tall and lean, wearing chinos and a hooded sweatshirt, and proffers a cold hand. He has just finished a week's retreat at the hermitage; later in the day, another monk will take his place.

Brother Patrick has given a great many tours of the place, and he points out its features: the carved wooden altar, the smoke-stained icons, the framed dedication from Paul VI to "il eremita Thomas Merton," a Jerusalem Bible left forlorn on an empty shelf.

The most striking appurtenances are two large plastic water jugs, empty and set in the doorway, ready for Brother Placid to tote back to the monastery. Each of the jugs is marked MERTON'S H_2O. Decades after he last dwelled there, the hermitage is still named after him with an easy familiarity. While he was there, he was Father Louis, a Trappist monk like all the rest. Now that he is gone, he is Thomas Merton, and the hermitage is MERTON'S forever.

A few years ago a peace activist published the journal he had kept during a retreat at the hermitage, turning the experience into a dialogue with Merton about the vocation of peacemaking. That is the approach taken by Merton's readers generally. His books allow us to gain entry to his hermitage, so to speak, to venture forth with him into the cloister or the woods or the ideal monastery of his imaginings, and to retreat there awhile in the company of a "spiritual master."

He invited this approach to his work, but he knew its dangers. When his journals were published twenty-five years after his death, Volume 6, his account of his romance with Margie, was presented as the most revealing; but perhaps the most telling passage in the seven volumes is about "ex-Fr. R. from Georgia, apostate after twelve years." This ex-Fr. R. had written to Merton to say that the strength of Merton's faith was what had made him become a monk and had kept him a monk all those years. Merton was enraged. "This model religious never really believed in God—as he has at last discovered. And a good thing that he has, for he has now taken the first step towards believing. He entered the monastery on somebody else's faith and lived there on somebody else's faith and when he finally had to face the fact that what was required was his own faith he collapsed. As many others could, or will, collapse when they find out how they stand."

Those words are as angry as anything Merton ever wrote. His anger, and his suspicion that ex-Fr. R. was only one of many such admirers, suggests how great his concern was. He was afraid that his writing legitimized other people's bad faith. The meaning of his life was to seek God and to urge others to go and do likewise, to describe for others the places where God might be met; and yet he knew that his gift of radical identification with others, and his way of inspiring others to identify with him, could lead his readers to see him as a surrogate believer—lead us to bury our unbelief in his belief, to remain religious novices sitting humbly in the presence of the master.

An hour's walk in the French Quarter puts *The Moviegoer* and the essays that led up to it in a different, a local, light. The alienation Walker Percy described is the everyday atmosphere here, where the real and the phony, the beautiful and the tacky, the antique and the ephemeral mingle as nowhere else in America.

Jackson Square is deserted. Inside the cathedral there is a warning sign— CATHEDRAL VISITORS ARE NOT TO GO ABOUT THE CHURCH WITHOUT A GUIDE—but there are no guides in sight this morning. Outside, on St. Peter Street, the tourist emporiums are already open for business in the ground floors of the old houses: Reverend Zombie's Voodoo Shop, the Cigar Factory, the Fatted Calf, the Velvet Dog. One saloon advertises a 3-for-1 Happy Hour all day long.

Past the weather-beaten doors of Preservation Hall the street changes. Suddenly the dwellings are low and impermanent, antebellum tinderboxes. The street runs long out toward the horizon; the sky is close. The windows are shuttered. There is nobody around. It might be the main street in a frontier town, or the movie set for such a street in Hollywood.

Covington is a different place altogether, just as Percy said it was. It is not quite the nonplace he described, though. The little town across Lake Ponchartrain, the "backwater of a backwater," is now an ordinary thriving suburb, with fast-food outlets and muffler shops lining the route from the causeway into town. The main street is now the Historic District. The muffalata on the passenger seat might have come from another country.

Percy owned three houses here over the years. The first is a wooden structure hidden from the road by trees and Spanish moss. The second is a brick English château, symmetrical down to the double chimneys—a new-money château, Lancelot Lamar might have called it. Alongside it is the gabled "Cajun cottage" where Percy lived the last years of his life. Inside, a fire roars in the grate. Mrs. Percy is watching the Weather Channel, tracking a coming storm. She mentions her husband only upon passing a wall of family photographs, remarking that his accomplishment isn't much appreciated in Covington. There was a plan to name the high school after him, but it didn't work out: a teacher blocked it, whereupon one of Percy's brothers challenged him to a duel.

St. Joseph's Abbey is a few minutes' drive away, a blond brick church with a cemetery behind it, a thicket of martial silver crosses. Night is falling, and the only way to make out who is buried where is to drive the car up close and leave the headlights on. The marker for Walker Percy gives his name and dates, that is all.

Here, now, it is easy to see why he wanted to be buried behind the monastery. For one thing, the setting is a perfect blend of Southern and Catholic: the church, the crusader crosses, the Spanish moss, the trees gothically silhouetted against the sky. For another, a monk's life and death are the opposite of the eminence which, he knew, would pursue him in death as it had in life.

In *Lost in the Cosmos* Percy described reading a piece about "Fifty Ways to Make a Coffee Table" in a house-and-garden magazine. The point of the piece was that with a little ingenuity just about any object can be turned into a coffee table—a cypress stump, a lobster trap, a cobbler's bench, a hayloft door, a stone slab from an old morgue—and that a coffee table made from a found object is better than "a table designed as such, that is, a horizontal member with four legs." Why is this? Percy asked. The reason, he loquaciously proposed, is "that the self in the twentieth century is a voracious nought which expands like the feeding vacuole of an amoeba seeking to nourish and inform its own nothingness by ingesting new objects in the world but, like a vacuole, only succeeds in emptying them out."

That is not as complicated as it sounds. In Percy's view, the modern self is essentially empty—a "nought." The self goes forth in the world in order to fill itself, but swamps the world with its search for selfhood instead. As a result, the self assigns the highest value to the things it cannot swamp with selfhood, things that fill the self and remain undiminished—that have themselves left over. We prize an antique, for example, not because it is sturdy or well-made but "because it is an antique and as such is saturated with another time and another place and is therefore resistant to absorption by the self." Any old thing can make us feel full; but the things of the world that can be swamped by our selves and remain standing, alone, integral, lasting—these are the things worth marveling at, and the self seeks to lose itself in them.

Well-born, successful, admired in his lifetime, gracious in his celebrity, an ordinary man in spite of it all, Percy knew he was liable to be prized as an antique—a dead eminence with which his readers would saturate themselves in order to fill their "nought" of self. He was especially vulnerable to eminence in New Orleans, place of history and legend, and he must have dreaded the thought of the house where he wrote *The Moviegoer* becoming a stop on literary walking tours, of a tavern in the Quarter serving a mixed drink called Love in the Ruins, of the students at Walker Percy High School wearing sweatshirts with his name emblazoned on them. Such eminence would undo the work of his adulthood, which was to find rather than fill himself—to carry out the search that his work describes and urges upon the reader, the search that brought him back to life.

The best time to see Flannery O'Connor country is at sunset, a striking hour in middle Georgia. You will pass the farm on the way into town, marked by a chain suspended between two poles and dangling a NO TRESPASSING sign. Keep on into Milledgeville: the small college, the main street—courthouse, bicycle shop, tattoo parlor—and, a few blocks away, the pillared white house where O'Connor lived until she left Georgia for Iowa. An old-fashioned dining room near the college serves good country food. Behind the red-brick Catholic church you will find Flannery O'Connor Hall, which, this week, a sign says, is holding a session for RETURNING CATHOLICS.

Idle through Milledgeville for a few minutes, enjoying its small-town ease. Then, as the post office closes and the silverware is laid out in the dining rooms of the big houses, drive back out of town on Highway 441, coming to a stop in the vicinity of the Holiday Inn on the right side of the road, a favored stopping place of the twenty-first-century pilgrim.

The farm is across the highway and up the hill. There is no need to trespass. Simply watch the sunset. You have seen it already in your mind's eye. The farmhouse is exactly as described in the stories: the white siding, the screened porch, the water pump, the broken-down barnlike shelters for beasts and help. So are the surroundings. The trees are arrayed in a fortress line, dividing earth from sky. Sure enough, even the meanest of them sparkles. And as the sun goes down, blood orange, it seems to sit atop the trees a moment, then abruptly fall below, throwing into darkness a few ragged figures who look like trees, but walking.

Take it all in—you are at Andalusia. Then stand back and try to see it afresh, pushing past the image implanted by O'Connor's fiction. Keep looking until the white farmhouse looks like a farmhouse out of your own experience, or from a story of your own devising.

The aim of the fiction writer is to make the reader see—"to render the highest possible justice to the visible universe," O'Connor said, quoting Joseph Conrad—in order to render justice to the invisible one, which is the object of religious belief. She sought to communicate her vision to the reader as fully as possible. Yet she troubled to make clear that she didn't mean to impose her vision on the reader: "You may think from all I say that the reason I write is to make the reader see what I see, and that writing fiction is primarily a missionary activity," she said. "Let me straighten this out." Rather, she sought, through art, to see with something like objectivity, so that she and the reader might see the same thing—so that we might see what she saw, but with our own eyes.

They are writers firmly embedded in posterity now. The cause for Dorothy Day's canonization is on track in Vatican City. Monastic life today is quite unlike the life of silent austerity and privation that Thomas Merton described. The happy anomie that Walker Percy made out to be a sickness in *The Moviegoer* has been endorsed as the spirit of a generation. Flannery O'Connor has been dead longer than she was alive.

What they saw, what they knew, what they believed, what they wrote about—in the eyes of the reader of the present age it all appears distinctly different than it did to their eyes. But they knew that it would, and anticipated the change, writing for readers quite unlike themselves.

When Elizabeth Hester ceased to believe, to take an example, O'Connor forbade her, in a peremptory letter, to write a review of the introductory essay she'd written about Mary Ann Long's life. "The introduction is about the things that hold us fast in Christ when Christ is taken to be divine," O'Connor told Hester. "It is worthless if it is not true."

It is true, or it is worthless: so starkly put, the would-be-believer's dilemma has an appealing clarity. But that way of putting it is actually less clear than the way of the essay itself, where, rather than drawing a line between believer and unbeliever, O'Connor invites the skeptical reader to see in Mary Ann's life the shadow of the life of Christ looming behind it.

We are all skeptics now, believer and unbeliever alike. There is no one true faith, evident at all times and places. Every religion is one among many. The clear lines of any orthodoxy are made crooked by our experience, are complicated by our lives.

Believer and unbeliever are in the same predicament, thrown back onto themselves in complex circumstances, looking for a sign. As ever, religious belief makes its claim somewhere between revelation and projection, between holiness and human frailty; but the burden of proof, indeed the burden of belief, for so long upheld by society, is now back on the believer, where it belongs.

This is the significance of a piece of writing that makes a case for the Communion of Saints by way of one girl's short, hard, complicated life—and, perhaps, the significance of the religious faith that makes its case through the account of God's experience of life on earth as a certain person at a particular place and time. There is no way to seek truth except personally. Every story worth knowing is a life story.

In their different ways, the four writers this book is about sought the truth personally—in charity, in prayer, in art, in philosophy. Their writing was the most personal way of all, for in the act of reading and writing one stranger and another go forth to meet in an encounter of the profoundest sort. In this encounter, there are no self-evident truths. Nothing can be taken for granted or asserted outright. The case must be made to each of us individually, with fierce attention on both sides; we must be persuaded one at a time.

Perhaps that doesn't tell us much; but it is enough, and perhaps a little modesty is a good thing, a useful check on our strivings. Like it or not, we come to life in the middle of stories that are not ours. The way to knowledge, and self-knowledge, is through pilgrimage. We imitate our way to the truth, finding our lives—saving them—in the process. Then we pass it on.

The story of their lives, then, is also its meaning and its implication for ours. They saw religious experience out before them. They read their way toward it. They believed it. They lived it. They made it their own. With us in mind, they put it in writing.

NOTES

INDEX

Notes

Biography is a secondhand art par excellence, an effort to find the path or pattern in another person's life, and Dorothy Day, Thomas Merton, Walker Percy, and Flannery O'Connor have attracted biographers who practice the art with uncommon sympathy and devotion. Michael Mott's *The Seven Mountains of Thomas Merton* (Harvest, 1984), James Forest's *Living with Wisdom: A Life of Thomas Merton* (Orbis, 1991), and Monica Furlong's *Merton: A Biography* (Harper & Row, 1980; Bantam, 1981); Jay Tolson's *Pilgrim in the Ruins: A Life of Walker Percy* (Simon & Schuster, 1992; North Carolina, 1994), Patrick H. Samway, S.J.'s *Walker Percy: A Life* (Farrar, Straus and Giroux, 1997), and Bertram Wyatt-Brown's *The House of Percy: Honor, Melancholy, and Imagination in a Southern Family* (Oxford, 1994); William D. Miller's *Dorothy Day: A Biography* (Harper & Row, 1982), Jim Forest's *Love Is the Measure: A Biography of Dorothy Day* (Paulist, 1986; Orbis, 1997), Robert Ellsberg's *By Little and By Little: The Selected Writings of Dorothy Day* (Knopf, 1983), Robert Coles's *Dorothy Day: A Radical Devotion* (Perseus, 1987), and Nancy L. Roberts's *Dorothy Day and the "Catholic Worker"* (State University of New York, 1984); Sally Fitzgerald's exemplary presentations of Flannery O'Connor's writing: for many years these books have furthered the dialogue between writer and reader, between the work and the life.

Considering the merits of these books, and the existence of a vast secondary literature about each of the four writers, I decided early on to forgo documentary and archival efforts—the biographer's approach—and instead to draw on and appraise readily available materials, hoping to fashion a fresh work from them. Such an approach has had, among other advantages, a certain fidelity to the pattern of pilgrimage the book describes, which is not a pattern of research or documentation but one of reading and writing.

Most of my debts are acknowledged in the main text or in the explanatory notes that follow, but particular thanks are due to Robert Giroux; Lydia Wills; Roger

Straus and Jonathan Galassi; Cecily Parks, James Wilson, Debra Helfand, and Chandra Wohleber; Susan Mitchell and Jonathan Lippincott; Louise Florencourt, Ben Camardi, Mary Bernice Percy, Phil Runkel, and Patrick Hart; Christine Wiltz, Anne Stringfield, and T. Cat Ford; Paul Baumann, Lawrence Joseph, Andrew Krivak, and Alexander Star.

After the book was written but before it was complete, two boys were born—Leonardo and Pietro—and it is a blessing that the family to whom the book is dedicated now includes them.

PROLOGUE: *On Pilgrimage*

ix The title is a reference to Dorothy Day's *Catholic Worker* column, called "On Pilgrimage" beginning in 1946.

ix The photograph of Flannery O'Connor, taken by Joe McTyre for the *Atlanta Journal*, appeared on the back cover of the clothbound edition of *The Habit of Being* (Farrar, Straus and Giroux, 1979); another, slightly better photograph from the same moment appears on a postcard. Thomas Merton is pictured in his habit in photographs from every stage of his monastic career. Walker Percy's preppie demeanor is apparent in all the photographs taken of him in the seventies and eighties. The photograph of Dorothy Day, by Bob Fitch, was reproduced on the cover of the Harper & Row edition of *The Long Loneliness*.

ix No one has placed the four of them in context all together. Separately, they have been depicted as exceptional Catholic figures in a number of books, from Martin E. Marty's *Pilgrims in Their Own Land: 500 Years of Religion in America* (Penguin, 1985), to the Jesuit priest Mark S. Massa's *Catholics and American Culture: Fulton Sheen, Dorothy Day, and the Notre Dame Football Team* (Crossroad, 1999), which has chapters on Day and Merton. "Go and do likewise" is the imperative conclusion to the Gospel story of the Good Samaritan, found in Luke, Chapter 10.

x The theme of pilgrimage is used to organize Marty's history of religion in America; he prefaces the book with a quotation from Jacques Maritain, who observed, in *Reflections on America*, that "Americans seem to be in their own land as pilgrims, prodded by a dream. They are always on the move—available for new tasks, prepared for the possible loss of what they have. They are not *settled, installed.*" In books about the four writers, the theme is ubiquitous, most often in casual use, most emphatically in Tolson's biography, which is called *Pilgrim in the Ruins*. The definition of a pilgrimage is derived, especially, from William James's distinction between doctrine and experience in *The Varieties of Religious Experience*, as well as from Kierkegaard's *Philosophical Fragments* (trans. David Swensen; Princeton, 1962), which is organized around the distinction between "the contemporary disciple" and "the disciple at second hand," a distinction that I first explored in an essay about St. Thomas the Apostle in *A Tremor of Bliss: Contemporary Writers on the Saints* (Harcourt, Brace, 1994). Day discussed the meaning of books in her life at length in interviews with Robert Coles recounted in *Dorothy Day: A Radical Devotion* (Perseus, 1987), likening great writers to "her spiritual kin"; the quotation is drawn from Coles's introduction to *The Long Loneliness* (Harper San Francisco, 1997).

xi James Wood ponders the relation of religious and literary modes of belief in *The Broken Estate* (Random House, 1999).

xii Harold Bloom introduces the idea of "the anxiety of influence" in the book by that title (Yale, 1973; 2nd ed., 1997). In *The American Religion* (Touchstone, 1993), Bloom both calls for and essays what he calls "religious criticism." Defining it, he suggestively remarks that

> its function, like that of all criticism, is to build bridges across gaps, to explain in particular the very curious relations that generally prevail between theology and actual religious experience, in whatever faith. Where threads move across denominational lines, as in the American Religion, then the function of religious criticism becomes more complex. Theologies will fall away, and the varieties of religious experience will begin to suggest subtler demarcations, keener sounds than earlier could have been apprehended.

xii Lionel Trilling's lament about the absence of representative figures, written as the introduction to the Harcourt, Brace edition of *Homage to Catalonia*, appeared in *Commentary* in March 1952 and in Trilling's book *The Opposing Self* in 1955 as "George Orwell and the Politics of Truth"; it is reprinted in *The Moral Obligation to Be Intelligent: Selected Essays* (Farrar, Straus and Giroux, 2000). In his concern Trilling intentionally or inadvertently echoes Emerson, whose *Representative Men* had been published a century earlier (1850).

xii Faulkner's remark about "oratory out of solitude" is quoted by Alfred Kazin in *Bright Book of Life: American Novelists and Storytellers from Hemingway to Mailer* (University of Notre Dame, 1980). Percy called Covington, Louisiana, a "pleasant nonplace" in "Why I Live Where I Live," an essay published in *Esquire* in April 1980 and included in the posthumous volume of Percy's essays, *Signposts in a Strange Land* (ed. Patrick Samway; Farrar, Straus and Giroux, 1991); he described the nature of writing as communication and discussed the writer's need for "a commonwealth of other writers" in a talk about Herman Melville included in the same book.

xiv Merton sought to define sapiential, or wisdom, literature in " 'Baptism in the Forest': Wisdom and Initiation in William Faulkner," a 1967 essay published in *The Literary Essays of Thomas Merton* (ed. Patrick Hart; New Directions, 1981).

xiv The title is drawn from O'Connor's story "The Life You Save May Be Your Own," in *The Complete Stories* (Farrar, Straus and Giroux, 1971), the way O'Connor drew titles of several of her works from other works. O'Connor called that story "The World Is Almost Rotten"; the title "The Life You Save May Be Your Own" was suggested to her by Sally and Robert Fitzgerald, as indicated in her letter to them of December 20, 1952, in the Library of America edition. Her letter to them of January 25, 1953, and the note to it in the Library of America edition make clear that the Fitzgeralds also supplied her with the title of "A Good Man Is Hard to Find," the title of a song popularized by Bessie Smith, by sending her a newspaper clipping showing a seven-year-old girl singing the song at a talent show; she replied: "My mamma says what do I think is funny about the enclosed clipping? It kills me." The title *The Violent Bear It Away* is drawn from Luke, Chapter 10. The title of the story "Everything That Rises Must Converge" is drawn from Teilhard de Chardin, as reported in the *New York Times*'s obituary for O'Connor, published August 4, 1964: "A collection of stories to be published next February by Farrar, Straus & Co., is entitled *Everything That Rises Must Converge*. This is a line from the writings of the late Jesuit anthropologist and philosopher, Pierre Teilhard de Chardin."

1. *Experience*

3 Dorothy Day's recollection of the San Francisco earthquake appears in *The Long Loneliness*. At the time, she was the third of four children; a fifth, her brother John, was born after the family moved to Chicago.

5 The early religious history of America is based on Marty's *Pilgrims in Their Own Land*; Charles R. Morris's *American Catholic* (Times Books, 1997); and Paul Johnson's *A History of Christianity* (Penguin, 1978), as well Henry James's review of *The Jesuits in North America in the Seventeenth Century*, by Francis Parkman, in the "American Writers" section of the Library of America edition of James's works (1984), and Richard Rodriguez's recasting of American history in *Days of Obligation: An Argument with My Mexican Father* (Viking, 1992). Morris reports, in his chapter called "An American Church," that in 1900 there were 12 million Catholics in a population of 100 million.

6 William James defines religion in Lecture II of *The Varieties of Religious Experience*. In the first lecture, mindful of the skeptical bent of his audience, he proposes that the Bible might be judged truthful and valuable even by unbelievers—"if only it be a true record of the inner experiences of great-souled persons wrestling with the crises of their fate." James distinguishes between " 'once-born' and 'twice-born' characters" in Lectures IV and V, and between the "sick-souled" and the "healthy-minded" there and also in Lectures VI and VII. James's religious experience is described briefly in Martin E. Marty's introduction to the Penguin edition, and in greater detail in the "Religious Variations" chapter of R.W.B. Lewis's *The Jameses: A Family Narrative* (Farrar, Straus and Giroux, 1991); Marty remarks on James's "usual clipping, filing, and storing of data."

6 Henry Adams's conversion is described in the introduction to the Mentor edition (1961) of *Mont-Saint-Michel and Chartres*, by Ernest Samuels, who quotes Adams's characterization of himself, in a letter to a friend, as a Christian anarchist. In Chapter 2, about the *Song of Roland*, Adams remarks, by way of an aside, "The passion for pilgrimages was universal among our ancestors as far back as we can trace them. For at least a thousand years it was their chief delight, and it is not yet extinct. To feel the art of Mont-Saint-Michel and Chartres we have got to become pilgrims again." He presents the book not as the record of a pilgrimage, but as an actual pilgrimage, which the reader is invited to join. His preface concludes, "The party, then, with such variations of detail as may suit its tastes, has sailed from New York, let us say, early in June for an entire summer in France. One pleasant June morning it has landed at Cherbourg or Havre and takes the train across Normandy to Pontorson, where, with the evening light, the tourists drive along the *chaussée*, over the sands or through the tide, till they stop at Madame Poulard's famous hotel within the Gate of the Mount"—and there the text proper begins. Looking upon the church at Mont-Saint-Michel, and inviting the "tourist" to do likewise, Adams remarks: "One needs to be eight centuries old to know what this mass of encrusted architecture meant to its builders, and even then one must still learn to feel it. The man who wanders into the twelfth century is lost, unless he can grow prematurely

young." By the next page, he is writing from the point of view of the Norman, observing, as he looks out toward Normandy, that "so familiar, so homelike are they, one can almost take oath that in this, or the other, or in all, one knew life once and has never so fully known it since"—a passage that Thomas Merton, recollecting his French boyhood in his autobiography, echoes with uncanny fidelity.

7 Merton describes his family and early life in Chapter 1 of *The Seven Storey Mountain* (Harcourt, Brace, 1948) and recounts his trip to France with his father in Chapter 2. Michael Mott, halfway through his biography (at the beginning of the "Mount Purgatory" chapter), remarks, "It would be hard to exaggerate the importance of place for Thomas Merton."

9 The evocation of immigrant Catholicism is grounded in the religious histories cited above, and also especially on *The Madonna of 115th Street: Faith and Community in Italian Harlem, 1880–1950*, by Robert Anthony Orsi (Yale, 1985).

10 Walker Percy's lineage and early life are discussed at length in Tolson's and Samway's biographies (the latter in a detailed appendix including family trees and the like), and also, with impressive thoroughness and insight, by Bertram Wyatt-Brown in *The House of Percy*. The fundamental texts for all these accounts are William Alexander Percy's memoir, *Lanterns on the Levee: Recollections of a Planter's Son* (Knopf, 1941), and Walker Percy's recollection of the "legend" of Will Percy in the introduction to the LSU Press reprint (1973), also published as "Uncle Will" in *Signposts in a Strange Land*. Will Percy describes his religious experiences in the chapters "Learning from Teachers" (in which he is converted) and "Sewanee" (in which he loses his faith, in effect, on his way down the mountain). Tolson's biography includes a picture of the renovated Percy mansion; Wyatt-Brown's book features a photograph of the medieval knight on the jacket.

12 The story of Mary Flannery O'Connor's encounter with a Pathé News photographer is told in "The King of the Birds," published in *Mystery and Manners*; the newsreel feature, called "Unique Chicken Goes in Reverse," is in the collection of O'Connor materials in the Ina Dillard Russell Library at the Georgia College and State University in Milledgeville. The most reliable source of information about O'Connor's early life is Sally Fitzgerald's "Chronology" in the Library of America edition of O'Connor's works, which gathers together information scattered elsewhere—in Fitzgerald's explanatory commentary in *The Habit of Being* and her introductory essay to *Three by Flannery O'Connor*; in Robert Fitzgerald's recollection of O'Connor in *Everything That Rises Must Converge* and Robert Giroux's recollection in *The Complete Stories*; and in O'Connor's own essays and letters, especially those to Elizabeth Hester. The remark about the "prophet-freak" as an image of the novelist is in the "On Her Own Work" section of *Mystery and Manners*. In "The Catholic Novelist in the Protestant South," O'Connor, speaking of the novelist, remarked, "His interest and sympathy may very well go—as I know my own does—directly to those aspects of Southern life where the religious feeling is most intense and where its outward forms are farthest from the Catholic, and most revealing of a need that only the Church can fill. . . . Descending within his region, he discovers that it is with these aspects of Southern life that he has a feeling of kinship strong enough to spur him to write."

14 Day's school years, in Chicago and then in Urbana, are detailed in Miller's biography, in James Forest's biography, and in Robert Ellsberg's biographical essay in *By*

Little and By Little, as well as in *The Long Loneliness*, in which Day recalls her father's strictness; describes venturing into the West Side Chicago of Upton Sinclair's novels; quotes her own letter to her friend Henrietta, "who was deeply religious and deeply sentimental"; and describes her effort "to overcome my religious sense." Day's earlier recollection of those years in *From Union Square to Rome* is available in the "Dorothy Day Library on the Web" at www.catholicworker.org. The notion of Tolstoy and Dostoevsky as the two halves of the Slavic soul is derived from Nikolai Berdyaev's *Dostoevsky* (trans. Donald Attwater; Living Age/Meridian, 1957), which was well-known among the Catholic Workers. Gorky's image of Tolstoy, from *Reminiscences* (1921), is quoted by Harold Bloom in *The Western Canon*. Day's account of reading—rereading—Dostoevsky's novels in New York is in *From Union Square to Rome*, reprinted in Robert Ellsberg's anthology. Here, as elsewhere in her recollections of her early life, the one autobiography is a precursor to the other, at once a draft and an aide-mémoire, less lyrical, more matter-of-fact and emphatic—more a work of traditional apologetics, meant to convince the reader of the truth of the Catholic faith. The remark about the "mystic gripping melody of struggle, a cry for world peace and human brotherhood" is Day's own quotation from *The Call*; the biblical quotation is from Psalm 126 in the Authorized Version. Recalling her jail time in *The Long Loneliness*, Day remarks, "When I first wrote of these experiences I wrote even more strongly of my identification with those around me. I was that mother whose child had been raped and slain. I was the mother who had borne the monster who had done it. I was even that monster, feeling in my own breast every abomination. Is this exaggeration?" She concluded that it was not.

18 Will Percy's request to Shelby Foote is found in "Uncle Will," in *Signposts in a Strange Land*. Samway's biography is strongest on Percy's high school years, Tolson's on Percy's inner life and his friendship with Foote (the photograph of the two of them with Phinizy Percy in Greenville is printed there). Father Samway describes Percy's visit to the World's Fair and his receiving *The Brothers Karamazov* as a Christmas gift. Percy recalls reading *The Brothers Karamazov* in two interviews in *Conversations with Walker Percy* (eds. Lewis A. Lawson and Victor A. Kramer; University Press of Mississippi, 1985)—one with Marcus Smith, from 1976, the other with John Griffin Jones, from 1983—and recalls his and Foote's "long Dostoevskian conversations" in a 1967 interview with Ashley Brown (for *Shenandoah*) reprinted in the same book. Foote reports on "winding up my fifth or sixth rereading of Dostoevsky's BROTHERS" in a letter of June 29, 1977, in *The Correspondence of Shelby Foote & Walker Percy* (ed. Jay Tolson; DoubleTake Books, 1997); in an earlier letter, of September 19, 1971, Percy reports that a faculty member at Vanderbilt has proposed inviting him and Foote to the campus to undertake some public "arguing about Dostoevski-vs-Tolstoy."

20 Merton's recollections of St. Antonin are found in *The Seven Storey Mountain*; his remark about those years as "my whole life" in a journal entry of March 23, 1941, is published in Volume 1 of Merton's journals, *Run to the Mountain* (ed. Patrick Hart; Harper San Francisco, 1995). On that day Merton, fearing that he would be drafted, went for a reflective long walk in the woods surrounding St. Bonaventure, where the terrain reminded him of France and of his father. Their house in St. Antonin is described and pictured in Michael Mott's biography; Mott reports that Merton's initials, which he evidently scratched into the mortar, are still there.

22 The drafting of the Baltimore Catechism and the emergence of the parochial school system are recounted by Charles R. Morris in *American Catholic*, and the rise and fall of a "separate" Catholic culture is the theme of the book. D. H. Lawrence describes the "complex escape" undertaken by American writers in *Studies in Classic American Literature* (1923; Penguin, 1977), especially the chapter called "The Spirit of Place"; William Carlos Williams devotes an essay to Père Sebastian Rasles in *In the American Grain* (1925; paperback edition, New Directions, 1956).

23 The photograph taken of Flannery O'Connor on her First Communion Day is in the O'Connor Collection in Milledgeville. "A Temple of the Holy Ghost," from *A Good Man Is Hard to Find and Other Stories*, is a story which O'Connor considered unjustly overlooked. "Nobody ever notices it," she told Elizabeth Hester in a letter (August 4, 1962). "It is never anthologized, never commented upon." Early in their correspondence (December 16, 1955), it was her own exegesis of the story, and particularly its imagery of the sun "like an elevated Host drenched in blood," that led her to tell the story, now notorious, of her exchange with Mary McCarthy over the significance of the Eucharist.

26 Day's recollections of the war years are found in the "Freelance" chapter of *The Long Loneliness*. In writing the book, Day revised *From Union Square to Rome*, the way Malcolm Cowley revised *Exile's Return* (Viking, 1934), for republication in 1951. Although the *Catholic Worker*, on account of its name, is generally said to have been modeled on the Communist *Daily Worker*, its blend of literary sophistication and radical politics seems to owe as much to *The Masses*, a magazine whose influence is discussed by Christine Stansell in *American Moderns* (Metropolitan Books, 2000), and especially insightfully by Barry Lewis in *A Walk in Greenwich Village*, a program which aired on PBS in 2000. The site of the Golden Swan, aka the Hell Hole, at the corner of Sixth Avenue and West Fourth Street, is now a pocket park named for the place. Day's relationship with Eugene O'Neill became a subject of discussion after O'Neill's 1943 play *Moon for the Misbegotten* was produced on Broadway: it was said that the character of Josie Hogan was fashioned after Day. In response, Day wrote a statement called "Told in Context": although she insisted that the story of their relationship had changed through ceaseless retelling, as in a game of telephone, she didn't actually correct the story so much as digress around it, stressing her gratitude to O'Neill for "an intensification of the religious sense that was within me" and concluding that, although O'Neill had died apostate, she was praying for his soul anyway, for "God accepts all our prayers" and "there is no time with God." The controversy, such as it was, is treated at length in Miller's biography.

29 Day's prayers, at the end of the chapter, are drawn from two separate passages. The first comes from the Hell Hole episode in *The Long Loneliness*; the second, from Day's account of her work at King's County Hospital early the next year, has been placed in this context for dramatic effect.

2. *The Downward Path*

30 Merton recalls learning of his father's mortal illness in Chapter 3 of *The Seven Storey Mountain*, called "The Harrowing of Hell." In their biographies Michael Mott and then James Forest treat Merton's reckless life at length. In hers (*Merton: A*

Biography, Harper & Row, 1980), Monica Furlong, though she seems not to have known that Merton evidently fathered a child at Cambridge, conveys a sense of riotous living at least as well as the others.

31 Merton and Day are often casually compared, and at least one full-length comparative study is in progress, though Daniel Berrigan overstated the case when, introducing *The Long Loneliness* (for Harper & Row; since replaced with an introduction by Robert Coles), he remarked on "her great friends Thomas Merton and Peter Maurin." The notion of "sinning one's way to God" and "the downward path" go back, in spirit, all the way to Augustine. Its fiercest modern expression, perhaps, is in Baudelaire's *Flowers of Evil*, an antithesis to the Psalm, to which Day alludes in *From Union Square to Rome* and to which Merton alludes in *The Seven Storey Mountain*; in the latter, Merton's citation of Baudelaire's famous address to the reader—"*Hypocrite lecteur, mon semblable, mon frère*"—suggests the identification which, for him, is at the root of literature; in his reading and his writing, he sees writer and reader as doubles, as twins.

32 The notion of a Jamesian "figure in the carpet" is derived from James's 1896 tale of that title. Michael Mott, in his biography, casually refers to Merton as "a rebel who won and kept a reputation for obedience," for example. Merton himself describes sin as rebellion in *The Seven Storey Mountain* and elsewhere.

32 Merton, deprecating his worldly past, called Chapter 2 of his autobiography "Our Lady of the Museums," but it is in Chapter 3, especially, in which he reads *Ulysses* and visits the churches of Rome, that the role of art in the intensification of his religious sense becomes clear.

33 The echoes of Augustine in *The Seven Storey Mountain* were first remarked upon by the "radio priest" Fulton J. Sheen, who, asked to comment on the book, described it as "a twentieth-century form of the *Confessions of St. Augustine*." But the connection had already been drawn by Merton himself, who in Chapter 4 of the book recalls being told, by his mentor Dan Walsh, that he is less a Thomist than an Augustinian—"that my bent was not so much towards the intellectual, dialectical, speculative character of Thomism, as towards the spiritual, mystical, voluntaristic and practical way of St. Augustine and his followers." H. G. Wells's comment comparing *A Portrait of the Artist* to a "mosaic of jagged fragments" appeared for many years on the Penguin edition.

34 Day's description of her work at Kings County Hospital is drawn from Chapter 8 of *From Union Square to Rome*, though the phrase "the sacrament of duty" comes from *The Long Loneliness*. The revision of her recollections from the earlier book to the later one is a telling example of her development as a writer: though the particulars of the experience are similar in the two books, and some sentences are nearly identical, in the later book the experience is presented in the second person, so as to elicit the reader's identification ("You stood when a head nurse entered the ward") and then continued in the first-person plural, so as to invite the reader to share in the experience ("From the first, in addition to bed-making and care of the ward, we were given nursing to do, straight nursing, which delights every woman's heart"). The whole experience, called "the rigorous life" in the earlier book, is summed up with the term "the sacrament of duty," which is clear, simple, memorable, Scholastic-seeming, all the better to stick in the reader's mind and call forth the reader's imitation. Characteristically—for her humility is part of her art of persuasion—

Day attributes the term to the nurse who was her supervisor, then adds, "She might not have used those words, but that was the tenor of her talk and I have never forgotten it."

34–9 The account of her exploits in this section follows the account given in *The Eleventh Virgin*, by way of Day's biographers. Because all of them—Miller, her authorized biographer; Forest, her associate; Ellsberg, her best anthologist—regard the novel as essentially true to the facts of Day's own life, their accounts are treated as essentially factual here and are made the basis of this one. The parallels between the novel and Day's life have been examined closely by two scholars at Brown University, Keith Morton and John Saltmarsh. Ellsberg, who knows Day's writings as well as anyone, in conversation assented to the assertion that Day never mentioned her abortion in her nonfiction writing. Her remark that she once sought for every copy of *The Eleventh Virgin* to be destroyed is found in Robert Coles's *A Radical Devotion*. Her recollections of Chicago are drawn from the chapter called "A Time of Searching" in *The Long Loneliness*, that of buying a "little manual of prayers" in New Orleans from *From Union Square to Rome*.

40 There is nothing to prove that Merton's boathouse rendezvous, recalled in his journal on December 30, 1965, was a rendezvous with the woman with whom he had conceived a child, as Michael Mott and James Forest suggest, but the context (which they leave out) makes it a very plausible conjecture. "Sex is one thing on my mind," Merton wrote in the journal that day, "as something I did not use maturely and well." Reviewing his life from the vantage point of age fifty, he remarked, "I suppose I regret most my lack of love, my selfishness and glibness (covering a deep shyness and need of love) with girls who, after all, did love me I think, for a time." In the published journal, *Dancing in the Water of Life* (ed. Robert E. Daggy; Harper San Francisco, 1997), the recollection ends with an ellipsis, suggesting that controversial material has been quietly excised.

40 In his biography, Michael Mott conjectures that there was a party at Cambridge during which a mock crucifixion was performed, with Merton as the Christ figure, an experience which left him with a scar on the palm of his right hand, a scar noted by the naturalization authorities when Merton sought U.S. citizenship in 1951. Unpublished manuscript pages from *The Seven Storey Mountain*, photocopies of which were given to me by Robert Giroux, seem to bear out Mott's conjecture. At the top of a fresh page—a passage following on another—Merton writes:

> And yet I hesitate even to talk of the truth of this crucifixion, because that statement has at least a certain dramatic character about it, and therefore makes the affair seem interesting. And that is the lie that I want to avoid. . . . For there is nothing so dull and tedious and uninteresting and unworthy of historical record, in itself, as sin: but above all is this true of the sins of adolescents who have just entered a university and have got the idea that lust is life, and mean to prove that they are alive. The one thing that needs to be said, the one truth, is that we were all dead, and most of us were already in hell. And that hell is much too complicated for me to harrow now.

41 Mott's is the most thorough account of the circumstances in which Merton left England for America, and it is Mott who reports the specifics of Merton's will and links

Merton's last night in England with a similar incident in Merton's *Journal of My Escape from the Nazis*, a novel first published the year after his death by New Directions under the title *My Argument with the Gestapo*. Merton mused on the Blitz of London in his journal on October 27, 1940. The prayer in prose to the Mother of God, part hymn, part entreaty, concludes Chapter 3 of *The Seven Storey Mountain*.

42 Day describes the Staten Island beach cottage in *From Union Square to Rome*, apparently reprinting verbatim a journal entry of the time, and recalls her reading there in *The Long Loneliness*. Malcolm Cowley reported on the war between the bohemians and the radicals in Part II of *Exile's Return*. The early years of Allen Tate and Caroline Gordon are described in *Allen Tate: Orphan of the South*, by Thomas A. Underwood (Princeton, 2001), and in two biographies of Gordon: *Close Connections: Caroline Gordon and the Southern Renaissance*, by Ann Waldron (Putnam, 1987), and *The Underground Stream: The Life and Art of Caroline Gordon*, by Nancylee Novell Jonza (Georgia, 1995). There is a concise history of the Fugitives in the entry on the Agrarians in the *Encyclopedia of Southern Culture* (eds. Charles Reagan Wilson and William Ferris; North Carolina, 1989).

45 Day's portrait of Forster Batterham in *The Long Loneliness* is "overly romantic," Miller suggests in his biography, giving prosaic details of Batterham and his family. In *From Union Square to Rome* he is depicted sketchily and given the name "Fred."

48 Gordon's response to Day's pregnancy is related in Miller's biography, the circumstances of her own pregnancy and subsequent marriage in Underwood's biography of Tate, Batterham's feelings about pregnancy in *The Long Loneliness*. Day's journal entries from the period are reprinted, apparently verbatim, in *From Union Square to Rome*, then simply recast in the past tense, like leftover food or secondhand clothing, and reused in *The Long Loneliness*.

50 John Day's view of the church is found in Miller's biography. Describing her pregnancy in *The Long Loneliness*, Day singles out *The Imitation of Christ* as the book she read most attentively. She says nothing about it in the earlier biography; the theme of books and their influence is one she understood better, and gave greater emphasis, after she became a writer of books herself. The translation of the *Imitation of Christ* quoted here is by Harold C. Gardiner, S.J. (Image, 1955).

52 The story of Sacco and Vanzetti is told, from different perspectives, in *The Twentieth Century: A People's History*, by Howard Zinn (Harper Perennial, 1998); in *La Storia: Five Centuries of the Italian American Experience*, by Jerre Mangione and Ben Morreale (Harper Perennial, 1993); in Edmund Wilson's *The Twenties* (where John Dos Passos is quoted); and by Malcolm Cowley in *Exile's Return*. Day's own reactions to the trial and execution are scattered in the final pages of the "Love Overflows" chapter of *The Long Loneliness*.

53 Day published several accounts of childbirth; the best, written on the spot at Bellevue Hospital, was published in *The New Masses* and is reprinted in *By Little and By Little*. Her vividest recollection of the first days of motherhood is found in the preface to *Therese*, her book about Thérèse of Lisieux (Templegate, 1979). Her story of Sister Aloysia is told in *The Long Loneliness*. Her condemnation of Charles Schwab is in *From Union Square to Rome*, as is her account of her ferry ride from Manhattan to Staten Island to be baptized—perhaps the strongest writing in that, her first autobiography. Her question about the saints is drawn from a recollection of her teen years in *From Union Square to Rome*; the placing of it in her mind here, and

the setting of her disquiet on the beach, is an instance of artistic license. Fritz Eichenberg's woodcut opens the "Time of Searching" chapter of *The Long Loneliness*.

3. Seeking the Real

59 The role of the Depression-era documentary workers was insightfully assessed by Henry Mayer, biographer of Dorothea Lange, in "Famous Men," an essay published in the *New York Times Book Review* (May 14, 2000). Mayer asserts that *Let Us Now Praise Famous Men*, thought today to be the apotheosis of Depression documentation, was meant by James Agee and Walker Evans "to be a counterfoil to a well-established documentary genre that they considered too closely allied to the politics of the New Deal," and quotes Evans's characterization of their working method as one of "distant harmony."

60 Walker Percy's recollections of the WPA years with Uncle Will are drawn from "Uncle Will" and "Uncle Will's House," both collected in *Signposts in a Strange Land*.

61 Flannery O'Connor once described her subject as "The Poor." Her Depression childhood is detailed in Sally Fitzgerald's chronology in the Library of America edition and in Robert Fitzgerald's introduction to *Everything That Rises Must Converge*. "A Temple of the Holy Ghost," "A View of the Woods," and "A Circle in the Fire" all appear in *The Complete Stories*.

62 Day recalls her first years as a Catholic in the preface to *Therese*, as well as in *The Long Loneliness*. Forest's biography gives the best secondary account, beginning, "The five years following Dorothy's entrance into the Catholic Church centered on her search to find something that didn't exist: a way of supporting herself and Tamar through work which joined her religious faith, her commitment to social justice, and writing." Her questioning of whether Catholics really believe each person is a temple of the Holy Ghost is found in *From Union Square to Rome*; her reports on life in Mexico appeared in *Commonweal* in 1930 and are republished in *Dorothy Day: Writings from "Commonweal,"* ed. Patrick Jordan (Liturgical Press, 2002); her description of New York during the Depression is from *Loaves and Fishes* (Harper & Brothers, 1963). Her description of the poor people's march on Washington is from *The Long Loneliness*. Miller, in his biography, discusses her whereabouts during 1930 and 1931.

67 Peter Maurin's arrival—some days after Day's return from Washington—is described in *Loaves and Fishes*, but her biographers all tell the earlier, more colorful version of the story, in which he is waiting at her apartment when she returns from the capital. *Loaves and Fishes* (subtitled *The Story of the Catholic Worker Movement*) grew out of Day's long intention to write a whole book about Maurin, and the later telling of the story shifts the emphasis away from Day—her conversion, her loneliness, her search for a vocation—and onto Maurin. Her characterization of Maurin as "a genius, a saint, an agitator, a writer, a lecturer, a poor man, and a shabby tramp, all at once" is quoted in Miller's biography; her account of his history and her synopsis of his philosophy is from the "Peasant of the Pavements" chapter of *The Long Loneliness*; her biographers, James Forest in particular, have checked and filled in the details. The characterization of poverty as Lady Poverty, to whom the poor man is espoused, is from the portrait of St. Francis of Assisi in Dante's *Paradiso*.

The Catholic boys' camp on Mt. Tremper is now the Zen Mountain Monastery; a huge carved wooden cross still presides over the zendo, inside and out.

70 Day tells of the influence of Rose Hawthorne Lathrop's biography on her in *Loaves and Fishes*; in this account, her reading of this woman's life, as much as her participation in the march on Washington or her prayers at the Cathedral of the Immaculate Conception, emboldened her to found a Catholic social movement. And it is clear, from all her accounts of their early days together, that Maurin regarded her as a figure out of a book no less than she did him—and that his grand sense of her potential goaded her into action.

71 *From Union Square to Rome* ends with Day's conversion, but in her two later memoirs, the climax is the founding of the *Catholic Worker*. In his biography, Jim Forest describes Day's becoming "a Christian missionary not to heathens but to fellow Christians, hoping to convert them to a faith they thought was theirs already."

72 Day's articles from the first issue of the paper are reprinted in A *Penny a Copy: Readings from "The Catholic Worker"* (ed. Thomas C. Cornell and James H. Forest; Macmillan, 1968); Peter Maurin's program is presented in *Loaves and Fishes*, where Day ponders his curious absence from the scene on May Day 1933. The movement's founding is set in historical context and the paper discussed in terms of mid-century "advocacy journalism" in *Dorothy Day and the "Catholic Worker,"* by Nancy L. Roberts (State University of New York Press, 1984). Working from material buried deep in the archives of the Catholic Worker Collection at Marquette University in Milwaukee—a 1933 missive entitled "Techniques of Action," and a 1935 letter to the Brooklyn diocesan newspaper, the *Tablet*—Roberts emphasizes Day's determination through the paper "to influence the thought of its readers," and observes, "Day further defined good journalism as the reporting of *eyewitness* events, 'not just taking the word of other papers and rewriting accounts.' Catholic Workers (including the paper's reporters) were present at such affairs as strikes and picketing, she wrote, because 'we think that lay apostles should bring their beliefs to the man in the street. . . .' This is a clear call for activist reporting." It is also a clear call for firsthand experience.

73 The photographs of the Catholic Workers on Union Square are reproduced in *Loaves and Fishes*. Thomas Merton's New York years dominate the long middle section of *The Seven Storey Mountain*, to such a degree that the book is, all other concerns aside, an evocation of New York literary and intellectual life, a cousin to Cowley's *Exile's Return* and Alfred Kazin's *Starting Out in the Thirties* (Atlantic–Little, Brown, 1965). The New York setting sits uncomfortably in Michael Mott's "seven mountains" scheme, in which a mountain is made to symbolize each stage of Merton's life. Mott might have made use of the rocky outcropping where the Cloisters is sited.

74 Reginald Marsh's etching *Tattoo–Shave–Haircut* (1932) illustrates the entry for BOWERY in *The Encyclopedia of New York* (ed. Kenneth T. Jackson; Yale, 1995), a book which, unforgivably, has only a single-sentence entry for CATHOLIC WORKER. Marsh's painting *Twenty Cent Movie* illustrates the encyclopedia's entry for MOVIE THEATERS.

75 The recollection of Merton's wardrobe is drawn from *The Man in the Sycamore Tree* (Doubleday, 1970), by Edward Rice, a classmate of Merton's at Columbia, who recalled, "He was invariably dressed like a businessman, in a neat suit and a double-breasted chesterfield topcoat." The book includes several photographs of Merton in business dress.

76 The analysis of Dante's account of pilgrimage owes something to Harold Bloom's chapter on Dante in *The Western Canon*, and also to Dorothy Sayers's introduction

to her translation of the *Purgatorio* (Penguin, 1955). Today, the translation of Dante is an act of faithful imitation akin to pilgrimage, called forth not so much by the reader's need to encounter Dante in a particular mode of contemporary English as by the poet's need to imitate Dante in a deep sense by recasting Dante's pilgrimage in his or her own idiom. Dante serves today's poets as a kind of Virgil—a guide figure with access to the the the treasures of antiquity and medieval Christendom alike.

77 Walker Percy's college years are treated in Tolson's and Samway's biographies, as one might expect, the two books running in parallel and intermittently converging. Samway's is a detailed account of classes taken and student activities participated in (as well as events on campus of only tangential interest). Tolson's is a portrait of a young man searching for "absolutes, certainty, authority," which he found in science. Tolson contrasts the searching Percy with the rebellious Foote, though not so sharply as Percy is contrasted with Merton here. Tolson's biography also reproduces the photograph of Percy outside the Carolina Theater and includes Roy Percy's recollection of his brother's powers of concentration when reading a book. Percy himself defines the searcher and the search in many of his essays and talks, particularly "Physician as Novelist" in *Signposts in a Strange Land*, as well as in *The Moviegoer*. In "Physician as Novelist," he characterized the novel as "squarely in the oldest tradition in Western letters: the pilgrim's search outside himself, rather than the guru's search within." In "The Man on the Train," he described the search in everything but name, and the recognition of the alienation of man's anxious questings as a search, and of the search as a pilgrimage, is what engendered *The Moviegoer*.

77 Merton characterizes the twentieth-century man as a rebel and himself as a twentieth-century man in the "Harrowing of Hell" chapter of *The Seven Storey Mountain*, citing the rebel of Baudelaire's *Flowers of Evil*. Curiously, even as he longed all his life to find himself by losing himself, Merton gave no special attention to the biblical adage in which the process is made explicit, instead resorting again and again to more recondite medieval or mystical formulations.

78 Percy's analysis of the appeal of movies is found in Robert Coles's profile of him for the *New Yorker* (October 12 and October 19, 1978); his recollections of sitting on the porch of the fraternity house emerged in an interview with Dannye Romine (1980), reprinted in *Conversations with Walker Percy*.

79 Merton's principal recollection of Mark Van Doren is found in *The Seven Storey Mountain*; his later recollection is made in his journal, September 29, 1957, published in Volume 4 of his journals, *A Search for Solitude* (ed. Lawrence S. Cunningham; Harper San Francisco, 1996).

80 Etienne Gilson's *The Spirit of Medieval Philosophy*, published in 1936 by Charles Scribner's Sons—which perhaps explains its placement in the window of the Scribner's bookshop on Fifth Avenue—is reprinted by the University of Notre Dame Press (1991). The argument for medieval philosophy, specifically medieval Christian philosophy, as "real" philosophy is made in the opening chapter or lecture, "The Problem of Christian Philosophy." The expectations for the Gifford lecturers are discussed at length in Alasdair MacIntyre's Gifford lectures, published as *Three Rival Versions of Moral Enquiry: Encyclopedia, Genealogy, and Tradition* (Notre Dame, 1990).

82 The concern for "scientific medicine" at Columbia's College of Physicians and Surgeons is touched upon in Tolson's biography, as it was by Percy himself in "Physician as Novelist." In an interview about Percy's meeting with Thomas Merton, conducted in 1984 by Victor A. Kramer and Dewey Weiss Kramer, Percy remarked

on their shared experience of "Columbia University agnosticism." The account of Percy's excursions to distant points of New York City is from the unpublished draft manuscript "Confessions of a Movie-goer," quoted by Samway, who in this instance reads fiction as autobiography. "Young Nuclear Physicist" was published in the *Oxford American* (January/February 1999); in an introduction, Shelby Foote confidently declared that the story "was written in the late summer or early fall of 1937" and that, though it "appears to be a short story . . . a closer look shows the undertaking to be quite something else; nothing less, in fact—whether he knew it or not when he began and then abandoned it—than the first-draft opening pages of a novel." Samway obliquely suggests that it was written three years later.

84 Of the two biographers, Samway gives Percy's program of psychoanalysis the more strenuous analysis and quotes from Will Percy's letter to Walker Percy; Tolson quotes from a 1943 paper in which Janet Rioch describes a case he takes to be Percy's. Both biographers are confident that Harry Stack Sullivan's visit to Will Percy's house in Greenville came after Walker Percy had graduated from college and shortly before he began analysis in New York. But Percy himself, in "Uncle Will's House," recalls the visit in the context of childhood recollections—"Children notice things first, people later," the run of recollections begins—so the visit is placed here in Chapter 1, not Chapter 3.

84 Merton's master's thesis, "Nature and Art in William Blake: An Essay in Interpretation," was published as an appendix to *The Literary Essays of Thomas Merton*. Jacques Maritain's story is told by Robert Ellsberg in *All Saints*. The remark about the "true mystic," from *The Life of William Blake*, by Mona Wilson (Jonathan Cape, 1932), is quoted by Merton in a notebook now in the collection of the Friedsam Memorial Library at St. Bonaventure University and cited in Michael Mott's biography. Bramachari's story, told in *The Seven Storey Mountain*, is retold, to take one example, in Rice's *The Man in the Sycamore Tree*.

88 The rise and spread of the *Catholic Worker* is described in *Loaves and Fishes*; circulation figures, reported in each issue of the newspaper, are presented in a table by Roberts in *Dorothy Day and the "Catholic Worker."* Day's account of its transformation from newspaper to social movement is given in *Hard Times: An Oral History of the Great Depression*, by Studs Terkel (Avon, 1971).

90 Joyce's notoriety as an apostate is conveyed in Richard Ellmann's biography (new and revised edition, corrected, Oxford, 1983), in Edmund Wilson's *Axel's Castle* (Scribner's, 1931; Flamingo, 1984), and in Anthony Burgess's *ReJoyce* (Norton, 1968, 2000) and *Little Wilson and Big God* (Grove Weidenfeld, 1986).

91 Merton read *Gerard Manley Hopkins*, by G. F. Lahey, S.J. (Oxford, 1930); he evidently misspelled Lahey's name in *The Seven Storey Mountain*. Hopkins's life story is told in brief in *Lives of the Poets*, by Michael Schmidt (Vintage, 2000) and in Robert Ellsberg's *All Saints*, and at somewhat greater length in *John Henry Newman: A Biography*, by Ian Ker (Oxford, 1988).

4. Another World

94 Flannery O'Connor's cartoons, discussed in Robert Fitzgerald's introduction to *Everything That Rises Must Converge* and Sally Fitzgerald's chronology in the Library of America edition, are in the O'Connor Collection in Milledgeville.

94 Edward Francis O'Connor's background and early life are summarized in *Flannery O'Connor: A Life*, by Jean W. Cash (Tennessee, 2002). The sketch called "Biography" is in the Flannery O'Connor Collection in Milledgeville. O'Connor's creation of an attic studio is remarked upon in the Library of America chronology. The view from the back bedroom of the house in Savannah and the physical character of the attic of the Cline house are firsthand observations, one taken from inside the house, one from the outside. Her recollection of Peabody High is from a letter to Elizabeth Hester, of August 28, 1955; her description of her juvenilia from the chronology to the Library of America editions, her explanation of lupus from a letter to Hester of July 28, 1956, in which she explained that she, like her father, had lupus.

96 The analysis of representation of Christendom, and especially medieval Christendom, as an "other" world is stimulated especially by Norman Cantor's brilliant study *Inventing the Middle Ages* (Quill, 1992); other sources are *The Inklings*, by Humphrey Carpenter (Ballantine, 1981); Michael Schmidt's *Lives of the Poets*; *Eliot's Early Years* and *Eliot's New Life*, by Lyndall Gordon (Noonday, 1988); and Peter Ackroyd's *London: A Biography* (Nan A. Talese, 2001). A lecture and walking tour led in 1986 by Michael Slater at the Division of Extra-mural Studies, University of London, situated Eliot in London and the London of the war in Eliot's imagination.

98 The account of Merton's year in Greenwich Village and upstate New York is drawn equally from his autobiography and his journal, published as *Run to the Mountain*. The house in Olean is characterized briefly but vividly by Michael Mott in his biography. The house on Perry Street still stands, shorn of its balcony.

99 Dorothy Day's article "To Christ—to the Land!" published in the *Catholic Worker* in January 1936, appears in *By Little and By Little*. Day's remark about the Staten Island farm is found in Miller's biography. The divide between the "workers" and the "scholars"—best described by Day herself in *Loaves and Fishes*—is thought to exist in the Catholic Worker movement today.

100 Robert Ellsberg, in the introduction to *By Little and By Little*, characterizes the Catholic Worker communities memorably: "In contrast to many intentional communities, with members carefully screened for personal and ideological compatibility, the Worker community consisted of whoever showed up at the door. The result was often an assemblage of characters that seemed drawn from a novel by Dostoevsky. On hand in most Catholic Worker houses was a similar cast of pilgrims, scholars, and 'holy fools,' the young and old, workers, loafers, and everything in between. . . . The basis for community was not an ideal to be achieved, but the recognition of a reality already accomplished in Christ—the fact that all, whether clever or dull, fit or infirm, beautiful or plain, were 'members of one another.' "

100 James Forest, who gives a detailed account of the vicissitudes of the different Catholic Worker farms in his biography, also details the activities of the Catholic Workers at St. Joseph's House and the nature of the Friday-night meetings. He and Ellsberg both stress the movement's opposition to anti-Semitism and German militarism; Miller, sentimentally stretching the point, writes of Day (in "The Coming of the War") that "she was, in a social sense, practically Jewish."

101 Eric Hobsbawm's remark about the remoteness of the Spanish Civil War is found in *The Age of Extremes: A History of the World, 1914–1991* (Vintage, 1996). Auden's *Spain* (quoted by Hobsbawm) is insightfully commented upon in *Early Auden*, by Edward Mendelsohn (Noonday, 1999). Day's letter explaining the "CW Stand on

the Use of Force," published in the paper in September 1938, is reprinted in *A Penny a Copy*. The distinction between the Chicago Catholic Worker and the New York one was explained to me by Ed Marciniak, a founder of the Chicago house, in a personal interview in July 1998.

103 Merton dramatizes his practice of the *Spiritual Exercises* of St. Ignatius in *The Seven Storey Mountain*; the history of their use is detailed in *Modern Spiritual Exercises: A Contemporary Reading of the Spiritual Exercises of St. Ignatius*, by David L. Fleming, S.J. (Image, 1983). Merton describes his anxiety as a new author in the autobiography; the journal is a record of it. He invoked the Holy Ghost as a muse on Ascension Thursday, May 18, 1939, looking forward to Pentecost the following week; he calls the Holy Ghost the Holy Spirit. His sketch of himself on the balcony on Decoration Day is reproduced in *Run to the Mountain*. His verbal sketch of himself on the balcony is from the second Saturday in September, 1939, as his remark about confessions indicates.

106 Walker Percy's visit to Caroline Gordon and Allen Tate is remarked on by Patrick Samway; Jay Tolson touches on Professor William Carson von Glahn's influence and describes Will Percy as "hard at work on a memoir" in the summer of 1939. Percy evokes the appeal of the "beautiful theater of disease" as compared to the "arts and crafts of the bedside manner" in "From Facts to Fiction," a 1966 essay published in *Signposts in a Strange Land*.

107 Merton's hospital stay and his pilgrimage to Cuba make up an entire section of *Run to the Mountain* but are most vividly described in *The Seven Storey Mountain*, the memories ripened by recollection. His rumination on Ad Reinhardt is in the journal entry dated January 5, 1940. The preconciliar understanding of priestly vocation is discussed insightfully in *The Other Side of the Altar*, by Paul E. Dinter (Farrar, Straus and Giroux, 2003).

113 Day's journal entries for *House of Hospitality* are excerpted in *By Little and By Little*, her father's characterization of her as a "Catholic crusader" in Miller's biography (at the end of the "Spreading Personalism" chapter), the movement's demands on her in Forest's biography. *From Union Square to Rome* is available, in full, at *www.catholicworker.org*. The 1940 statement of "Aims and Purposes" appears in *By Little and By Little*; "Our Stand" is quoted at length in Miller's biography; Day's call for a movementwide retreat in Forest's biography, her impatience for solitary retreats in Miller's biography, Pacifique Roy's approach in *Loaves and Fishes*. Day recalled the prewar movementwide retreat in her column for July/August 1947, which Miller quotes at length. Her note about turning away from current events is quoted by Miller—confusingly, some pages before he describes the communal retreat and the Blitz of London, which in all likelihood prompted it.

117 Quite early in World War II—November 21, 1939—Thomas Merton concluded in his journal that it was "a new kind of war"; he remarked on the "vile combat of bombs against bricks" on November 28, 1940. He explained his objections to war in the clearest possible terms in the "True North" chapter of *The Seven Storey Mountain*, so as to cut through the obfuscation of religious and secular arguments alike— which had been compounded, in the intervening years, by the bombing of Hiroshima and Nagasaki. The passage begins:

> God was asking me . . . to signify where I stood in relation to the actions of governments and armies and states in this world overcome with the throes of its

own blind wickedness. He was not asking me to judge all the nations of the world, or to elucidate all the moral and political motives behind their actions. He was not demanding that I pass some critical decision defining the innocence and guilt of all those concerned in the war. He was asking me to make a choice that amounted to an act of love for His Truth, His goodness, His charity, His Gospel, as an individual, as a member of His Mystical Body. He was asking me to do, to the best of my knowledge, what I thought Christ would do.

118 Merton's evocation of St. Bonaventure as a medieval place is from *The Seven Storey Mountain*; his description of his image-adorned room there from a journal entry of November 27, 1940; his remark about Kierkegaard from one of January 11, 1941, a line of thought begun November 29, 1940. In the observation that "radios are forcing men into the desert," from December 2, 1940, the voice of *The Seven Storey Mountain*—public, a shade grandiose, confident in its pronouncement on the present age, taking personal experience as representative of those of modern people generally—is heard for the first time. Merton described the speech he gave on the radio December 18, 1940, and the vow he made to the Selective Service March 4, 1941. James Forest in *Living with Wisdom* summarizes the significance of the Franciscan "third order" and the obligations attached to it.

119 Merton's encounter with the legend of the Cistercians, through the *Catholic Encyclopaedia*, is recounted dramatically in *The Seven Storey Mountain*. So is his journey to Gethsemani for a Holy Week retreat; this is described, in entirely different terms, in the journal, beginning April 5, 1941—twenty-eight pages in *Run to the Mountain*. His stop in New York, passed over altogether in the autobiography, is described in the journal and in Michael Mott's biography. His remark to Robert Giroux in the Scribner's bookstore is drawn from Giroux's introduction to the Fiftieth Anniversary Edition of *The Seven Storey Mountain* (Harcourt, Brace, 1998).

127 Merton's plan for an anthology of religious poetry is in his journal, July 27, 1941; the remark about Francis Thompson in the journal, August 21, 1941.

127 Merton's recollection of the speakers in a lecture series at St. Bonaventure—including "one from *The Catholic Worker*"—is in the chapter of *The Seven Storey Mountain* called "The Sleeping Volcano." Baroness Catherine de Hueck Doherty's life story is told briefly in *All Saints*, by Robert Ellsberg. Three decades later, the passages on Harlem in *The Seven Storey Mountain* elicited the admiration of Eldridge Cleaver, then an inmate in solitary confinement in Folsom Prison in California. Cleaver wrote in *Soul on Ice* (McGraw-Hill, 1968):

> Despite my rejection of Merton's theistic world view, I could not keep him out of the room. He shouldered his way through the door. Welcome, Brother Merton. I give him a bear hug. Most impressive of all was Merton's description of New York's black ghetto—Harlem. I liked it so much I copied out the heart of it in longhand. Later, after getting out of solitary, I used to keep this passage in mind when delivering Black Muslim lectures to other prisoners. . . . For a while, whenever I felt myself softening, relaxing, I had only to read that passage to become once more a rigid flame of indignation. It had precisely the same effect on me that Elijah Muhammad's writings used to have, or the words of Malcolm X, or the words of any spokesman of the oppressed in any land.

131 Merton's recollection of the Trappist drowned to the world is from his first visit to Gethsemani as described in the "True North" chapter of *The Seven Storey Mountain*.

131 Day's editorial "Our Country Passes from Undeclared War to Declared War; We Continue Our Christian Pacifist Stand," published in the January 1942 *Catholic Worker*, is reprinted in *A Penny a Copy* and *By Little and By Little*. Day on several occasions described going to the old cathedral to write important pieces, and artistic license has been taken in situating her there in this instance.

5. *Independents*

132 Will Percy's peroration on the "one good life" and on the hazards of life without religion is found in the chapter "For the Younger Generation" in *Lanterns on the Levee*. The circumstances of the book's publication are recounted by Bertram Wyatt-Brown in *The House of Percy*. The *New York Times* review is quoted on the cover of the Louisiana State University Press paperback edition. The book is addressed to its readers as a "pilgrim's script" in an italicized Foreword, and is dedicated not only to Walker Percy and his two brothers but also to "Adah, Charlotte & Tom," who were (Patrick Samway reports) three close friends of Will Percy's generation. Bertram Wyatt-Brown touches on the similarities between the book, the *Meditations* of Marcus Aurelius, and *The Education of Henry Adams*. Percy himself, in an interview with Zoltan Abádi-Nagy conducted for the *Southern Literary Journal* (Fall 1973), declared that "I have an uncle whose hero was Marcus Aurelius."

134 Walker Percy's work as an intern at Bellevue is described in the two biographies and also in his essay "From Facts to Fiction," in which he remarks, "Now I was one of them."

134 Edward O'Connor's death is explained in Robert Fitzgerald's introduction to *Everything That Rises Must Converge* and Sally Fitzgerald's chronology in the Library of America edition. O'Connor recalled her father and remarked on his speeches in a letter to Elizabeth Hester of July 13, 1956. She described—defined—the independent in a letter to William Sessions of September 13, 1960. In a letter to Sister Mariella Gable of May 4, 1963, she amplified the point: "The prophet is a man apart. He is not typical of a group. Old Tarwater is not typical of the Southern Baptist or the Southern Methodist. Essentially, he's a crypto-Catholic. When you have a man alone with his Bible and the Holy Ghost inspires him, he's going to be a Catholic one way or another, even though he knows nothing about the visible church. His kind of Christianity may not be socially desirable, but it will be real in the sight of God." Of O'Connor's own independence, Alfred Kazin, in *Writing Was Everything* (Harvard, 1995), observed, "There is a severity, a compactness, to her faith exactly like the tone she takes to her characters. Everything is all of a piece with her, which is the last thing I would say about most of the people I know (especially the writers)." He follows his analysis of O'Connor with some reflections on Czeslaw Milosz.

135 O'Connor remarked that she had her father's disposition in the letter to Hester of July 13, 1956. Sally Fitzgerald suggests that he was her best friend in the essay "Flannery O'Connor: Patterns of Friendship, Patterns of Love," published in the *Georgia Review* (Fall 1998). O'Connor recalled "just 'hanging out' in high school" in "The

Teaching of Literature," and the method of teaching literature in a letter to Cecil Dawkins of October 27, 1957; the approach is mocked and rebutted in "The Teaching of Literature" and "Total Effect and the Eighth Grade," both published in *Mystery and Manners*.

136 O'Connor's playfully mocking description of the Georgia State College for Women comes from a letter to Betty Boyd Love postmarked September 20, 1952. Her activities there are documented in Sally Fitzgerald's chronology and in several photographs in the Flannery O'Connor Collection in Milledgeville: a photograph of her with the staff of the *Corinthian* (for all her supposed shyness, she is seated in the middle of the group, obviously in charge, and staring straight at the camera); a photograph evidently taken for the yearbook, in which her face is flattened and her eyes made angular in the catlike way later suggestive of wisdom. Her romance with John Sullivan, such as it was, is described by Sally Fitzgerald in "Patterns of Friendship, Patterns of Love." The nature of her scholarship to the University of Iowa is described there and in Robert Giroux's introduction to *The Complete Stories*.

137 Bertram Wyatt-Brown, working with greater distance from Percy than Percy's biographers could achieve and a lesser need to sustain a narrative, often moves quickly to penetrating insight, and the thousand-word synopsis of Percy's bout with tuberculosis in *The House of Percy* is more revealing than the chapters devoted to it in the two biographies, which are fruitfully thick with detail nonetheless. Percy's life as a "hermit" at Saranac Lake, recalled by Shelby Foote, is quoted in Robert Coles's *Walker Percy: An American Search*, as is his recollection that he had "nothing to do but read and think"; the image of his uncashed government checks is from Tolson.

137 Percy remarked on fiction as a key to the human "predicament" in an interview with John Griffin Jones for Volume 2 of *Mississippi Writers Talking* (University Press of Mississippi, 1983). He discussed Sartre's influence in many interviews and essays, most incisively in "The State of the Novel: Dying Art or New Science?" reprinted in *Signposts in a Strange Land*. Likewise Dostoevsky: in *Conversations with Walker Percy*, the index entry for the Russian author is as extensive as those for William Alexander Percy and Flannery O'Connor; the remark about Dostoevsky's characters comes from the interview with John Griffin Jones. Although his biographers stress Thomas Mann's influence, Robert Coles gives it special emphasis; in conversation with me he declared, "If you want to understand Percy, read *The Magic Mountain*, and if you've read it, read it again." Percy's assessment of the modern novel is found in an interview with Marcus Smith, conducted for the *New Orleans Review* in 1976 and reprinted (as are all the other interviews cited here) in *Conversations with Walker Percy*; his view of "the nature and destiny of man" is in "From Facts to Fiction," reprinted in *Signposts in a Strange Land*.

138 Percy's recuperation at Trudeau is described vividly by Tolson, the ritual of "cousining" by Samway, the relative health and enthusiasm of the other tubercular doctors by Tolson.

139 There is a photograph of the first Catholic Workers in *Loaves and Fishes*, on the stoop outside Dorothy Day's apartment. Two photographs of Day and the Catholic Workers outside Houses of Hospitality are reproduced in Miller's biography, as is a group photograph taken at the Easton Farm; another photograph from the same day appears in *Love Is the Measure*. Of the portrait photographs of Dorothy Day alone, the earliest, from about 1938, is reproduced in *Dorothy Day and the "Catholic*

Worker"; two others, taken perhaps five years apart, appeared in *Commonweal* in 1997, illustrating Patrick Jordan's article "An Appetite for God: Dorothy Day at 100."

139 Day's description of bus stations is quoted by Miller in the "Rearing a Daughter" chapter of his biography. Her observation that love "is the laying down of one's life for one's friend" from February 1942, her argument against the conscription of women from January 1943, her confession of her loneliness from June 1944. Her breakfast meeting with Forster Batterham is mentioned in Miller's biography; Tamar's marriage to David Hennessy is described in Day's column for May 1944 and in *Love Is the Measure*.

141 Percy's misadventures after his release from the sanatorium are documented in Tolson's and Samway's biographies. His remark about having no home is from Robert Coles's *New Yorker* profile, his remark about having washed up on shore from an interview conducted by Linda Whitney Hobson in 1981 and quoted by Samway. Of his many explanations of Kierkegaard's role in his life, the most detailed is in an interview with Bradley R. Dewey in 1974, published in the *Journal of Religion* and reprinted in *Conversations with Walker Percy*. His account of existentialism is from "Diagnosing the Modern Malaise," a 1977 talk reprinted in *Signposts in a Strange Land*.

143 The list of things forbidden in a Trappist monastery is drawn from *The Seven Storey Mountain*; Michael Mott explains the dread "particular friendships"; James Forest reports other lurid proscriptions in the "Brother Louis" chapter of *Living with Wisdom*. Merton's description of his "small box" comes from the autobiography; his letter to Mark Van Doren of April 14, 1942, is published in *The Road to Joy: Letters to New and Old Friends* (ed. Robert E. Daggy; Farrar, Straus and Giroux, 1989; Harvest, 1993). His account of the monastery as a school opens the final chapter of *The Seven Storey Mountain*; his observations that he was born and would die a writer are from "First and Last Thoughts: An Author's Preface" to *A Thomas Merton Reader* (ed. Thomas P. McDonnell; Doubleday, 1961; rev. ed. Image, 1974). The circumstances of the publication of *Thirty Poems* are detailed by Michael Mott, whose biography emphasizes Merton's life as a poet; the rules against an author photograph and the like—which were formally reiterated upon the publication of Merton's second book, *A Man in the Divided Sea*—are reported by James Forest.

145 O'Connor's muskrat fur coat is remarked upon by Sally Fitzgerald in her introduction to *Three by Flannery O'Connor*; O'Connor is shown wearing it in a photograph in the Flannery O'Connor Collection in Milledgeville and reproduced to accompany "The Coat" in *DoubleTake* (Summer 1996). Her reason for changing her name—"Who was likely to buy the stories of an Irish washwoman?"—is given by Richard Gilman in "On Flannery O'Connor," published in the *New York Review of Books* (August 21, 1969) and reprinted in *Conversations with Flannery O'Connor* (ed. Rosemary M. Magee; University Press of Mississippi, 1987). The story of her arrival at the Iowa Writers' Workshop is told by Robert Giroux in his introduction to *The Complete Stories*. Her impressions of Iowa City, including its zoo, are from a letter to Elizabeth Hardwick and Robert Lowell of February 1, 1953, in the Library of America edition; her course work, rooming situation, and letters to her mother are detailed in Sally Fitzgerald's chronology. Her remark on what inspires the beginning writer is made in "Some Aspects of the Grotesque in Southern Fiction" in *Mystery and Manners*; the image of the loaves and fishes is from a letter to Elizabeth

Hester of March 24, 1956; her account of her reading in fiction at Iowa is from a letter to Hester of August 28, 1955.

147 The quotations from Cleanth Brooks and Robert Penn Warren's *Understanding Fiction* are taken from the first edition (Appleton-Century-Crofts, 1943); the book is dedicated to Donald Davidson, a Fugitive and Agrarian, who would review *The Violent Bear It Away* for the *New York Times Book Review* in 1960. O'Connor's claim that she was "congenitally innocent of theory" is from the Author's Note to the second edition of *Wise Blood* (Farrar, Straus and Cudahy, 1962), her insistence that "nobody has ever gotten away with much" from "The Nature and Aim of Fiction," in *Mystery and Manners*. In the same essay she declared, "I am not, of course, as innocent as I look."

148 "The Coat" was first published in *DoubleTake* (Summer 1996). O'Connor's thesis stories are presented as the first six stories in *The Complete Stories* and in the "Stories and Occasional Prose" section of the Library of America edition, where their inclusion, rather than that of several essays left out of the volume, seems an editorial misjudgment. O'Connor's remark about "manners under stress" is found toward the end of "The Catholic Novelist in the Protestant South," in *Mystery and Manners*.

149 Dorothy Day's rumination on the Desert Fathers is found in an article entitled "On Retreat," published in the *Catholic Worker* (July/August 1943); her retreat on Long Island and her letter to the abbot of Gethsemani, Frederic M. Dunne, are described in Miller's biography. Day's editorial in response to the bombings of Hiroshima and Nagasaki, "We Go on Record—," is one of her best-known pieces; published in the paper in September 1945, it is reprinted in *A Penny a Copy* and *By Little and By Little*. Day's warning that "now destruction hangs over New York and London" was published in the *Catholic Worker* in November 1945; her article from June 1946, "Love Is the Measure," is one of the best distillations of her point of view; both are reprinted in *By Little and By Little*. Her paraphrase of St. Teresa of Avila and St. Catherine of Siena, also often cited, is from the *Catholic Worker* (February 1946).

150 Merton's letter of March 1, 1946, to James Laughlin, quoted by Michael Mott and James Forest, is published in *Thomas Merton and James Laughlin: Selected Letters* (ed. David D. Cooper; Norton, 1997). Merton described the typescript as 650 pages of "straight autobiography" in a letter to Laughlin of August 17, 1946. The story of how it made its way to the publisher is told by Robert Giroux in his introduction to the Fiftieth Anniversary Edition.

151 O'Connor's acquisition, by inheritance, of Grey Quail Farm is described in Sally Fitzgerald's chronology, the Rinehart-sponsored fellowship in Robert Giroux's introduction to *The Complete Stories*. She described Jacques Maritain's *Art and Scholasticism* (with *The Frontiers of Poetry*; trans. Joseph W. Evans; Scribner's, 1962) as "the book I cut my teeth on" in a letter to Elizabeth Hester of April 20, 1957, and recommended it to Cecil Dawkins in a letter of May 19, 1957, emphasizing the practical intellect; she quoted St. Thomas's "very cold and very beautiful definition" of art as "reason in making" in "The Nature and Aim of Fiction," in *Mystery and Manners*. "Christian Art" is the eighth chapter of *Art and Scholasticism*. Shrike brandishes an irreverent newspaper clipping in the second chapter of Nathanael West's *Miss Lonelyhearts* (published with *The Day of the Locust*; New Directions, 1969).

152 O'Connor described her exaggerated technique, of which Hazel Motes is the first example, in "The Fiction Writer and His Country": "To the hard of hearing you shout, and for the almost-blind you draw large and startling figures." "The Train" is

published in *The Complete Stories*. Sally Fitzgerald discusses some of the intermediate revisions of *Wise Blood* in her introduction to *Three by Flannery O'Connor*. O'Connor described Motes as an "admirable nihilist" in a letter to Ben Griffith, March 3, 1954. The aspirations for a Catholic "renascence" were expressed in the journal of that title. *The Diary of a Country Priest* was published in English translation in 1937 (Macmillan), *Thérèse* in 1947 (Holt). François Mauriac's story is told in *All Saints*, by Robert Ellsberg. Graham Greene and Evelyn Waugh, and the relation between them, are the subject of a chapter of *Our Age: The Generation That Made Post-War Britain*, by Noel Annan (Fontana, U.K., 1991), delivered as a lecture at the University of London (Summer 1986). Evelyn Waugh explains his motives in the introduction to the Penguin edition of *Brideshead Revisited* (1962).

155 O'Connor described the experience of faith and doubt in a letter to Alfred Corn, May 30, 1962. She concluded a subsequent letter (July 25, 1962) in Percy-like terms, telling Corn, a college student, "Sometime when you are going to Emory, stop and pay me a visit. I would like to fit your face to your search." She explained the "conflict between an attraction for the Holy and the disbelief in it" in a letter to John Hawkes, September 13, 1959, and remarked that "belief, in my own case anyway, is the engine that makes perception operate" while introducing "A Good Man Is Hard to Find" at Hollins College, October 14, 1963; the remark is quoted in the section "On Her Own Work" of *Mystery and Manners*. She defined "wise blood" in a remarkable letter to Carl Hartman, March 2, 1954, in the Library of America edition; the scene in which Hazel Motes strikes Enoch Emery with a rock concludes Chapter 5 of *Wise Blood*.

156 Walker Percy explains the ways in which Covington, Louisiana, represents the ordinary in "Why I Live Where I Live," published in *Esquire* in April 1980 and reprinted in *Signposts in a Strange Land*. His cross-country trip with Shelby Foote is vividly evoked in Jay Tolson's biography; Patrick Samway locates the hotel they stayed in as near the cathedral. Foote's warning is drawn from a letter of some years later—November 8, 1951—published in *The Correspondence of Shelby Foote and Walker Percy*. Percy's peregrinations after the war included several awkward romances, described by Bertram Wyatt-Brown in *The House of Percy*. Percy's thoughts of marriage are quoted by Tolson; Samway quotes Percy's remarks to Bunt Townsend and his telegram proposing marriage.

158 Percy's marriage and honeymoon at Sewanee are described in both biographies, as is his conversion to Catholicism, which Tolson explores more insightfully than does Samway, a Jesuit priest. Samway tells of the influence of a Catholic fraternity brother and a Catholic doctor with tuberculosis. Percy's own blunt explanation of why he believed is found in the "Self-Interview" in *Signposts in a Strange Land*, where he says what attracted him was "Christianity's rather insolent claim to be true, with the implication that the other religions are more or less false." His description of the novel as "an instrument of exploration and discovery" is from "Diagnosing the Modern Malaise," in *Signposts in a Strange Land*.

6. The School of the Holy Ghost

162 Dorothy Day's recollection of the time Peter Maurin went missing is quoted in the "Middle Years" chapter of Miller's biography; her likening of him to St. Francis is

from *The Long Loneliness*, as are the recollections of his decline and of the Workers' attempt to tape-record his voice.

163 Robert Giroux recalls his efforts on behalf of *The Seven Storey Mountain* in his introduction to the Fiftieth Anniversary Edition. Waugh's postwar success is thrillingly recounted in *Evelyn Waugh: The Later Years*, by Martin Stannard (Norton, 1992); *The Brideshead Generation*, by Humphrey Carpenter (Houghton Mifflin, 1990), is readable and vivid but less dramatic. The pairing of Waugh and Graham Greene is described (and penetrated in the deepest sense) by Noel Annan in *Our Age*, but Annan stresses the differences rather than the underlying similarities. Waugh's review of *The Heart of the Matter*, published in *Commonweal* in July 1948, is reprinted in Waugh's *Essays, Articles, and Reviews* (Methuen, 1983) and in *Commonweal Confronts the Century* (Touchstone, 1999). Waugh's letter to Clare Boothe Luce is quoted in Stannard's biography.

166 Dorothy Day's journal entry for September 19, 1948, is in *On Pilgrimage*, published by Catholic Worker Books. It has been reprinted by Eerdmans (1999) with a foreword by Michael O. Garvey and an introductory essay by Mark and Louise Zwick of Casa Juan Diego, the Catholic Worker House of Hospitality in Houston. The abbot of Gethsemani's remark about the Catholic Worker being a "companion order in the world" is found in *Loaves and Fishes*; the complaints about modern life are also from *Loaves and Fishes*. (*On Pilgrimage* includes Day's appraisal of Albert Camus; apparently she was the first of the four writers depicted here to encounter him through his books.)

167 Evelyn Waugh's visit, and his lunch with Dorothy Day, is recounted in *Evelyn Waugh: The Later Years*, and in *Loaves and Fishes*, but not in *On Pilgrimage*. His visit to the Abbey of Gethsemani is described in Merton's journal, dated November 30, 1948, published in *Entering the Silence* (ed. Jonathan Montaldo; Harper San Francisco, 1996) and in Mott's biography. Merton's letters to Waugh are published, along with a synopsis of Waugh's replies, in *The Courage for Truth: Letters to Writers* (Farrar, Straus and Giroux, 1993). Waugh's *Life* article, "The American Epoch in the Catholic Church," is reprinted in Waugh's *Essays, Articles, and Reviews*.

169 The publication of *The Seven Storey Mountain* is described in Robert Giroux's introduction to the Fiftieth Anniversary Edition, and in Mott's biography.

170 O'Connor explained her working habits in a letter to Elizabeth McKee, July 21, 1948, and in one to Paul Engle, April 7, 1949, both quoted in the introduction to *The Complete Stories* and published in *The Habit of Being*; she recalled parties at Yaddo and the colony's view of "Experience" in a letter to Cecil Dawkins, December 19, 1959; the animals underfoot in a letter to Dawkins, July 19, 1962, the place generally in a letter to Dawkins, August 1, 1962; and the conversations among the guests in a letter to Elizabeth Hester, August 4, 1962, and one to Dawkins, September 6, 1962. She recollected meeting Alfred Kazin in letters to Elizabeth McKee, January 20, 1949, and to Ben Griffith, May 7, 1956. Sally Fitzgerald describes O'Connor's churchgoing habits in the Library of America chronology and in "Patterns of Friendship, Patterns of Love."

171 Robert Lowell's early manhood is recounted in several biographies: *Robert Lowell: A Biography*, by Ian Hamilton (Vintage, 1983); *The Lost Puritan*, by Paul Mariani (Norton, 1994); *The Interior Castle: The Art and Life of Jean Stafford*, by Ann Hul-

bert (Knopf, 1992); *Jean Stafford: The Life of a Writer,* by David Roberts (St. Martin's, 1988); and he is recalled especially vividly in *Poets in Their Youth,* by Eileen Simpson (Noonday, 1990), which also has a great deal to say about Stafford's life and career.

171 Lowell had (coolly) reviewed Thomas Merton's *Thirty Poems* in the Catholic press, and in a journal entry of December 16, 1947 (expanded upon in *The Sign of Jonas*), Merton offhandedly reviewed Lowell's book *Lord Weary's Castle,* which Robert Giroux had sent to him, saying, "He makes no false steps. . . . I'd like to write to him but I guess it would be smarter if I didn't." O'Connor recalled her time with Lowell and his return to the Church in a letter to Elizabeth Hester, April 21, 1956, describing him as "one of the people I love."

172 The story of the conflict at Yaddo has been told so often as to exaggerate its importance. Lowell's remarks are quoted in Hamilton's and Mariani's biographies. O'Connor's plans to meet publishers and her agent in New York are set out in her letters of early 1949. The story of her conflict with John Selby is recounted most memorably in Robert Giroux's introduction to *The Complete Stories.* O'Connor expressed her impatience with "the Brothers Rinehart" in a letter to Elizabeth McKee, January 28, 1949; the agent's dealings with Harcourt, Brace are summarized in a letter of February 3; O'Connor told McKee, "I am very much pleased about what you have done with the manuscript." O'Connor described John Selby's letter in a letter to McKee, February 17, 1949, and in one to Paul Engle, April 7, 1949. She had described her work as "formless stuff" in a letter to McKee of July 21, 1948. The "Author's Note" to *Wise Blood* was written in 1961.

174 Lowell's return to the Church is described in the biographies of him; O'Connor's visit to the Fitzgeralds in Sally Fitzgerald's "Patterns of Friendship, Patterns of Love" and in Robert Fitzgerald's introduction to *Everything That Rises Must Converge,* where it is euphemized with old-fashioned faux down-home formality: "A friend of ours brought her to our apartment in New York to bear him out in something he had to tell, and this she did with some difficulty, frowning and struggling softly in her drawl to put whatever it was exactly the way it was." Robert Giroux recalls meeting O'Connor, and giving her a copy of *The Seven Storey Mountain,* in his introduction to *The Complete Stories.* She calls him "my good editor" in a letter to Elizabeth Hester, May 16, 1959, as published in the Library of America edition.

175 Lowell's manic break, and Robert Fitzgerald's reaction to it, is described in the two Lowell biographies; Mariani paraphrases Allen Tate's conjecture that Lowell "would probably become a monk like Thomas Merton."

176 Fitzgerald's musings on God's power are from a letter to Allen Tate and Caroline Gordon, March 4, 1949, quoted by Ian Hamilton. O'Connor recalled her stint at the YWCA in a letter to Elizabeth Hester, September 8, 1962; Sally Fitzgerald describes it in the chronology to the Library of America edition. O'Connor's performance at dinner with Mary McCarthy is evoked in Mariani's biography, as well as in O'Connor's letter to Elizabeth Hester of December 16, 1955; it is rarely remarked upon that on another occasion—a letter to Hester of February 21, 1957—O'Connor defended McCarthy against hostile reviewers the way she might have defended herself: "They all—all the bright boys—love to take potshots at her because she is so much smarter than they are." Lowell's remark to Hardwick is found in Robert Fitzgerald's notes, quoted by Hamilton.

176 O'Connor's reaction to Lowell's manic episode is found in a letter to Elizabeth Hester, May 14, 1960, which begins, "Let me right now correct, stash & obliterate this revolting story about Lowell introducing me as a saint," and goes on, "I was too inexperienced to know he was mad, I just thought that was the way poets acted." Ian Hamilton reports that Allen Tate, in a telephone conversation with Elizabeth Hardwick, castigated her and O'Connor for "indulging" Lowell, as inexperienced women were wont to do.

178 O'Connor's months alone in New York are recounted in Robert Fitzgerald's introduction to *Everything That Rises Must Converge*, in "Patterns of Friendship, Patterns of Love," and in the Library of America chronology; the latter two accounts are based on O'Connor's letters to Betty Boyd, November 5, 1949, and to Janet McKane, June 5, June 19, and July 9, 1963. O'Connor announced her move to "the rural parts of Connecticut" in a letter to Betty Boyd, August 17, 1949. "The Enduring Chill," written in 1957, is in *The Complete Stories*.

179 Dorothy Day's description of Mott Street is quoted in Miller's biography; the publication snarls of *On Pilgrimage* and the "war between the clergy and the laity" in her column for April 1949; Peter Maurin's death in *The Long Loneliness*; the squabbles over his funeral in her column for October 1949. James Forest reports in *Love Is the Measure* that Peter Maurin's death was acknowledged far and wide.

182 Waugh's swift ripening to old age is described by Martin Stannard in *Evelyn Waugh: The Later Years*.

182 O'Connor's life in Connecticut is described in Robert Fitzgerald's introduction to *Everything That Rises Must Converge* and Sally Fitzgerald's introduction to *The Habit of Being*, her essay "Patterns of Friendship, Patterns of Love," and her Library of America chronology. O'Connor reported on Enoch Emery's exploits in an undated letter of 1950 to Robie Macauley, and described Philip Hughes's history of the Reformation in an undated 1952 letter to the Fitzgeralds. She remarked on Robert Lowell's *The Mills of the Kavanaghs* in a letter to the Fitzgeralds, September 21, 1951, in the Library of America edition (apparently she took the typescript to Georgia and tried to read it there). She recalled reading *Oedipus Rex* in a letter to Ben Griffith, February 13, 1954.

183 Walker Percy's efforts to become a novelist are described in Tolson's biography ("A Second Apprenticeship") and Samway's biography ("The Apprenticeship Years: Writing *The Charterhouse* 1947–53"). The synopsis of *The Charterhouse*, the manuscript of which Percy destroyed, is based especially on Tolson. Percy's dismissal of his two unpublished novels is from "Physician as Novelist," in *Signposts in a Strange Land*; he describes "two novels, one a bad imitation of Thomas Mann, the other a worse imitation of Thomas Wolfe—which is very bad indeed." Samway suggests *The Charterhouse* was the "Wolfean" one, but it is hard to know for sure. Tolson suggests that Percy read Pascal before he set about becoming a novelist. Because Walker Percy's early letters to Shelby Foote are lost, Foote dominates the 1997 book of their correspondence, and seems even more domineeringly self-assured than he must have been.

184 Merton's reflections upon his seven years as a Trappist are taken from his journal, December 13, 1949, published in *Entering the Silence*. His notoriety as the "literary Trappist," a subject of running commentary in the journal, is summarized by Mott, Forest, and Giroux, and by Merton himself in "First and Last Thoughts: An Author's

Preface" to *A Thomas Merton Reader*. Mott, who describes the process whereby Merton's mail was answered, also makes vivid the significance of the book vault and the key that symbolized it. The remark about fan mail is from his journal, February 9, 1949. *The Seven Storey Mountain* was described as "the odyssey of a soul" in the review in the *Saturday Review of Literature*, quoted on the cover of the paperback edition. Merton's remarks in *Seeds of Contemplation* are drawn from the Dell paperback, his image of a "one-man hermitage" from the journal, June 27, 1949.

187 Day's account of the ferry ride to Staten Island—a ride she took dozens of times—is from *Loaves and Fishes*. Day's visit to the Tates in Princeton in May 1950, which gave rise to Gordon's description of Day, is recounted in Ann Waldron's *Close Connections: Caroline Gordon and the Southern Renaissance*, as are Gordon's visits to St. Joseph's House and Maryfarm. Robert Giroux confirmed Gordon's impressions in a firsthand account of the Princeton gathering. Allen Tate's catechumenate is described in Nancylee Novell Jonza's *The Underground Stream: The Life and Art of Caroline Gordon*, but not in Thomas A. Underwood's *Allen Tate: Orphan of the South*, which concludes in 1938. Malcolm Cowley's revision of *Exile's Return* is explained in the prologue to the revised edition; the epilogue carries the colophon "Sherman, Connecticut, March 1951," and the book (the copyright page indicates) was published in June. Day's impressions of Maryfarm and her attraction to the farm on Staten Island are described in the "Back to Staten Island" chapter of Miller's biography, as are the circumstances in which she received a thousand-dollar advance from Harper & Brothers.

190 Robert Fitzgerald recalled O'Connor's careful revision of *Wise Blood* in the introduction to *Everything That Rises Must Converge*. The term "realist of distances" is introduced in "Some Aspects of the Grotesque in Southern Fiction" in *Mystery and Manners*; the image of Christ lurking in the trees is emphasized in the Author's Note to the second edition of *Wise Blood*; the "pin point of light," in the last paragraph of the novel. O'Connor's effortful further revision is described by Robert Fitzgerald in his introduction and by Sally Fitzgerald in the Library of America chronology; the image of O'Connor as a "shriveled old woman" is from Sally Fitzgerald's headnote to the letters of 1950–1952 in *The Habit of Being*.

191 O'Connor described her hospital stay in a letter to Betty Boyd Love, December 23, 1950. She described the interpenetration of her own character and Hazel Motes's in a letter to Elizabeth Hester, November 25, 1955; she likened sickness to a place in a letter to Hester of June 28, 1956.

192 Sally Fitzgerald proposed the presence of "an unusually strong sense of active destiny" in O'Connor's life in "Patterns of Friendship, Patterns of Love"; the conclusion of this section is an amplification, unconscious but doubtless intentional, of a remark of Sally Fitzgerald's in the introduction to *The Habit of Being*: "Here [in Georgia] her mature life began."

193 Caroline Gordon's role in the final revisions of *Wise Blood* is described in Sally Fitzgerald's offprint "A Master Class: From the Correspondence of Caroline Gordon and Flannery O'Connor," published in the *Georgia Review* (Vol. 33, No. 4)— which is not an essay so much as a gathering together of quotations from their letters to each other joined with interstitial material. O'Connor's letters to others and the two biographies of Caroline Gordon also remark on the story. O'Connor's September 1951 letters to the Fitzgeralds about *Wise Blood* are published in *The Habit of*

Being; her two passages from an unsent letter of thanks are published in "A Master Class."

194 Walker Percy's correspondence with Caroline Gordon is presented in the two Percy biographies and in the two Gordon biographies. Gordon's letters to her friend Brainard Cheney are quoted at length by Patrick Samway, as is Gordon's sharp criticism of the limitations of *Wise Blood.* Percy compared *The Charterhouse* and *Wise Blood* in a 1980 interview with Ben Forkner and J. Gerald Kennedy, published in *Conversations with Walker Percy.* (There he also had a good deal to say about O'Connor's stories, especially "A Good Man Is Hard to Find," "The Artificial Nigger," and "Everything That Rises Must Converge.") The background to the discussions of Catholicism and literature of which Gordon was a part is given in *Walker Percy: The Last Catholic Novelist,* by Kieran Quinlan (Louisiana State University, 1996).

197 Gordon's praise for Percy's revision of *The Charterhouse* is quoted by Jay Tolson; her remark about the Holy Ghost by Ann Waldron in *Close Connections: Caroline Gordon and the Southern Renaissance.* Gordon's notion for a "School of the Holy Ghost" is described, and her letter quoted, by Samway; her description of the retreat at Maryfarm as "the finest experience I ever had" by Waldron.

7. The Stranger

201 The publication date of *Wise Blood* is given in the Library of America chronology; the party is described in O'Connor's letter to Betty Boyd Love, May 23, 1953. Photographs taken at the party are in the Flannery O'Connor collection in Milledgeville, as is Robert Giroux's correspondence with Evelyn Waugh about the novel. (In full, Waugh's letter read: "Thank you for sending me WISE BLOOD, which I read with interest. You want a favorable opinion to quote. The best I can say is: 'If this is really the unaided work of a young lady, it is a remarkable product.' End quote. It isn't the kind of book I like much, but it is good of its kind. It is lively and more imaginative than most modern books. Why are so many characters in recent American fiction sub-human? Kindest regards. E. W.") Regina O'Connor's query is found in O'Connor's letter to the Fitzgeralds of April 1952.

202 Camus's expression of alienation and estrangement is found in *The Myth of Sisyphus* (Eng. trans., Knopf, 1955). The quotations from *Wise Blood* are taken from the second edition (Farrar, Straus and Cudahy, 1962), which, apart from the Author's Note, is no different from the first. The "catch-all" of Motes's maxims of unbelief is drawn from his various sermons in the novel. Caroline Gordon pointed out the spotlit quality of the novel in her editorial letter to O'Connor, quoted by Sally Fitzgerald in "A Master Class." Iris Murdoch describes modern fiction by means of philosophical and religious categories in "Existentialists and Mystics," a 1970 essay and the title essay of a posthumous collection of her incidental work (ed. Peter Conradi; Allen Lane/Penguin, 1997). *The Picaresque Saint: Representative Figures in Contemporary Fiction,* by R.W.B. Lewis (Lippincott, 1959), also informs the analysis of Hazel Motes in this section. Morris Dickstein's *Leopards in the Temple: The Transformation of American Fiction 1945–70* (Harvard, 2002) is an incisive account of the major writers and themes of the postwar period.

206 *Time's* review was published June 9, 1952; the *New Republic's,* by Isaac Rosenfeld,

was summarized by O'Connor in a letter to Robert Fitzgerald, July 1952. Harold Bloom defines the combination of strength and strangeness as the mark of great literature in *The Western Canon*. O'Connor explained the purposes of a jagged style in "Some Aspects of the Grotesque in Southern Fiction," in *Mystery and Manners*, and singled out Hazel Motes's integrity as his characteristic virtue in the "Author's Note to the Second Edition" of *Wise Blood*.

208 Thomas Merton recounts the monastery fire watch in the celebrated essay by that name, published first as the epilogue to *The Sign of Jonas* (Harcourt, Brace, 1953), then in the journal published as *Entering the Silence*, where the *Sign of Jonas* epilogue material ("composed on the typewriter," a note explains) includes a more general celebration of Gethsemani and monastic life. Michael Mott explains the circumstances in which Merton revised the journal for *The Sign of Jonas*.

210 Merton's application for U.S. citizenship is described in the journal and in *The Sign of Jonas*, both entries dated June 23, 1951; his efforts in contemplative prayer, an ongoing theme of the journal, public and private, conclude in the entry for February 26, 1952.

210 Dwight Macdonald's profile of Dorothy Day was published in the *New Yorker*, October 4 and October 11, 1952. Day's journal is quoted in Miller's biography; Michael Harrington's review of *The Long Loneliness* is characterized by Tom Sullivan in Nancy Roberts' *Dorothy Day and the "Catholic Worker"*; Sullivan's warning about the *New Yorker* is found in Miller's biography. The analysis of the rhetoric of *The Long Loneliness* is indebted to the insights of the Reverend Michael Baxter of the University of Notre Dame, elicited in conversation in July 1998.

212 Day's travels are chronicled in her *Catholic Worker* columns for November 1951 and May and June 1952; her call for saints and heroes is in an article for the January 1953 issue, which she concludes by quoting John Wesley (whom she had read in childhood) on the call to pilgrimage.

212 The early history of Holy Ghost monastery—vividly evoked by Thomas Merton in his history of Cistercian monasticism, *The Waters of Siloe* (Harcourt, Brace, 1949)— is related in detail in *Open to the Spirit: A History of the Monastery of the Holy Spirit*, by Dewey Weiss Kramer, a short book available at the monastery. Day describes visiting there in her June 1952 column. Day's visit to Caroline Gordon in Minnesota is described in Nancylee Novell Jonza's *The Underground Stream: The Life and Art of Caroline Gordon*; Day's appraisal of the School of the Holy Ghost is in Ann Waldron's *Close Connections: Caroline Gordon and the Southern Renaissance*. Gordon's description of *The Malefactors* as a story of the journey of faith is quoted in Jonza's biography; her assessment of Percy as a formidable Southern writer is in Samway's biography.

214 Both biographies of Percy give ample attention to Shelby Foote's objections to the counsel of Gordon and Allen Tate and his distaste for Percy's religiosity. In a letter not published in the volume of Foote-Percy correspondence, one that Patrick Samway quotes at length (but doesn't cite in his end notes), dated July 20, 1952, Foote told Percy that he did "look with horror at your approach in some respects— especially your desire to be 'wise' in that bloodless way. It's ruinous, nothing less." Percy's remark about the School of the Holy Ghost is related by Samway, his purchase of a Lincoln Town Car by Tolson, his contacts with Sue Brown Jenkins by both biographers.

214 Percy describes his prolonged encounter with the existentialists in many interviews, most tellingly Ashley Brown's for *Shenandoah* (1967), Bradley R. Dewey's for the *Journal of Religion* (1974), and John Griffin Jones's for *Mississippi Writers Talking* (1983), all reprinted in *Conversations with Walker Percy*, and in Robert Coles's *New Yorker* profile. Marcel's comments are drawn from *Homo Viator: Introduction to a Metaphysic of Hope* (trans. Emma Crawford; Harper & Row, 1962).

215 O'Connor described her visit to Connecticut in letters to Robert Giroux, Sally Fitzgerald, Robert Fitzgerald, and Elizabeth McKee, all of July 1952, and in a letter to Robert Lowell and Elizabeth Hardwick of March 17, 1953; she alluded to her diagnosis and asked for *Art and Scholasticism* to be returned to her in two undated letters from that summer. She described whipping Benedict Fitzgerald in a letter to Caroline Gordon, September 11, 1952, in the Library of America edition. She described taking up painting in a letter to the Fitzgeralds of the summer of 1953 and ordering *Moby-Dick* and *The Idiot* in a letter to the Fitzgeralds of February 1, 1953; she thanked Ashley Brown in a letter of May 22, 1953, in the Library of America edition.

217 Caroline Gordon had described O'Connor's characters as freaks in a letter of St. Didacus's Day, 1951; O'Connor reported that she was trying to get away from freaks in a letter to Gordon of September 11, 1952, in the Library of America edition. "The Life You Save May Be Your Own" is in *The Complete Stories*; O'Connor thanked the Fitzgeralds for suggesting the title—"your title," she called it—in a letter of December 20, 1952. O'Connor reported buying peafowl in letters to the Fitzgeralds, late summer 1952, and Robie Macaulay, October 28, 1952, and told the story of their acquisition in "The King of the Birds," in *Mystery and Manners*.

219 Merton described the "fixed-up shanty" he called St. Anne's in his journal, beginning with the entry of September 3, 1952, published in *A Search for Solitude* (ed. Lawrence S. Cunningham; Harper San Francisco, 1996); the quotations are from the entries dated December 29, 1952, and February 9 and 16, 1953. The journal for that period also describes his "stability crisis."

220 O'Connor reported on Erik Langkjaer's first visit to Andalusia in a letter to the Fitzgeralds of May 7, 1953; Langkjaer recalled it in a taped conversation which Christopher O'Hare shared with me. Sally Fitzgerald describes their romance in "Patterns of Friendship, Patterns of Love." O'Connor called herself Grimrack and described her baldness in letters to the Fitzgeralds of December 20, 1952, and January 25, 1953; asked them about the "Conversations at Newburgh," June 7, 1953; recalled ordering "some back issues" of *The Third Hour* in a letter to Elizabeth Hester, August 28, 1955. She recalled receiving a prayer card in the mail from the *Catholic Worker* "a couple of years ago" in a letter to Hester, January 17, 1956, which suggests that she was already on the paper's mailing list—was a subscriber, that is.

221 Dorothy Day published "Little by Little" in the *Catholic Worker* (April 1953) and revised it as "The Faces of Poverty" for *Loaves and Fishes*.

222 O'Connor described her self-portrait in an undated letter to the Fitzgeralds, which Sally Fitzgerald places in the summer of 1953; the photograph of it is in the Farrar, Straus and Giroux archives. She recounted her trip to Connecticut in a letter to Robie Macaulay, October 13, 1953; quipped about "the continental tour" in the letter to the Fitzgeralds of June 7, 1953; and remarked on her friends' travels in a letter to them of September 1953. "The Displaced Person" is in *The Complete Stories*; her

visit to the Cheneys is recorded in the Library of America chronology. O'Connor's treatment of love, sacred and profane, is explored in depth by Richard Giannone in *Flannery O'Connor and the Mystery of Love* (Illinois, 1989; Fordham, 1999); he discusses the stories treated here in chapters entitled "Looking for the Good Man" and "Finding the Good Man."

224 Erik Langkjaer's intentions are reported in the Library of America chronology and in "Patterns of Friendship, Patterns of Love"; O'Connor's intensive rewriting of "The Displaced Person" in the "Note on the Texts" section of the Library of America edition. O'Connor described herself as a "great admirer" of Conrad in a letter to Elizabeth Hester, August 28, 1955. Dorothy Day developed her view of the stranger as Christ in one of her strongest pieces, "Room for Christ," published in the *Catholic Worker* in December 1945 and reprinted in *By Little and By Little*.

225 The travails of *The Gramercy Winner* are described in the two biographies of Walker Percy, each of which summarizes the novel, a manuscript of which is in the library of the University of North Carolina. The passage about "Willy" Grey is quoted from Patrick Samway's summary. Tolson's biography includes a photograph of Percy, wearing a tuxedo, circa 1955; other photographs show him wearing plain clothes. The paperback edition of *Philosophy in a New Key* was published by the New American Library in 1948; the cover described here is on the fifth printing, May 1953. Percy recalled the experience of reading the book to Marcus Smith in a 1976 interview reprinted in *Conversations with Walker Percy*; his review, "Symbol as Need," published in *Thought* in September 1954, is reprinted in *The Message in the Bottle*; he mentioned the twenty-five offprints to John Griffin Jones in the interview for *Mississippi Writers Talking*, reprinted in *Conversations*.

229 Merton's reputation as the "literary Trappist" was the subject of "Thomas Merton: Modern Man in Reverse," by Dom Aelred Graham, in the *Atlantic Monthly* (January 1953). Merton complained about the St. Bernard assignment in his journal, August 28, 1952, and derided his early work and "professional spirituality" in an entry of October 22, 1952, both published in *The Search for Solitude*. *Bread in the Wilderness* was published in 1953 (Michael Mott reports), *The Last of the Fathers* in 1954, *No Man Is an Island* in 1955, *The Living Bread* in 1956, *The Silent Life* in 1957; a work called *Existential Communion* was rewritten and published in 1962 as *The New Man*. Merton's journal goes silent between March 10, 1953, and July 17, 1956, and again between September 12, 1956, and April 4, 1957.

230 O'Connor's correspondence with Erik Langkjaer is described by Sally Fitzgerald in "Patterns of Friendship, Patterns of Love"; his plan to work on a communal farm in the notes section of the Library of America edition; her work on "Good Country People" in the chronology. O'Connor recalled its quick composition in a letter to Elizabeth Hester of June 1, 1956; recounted the process in "Writing Short Stories," in *Mystery and Manners*; described its protagonist as "a projection of myself . . . presumably only a projection" in a letter to Hester of September 30, 1955; and engaged in disputation over its autobiographical aspect in letters to Hester of May 19 and August 24, 1956, discussing the lack of "technical control" in the latter. The story itself is in *The Complete Stories*. O'Connor's letter to Langkjaer of May 23, 1955, is in the Library of America edition; her switch in pronoun is remarked upon by Sally Fitzgerald in "Patterns of Friendship, Patterns of Love." Fitzgerald quotes Langkjaer as recalling that O'Connor was "mildly" in love with him, but then suggests that the

attachment was strong enough to prompt Langkjaer to leave the country alto-gether—that Langkjaer, in order to avoid a misunderstanding, "removed himself gently from the scene and returned to Denmark." O'Connor herself, describing Helene Iswolsky, recalled that "I used to go with her nephew" in a letter to Hester, August 28, 1955.

234 O'Connor characterized herself as a "hillbilly Thomist" in a letter of May 18, 1955. A videotape of *Galley Proof* is in the Flannery O'Connor Collection in Mil-ledgeville; a transcript is published in *Conversations with Flannery O'Connor*. O'Con-nor touched on her New York trip in letters to Catharine Carver, May 24, 1955, and Elizabeth McKee, June 29, 1955, and recounted the weekend in Connecti-cut to the Fitzgeralds in a letter of June 10, 1955, an outing also described by Ann Waldron in *Close Connections*. Gordon's review of *A Good Man Is Hard to Find* was published in the *New York Times Book Review* (June 12, 1955).

236 The Catholic Worker's direct action outside City Hall, which Day described in the paper in July–August 1955, is a set piece in Jim Forest's *Love Is the Measure*. A pho-tograph of Day being ushered into a paddy wagon—from that year or one subse-quent—appears in *Loaves and Fishes*. Ammon Hennacy's story is a staple of the biographies, and Miller's account is particularly detailed. Day herself wrote about him at length in an article for *The Third Hour*—the magazine published by Helene Iswolsky, the Russian "aunt" of Erik Langkjaer.

238 Day's visit to Caroline Gordon is recounted in *Close Connections*; Day's reception of the manuscript of *The Malefactors* is in Miller's biography, as is her correspondence about it. *The Malefactors*, now out of print, was published by Harcourt, Brace in 1956, and edited by Denver Lindley, who had just become (through attrition) Flan-nery O'Connor's editor as well. Day's appraisal of the novel is a topic of O'Connor's letter to the Fitzgeralds, February 6, 1956; O'Connor declined to praise the book in a letter to Lindley, January 15, 1956, criticized it in a letter to the Fitzger-alds of January 22 (which was excised by Sally Fitzgerald before publication in *The Habit of Being*), discussed its merits and drawbacks in letters to Elizabeth Hester of March 10 and May 19, and proposed reviewing it for the *Bulletin* in a letter to Eileen Hall of March 10. Mindful of the book's controversial aspect, she wrote: "Don't feel you have to review the Gordon book"—assign a review of it, that is—"if you think it would cause the *Bulletin* embarrassment or trouble. I will certainly understand. Most of your readers wouldn't like *The Malefactors* if it were reviewed favorably by Pius XII." Her remark about "My dog, Spot," is from an unpublished letter to Lind-ley of January 31, 1956, in the O'Connor Collection in Milledgeville; her review is reprinted in *The Presence of Grace and Other Book Reviews by Flannery O'Connor* (compiled by Leo J. Zuber; ed. Carter W. Martin; Georgia, 1983).

240 Day's account of the 1956 action is from the *Catholic Worker* (July/August 1956). The account of the Montgomery bus boycott is drawn especially from the docu-mentary television series *Eyes on the Prize*. Day's plan to go to Montgomery is from her column for October; O'Connor's remarks about racial conflict were made in let-ters to Erik Langkjaer, May 23, 1955, in the Library of America edition, and to Eliz-abeth Hester, May 19, 1956; her remarks about "The Artificial Nigger" are in two letters to Maryat Lee, June 28 and March 10, 1957, and in one to Ben Griffith, May 4, 1955. The story itself is in *The Complete Stories*; her revisions are described in the Library of America chronology. O'Connor expressed her suspicion of reform-

ers from other parts of the country in an interview with C. Ross Mullins for *Jubilee*, June 11, 1963, reprinted in *Conversations with Flannery O'Connor*, and referred to the "tragedy of the South" in a letter to Hester, September 6, 1955.

244 Dorothy Day described her trip to the South in *Catholic Worker* columns for November 1956, December 1956, and January 1957. She described her trip to Koinonia in a series of letters published in the May 1957 issue; Flannery O'Connor remarked on them, and on Day, in a letter to Elizabeth Hester, May 4, 1957.

247 Walker Percy's views on race relations are found in "Stoicism in the South" (*Commonweal*, July 6, 1956); "A Southern View" (letter to the editor of *America*, July 20, 1957); and "The Southern Moderate" (*Commonweal*, December 13, 1957), all reprinted in *Signposts in a Strange Land*. "The Man on the Train" is published in *The Message in the Bottle*.

8. *Counterparts*

254 Thomas Merton's "Vision in Louisville" (as it is called on a cast-iron sign which now stands at the corner of Fourth Street and Muhammad Ali Boulevard in Louisville) is a set piece in James Forest's biography; Michael Mott touches on the differences between the account in Merton's journal and the one published in *Conjectures of a Guilty Bystander* (Doubleday, 1966). Although the differences are considerable, the most significant change was effected by the passage of time: in 1966, the "Vision" seemed to incarnate the themes of church renewal and openness to the world made current by the Second Vatican Council.

255 Merton's excursions from the monastery are described in the journals published as *A Search for Solitude*, as are his visit to Minnesota (which his biographers give great significance), his enthusiasm for Russian writers, his dreams of Sophia, and his insights into Martin Buber, these last entries made April 20 and April 24, 1958. *I and Thou* (trans. Ronald Gregor Smith) was published in a new edition by Scribner in 1957. Of the many reappraisals of J. F. Powers's work, the most persuasive is by Donna Tartt (*Harper's*, July 2000).

258 Walker Percy's purchase of a house in New Orleans is described in the two Percy biographies. His remark about "secure anonymity" is from "The Southern Moderate," about the "zone crossing" in "The Man on the Train."

258 Merton's letters to Boris Pasternak are published, and Pasternak's replies summarized, in *The Courage for Truth: Letters to Writers* (ed. Christine M. Bochen; Farrar, Straus and Giroux, 1993; Harvest, 1994). Merton related Pasternak's story in "The Pasternak Affair in Perspective," published in *Thought* (Winter 1959–1960). "Last week, I stayed awake until 4 a.m. after reading too stimulating an article by Thomas Merton, 'The Pasternak Affair in Perspective,' " Dorothy Day remarked in her column for February 1960 (reprinted in *By Little and By Little*) and went on to quote the final paragraphs. The article was revised and published in Merton's *Disputed Questions* (Farrar, Straus and Cudahy, 1960), which, in a postscript to the book, reprints Pasternak's last reply to Merton; Merton's remark on Pasternak's death is from his journal, June 1, 1960, published in *Turning Toward the World* (ed. Victor A. Kramer; Harper San Francisco, 1996).

261 Czeslaw Milosz's *The Captive Mind* (trans. Jane Zielonko; Knopf, 1953) was published with a new foreword in 1981. Merton's letters to Milosz are published in *The Courage for Truth*; the complete correspondence is published in *Striving Towards*

Being: The Letters of Thomas Merton and Czeslaw Milosz (ed. Robert Faggen; Farrar, Straus and Giroux, 1997); Milosz's critique of Merton's work is in an undated letter of 1959; Merton's account of Christianity is in a letter of September 12, 1959, which precedes the Milosz letter in the correspondence.

264 "You Can't Be Any Poorer Than Dead" was published in *New World Writing* (October 1955) and reprinted in *The Complete Stories*. O'Connor reported her trouble with the novel and her pleasure with a story in a letter to Elizabeth Hester, January 1, 1956; she characterized her talk on the short story as a "yammer" in a letter to Hester, February 25, 1956, and denounced a "silly" lesbian interpretation of "A Temple of the Holy Ghost" in two letters to the interpreter, Beverly Brunson, September 13, 1954, and January 1, 1956, both in the Library of America edition. The second letter begins as an apology for the first, as though O'Connor had made a firm purpose of amendment on New Year's Day; but she reiterated her view of lesbianism as a form of "uncleanness," declaring, "This is not rudeness; this is just my point of view." She wrote to Andrew Lytle September 15, 1955, and to Ben Griffith July 9, 1955, in the latter instance continuing a correspondence beginning in 1954. The editor who compared her sales to Thomas Merton's was Catherine Carver, not Robert Giroux, in an unpublished letter in the O'Connor Collection in Milledgeville.

265 O'Connor's first letter to Elizabeth Hester, of July 20, 1955, is printed in full here. O'Connor first remarked on Hopkins's correspondence October 20, 1955, using the past tense—"Hopkins said"—which suggests that she had read it some time earlier. In her second letter to Hester, on August 2, 1955, O'Connor remarked, "I may seem to force on you a correspondence that you don't have time for or that will become a burden"—which suggests that she already conceived of their letters as a correspondence, very likely a complex one, undertaken at her initiative as much as Hester's. She described writing for people "who think God is dead" in the letter of August 2, and described work—fiction—written for "public consumption" in "The Nature and Aim of Fiction" and paraphrased Arthur Koestler's remark about the writer's willingness to "swap" present readers for future ones in "Catholic Novelists and Their Readers," both in *Mystery and Manners*. She remarked on letters in the section of her will, drafted in 1958, in which she appointed Robert Fitzgerald her literary executor; a photocopy is in the Farrar, Straus and Giroux files. She proposed that the honorific "Miss" be dropped in a letter to Hester of October 12, 1955.

267 Hester was referred to as "A" in O'Connor scholarship until her death at age seventy-five in 1998 by a gunshot wound—a suicide. Her death and life—which included a long correspondence with the novelist Iris Murdoch—were described in the *Atlanta Journal and Constitution* in two articles: by Joel Groover (December 30, 1998), and by Bo Emerson (March 28, 1999). William Sessions, a mutual friend of O'Connor's and Hester's, is preparing an edition of her letters. Sally Fitzgerald, in her introduction and headnotes to *The Habit of Being*, depicted Hester as first among equals in O'Connor's correspondence, a precedent followed by many scholars. Robert Giroux, who as editor of *The Habit of Being* suggested that she be identified as "A," insisted, in conversation, that he did not have Hawthorne in mind: he was thinking of "Anonymous."

267 O'Connor described feeling like an "anthropoid ape" in a letter to Hester written on September 24, 1955; recalled reading "Slop" on August 28; described reading the *Summa* in bed on August 9; described her study as a "rat's nest" on October 12; pic-

tured Hester as "7 ft. tall" on October 12; pictured Hester as her own size on October 20 (and remarked on the photograph of herself alongside her self-portrait) and as "a ginger beer bottle" on October 30, also remarking on her own prettiness gone "a mite sour." She discussed Céline and Nelson Algren in letters beginning October 28, 1955; derided the notion that the Incarnation, and religious faith generally, must be "emotionally satisfying" on September 6, 1955, also seeking to distinguish between Catholic principle and Church policy; remarked on her "celebrity" on December 16; and described her "letter-writing duties"—"every Tuesday come fire pestilence or plague I write to my 86 year old cousin in Savannah"—April 21, 1956; the full letter is published in the Library of America edition.

269 She insisted that she had "consented to be in love" in the letter of August 24, 1956; declared that she did not "lead a holy life" on August 2, 1955; acknowledged her lack of worldly experience on August 9 and August 28; called resistance to faith "the devil's greatest work of hallucination" on August 9; and dubbed herself a "besieged defender of the faith" on January 17, 1956. She remarked on reading about Simone Weil in *The Third Hour* on August 28, 1955; asked whether Hester knew Weil's work on August 2; and described reading some Weil books Hester had sent—and finding some of Weil "ridiculous"—September 24; one was *Waiting for God* (trans. Emma Crawford; Harper, 1973, published in 1951, with a biographical note and an introduction by Leslie A. Fiedler that may have provoked O'Connor as much as the text proper did. She professed her inability to "dominate" Weil—"Miss Weil"—and called her remarks a "tribute" on September 30, 1955; the order of the remarks is reversed here. She remarked on where Weil had "started from" on October 30, 1955. The story she was writing is "Greenleaf," in *The Complete Stories*.

272 O'Connor responded to the news of Hester's baptism—and to the photograph of her—on January 17, 1956; described sending her "Greenleaf" on March 10 and ordering *A Short Breviary* on May 19; and anticipated Easter on March 24.

273 Dorothy Day sought to "restate our position" in the Fall Appeal published in the *Catholic Worker* in November 1955 (reprinted in *A Penny a Copy*) and remarked on the cost of poverty (and numbered the meals served) in the October 1958 appeal. The economics of the paper are discussed in detail by Nancy L. Roberts in *Dorothy Day and the "Catholic Worker"*; Flannery O'Connor delighted in its "ideal subscription rate" in a letter to Elizabeth Hester, September 28, 1956. Robert Ellsberg explains the movement's principles in the introduction to *By Little and By Little*; Day derided a "businesslike" approach in a column of February 1934 (reprinted in *By Little and By Little*) and explained the refusal to incorporate in the paper in September 1942. She explained the Catholic Worker's dispute with the New York City fire marshal in the November 1955 appeal and told the story of the old woman and her poor son in the November 1957 appeal.

276 Walker Percy's essay "The Coming Crisis in Psychiatry," published in *America* (January 5 and January 12, 1957), is reprinted in *Signposts in a Strange Land*; "Metaphor as Mistake," from the *Sewanee Review* (Spring 1958), is published in *The Message in the Bottle*, as is "The Loss of the Creature," which first appeared in *Forum* (Fall 1958), a journal edited by Donald Barthelme.

279 The Catholic Workers' direct action of 1957 and Dorothy Day's jail sentence are vividly described in *Love Is the Measure*, with James Forest pointing out that the Women's House of Detention was not far from the old Hell Hole. Day herself de-

scribed the episode in articles for *Commonweal* and *Liberation* as well as in her own paper; Robert Ellsberg has blended them artfully under the title "Visiting the Prisoner" in *By Little and By Little*. Of voluntary jail time Day remarked, "It is a gesture, perhaps, but a necessary one." The remark is echoed by Flannery O'Connor's remark, in "Novelist and Believer," that the religious novelist may find that "instead of reflecting the image at the heart of things, he has only reflected our broken condition and, through it, the face of the devil we are possessed by. This is a modest achievement, but perhaps a necessary one."

280 Day's struggle to write *Therese* is recounted in William D. Miller's biography. She recalled her first impressions of St. Thérèse of Lisieux most vividly in her introduction to the book; the afterword is one of her keenest expressions of her own point of view—about poverty, sanctity, ordinariness, suffering, and the bonds among them.

281 Flannery O'Connor remarked on "St. Theresa Lisieux" in a letter of February 6, 1956, to J. H. McCown, S.J., who is given a cloying portrait in Patrick Samway's biography of Walker Percy; her review of two books about the saint for the *Bulletin* is reprinted in *The Presence of Grace*. She explained her view of sickness to Elizabeth Hester, and recalls Hester's visit, in a letter of June 28, 1956; remarked on her deprivations to Hester, April 6, 1957; called reviewing for the diocesan paper a "mortification" in a letter to Hester, February 25, 1956, and described counseling a student at the Iowa Writers' Workshop in a letter to Hester, February 11, 1956.

282 Friedrich von Hügel's *Letters to a Niece*, published in 1928, are in print with Regent College Publishing, Vancouver; his story is told by Robert Ellsberg in *All Saints*. O'Connor first mentioned Von Hügel in a letter to Elizabeth Hester, November 10, 1955; remarked on ordering the volume of *Letters* on November 25; and summarized her *Bulletin* review on May 5, 1956: "According to me it is absolutely finer than anything I've seen in a long long time. You can read one letter a night without straining yourself much." Recommending the book to T. R. Spivey on May 25, 1959, she warned him that "all the 'darling Gwen-childs' have to be ignored."

283 O'Connor recounted her meeting with Phinizy Spalding in a letter to Elizabeth Hester, August 9, 1957, and explained his relationship to Walker Percy on August 24. In calling Walker Percy "our mutual admiration," she implied that they both already admired his work, most likely the essays "Stoicism in the South" (*Commonweal*, July 6, 1956), and "The Man on the Train" (*Partisan Review*, Fall 1956).

283 Foreign editions of *A Good Man Is Hard to Find* are detailed in the chronology to the Library of America edition. She announced the planned trip to Lourdes in a letter to Elizabeth Hester, November 2, 1957, and in one to the Fitzgeralds, November 4, 1957, in the Library of America edition; the quotation is from the latter. She explained her motives in a letter to the Fitzgeralds, February 26, 1958. She called it a "pilgrumidge" in a letter to the Fitzgeralds, December 4, 1957, and described the run-up to it in a succession of letters, as follows: to Hester, November 16; to Hester, December 14; to Cecil Dawkins, January 17, 1958; to the Fitzgeralds, February 11, February 26, March 11, March 21, and April 14; to Ashley Brown, April 14. The emergence of Lourdes as a place of pilgrimage is discussed with great insight by Ruth Harris in *Lourdes: Body and Spirit in the Secular Age* (Viking, 1999). Harris's discussion of the relation of Lourdes, in rural southern France, to Paris, in the developed north, is especially rich in implications.

285 Sally Fitzgerald remarked expansively that O'Connor "dreaded" a miracle cure "in

those circumstances" in a note in *The Habit of Being*, commenting on a letter to Elizabeth Hester, May 17, 1958; O'Connor had remarked that Fitzgerald had a "hyperthyroid moral imagination." Fitzgerald's own remarks about grace, which O'Connor paraphrases, are akin to Robert Fitzgerald's remarks about grace during Robert Lowell's manic episode in 1950. O'Connor remarked on her "magnificent fortitude" to the Fitzgeralds, February 11, 1958, and explained that she was going to Lourdes as "a pilgrim not a patient" in the letter to Hester of December 14, 1957. She remarked on the artist's calling to "contemplate experience" in "The Nature and Aim of Fiction," in *Mystery and Manners*.

286 O'Connor described the pilgrimage itself in letters to Elizabeth Hester, May 5, 1958; the Fitzgeralds, May 11; Hester, May 17; Ashley Brown, May 28; Elizabeth Bishop, June 1. The last, printed in full in the Library of America edition, is a letter unusual in its sobriety and exactness of description. She had likened herself to a "structure with flying buttresses" in a letter to Hester, April 7, 1956. The details of the grotto and its procedures are drawn from Ruth Harris's *Lourdes*.

287 O'Connor's brief stopover in New York en route from Europe was recalled in conversation by Roger Straus; her remark about being a "hermit novelist" is in a letter to Maryat Lee, June 28, 1957. Her sense of herself as such a character is fruitfully explored by Richard Giannone in *Flannery O'Connor: Hermit Novelist* (Illinois, 2000). She described her time alone at Andalusia in a letter to Elizabeth Hester, April 4, 1958; her driver's education to Hester, July 19, her "hearse-like" car to Hester, August 30; her Cousin Kate's illness, and the state of her own bones, to Hester, November 22. The cousin's death "in late November" is reported in the Library of America chronology.

288 O'Connor reported on her struggle with *The Violent Bear It Away* in letters to Elizabeth Hester, May 17, 1958, and December 23, and explained her need to "bend" the novel so as to elicit "awe and mystery" in "Novelist and Believer," in *Mystery and Manners*. She announced its completion in letters to Hester, January 31, 1959, and the Fitzgeralds, January 1, February 15, and March 24; the quote is from the last letter.

289 Walker Percy recalls the "breakthrough" of *The Moviegoer* in "From Facts to Fiction," in *Signposts in a Strange Land*, and in "Physician as Novelist" describes the nature of the breakthrough, and of Binx Bolling's story, as "the pilgrim's search outside himself." Jay Tolson and Patrick Samway detail the different iterations of the manuscript in their biographies. Tolson introduces Shelby Foote's remark about New Orleans having "everything," from a letter of May 1951 (since published in *The Correspondence of Shelby Foote & Walker Percy*), and examines the importance of point of view in the novel; Samway offers the insight that Percy, away from his library, wrote differently than he might have otherwise. *The Moviegoer* (Knopf, 1961) is now a Vintage paperback. Flannery O'Connor's remark about the writing of fiction as an act of self-knowledge is drawn from the transcript of her appearance on *Galley Proof* in *Conversations with Flannery O'Connor*, Percy's from "Physician as Novelist." In the Percy passage, the pronouns are suggestively ambiguous; Percy, who in the novel paradoxically used the first person to achieve some distance between himself and his protagonist, in the essay paradoxically uses the third person to collapse that distance, to conflate his pilgrimage and Binx Bolling's.

293 Thomas Merton's obsession with an imagined, ideal monastery is a theme—*the*

theme—of his journals of the later fifties, published in A *Search for Solitude*. Pius XII's death and Angelo Roncalli's election as John XXIII are related in *Pope John XXIII*, by Thomas Cahill (Lipper/Viking, 2002); John's pilgrimage to Assisi and Loreto was described in a draft of Cahill's *Pope John XXIII*. Merton remarked on Pius's death in his journal, October 12 and 15, and on John's character, November 9; his letter to the pope of November 12 is published in *The Hidden Ground of Love*. James Forest, in his biography, underscores the significance of the stole sent in reply. Merton's letter to Robert Lax, April 2, 1959, is published in *When Prophecy Still Had a Voice: The Letters of Thomas Merton and Robert Lax* (ed. Arthur W. Biddle; University of Kentucky, 2001).

296 Merton's characterization of Lax as a "natural contemplative" is from *The Seven Storey Mountain*. Merton remarked on Lax and Reinhardt's visit, and then Robert Giroux's, in his journal, May 3, 1959, saying little more than this: "The thing is, when people come to see me, they are not really edified. I have to face this fact—it is disturbing. It is that I am not really a monk and not really a Christian."

296 Giroux recalled the visit to Gethsemani vividly in his introduction to *The Complete Stories* of Flannery O'Connor. His account of his visit to Andalusia on the same trip is based on his recollections in *The Complete Stories*, as well as his recollections in conversation, which diverge somewhat from O'Connor's account in letters to Caroline Gordon, May 10, 1959; to Elizabeth Hester, May 16, as published in the Library of America edition, in which she suggests that Giroux visited the monastery by himself before coming to Milledgeville; and to Hester, May 30, in which she reports that "we did finally get to the monastery" for the first time.

298 Dorothy Day's account of Jack English's first Mass was published in the *Catholic Worker* (March 1959); Day's appraisal of *The Seven Storey Mountain* is quoted in Miller's biography.

299 Dorothy Day's letters and notes to Thomas Merton are unpublished, and are quoted here with the permission of the Catholic Worker Collection at Marquette University, Milwaukee, and made available through the Thomas Merton Studies Center at Bellarmine College, Louisville. Merton's letters are published, with excisions here and there, in *The Hidden Ground of Love*. Day's first card is dated June 20, 1959; her second is marked the Feast of the Sacred Heart, which falls in early summer. Merton's reply is dated July 9, 1959. Day's next letter is dated December 23, 1959; Merton's, February 4, 1960.

9. *Convergences*

302 Faulkner's remark about "oratory out of solitude" is cited by Alfred Kazin in "The Secret of the South: Faulkner to Percy," a section of *Bright Book of Life*, a consideration of postwar Southern fiction that also touches on Flannery O'Connor. The elements of Binx Bolling's philosophy in *The Moviegoer* repeat concepts found especially in "The Man on the Train" and in Kierkegaard's *Either/Or* and *Repetition*. Morris Dickstein has nothing to say about *The Moviegoer* in his study *Leopards in the Temple*, but he usefully situates *Rabbit, Run* and *Revolutionary Road* in the context of the "road" novel, epitomized by Jack Kerouac's classic, and brings out themes similar to those emphasized here. Richard Ford (quoted in Jay Tolson's biography) has observed that *The Moviegoer* describes "the rough traverse from the

Fifties to the Sixties"; in greater retrospect, the novel seems to describe the traverse from the postwar period to the period bracketed by the Cuban missile crisis and the destruction of the World Trade Center. Flannery O'Connor remarked on the contemporary "sub-religion" in "Novelist and Believer," in *Mystery and Manners*.

307 O'Connor described a reporter and photographer's visit to Andalusia in a letter to Elizabeth Hester, October 3, 1959, remarking that she typed answers to prospective questions in advance. *Conversations with Flannery O'Connor* reprints two articles from the *Atlanta Journal and Constitution*, as well as two by Richard Gilman, one published pseudonymously in *The Sign* in 1960, the other in the *New York Review of Books* upon O'Connor's death in 1964. Contact sheets of photographs taken for the *Journal*, by Joe McTyre and Jay Leviton, are in the Farrar, Straus and Giroux archives. The side effects of O'Connor's lupus are described in the chronology in the Library of America edition.

308 *The Violent Bear It Away* was reviewed in the *New York Times*, February 24, 1960, and in *Time*, February 29, 1960. O'Connor predicted that the novel would be "pounced on" to Elizabeth Hester, July 25, 1959; writing to Hester, October 31, 1959, she worried that "it will be dammed and dropped, genteelly sneered at." She smarted over "idiot reviews" in letters to Hester, March 5, 1960, and Robert Giroux, March 6; she wished novels could be "deposited in a slot for the next century" in a letter to John Hawkes, October 14; she told Hawkes her concern about "where the next word is coming from," July 26, 1959.

309 O'Connor reported that she was "toying" with "The King of the Birds" in a letter to Cecil Dawkins, August 10, 1960; the essay is in *Mystery and Manners*. She described the genesis of her introductory essay to A *Memoir of Mary Ann* in the essay itself and in letters to Elizabeth Hester, April 30 and May 14, 1960, and Robert Giroux, September 29, 1960. She expressed her admiration for Nathaniel Hawthorne in letters to Ben Griffith, March 3, 1954, and Elizabeth Hester, August 28, 1955, and first remarked on the connection between Hawthorne and the Free Cancer Home on March 10, 1956. She described the arts festival at Wesleyan College in Macon in a letter to John Hawkes, October 9, 1960; a transcript of the panel discussion is reprinted in *Conversations with Flannery O'Connor*; at one point, O'Connor remarks that "Walker Percy wrote somewhere that his generation of Southerners had no more interest in the Civil War than in the Boer War. I think that is probably quite true," and her remark in the talk about "men in gray flannel suits" seems to echo Percy's description, in "The Man on the Train," of Charles Gray, the protagonist of *Point of No Return*, by John P. Marquand, author of *The Man in the Gray Flannel Suit*.

311 "Some Aspects of the Grotesque in Southern Fiction" is in *Mystery and Manners*; in the notes, Sally Fitzgerald reports that upon giving the talk O'Connor "asked that it be given only local distribution as she might 'sooner or later revise it for publication.'" As it is, the talk was published in 1966 in *The Added Dimension* (eds. Melvin J. Friedman and Lewis J. Lawson; Fordham); as the first of O'Connor's pieces of self-exegesis to receive wide distribution, it shaped the interpretation of her work in precisely the way that she hoped it would. This talk also includes O'Connor's observation that "I think the writer is initially set going more by literature than by life."

313 O'Connor described the nuns' literary abilities in a letter to Elizabeth Hester,

July 23, 1960, published in full in the Library of America edition, and sought Robert Giroux's advice in a letter of September 29, 1960. Dorothy Day recalled reading a life of Rose Hawthorne Lathrop in *Loaves and Fishes* and told the saint's story, concluding, "There are now half a dozen of those hospitals, run by the Dominicans, scattered around the country." O'Connor told the story in the Mary Ann essay, concluding, "There are now seven of their free cancer homes over the country."

314 The "Introduction to *A Memoir of Mary Ann*" is in *Mystery and Manners*. O'Connor reported on Caroline Gordon's critique of it—saying she agreed with it but thought the problem easily remedied—in a letter to Hester, November 25, 1959; in a letter to Hester, November 12, she remarked, "The introduction is quite opposite in tone to the book itself; which is I think as it ought to be." In considering the essay about Mary Ann Long an expression of O'Connor's view, her remark that the novelist's "prophet-freak is an image of himself" is apposite.

315 O'Connor sent the introduction and manuscript to Robert Giroux, December 8, 1960, with a letter published in full in the Library of America edition; described the imminent "inspection of my bones" to Maryat Lee the same day; and told Elizabeth Hester about a new story, December 24, also remarking on the "disintegration" of her bones. A note by Sally Fitzgerald in *The Habit of Being* identifies the story as "Parker's Back"; the title appears on the first page of the first draft of the story on file in the O'Connor Collection in Milledgeville.

315 The election of John F. Kennedy is seen as a turning point in American Catholicism by Garry Wills in *Bare Ruined Choirs* (Doubleday, 1972), Martin Marty in *Pilgrims in Their Own Land*, Mark Silk in *Spiritual Politics* (Simon & Schuster, 1988), Charles R. Morris in *American Catholic*, and Mark S. Massa in *Catholics and American Culture*, among many others. Walker Percy's pleasure is described in Jay Tolson's biography (where there is a forced comparison of John F. Kennedy and Binx Bolling); Dorothy Day recalled two Kennedys' visit to St. Joseph's House in *Loaves and Fishes*; Flannery O'Connor remarked on the election in a letter to Maryat Lee, November 19, 1960; Thomas Merton did so in his journal, November 9, published in *Turning Toward the World* (ed. Victor A. Kramer; Harper San Francisco, 1996).

316 Merton described fashioning the hermitage in a series of journal entries beginning October 3, 1960, and culminating December 2, 5, and 26; Mott draws the connection between the hermitage and the chapel at St. Antonin in his biography. Merton described the hermitage as a place for "passage out of this world," April 16, 1961, and remarked on the imperative to "enter into truth" there, September 30.

317 Merton wrote an introduction to *The Wisdom of the Desert* (New Directions, 1960) in the spring of 1959, but observed that "there is more to be done" on it in his journal, April 21, 1959. Dorothy Day, in a Christmas card, December 23, 1959, thanked him for "your beautiful book containing the beautiful news." The news, inscribed on the flyleaf, was very likely that he expected to be allowed to make a new foundation in Mexico; the book, most likely, was *What Ought I to Do?*—a limited edition (fifty copies) of the text of *The Wisdom of the Desert*, printed by his friend Victor Hammer in Louisville. Merton evidently did not reply. On January 22, 1960, Day wrote to Merton to tell him she had been kept awake by his "beautiful and profound" essay on Pasternak: "It was very exciting, all of it, and I thank you for writing it, and for sending us a copy. I carried it along with me on my trip west."

318 In a letter to Merton of June 4, 1960, which includes her account of the "disturbed

family," Day told Merton about a second ex-Trappist, now at the Catholic Worker, who was a "hero-worshipper" of Merton's, to the extent of going on pilgrimage to the home where Merton had lived on Long Island in the 1930s. She likened Catholic Workers to Dostoevsky characters explicitly: "Did you ever read 'Friend of the Family' . . . ? We have one such friend on Peter Maurin Farm this year. Also many an 'Honest Thief.' " Merton, replying August 17, explained that he especially liked Staretz Zosima in *The Brothers Karamazov* "and the little Jew in 'The House of the Dead,' the one with the prayers, the weeping, the joy." In her next letter, October 10, 1960, Day thanked him for having *Disputed Questions* sent to her.

319 *The Moviegoer's* rough road to publication is chronicled in Jay Tolson's and Patrick Samway's biographies; Stanley Kauffmann, in conversation, reiterated his version of events. Tolson quotes Brainard Cheney's comparison of the novel to *Notes from Underground* and *The Fall*; Samway indicates that Kauffmann coaxed the Biloxi material out of Percy. Percy explained the ending as a "salute" to Dostoevsky in interviews with John C. Carr (1971) and Zoltan Abádi-Nagy (1973), reprinted in *Conversations with Walker Percy.*

320 Flannery O'Connor's remarks about the grotesque are from her introduction to *A Memoir of Mary Ann*, in *Mystery and Manners*. She discussed Teilhard de Chardin with Robert Giroux during his May 1959 visit—as described in her letter to T. R. Spivey, May 25—and read his work the next year, describing it in letters beginning with one to Elizabeth Hester, January 2, 1960; she best expressed her enthusiasm for Teilhard ("The man comes through") in a letter to Thomas Stritch, September 14, 1961, which is quoted here. She described Teilhard's obedience in a letter to Hester, February 4, 1961. *The Divine Milieu* was published in an anonymous English translation by Harper & Row in 1960; O'Connor mailed a copy to Roslyn Barnes, January 23, 1961. O'Connor stated her conviction about love "in the loooong run" in a letter to Hester, August 28, 1955.

322 "Everything That Rises Must Converge" is in *The Complete Stories*. Sally Fitzgerald, in the "Note on the Texts" of the Library of America edition, reports that O'Connor had "just finished" the story when she wrote a letter to Elizabeth McKee, March 26, 1961. Robert Giroux, in the introduction to *The Complete Stories*, recalls having sent O'Connor a French anthology of Teilhard's work with a section entitled *Tous Ce Qui Monte Converge*. O'Connor wrote to Roslyn Barnes, March 29, 1961, and described receiving a television in a letter to Maryat Lee March 26.

324 O'Connor recalled the ill treatment of "stove-pipe blondes" in a letter to Elizabeth Hester, November 16, 1957; she best explained her misgivings about integration in an interview with C. Ross Mullins for *Jubilee* (June 1963), reprinted in *Conversations with Flannery O'Connor.*

325 The complexity of O'Connor's racial attitudes became especially clear upon the publication of the Library of America edition in 1988, as a number of O'Connor's letters, published in partial (and often partially altered) form in *The Habit of Being* in 1979, appeared presumably complete and unaltered.

O'Connor's view of integration is most succinctly conveyed by a remark she made in an interview with C. Ross Mullins for *Jubilee* in 1963, printed as an appendix to *Mystery and Manners* and published at greater length in *Conversations with Flannery O'Connor*. Her fondness for racial quips is exhibited in a letter to Maryat Lee, September 10, 1963, in the Library of America edition, and for amused paraphrase in letters to Sally Fitzgerald, November 11, 1953, in the Library of America edition; to Cecil Dawkins, November 8, 1960, in the Library of America edition; and to Elizabeth Hester, March 14, 1964. She remarked on purchasing "colored rental property" in a letter to the Fitzgeralds, January 4, 1954, offhandedly remarked that "as the niggers say, I have the misery" in a letter to Sally Fitzgerald, December 26, 1954, and lamented the presence of a "wealthy sitting Negro" at Andalusia to Hester, September 16, 1961. She declared her refusal to meet James Baldwin in Georgia in a letter to Lee, April 25, 1959, derided the "philosophizing prophesying pontificating kind" of black person in a letter to Lee of May 21, 1964, in the Library of America edition, adding her criterion for judging a black person there. Her unpublished remarks about a dislike of black people and a wish that they would return to Africa were paraphrased by Lawrence Janowski in an account—published in the *Critic* in 1994 as "For the Deaf, for the Blind"—of a conference about O'Connor's work held in Milledgeville that year. Sally Fitzgerald's remarks on O'Connor's friendship with Maryat Lee are found in the introduction to *The Habit of Being*; the extent of their correspondence has been documented by Georgia Newman of Winter Haven, Florida, in a doctoral dissertation entitled *"A Contrary Kinship": The Letters of Flannery O'Connor and Maryat Lee*. O'Connor remarked on an unimaginable conversation in a car in a letter to Lee, January 9, 1957, and referred to "dear old dirty Southland" in a letter of February 11, 1958, and one of April 21, 1961, in the Library of America edition. She remarked skeptically on Lee's impending marriage in a letter to Lee of May 19, 1957, and on her "bad prose" in a letter of August 21, 1958, and drew a skull and crossbones at the bottom of her letter to Lee of February 11, 1958.

328 The *Catholic Worker's* position on the revolution in Cuba, and the outcry it produced, is described in William D. Miller's and James Forest's biographies of Dorothy Day; Robert Ellsberg describes the FBI's scrutiny, which had gone on since the 1950s or earlier. Day described trying to write amid the turmoil of events in her column for May 1961 and wrote an article "About Cuba" for the July/August 1961 issue of the paper, remarking that she was sitting "in church" as she wrote.

329 That Day wrote a letter to Merton is suggested by his reply, July 23, 1961, in *The Hidden Ground of Love*. Merton called himself a "14th century man" in his journal, March 11, 1961; James Forest indicates that Merton read *The Rise and Fall of the Third Reich* and drew on it in writing "Chant to Be Used in Processions Around a Site with Furnaces," which was published in the *Catholic Worker* (July/August 1961) and is reprinted in *A Thomas Merton Reader*. Day's letter is dated the Feast of the Assumption; Merton remarked on the " 'mistake' " in his journal, September 23. The Catholic Worker who sought to make a Trappist retreat is James Forest, who went to work at St. Joseph's House in 1961, inspired by a visit in which Day, opening the mail, read a letter from Merton aloud. Forest became managing editor of the paper that fall and, as such, corresponded with Merton; their correspondence, presented in *The Hidden Ground of Love*, supplements the Merton–Day correspondence.

331 Merton replied to Day's letter, August 23, and sent her an excerpt from *New Seeds of Contemplation*, September 22. It was published in the November 1961 *Catholic Worker*. Merton sent the article published as "Shelter Ethics" to James Forest with a letter, October 29, calling the article "The Machine Gun in the Fallout Shelter"; he identified Jack English as one of the censors in a letter to Forest, November 14,

crediting English with getting the article cleared for publication. Merton's "Cold War Letters" are scattered throughout the five volumes of his correspondence; Cold War Letter 11, to "D.D.," is dated December 20, 1961.

334 Day described "the war between young and old" in her column for July/August 1962; James Forest tells the episode from a different perspective in his biography. Merton envied the Catholic Worker's "flexible and wide open setup" in a letter to Day, March 21, 1962; that she replied at once is suggested by his letter of April 9, which opened, "Thank you for your letter. There are certainly a lot of things I needed to know." In a letter to Forest, February 6—the feast of St. Dorothy (virgin and martyr, d. 313)—he remarked, "Today is Dorothy's feast and I am remembering her in a special way. Do please give her my congratulations and best wishes." Day discussed the "young and old" conflict further in a letter to Merton of June 4, 1962, and praised his Cold War Letters, which another peace activist had shared with her: "Your letters charmed me, there was such a diversity of interests, such a richness in them, all of which goes to increase our knowledge and love of God."

335 The story of how *The Moviegoer* came to receive the National Book Award is told in the two biographies of Walker Percy; both authors cite an article by Gay Talese in the *New York Times* (March 15, 1962). Patrick Samway mentions *Time*'s accolade and Jack English's correspondence with Percy; Jay Tolson makes clear that five days passed between news of the award and the ceremony, enabling Percy to write an assured speech, and quotes Percy's remark on the *Today* show about the Civil War. Both biographers describe his work on *Fall Out*. Percy's fear of "ten years" of writer's block is quoted by Tolson. His correspondence with Jack English, aka Father Charles, is remarked upon in a letter of Flannery O'Connor to Caroline Gordon, November 16, 1961.

337 Flannery O'Connor wrote to Walker Percy, March 29, 1962; she glossed his remark in "The Regional Writer," in *Mystery and Manners*.

338 O'Connor described her efforts to write the "Author's Note" to *Wise Blood* in a series of letters in late 1961 and early 1962, including a letter to John Hawkes, November 28, 1961. She sent the note to Robert Giroux, May 9, 1962, calling it "as much as I can get out of myself" in a letter to Cecil Dawkins, April 25. She remarked on Mauriac's *Mémoires Intérieurs* to Elizabeth Hester, February 4.

339 O'Connor's letter to Walker Percy, June 24, 1962, heretofore unpublished, is in the Flannery O'Connor Collection in Milledgeville. Benjamin B. Alexander of the Franciscan University of Steubenville has made a study of the correspondence among O'Connor, Percy, and Caroline Gordon. O'Connor reported that Gordon was a " 'lonesome old lady' " in a letter to Ashley Brown, February 13, 1961, as published in the Library of America edition.

339 O'Connor described the Cub Scouts' visit in a letter to Roslyn Barnes, June 29, 1962; Roslyn Barnes's in a letter to J. H. McCown, November 2, 1962; Mary Ann Long's parents' in a letter to Elizabeth Hester, August 4, 1962; Archbishop Paul J. Hallinan's in a letter to Hester, May 19, 1962. Her financial troubles are emphasized in the chronology to the Library of America edition; she outlined her "breadwinning expeditions" to John Hawkes, April 5, 1962, and described the "honored guest bidnis" to Cecil Dawkins, April 25. Her "inordinate fondness" for Thomas Stritch, nephew of the archbishop of Chicago, is reported by Sally Fitzgerald in "Patterns of Friendship, Patterns of Love." She told Hester of her "grief" over Hester's turning away from the Church in a letter of October 28, 1961, and described

Hester as "high as a kite" to Cecil Dawkins, January 10, 1962. She wrote the first of several letters to Alfred Corn, then a student at Emory University, May 30, 1962, and described her arduous return from Notre Dame to Thomas Stritch, May 7, 1962.

341 "The Lame Shall Enter First" is in *The Complete Stories*; O'Connor found fault with it in letters to Cecil Dawkins, January 10, 1962, and Elizabeth McKee, May 28; she worried that she had "exhausted my original potentiality" in a letter to J. H. McCown, March 4, 1962.

342 O'Connor reported on her speaking tour, and her exhaustion, in a letter to Maryat Lee, October 27, 1962. Richard Allen recalled touring New Orleans with Flannery O'Connor in conversation, December 2000; O'Connor described their doings to John Hawkes, November 24, 1962, and there characterized New Orleans as a city where "the Devil's existence is freely recognized."

343 Walker Percy's attendance at Flannery O'Connor's talk at Loyola of New Orleans is described in both Percy biographies. Samway paraphrases Percy's recollections from letters to Phinizy Spalding and Lewis A. Lawson; Tolson quotes the letter to Spalding (Percy had trouble with O'Connor's "deep Georgia accent") and his own interview with Percy. The account given here is based on the eyewitness account of Richard Allen, who attended. The talk O'Connor gave—"The Catholic Novelist in the Protestant South," with interpolations—is preserved in an audio recording (marked NEWMAN FORUM) in the O'Connor Collection in Milledgeville. Samway reports that Percy took away a typescript and referred to it for years.

343 The source of O'Connor's remark—"Why don't you make up another one?"—is unknown. Tolson does not quote the remark; Samway, who does, gives an indirect citation, to Ben Forkner and J. Gerald Kennedy's 1981 interview, reprinted in *Conversations*, where Percy says: "She wrote me afterwards one of her laconic letters saying, 'That was a good story. I hope you make up another one.' " His comment is confusing, however: the interviewers have asked him about *The Charterhouse*, not *The Moviegoer*, and he has just said, "I never really saw her." Also, he recalled the remark and the context differently in a letter to Shelby Foote, February 3, 1971: "As Flannery said to me before she died: why don't you make up another one?" This discrepancy—"wrote" versus "said," a statement versus a question—together with the scantiness of others' recollections of their meeting, seems to justify the taking of some artistic license in combining the two versions of the remark into one and introducing it here.

343 Day was called the "grand old lady of pacifism" in *Fuck You: A Magazine of Literature and the Arts*, quoted in Miller's biography; the magazine's history is related in *A Secret Location on the Lower East Side: Adventures in Writing, 1960–1980* (eds. Steven Clay and Rodney Phillips; New York Public Library and Granary Books, 1998). Day remarks on the "rediscovery of poverty" in *Loaves and Fishes*, cataloging her impressions of the changing poverty of America and relating her encounter with "The Insulted and the Injured." She explained what prompted her to write the book in her column for the July/August 1962 *Catholic Worker*; Robert Coles quotes her naming her favorite nonfiction writers in *Dorothy Day: A Radical Devotion*. The story of *The Other America* is told by Irving Howe in the introduction to the 1993 edition (Collier); Alan Wolfe assessed Michael Harrington's achievement in a review, for the *New Republic* (April 3, 2000), of *The Other American: The Life of Michael Harrington*, by Maurice Isserman (Public Affairs, 1999).

345 Day discussed her imminent pilgrimage to Cuba in her column for July/August 1962, and wrote a four-part account for the September, October, November, and December issues of the paper. She shared her aspirations with Thomas Merton on a notecard, July 23, 1962, and gave further details in a letter of August 23, in which she begged a favor of him—a letter of introduction for a Catholic Worker going on pilgrimage in Europe, "so that he can beg hospitality at monasteries for himself and friend along the way." She likened the Catholic Workers to forerunners of Vatican II in "The Council and the Mass" in the September 1962 issue. Thomas Merton reflected on the council in his journal, October 2, 1962; his "affairs," September 15; his "own country," October 1; the Cuban missile crisis, October 27 and November 6. John XXIII's role in averting the crisis is stressed in James Forest's biography of Merton and in Thomas Cahill's *John XXIII*.

347 Merton's Cold War Letter to Day—June 16, 1962—is in *The Hidden Ground of Love*. In her letter of March 17, 1963, she told him of her planned Roman pilgrimage, which she recounted in her column for June 1963, reprinted in *A Penny a Copy*. Merton remarked on the death of Pope John and the arrival of *Loaves and Fishes* in his journal, June 11, 1963; Day's praise for Merton's writing was the pretext for their correspondence—"Your books are treasures around the CW and keep circulating," she told him in her first letter; she remarked on the peace pilgrim Bob Steed, August 23, 1962, and the "lovely" girl Ellen, November 12, 1962, and March 17, 1963. Merton's comment about *Loaves and Fishes* is on the back cover of the paperback edition (Harper & Row, 1983). Upon receiving the book, August 28, he remarked in his journal, "And on the back of Dorothy Day's new book, another letter of mine. I am glad to help, but—too many letters. My silence would really be of greater value to all these people, to the causes and to myself. Yet there always seems to be a reason to give in."

349 Michael Mott reports on the whiteness of Gethsemani and tells of Brother Joshua, a black monk who listened to jazz on headphones there. Merton recounted meeting John Howard Griffin in his journal, March 4, 1963; and reading *The Fire Next Time* and *Nobody Knows My Name*, February 23, 1963. On February 24, 1965, he laconically observed: "Malcolm X, the Negro racist, has been murdered (I am sorry because now there is bitter fighting between two Muslim factions)."

349 Merton's "Letters to a White Liberal" are published in *Seeds of Destruction* (Farrar, Straus and Giroux, 1964). He remarked on the March on Washington in his journal, August 28 and September 3, 1963, published as *Dancing in the Water of Life* (ed. Robert E. Daggy; Harper San Francisco, 1997).

350 Flannery O'Connor delivered "The Catholic Novelist in the Protestant South" at Georgetown, October 18, 1963, as indicated in the "Note on the Texts" section of the Library of America edition. The text, published there and in Georgetown's alumni magazine, differs somewhat from the "master version" printed in *Mystery and Manners*.

351 O'Connor reported that she was "right enthusiastic about" "Revelation" in a letter to Cecil Dawkins, November 5, 1963; on November 9, she told Elizabeth Hester that she had "not decided yet if it is any good." She described Ruby Turpin as a "country female Jacob" to Maryat Lee, May 15, 1964, and told Janet McKane that "I've been reading Shakespeare myself lately," August 27, 1963. The story itself is in *The Complete Stories*.

356 Thomas Merton reported on the run of deaths culminating in President Kennedy's

in his journal, November 10, 16, 20, and 23, 1963; Flannery O'Connor remarked on the assassination in letters to Elizabeth Hester and to the Fitzgeralds, both November 23; Dorothy Day pondered it in her column for December 1963. Walker Percy's whereabouts on November 23 are described in the two biographies; Jay Tolson draws the connection to Sutter Vaught's cryptic remark about Kennedy in *The Last Gentleman*.

357 Merton recounted Father Charles's expedition to Gethsemani in his journal, November 16, 1963; discussed Dorothy Day's plans to visit Bardstown Hospital, December 3; and explained that Father Charles had asked for *The Moviegoer* in his first letter to Percy, of January 1964, published in *The Courage for Truth: Letters to Writers* (Farrar, Straus and Giroux, 1993; Harvest, 1994). Patrick Samway tells, in his biography, of the priest's alcoholism and his wont to phone Percy "at ungodly hours." Merton's letter to Day, December 4, 1963, is in *The Hidden Ground of Love*; in her undated reply, she reported that a "drifter" on the Catholic Worker farm was reading "your latest paperback," adding, "You will never know the good you do. I pray the Lord will continue his inspiration—it is truly your vocation."

357 Merton remarked on *The Moviegoer* in his journal, January 18, 1964. His own new book, a volume of poems, was entitled *Emblems of a Season of Fury*, and he discussed the meaning of "emblems" in his journal, December 1, 1963. Percy recalled his reaction to Merton's letter in the 1984 interview about Merton with Victor A. Kramer and Dewey W. Kramer, reprinted in *Conversations with Walker Percy*. Percy's reply is quoted in the two biographies, which report that Percy hung Merton's drawing over his desk; his remark likening *The Last Gentleman* to Dostoevsky's *The Idiot*—"Shelby, it's *The Idiot*, that's what I've written"—is quoted in Robert Coles's introduction to the Modern Library edition of the novel (Random House, 1997).

359 O'Connor reported the "howling success" of the fibroid surgery in a letter to Robert Fitzgerald, March 8, 1964; her suspicion that the surgery had "kicked up" the lupus to Elizabeth Hester, March 28; its side effects to Janet McKane, April 2; her way of working "one hour a day" to Maryat Lee, May 15.

359 The account of the writing of "Parker's Back" is based on a close reading of the many stages of manuscript filed, each draft or fragment in its own folder, in the O'Connor Collection in Milledgeville. The obvious change from one typewriter to another, and then from handwritten revisions to typewritten ones, suggests where the different drafts were written or revised.

361 O'Connor pointed out that she went to the hospital "as my own guest" in a letter to Cecil Dawkins, June 24, 1964, and described signing the contracts for *Everything That Rises Must Converge* in a letter to Elizabeth McKee, May 21; the signed contracts are in the Farrar, Straus and Giroux files.

361 Caroline Gordon recalled O'Connor's hiding a notebook under her pillow in the essay "An American Girl," written after O'Connor's death and published in *The Added Dimension*. Gordon identified the story O'Connor was working on as "Parker's Back." O'Connor, for her part, recounted Gordon's visit in a letter to Ashley Brown, June 15, 1964.

361 O'Connor described reading *The Voices of Silence*, by André Malraux (trans. Stuart Gilbert; Doubleday, 1953; Princeton, 1978), in a letter to Cecil Dawkins, January 28, 1960, and remarked on the book to Elizabeth Hester, October 6, 1962, saying that she didn't own it and "it may be out of print." She then exclaimed over a

book given as a gift from Hester in a letter of December 21, 1962, saying she was "altogether clobbered" to receive it, as "I thought it was out of print." Clearly that book was *The Voices of Silence*. The detail of "Christ in Glory" from Santa Sophia, on page 206 of the book, matches the description of the tattoo in "Parker's Back" precisely, and the style of "superb negation," as described by Malraux on the verso, matches the style of O'Connor's story, a style that "arose from a passionate desire to represent that which, rationally speaking, cannot be represented; to depict the superhuman through the human." O'Connor's friend William Sessions, in a paper published in *Flannery O'Connor and the Christian Mystery* (*Literature and Belief*, Vol. 17; Brigham Young, 1997), proposes that "the image of the Byzantine Christ that appears in O'Connor's 'Parker's Back' and on the body of its hero came, in all probability, from a postcard my wife Jenny and I sent Flannery from Greece in the summer of 1961"—but the image does not match the one described in the story; it lacks the "little blocks" the tattooist emphatically remarks on, and the eyes are not all-seeing but are looking off to the side. Even so, it may be that the postcard from Sessions put the idea of a "tattooed Byzantine Christ" in O'Connor's mind.

363 O'Connor reported on her blood transfusions in her letter to Cecil Dawkins, June 24, 1964; looked forward to her release from the hospital the next day in a letter to Janet McKane, June 19; and described the scene at Andalusia to Elizabeth Hester, June 27. She described working on an electric typewriter in her farmhouse study in letters to Catherine Carver, June 27 (mentioning "Judgement Day"); Thomas Stritch, June 27; and Robert Giroux, June 28. She sent the story to Hester with a letter, July 11, and to Carver, July 15, and reported that she was "still puttering" on it to Maryat Lee, July 21. She asked for prayers in a letter to Louise Abbot, May 28, 1964; Sally Fitzgerald, in the headnote to the "The Last Year" section of *The Habit of Being*, recalls receiving a similar letter. She addressed Maryat Lee as "Grace Bug" May 21, 1964, as "Marybat" June 23, as "Raycheek" July 10 (urging her to vote for Goldwater), and as "Raybat" July 21, in letters published in the Library of America edition. She remarked on Walker Percy's review of *Fox in the Attic* to Elizabeth Hester, July 17, 1964, quoted Gerard Manley Hopkins's poem "Spring and Fall" to Janet McKane, June 19, 1964, and quoted the prayer to St. Raphael to McKane, June 17, 1964; she had described receiving it from the Catholic Workers in a letter to Hester, January 17, 1956. She dismissed Caroline Gordon's criticism of "Parker's Back" in a letter to Hester, July 25, 1964.

365 O'Connor's death, funeral, and burial are detailed in the chronology in the Library of America edition. The *New York Times* published an obituary on August 4, 1964, and a note on the funeral on August 5, announcing a requiem Mass to be said at St. Patrick's Cathedral in New York. Caroline Gordon's posthumous assessment of O'Connor is in the essay "An American Girl," in *The Added Dimension*. Recollections of O'Connor (including many written for the *New York Review of Books*) were gathered and published in a special issue of *Esprit* (ed. J. J. Quinn, S.J.; Scranton, 1964), republished as *Flannery O'Connor: A Memorial* (Scranton, 1995). Thomas Merton's "Prose Elegy" for *Jubilee* (November 1964) was published in *Raids on the Unspeakable* (New Directions, 1966) and in the revised edition of *A Thomas Merton Reader* (Image, 1974). The *Esprit* memorial includes another recollection from Merton, three paragraphs long, in which he pronounced her a "great artist" and sought to explain why. "She had much to say that other writers could not tell us, and

that is why she is such a loss," he remarked. "But once she is lost to us, then her art and her books must be better studied and meditated in fear and trembling."

10. *Pilgrimage or Crusade?*

367 Dorothy Day described the scene at the corner of Mott and Kenmare Streets, and the changes in the neighborhood, in her column for the June 1964 *Catholic Worker*. Her room has been recalled by the Catholic Workers Eric Brandt and Patrick Jordan. Paul VI's characterization of the Church's mission is quoted by Xavier Rynne in *Vatican Council II* (Farrar, Straus and Giroux, 1968; Orbis, 1999), which details the bishops' discussions about religious liberty and Catholic-Jewish relations.

368 Thomas Merton recounted his trip to New York to meet D. T. Suzuki in his journal, June 12, 13, 15, 16, 17, and 20, and July 10, 1964, published in *Dancing in the Water of Life*; his letters to Suzuki were published in *The Hidden Ground of Love*; their dialogue about Zen Buddhism was published in Merton's *Zen and the Birds of Appetite* (New Directions, 1968). Michael Mott and Monica Furlong describe the Merton-Suzuki encounter in their biographies.

369 Merton discussed his life at the hermitage in his journal all through the fall of 1964, remarking on the sense of "walking on water" and of feeling "ripe," October 31; he wrote about lamplight, October 21. The retreat of peace activists at the hermitage is described by James Forest, who attended; by Michael Mott; and by Merton himself in letters to Forest and Daniel Berrigan, in *The Hidden Ground of Love*; he stated the perils of "projects and statements and programs," August 4, 1964; explained that "God writes straight on crooked lines," February 23, 1964, and urged a "freewheeling" approach, November 9, 1964. He described the retreat as "remarkably lively and fruitful" in his journal, November 19, 1964.

370 Merton's writing from the hermitage is found in *Raids on the Unspeakable* (notably "Rain and the Rhinoceros"), *Mystics and Zen Masters* (Farrar, Straus and Giroux, 1967), and *The Nonviolent Alternative* (ed. Gordon H. Zahn; Farrar, Straus and Giroux, 1980), as well as in his journal. "From Pilgrimage to Crusade," written for the journal *Cithara*, is published in *Mystics and Zen Masters*; Merton reported finishing it in his journal, August 2, 1964, and adding footnotes "as an afterthought," August 29.

372 Walker Percy's practice of narrating the television news for his daughter Ann is described by Jay Tolson in his biography. "Mississippi: The Fallen Paradise," published in *Harper's* in April 1965, is reprinted in *Signposts in a Strange Land*; the circumstances were recalled by Willie Morris in *New York Days* (Little, Brown, 1993). Percy spoke of joining the Committee of Southern Churchmen in the 1984 interview about Thomas Merton, reprinted in *Conversations with Walker Percy*; Jay Tolson describes the writing of "The Failure and the Hope," which is reprinted in *Signposts in a Strange Land*; Patrick Samway details the Percy family's pilgrimage to Lourdes.

374 Robert Fitzgerald's introduction appears in *Everything That Rises Must Converge* (Farrar, Straus and Giroux, 1965); the relationship of "Judgement Day" to "The Geranium" is explained in Robert Giroux's introduction to *The Complete Stories*; O'Connor's late revisions to the typescript were observed firsthand in the Farrar, Straus and Giroux offices.

376 The phrase "People of God" and the notion of the "Pilgrim Church" are emphasized in the Dogmatic Constitution on the Church, *Lumen Gentium,* from the
council's first session, of 1962, in *Vatican II: The Conciliar and Post Conciliar Documents* (ed. Austin Flannery, O.P.; Paulist, 1992). Avery Dulles, S.J., compares the
imagery of the Mystical Body with that of the People of God in *Models of the
Church* (Doubleday, 1978; expanded ed., Image, 1987).

376 The formation of the Catholic Peace Fellowship is described in *Disarmed and Dan-
gerous: The Radical Lives and Times of Daniel and Philip Berrigan,* by Murray Pol-
ner and Jim O'Grady (Basic, 1997). Dorothy Day recounted her pilgrimage to
Rome in her columns for October, November, and December 1965; James Forest
details the efforts surrounding Schema 13 in *Love Is the Measure.* Day's return to
New York is dramatized in *Divine Disobedience: Portraits in Catholic Radicalism,* by
Francine du Plessix Gray (Knopf, 1970); her presence at an antiwar rally in Union
Square is noted in James Forest's biography.

377 Roger LaPorte's self-immolation is discussed by Gray, by Polner and O'Grady, by
Forest in his biographies of Day and Merton, and in fictional form by Nicole D'En-
tremont, who knew LaPorte at the Catholic Worker. Forest's *Love Is the Measure* recounts the aftermath.

378 Thomas Merton expressed his view of LaPorte's act in a telegram, quoted in all the
biographies; in letters to James Forest and Daniel Berrigan, published in *The Hidden Ground of Love*; and in his journal, November 10, 1964: "What is happening? Is
everybody nuts?" he asked, but later added, "Afterwards I wondered if I had been too
hard on Jim and the Catholic Peace Fellowship." Day reflected on the whole affair
in an article in the November 1965 *Catholic Worker,* reprinted in *By Little and By
Little.*

379 Day's letter to Thomas Merton of November 15, 1965, was her third letter that year.
In a letter of June, she described troubles at the Catholic Worker and thanked him
again for his writings: "You certainly have used the graces and talents God has given
you. I am afraid I lack the discipline to do the work I ought to do, being occupied
with many Martha-cares." On August 11, she thanked him for his reply—a letter of
July 16, along with an article about Maximus the Confessor—and reported that Jim
Douglass, a Catholic peace activist, had given her five hundred dollars, encouraging
her to travel to Rome "to try to reach the bishops directly." Merton's reply to her November 15 letter is in *The Hidden Ground of Love,* as is his letter to Catherine de
Hueck Doherty, January 12, 1966.

381 Day's characterization of Daniel Berrigan to Merton, December 2, 1965, began
with the following: "I think all his writing and his speaking have done a wonderful
amount of good and, even now, his silence will cry out in what people consider his
exile to South America." Merton replied, December 20; observed that "we agree" in
his journal, December 7; and offered a tribute to her movement, December 29.

382 Percy's pilgrimage to the Holy Spirit Monastery (formerly Holy Ghost Monastery) is
described in the two biographies. Jay Tolson reports that Caroline Gordon read *The
Last Gentleman* at the monastery; Patrick Samway reports that Percy found Father
Charles "nutty" and indicates that Gordon, after leaving the monastery, went to see
Regina O'Connor in Milledgeville. Percy remarked on the "threadbareness of religious words" in a 1962 letter to Gordon, quoted by Tolson. Gordon's editorial letter
about *The Last Gentleman* is quoted by both biographers. Percy's reply is quoted by

Tolson; Percy's précis of the novel, by Samway. *The Last Gentleman* was published by Farrar, Straus and Giroux in 1966.

385 Michael Mott describes the renovation of the Abbey of Gethsemani in his biography; Merton described the removal of the steeple in his journal, April 20 and 22, 1966, published in *Learning to Love* (ed. Christine M. Bochen; Harper San Francisco, 1997); the two entries are conflated here. Mott gives a careful chronological account of Merton's affair with "S.," as he calls her; James Forest, forcing an interpretation of the affair as the fulfillment of Merton's dreams of the 1950s, calls his chapter "A Proverb Named Margie." Merton described the "struggle in my heart" in his journal, April 24; posed the "question of love," April 19; acknowledged that "I am in deep," April 27; welcomed Margie into the hermitage imaginatively, May 2; described making "love and love and love," May 20; and concluded that "it had to stop," May 21.

388 In the same entry, Merton mentioned having started "reading Walker Percy's novel." Caroline Gordon's comment on the book is quoted by Percy's two biographers. Merton's comment, quoted by both biographers, is in an unpublished letter to Robert Giroux, dated May 22, 1966.

389 Merton spoke of the "endless involvement" with Margie and resolved to "drop her," May 24; begged God "not to take away the gift of love," May 31; mentioned reading the Sufis, June 2; and remarked on *The Myth of Sisyphus*, June 17. Michael Mott explains Merton's agreement with his psychologist, James Wygal. Merton related his encounter with Margie at Wygal's office, June 12; the excised material was described in conversation by Robert Giroux. The abbot's demand for a "complete break" is described by James Forest. Merton pondered his fate as "a priest who has a woman," June 9, and reflected on "so many priests" doing as he did, June 2.

392 Merton's "Seven Essays on Albert Camus" are published in *The Literary Essays of Thomas Merton*. The longest of them, "The Plague: A Commentary and Introduction," includes a "Life of Albert Camus," the source of many of the remarks about Camus in this section. The description of Camus's work as "essentially meditative, imaginative, and symbolic" is from "Three Saviors in Camus: Lucidity and the Absurd"; the account of Camus's experience at Fiesole, from his *Notebooks*, is quoted in "Terror and the Absurd: Violence and Nonviolence in Albert Camus," as is the phrase "solidarity in revolt." Merton defined faith as "the fundamental revolt" and solitude as "the struggle for lucidity" in "A Midsummer Diary for Margie," published in *Learning to Love*. "Camus and the Church" was published in the *Catholic Worker* (December 1966) and reprinted in *A Penny a Copy*. Merton sent it to Dorothy Day with a letter, September 12, 1966.

392 Walker Percy's essay about the genesis of *The Moviegoer* is "From Facts to Fiction," in *Signposts in a Strange Land*; his letter to Shelby Foote, which Jay Tolson dates January or February 1967, is in *The Correspondence of Shelby Foote & Walker Percy*; Foote replied March 19. Tolson in his biography tells of Percy receiving *The Added Dimension* in the mail from Lewis A. Lawson; Samway gives the date as May 28, 1967. Percy's essay about "Novel No. 3" is "Notes for a Novel About the End of the World," in *The Message in the Bottle*.

395 Percy describes the Committee of Southern Churchmen's pilgrimage to the Abbey of Gethsemani in the 1984 interview with Victor A. Kramer and Dewey Weiss Kramer, reprinted in *Conversations with Walker Percy*. Tolson and Samway quote

different passages from Percy's thank-you letter; the two passages have been combined here. Merton replied, July 20, 1967; and sent another letter, August 24. *Love in the Ruins* was published by Farrar, Straus and Giroux in 1971; Samway reports that Percy "began typing the 'Journal of a Bad Catholic at a Time Near the End of the World,'" narrated by a John E. Smith, in March 1967.

397 Merton told of receiving Jacques Maritain and John Howard Griffin at the hermitage in his journal, October 13, 1966; Joan Baez, December 10, effusing over her as "a precious, authentic, totally human person . . . a manifestation given us for a while"; and Ralph Eugene Meatyard and friends, January 28, 1967. This visit—of the "three kings," as Merton told Robert Lax in a letter, January 18, 1967, in *When Prophecy Still Had a Voice*—was recalled in the essay "Tom and Gene," by Guy Davenport, who remarked, "The breakthrough in Tom's poetry came from a convergence of forces: reading Flannery O'Connor (whose stories are Christian mimes in a comic vernacular), *Mad* magazine, and the ads in *The New Yorker*, and a vision from the cargo cults of New Guinea." Merton described Thich Nhat Hanh's visit, May 31 and June 2, 1966, in the midst of his affair with Margie; his essay "Nhat Hanh Is My Brother," remarked on in the journal, October 18, 1966, is published in *The Nonviolent Alternative*; the photograph of the two monks, by John Heidbrink, appears in James Forest's biography.

398 Day remarked on the "wide repercussions" from Merton's Camus article in a letter, January 29, 1967, and added, "We get so overcome with visits that we are all overworked, and the mail piles up, as you well know." She praised his latest book, *Conjectures of a Guilty Bystander*. Her rejoinder to Cardinal Spellman, "'In Peace Is My Bitterness Most Bitter,'" published in the January 1967 *Catholic Worker*, is reprinted in *By Little and By Little*. Merton praised it in a letter of February 9, 1967, published in *The Hidden Ground of Love*.

399 The emergence of a strain of "militant nonviolence" within the Catholic peace movement is described in Francine du Plessix Gray's *Divine Disobedience*; in Garry Wills's *Bare Ruined Choirs*; in James Forest's biography of Merton; in *Disarmed and Dangerous*, the biography of Daniel and Philip Berrigan; and in Daniel Berrigan's autobiography, *To Dwell in Peace* (Harper & Row, 1987). Forest calls attention to Merton's affinity for tobacco farmers and Day's for the World War II veterans at the Catholic Worker and for her grandson Eric, an Army Ranger in Vietnam. Day worried about the peace movement in letters to Merton as early as 1965: in June that year, she reported that the movement "seems to be plagued" by drug addicts and promiscuous layabouts; on December 2, appraising Daniel Berrigan's actions to Merton, she said of the Catholic Worker: "We are not just talking to each other as so many in the pacifist movement do." She reported on the antiwar march in Manhattan in her column for the May 1967 *Catholic Worker*, on a "sit-in" in Washington in her column for the March/April issue, and on a "Mass Protest" at St. Patrick's in her column for February. She set out her objections to Daniel Berrigan's use of a coffee cup as a chalice (without naming him) in a "rambling" column for March 1966; the quotation from Merton's *Seasons of Celebration* precedes her remarks about the incident.

400 Day had shared her concerns about James Forest's commitment to Catholic fundamentals with Merton as early as 1962. "As for PAX, I am afraid the main reason it was formed was to take care of the fearful souls who do not wish to be associated with the Catholic Worker," she told him in her letter of August 23:

I don't know what will come of it. Jim Forest has the push but not the stuff as Peter Maurin would say. He jumps from this to that, and when he married out of the church and insisted marriage had to do with two people and the priest was but a witness, not needed in his case, one realized how little down to earth knowledge he had of the sacraments, of the life of grace, of the tremendous teaching of the Church. Now the marriage has been solemnized, but the girl has publicly stated she made promises she did not intend to keep, and that she intends to have no more children, etc. etc., and that, in a nutshell is why I am so cool to PAX.

The circumstances of Forest's separation and remarriage are explained in the headnote to Merton's letters to Forest of March 1967 in *The Hidden Ground of Love*; Day's letter to Forest is quoted at length in Miller's biography; Miller reports that Forest sent Day's letter to Merton and Daniel Berrigan, among others. Merton wrote a letter of advice to Forest March 21.

401 Day asked Merton to pray for Father Charles and for "a young girl named Barbara" in a letter, September 13, 1967; described the Little Brothers of Jesus—"They really know how to do nothing"—September 28; and remarked on the "wonderful good fortune" of a trip to Rome September 13.

401 Merton described the new "Aztec altar" at Gethsemani in his journal, August 20, 1967, and the arrival of "a letter from Rome," August 21, puzzling out the nature of the request and an appropriate response to it. "A Letter on the Contemplative Life" and "Contemplatives and the Crisis of Faith" are published, with an explanatory note, in *Thomas Merton: Spiritual Master* (ed. Lawrence S. Cunningham; Paulist, 1992). In his journal, August 21, 1967, Merton described writing the letter—"I put down the first things that came into my head, probably absurd and totally nonacceptable, a kind of Christian existentialist mish-mash which will please no one and which they probably won't understand." August 22, he described reading *As I Lay Dying* and a text on the Bantu prophets—which put Walker Percy in mind, prompting Merton's letter to Percy of August 24, published in *The Courage for Truth*; August 24, he described writing the "Message to Contemplatives," and made clear that it was, at least in part, written in response to Daniel Berrigan—whom he mentioned by name—and other Catholic activists. "I feel with the greatest seriousness that we are in for difficult times, for violence, confusion, nastiness, mess, blood, destructive maneuvers everywhere, in everything—in the Church and outside it! . . . ," he wrote. "And I feel that there is nothing I can do by talking about it, or trying to intervene in it. I have said what I know how to say and it wasn't much. . . . Better to stay out of it, not be used, do what I am really *supposed* to do and live the life that has been given me to live."

405 Merton's letter of advice to Daniel Berrigan, October 10, 1967, is published in *The Hidden Ground of Love*. The action of the radicals dubbed the Baltimore Four is described in *Divine Disobedience* and *Disarmed and Dangerous*. The political events of those months are recounted there and in *"Democracy Is in the Streets": From Port Huron to the Seige of Chicago*, by James Miller (Simon & Schuster, 1987; Harvard, 1994).

406 Merton recorded his reaction to the murder of Martin Luther King, Jr., in his journal, April 6, 1968, published in *The Other Side of the Mountain* (ed. Patrick Hart; Harper San Francisco, 1998); Day wrote about the murder, and the funeral, in her column for April 1968, reprinted in *By Little and By Little*.

407 Michael Mott's Merton biography is weighted heavily toward Merton's later years, and in it Merton's western journey is described at length. The journal Merton dedicated to the trip, "Woods, Shore, Desert," is published in *The Other Side of the Mountain*. His remark about the conversion of Christ of the Desert from a "dude ranch" is from *The Waters of Siloe* (Harcourt, Brace, 1949). He remarked on his yearning for "change and transformation" in the journal, May 30, 1968; on the Poor People's March, May 20; the general strike in Paris and the student uprising at Columbia University, May 22; the Catonsville action, May 22. Daniel Berrigan describes the action as removing "an abomination from the Earth" in a chapter of *To Dwell in Peace* entitled "Catonsville: The Fires of Pentecost."

408 Walker Percy's letter to *Commonweal* denouncing the Catonsville action is quoted in the two biographies. Dorothy Day's initial response to the action—"These actions are not ours"—is quoted in *Disarmed and Dangerous*. Thomas Merton's remarks on the action are scattered here and there: in a circular letter to friends of midsummer 1968, published in *The Road to Joy: Letters to New and Old Friends* (Farrar, Straus and Giroux, 1989; Harvest, 1993); in a letter to Mary Lanahan, June 24, 1968, published in *Witness to Freedom: Letters in Times of Crisis* (Farrar, Straus and Giroux, 1994; Harvest, 1995); in his journal, August 5, 1968; and, most comprehensively, in the "Note" for *Ave Maria* magazine, republished in *The Nonviolent Alternative*, a note the editor of the volume, Gordon C. Zahn, judges "inconclusive" (though it is Zahn's view that Merton's "disapproval would have grown more outspoken" in light of subsequent events). In the journal he kept on his Asian journey, September 29, 1968, Merton remarked on seeing copies of *Ave Maria* at the Precious Blood convent in Anchorage, "but I did not get to look at them to see if my statement on draft record burning was there." In a letter to W. H. Ferry, September 4, 1968, published in *The Hidden Ground of Love*, Merton confessed, "Many other things I have to skip—must write Dan—does mail reach Phil? I am under the impression mine doesn't." Father Berrigan himself, in a 1995 letter to Andrew Krivak, which Krivak shared with me, tells of finding peace at last in a letter from Merton to John Howard Griffin, written from Asia—evidently, the letter quoted at the end of the "Hermitage Years" section of Griffin's *Follow the Ecstasy* (Latitudes Press, 1983) in which Merton said: "If, in fact, I basically agree with them, then how long will I myself be out of jail? I suppose I can say 'as long as I don't make a special effort to get in'—which is what they did. All I can say is that I haven't deliberately broken any laws. But one of these days I may find myself in a position where I will have to."

412 Merton told Day about "a big thing coming up" in a letter of July 25, 1968. Day's announcement of Merton's imminent departure for the Far East is reported by Edward Rice in *The Man in the Sycamore Tree: The Good Times and Hard Life of Thomas Merton* (Doubleday, 1970). Merton described getting inoculated in his journal, July 19 and 27 and August 1, 1968; anticipated living out of a suitcase, September 1; described burning Margie's letters, August 20; and remarked on *Ulysses*, August 10.

412 Merton described his overnight trip to Washington in his journal, August 26, 1968; Michael Mott quotes the Indonesian ambassador's memory of Merton—"a memory of one of the very few people I have known in this world with an inner freedom which is almost total." Dorothy Day, in Washington that weekend for a conference on the Catholic liturgy, wrote Merton a note, August 19. Merton's circular letter of

September 1968 is published in *The Road to Joy*. Merton's last Mass in the hermitage was described by Patrick Hart in conversation, January 1, 2001; his attire is detailed by Michael Mott.

414 Merton chronicled his Asian journey in his journal, published first, with photographs and annotations, as *The Asian Journal of Thomas Merton* (eds. Naomi Burton Stone, Patrick Hart, and James Laughlin; New Directions, 1971), then in *The Other Side of the Mountain*. He remarked on a ruined church in Chicago, September 17, 1968, and on Georgia O'Keeffe, September 12; his remark about the lure of the "revolutionary mystique" is quoted in James Forest's biography. He described scouting sites in Alaska in his journal in a series of entries beginning September 18. Merton defined wisdom in "Baptism in the Forest: Wisdom and Initiation in William Faulkner," published in *The Literary Essays of Thomas Merton*. Merton's letter to Philip Berrigan, September 30, 1968, is published in *The Hidden Ground of Love*.

415 Merton described Bangkok in his journal, October 17, 1968, and Calcutta in a series of entries beginning October 19. His closing prayer at the "Spiritual Summit Conference" is an appendix to *The Asian Journal*. He described his journey to Dharamsala, November 1; the city itself, November 3; his meetings with the Dalai Lama, November 4, 6, and 8. A photograph of the two of them is reproduced in James Forest's biography.

417 Merton described his meeting with Chantral Rimpoche, November 16; his return to Calcutta, November 12; his visit to Darjeeling, November 13, 14, and 15; his encounter with the Kanchenjunga, November 17, 19, and 22. He described his pilgrimage to Madras, November 27 and 28; at the end of the passage, the order of his visits to the two churches has been reversed. He described his visit to Kandy and Polonnaruwa, November 29 and 30 and December 1 and 2, and largely in poetry, December 3. He recalled the visit in retrospect, December 4, and it is this entry from which the quotations are drawn.

421 The last entry in Merton's journal is dated December 8. The letter from Daniel Berrigan is described in a note in *The Hidden Ground of Love*, which includes Merton's letter to W. H. Ferry of December 5, 1968, dismissing the prospect of being interviewed for a *New Yorker* profile.

421 The talk Merton gave in Bangkok, entitled "Marxism and Monastic Perspectives," is an appendix to *The Asian Journal*. Michael Mott and James Forest describe the circumstances of the talk, and those of Merton's death; Mott alludes to rumors of suicide and of murder and calculates that Merton had just celebrated the twenty-seventh anniversary of his entry into the monastery.

11. *The Holiness of the Ordinary*

423 John Kennedy Toole's final expedition is described in *Ignatius Rising: The Life of John Kennedy Toole*, by René Pol Nevils and Deborah George Hardy (Louisiana State University, 2001). That Toole visited the Hearst mansion, Marilyn Monroe's grave, and Milledgeville is taken on the testimony of his mother, Thelma, and although the evidence is shaky, the biographers conclude that "there is no reason to discount Thelma's reconstruction of events." Emilie Griffin, a friend of Toole's, discussed the Toole "myth" in "Style and Zest: Remembering John Kennedy Toole," in *Image* (No. 24). The Paris-based scholar Karin Badt has made a number of fruitful

conjectures about Toole's legacy. A *Confederacy of Dunces* (Louisiana State University, 1980), published with a foreword by Walker Percy, is a Grove paperback.

424 *Mystery and Manners* was published by Farrar, Straus and Giroux on May 12, 1969. Flannery O'Connor had remarked on her hope of going to California in a letter to the Fitzgeralds, December 20, 1952, and is quoted describing her work as reporting on terrible beasts slouching toward Bethlehem to be born in *Conversations with Flannery O'Connor*. She expressed her wish to write a book on the subject of the "Christ-haunted" South at the arts festival in Macon in 1961; the panel discussion is transcribed in *Conversations with Flannery O'Connor*. In *Mystery and Manners*, she describes the "unbelieving age" as an age of "searchers and discoverers" in "Novelist and Believer"; describes the religious artist testing "the limits of mystery" and depicting fanatics who carry an "invisible burden" and act on "a trust beyond themselves" in "Some Aspects of the Grotesque in Southern Fiction"; insists on the need to draw "large and startling figures" in "The Fiction Writer and His Country"; she described the religion of the South as a "do-it-yourself religion" in a letter to John Hawkes, September 13, 1959. She remarks on "our fierce and fading manners" in "The Fiction Writer & His Country"; speaks of "strange skips and gaps" of the grotesque style in "Some Aspects of the Grotesque"; identifies the writer's true subject as "the mystery of our position on earth" in "The Teaching of Literature"; opines about "the Divine Life" in "The Nature and Aim of Fiction," about the mystery that life has "been found by God to be worth dying for" in "The Church and the Fiction Writer," and about the "ordeal" of writing a novel in "The Nature and Aim of Fiction," where she remarks that "I see from the standpoint of Christian orthodoxy."

426 The Catonsville Nine's evasions of the authorities are described in *Divine Disobedience* and *Disarmed and Dangerous*. Robert Coles conducted a series of interviews with Daniel Berrigan, while the latter was "underground," published as *The Geography of Faith* (Beacon, 1971).

426 Dorothy Day's column "Adventures in Prayer" is reprinted in *By Little and By Little*. Thomas Merton's *Contemplative Prayer* was published by Herder and Herder in 1969; *Thomas Merton on Peace* by Farrar, Straus and Giroux in 1971; *The Asian Journal of Thomas Merton* by New Directions in 1973, with a preface by Amiya Chakravarty; Edward Rice's *The Man in the Sycamore Tree: The Good Times and Hard Life of Thomas Merton* by Doubleday in 1970. Rice hints at the "fittingness" of Merton's death among the monks of Asia, and concludes the book, "A hippy said to me: 'Did he give out good vibrations?' 'Yes,' I said, 'he did.' " Douglas Steere called Merton a "spiritual masseur" in the introduction to *Contemplative Prayer*. Gordon Zahn (in *The Nonviolent Alternative*) argues past Merton's own written remarks about the Catonsville action to conclude that he would have offered "safe haven" to Father Berrigan at his hermitage.

428 Walker Percy developed the phrase "the holiness of the ordinary" in a 1989 essay by that title, published in *Boston College Magazine* and reprinted in *Signposts in a Strange Land*. Shelby Foote thanked Percy for sending *Mystery and Manners* in a letter of October 28, 1969, published in *The Correspondence of Shelby Foote & Walker Percy*. Percy announced the title of Novel No. 3 in a letter of August 4, 1970, declaring that he wasn't a Catholic writer "the way Flannery was." *Love in the Ruins* was published by Farrar, Straus and Giroux in 1971. Percy's talk "Concerning *Love in the Ruins*," published in *Signposts in a Strange Land*, was given under the auspices of the National Book Award organization.

428 Dorothy Day described her "mild heart failure" in a 1971 letter to Daniel Berrigan, quoted in Miller's biography. She bought the East First Street property in the spring of 1968 (Francine du Plessix Gray indicates in *Divine Disobedience*), and disputed with the IRS in April and May 1972, as reported in Forest's biography. Her call for a new St. Francis is from an article of May 1940, reprinted in *By Little and By Little*. Cesar Chavez's efforts are described by James Forest, who quotes Day's characterization of him from 1967; Day wrote about him in articles of January 1972 and December 1973, reprinted in *By Little and By Little*. Day's 1972 remark about "the wounded in the class struggle" was quoted by Nat Hentoff in the *Village Voice*, November 10, 1987. Day's remark to Thomas Merton about St. Joseph's House concludes an undated letter of 1967. Day's round-the-world trip is described in James Forest's biography; Forest quotes her notorious remark about the liabilities of the "saintly" tag. She described the "peace pilgrimage" to Washington in her column for May 1971. Bob Fitch's photograph of Day praying is reproduced in Forest's biography; other Fitch photographs are on the cover of that book and on the covers of the Harper & Row paperback editions of *The Long Loneliness* and *Loaves and Fishes*. Richard Avedon's portrait is on the cover of William D. Miller's biography.

430 Percy remarked on the pressure of Flannery O'Connor's request that he "make up another one" in a letter to Foote, February 3, 1971, quoted in both biographies; counted "sober old age as a windfall," July 9, 1971; and reported on the "watershed" in his life, October 17, 1973. The February 3, 1971, letter is silently abridged in the *Correspondence* volume; the *New York Observer*, in June 1996, printed a passage in which Percy explained his "hang-ups" about writing literary pornography: (1) as a Catholic, "I have Christ's word that if I give scandal to 'the little ones,' it would be better for me to be thrown into the sea with a millstone tied around my neck"; and (2) Pornography invariably arouses the reader and "if you have a hard-on, you are in no state to get the message about the human heart which Faulkner says art is all about." Percy reported on giving up whiskey in the letter of July 9, 1971, and on taking up golf in a letter of August 4, 1970; his teaching stints at LSU and Loyola are discussed at length in the two biographies; seven long interviews from the first half of the 1970s—nearly a hundred pages—are reprinted in *Conversations with Walker Percy*. *Lancelot* was published by Farrar, Straus and Giroux in 1977.

431 Day chronicled her pilgrimage to Soviet Russia in her columns for September and October/November 1971.

432 Farrar, Straus and Giroux issued a press release announcing Jimmy Carter's declaration of "Flannery O'Connor Day" in Georgia upon the presentation of O'Connor's papers to the library at Georgia College in Milledgeville; the O'Connor Collection includes a photograph of Governor Carter shaking hands with Regina O'Connor.

433 Percy described writing the introduction to the LSU edition of *Lanterns on the Levee* in the letter to Foote of October 9, 1973; the introduction is reprinted in *Signposts in a Strange Land*. His honorary degrees, his induction into the Academy of Arts and Letters, and his teaching duties are described in both biographies; his Great Books group and his work with a group of nuns to integrate real estate in Covington are related in detail by Patrick Samway, who treats Percy's later years thoroughly.

433 The seventy-fifth-birthday tributes to Dorothy Day are described in James Forest's biography. Day's remarks about "women's lib" are quoted in Miller's biography, those about the lack of traditional piety in James Forest's biography.

433 Day described what is now known as her "last arrest" in "A Brief Sojourn in Jail," published in the September 1973 *Catholic Worker*; Bob Fitch's photograph is on the cover of *Love Is the Measure*. She defined Catholic Workers as "holy fools" in a column for May 1974; as anarchists, July/August 1977; and as demonstrators of the "providence of God" in the Fall Appeal for 1977.

434 Patrick Jordan and Robert Ellsberg, in conversation, described the Catholic Worker as a Catholic experience of a kind that they had not encountered before. Ellsberg describes Day's "intense, haunting beauty" in the introduction to *By Little and By Little*; Jordan recalled spying her listening to the opera in "An Appetite for God," in *Commonweal* (October 24, 1997). Eric Brandt described painting Day's room in conversation. Robert Coles recalls his visits to the Catholic Worker in his introduction to *The Long Loneliness*; tells the story of his own search in the preface to *Dorothy Day: A Radical Devotion*; recalls going "to say thank you" and hearing her on "her great loves" in a column in *America* (January 17, 1998); quotes Day on Silone and Orwell in the chapter of *A Radical Devotion* about "Her Spiritual Kin"; and recalls trying to persuade her to read *The Moviegoer* in the *America* column. Jay Tolson and Patrick Samway describe Coles's interviewing Walker Percy for the *New Yorker* profile, pointing out that the friendship began when Percy reviewed a volume from Coles's *Children of Crisis* series for the *New York Times*; Tolson emphasizes the awkwardness of their encounter. The profile, published in the *New Yorker* in two parts, October 2 and October 9, 1978, was republished as *Walker Percy: An American Search* (Little, Brown, 1978), with an introduction in which Coles explains how he came to admire Percy's writing.

436 Alice Walker recounts her pilgrimage to Andalusia in the essay "Beyond the Peacock: Reconstructing Flannery O'Connor," published in *In Search of Our Mothers' Gardens* (Harcourt Brace Jovanovich, 1983).

438 Dorothy Day acknowledged her retirement from daily work in her column for March 1975, reprinted in *By Little and By Little*; she described the Catholic Worker as "a school, a work camp" and its work in the same column. James Forest details the purchase of cottages at Spanish Camp. Several of the cottages were later destroyed—Day's cottage by a real-estate developer after a long property fight described in "Material Battle for a Spiritual Place," by Dan Barry (*New York Times*, November 24, 1997), and "Sacking a Saint," by Wayne Barrett (*Village Voice*, May 8, 2001), some others by two teenage arsonists ("Metro News Briefs," *New York Times*, April 10, 2002).

439 The provision for royalties in Thomas Merton's will is reported in Michael Mott's biography. *Contemplation in a World of Action* was published by Doubleday in 1971; *A Vow of Conversation* by Farrar, Straus and Giroux in 1988; *The Collected Poems of Thomas Merton* by New Directions in 1977; Monica Furlong's *Merton: A Biography* in 1980; John Howard Griffin's *Following the Ecstasy* in 1983; Michael Mott's *The Seven Mountains of Thomas Merton* in 1984; James Forest's *Living with Wisdom* in 1991. *Ishi Means Man* was published by the Unicorn Press in 1976, with a wood-block print by Rita Corbin. Dorothy Day praised Merton's retreat tapes in her column for March 1973.

439 The purchase and renovation of Maryhouse are detailed in William A. Miller's biography, where Day is quoted on the symbolism of the place. Day described the view from her window in her column for July/August 1976; her remark about prayer is quoted in James Forest's biography.

440 The 1976 Eucharistic Congress is described in Miller's and Forest's biographies; Day's talk was published as "Bread for the Hungry" in the September 1976 *Catholic Worker*. She described her reading in her journal notes, published in the paper and quoted in Forest's biography.

440 Percy's struggles with *Lancelot* and with life generally are described by Jay Tolson and Patrick Samway, who approach his midlife crisis gingerly, and by Percy himself, who is blunt. Writing to Shelby Foote, Percy described being in the "horse latitudes," October 6, 1972; a "low-grade fever and malaise" that suggested hepatitis, July 27, 1974; his "liver mending," September 9, 1974 ("Back *up* to my *normal* depression," he added); his restlessness upon turning sixty and finishing *The Message in the Bottle*, April 8, 1975. He remarked upon "Percy, O'Connor, and Foote," May 1, 1975; and upon the alternatives to "Shelley 5 hrs per day," October 9, 1975. Percy's acquisition of an artist's studio, his friendship with Lyn Hill, and the Sons and Daughters of the Apocalypse are described in the two biographies, as is a Jung discussion group with Percy and Lyn Hill as members. Tolson describes the lost weekend in Las Vegas, arguing that it stimulated the writing of *Lancelot*. Percy discussed the portrait of him by Lyn Hill ("an artist friend of mine") in the self-interview "Questions They Never Asked Me," published in *Esquire* (December 1977) and reprinted in *Signposts in a Strange Land*.

442 Percy told the story of how *A Confederacy of Dunces* came to be published in a foreword to the novel (Louisiana State University, 1980), reprinted in *Signposts in a Strange Land*. His two biographers fill out the story, which has gained the stature of a legend in New Orleans.

444 Dorothy Day's journal notes from "our Staten Island headquarters" were published in the July/August 1977 *Catholic Worker*; excerpts are reprinted in *By Little and By Little*. James Forest recalls the visitors to her bedside in his biography, and recalls her piety in the "Personal Remembrance" appended to it. Patrick Jordan described the validation her faith seemed to provide in "An Appetite for God." Daniel Berrigan depicted her as "served, reverenced, cherished, protected," in his eloquent and moving introduction to the Harper & Row edition of *The Long Loneliness*, since supplanted by an edition with an introduction by Robert Coles.

445 Percy explained *Lancelot* in 1977 interviews with Herbert Mitgang and William Delaney, reprinted in *Conversations with Walker Percy*; "Questions They Never Asked Me" is reprinted there and in *Signposts in a Strange Land*. Robert Coles's profile of Percy was published in the *New Yorker* (October 2 and October 9, 1978); Percy remarked on it in a letter to Shelby Foote, January 29, 1979, in the *Correspondence* volume. Percy described his plans for a Swiftian satire and a novel about the "new consciousness" in a letter to Foote, February 8, 1977, and pronounced the dramatic monologue "an uncongenial form" in a letter to Foote, March 4, 1978. He described how *The Second Coming* came about, September 15, 1979; the letter of February 8 indicates that Foote had suggested he write a sequel. *The Second Coming* was published by Farrar, Straus and Giroux in 1980.

449 Day's reflections in her journal, published in the February 1979 *Catholic Worker*, are reprinted in *By Little and By Little*. James Forest reports that she prayed the prayer of St. Simeon: "Now let thy servant depart in peace."

449 *The Habit of Being: Letters of Flannery O'Connor* (as the jacket reads) was published by Farrar, Straus and Giroux in 1979. Sally Fitzgerald, introducing the volume, wrote, "There she stands, a phoenix risen from her own words . . ." O'Connor

remarked on keeping carbon copies in a number of letters, such as one to Beverly Brunson, January 1, 1955, in the Library of America edition: "I keep copies to keep myself from writing the same thing twice and for other conventional reasons." Percy sent the book to Shelby Foote with a letter, April 18, 1979; declared "I don't want to write another novel," August 29, and described the work he was calling *Novum Organum*, September 10, 1980. O'Connor had described writing a novel as "a terrible experience" in "The Nature and Aim of Fiction," in *Mystery and Manners.*

451 Day's journal notes for March and April 1980 were published in the September 1980 *Catholic Worker*. The summer and the deaths in her family are detailed in James Forest's biography, and her wistful recollection of bus rides is quoted there.

451 Day's death is recounted in Miller's and Forest's biographies, as well as in Robert Ellsberg's introduction to *By Little and By Little* and Nancy L. Roberts's *Dorothy Day and the "Catholic Worker."* Her interest in the news of the earthquake in Sicily is recalled by her friend Eileen Egan in James Forest's biography; Ignazio Silone's remark about earthquakes is quoted by Alexander Stille in the introduction to Silone's *Abruzzo Trilogy* (Steerforth, 2000). The account of her funeral is based on Miller's and Forest's reports, as well as the personal recollections of Geoffrey Gneuchs, the Right Reverend Paul Moore, and Kenneth L. Woodward. The *New York Times* published an obituary on December 1, 1980; *Commonweal's* appreciation, by David J. O'Brien, is quoted on the cover of *By Little and By Little.* Day's explanation of the meaning of her life is quoted in Robert Coles's introduction to the Harper San Francisco edition of *The Long Loneliness.*

453 The likening of Walker Percy to a "last gentleman" is commonplace; e.g., Kieran Quinlan's book *Walker Percy: The Last Catholic Novelist* (Louisiana State University, 1996). Scholarly attention to Percy, such as Lewis A. Lawson's, is described in the two biographies: Samway reports on the appraisal of Percy's papers; Tolson relates how Samway's biography came about, and vice versa. Garry Wills described a "brilliant crew" of Catholic novelists in a 1972 article for the *New York Times Magazine*, reprinted as "The Catholic Seventies" in *Bare Ruined Choirs.*

453 The success of *A Confederacy of Dunces* relative to *The Second Coming* is described in the two Percy biographies. Percy diagnosed the age's "semiotic breakdown" in a letter to Shelby Foote, May 21, 1979. *Lost in the Cosmos* was published by Farrar, Straus and Giroux in 1983.

455 Percy gave the talk published in *Signposts in a Strange Land* as "Diagnosing the Modern Malaise" during a Chekhov festival held at Cornell University in 1977. The annual Phinizy Lecture at the University of Georgia, arranged by Percy's cousin Phinizy Spalding, was published as "Going Back to Georgia" in *Signposts in a Strange Land*. Percy spoke of O'Connor as a "dear friend" in his February 23, 1990, letter to Bruce Springsteen, published in *DoubleTake* (Spring 1998), and spoke of her at length in the 1981 interview with Ben Forkner and J. Gerald Kennedy, reprinted in *Conversations with Walker Percy.* His Eudora Welty lecture was published privately by Faust Publishing and reprinted in *Signposts in a Strange Land* as "Novel-Writing in an Apocalyptic Time."

456 *The Thanatos Syndrome* was published by Farrar, Straus and Giroux in 1987. Patrick Samway points out that Father Smith's peroration is rooted in O'Connor's remark about "tenderness," and argues convincingly that Father Charles of Holy Ghost Monastery (aka Jack English of the Catholic Worker) is a model for Father Smith;

Samway also reports on the financial success of the novel. Percy's attenuated book tour is described in both biographies.

459 "If I Had Five Minutes with the Pope," published in *America*, is reprinted in *Signposts in a Strange Land*. Percy's friend Nikki Barranger, in conversation, explained why Percy didn't attend the Mass celebrated by the pope at the Superdome in New Orleans. "Culture, the Church, and Evangelization" is published in *Signposts*. The photograph of Percy and John Paul appears in Tolson's biography. Percy described *Contra Gentiles* as "a somewhat smart-ass collection of occasional pieces" in a letter to Shelby Foote, July 29, 1989. "A 'Cranky Novelist' Reflects on the Church," Percy's letters to the *New York Times* about abortion, "Why Are You a Catholic?" and the foreword to *The "New" Catholics* are all published in *Signposts*.

460 Percy latinately diagnosed cancer in a letter to Shelby Foote, June 8, 1989, and discussed Chekhov's story "The Bishop" in a letter, June 12, 1989; his commencement address to the monks of St. Joseph's Abbey is "A 'Cranky Novelist' Reflects on the Church." Tolson describes Percy's writing a piece about the Waffle House, and quotes the piece at length; "The Holiness of the Ordinary," written for *Boston College Magazine*, is reprinted in *Signposts*. Tolson reports that Percy had become a Benedictine oblate "several years earlier," Samway that Percy and his wife did so in "mid-February" 1990.

461 Percy wrote to Bruce Springsteen on February 23, 1990. Tolson, in his biography of Percy, gives the circumstances; surprisingly, Samway (who was once an editor of *America*) does not. The letter, when published in *DoubleTake* (Spring, 1998), bore the date February 23, 1989; in it, however, Percy remarks that "I have cancer and am taking radiation for it"; given that Tolson and Samway both place Percy's radiation treatments in early 1990, it is reasonable to conclude that Percy wrote the letter in the last months of his life. To begin this "fan letter of sorts," Percy, surely overstating the case, told Springsteen, "I've always been an admirer of yours, for your musicianship and for being one of the few sane guys in your field." He then overstated his friendship with O'Connor in the same way—"The whole time I knew her, she was dying of lupus . . ."—and for the same reason, to emphasize his identification with another Catholic artist.

Springsteen remarked on both Percy and O'Connor in a 1997 interview with Percy's nephew Will (published in *DoubleTake*, Spring, 1998, alongside Walker Percy's letter). Of O'Connor, whose work he recalled having read in his late twenties—"right prior to the record *Nebraska* (1982), I was deep into O'Connor"—Springsteen observed: "There was something in those stories of hers that I felt captured a certain part of the American character that I was interested in writing about. They were a big, big revelation. . . . There was some dark thing—a component of spirituality—that I sensed in her stories, and that set me off exploring characters of my own." Speaking of Percy, Springsteen used his characteristic vocabulary of restlessness and displacement: "It's all there in your uncle's essay 'The Man on the Train,'" he told Will Percy, "about the 'wandering spirit' and modern man—all that's happened since the Industrial Revolution when people were uprooted and set out on the road into towns where they'd never been before, leaving families, leaving traditions that were hundreds of years old. . . . I think that we're all trying to find what passes for a home, or creating a home of some sort, while we're constantly being uprooted by technology, or by factories being shut down."

462 Percy's funeral is described in the two biographies. Robert Giroux's remarks at the Church of St. Ignatius Loyola in New York were published in chapbook form by Farrar, Straus and Giroux in 1991, along with the remarks of the other speakers: Eudora Welty, Wilfrid Sheed, Mary Lee Settle, Stanley Kauffmann, Shelby Foote, and Patrick Samway.

EPILOGUE: *The Life You Save May Be Your Own*

463 Carmen Trotta described and displayed St. Joseph's House to me in August 1998, and reflected at length on the nature of the Catholic Worker today, as did members of Houses of Hospitality in Houston; Chicago; Rockford, Illinois; Syracuse, New York; and Los Angeles. *Dorothy Day*, starring Moira Kelly and Martin Sheen, was released in 1996. Various opinions on the prospect of Day's canonization, including Daniel Berrigan's, were gathered in *Salt* (November/December 1987). The recollections read into the *Congressional Record* were Patrick Jordan's, published in *Commonweal* as "An Appetite for God"; Senator Daniel Patrick Moynihan sponsored the effort. A listing of all the Catholic Worker houses was published in the May 1996 *Catholic Worker.*

464 The conflict over Day's impending canonization is the subject of my article "Patron Saint of Paradox," published in the *New York Times Magazine* (November 8, 1998).

466 Patrick Hart welcomed me to the Abbey of Gethsemani on December 31, 2000. The peace activist who made a literary retreat at Merton's hermitage is John Dear, S.J.; John Howard Griffin made a similar retreat.

468 Christine Wiltz showed me around New Orleans; Nikki Barranger served as guide to Covington, providing an introduction to Mrs. Walker Percy and identifying Percy's grave behind St. Joseph's Abbey. Percy called Covington a "backwater of a backwater" in "Why I Live Where I Live," reprinted in *Signposts in a Strange Land.* Percy's riff about a coffee table appears in *Lost in the Cosmos.*

470 Louise Florencourt discussed Flannery O'Connor with me at a restaurant in Milledgeville. O'Connor quoted from Joseph Conrad's preface to The *"Nigger" of the Narcissus*, and commented on it, in "The Nature and Aim of Fiction," in *Mystery and Manners*; she forbade Elizabeth Hester to write about the introduction to *A Memoir of Mary Ann* in a letter, October 28, 1961.

Index

Romanticism, xii, 86, 441
"Root of War, The" (Merton), 332
Roosevelt, Franklin D., 172
Roy, Pacifique, 116
Royal Canadian Air Force, 143–45
Russian Revolution, 14, 17, 101
Ruysbroeck, Jan van, 330

Sacco, Nicola, 52, 55–57, 101, 175, 279
St. Bonaventure's (college), 99, 113, 117–21
St. John's Abbey (Minnesota), 213
St. Elizabeth's Hospital (New York), 108, 191
St. Joseph's House (New York), 116, 168, 211, 237, 318, 399, 430, 432, 434, 452, 463–64; conflict between young and old at, 334, 343; Day's absences from, 212; English at, 298; founding of, 88; Friday-night discussions at, 100; fundraising for, 273, 275; Gordon at, 187; Harrington at, 344; Kennedy brothers at, 315; Maryhouse as companion place to, 439–40; Merton's admirers at, 298–99, 348; move to First Street of, 429; Moyers at, 433; peace movement and, 376–78, 397; wake for Maurin at, 180
Salinger, J. D., 202, 275
Samway, Patrick, 126, 159, 289, 458
Sandburg, Carl, 60
San Francisco earthquake (1906), 3–4, 6, 254
Santayana, George, 78
Sartre, Jean-Paul, 137–38, 154, 214, 366
Saturday Evening Post, 157
Saturday Review, 194
satyagraha (Gandhian nonviolence), 294, 299
Schmidt, Michael, 97
Scholasticism, 150–52, 159, 277
Schwab, Charles, 54
Scopes trial, 23
Scott, Walter, 11
Scotus, Duns, 91
Scribner's, 214

Seamen's Strike, 89
Seasons of Celebration (Merton), 400
Second Coming, The (Percy), 447–50, 453, 456
Second Vatican Council, see Vatican II
Seeds of Contemplation (Merton), 185, 186, 331–32
Selby, John, 173, 174, 193
semiotics, 450
Sessions, William, 286, 312n
Seven Storey Mountain, The (Merton), 74, 82, 87, 98, 110–11, 121, 124, 129, 144, 150–51, 175, 208, 329, 419, 426, 427; aftermath of father's death described in, 30–31; Augustine's influence on, 33, 40; as best-seller, x, 169–70; Catholic Workers and, 188–89, 298; censored by Trappist superiors, 31, 113; childhood travels recounted in, 8; as conversion story, 93; Dante's influence on, 40, 76, 108; excerpts from, 166; Joyce's influence on, 90; monastic revival inspired by, 184; poem concluding, 402; publication of, xii, 151, 169, 213; Van Doren in, 79; Waugh's editing of, 163–66, 168
Sewanee Review, 264, 276, 341, 364
Sewanee University, 158
Shakers, 23, 371, 406
Shakespeare, William, 10, 78–80, 189, 277n, 304, 313, 353
Sheed and Ward, 172
Sheen, Fulton J., 159, 163, 169
Shelley, Percy Bysshe, 441
Shenandoah (journal), 216
Sickness unto Death, The (Kierkegaard), 304
Sign, The (magazine), 308
Sign of Jonas, The (Merton), 210, 263, 386
Signs (Merleau-Ponty), 357
Silent Life, The (Merton), 230
Silone, Ignazio, 344, 435, 451, 452
Sinclair, Upton, 15, 52
Singer, Isaac Bashevis, 335
Sisters of Charity, 54
Sitwell, Edith, 296, 297
60 Minutes, 433

works by, 31, 113, 310, 332; Day and,
245, 318, 331, 333, 348; English and,
189, 213, 298; female, 407, 422; habits
worn by, ix, 189, 413, 421, 427; in Italy,
39, 220, 401, 402; Lowell and, 172,
175; O'Connor and, 382; Percy and,
395; religious experience in retreats of,
466; Waugh on, 165; *see also* Cistercians; Holy Ghost Monastery; Our Lady
of Gethsemani, Abbey of
Trilling, Lionel, xii
Trotsky, Leon, 17, 432
True Humanism (Maritain), 236–37
Truman, Harry S., 149
Tulane University, 342
"Turkey, The" (O'Connor), 148
Turgenev, Ivan, 146, 193
Twain, Mark, 235, 457

Ulysses (Joyce), 33, 41, 90, 105, 177, 412
Understanding Fiction (Brooks and War-
ren), 146, 148
Unitarians, 5–6, 97
United Farm Workers, 429, 433–34
United Nations, 377, 399
Updike, John, 306

Vanderbilt University, 44
Van Doren, Mark, 79–80, 129–30, 143,
144
Vanzetti, Bartolomeo, 52, 55–57, 101,
175, 279
Varieties of Religious Experience, The
(James), 6, 51, 81
Vassar College, 176
Vatican II, 320, 335, 340, 346, 358, 368,
375–77, 385, 400, 425, 459, 466
Victorianism, 32, 91, 134
"View of the Woods, A" (O'Connor),
62
Vietnam War, 395; opposition to, 368,
376–80, 397–99, 405–6, 408–11, 414,
429
Viking Press, 214
Vile Bodies (Waugh), 122

Violent Bear It Away, The (O'Connor), 14,
135n, 287–89, 297, 307–9, 327, 337,
341
Virgil, 76, 79, 97
Virginia, University of, 82
Voices of Silence, The (Malraux), 361, 363
Vow of Conversation, A (Merton), 430

Waiting for God (Weil), 271
Waldron, Ann, 213, 236, 238n
Walker, Alice, 436–38
Wallace, Mike, 433
Wall Street Journal, 379
Walsh, Dan, 112
War Resisters League, 236
Warren, Robert Penn, 147–48, 152, 171
Washington Post, 392
Waugh, Evelyn, 122, 146, 154, 163–69,
181–82, 185, 188, 190, 201
Weil, Simone, 271–72
Wells, H. G., 33
Welty, Eudora, 146; lecture, 455
Wesley, John, 212
West, Nathanael, 152
Wheelock, John Hall, 214
White Citizens' Councils, 372
"Why I Live Where I Live" (Percy), 159
"Wildcat" (O'Connor), 148
Williams, William Carlos, 22, 414
Wills, Garry, 453
Wilson, Edmund, 176
"Wisdom of the Desert, The" (Merton),
317
Wise Blood (O'Connor), xii, 14, 152–55,
183, 210, 213, 216, 234, 242, 288, 306,
307, 328; conflict with Rinehart over,
173–74, 193; contract with Harcourt,
Brace for, 182, 193; excerpts from, 178;
French translation of, 283; Gordon's
comments on, 193–99, 239; preface to
1962 reprint of, 337–39; publication of,
201–2; reviews of, 201, 206; revisions
of, 189–91; synopsis of, 202–8
Wobblies, 37
Wolfe, Thomas, 146, 250, 253, 433
Women Strike for Peace, 347, 348